**EXPLORING CULTURES**
**A Prentice Hall Series in Anthropology**

*Crossing Currents: Continuity and Change in Latin America*
Michael B. Whiteford and Scott Whiteford

*Europe in the Anthropological Imagination*
Susan Parman

*Globalization and Culture Change in the Pacific Islands*
Victoria S. Lockwood

*The Legacy of Mesoamerica: History and Culture of a Native American Civilization*
Robert M. Carmack, Janine Gasco, and Gary H. Gossen

# Globalization and Culture Change in the Pacific Islands

Edited by

## Victoria S. Lockwood
*Southern Methodist University*

PEARSON
Prentice
Hall

Upper Saddle River, New Jersey 07458

*Library of Congress Cataloging-in-Publication Data*

Globalization and culture change in the Pacific Islands / edited by Victoria S. Lockwood.
   p. cm.—(Exploring cultures)
  Includes index.
  ISBN  0–13–042173–1
   1. Ethnology—Oceania.  2. Globalization—Oceania.  3. Culture diffusion—Oceania.  4.
Social change—Oceania.  5. Oceania—Social conditions.  6. Oceania—Ethnic relations.  7.
Oceania—Politics and government.  I. Lockwood, Victoria S.  II. Series.

GN663.G56 2004
306'.0995—dc21

2003049816

**AVP/Publisher:** Nancy Roberts
**Editorial Assistant:** Lee Peterson
**Senior Marketing Manager:** Marissa Feliberty
**Marketing Assistant:** Adam Laitman
**Production Editor:** Joan Stone
**Manufacturing Buyer:** Ben Smith
**Cover Art Director:** Jayne Conte
**Cover Design:** Kiwi Design
**Illustrator (Interior):** Mirella Signoretto
**Image Permission Coordinator:** Craig A. Jones
**Composition:** Interactive Composition Corporation
**Printer/Binder:** Hamilton Printing Company
**Cover Printer:** Coral Graphic Services, Inc.
**Typeface:** 10/11 New Baskerville

Acknowledgments for articles and photographs from other sources and reproduced, with permission, in this textbook appear on the acknowledgments page for that chapter (or on page 476).

Pearson Education LTD.
Pearson Education Singapore, Pte. Ltd
Pearson Education, Canada, Ltd
Pearson Education–Japan
Pearson Education Australia PTY, Limited
Pearson Education North Asia Ltd
Pearson Educación de Mexico, S.A. de C.V.
Pearson Education Malaysia, Pte. Ltd
Pearson Education, Upper Saddle River, NJ

10 9 8 7 6 5 4 3 2 1
ISBN 0-13-042173-1

Dedicated to my son, Henry

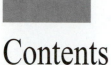
= exam #1

# Contents

## PART IV    IDENTITIES AND CULTURAL REPRESENTATIONS

# 1

# The Global Imperative
# and Pacific Island Societies

**Victoria S. Lockwood**

*Southern Methodist University*

Globalization has become the hallmark of the twenty-first century as it articulates a new form of social organization—an increasingly borderless world where flows of capital and new technologies are propelling goods, information, people, and ideologies around the globe in volumes, and at speeds, never previously imagined. These flows generate an "interconnectedness . . . a world full of movement and mixture, contact and linkages, and persistent cultural interaction and exchange" (Inda and Rosaldo 2002:2; see also Appadurai 1991). Through interconnections, "people become increasingly aware of the extent to which their well-being is dependent on events and trends elsewhere in the world" (Rosenau 2002:71). Moreover, with the global expansion of media, telecommunications, information technology, and the Internet, and with unprecedented numbers of people migrating internationally, people in different parts of the world are exposed to the lifestyles and cultural visions of others very different from themselves. As a result, cultures, societies, and identities around the world are rapidly being transformed.

The complexity and scale of these processes oftentimes precludes an understanding of precisely how the forces of globalization are experienced and shaped by real people in the world's many culturally diverse regions. Anthropologists have sought to redress that gap: "What anthropology offers that is often lacking in other disciplines is a concrete attentiveness to human agency, to the practices of everyday life, in short, to how subjects mediate the processes of globalization" (Inda and Rosaldo 2002:5). In other words, they seek to "ground" globalization by focusing on the *juncture* of the local and global, examining the many ways that particular local communities and cultural groups participate in and are affected by these interconnections (see Burawoy 2000). In this way, we can gain a greater understanding of "how globally extensive social processes configure lives lived locally" (Foster 1999:148).

This volume will contribute to our understanding of what globalization looks like from the vantage point of people in one peripheral world region, Oceania (see Lederman 1998). In this introduction, I first describe the key processes and trends that generate global integration and outline the ongoing debates over globalization's potential impacts on societies around the world. I then turn specifically to the Pacific Islands, describing how the particular sociocultural, economic, and political conditions prevailing in this part of the world shape the major types and directions of transnational flows. The case studies in this volume then describe and analyze how Pacific Islanders, peoples distant from the capitalist core and often peripheral to its interests, perceive and interact with those flows and connections and how they impact their lives.

## GLOBAL PROCESSES AND TRENDS

One of the major dynamics that drives contemporary global flows is the aggressive worldwide expansion of capitalism through free market trade and neoliberal policies—the new ideology of "unleashed capitalism" (see Galbraith 1999). According to this ideology, free trade without government interference, increasing privatization, and deregulation are the catalysts that will spur a new era of economic growth. Neoliberal economists and business leaders propose that such policies will lead to the creation of new jobs and widespread improvements in incomes and standards of living around the world (Scott 2002).

In this global capitalist economy, world trade policies, currencies, and loans to developing countries are regulated by international institutions such as the World Bank, the International Monetary Fund (IMF), and the World Trade Organization (WTO), and by international agreements such as the General Agreement on Tariffs and Trade (GATT). World trade has expanded greatly, "from $124 billion in 1948 to $10,722 billion in 1997, a seventeen-fold increase in the volume of economic transactions" (Robbins 2002:366). Some of that trade has been promoted by recently integrated regional markets, such as the North American Free Trade Agreement (NAFTA) and the European Economic Union (EU).

One of the key processes in greater economic integration over the last several decades has been a dramatic rise in direct foreign investments, which have risen to $644 billion in 1998. Much of that foreign investment in manufacturing, real estate, tourism, banking, and natural resource extraction (mining, and so on) is made by powerful transnational corporations (see Trouillot 2001; Robbins 2002). Manufacturing and some service-related industries are increasingly relocated from wealthy industrialized countries with high labor costs to parts of the developing world where labor or production is cheaper. One indicator of the increasing power of transnational corporations is that a list of the world's top 100 financial entities includes 51 nation states (the United States and others) and 49 transnational corporations (for example, General Motors, Wal-Mart, Exxon Mobil, Mitsubishi, and others) (Robbins 2002:123).

Labor is also highly mobile, flowing in and out of regions depending on relative demand and price. People stream mainly out of relatively impoverished regions to find jobs in the "capitalist core," the relatively wealthy, industrialized nations. Many serve as a pool of semiskilled and unskilled labor. Robbins (2002:119) estimates that there are now about "100 million people who live and work in countries of which they are not citizens." While some of these are political refugees, the vast majority are "economic migrants." They include nurses who are imported from India to work in American hospitals (George 2000), as well as large numbers of Mexican workers who come to the United States illegally. Many migrants resist unqualified assimilation into their host nations and maintain "transnational" lives that bridge two societies (see Basch et al. 1994; Kearney 1995; Brettell and Hollifield 2000). One consequence of population mobility is that highly distinct cultures come into close daily contact with each other, often competing for the same jobs, housing, and other opportunities. That competition often generates social conflict that is shaped and exacerbated by racial and ethnic differences and inequalities.

There has also been a trend toward greater global political integration. Since the end of World War II, international institutions such as the United Nations and World Court increasingly "intervene" in what many nation states consider their internal affairs; peace-keeping missions in the former Yugoslavia and Sierra Leone are examples. They also establish international standards, such as the U.N. Declaration on Human Rights and bans on child labor. There are also growing numbers of international nongovernmental agencies (NGOs) such as the Red Cross and Amnesty International that operate around the world. Some argue that such political institutions undermine the sovereignty, self-determination, and political autonomy of nation states (see Hannerz 1997; Trouillot 2001).

In addition, various social movements are increasingly operating on a global scale, building international memberships and playing a more significant role in policy discussions about international affairs. The environmental movement is today promoted by a number of highly internationalized groups and NGOs (for example, World Wildlife Fund, Greenpeace). Other issues attract widespread support as well. In 1997, Jody Williams won the Nobel Peace Prize for organizing 1,000 different human rights and arms control groups on six continents into an International Campaign to Ban Landmines; she did this mainly through e-mail (Friedman and Ramonet 2002).

Another phenomenon is the active worldwide expansion of relatively new kinds of religious movements, many of which are fundamentalist in their belief systems. The two major movements, Islamic fundamentalism among Muslims and Protestant fundamentalism among Christians, have grown at unprecedented rates in recent years and are actively integrating diverse peoples into their belief systems. Some analysts see the rise of fundamentalist movements as a form of protest or resistance against the global expansion of capitalism and the materialist values and lifestyles which accompany it (see Ernst 1996; Robbins 2002).

## The Historical Context: Capitalism, Western Imperialism, and Colonialism

Although many people think of "globalization" as a recent phenomenon, the economic and political processes that created it and serve as its foundations have deep historical roots. Tomlinson argues that globalization is "the continuation of a long historical process of western 'imperialist' expansion—embracing the colonial expansions of the sixteenth to the nineteenth centuries—and representing an historical pattern of increasing global hegemony" (1997:143–144). At the core of Western expansion, both historically and today, is the expansion of capitalism, a historically specific form of political economic relations that evolved and gained ascendancy in the seventeenth and eighteenth centuries in Europe. Since that time, "capitalism has always been transnational," impelled by its own internal logic, a drive to accumulate capital and expand, or to stagnate and collapse (Trouillot 2001).

Propelled by the industrial revolution and the need for raw materials and markets, Europeans first dominated and integrated distant peoples and cultures into global-scale political economic relations during the colonial era. They created an international division of labor where colonized peoples provided the cheap labor and raw materials for European expansion, wealth accumulation, and industrialization, while peripheral colonized regions stagnated and were forcibly introduced to Western institutions and Christianity (see Wallerstein 1974; Wolf 1982).

Today, the major push for capitalist expansion and globalization comes from the wealthy, industrialized, "core" nations of the United States, Europe, and Japan, who reap most of their benefits. There are a small number of Newly Industrializing Countries (NICs)—such as South Korea, Hong Kong, Taiwan, and Brazil—that have growing manufacturing and industrial sectors. The rest of the "developing" world—nations integrated into the capitalist world system through colonialism or neocolonialism—is "mired in poverty, debt, and economic malaise" (A. Gordon 1996) and often suffers from ethnic conflict and political instability. Its economies are usually agricultural, and exports are mainly primary products and sometimes laborers to wealthier industrialized nations. At the same time, these nations are often dependent on imports of manufactured and consumer items. Because of their peripheral and dependent economic position, they find it difficult to shape the terms on which they participate in the global political economy, and they often struggle to find a niche in it at all.

Thus, "there is no egalitarian global village" and the world is not a level playing field (Hannerz 1997:107). Flows of capital, goods, and people do not travel in the same ways or in the same quantities in various regions of the world (see Trouillot 2001). The flow of capital is particularly selective; in 1997 about 70 percent of direct foreign investment "went from one rich country to another, 8 developing countries received about 20 percent, and the remainder was divided among more than 100 poor nations" (Scott 2002:74). Africa, for instance, received only 1.5 percent of total foreign investment in 1995 (Robbins 2002:99). Areas of the world struggling with political instability and/or ethnic conflict are generally shunned by transnational capital.

And the world labor market is also highly differentiated by region, with most labor flowing from the poorer developing regions to the wealthier industrialized nations where wages are higher. Similarly, most manufactured goods are produced in the core and are consumed by their wealthy populations, although transnational corporations aggressively market their goods and services into even the most peripheral and remote regions. In general, goods, information, and media follow the path of capital and flow from Western countries to non-Western countries, although some would argue that new modes of communication like the Internet create channels that are less bounded by the constraints that structure commodity and other flows.

## THE POTENTIAL IMPACTS AND OUTCOMES OF GLOBALIZATION

The potential impacts of globalization are much debated. Some analysts argue that globalization will promote economic development in poor nations and contribute to global equity, while others say that it will simply exacerbate existing inequalities between rich and poor nations. In other words, how will the various costs and benefits of globalization be distributed? Another major issue concerns whether or not the processes of globalization will promote Western (or American) cultural hegemony and make the world over in the image of the West, or if cultural diversity can flourish despite greater global integration.

Neoliberal economists propose that globalization will promote the diffusion of capital, technology, innovations, and consumer goods around the world and ultimately create jobs and bring greater prosperity to all. They argue that free trade is the key to promoting economic growth in impoverished areas, and that development will ultimately lead to greater equity and income convergence around the globe (see Rosenau 2002). They also argue that globalization will prevail over the cultural and political protectionism and fragmentation that seems to be on the rise around the world; in their view, capitalism is an economic engine that cannot be stopped.

Critics of globalization contend that those who favor this position are economic determinists who fail to see the importance of non-market factors in shaping social processes. They argue that it "inexorably leads to the concentration of wealth and economic power in the hands of a small group," enriching the powerful capitalist nations and impoverishing the developing world (Friedman and Ramonet 2002:88; see also Scott 2002). Indeed, Ramonet notes that "during the last 15 years of globalization, per capita income has decreased in more than 80 countries, or in almost half the states in the world" (Friedman and Ramonet 2002:88).

Indeed, in the competition to secure a niche in the global economy, poor, less-developed nations who lack capital, technology, and developed infrastructures find it difficult to compete with the developed industrial nations. International trade in the developing world's "traditional advantages"—primary commodities (agriculture and minerals)—has shrunk from 70 percent in 1900 to 20 percent today (Scott 2002:73–74). Scott contends that poor countries are also disadvantaged because the "rich countries insist on barriers to immigration and agricultural imports . . . and poor nations have been unable to attract much foreign capital" (2002:73). Moreover, "opportunities for growth in the world market have shifted from raw or semiprocessed commodities toward manufactured goods and services—and within these categories, toward more knowledge-intensive segments. This trend obviously favors rich countries over poor ones" (Scott 2002:75). Thus critics contend that while "free trade" may benefit developed, industrialized nations, it will not promote development in poor nations (see Galbraith 1999).

Some argue that the developing nations' inability to benefit from globalization is their own fault. They cite political instability, infrastructural inadequacies, non-Western institutions and values ("institutional deficiencies"), government corruption, ethnic conflict, and high rates of population growth in these nations as the real causes of their underdevelopment. Lacking capital, technology, and a well-educated workforce, developing nations are poorly positioned to capitalize on the "opportunities" global flows might bring their way (Scott 2002:78).

But others argue that most political and economic problems in developing nations were created by Western domination and capitalist exploitation during the colonial era, and that postcolonial nations are struggling to emerge from the backwater of colonialism (for example, Lappe and Collins 1977). Moreover, many developing nations have huge international debts and have been required by the IMF and World Bank to undertake structural adjustment policies that limit government spending and social welfare programs, exacerbating the difficult situations of the poor in these countries.

Critics also object to globalization for a number of other reasons:

> Globalization has little to do with people or progress and everything to do with money. Dazzled by the glimmer of fast profits, the champions of globalization are incapable of taking stock in the future, anticipating the needs of humanity and the environment, planning for the expansion of cities, or slowly reducing inequalities and healing social fractures. (Ramonet in Friedman and Ramonet 2002:84)

They argue that globalization and neoliberal economics focus on growth and profits while workers, communities, and environments suffer and "economic justice" is ignored (see Broad 2002:13). International environmental groups have fought against transnational corporations' development initiatives and quest for profits that destroy the world's rainforests, pollute the air, contribute to global warming, destroy ecosystems, and promote loss of biodiversity. Organized labor has also been at the forefront of the assault on globalization, arguing that it sacrifices workers' rights, jobs, and livelihoods to the quest for profits. In 1999, the AFL-CIO and other unions played an important role in organizing the massive demonstrations against the World Trade Organization that took place in Seattle (Winthrop 2000).

Moreover, antiglobalization, "protectionist," and "nationalist" thinkers worry that globalization will lead to a loss of local and national autonomy. They appeal to economic nationalism, arguing that national sovereignty should be protected and that nations should not "cede political authority to multilateral bodies that can undermine national law" (Broad 2002). They also argue that countries should be able to protect their domestic industries and products from international competition and protect their workers' jobs from relocation overseas or being overtaken by foreign migrant labor (see Broad 2002).

## The Globalization of Culture: Homogeneity or Diversity?

Another antiglobalization debate is concerned about the increasing "McDonaldization" of the world, the loss of cultural diversity, and the increasing Western cultural hegemony that appears to be at the root of these processes (see Appadurai 1990). Whereas prior to the colonial era and the expansion of capitalism there were several thousand distinct cultures in the world, today there are only about 200 (Scupin 2000). Few would dispute that the history of humanity has been one of powerful groups subordinating weaker groups and forcing not only their political-economic control on others but also their cultures and religions. But this process greatly accelerated and achieved a truly global scale when European colonizers saw it as the "white man's burden" to force their institutions (including capitalism), way of life, and religious beliefs (Christianity) on the "uncivilized heathens" in other parts of the world.

Since the colonial era, the expansion of capitalism has been accompanied by a steady export of Western culture to the developing world. Some have argued that "the traffic in culture moves primarily in one direction: sometimes it is seen to move from the First World (or West/center) to the Third World (or rest/periphery), other times more specifically from the United States to the rest of the world" (Inda and Rosaldo 2002:13–14). This includes not only Western commodities and goods but also Western political culture (democracy), Western worldview (a techno-scientific view of the world) and Western values (economic rationality, individualism, competition, consumerism). The export of Western media, television programs, and popular culture/music promote the "large-scale transfer of meaning systems and symbolic forms" (see Hannerz 1997:107). The developing nation (peripheral state) in the global system:

> to provide for the material welfare of its citizenry and to stay in business as a competitor within the international system, . . . has had to be heavily involved in the wholesale importation of culture from center to periphery. As it reconstructs society within its territory into a form which is more or less globally recurrent, institutions are introduced which are fundamentally inspired by and modeled on those of the world system centers. (Hannerz 1997:118)

But there are many reasons to be cautious about the possibility of a monolithic Western culture remaking the world in its image. This perspective greatly simplifies highly complex cultural interactions generated by globalization and ignores the many forces out there in the world that are either actively rejecting Western cultural and political hegemony and/or working to assert their own locally meaningful cultural systems. The growing number of ethnic and nationalist conflicts are organized around the notion of cultural and religious differences, of "us" and "them," and are movements that strive to differentiate, instead of integrate, competing populations. Barber (1992) calls ethnic and nationalist movements "centrifugal whirlwinds" that are actively fragmenting the world at the same time that the forces of globalization are integrating it. Nation states like the Soviet Union and Yugoslavia, for example, disintegrated overnight into mutually hostile, culturally and politically distinct fragments (see Barber 1992).

Moreover, religious nationalism in the form of Islamic fundamentalist states (Iran, Sudan, and, increasingly, Egypt), Palestinian nationalism, and Hindu nationalism in India strongly assert both religious, nationalistic, and particular cultural agendas (see Juergensmeyer 1993), and are often anti-Western. Similarly, many of the growing number of ethnic conflicts and ethnically based, nationalist secessionist movements around the world—Rwanda, the Kurds, Kashmir, and others—are actively utilizing ethnic, cultural, linguistic, and religious difference and identity politics as rallying cries in their often violent competitions with other groups for land, resources, and power. Various indigenous and ethnic revitalization movements, such as the sovereignty movements of the Hawai'ians, Maori, Australian Aborigines, and others, similarly use identity politics to claim restitution against dominant groups.

These "fragmenting" trends all prioritize the local over perceived threats from outside. But Friedman contends: "Ethnic and cultural fragmentation and modernist homogenization are not two arguments, two opposing views of what is happening in the world today, but two constitutive trends of global reality" (J. Friedman 2002:233). Rosenau summarizes these two simultaneous and dialectical processes:

> The boundary expanding dynamics of globalization have become highly salient precisely

because recent decades have witnessed a mush-rooming of facilities, interests, and markets through which a potential for worldwide spread can be realized. Likewise, the boundary-contracting dynamics of localization have also become increasingly significant, not least because some people and cultures feel threat-ened by the incursions of globalization . . . Globalization does intrude; its processes do shift jobs elsewhere; its norms do undermine traditional mores. Responses to these threats can vary considerably. At one extreme are adap-tations that accept the boundary-broadening processes and make the best of them by inte-grating them into local customs and practices. At the other extreme are responses intended to ward off the globalizing processes by resorting to ideological purities, closed borders, and eco-nomic isolation. (Rosenau 2002:69)

Around the world one finds that instead of Western homogenization, there has been in-stead a great deal of selective adoption and rejection, customization, and "cultural cre-olization" (Hannerz 1992). Foreign ideas and goods are typically interpreted in the cultural terms of the receiving society, and their meanings become transformed in the process (see Liebes and Katz 1990; Michaels 2002). The periphery reshapes "metropolitan cul-ture to its own specifications" generating "new forms that are more responsive to, and at the same time in part outgrowths of, local everyday life" (Hannerz 1997:124). This creolization is a "jelling and blending, the emergence of something integrated and co-herent out of the mixture of elements . . . previously separate." (Foster 1999:150)

For example, in Nigeria, Muslim Hausa have zealously incorporated popular movies from Hindu India into their lives, decorating their offices, businesses, and taxis with stick-ers and posters of the films and singing Indian love songs. Larkin (2002) argues that the themes presented in these films resonate with Hausa lives in ways that other films, par-ticularly the American films that dominate the global film industry, do not. This does not mean that the Nigerian Hausa are becoming more like the Indians; it means that the

Hausa have taken something foreign, found key aspects appealing, and integrated it into their own culture. This particular example also illustrates how dominant cultural flows in some regions—notably Africa and Asia—may not be from the West but from China, India, or Japan (Inda and Rosaldo 2002).

Moreover, even if "center mostly speaks, while the periphery principally listens . . . this does not mean that the periphery does not talk back at all" (Inda and Rosaldo 2002:18). Through flows of media, tourists, and mi-grants to Western countries, the foods, music, and religions of non-Western societies are brought to the West and incorporated into Western lives, as well.

## THE PACIFIC REGION

It is difficult to generalize about any particu-lar "region" of the world. Anthropologists and other social scientists identify particu-lar regions of the world because—broadly speaking—the peoples and societies of that re-gion share aspects of a common heritage, as well as cultural patterns, that distinguish them from other regions. This is certainly true of Oceania (see Figure 1.1), whose indigenous Melanesian, Polynesian, and Micronesian is-landers are the descendants of peoples who migrated out of Southeast Asia. New Guinea was settled as early as 40,000 years ago, and then later waves of migrants began to move out into island Oceania about 6,000–7,000 years ago. The easternmost islands of Polynesia (and New Zealand) were finally settled only about 800 A.D.

Over time, the peoples who settled the Melanesian islands in the southwestern Pacific, the Polynesian islands in the eastern Pacific, and the Micronesian islands in the northern Pacific all developed cultural pat-terns and adaptations specific to those cul-tural groups (see Figure 1.2). But even within each of these broad cultural groups, there is great cultural and linguistic diversity. Island societies evolved and changed over time and then were transformed in different kinds of ways by various colonizers and missionaries. Thus, in the Pacific region, as elsewhere, a

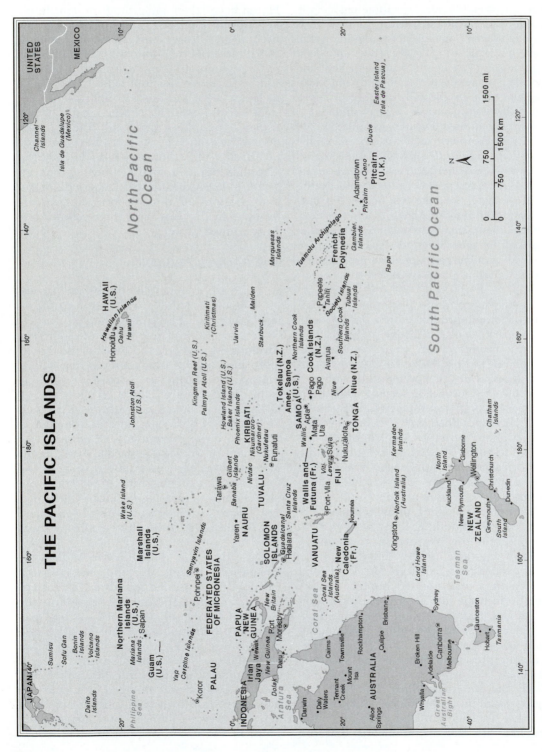

**Figure 1.1** The Pacific Islands

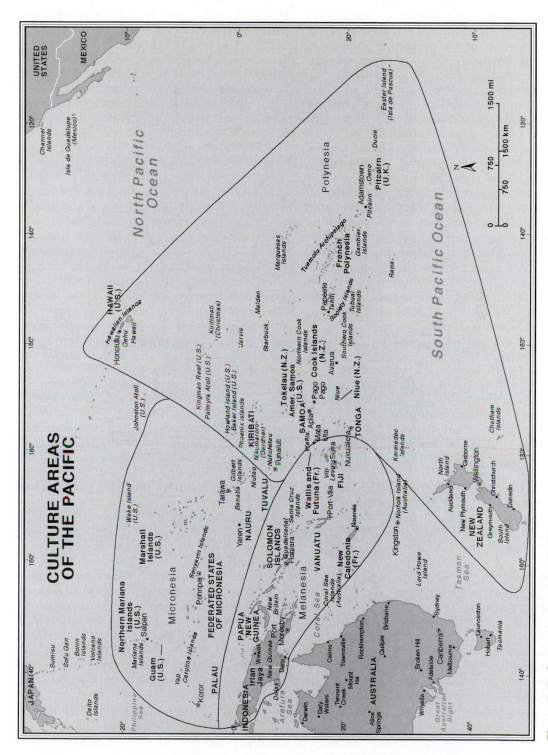

**Figure 1.2** Culture Areas of the Pacific

wide range of highly variable cultural, environmental, and historical factors shape the contemporary conditions under which individual societies participate in global interconnections and networks.

Foster has suggested that in the global era, we can gain important insights into particular regions by understanding them "not as homogeneous units, but as historically distinctive configurations of flows within a global network of flows" (1999:147; see also Lederman 1998). Thus, particular regions or subregions may be characterized by the distinctive kinds, quantities, and directions of their global flows—of finance capital, emigrant labor, tourists, consumer commodities, media, and so on. They may also differ in the ways that their populations participate in those flows, as well as in various kinds of global connections—foreign political affiliations, global religious communities, international social movements, transnational families, and so on.

To understand the distinctive "configurations" of global flows and connections in the Pacific Islands, we must first locate their historical roots in the region's particular European colonial encounter and then trace their evolution and current expression in contemporary island societies. In tracing that process, it is important to understand not only what has motivated foreign interests in the region but also what motivates islanders as they encounter globalizing forces, and how their particular cultural lenses shape the ways they choose to interact with those forces (see Borofsky, chapter 2; Borofsky 2000; Hanlon and White 2000).

## THE HISTORICAL FOUNDATIONS OF GLOBAL PROCESSES IN THE PACIFIC

The Pacific Islands comprise thousands of islands and atolls and a population of about nine million people, not counting the nonindigenous populations of Hawai'i and New Zealand. About seven million people live on the large Melanesian island of New Guinea, today divided in half between the independent nation of Papua New Guinea (PNG) and

Papua (formerly Irian Jaya, renamed in 2000, a territory of Indonesia; see the *Jakarta Post* 2002). The remaining two million Pacific Islanders live on the many smaller islands and atolls scattered across the Pacific Ocean, a vast area spanning one-third of the globe.

Polynesians inhabit the islands in the eastern Pacific within the triangle formed by Hawai'i in the north, Easter Island in the east, and New Zealand in the south; they also include Tonga, Western Samoa, American Samoa, the Cook Islands, French Polynesia (Tahiti and nearby islands), and the small islands of Tuvalu, Tokelau, Niue, and Wallis and Futuna (see Figure 1.2). Most Polynesian societies (see Feinberg and Macpherson 2002:101–179) were organized as stratified chiefdoms structured genealogically by cognatic (nonunilineal) kinship. Chiefs and their families were at the apex of the hierarchy and possessed the most *mana,* supernatural power. Chiefs interceded with the gods and spirits to bring prosperity and fertility to their communities of farmers, fishermen, and seafarers. Taro, tree crops, and fish were staple foods. On the larger volcanic islands, warfare was common as chiefs sought to expand their territories and power.

Micronesians inhabit the small islands and many atolls of the northwest Pacific, on Palau, Guam, the Northern Marianas, the Marshall Islands, the Federated States of Micronesia, Kiribati, and Nauru (Figure 1.2). In many ways, their societies were similar to those of Polynesia, although the resource-poor atolls of this subregion supported smaller-scale and less sociopolitically complex communities (see Kiste and Marshall 1999). They were also organized by kinship, but many Micronesian societies adhered to matrilineal principles of descent and property transmission. Councils of elders were often the primary political authorities in small communities. Coral soils were poor and fresh water (on atolls) was scarce so Micronesians depended heavily on sea resources. Both Micronesians and Polynesians excelled as seafarers.

The highly culturally and linguistically diverse Melanesian peoples (see Sillitoe 1998; Strathern and Stewart 2002:11–98) live on the islands of the southwest Pacific, in New Guinea, the Solomon Islands, New Caledonia, Vanuatu, and Fiji (see Figure 1.2). They had a significantly more informal sociopolitical organization and lived in villages organized around kinship (patrilineal, matrilineal, or cognatic). In these politically acephalous societies, men competed with each other through various kinds of ceremonial exchange and resource redistribution to achieve social prestige and political influence; success in warfare was also important in some areas (see Roscoe 2000). Most villagers practiced horticulture (mainly yams and other starchy crops) and raised pigs, while in coastal and lowland areas, arboriculture (sago palms) and fishing were important. Beliefs in ancestral and nature spirits animated a rich religious life that also included male cults. Many are known for their relatively extreme forms of gender stratification and beliefs in female pollution. Melanesian societies, particularly those in the interior of New Guinea, have been the least exposed to Western influences, and thus their lives are more "traditional" than other Pacific Islanders.

## COLONIALISM AND ITS LEGACY

Most island groups had already experienced a century or more of invasive and culturally destructive contact from European explorers, sailors, whalers, and missionaries before they were officially colonized in the mid-1800s (with the exception of Spain in the Marianas) (see Oliver 1989). Europeans sought the islands' sandalwood, trepang (sea cucumbers), copra, and whales and offered islanders guns, iron tools, cloth, tobacco, and alcohol in exchange. Many islands experienced high rates of Western-disease-related depopulation, as well as the depredations linked to slave raiding and increasing violence from introduced firearms and alcohol. Missionaries and other European intruders also introduced Western institutions, values, and Christianity.

"Christian missions penetrated the villages of the Pacific earlier, more deeply, and more effectively than did the colonial states" (Otto and Thomas 1997:9; see also Barker 1990). Missionaries from various denominations,

including Catholics, Methodists, Anglicans, Presbyterians, Lutherans, and others, competed with each other to establish missions and convert native populations (see Hezel 1995). Oftentimes, missionaries were the first to establish schools and provide health services for native populations, and sought to protect them from the worst forms of colonial exploitation (labor indenture, and so on) (Barker 1990:7). They also came to be important middlemen, serving as models and providing perceptual frameworks for how indigenous populations should understand their relationship with the powerful Westerners and the outside world (see Barker, chapter 25).

Christianity was adapted, remade, and blended with local worldview as islanders integrated it into their lives (see Boutilier et al. 1978; Douglas 2002). It was oftentimes practiced simultaneously with long-standing beliefs in nature, ancestral, or other kinds of supernatural beings or forces (Swain and Trompf 1995; Barker 1990, 1999a), as well as with cargo cult or millenarian ideologies (Loeliger and Trompf 1985; Trompf 1987). Across the Pacific today, Christianity plays a major role in islanders' lives. Community leaders are also church leaders, emerging national elites have strong church connections, and Christian ideology/morality has become a cornerstone of Pacific Islanders' identities (see White 1991; Smith 1994).

### European Imperialism

During the colonial era, several of the largest islands were taken over to become white settler colonies. British colonists took New Zealand from the indigenous Maori (Polynesians) (van Meijl 1997:400–402) and American planters overran Hawai'i (Laenui 1997); in both cases, the indigenous populations rapidly dwindled and became a small, marginalized minority group. New Caledonia was first used by France as a penal colony and then was gradually populated by large numbers of French settlers who put the indigenous Melanesian Kanak population on reservations. They took the island's fertile agricultural lands and began to mine its rich nickel deposits.

In addition to New Caledonia, the French took Tahiti and the surrounding island groups (French Polynesia), as well as the small islands of Wallis and Futuna (near Fiji). An attempted plantation economy on Tahiti largely failed, although large numbers of Chinese had been imported as laborers. France also agreed to govern Vanuatu in a joint colonial condominium with Britain.

Unlike Britain, which agreed to the gradual emancipation of its colonies, France has insisted on retaining its colonies and incorporating them into the French state. Today, New Caledonia, French Polynesia, and Wallis and Futuna are French overseas territories, and islanders are French citizens. French Polynesia is the site of French military bases and nuclear testing installations (although active testing ended in 1996). The only French colonial possession in the Pacific that is independent today is Vanuatu; after a nationalist struggle that was opposed by France, it finally achieved independence in 1980 (Robie 1989).

Britain took colonial control of Fiji, Tonga, the Cook Islands, Niue, Tokelau, and the northern Gilbert and Ellice Islands (today, Kiribati and Tuvalu). The Fiji islands became a major sugar producer and its European plantations imported over 60,000 laborers from India. Britain also controlled the southern Solomon Islands and the southeastern part of New Guinea. The British government handed control of its New Guinea possession to Australia in 1906, which renamed it Papua (now part of Papua New Guinea). Similarly, New Zealand administered the former British colonies of the Cook Islands, Niue, and Tokelau. Britain granted independence to Fiji and Tonga in 1970, to Tuvalu in 1978, and to Kiribati in 1979. In contrast, the New Zealand-administered islands chose to maintain a political affiliation with it; today, the Cook Islands and Niue are "self-governing in free association" with New Zealand, while Tokelau is a territory of New Zealand.

In the northern Pacific, Spain claimed the Marshall, Caroline, and Mariana Islands of Micronesia early in the 1500s, but it only exercised any real control over the larger islands of Guam and Saipan. When Spain was defeated in the Spanish-American War in 1898, the United States took Guam and Spain ceded its interests in the other Micronesian islands to Germany. The Germans had also acquired Western Samoa, the northeastern part of New Guinea, and phosphate-rich Nauru.

The western half of New Guinea was claimed by the Dutch, who also controlled the nearby Indonesian islands as the Dutch East Indies. When Indonesia became independent, it insisted on retaining control over all of the former colony (see Denoon, Mein-Smith, and Wyndham 2000:391–392), and various Western nations who might have supported the area's independence failed to do so. Today the western half of New Guinea, Papua, is a territory of Indonesia.

The United States claimed Hawai'i and American Samoa, both of which had excellent deep-water ports, while Hawai'i also boasted a flourishing plantation economy. The United States fully incorporated Hawai'i as the fiftieth state, while American Samoa remains a U.S. territory. Chile claimed Easter Island, several thousand miles directly to its west.

Germany lost its Pacific possessions after its defeat in World War I. Japan assumed control over the Micronesian islands and actively sought to develop agriculture and industries there. Germany's other possessions, Western Samoa, northeastern New Guinea, and Nauru, became League of Nations–mandated territories. Western Samoa was administered by New Zealand, and northeastern New Guinea (now a part of Papua New Guinea) and Nauru were administered by Australia. In Western Samoa an indigenous elite of half-castes (Samoan/European) became a major force agitating for independence (see Shankman, chapter 22) and it was granted in 1962. Nauru received independence in 1968 and Papua New Guinea in 1975.

With Japan's defeat in World War II, the United States assumed control over Micronesia as a United Nations Trust Territory. Many of the major Japanese-American battles had been fought in the islands of Micronesia and Melanesia and the islands had been devastated. After the war, the United States removed islanders from Bikini and Enewetak in the

Marshalls and used the atolls to test nuclear bombs. Both the war and nuclear testing have left a painful legacy (see White and Lindstrom 1989; Lindstrom and White 1991; Poyer, Falgout, and Carucci 2001). Today, the United States maintains military bases and missile ranges in Micronesia, and it holds Guam as a territory and the Northern Marianas as a commonwealth. It has also worked to keep other militarily useful and strategically located Micronesian islands (mainly Palau and the Marshall Islands, but also the Federated States of Micronesia) in political "association" with it even though these island groups are now technically "independent."

Despite the number of Pacific island societies that have recently been granted independence, one is struck by the significant number still firmly attached in neocolonial relationships (see Figure 1.3). Otto and Thomas conclude that it is difficult to talk about the "colonial aftermath" in the Pacific (1997:4). Perhaps more than any other factor, the islands' geostrategic location—and their use by powerful Western nations seeking a global military/strategic presence (and security)—has been central to determining their political statuses.

## THE GLOBAL ERA: PACIFIC ISLANDS AND ACCELERATED GLOBAL FLOWS

In broad terms, three key factors play an important role in shaping the options islanders have available to them in an increasingly globalized world. The first is *the political status of particular island societies* (see Figure 1.3), whether they are independent or still attached to a foreign nation, and the nature of their political relationships with that nation as well as with the other Western and Pacific Rim nations (see Nero 1997a, 1997b; Bertram 1999a). These political relationships establish the conditions for significant capital flows to islands in the form of foreign aid, development subsidies, and commercial investments. They also provide opportunities for islanders' transnational migration and shape the degree to which Pacific nations exercise political sovereignty in the global community.

The second major factor is *whether islands have natural or other exploitable resources* of interest in either regional markets or the global economy. For the most part, the "terrestrially challenged" (see Adams, Dalzell, and Ledua 1999) islands and atolls of Polynesia and Micronesia are resource poor and have fragile environments that are vulnerable to extreme weather conditions (typhoons, hurricanes, rising sea levels caused by global warming, and so on) (Rapaport 1999). They are also distant from major markets and produce only small quantities of mostly agricultural exports (coconut products, fruits, and so on). For these many reasons, their development potential is limited. But on a more positive note, they can claim several economic assets: a natural tropical beauty (and "paradise" image) that appeals to tourists, and control over the marine resources in the 200-mile exclusive economic zones surrounding their islands (see Figure 1.4). And of course, a number of these islands also have their geostrategic utility to Western nations to use as a political and economic bargaining chip.

In contrast, several of the larger Melanesian islands have important natural resources that attract foreign investment and development capital. New Guinea has minerals (gold, copper, nickel) and timber, as well as petroleum and natural gas. The Solomon Islands and Fiji have timber and may also have mineral deposits. New Caledonia has nickel and may also have other minerals.

And the third major factor shaping islanders' participation in global flows and connections is *their drive to shape their own cultural identities and political destinies*. Villagers in Papua New Guinea, for example, have agreed to multinational consortiums building mines in their areas, but they have demanded that compensation and environmental reparation be on their terms. When France resumed nuclear testing in French Polynesia in 1995, Tahitians rioted and protested, not only bringing international censure on France but also causing it to terminate the tests. And in many Pacific nations, where Westernizing influences have become more pervasive every day, indigenous cultural

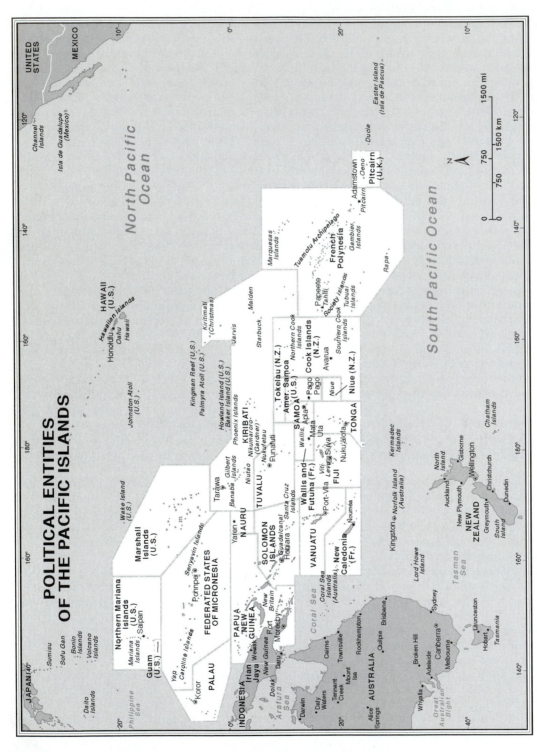

**Figure 1.3**  Political Entities of the Pacific Islands

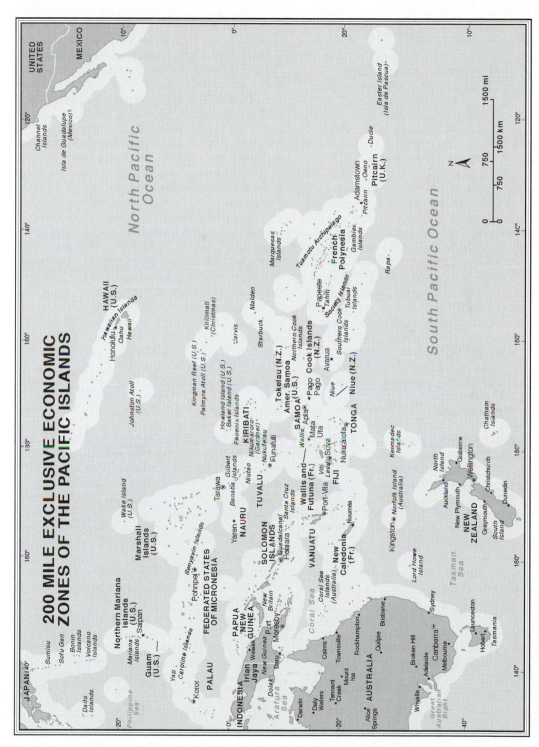

**Figure 1.4** 200-mile Exclusive Economic Zones of the Pacific Islands

revitalization movements are thriving—statements that islanders will shape their own cultural identities.

## GLOBAL POLITICAL AFFILIATIONS, FOREIGN INFLUENCE, AND AID

In many of the cases of islands politically attached to foreign nations—the American territories and "associates" in Micronesia, France's territories (French Polynesia, New Caledonia, Wallis and Futuna), and New Zealand's affiliates (the Cook Islands, Niue, and Tokelau)—islanders have generally agreed, sometimes through plebiscites and sometimes not, to maintain these foreign political affiliations. In the cases of France and the United States, islanders "rent" their islands to these foreign powers for military/strategic uses in exchange for substantial amounts of financial aid and subsidies. In the case of New Zealand, its financial largesse for its tiny island affiliates appears to be predominantly paternalistic, although it does benefit from the labor these islands export. In contrast to the politically affiliated islands, independent island nations receive significantly less foreign assistance and have lower standards of living and social welfare.

Aid from these nations not only sustains island governments and public/social services (education, health care, and so on) but also provides government employment (often the major employer on these islands) and a relatively high standard of living. In virtually all of these island societies, the value of Western imports far exceeds local exports; affiliated islands are dependent on aid to make up the difference, although remittances from transnational relatives living abroad may also be an important supplement.

Some scholars have argued that the end of the Cold War would reduce the strategic value of Pacific Islands as "buffers" between East and West and as military outposts of Western nations, and that "aid fatigue" would set in (see Connell, chapter 15). But in this new age of global terrorism, "rogue" states, and political uncertainty, this does not appear to be the case. Moreover, the United States

perceives the Pacific Islands to be important to its commercial interests in Asia. A recent report to Congress stated: "The more the United States gets connected to the larger Pacific Rim countries via trade and investment, the more important it becomes to keep the Pacific Ocean economies prosperous and secure" (U.S. House of Representatives 2002). Nevertheless, total amounts of U.S. aid to some island groups, particularly the less militarily important, will undoubtedly slowly decline in the coming years.

In Micronesia, the people of the Northern Marianas (a U.S. commonwealth) and Guam (a U.S. territory with a major American military base) are American citizens. The U.S. "associated" states of Palau, the Federated States of Micronesia (Yap, Chuuk, Pohnpei, and Kosrae), and the Marshall Islands maintain their own citizenship yet have free access to the United States. "They are self-governing and control their foreign affairs (unless contrary to U.S. defence interests), but the association can only be terminated bilaterally" (Nero 1997a:363).

Between 1986 and 2001, the Federated States of Micronesia received about $1.3 billion from the United States as part of its Compact of Free Association, or $639/year/capita (see Tables 1.1 to 1.3). Palau (population about 19,100), which is used for American military facilities, received $155.8 million in 1995, or $8,160 per capita; its gross domestic product, in contrast, is only about $129 million a year. The Marshall Islands receive about $65 million per year, or $918 per capita; its Kwajalein Missile Testing Range has become increasingly important to the United States as it places greater emphasis on missile defense systems (Pacific Islands Report 1998).

Both the Federated States of Micronesia and the Marshall Islands are presently renegotiating their compacts that expired in 2001. Future U.S. funding in the Marshall Islands, for example, will probably stabilize at about $33–35 million annually but decline slowly over the next twenty years. Funding for the Federated States of Micronesia (FSM) will start at $76 million annually and decline

**Table 1.1** Overview of Melanesian Societies[a]

| Society | Political Status | Capital | Population Size | Pop. Growth Rate | Urban Pop. | Global Economy | GDP[b] | GDP/ Capita[b] | Annual Foreign Aid (Major Donors) | Foreign Aid/ Capita | Major Ethnic Groups |
|---|---|---|---|---|---|---|---|---|---|---|---|
| *Papua New Guinea* | Independent, 1975, from Australia | Port Moresby | 4,790,800 | 2.3% | 15% | Minerals; gas; timber; coffee; palm oil | $12.2 billion | $2,500 | $400 million (1999) (Australia) | $80 | Melanesian |
| *Papua (Irian Jaya)[c]* | Territory of Indonesia | N/A | 2,111,500 | 2.8% | 25% | Minerals; gas; oil; timber; nutmeg; coffee | $2.1 billion | $1,074 | ? (Indonesia) | ? | Melanesian; Indonesian |
| *Solomon Islands* | Independent 1978, from Britain | Honiara | 447,900 | 3.4% | 13% | Timber; fish; palm oil; cocoa; copra | $900 million | $2,000 | $47 million (1999) (Australia, Japan, N.Z., China) | $98 | Melanesian |
| *Vanuatu* | Independent 1980, from Britain/France | Port-Vila | 199,800 | 3.0% | 21% | Copra; beef; cocoa; tourism; offshore financial services | $245 million | $1,300 | $45.8 million (1995) (Australia, U.K, France, N.Z.) | $254 | Melanesian |
| *New Caledonia* | Territory of France | Noumea | 212,700 | 1.8% | 71% | Nickel; tourism; fish | $3 billion | $15,000 | $880 million (France) | $4,296 | Melanesian 43% European 37% Polynesian 12% |
| *Fiji* | Independent 1970, from Britain | Suva | 824,700 | 1.6% | 46% | Sugar; tourism; garments; gold; timber; fish | $6 billion | $7,300 | $40.3 million (1995) (Australia; New Zealand) | $48 | Fijian 51% Indo-Fijian 44% |

[a]Information on population size, population growth rate, and urban population from the South Pacific Commission. http: www.spc.org.nc/demog/pop_data2000.html Other information compiled from the CIA World FactBook, *Country Profiles* (http://www.cia.gov/cia/publications/factbook/geos).

[b]Calculated as purchasing power parity.

[c]Information on Papua (Irian Jaya) from *The Jakarta Post* ("Irian Jaya: Facts and Figures"): http://www.the jakartapost.com/special/os_8_facts.asp. (accessed April 28, 2002).

**Table 1.2** Overview of Polynesian Societies[a]

| Society | Political Status | Capital | Population Size | Pop. Growth Rate | Urban Pop. | Global Economy | GDP[b] | GDP/ Capita[b] | Annual Foreign Aid (Major Donors) | Foreign Aid/ Capita | Major Ethnic Groups |
|---------|-----------------|---------|-----------------|------------------|------------|----------------|--------|----------------|-----------------------------------|---------------------|---------------------|
| French Polynesia | Territory of France | Papeete | 233,000 | 1.6% | 53% | Tourism; pearls; coconut products; vanilla | $2.6 billion | $10,800 | $367 million (France) | $1,448 | Tahitian 78% Chinese 12% European 10% |
| American Samoa | Territory of the U.S. | Pago Pago | 64,100 | 2.9% | 48% | Tuna fishing and processing | $500 million | $8,000 | $40 million (1994) (U.S.) | $689 | Samoan 89% Other 11% |
| Samoa (Western) | Independent 1962, from New Zealand | Apia | 169,200 | 0.6% | 21% | Coconut products; fish; remittances; tourism | $571 million | $3,200 | $42.9 million (1995) (New Zealand) | $268 | Samoan 93% Other 7% |
| Tonga | Independent 1970, from Britian | Nuku'olofa | 100,200 | 0.6% | 32% | Agricultural products; tourism; remittances; fish | $225 million | $2,200 | $38.8 million (1995) (U.K., Australia) | $372 | Tongans |
| Cook Islands | Self-Governing in Free Assoc. w/New Zealand | Avarua | 18,700 | −0.5% | 59% | Copra; fruits; fish; tourism; remittances; garments | $100 million | $5,000 | $13.1 million (1995) (New Zealand) | $636 | Cook Isl. 81% Others 19% |
| Tuvalu | Independent 1978, from Britain | Funafuti | 9,900 | 0.9% | 42% | Leased internet name; stamps; remittances; fishing licenses | $11.6 million | $1,100 | $13 million (1999) (Australia, Japan) | $1,183 | Tuvalans |
| Tokelau | Territory of New Zealand | None | 1,500 | 0.0% | N/A | Copra; handicrafts; stamps; remittances | $1.5 million | $1,000 | $3.8 million (1985) (New Zealand) | $2,629 | Tokelauans |
| Niue | Self-Governing/ in Assoc. w/NZ | Alofi | 1,900 | −3.1% | 35% | Stamps; remittances; coconut products | $4.5 million | $2,800 | $8.3 million (1995) (New Zealand) | $3,908 | Niueans |
| Wallis and Futuna | Territory of France | Mata-Utu | 14,600 | 0.7% | 0% | Copra; fishing licenses; remittances | $30 million | $2,000 | Assistance from France | ? | Wallisean and Futunan |

[a]Information on population size, population growth rate, and urban population from the South Pacific Commission. http: www.spc.org.nc/demog/pop_data2000.html Other information compiled from the CIA World Fact Book, *Country Profiles* (http://www.cia.gov/cia/publications/factbook/geos).
[b]Calculated as purchasing power parity.

**Table 1.3** Overview of Micronesian Societies[a]

| Society | Political Status | Capital | Population Size | Pop. Growth Rate | Urban Pop. | Global Economy | GDP[b] | GDP/Capita[b] | Annual Foreign Aid (Major Donors) | Foreign Aid/Capita | Major Ethnic Groups |
|---|---|---|---|---|---|---|---|---|---|---|---|
| *Palau (Belau)* | Independent in Assoc. w/U.S. | Koror | 19,100 | 2.2% | 71% | Tourism; fish; copra | $129 million | $7,100 | $155.8 million (1995) (United States) | $8,160 | Palauan 70% Asian 28% |
| *Guam* | Territory of the U.S. | Hagatna | 148,200 | 1.0% | 38% | U.S. military; tourism; fish; handicrafts | $3.2 billion | $21,000 | $143 million (1997) (United States) | $907 | Chamorro 47% Filipino/ Asian 43% Amer./Europ. 10% |
| *Federated States of Micronesia* | Independent in Assoc. w/U.S. | Palikir | 118,100 | 1.9% | 27% | Fish; garments; bananas; black pepper | $263 million | $2,000 | Approx. $86 million (United States) | $639 | Micronesian |
| *Northern Marianas* | Commonwealth of the U.S. | Saipan | 76,700 | 5.5% | 90% | Tourism; garments | $900 million | $12,500 | ? (United States) | ? | Chamorro Micronesians Asians |
| *Marshall Islands* | Independent in Assoc. w/U.S. | Majuro | 51,800 | 2.0% | 65% | Fish; coconut products | $105 million | $1,670 | $65 million (United States) | $918 | Micronesian |
| *Kiribati* | Independent 1979 from Britain | Tarawa | 90,700 | 2.5% | 37% | Copra; fish; fishing licenses; remittances | $76 million | $850 | $15.5 million (1995) (U.K., Japan, Australia, N.Z.) | $182 | Micronesian |
| *Nauru* | Independent 1968 from Britain | Yaren District | 11,500 | 1.8% | 100% | Phosphates; off-shore banking | $59 million | $5,000 | $2.25 million (1996) (Australia) | $186 | Nauruan 58% Pac. Islanders 26% Chinese & Eur. |

[a]Information on population size, population growth rate, and urban population from the South Pacific Commission. http:www.spc.org.nc/demog/pop_data2000.html Other information compiled from the CIA World Fact Book, *Country Profiles* (http://www.cia.gov/cia/publications/factbook/geos).
[b]Calculated as purchasing power parity.

slowly (Pacific Islands Report 2002a, 2002b). These island groups also will receive about $35 million per annum in various federal services, and will benefit from monies placed in a trust fund each year by the United States for the islands' future support ($16 million for the FSM and $7 million for the Marshall Islands). (Tables 1.1, 1.2, and 1.3 summarize the major socioeconomic attributes of Pacific island societies, including aid received and major donors.)

The pattern is similar in the French territories, with France's financial benevolence increasing as local populations periodically build opposition to its presence and, in the case of French Polynesia, its nuclear testing activities. French Polynesia receives about $367 million per year from France ($1,448 per capita) in exchange for renting its islands for French military bases and nuclear testing installations (see Lockwood 1993a). Aid to New Caledonia is about $880 million a year, or $4,296 per capita. During the 1980s, the indigenous peoples of New Caledonia, the long-marginalized *Kanaks* (about half the total population), sought independence from France, and extended violence between them and the French settlers broke out. In 1988, French troops were brought in to control the militants. France subsequently agreed to divide the territory into three provinces, two of which would ultimately elect Kanak governments (Nero 1997a:363).

The tiny islands of Niue (population about 2,100) and Tokelau (population about 1,400) annually receive about $3,908 and $2,629 per capita, respectively, from New Zealand. In these cases, the islands' major economic activity, after receiving aid from New Zealand and remittances from transnationals abroad, is selling postage stamps and a few coconut or other agricultural products. In 2001, Niue's exports were valued at $117,500, while its imports were valued at $4.1 million (see CIA World Factbook 2001). The aid dependency of these small islands is staggering.

Many of the small Polynesian and Micronesian "microstate" economies appear to fit the MIRAB model (Migration, Remittances, Aid, and Bureaucracy) articulated by Bertram

and Watters (1985; see also Bertram 1986, 1999b). These islands have high rates of *out-migration, remittance* and *foreign aid* dependency, and well-developed government *bureaucracies* and public sectors financed by that foreign aid. But Nero (1997b:442) argues that remittances should not be understood as charity to home communities because it is the real labor of family members that produces them. She goes on to say that to "label this as dependency is belittling." Indeed, host countries are themselves often dependent on the availability of inexpensive imported labor. And Poirine (1998:65) contends that such island nations are simply making use of the only comparative advantages they have, their labor (which they export) and their global "geostrategic services." The key questions concerning MIRAB economies are whether they are economically sustainable—will migrants continue to remit and will foreign donors continue to pay?—and whether such a model can contribute to island economic development.

But the independent Pacific nations also receive significant amounts of aid (and investment) from powerful Pacific Rim nations like Australia, New Zealand, Japan, China, Taiwan, and South Korea. Australia and New Zealand dominate the southern Pacific politically and are the major aid donors and trading partners for most islands (with the exception of the French-held islands); Australia is particularly enmeshed in the internal affairs of PNG and some of the other Melanesian islands. Not surprisingly, Australian-based multinational consortiums are often involved in exploiting the mineral and timber resources of these island nations.

Both Japan and China have sought to gain economic and political prominence in the region by generously bestowing aid, building public works, and providing disaster relief for struggling island nations. The Japanese have long dominated highly lucrative commercial fishing in the region and have also invested heavily in developing tourism in Micronesia and the thriving black pearl industry in French Polynesia (Rapaport 1995). And although the aid supplied by China is small compared to that of Australia, New Zealand,

and Japan, it has nevertheless sought, according to one recent analysis, to "become the heavyweight of the Asia-Pacific" and to sideline Taiwanese interests in the region. Its growing list of accomplishments in the region include building government offices in Samoa and the parliament in Vanuatu, and planning to build the foreign ministry building in Port Moresby (PNG) and a stadium in Suva (Fiji) for the 2003 South Pacific Games (Time International 2001b).

## ISLAND ECONOMIES, GLOBAL CAPITAL, AND GLOBAL COMMODITIES

The larger Pacific Island nations have sought to develop the natural resources they possess and, in the cases of the smaller, resource-poor islands, to find specialized niches in the global economy that they might profitably exploit. Most often, however, the capital and technology required for development—of mines, timber resources, commercial fishing, tourist resorts, garment factories, and so on—come from outside the region in the form of foreign investments and foreign-owned enterprises. In most cases, only a small percentage of the value of local resources is retained by Pacific Island nations.

While the larger Melanesian islands export minerals, timber, and some fish, most of the islands export only small quantities of coconut products, handicrafts, fruits, fish, and stamps. Papua New Guinea exports some coffee, Vanuatu exports beef and cocoa, Fiji exports sugar, and French Polynesia exports black pearls. Island nations' trading partners are predominantly their former (or current) colonial administrators, and very little trade takes place regionally between island nations.

At the same time, the islands are a growing market for the manufactured and consumer items produced by Western nations and Pacific rim countries. With their relatively high incomes provided by foreign aid and remittances (mainly in Micronesia and Polynesia), islanders have become dependent on imported foods and consumer items. On the remote outer islands of French Polynesia where islanders mix some wage employment

with farming and fishing, they are able to purchase an impressive range of imports: Pampers diapers, French wines, New Zealand canned butter, tortilla chips and salsa, and many others; they also drive Toyota trucks and watch Sony television sets (Lockwood 1993b, 2002). But even in the less-affluent highlands of Papua New Guinea, marketing agents employed by Australian firms travel to reach remote villages to introduce villagers to Coca-Cola, Colgate toothpaste, and imported rice (Aspire Films 1996). And as in other parts of the developing world, aggressive marketing by transnational corporations has succeeded in making alcohol and tobacco products the region's major imports and contributed to major social and health problems (see Marshall, chapter 12). The adoption of imported Western foods—many of which are high in fats and processed sugars—has contributed to rapidly growing rates of heart disease and diabetes among islanders (see Leslie, chapter 23).

### Extraction of Natural Resources: Mining and Logging

With globalization has come an intensified extraction of natural resources, particularly minerals and timber, by transnational corporations (often consortiums) usually based in Australia, the United Kingdom, Canada, or the United States. In Papua New Guinea and the Solomons, mining and logging revenues have significantly bolstered national export earnings and GDPs, and corporations are often willing to provide services to impacted communities that have never seen such amenities. "Islanders desire for roads, electricity and education contributes to their tolerance of forestry and mining projects" that often severely disrupt communities (Nero 1997a:373).

The island of New Guinea is rich in gold, silver, and copper (and natural gas and oil), producing between 2 and 3 percent of the world's gold and copper in 1994 (see Banks and McShane 1999:382). Its "world class" mines include the Panguna Copper Mine in Bougainville (now closed), the Ok Tedi Mine (copper, gold, silver), and the Porgera Mine (gold). Minerals provide about 72 percent of the nation of Papua New Guinea's export earnings and it is also now pushing for development of a Papua New Guinea-Australia oil pipeline (CIA World Factbook 2002). Fiji and New Zealand also have minor gold deposits. New Caledonia and Nauru have been major world producers of nickel and phosphate, respectively, for decades. Although Nauru boasts a high standard of living because of its phosphate earnings, it has experienced losses from poor international investments and suffers from extensive environmental damage. In the early 1990s, Nauru islanders took their demands for compensation to international courts and received a settlement from Australia.

The anticipated mineral, gas, and oil riches of Papua, a territory of Indonesia, have caused the Indonesian government to violently suppress a Melanesian separatist/independence movement that formed in the early years of Indonesian rule and has attracted increasing popular support since the downfall of the Suharto regime. To calm the situation, Indonesia has offered the territory a greater share of the revenue from its natural resources and has pledged "to allow wider scope for expression of Papua's culture" (Mapes 2002). Indonesia is currently in the planning stages of "a $2 billion plan by British [Petroleum] energy company BP PLC to develop a huge natural-gas project in the territory" (Mapes 2002). The large American transnational corporations ExxonMobil and Freeport McMoRan Copper and Gold already operate in Papua, guarded by Indonesian soldiers who often clash with local residents (Mapes 2002).

The environmental damage caused by the large open-pit mines such as Panguna (Bougainville), Porgera, and Ok Tedi in Papua New Guinea has been extensive. The mines produce hundreds of thousands of tons of waste from processed ore (tailings), which is disposed of on land or in the rivers (Banks and McShane 1999:389; Macintyre and Foale, chapter 9). Waste dumping has left the Ok Tedi river biologically dead, and

the Fly River has also been adversely affected. In 1996, a six-billion-dollar class action suit was brought in a New Orleans court on behalf of the area's Amungme people against Freeport (Ok Tedi Mine, Papua, Indonesia). The suit demanded compensation for environmental and cultural destruction (Denoon 1997:388).

Thus, these riches have proven to be an extremely mixed blessing (Banks and McShane 1999). In almost all cases, major disputes between local populations and mining corporations have erupted over land and mineral ownership claims and over environmental damage and compensation claims. Grievances against the Panguna Gold and Copper Mine were a critical element in the development of Bougainville's ethnonationalist secessionist movement from Papua New Guinea (Regan 1998) (see below). The nickel mines of New Caledonia have also been the site of anti-French resistance movements of the indigenous *Kanaks*.

The exploitation of forest resources by logging companies from Japan, Malaysia, Singapore, and China is another important source of export revenues in the Solomon Islands, Papua New Guinea, and Vanuatu. In the Solomons, logging generates 50 percent of all export revenue and 31 percent of all government revenue (Clarke et al. 1999:361), but timber is being harvested at unsustainable rates and this is degrading island environments (Macintyre and Foale, chapter 9). In their efforts to participate more fully in commercial agriculture and export, islanders themselves have deforested extensive areas, and overused chemical fertilizers and insecticides, and contributed to environmental degradation and pollution (Clarke et al. 1999).

Macintyre and Foale (chapter 9) have examined Melanesian views on environmental conservation in the contexts of the Lihir (New Ireland, PNG) gold mine and of logging in the western provinces of the Solomon Islands. They conclude that although villagers understand environmental issues, they prefer immediate economic gains to long-term environmental conservation. In contrast, Barker (chapter 25) discusses how

Maisin (PNG) villagers—with the support of missionaries, NGOs, and environmentalists—have protested logging in their area. "They want to be part of the global Christian community; they feel pride at being one of the "tribal" peoples who have the wisdom to save the rain forest." But like the people of Lihir, they expect an economic pay-off from their work with the environmentalists and NGOs.

## Marine Resources

Fish and other sea resources have been an important component of islanders' diets and subsistence economies for many centuries. Islanders fish mainly for local consumption, while commercial/industrial fishing fleets, mostly purse-seiners from the United States, Japan, Taiwan, and Korea, are exploiting the regions' fish resources. Only the Solomon Islands and Fiji have been able to develop their own fledgling commercial fishing industries, and Pacific Island fishing vessels take only about 7 percent of the total catch in the region (Adams, Dalzell, and Ledua 1999).

The western Pacific yields about 1,000,000 tons of tuna per year, valued at $1.6 billion. Even so, the Pacific Ocean remains a largely untapped resource; its fisheries provide only about 2 percent of total world production, and half of that is pelagic tuna. Much of the Pacific tuna is processed in the canneries of American Samoa and the Solomon Islands (a highly successful joint venture of the Solomon Islands and the Japanese Taiyo Fishery Company: Nero 1997a:379).

Many Pacific Islands license rights to fish in their waters to foreign fleets, receiving only about 5 percent of the catch value (Nero 1997a:378). Nevertheless, this can constitute a major source of island revenue, particularly in the Solomons, Fiji, and Palau. The U.N. Convention on the Law of the Sea states that nations control the exclusive economic zone (EEZ) within 200 miles of their coastlines (Figure 1.4). Pacific Island nations played a major role in developing the EEZ concept in the United Nations, and Fiji was the first to ratify the convention in 1982. And Pacific Island nations have joined together to create the regional Forum Fisheries Agency to oversee ocean resource exploitation and to protect their interests against foreign fishing nations (see Adams, Dalzell, and Ledua 1999).

## Tourism

As noted above, the tropical beauty of many Pacific Islands and their enduring place in the Western imagination as "paradises" (see Borofsky, chapter 2) has generated great potential for regional tourism development (see Hall and Page 1996). The region receives about 10,000,000 visitors a year, more than half of whom visit Hawai'i. The other major tourist "honey pots" are New Zealand, Guam, Saipan, Fiji, and Tahiti (Fagence 1999). Guam and Saipan attract large numbers of visitors from Japan, Taiwan, and other parts of East Asia. Pacific tourism has grown, and the region is expected to outperform other regions in the next decade (Fagence 1999:396).

In the "honey pots," much of the capital investment in tourist facilities is made by large, transnational corporations such as Hyatt, Radisson, Club Med, and others. Only in the smaller islands, like the Cook Islands, is there a stronger presence of small hotels operated by local enterprises and families. Even though many of the larger tourist operations are foreign-owned, they nevertheless generate employment for islanders and contribute to island nations' GDP. In the smaller island economies, like Vanuatu and Samoa, tourism contributes 16 percent of GDP and 37 percent in the Cook Islands. Many of these small islands are focusing on developing locally owned, specialized niche tourism such as ecotourism, adventure tourism (such as the diving tours of Palau), or cultural tourism (such as the Sepik River cruises described by Silverman in chapter 20).

Although tourism may be one of the few development options available to resource-poor island nations, it presents a number of potential challenges that these nations must confront. In many cases, foreign corporate owners repatriate profits and tourism contributes little to island economic development. It is also a capital-intensive and fickle industry, one that is highly susceptible to events taking place outside of the region (Fagence 1999:395). Tourist visits from Japan and elsewhere in Asia, for example, dropped dramatically during the East Asia economic crisis in the 1990s, and most international travel declined sharply after the September 11 terrorist attacks. Tourism also contributes to environmental damage and pollution and increasing incidences of crime, prostitution, and drug abuse (see Fagence 1999).

In addition, tourism promotes the "commercialization of culture," where island cultures become commoditized, degraded, and "sold" to tourists as entertainment. But Silverman (chapter 20) argues that tourism can have positive, creative impacts on local cultures, as well. He describes the interactions of Papua New Guinea villagers with the Europeans who cruise the Sepik River hoping to make contact with the primitive "Other" and buy their "primitive" art. In this case, the tourist presence has encouraged the creative development of new art forms. Whether ultimately positive or negative, tourists from vastly different cultures set in motion major changes in host societies.

## Small Islands' Global Economic Strategies

Many of the resource-poor small Pacific Islands are creatively maximizing their available options to generate income. Tuvalu leased its Internet domain name, "tv," to a Canadian company for $50 million dollars over the next decade (BBC News 2000); this is a significant amount of money for a country of about 11,000 people with a GDP of only about $12 million per year. Others have earned sizable revenues from the sale of national postage stamps, and many sell local agricultural (mainly coconut) products or handicrafts. Tonga—which has no satellites—decided to lease its international allocation of satellite parking slots in earth's orbit to acquire income (Marcus 1993). Vanuatu, the Cook Islands, Nauru, and Niue (and others) have licensed off-shore banking and financial operations in their islands (see Mitchell, chapter 21). Niue was to collect $1.6 million in off-shore licensing fees in 2001 (again, a large amount for a small island). But U.S. banks stopped payments from international businesses when Niue was blacklisted for failing to curtail money laundering (East-West Center 2001). Other Pacific nations have been blacklisted as well.

And still others, including Fiji, the U.S. Commonwealth of the Northern Marianas Islands (CNMI), and the Cook Islands, have become major sites for foreign-owned garment factories, relocated to the islands to benefit from cheap labor. In Saipan (CNMI), garment factories owned by Chinese, Hong Kong, and South Korean companies produce clothing for U.S. retailers, including the Gap, Sears, and Nordstrom. They employ about 12,000 imported Chinese laborers who sew "Made in the U.S.A." tags into their garments. Seventeen major U.S. clothing retailers recently settled a class action suit by garment workers claiming sweatshop conditions (Global Exchange 2000).

And in some cases, islands have benefited from special trade concessions for their particular export products granted by their former or current colonial administrators, allowing them to be more competitive. The Lome Convention gave Pacific Islands' agricultural exports preferential access to the European (EU) market, a relationship that "sustained an entire social system of small-farm sugar production by mostly Indo-Fijian tenant farmers" (Firth 2000:187). Both the garments produced in the Northern Marianas and the tuna canned in American Samoa enter the U.S. exempt from duty and quota restrictions. And the Cook Islands have preferentially supplied fruits and vegetables to New Zealand. But as such trade concessions increasingly conflict with World Trade Organization rules about "free trade," many have been reduced or eliminated. Nero notes that the loss of the Cook Islands' New Zealand niche has contributed to its recent agreement to allow off-shore banking, and for increasing waves of out-migration (1997a:370).

## POPULATION MOBILITY AND TRANSNATIONALISM

Like most developing regions of the world, the Pacific Islands have experienced two major types of population movement in the last several decades, extensive rural to urban migration (and rapid urban growth) and, in the cases of some islands in Polynesia and Micronesia, high rates of international emigration and transnationalism.

### Rural to Urban Migration and Rapid Urbanization

Most of the region's few major towns and cities started out as colonial port towns and trading centers. Today they are centers of "global modernity" (Doumenge 1999:324) and global "connections"—local and transnational commerce, tourism, and media/telecommunications—and local government administration. Rural and outer-islanders flock to them seeking jobs and the critical government services (health, educational, and social services) that are often concentrated there. Rates of urbanization across the region are noted in Tables 1.1, 1.2, and 1.3 (pages 17–19).

The region's few urban centers have grown at astounding rates, creating population densities in some of the atoll states as high as those of major Asian cities (Connell 1999). In many Micronesian nations, towns typically contain more than half of the island population (for example, Majuro, Saipan, Koror) (see Doumenge 1999:318). The town of Ebeye in the Marshall Islands, for example, has a population of about 8,000 people who live at a density of 60,000 people per square mile (Connell 1999:330). Outside of New Zealand and Hawai'i, the largest city in the region is Port Moresby, whose current population of 250,000 has quadrupled since 1970. But few cities have an infrastructure that can provide water, sanitation, and consumer waste disposal for their rapidly growing populations (Connell 1999; Doumenge 1999). In some cases (Micronesia), sewage is dumped in lagoons, contributing to outbreaks of cholera.

Most regional towns also suffer from high rates of unemployment and urban poverty (Bryant 1993; Doumenge 1999). In Port Moresby, for example, one-third of the working population is unemployed. Mitchell (chapter 21) describes how the large numbers of impoverished and unemployed young people in Port Vila, Vanuatu, "kill time" by idly wandering the streets and "eye-shopping" in the windows of expensive boutiques that cater to cruise ship tourists and the highly paid staffs of the off-shore banking firms located there.

### Transnationalism

Pacific Islanders seeking jobs, educational opportunities, and a higher standard of living have also left for New Zealand, Australia, the United States, France, and Canada. Citing recent census data, Lee (chapter 8) notes that there are now approximately 365,000 Pacific Islanders living in the United States, 202,000 in New Zealand, and 164,000 in Australia. In the cases of Tonga and Samoa, there are now as many Tongans and Samoans living in foreign countries as there are living on their home islands. Other islands with high out-migration rates include the Polynesian Cook Islands, Niue, and Tokelau, and the Micronesian islands of Guam and the Federated States of Micronesia. In the cases of Niue and Tokelau, the overseas population is almost two to three times the size of the remaining home population; there are, for example, about 52,500 Cook Islanders living in New Zealand alone, while the home population is about 19,000 (Government of New Zealand 2001). For the most part, Melanesian societies, which are more rural, less urbanized, and have stronger agricultural economies, have little emigration.

Specific international migration patterns are determined mainly by on-going relationships between island nations and their former colonial administrators (Lee, chapter 8). Guamanians and American Samoans have open access to the United States, as do the citizens of the Northern Marianas and of the

U.S. "associated" states (Federated States of Micronesia, Marshall Islands, and Palau). Today the overseas Palauan population, for example, is estimated at 7,000, while the home population has stabilized at 13,000 (Nero, Murray, and Burton, chapter 14). Many Micronesians use their connection to the United States to move to Guam, Saipan, or Hawai'i. Similarly, western Samoans have access to New Zealand, and the Cook Islanders', Niueans', and Tokelauans' connections to New Zealand also open it to islanders' transnational migration.

In contrast to the general regional pattern of out-migration, certain areas of Micronesia, notably Palau and the U.S. Commonwealth of the Northern Marianas, have been the recent recipients of influxes of foreign labor, mostly from East Asia (Nero 1997a). In these cases, large sums of money from the United States have fueled local economic growth and a demand for skilled and domestic workers. Both Guam and Saipan have large foreign (and American) populations, and islanders are minorities in their own land. In Palau today, 24 percent of the population is composed of foreign workers (mainly Filipinos) and they make up 37 percent of the workforce. While foreign workers have contributed to island development, many islanders feel that their presence is having a problematic impact on the Palauan way of life (see Nero, Murray, and Burton, chapter 14).

Papua (territory of Indonesia) is another exception to the major pattern of regional out-migration. In its efforts to secure the rebellious Papua as a part of Indonesia, the Indonesian government has resettled large numbers of families from the more densely settled Indonesian islands to Papua (see the *Jakarta Post* 2002). These settlers often displace indigenous communities and generate conflict (Denoon 1997:386).

The impacts of Pacific Islander migration and transnationalism on both the sending and receiving communities, as well as on island cultures, have been extensive (see Connell 1987a, 1987b, 1990; Spoonley 1990; Ahlburg 1991; James 1991; McCall and Connell 1993; Shankman 1993; Connell and

Brown 1995; Bedford 1997; Brown 1998). Researchers have looked at the consequences of population loss on home islands, the oftentimes problematic experiences of islanders living abroad, including racism and discrimination, and the role remittances may (or may not) play in island economies. Islanders' migration motives, strategies, and decision-making processes (see Macpherson, chapter 10) and, in some cases, maintenance of what some scholars have called transnational "kin corporations" have also been described (Marcus 1993).

Transnationalism (Basch et al. 1994; Kearney 1995) among Pacific Islanders, notably Tongans and Samoans, oftentimes differs from the transnationalism of other migrants around the world in several key ways. First, the extensive and tightly held kin relationships of Pacific Islanders appear to foster tenacious and long-enduring transnational kin networks and ties to home to an extent not found among other transnational groups (see Lee, chapter 8). And second, these ties also appear to foster an enduring pattern of significant remittances not found elsewhere; 60 percent of the GDP of Tonga, for example, is generated by remittances.

As a result of transnationalism and remittances, islanders become enmeshed in extensive kinds of international exchanges. Tongan women, for example, work long, hard hours to produce traditional craft and textile items, and other items of traditional wealth (*koloa*), to send to relatives overseas (see Leslie, chapter 23; James 1997). Indeed, Leslie argues that they sacrifice their health to be able to acquire the cash they need to pay their children's school fees and to foster networks of beneficial social relationships overseas.

But both Lee (chapter 8) and Macpherson (chapter 10) argue that transnational ties may be weakening and taking new forms, particularly for young foreign-born islanders who may not speak their home language or know its culture well, and who are choosing to participate in new kinds of identities. As they adapt to new lives overseas, they alter their "traditional" cultural practices. When these practices are shared with relatives at home as well as others from their islands living in different parts of the world, it generates a new form of deterritorialized, "globalized" island culture (see Macpherson, chapter 10). Indeed, Hess (chapter 11) suggests that the Marshallese, both those at home and those living in Orange County, California, perceive their communities to be in fact "global" communities not bounded by territorial borders.

## BUILDING POSTCOLONIAL NATION STATES

In many respects, most new Pacific Island nation states are best described as weak nations with undeveloped national identities and political infrastructures (Wesley-Smith 1999). Many financially strapped and aid-dependent Pacific states often find it difficult to provide social services, security, and basic infrastructure for their rapidly growing and urbanizing populations. Both PNG and the Solomons have faced potential bankruptcy; PNG has received loans from the International Monetary Fund and World Bank to stay afloat and both governments have been the targets of charges of corruption and illegal use of public funds (see Nelson 1999). Papua New Guinea, the Solomon Islands, and Fiji have also been plagued by intractable ethnic conflicts and violence. Others are deterritorialized through high rates of emigration and transnationalism, or become subject to powerful transnational corporations seeking to exploit their national resources.

The inability of the Papua New Guinea government to provide social services was readily apparent when a devastating tsunami struck near Aitape (West Sepik Province) in 1998, decimating coastal villages. Most of the relief effort was organized by local Catholic missions and the large numbers of international aid organizations that flocked to the area and then began to compete with each other to provide services. This process only further disrupted villagers' lives and left them disillusioned and dissatisfied (see Welsch, chapter 13).

As new Pacific states work to consolidate their postcolonial political infrastructures, it

is not surprising that they have increasingly turned for guidance to the imported Western democratic and parliamentary models (and legal systems) of their former colonizers (see Kaplan, chapter 4). And many have incorporated Christianity into those models, as well. Barker (1999b:116) notes, for example: "The Papua New Guinea constitution gives equal recognition to ancestral traditions and Christianity . . . while Fijian nationalists found justification for the [recent] military coups in biblical stories, which they relocate to their own islands (Rutz 1995)." But while in Tonga the traditional monarchy has come under increasing attack from a growing prodemocracy movement (Campbell 1999), in Fiji, chiefs have effectively denounced democracy by leading several political coups to depose democratically elected governments headed by individuals of Indian descent (see Kaplan, chapter 4). Lal (1997:415) suggests that democracy may be "a foreign flower unsuited to the Fijian soil."

But island nations fashioning postcolonial identities also strive to distance themselves from Western cultural hegemony and to assert their "authentic" identities by turning to aspects of their "traditional" indigenous culture (*kastom* or custom) (see Anderson 1983; Jolly 1992, 1997; LiPuma 1997; Otto and Thomas 1997). Peripheral states are thus often simultaneously, "large scale importers of culture from the center and guardians of either more or less authentic traditions from the periphery" (Hannerz 1997:128; see also Jolly 1992). But sometimes, democratic values and institutions and Western legal codes clash with longstanding "traditional" institutions and values. This has been true in the case of Vanuatu, where the constitution speaks of women's emancipation and equality but island chiefs work to reinforce the subordination of women characteristic of "traditional" society (Jolly 1994, 1997).

Similarly, one can see the inconsistency between Western and indigenous models in the rise in crime and "raskolism" (gangs) in Papua New Guinea. While the PNG government defines raskolism as "crime" (following Western legal models), traditional village culture defines it as "warfare," justifiable actions against long-standing clan and tribal enemies (see Roscoe, chapter 3). Growing poverty and socioeconomic inequalities, as well as the inability of the police to deal with raskolism, have all promoted and exacerbated this major social problem.

As this example suggests, most nation states have retained aspects of their indigenous legal and dispute settlement systems while adopting Western systems, generating "schizophrenic worlds" (see Scaglion, chapter 5). Scaglion notes: "Customary legal practices often operate quite well in the small face-to-face contexts in which they developed, but they prove to be inadequate for coping with the demands of modern nation-states in a globalizing world."

Poorly developed senses of "national" identity and consciousness are also characteristic of many states artificially created out of colonialism, but this seems particularly severe in many new Melanesian states (see Babadzan 1988; Linnekin and Poyer 1990; Foster 1991; Otto and Thomas 1997). Colonial rulers arbitrarily grouped island peoples who had been politically autonomous and were culturally and linguistically distinct before contact into single colonial states. Colonial powers also frequently pitted different ethnic groups against each other to maintain their own control, establishing a pattern of interethnic hostility and competition (see Howard 1989). In these cases, the citizens of new states had "never previously had to think of themselves as one people," nor did they have to band together to fight for independence as it was simply handed to them "on a silver platter" (with the exception of Vanuatu) (see Jourdan, chapter 6). To attain legitimacy and stability, postcolonial states like the Solomons have consciously sought to generate an emotional attachment to, and identification with, the state through a shared language (a Pidgin English) and national educational system, Independence Day celebrations, national sports teams, and a shared popular culture (see Jourdan, chapter 6).

One of the strategies adopted by the Papua New Guinea government to promote a shared national identity among its highly diverse peoples was to require that all commercial advertising be locally produced using local talent (see Foster, chapter 7). Foster says:

> This is not only a question of cultural imperialism, of resisting "Coca-Colonization"—the flow of images, and objects emanating from various dominant regional centers. It is equally a question of the instrumental effects of mass-consumption practices in nation making, that is, the question of the potential for advertisements to present constructs of "the nation" and perforce to define the terms of membership in "the nation."

Thus, advertisers present images of Papua New Guineans traveling on "their National Airline" (Air Niugini) or preparing and drinking coffee grown locally ("How PNG People Make and Enjoy PNG Coffee"), promoting a sense of shared belonging to the PNG nation.

## Regional Organizations and Governance

Pacific Island states' political agendas and statuses in international arenas have been bolstered by their participation in several strong and effective regional organizations. In 1971, the South Pacific Forum (now the Pacific Islands Forum Secretariat) was created by Pacific Island nations when the South Pacific Commission (created during the colonial era) refused to act on the growing regional sentiment for a nuclear-free Pacific. The Forum has sixteen island nation members today, which include the Pacific's independent nation states, Australia, and New Zealand and it is undoubtedly the most influential regional body (see Pacific Islands Forum Secretariat 1998). It is concerned with many aspects of regional trade and development, environmental issues, and relief efforts for natural disasters. It organizes island nations' economic ministers to address issues of regional economic development, and to work with major international economic organizations like the Organization for Economic Cooperation and Development (OECD) and the European Union (EU) to promote Pacific economic interests.

The forum was created and gained vitality as a regional body in the context of the first major issue to galvanize regional political activism, the nuclear testing taking place in the islands. Since World War II and the United States' testing of nuclear bombs in Micronesia after the war, islanders have been adamant in their opposition to any kind of nuclear presence (see chapter 18 by Poyer, Falgout, and Carucci and chapter 24 by Carucci). Many Pacific nations, including New Zealand, supported a South Pacific Nuclear Free Zone, and this stance has been written into the constitutions of many island states. But a Nuclear Free Zone had implications not only for France's on-going nuclear testing in French Polynesia but also for U.S. military activities in the region (Firth and von Strokirch 2000:356). It was only when France's resumption of testing in 1995 generated riots that France agreed to end testing and signed a nuclear test ban treaty supported by both islanders and other Western nations (but did not affect U.S. nuclear ships or missile testing).

Other influential regional institutions include the Pacific Conference of Churches and the University of the South Pacific (in Suva, Fiji and funded by a number of island nations). In 1982, the South Pacific Regional Environment Programme (with members from all Pacific nations and territories, as well as the United States, France, New Zealand, and Australia) was initiated to protect Pacific environments and promote sustainable development (U.S. Department of State 2002). Island nations have sought to foster greater regional identity and cohesion through activities such as the South Pacific Games and the Pacific Festival of Arts.

## Ethnic Conflict and Nationalist Struggle

As in many regions of the developing world, ethnic tensions and violence have become critical issues in some Pacific island nations since independence. The region's major conflicts on the island of Bougainville (Papua New Guinea), on Guadalcanal in the Solomon Islands, and in Fiji all have their roots in colonial era policies. But most important, they have been exacerbated by globalizing processes that have destabilized these communities and opened doors for the expression of ethnic competition and violence.

Soon after PNG independence in 1975, a secessionist threat by Bougainville, an island in the northern Solomons whose ethnic groups see themselves as distinct from those in its nation state of Papua New Guinea, was minimized when the new government created a system of local provincial governments. But in the 1990s, grievances by the Bougainville population against the Panguna copper and gold mine, a large enterprise run by Australia-based Conzinc Riotinto (one of the largest mining multinationals) were growing and they reactivated that sentiment. Over time, those grievances were the catalyst for the development of a violent, secessionist movement against the national government (see May and Spriggs 1990; Wesley-Smith and Ogan 1992; Regan 1998). The Bougainville provincial government and local landowners had long claimed that the PNG government had deprived them of their fair share of royalties from the mine and failed to pursue their claims against the multinational for environmental damage. When the Bougainville Revolutionary Army shut down the mine in 1990, the Papua New Guinea Defense Force responded brutally. After years of bloody violence, peace negotiations are now underway and it appears that Bougainville may gain its own "autonomous" government and possibly even independence (Asia Times Online 2002).

In the case of Guadalcanal, when the Solomon Islands were granted independence in 1978, the withdrawal of British rule left a power vacuum among the islands' various ethnic groups. Suspicious of each other and contentious for power, they sought political autonomy for their particular islands. Ethnic tensions escalated in 1999 between residents of Guadalcanal, the island where the capital city of Honiara is located, and the thousands of ethnically distinct Malaitans who had settled in the city since World War II. Land disputes and resentment over the newcomers' relative economic success in the new commercial economy have caused the people of Guadalcanal to launch a violent campaign to expel about 20,000 Malaitans from their island. In 2001, ethnic violence and charges of government corruption led to a coup.

In contrast to the situations on Bougainville and Guadalcanal, ethnic conflict in Fiji is between indigenous Fijians and Indo-Fijians, descendants of the indentured Indian laborers brought to the island by the colonial British to work in the sugarcane plantations (Kaplan 1993). Fijians have sought to limit the political power and economic clout of Indo-Fijians, reserving political power for themselves. Democratically elected coalition governments led by Indo-Fijians have been overthrown in several recent political coups and Fijian chiefly-led governments installed (see Kaplan, chapter 4). As a result, Western nations slashed their aid to Fiji and imposed international sanctions and the island economy continues to decline.

## THE GLOBAL ENVIRONMENT

The Pacific Islands are the first major victims of global warming, a phenomenon that many researchers link to the industrialized nations' zealous burning of fossil fuels and the emission of carbon dioxide into the atmosphere. This produces a "greenhouse effect" that warms the earth and leads to rising sea levels and disturbed weather patterns. Although not all researchers agree on the precise causes, consequences, and magnitude of global warming, most concur that rising sea levels are threatening the very existence of many low-lying atoll societies only a few meters above sea level (for example, Tuvalu, Tokelau, Kiribati, and the Marshall Islands). Shifts in weather patterns have also caused droughts, increasingly frequent and violent tropical storms, coastal erosion, and the deterioration of coral reefs. "Many Pacific island nations . . . stand at the global warming equivalent of 'ground zero'" (Lobe 2001; see also Bullfrog Films 2000).

The Pacific Island nation of Tuvalu (population about 10,500) exemplifies the current plight of these small atoll societies (see

Connell, chapter 15; Chambers and Chambers 2001). Its limited economy and threat of gradual inundation have caused many Tuvaluans to migrate to New Zealand, and the Tuvalu government is trying to convince New Zealand to accept more as "environmental refugees." Tuvalu has hired two law firms, one in the United States and one in Australia, to explore legal action, force the industrial nations to assume responsibility for global warming, and fight for international compensation (Kriner 2002).

## A SECOND WAVE OF GLOBAL RELIGIOUS INTEGRATION

As a global religion, Christianity has "brought the world to Pacific islanders and encouraged their entry onto the world stage" (Barker 1990:21). Today, islanders participate as active and devout members of various global Christian religious communities. But there are tensions between local and global churches (Barker 1990:4). Pacific churches struggle to fund their theological colleges and train clergy to "world" standards, and to fund the regional and international cooperative and educational bodies deemed important by the World Council of Churches. Many are in debt to central church administrations in the United States and elsewhere (Forman 1985). But the most significant challenge has been the widespread appeal of various Protestant fundamentalist sects, a "second wave" of Christianity that has inundated the region recently (Forman 1990:29; Ernst 1996; Harmon 1998; Barker 1999b).

These sects have been called "New Religious Movements" by Ernst (1996), a political scientist who analyzed their rapid growth in Pacific societies for the Pacific Conference of Churches. Many of these groups adhere to evangelical, either fundamentalist or pentecostal (or charismatic), belief systems. They include the Seventh-Day Adventists, Jehovah's Witnesses, and Assemblies of God, as well as dozens of other smaller groups. In addition, islanders have also been attracted in significant numbers to the Church of Latter Day Saints (Mormons).

Most of these various groups have their origins and central administrations in the United States.

Over the last thirty years in Oceania, membership in these churches has expanded directly at the expense of mainline Christian groups. Membership has grown to approximately 28 percent of the population in Tonga (20 percent of which is Mormon, the highest proportion of Mormons in any country [Forman 1989]), 38 percent in the Marshall Islands, 19 percent in Samoa, and 12 percent in Fiji (Ernst 1996:5, 281). There are today twice as many Seventh-Day Adventists in Papua New Guinea than in Australia and New Zealand combined (Westermark, chapter 26).

While there is great variability in the particular belief systems of these churches, they share certain patterns (see Ernst 1996). Many adhere to a strongly literal interpretation of the Bible, a belief in the premillennial second coming of Jesus, a desire to resurrect "traditional values," and a rigid moral and social code with a simplified distinction between good and evil. Adherents generally display a disinterest in broader political issues other than those that concern their specific beliefs, and they are generally intolerant of other religious groups (Ernst 1996:281).

Both Ernst (1996) and Robbins (2002) link the worldwide growth of religious fundamentalism to increasing alienation from materialistic, capitalist society that many evangelical and fundamentalist groups associate with moral decay. Fundamentalism is seen as a radical counterforce to modernization (Ernst 1996). In developing Pacific nations, as elsewhere in the developing world, islanders are dissatisfied and disillusioned with their relative poverty, the "crisis" (lack) of development, and the perceived failures of "modernization" and capitalism to deliver the good life. They also appear to be dissatisfied with the conservative, mainline Christian churches for not being more in tune with islanders' rapidly changing lives and identities (Ernst 1996:268–285), and they search for a more intensely personal religious experience. It is also important to note that some of the belief systems of the new sects resonate well with the aspects of the historical consciousness and identity of some Pacific Island groups and thus have a compelling appeal to them. This phenomenon has been described for the case of Mormonism and the New Zealand Maori by Underwood (2000), and for Seventh-Day Adventism and the Agarabi (Papua New Guinea) by Westermark (chapter 26).

The spread of fundamentalist sects has a number of important implications for island societies, as they are powerful forces for social and cultural change (see Westermark, chapter 26; T. Gordon 1990; Ernst 1996; Time International 2001a). But exactly how they will affect islanders' lives and identities is much debated (see Barker 1999b).

## IDENTITIES

In almost all respects—religious, political, and cultural—Pacific islanders' identities have been evolving and taking new forms as they become increasingly caught up in globalizing forces. Today, islanders are not only faced with the necessity of defining and articulating "national" identities in multiethnic and multicultural nation states, they are also faced with redefining their cultural and social identities as their lives and communities are barraged by change. Not surprisingly, "cultural and national identities—and categories such as 'indigenous'—are ambiguous and contested" (Linnekin 1997:397). "Custom is neither fixed nor unconsciously experienced: its definitions and evaluations are constantly debated" (Lindstrom 1997:408). But as one Pacific Islander eloquently notes, this is, in fact, not new:

> Our cultural identities are always in a state of becoming, a journey in which we never arrive; who we are is not a rock that is passed on from generation to generation, fixed and unchanging. Cultural identity is a process. (Hereniko 1997:428–429)

One can, however, date the start of a "modern" global era of heightened volatility in the processes of identity change to the massive upheaval in the region caused by World War II.

The sheer magnitude of the destruction and suffering that many islanders experienced, as well as the intensity of their interactions with Japanese and American soldiers and with the outside world, forever changed their senses of themselves (see White and Lindstrom 1989; Lindstrom and White 1991; Poyer, Falgout, and Carucci 2001). Indeed, Poyer, Falgout, and Carucci (chapter 18) argue that Micronesian identities have been transformed irrevocably by those processes, and that they developed an increasingly global identity and worldview at that time. Carucci (chapter 24) has described how the testing of nuclear bombs on Bikini and Enewetak (Marshall Islands) deprived the dislocated islanders of those things that were most fundamental to defining who they were as people, their ancestral lands and customary foods. The tragedies of that era remain etched in islanders' memories and are now a part of who they are.

Islanders are self-consciously aware that the forces shaping evolving identities today are different from those of earlier eras. Hereniko (1997), for example, describes Rotuman Islanders' (near Fiji) views on history and identity, describing how they divide history into three phases: a time of darkness (precolonial, pre-Christian), a time of light (Christian/colonial), and "new time" (the current postcolonial era). He says that "cultural identity was contested during the time of darkness, was transformed (with certain elements suppressed) during the time of light, and is *negotiable* in the new time" (1997:429; italics added).

That negotiation takes place among a myriad of choices and *options* that islanders must navigate as their lives take new forms. With the globalization of media and popular culture and the growth of tourism and transnationalism in the region, islanders are exposed to "an exotic array of life-styles and persuasions," and "they face dilemmas of affiliation and self-definition" (Linnekin 1997:398). In islanders' rapidly changing worlds, those things that once provided cultural definitions of self, identity, and personal worth—gender roles and ideology, principles of family and kinship,

work roles, avenues to social prestige and status, and so on—are all being transformed by the rapidly modernizing and globalizing world. Islanders' senses of who they are and what they want changes when they attend high schools and universities, abandon farming and fishing for urban jobs, watch foreign television shows, create "traditional" art to appeal to foreign tourists (see Silverman, chapter 20), and migrate to foreign countries.

At the same time, modernization and the spread of capitalist relations of production, as well as the concentration of jobs in cities and oftentimes rural and outer-island stagnation, have promoted the growth of new kinds of socioeconomic inequalities. Educated urbanites distinguish themselves from the more "traditional" islanders/villagers who live on outer islands or in rural areas. Socioeconomic inequalities and class distinctions are rapidly emerging and islanders are increasingly defining themselves in terms of those distinctions (Gewertz and Errington 1999).

Yet, as island societies evolve and respond to change, islanders do not necessarily relinquish important values and perspectives embedded in their long-standing cultural beliefs and traditions. Instead, they creatively fashion new identities that merge both the local and the global. As previously mentioned, this is a process of creolization, a "jelling and blending, the emergence of something integrated and coherent out of the mixture of elements . . . previously separate" (Foster 1999:150). How does this happen?

When the Chambri of the Eastern Sepik (Papua New Guinea) leave their rural villages for the squatter settlements of urban Wewak, they attempt to create what they consider "modern" selves through the consumption of Western imports and new kinds of personalized religious experiences (see Gewertz and Errington, chapter 16). But ultimately, their new desires and identities reflect a sometimes contradictory mix of both the "traditional" and the "modern."

Tahitians' sense of place and identity is rooted in the lands that have nurtured and sustained them for many generations (see Kahn, chapter 17). But to France, this "place"

(French Polynesia) is a site for testing destructive nuclear bombs, as well as a "tropical paradise" of scantily clad native women promoted in the international media for a growing tourist industry. Kahn concludes that it is at the "intersection of global politics, mass media, and local beliefs . . . that Tahitians live their social lives on a daily basis and gain a sense of who they are."

Islanders' struggles with their national identities and sense of ethnic pride are expressed in the burgeoning quantities of "identity merchandise" produced and sold across the Pacific Islands (see Linnekin, chapter 19). These are various kinds of consumer goods, such as T-shirts and milk bottle caps (pogs), that depict traditional cultural symbols for the purpose of defining and evoking ethnic pride. Popular T-shirts in Samoa, for example, often depict a powerful, conquering traditional warrior and the caption reads "Samoan Pride." Identity merchandise not only generates a sense of "belonging" to certain cultural groups but also clarifies and defines the key cultural values and stances of those groups.

## THE FUTURE OF GLOBALIZATION IN THE PACIFIC

As the previous discussion suggests, Pacific Island nations face a number of critical challenges. At the present time, all of the major global economic players in the region—"aid donors, international financial institutions, banks, and investors . . . agree that salvation for the economies in the region lies in opening themselves up to international forces" (Firth 2000:184). In addition, both Australia and the EU have specifically argued that "the globalization agenda [is] a cure for the ills of the Pacific Islands" (Firth 2000:184). And at the 1998 South Pacific Forum meeting, Pacific nations agreed that promoting the private sector and investment, as well as reduced government spending, were the keys to greater prosperity in the region (Firth 2000).

Yet, at the Sixth Pacific Islands Conference of Leaders in 1998, some Pacific Islands' leaders responded to globalization in highly ambivalent terms (East-West Center 2001).

Clearly Pacific Island nations feel that they must conform to the models of governance (that is, democracy) advocated by the dominant Western nations/aid donors in the region, and to follow the neoliberal economic guidelines set up by global financial institutions and those same Western nations (see Firth 2000). But island leaders seem to be increasingly concerned about their ability to maintain the integrity of their cultures and traditions, and are less convinced that the benefits of globalization that are supposed to accrue to their nation states will actually do so.

A government official from Kiribati stated, for example, that globalization "goes against our culture and traditions. Globalization seems to be a one-way street, benefiting only the economically strong" (East-West Center 2001). The premier of Niue, who had just learned that U.S. banks had blocked his nation's receipt of international payments for their off-shore banking licenses, said: "I feel like my own small nation was kicked in the stomach by the powers of the world. Define this globalization. Who are the beneficiaries?" (East-West Center 2001). And one analyst at the meeting from the University of Hawai'i concluded: "The new rules of globalization are being set by people who don't care about small places."

Indeed, what is the future of peripheral nation states in global society when they have few, if any, "comparative advantages" that would secure them a niche in the global economy? Pacific Island nations are wondering if "their small and isolated countries would . . . be left to survive entirely without protection in an increasingly free-trade world" (Firth 2000:186). Consequently, they have pushed for recognition as "vulnerable" economies (small, isolated, prone to natural disasters) in their trade negotiations with the EU and others (Firth 2000).

But most Pacific Island leaders, instead of criticizing globalization, have sought ways to become more integrated into the global economy, generate foreign investment, and build their private sectors. For them, solving the problems created by rapidly growing and urbanizing populations, lack of capital and infrastructure, and aid-dependency lies in internationalizing their economies. In these strategies, Pacific Island nations are much like many other developing nations around the world, and because the ultimate outcomes of such strategies are difficult to predict, they also share unknown futures.

But islanders, particularly those in Micronesia and Polynesia (and the smaller islands of Melanesia), also seem to be different from other peoples in their attitudes about their place in the global scheme of things. Hau'ofa (1994) argues that virtually since the first settling of the islands, islanders had little choice but to minimize their "terrestrial challenges" and limited resource bases by gaining access to the resources beyond their shores. They did this by sailing the open ocean to establish intense connections and exchange networks between themselves and both neighboring and distant islands. According to Hau'ofa, islanders have always perceived themselves more in "global" terms than in localized terms. It was the Europeans who drew the boundaries around islands, causing the islands and ocean to shrink (see also Hess, chapter 11).

Hau'ofa suggests that the Pacific's new nation states are no longer constrained by these colonial era boundaries and that their populations, as well as their cultures and resources, are once again traversing the ocean freely. Indeed, particularly in Micronesia and Polynesia, islanders are moving readily between their islands, regional urban centers, and international locales, making new homes, and maximizing their access to the range of resources (education, economic opportunities, and so on) that the world offers. In this way, "The world of Oceania . . . encompasses the great cities of Australia, New Zealand, the United States, and Canada. It is within this expanded world that the extent of peoples' resources must be measured" (Hau'ofa 1994:157). If one looks at Pacific Island societies this way, they are no longer tiny, no longer isolated, and no longer poor.

Thus the future of these island nations may lie in their propensity to seek global connections beyond themselves, and to perceive themselves in global terms. It may also lie in the openness of the Pacific Islands' indigenous cultures—long known for their hospitality and generosity—to the possibilities inherent in other peoples and cultures. Hau'ofa (1994) sees a future in which there is greater sharing of a pan-Pacific identity and greater regional integration, and in which islanders increasingly assume the role of environmental stewards (and beneficiaries) of the Pacific Ocean's immense, untapped resources.

## ACKNOWLEDGMENTS

I am very grateful to a number of colleagues who made their expertise on different areas and topics in Pacific anthropology available to me and generously provided critical comments and suggestions on this introduction. They are John Barker, Jim (Paul) Roscoe, Mac Marshall, Karen Nero, and George Westermark.

## REFERENCES

Adams, Tim, Paul Dalzell, and Esaroma Ledua. 1999. "Ocean Resources." In *The Pacific Islands: Environment and Society*. Moshe Rapaport, ed. Pp. 366–381. Honolulu: Bess Press.

Ahlburg, Dennis. 1991. *Remittances and Their Impact: A Study of Tonga and Western Samoa*. Canberra: National Centre for Development Studies, Research School of Pacific Studies, Australian National University.

Anderson, Benedict. 1983. *Imagined Communities: Reflections on the Origin and Spread of Nationalism*. London: Verso.

Appadurai, Arjun. 1990. "Disjuncture and Difference in the Global Cultural Economy." *Theory, Culture, and Society* 7:295–310.

———. 1991. "Global Ethnoscapes: Notes and Queries for a Transnational Anthropology." In *Recapturing Anthropology*. R. G. Fox, ed. Pp. 191–210. Santa Fe, N.M.: School of American Research.

Asia Times Online. 2002. "Bougainville's Panguna Mine to Remain Closed." *Asia Times Online*, April 12, 2002. http://www.atimes.com/oceania/DD12Ah02.html (accessed April 29, 2002).

Aspire Films. 1996. *Advertising Missionaries*. Aspire Films and Ellipse Programme. Produced by ABC Australia and France 3, RTSR in association with the Australian Film Finance Corporation and the Centre National de la Cinematographie. New York: First Run/Icarus Films.

Babadzan, Alain. 1988. "Kastom and Nation Building in the South Pacific." In *Ethnicities and Nations: Processes* of Interethnic Relations in Latin America, Southeast Asia, and the Pacific. R. Guilieri, F. Pellizi, and S. Tambiah, eds. Pp. 199–228. Austin: University of Texas Press.

Banks, Glenn, and France McShane. 1999. "Mining." In The Pacific Islands: Environment and Society. Moshe Rapaport, ed. Pp. 382–393. Honolulu: Bess Press.

Barber, Benjamin R. 1992. "Jihad vs. McWorld." The Atlantic Monthly 269(3):53–65.

Barker, John. 1999a. "Oceanic Religion." In The Pacific Islands: Environment and Society. M. Rapaport, ed. Pp. 234–245. Honolulu: Bess Press.

———. 1999b. "Recent Changes in Pacific Island Christianity/Les Mutations Recentes du Christianisme en Oceanie." The New Pacific Review/La Nouvelle Revue du Pacifique 1(1):116–127, 108–117.

Barker, John, ed. 1990. "Christianity in Oceania: Ethnographic Perspectives." ASAO Monograph No. 12. Lanham, Md.: University Press of America.

Basch, Linda, Nina Glick Schiller, and Cristina Blanc. 1994. Nations Unbound: Transnational Projects, Postcolonial Predicaments, and Deterritorialized Nation States. Amsterdam: Gordon and Breach.

BBC News (Sci/Tech). 2000. "Net Gains for Tuvalu." http://news.bbc.co.uk/1/hi/sci/tech/1067065.stm (accessed August 4, 2002).

Bedford, Richard. 1997. "Migration in Oceania: Reflections on Contemporary Theoretical Debates." New Zealand Population Review 23:45–64.

Bertram, I. Geoffrey. 1986. "Sustainable Development in Pacific Micro-Economies." World Development 14(7): 809–822.

———. 1999a. "Economy." In The Pacific Islands: Environment and Society. Moshe Rapaport, ed. Pp. 258–269. Honolulu: Bess Press.

———. 1999b. "The MIRAB Model Twelve Years On." The Contemporary Pacific 11(1):105–138.

Bertram, Geoffrey, and R. F. Watters. 1985. "The MIRAB Economy in South Pacific Microstates." Pacific Viewpoint 26(3):497–519.

Borofsky, Robert, ed. 2000. Remembrance of Pacific Pasts: An Invitation to Remake History. Honolulu: University of Hawai'i Press.

Boutilier, James, Daniel Hughes, and Sharon Tiffany, eds. 1978. Mission, Church and Sect in Oceania. ASAO Monograph No. 6. Ann Arbor: University of Michigan Press.

Brettell, Caroline, and James Hollifield, eds. 2000. Migration Theory: Talking Across the Disciplines. New York: Routledge.

Broad, Robin. 2002. Global Backlash: Citizen Initiatives for a Just World Economy. Lanham, Md.: Rowman and Littlefield.

Brown, Richard. 1998. "Do Migrants' Remittances Decline over Time? Evidence from Tongans and Western Samoans in Australia." The Contemporary Pacific 10(1):107–151.

Bryant, Jenny. 1993. Urban Poverty and Environment in the South Pacific. Armidale, Australia: University of New England, Department of Geography and Planning.

Bullfrog Films. 2000. Rising Waters: Global Warming and the Fate of the Pacific Islands. Produced and written by Andrea Torrice. National Film Board of Canada. Oley, Pa.: Bullfrog Films.

Burawoy, Michael. 2000. "Grounding Globalization." In Global Ethnography: Forces, Connections, and Imaginations in a Postmodern World. Michael Burawoy, J. Blum, S. George, Z. Gille, T. Gowan, L. Haney, M. Klawiter, S. Lopez, S. O'Riain, and M. Thayer, eds. Pp. 337–350. Berkeley: University of California Press.

Campbell, Ian. 1999. "The Democracy Movement and the 1999 Tongan Elections." Journal of Pacific History 34(3):265–272.

Chambers, Keith, and Anne Chambers. 2001. Unity of Heart: Culture and Change in a Polynesian Atoll Society. Prospect Heights, Ill.: Waveland.

CIA World Factbook. 2002. Country Profiles (Pacific Islands). http://www.cia.gov.cia/publications/factbook/geos. html (accessed March 2002).

Clarke, William, H. Manner, and R. Thaman. 1999. "Agriculture and Forestry." In The Pacific Islands: Environment and Society. Moshe Rapaport, ed. Pp. 353–365. Honolulu: Bess Press.

Connell, John. 1987a. Migration, Employment and Development in the South Pacific. Noumea: South Pacific Commission.

———. 1987b. "Paradise Left? Pacific Island Voyagers in the Modern World." In Pacific Bridges: The New Immigration from Asia and the Pacific Islands. James Fawcett and B. Carion, eds. Pp. 375–404. New York: Center for Migration Studies.

———. 1999. "Urban Dilemmas." In The Pacific Islands: Environment and Society. Moshe Rapaport, ed. Pp. 326–335. Honolulu: Bess Press.

Connell, John, ed. 1990. Migration and Development in the South Pacific. Canberra: National Center for Development Studies, Research School of Pacific Studies, Australian National University.

Connell, John, and Richard Brown. 1995. "Migration and Remittances in the South Pacific: Towards New Perspectives." Asian and Pacific Migration Journal 4(1):1–34.

Connell, John, and John Lea. 1995. Pacific 2010: Urbanization in Polynesia. Sydney: National Centre for Development Studies, Australian National University.

Denoon, Donald. 1997. "Redefining Mineral Sources." In The Cambridge History of the Pacific Islanders. D. Denoon, S. Firth, J. Linnekin, M. Meleisea, and K. Nero, eds. Pp. 383–389. Cambridge: Cambridge University Press.

Denoon, Donald, Philippa Mein-Smith, and Marivic Wyndham. 2000. A History of Australia, New Zealand, and the Pacific Islands. Oxford: Blackwell.

Dibblin, Jane. 1988. *Day of Two Suns: US Nuclear Testing and the Pacific Islanders.* London: Virago Press.

Douglas, Bronwen. 2002. "Christian Citizens: Women and Negotiations of Modernity in Vanuatu." *The Contemporary Pacific* 14(1):1–38.

Doumenge, Jean-Pierre. 1999. "Urbanization." In *The Pacific Islands: Environment and Society.* Moshe Rapaport, ed. Pp. 315–325. Honolulu: Bess Press.

East-West Center. 2001. Pacific Leaders Criticize Globalization, Ask for Help. EWC in the News. http://eastwestcenter.org/events-en-detail.asp? news_ID=16 (accessed March 25, 2002).

Ernst, Manfred. 1996. *The Role of Social Change in the Rise and Development of New Religious Groups in the Pacific Islands.* Hamburg: LIT Verlag.

Fagence, Michael. 1999. "Tourism." In *The Pacific Islands: Environment and Society.* Moshe Rapaport, ed. Pp. 394–404. Honolulu: Bess Press.

Feinberg, Richard, and Cluny Macpherson. 2002. "The Eastern Pacific." In *Oceania: An Introduction to the Cultures and Identities of Pacific Islanders.* Andrew Strathern et al., eds. Pp. 101–179. Durham, N.C.: Carolina Academic Press.

Firth, Stewart. 2000. "The Pacific Islands and the Globalization Agenda." *The Contemporary Pacific* 12(1):178–192.

Firth, Stewart, and Karin von Strokirch. 2000. "A Nuclear Pacific." In *The Cambridge History of the Pacific Islanders.* D. Denoon, S. Firth, J. Linnekin, M. Meleisea, and K. Nero, eds. Pp. 324–358. Cambridge: Cambridge University Press.

Forman, Charles. 1985. "Playing Catch-Up Ball: The History of Financial Dependence in Pacific Island Churches." In *Missions and Missionaries in the Pacific.* Char Miller, ed. Pp. 91–188. New York: Edwin Mellen Press.

———. 1989. "Mormons and Others in Pacific Islands." *International Review of Mission* 78(309):102–104.

———. 1990. "Some Next Steps in the Study of Pacific Island Christianity." In *Christianity in Oceania: Ethnographic Perspectives.* ASAO Monograph No. 12. John Barker, ed. Pp. 25–32. Lanham, Md.: University Press of America.

Foster, Robert. 1991. "Making National Cultures in the Global Ecumene." *Annual Review of Anthropology* 20:235–260.

———. 1999. "Melanesianist Anthropology in the Era of Globalization." *The Contemporary Pacific* 11(1): 140–159.

Friedman, Jonathan. 1994a. *Cultural Identity and Global Process.* London: Sage Publications.

———. 1994b. *Consumption and Identity.* Chur, Switzerland: Harwood.

Friedman, Thomas, and Ignacio Ramonet. 2002. "Dueling Globalizations: A Debate Between Thomas L. Friedman and Ignacio Ramonet." In *Global Issues 02/03.* Michael Jackson, ed. Pp. 80–88. Guilford, Conn.: McGraw-Hill/Dushkin.

Galbraith, James K. 1999. "The Crisis of Globalization." *Dissent Magazine,* summer 1999:12–16.

George, Sheba. 2000. "Dirty Nurses and Men Who Play: Gender and Class in Transnational Migration." In *Global Ethnography: Forces, Connections, and Imaginations in a Postmodern World.* Michael Burawoy et al., eds. Pp. 144–174. Berkeley: University of California Press.

Gewertz, Deborah, and Fred Errington. 1999. *Emerging Class in Papua New Guinea: The Telling of Difference.* Cambridge: Cambridge University Press.

Global Exchange. 2000. Some Large Retailers Settle Suit over Sweatshops in U.S. Islands. http://www.globalexchange.org/economy/corporations/saipan/pr032800.html (accessed July 17, 2002).

Gordon, April. 1996. *Transforming Capitalism and Patriarchy: Gender and Development in Africa.* Boulder, Colo.: Lynne Rienner.

Gordon, Tamar. 1990. "Inventing the Mormon Tongan Family." In *Christianity in Oceania: Ethnographic Perspectives.* ASAO Monograph No. 12. John Barker, ed. Pp. 197–219. Lanham, Md.: University Press of America.

Government of New Zealand. 2001. http://www.stats.govt.nz/domino/external/web/prod_serv.nsf/htmldocs/2001+Census+of+Population+and+Dwellings+−+Cultural+diversity+tables.

Hall, C. Michael, and Stephen Page, eds. 1996. *Tourism in the Pacific: Issues and Cases.* London: International Thomson Business Press.

Hanlon, David, and Geoffrey White, eds. 2000. *Voyaging Through the Contemporary Pacific.* Lanham, Md.: Rowman and Littlefield.

Hannerz, Ulf. 1992. "The Global Ecumene as a Network of Networks." In *Conceptualizing Society.* Adam Kuper, ed. Pp. 34–56. New York: Routledge.

———. 1997. "Scenarios for Peripheral Cultures." In *Culture, Globalization and the World System: Contemporary Conditions for the Representation of Identity.* Anthony King, ed. Pp. 107–128. Minneapolis: University of Minnesota Press.

Harmon, Jeff B. 1998. "Ignoring the Missionary Position." *New Statesman* 127(4399):20–21.

Hau'ofa, Epeli. 1994. "Our Sea of Islands." *The Contemporary Pacific* 6(1):148–161.

Hereniko, Vilsoni. 1997. "Pacific Cultural Identities." In *The Cambridge History of the Pacific Islanders.* D. Denoon et al., eds. Pp. 428–437. Cambridge: Cambridge University Press.

Hezel, Francis X. 1995. "The Church in Micronesia (Jesuits' Missionary Work)." *America* 172(5):23–24.

Howard, Michael. 1989. "Ethnicity and the State in the Pacific." In *Ethnicity and Nation-Building in the Pacific.* M. Howard, ed. Pp. 1–49. Tokyo: United Nations University.

Inda, Jonathan X., and Renato Rosaldo. 2002. "A World in Motion." In *The Anthropology of Globalization.* Jonathan Inda and R. Rosaldo, eds. Pp. 1–34. Oxford: Blackwell.

Jakarta Post. 2002. "Irian Jaya: Facts and Figures." The Jakarta Post.com. http://www.thejakartapost.com/special/os_8_facts.asp (accessed April 28, 2002).

James, Kerry. 1991. "Migration and Remittances: A Tongan Village Perspective." *Pacific Viewpoint* 32(1):1–23.

———. 1997. "Reading the Leaves: The Role of Tongan Women's Traditional Wealth and Other 'Contraflows' in the Processes of Modern Migration and Remittance." *Pacific Studies* 20(1):1–27.

Jolly, Margaret. 1992. "Specters of Inauthenticity." *The Contemporary Pacific* 4(1):49–72.

———. 1994. *Women of the Place: Kastom, Colonialism, and Gender in Vanuatu.* Amsterdam: Harwood.

———. 1997. "Woman-Nation-State in Vanuatu: Women as Signs and Subjects in the Discourses of Kastom, Modernity, and Christianity." In *Narratives of Nation in the South Pacific.* Ton Otto and Nicholas Thomas, eds. Pp. 133–162. Amsterdam: Harwood.

Juergensmeyer, Mark. 1993. *The New Cold War? Religious Nationalism Confronts the Secular State.* Berkeley: University of California Press.

Kaplan, Martha. 1993. "Imagining a Nation: Race, Politics, and Crisis in Post-Colonial Fiji." In *Contemporary Pacific Societies: Studies in Development and Change.* V. Lockwood, T. Harding, and B. Wallace, eds. Pp. 34–54. Englewood Cliffs, N.J.: Prentice Hall.

Kearney, Michael. 1995. "The Local and the Global: The Anthropology of Globalization and Transnationalism." *Annual Review of Anthropology* 24:547–565.

Kiste, Robert C., and Mac Marshall, eds. 1999. *American Anthropology in Micronesia: An Assessment.* Honolulu: University of Hawai'i Press.

Kriner, Stephanie. 2002. Tiny Pacific Islands to Sue over Global Warming. Posted on March 15, 2000, www.disasterrelief.org (accessed April 24, 2001).

Laenui, Poka. 1997. "Repression and Renaissance in Hawai'i." In *The Cambridge History of the Pacific Islanders.* D. Denoon et al., eds. Pp. 403–407. Cambridge: Cambridge University Press.

Lal, Brij. 1997. "Coups in Fiji." In *The Cambridge History of the Pacific Islanders.* D. Denoon et al., eds. Pp. 415–419. Cambridge: Cambridge University Press.

Lappe, Frances Moore, and Joseph Collins. 1977. "Why Can't People Feed Themselves?" In *Food First: Beyond the Myth of Food Scarcity.* Pp. 99–111. New York: Random House.

Larkin, Brian. 2002. "Indian Films and Nigerian Lovers: Media and the Creation of Parallel Modernities." In *The Anthropology of Globalization.* Jonathan Inda and Renato Rosaldo, eds. Pp. 350–379. Oxford: Blackwell.

Lederman, Rena. 1998. "Globalization and the Future of Culture Areas: Melanesianist Anthropology in Transition." *Annual Review of Anthropology* 27:427–449.

Liebes, Tamar, and Elihu Katz. 1990. *The Export of Meaning: Cross-Cultural Readings of* Dallas. New York: Oxford University Press.

Lindstrom, Lamont. 1997. "Custom Remade." In *The Cambridge History of the Pacific Islanders.* D. Denoon et al., eds. Pp. 407–415. Cambridge: Cambridge University Press.

Lindstrom, Lamont, and Geoffrey White, eds. 1991. *Island Encounters: Black and White Memories of the Pacific War.* Washington, D.C.: Smithsonian Institution Press.

Linnekin, Jocelyn. 1997. "The Ideological World Remade." In *The Cambridge History of the Pacific Islanders.* D. Denoon et al., eds. Pp. 397–400, 424–428. Cambridge: Cambridge University Press.

Linnekin, Jocelyn, and Linette Poyer, eds. 1990. *Cultural Identity and Ethnicity in the Pacific.* Honolulu: University of Hawai'i Press.

LiPuma, Edward. 1997. "History, Identity, and Encompassment: Nation-Making in the Solomon Islands." *Identities* 4(2):213–244.

Lobe, Jim. 2001. Environment—Pacific Islands: Climate Change to Hurt Economies—Big Time. World News: Interpress Service. http://www.oneworld.org/ips2/nov00/02_40_005.html (accessed March 13, 2002).

Lockwood, Victoria. 1993a. "Welfare State Colonialism in Rural French Polynesia." In *Contemporary Pacific Societies: Studies in Development and Change.* V. Lockwood, T. Harding, and B. Wallace, eds. Pp. 81–98. Englewood Cliffs, N.J.: Prentice Hall.

———. 1993b. *Tahitian Transformation: Gender and Capitalist Development in a Rural Society.* Boulder, Colo.: Lynne Rienner.

———. 2002. "Poverty in Paradise: Development and Relative Income Poverty in Rural Tahitian Society." *Human Organization* 61(3):210–225.

Loeliger, Carl, and Gary Trompf, eds. 1985. *New Religious Movements in Melanesia.* Suva, Fiji: University of the South Pacific and the University of Papua New Guinea.

Mapes, Timothy. 2002. "Indonesian Military May Threaten Political Unity, BP Gas Investment." *The Wall Street Journal,* April 19, 2002.

Marcus, George. 1993. "Tonga's Contemporary Globalizing Strategies: Trading on Sovereignty Amidst International Migration." In *Contemporary Pacific Societies: Studies in Development and Change.* V. Lockwood, T. Harding, and B. Wallace, eds. Pp. 21–33. Englewood Cliffs, N.J.: Prentice Hall.

May, R. J., and Matthew Spriggs, eds. 1990. *The Bougainville Crisis.* Bathurst, Australia: Crawford House Press.

McCall, Grant, and John Connell, eds. 1993. *A World Perspective on Pacific Islanders Migration: Australia, New Zealand, and the U.S.A.* Sydney: Centre for South Pacific Studies, University of New South Wales.

Michaels, Eric. 2002. "Hollywood Iconography: A Walpiri Reading." In *The Anthropology of Globalization.*

Jonathan Inda and R. Rosaldo, eds. Pp. 311–324. Oxford: Blackwell.

Nelson, Hank. 1999. "Crises of God and Man: Papua New Guinea Political Chronicle 1997–99." *Journal of Pacific History* 34:259–264.

Nero, Karen. 1997a. "The Material World Remade." In *The Cambridge History of the Pacific Islanders*. D. Denoon, S. Firth, J. Linnekin, M. Meleisea, and K. Nero, eds. Pp. 359–382, 389–396. Cambridge: Cambridge University Press.

———. 1997b. "The End of Insularity." In *The Cambridge History of the Pacific Islanders*. D. Denoon, S. Firth, J. Linnekin, M. Meleisea, and K. Nero, eds. Pp. 439–467. Cambridge: Cambridge University Press.

Oliver, Douglas. 1989. *The Pacific Islands*, 3rd ed. Honolulu: University of Hawai'i Press.

Otto, Ton, and Nicholas Thomas, eds. 1997. *Narratives of Nation in the South Pacific*. London: Harwood.

Pacific Islands Forum Secretariat. 1998. Home Page. http://www.forumsec.org.fj/ (accessed July 22, 2002).

Pacific Islands Report. 1998. "U.S. Military Says Marshall Islands Will Grow in Importance." Pacific Islands Report (Radio Australia), Pacific Islands Development Program/East-West Center, University of Hawai'i at Manoa. http://166.122.164.43/archive/1998/November/11-16.htm (accessed July 14, 2002).

———. 2002a. "Marshall Islands Government Wants Compact Deal by September." Pacific Islands Development Program/East-West Center. http://pidp.eastwestcenter.org/pireport/2002/August/08-21-09.htm.

———. 2002b. "Compact of Free Association Negotiations: Fulfilling the Promise." Pacific Islands Development Program/East-West Center. http://166.122.164.43/archive/2002/July/07-17-cofa.htm (accessed August 25, 2002).

Poirine, Bernard. 1998. "Should We Hate or Love MIRAB?" *The Contemporary Pacific* 10(1):65–105.

Poyer, Lin, Suzanne Falgout, and Laurence Carucci. 2001. *The Typhoon of War: Micronesian Experiences of the Pacific War*. Honolulu: University of Hawai'i Press.

Rapaport, Moshe. 1995. "Pearl Farming in the Tuamotus: Atoll Development and Its Consequences." *Pacific Studies* 18(3):1–25.

———. 1999. "Mobility." In *The Pacific Islands: Environment and Society*. Moshe Rapaport, ed. Pp. 270–281. Honolulu: Bess Press.

Regan, Anthony J. 1998. "Current Developments in the Pacific (Mining in Papua New Guinea)." *Journal of Pacific History* 33:269–286.

Robbins, Richard H. 2002. *Global Problems and the Culture of Capitalism*. Boston: Allyn and Bacon.

Robie, David. 1989. *Blood on Their Banner: Nationalist Struggles in the South Pacific*. London: Zed Books.

Roscoe, Paul. 2000. "New Guinea Leadership as Ethnographic Analogy: A Critical Review." *Journal of Archaeological Method and Theory* 7:79–126.

Rosenau, James N. 2002. "The Complexities and Contradictions of Globalization." In *Global Issues 02/03*. Robert Jackson, ed. Pp. 68–72. Guilford, Conn.: McGraw-Hill/Dushkin.

Rutz, H. J. 1995. "Occupying the Headwaters of Tradition: Rhetorical Strategies of Nation Making in Fiji." In *Nation Making: Emergent Identities in Postcolonial Melanesia*. R. Foster, ed. Pp. 71–94. Ann Arbor: University of Michigan Press.

Scott, Bruce R. 2002. "The Great Divide in the Global Village." In *Global Issues 02/03*. Michael Jackson, ed. Pp. 73–79. Guilford, Conn.: McGraw-Hill/Dushkin.

Scupin, Raymond. 2000. *Cultural Anthropology: A Global Perspective*. Upper Saddle River, N.J.: Prentice Hall.

Shankman, Paul. 1993. "The Samoan Exodus." In *Contemporary Pacific Societies: Studies in Development and Change*. V. Lockwood, T. Harding, and B. Wallace, eds. Pp. 156–170. Englewood Cliffs, N.J.: Prentice Hall.

Sillitoe, Paul. 1998. *An Introduction to the Anthropology of Melanesia: Culture and Tradition*. Cambridge: Cambridge University Press.

Smith, Michael French. 1994. *Hard Times on Kairiru Island: Poverty, Development, and Morality in a Papua New Guinea Village*. Honolulu: University of Hawai'i Press.

Spoonley, P. 1990. "Polynesian Immigrant Workers in New Zealand." In *Labour in the South Pacific*. C. J. Moore, J. Leckie, and D. Munro, eds. Pp. 155–164. Townsville: James Cook University, Queensland.

Strathern, Andrew, and Pamela Stewart. 2002. "The South-West Pacific." In *Oceania: An Introduction to the Cultures and Identities of Pacific Islanders*. Andrew Strathern et al., eds. Pp. 11–100. Durham, N.C.: Carolina Academic Press.

Swain, Tony, and Garry Trompf. 1995. *The Religions of Oceania*. London: Routledge.

Time International. 2001a. "Defending the Faith: Christianity Has Deep Roots in Samoa, but the Established Churches Are Facing Keen Competition from Younger, More Zealous Creeds." *Time International*, August 20, 2001, 158(7/8):46.

———. 2001b. "How to Win Friends . . . Beijing Is Courting Tiny Pacific Nations." *Time International*, June 4, 2001, 157:34.

Tomlinson, John. 1997. "Internationalism, Globalization, and Cultural Imperialism." In *Media and Cultural Representation*. Kenneth Thompson, ed. Pp. 117–162. London: Sage.

Trompf, Garry W. 1987. *The Gospel Is Not Western: Black Theologies from the Southwest Pacific*. Maryknoll, N.Y.: Orbis Books.

Trouillot, Michel-Rolph. 2001. "The Anthropology of the State in the Age of Globalization." *Current Anthropology* 42(1):125–138.

Underwood, Grant. 2000. "Mormonism, the Maori, and Cultural Authenticity." *Journal of Pacific History* 35(2):133–146.

U.S. Department of State. 2002. South Pacific Regional Environment Programme. Under Secretary for

Global Affairs. http://www.state.gov/g/oes/ocns/rsp/cta/sprep/ (accessed July 15, 2002).

U.S. House of Representatives, Committee on International Relations. 2000. *Toward a Prosperous Pacific: A Report on the Pacific Island Economies.* Presented by Wali Osman, Bank of Hawai'i Senior Fellow, East-West Center, July 23, 2002. http://www.house.gov/international_relations/osma0723.htm

Van Meijl, Toon. 1997. "Encapsulated Communities: The Treaty of Waitangi Reconsidered." In *The Cambridge History of the Pacific Islanders.* D. Denoon et al., eds. Pp. 400–403. Cambridge: Cambridge University Press.

Wallerstein, Immanuel. 1974. *The Modern World System: Capitalist Agriculture and the Origins of the European World Economy in the Sixteenth Century.* New York: Academic Press.

Wesley-Smith, Terence. 1999 "Changing Patterns of Power." In *The Pacific Islands: Environment and Society.* M. Rapaport, ed. Pp. 144–155. Honolulu: Bess Press.

Wesley-Smith, Terence, and Eugene Ogan. 1992. "Copper, Class, and Crisis: Changing Relations of Production in Bougainville." *The Contemporary Pacific* 4(2):245–267.

White, Geoffrey. 1991. *Identity Through History: Living Stories in a Solomon Islands Society.* Cambridge: Cambridge University Press.

White, Geoffrey, and Lamont Lindstrom, eds. 1989. *The Pacific Theatre: Island Representations of World War II.* Honolulu: University of Hawai'i Press.

Winthrop, Rob. 2000. "The Real World After Seattle: Trade and Culture." *Practicing Anthropology* 22(2): 38–39.

Wolf, Eric. 1982. *Europe and the People Without History.* Berkeley: University of California Press.

# 2

# Need the Pacific Always Be So Pacific?

**Robert Borofsky**

*Hawaii Pacific University*

## THE PROBLEM

A perennial problem faces people writing about the Pacific. A little investigation indicates that the Pacific offers a host of thoughtful research possibilities. Polynesia, for example, is one of the few areas of the world where effective comparisons can be conducted on a regional scale. The reason: Its varied archipelagoes are analyzable as variations on underlying regional ancestral patterns and almost all of its diverse archipelagoes have been reported on in depth. Comparisons, therefore, can be not only broad but also inclusive—drawing together all of the region's varied archipelagoes. Kirch writes, "There are probably few areas in the world where the potential for studying the growth and development of complex, stratified social and political systems is as great as among the islands of Polynesia" (1984:ix). We see this in two landmark works. Sahlins (1958) explains the region's varied social stratification in terms of ecological diversity; Goldman (1970) explains it in terms of cultural dynamics implicit in the region's shared ancestral traditions. Both comparisons proceed ethnographically—archipelago by archipelago—to encompass the major Polynesian groups. Comparisons in other parts of the globe rarely, if ever, combine such breadth—a total region—with such depth—an ethnographic account of every major group in that region (see, for example, Spier 1921; Murdock 1949; Nadel 1952; Eggan 1955, 1968; Wolf 1957, 1982; Durkheim and Mauss 1963).

The cultural diversity of Melanesia is stunning. Perhaps 20 percent of the world's languages lie within the confines of a single island, New Guinea. And the cultural formations are not the stereotypical ones we are familiar with—in which the organization of land, society, politics, economics, and language overlap in the model of Western nation states. James Clifford writes: "Places like Papua New Guinea, Vanuatu, and New Caledonia are exemplary contexts for thinking about the fractured, sutured, overlaid, incredibly diverse, and yet hooked-up complexes of local, regional, national, and transnational forms, the articulated sites of an unfinished (post)modernity"

(2000:94). The Pacific, he continues, is "a very clear laboratory for looking at processes now taking place in Europe and elsewhere. There are all sorts of complex couplings and uncouplings going on" (2000:96). The different cultural elements we traditionally group together, based on our own history, overlap and diverge in a host of varied, fluid ways, Clifford is suggesting. They represent, if anything, the dynamic, changing cultural formations we are coming to associate with globalization—as nation states become reconfigured in new forms.

The Pacific also offers one of the most, if not the most, regionally condensed historical time-lines of the global changes that have taken place in recent millennia—from human settlement to European contact to colonialism to postcolonialism. This results, particularly for events surrounding and following European contact, in a treasure trove of ethnographic materials. By the time most Europeans and Americans reached the region and began their domination of it, Enlightenment efforts at clear, empirical accounting of what they saw, what others did, dominated official records. "As a result," the historian Alfred Crosby observes, "students of history interested in microcosmic case studies of exploration, cultural contact, colonial control, and post-colonial politics will find much insight in turning to the Pacific" (Borofsky 2000:back cover). The highlands of New Guinea, we might note in this regard, were only really explored in the 1930s. Consequently, we can gather personal accounts from people on both sides who lived through the "first encounter" process—unlike in the Americas, Africa, or Asia. The transformations that took centuries in many regions came in a rush in the Pacific. Albert Kiki (1968) subtitled his autobiography "Ten Thousand Years in a Lifetime." One more historical point: Hawai'i offers one of the richest collections in the world of indigenous voices, embodied in Hawai'ian language newspapers, discussing the European encounter of the eighteenth century. Here, as in few places, we can study in great detail how an indigenous group, in all its diversity and all its

complexity, responded to the onslaught of Western imperialism.

What the Pacific possesses, then, is the materials for placing globalization in perspective. We can take a broad, comparative focus— exploring one archipelago's responses in respect to another, knowing that the underlying cultural formations of both groups are related. We can perceive today's splitting asunder of the cultural and political formations that once seemed the "normal" state of things, before globalization, as far more historically contingent. The cultural dynamics we have come to associate with globalization have probably existed in Melanesia for centuries (perhaps even millennia). And we are able to place in context recent changes—and, perhaps more important, indigenous responses to such changes—through a rich historical record that charts earlier political/economic/cultural transformations.

Yet, despite such notable academic assets, the Pacific appears to be one of the less academically noted regions of the world. Comparatively few study or publish on it. Let me offer illustrative Internet data to buttress these statements. (Readers need note that these data are time sensitive; I am referring to data collected on February 19, 2001.) One obvious search topic is "centers for study." If we use the *Google* search engine, we find that "Center for Latin American Studies" has roughly 8,570 references (that is, URLs listed), "Center for Africa Studies" roughly 2,580 references, and "Center for Asian Studies" roughly 2,830 references. (The "roughly" refers to the fact that these numbers appear rounded off by the search engine.) Searching under "Center for Pacific Studies" is complicated. In mainland United States, the "Pacific" refers to the Pacific Rim of China, Japan, and the west coast of North America, as well as the islands in between. For anthropologists, the "Pacific" generally refers to the one-third of the globe that contains the Pacific Ocean plus the islands therein. (A subject search on Amazon.com for the "Pacific" turned up—in the top ten "most available" category—such books as *Choose California for Retirement, Moon Handbooks:*

*Pacific Mexico,* and *100 Classic Backcountry Ski & Snowboard Routes in Washington.* The only anthropologically "Pacific" book in the top ten was *Kauai Underground Guide.*) To get the anthropological sense of "Pacific," we need to focus our Internet investigations on "Pacific Islands." A *Google* search for "Center of Pacific Islands" produces 412 references. If we focus on a more generalized topic, "regional studies" (rather than "centers for regional studies"), we arrive at the following data using the Google search engine: "Latin American Studies" roughly 159,000 references, "African Studies" roughly 170,000 references, "Asian Studies" roughly 473,000 references, and "Pacific Island Studies" roughly 11,900 references. If we use, instead, the *Yahoo* search engine (which is "powered by *Google*"), we arrive at the following figures, counted, this time, in Web pages: "Center for Latin American Studies," roughly 4,030 Web pages; "Latin American Studies," roughly 74,600 Web pages; "Center for African Studies," roughly 1,210 Web pages; "African Studies," roughly 79,800 Web pages; "Center for Asian Studies," roughly 1,330 Web pages; "Asian Studies," roughly 223,000 Web pages; "Center for Pacific Island Studies," 306 Web pages; and "Pacific Island Studies," 473 Web pages.

Turning to books, again being aware of the date-sensitive nature of these figures (I am dealing with data collected on February 19, 2001), a subject search of Amazon.com produced the following: 6,750 subject matches for Latin America, 22,362 for Africa, 10,174 for Asia, and 177 for Pacific Islands. In terms of organizational membership, the Latin American Studies Association claims approximately 4,800 members, the African Studies Association over 3,000 members, and the Association of Asian Studies roughly 7,800 members. There is no Pacific Island Studies Association in the same overarching sense as for these other regions. But adding the two largest scholarly groups concerned with the Pacific Islands together—the Association of Social Anthropologists in Oceania (341 members) and the Pacific History Association (180 members)—and ignoring the considerable overlap in membership, we arrive at 521 members.

## POSITIVE IMAGES

Why the lack of academic attention, especially given the region's rich and exciting intellectual dynamics? It relates, I would suggest, to another particularity of the region. While many regions of the world have been depicted in positive, even paradisaical, terms by Western writers, the Pacific—especially Polynesia—is the only region that has retained its positive image over a lengthy period of time. From the mid-eighteenth century to the beginning of the twenty-first century, parts of the Pacific have been portrayed in almost mythical terms—as the "South Seas," a place rich in islands of easy living, gentle weather, and, not infrequently, sexual liaisons.

Let me be careful here. I will be making certain generalizations and buttressing them with supporting quotes. But there are other quotes (and generalizations) that we might make that qualify and limit these assertions. The explorer image of Tahiti as a land of "noble savages," for example, can be counterbalanced by the London Missionary Society's subsequent view of the island as a realm of "ignoble savages." "Instead of island societies being seen as remnants of some former golden age, of primeval harmony," Howe writes, "they were depicted [by the missionaries] as degraded and brutish. For evangelicals, the idea of a noble savage was a contradiction in terms—the savage could never be noble" (1984:112).

My intention is not to ignore the gamut of opinions that exists for the region, for Polynesia, or, for that matter, Tahiti. But I want to emphasize that positive images keep on appearing through time and, importantly, these are the ones that tend to dominate today in vast stretches of the Pacific. Without doubt, different people describe certain islands in different ways. But time and again, despite such variation, there is a tendency to wax poetic about the positive qualities of the South Seas, typified most notably perhaps by Tahiti but also ramifying out to a host of other islands in other archipelagoes as well.

Let me start with examples from the Enlightenment explorers of the eighteenth century. In the process of the British "discovering" Tahiti, the master of Wallis's ship, George Robertson, records on July 5, 1767: "Our honest-hearted tars ... made ... some little presents which gained the hearts of the Young Girls, and made them give our men a signal." Later he calls it "a new sort of trade ... but it might be more properly called the old trade" (1973:69, 73). Arriving at Tahiti in 1768, Bougainville comments on the "agreeable features [of the women who] are not inferior to most European women; and who in point of beauty of the body might with much reason, vie with them all. . . . [the Tahitian men] pressed us to choose a woman . . . It was very difficult, amidst such a sight, to keep at their work four hundred young French sailors." Later he writes: "I thought I was transported into the garden of Eden . . . people there enjoy the blessings which nature showers liberally down upon them. We found companies of men and women sitting under the shade of fruit-trees . . . every where we found hospitality, ease, innocent joy, and every appearance of happiness amongst them" (1772[1967]:218, 228, though compare Kahn 2000:12). On Cook's second voyage to Tahiti in 1773–1774 (see Cook and King 1784), Foster writes of "the great happiness which reigns at O-Taheitee and the Society-isles. All the inhabitants are of an agreeable temper, and lovers of mirth and joy; I never saw any one of a morose, peevish, discontented disposition in the whole nation." And generalizing further, he suggests, "the inhabitants of the islands in the South Sea, though unconnected with highly civilized nations, are more improved in every respect" (1996[1778]:345, 191). "Tahiti came to stand for the South Seas," Daws writes. He continues, "and the South Seas came to stand for release from the constraints of civilized life, for the life of nature, for freedom and delight" (1980:4).

Regarding the 1789 Bounty mutiny, Bernard Smith observes,

> did much to sustain in the minds of Europeans a romantic view of Pacific Island life. For the mutiny provided a clear case of men born and reared in a civilized society deliberately choosing to live permanently among native people ... the mutineers chose to accomplish in real life an ideal that lay close to the romantic view of life—the desire to live in intimate and continuous contact with nature. (1960:248; compare Dening 1992; Smith 1992:61)

If we wish to move beyond Tahiti, there are a plethora of positive remarks regarding other Pacific islands as well during this period. Here is Samwell during Cook's third voyage, January 23, 1778, at Kealakekua Bay, Hawai'i: "We found all the Women of these Islands ... would almost use violence to force you into their Embrace Regardless whether we gave them anything or not" (in Beaglehole 1967(2): 1085; compare La Pérouse's comments at Maui in 1786, 1799[1968]:347). And the official Admiralty (1784) version of Cook's third voyage observes (following Cook's murder!):

> Notwithstanding the irreparable loss we suffered from the sudden resentment and violence of these people, yet, in justice to their general conduct, it must be acknowledged that they are of the most mild and affectionate disposition. . . . They appear to live in the utmost harmony and friendship with one another. The women, who had children were remarkable for their tender and constant attention to them; and the men would often lend their assistance in those domestic offices, with a willingness that does credit to their feelings. (Cook and King 1784(3):129–130)

Of Tonga, Samwell wrote in May, 1777:

> In Countrys like these situated in the most delightful Climates ... spontaneously producing the most delicious fruits in the great plenty ... where all is beautiful all is lovely ... Where man lives in the State most agreeable to his Nature ... where nothing but Benevolence Love & Charity dwell, where even-handed Justice holds her distinguished Seat where Happiness for ever reigns. (cited in Beaglehole 1967:1021–1022)

Moving on to Palau, Smith observes that Keate's (1788) account of the "Pelew Islands" "finds the islanders noble not because of their admirable physique, or their freedom from social constraints, but because they possess good sense and good hearts" (1960:97). Here is Keate on Abba Thule:

> With regard to the excellent man, who ruled over these sons of Nature, he certainly, in every part of his conduct, showed himself firm, noble, gracious, and benevolent; there was a dignity in all his deportment, a gentleness in all his manners, and a warmth and sensibility about his heart, that won the love of all who approached him. (1788[1960]:261)

What is so intriguing is that these positive images did not end with increased contact. They wavered at times perhaps, but they continued to come back, time and time again. Here is how Daws puts it in *A Dream of Islands:*

> For a brief moment in the eighteenth century the savage, and especially the Polynesian, had seemed to offer the white man a vision of what it might be like to go naked in the world once more. The idea of some sort of earthly paradise in the South Seas in fact lived on into the nineteenth century. It was by its nature inextinguishable, irrepressible. The nineteenth century repressed it. It returned, only to be repressed again, only to return once more. (1980:20)

We might note, in this regard, *The Marriage of Loti,* a widely popular French novel of the late nineteenth century by Pierre Loti. He writes of a romantic tryst in Tahiti: "Loti was beginning to realize that he was experiencing toward [Rarahu, a young Tahitian women] a feeling that was no longer commonplace. Already he had feelings for her that came from the heart. . . . It seemed very possible to Loti that this adventure, begun by chance . . . might leave profound and durable traces on his whole life" (1976[1880]:52). And there is Paul Gauguin (inspired by *The Marriage of Loti,* it turns out). Kahn observes that Gauguin

> continues to be regarded as a symbol of the simple rejection of European civilization and the embracing of South Seas primitivism. Ever since Gauguin, European painters have flocked

to Tahiti to re-create Gauguin-like images on canvases of their own (Jacques Boullaire, Pierre Heyman, Jean Masson, and Yves de Saint-Font, to name only a few). (2000:13)

We might also turn to Mark Twain writing about Hawai'ians in 1866: "They are amazingly unselfish and hospitable. To the wayfarer, who visits them they freely offer their houses, food, beds, and often their wives and daughters" (1975[1866]:282).

We need only walk into a movie theater or pick up a travel magazine today to see these images continue. Who can forget, if one is old enough, such movies as "Blue Hawaii" (with Elvis Presley) or "Gidget Goes Hawaiian," or, earlier still, "South Pacific"? We might also turn to the Hawai'ian Visitors Bureau's Web site, where we can read:

> The Hawaii of Your Imagination Still Exists. And it's available right now . . . *in Hawaii.* For most of us, Hawaii begins to weave her spell with some little glimmer of awareness. A friend describes a sunset off Waikiki. We hear the twang of a steel guitar. Or we open a magazine and there it is . . . Golden beaches and golden people. Sun, sand, sea, and surf . . . And somewhere between the blue skies and the palm trees . . . we're hooked.
>
> The Hawaiian Islands are one of the most beautiful places on earth. The weather is friendly . . . every day is a beach day . . .
>
> The environment is friendly. The physical beauty of Hawaii is almost unparalleled. . . . There are no strangers in Paradise. Perhaps the most beautiful part of Hawaii is the genuine warmth of our people. We call it the spirit of Aloha.

Margolis, in the Sierra Club's *Adventuring in the Pacific,* provides a somewhat more balanced view:

> One place . . . has long loomed—in the Western imagination, at least—as the ultimate paradise, universally longed for, so that you have only to say the words South Sea island and the image appears in the mind's eye: a small and very distant island set in the middle of a serene blue ocean and ringed by white-sand beaches. Palm trees stride these beaches, and their green fronds sway in the breezes made fragrant by

extravagantly colored and perfumed flowers. . . . An island whose inhabitants live in innocence and harmony—healthy, beautiful, untroubled. A place whose very existence constitutes an important message for the world, a refuge for the defeated, a haven for dreams. (1995:1–2)

There never was and is not now such a place. Although the description holds true for many islands in the Pacific, it is not the whole truth. Not that the whole truth will destroy the hold these islands continue to have on the imagination. Travel agents confirm what psychologists have studied: Almost any outbreak of dreadful world news is quickly followed by a flurry of inquiries about travel in the Pacific. There seems no end to the human need for this elusive paradise.

As I said earlier, I want to be careful. It is easy, with a swosh of telling quotes, to pretend I have proven my point. It is more complicated than that. Following a style common in certain circles, it is tempting to offer a few exemplary excerpts and suggest that they speak for the hundreds or thousands of other texts that remain uncited. There is fancy footwork in this that needs to be acknowledged.

Still, whatever the ambiguities, whatever the diversity of opinions that remain uncited, there is no disputing two facts. (I think it is safe to use the word in this context.) First, the Enlightenment explorers persistently perceived Pacific people in positive, indeed romantic, terms. And second, today many of these same images continue. That is what is so unusual. The images continue: Despite all the contact, despite all the colonization, despite the centuries of time, they continue.

## CONTRASTING CASES

Rest assured, that is not the case with many other places Europeans wrote so gloriously about during the early days of contact. Take China, for example. Here is how Baudet, in *Paradise on Earth: Some Thoughts on European Images of Non-European Man,* describes early European attitudes toward China:

The Jesuits, who introduced [the Chinese] . . . to Europe, were so vastly impressed by them that they were in danger of losing sight of their own missionary purpose. . . . fired with zeal and admiration, they informed the West of this extraordinary . . . country and built up an image of an East perfect in every way . . . China was seen through the eyes of the Jesuits as an immense, remarkable land of perfect peace. . . . The Far East became the source of inspiration . . . the Chinese style was by definition synonymous with perfect beauty. (1965:43–44)

Adas, writing about this same contact period, notes:

If much of what European travelers found in India lived up to the subcontinent's advance billing, what they encountered in China exceeded even the most effusive pre-expansion descriptions of Cathay or the Land of the Great Khan. In the decades of the first overseas expeditions, the hyperbolic descriptions of Marco Polo, who [it is believed] had actually visited China, and John Mandeville, who had not, had come to be mistrusted and regarded as excessive. . . . The early reports of Portuguese sailors, however, and later accounts by Jesuit missionaries of varying nationalities indicated that, if anything Polo and Mandeville had been too sparing in their praise of Chinese achievements. . . . Explorers and missionaries remarked on the extent to which tranquillity prevailed in a society where the power of fractious nobles had been broken, religious strife . . . was unknown, crime was checked by strict laws and hard penal codes, and vagabonds were rarely seen. (1989:43–44)

Adas continues:

No culture or civilization has been as lavishly praised or as widely acclaimed as a model to be emulated as was Qing China in the first half of the eighteenth century. . . . Some of the most prominent thinkers of the age, including Leibniz, Voltaire, and Quesnay, looked to China for moral instruction. (1989:79)

But all this changed with time, or (to phrase it another way) with more extensive economic contact. The "varying strains of French criticism of China were brought together," Adas reports, "in Pierre Sonnerat's multivolume account of his travels in Asia, first published in 1782. The son of a wholesale merchant, Sonnerat shared Anson's hostility toward the Qing bureaucracy and its restrictive policies regarding foreign commerce. He stridently dismissed notions of China as a benevolent despotism, declaring that taxes in the empire were oppressive, the mandarin bureaucrats harsh and corrupt, the populace as a whole poverty-stricken, superstitious, and servile. Sonnerat confirmed Anson and Lange's charges of merchant harassment and Goslier's image of a cowardly people that could be conquered by a handful of British solders" (1989:93). When we think of the West's military conflicts with China, particularly the Opium War (1839–1842) and the Boxer Rebellion (1899–1900), it is clear that whatever glowing respect Europeans once showered on China and the Chinese during the eighteenth century, that respect had significantly diminished by the latter part of the nineteenth century. No longer was China perceived—nor is it today—as a model of all that is best in political governance and human society.

Take another example: the Indians of the New World, or, since this is a fairly wide spread, the Indians of the northeast United States. McGregor observes:

> The first responses to the New World were . . . inherited ones . . . as Richard Slotkin points out . . . the earliest views of the continent were inevitably set forth "in the conventional terms of utopian treatise-fiction, arcadian poetry, and the chivalric romance-epic." Under the stimulus of great expectations, to those literary conventions were added the paradisaical images of Christian tradition, revitalized by the Protestant millennialism. . . . The resulting synthesis combined Eden with Arcadia, Elysium, Atlantis, Tirananogue, and all the other enchanted gardens of antiquity to produce a vision of abundance and felicity. . . . Columbus's own identification of the New World with the terrestrial paradise, far from idiosyncratic, set the tone for the whole period. (1988:30–31; compare Campbell 1988:180)

Vasco de Quiroga wrote in 1535: "with much cause and reason is this [land] called the New World, not because it is newly found, but because in its people and in almost everything it is like as was the first and golden age" (Davis 2000:96). There are literally hundreds of writers we might quote to lend further credence to these statements. But let me cite Montaigne for the pleasure of his prose and the fact that his 1578–1580 piece "Of Cannibals" (cited here) is often referred to as a foundational work for anthropology:

> I think there is nothing barbarous and savage in that nation [he is referring to Villegaignon's landfall in Brazil in 1557], from what I have been told, except that each man calls barbarous whatever is not his own practice . . . for it seems to me that what we actually see in these nations surpasses not only all the pictures in which poets have idealized the golden age and all their inventions in imagining a happy state of man, but also the conceptions and the very desire of philosophy. They could not imagine a naturalness so pure and simple as we see by experience; nor could they believe that our society could be maintained with so little artifice and human solder. This is a nation . . . in which there is . . . no name for a magistrate or for political superiority, no custom of servitude, no riches or poverty . . . no care for any but common kinship, no clothes . . . The very words that signify lying, treachery, dissimulation, avarice, envy, belittling, pardon—unheard of. (1943[1588]:152–153)

But, as one might suspect, such prose did not last in the give and take of colonist-Indian relations. After the first decades of contact, after colonial expansion came to threaten Indian lands and political economies, conflicts set in. Focusing on the American northeast, there was, for example, the Pequot War of 1637 (which threatened colonists in Connecticut) and King Philip's War of 1675–1678 (which threatened most of New England). Lepore refers to the latter, given the proportion of wounded and killed to the total colonial population, as the bloodiest war in American history (see 1998:book flap). Here is how Saltonstall in 1676 described the Indians' work:

> In Narraganset not one House left standing . . . At Providence, not above three . . . And as to Persons, it is generally thought, that of the

English there hath been lost . . . above Eight Hundred since the War began: Of whom many have been destroyed with exquisite Torments and most inhuman Barbarities; the Heathen rarely giving Quarter to those that they take. (in Lepore 1998:71)

Lepore continues:

Nearly all that was English has been destroyed— English houses, English farms, English crops, English livestock, English bodies. The tamed wilderness has become wild once again. . . . Thousands of colonists have suffered; hundreds are dead. As one frantic colonist reported, "Many of our miserable inhabitants lye naked, wallowing in their blood, and crying, and whilst the Barbarous enraged Natives . . . are . . . flaming forth their fury . . . burning Houses, and torturing Men, Women, and Children; and burning them alive." (1998:72)

Both sides, I might note, acted with much savagery. When King Philip's nine-year-old son was captured, for example, the question arose as to whether he should be killed—the sins of the father being visited on the son. While acknowledging that Deuteronomy 24:16 was against such action, the colonist Cotton suggested:

We humbly conceive, that the children of notorious traitors, rebels and murtherers, especially of such as have been principall leaders and actors in such horrid villanies . . . May bee involved in the guilt of their parents, and may . . . be adjudged to death, as seems evident, by the Scripture. (Lepore 1998:151, spelling in the original form)

The colonists, in the end, tempered their malevolence slightly (having already massacred hundreds of Indians). After leaving the nine-year-old in a small dark cell for some time, they sold him into slavery.

By the 1830s—when the Indians of the northeast had been marginalized on reservations or mostly killed off and King Philip's war was a distant memory—another view arose of the northeast Indians. Crane writes: Washington "Irving, literally turned inside out the old Puritan views of King Philip, and thereby fathered a brood of writers who, until

about 1860, were to embellish the tale of this sachem until it became in popularity the northern counterpart of the romantic Pocahontas story of Virginia. Philip emerged as a freedom-loving patriot defending his homeland" (1952:47). In 1829, at roughly the time James Fenimore Cooper was starting to achieve success with his adventure stories (such as *The Last of the Mohicans,* published in 1826), the play "Metamora; or, the Last of the Wamoanoags" opened. It was widely popular, so much so in fact that it became one of the most widely produced plays of the nineteenth century (Lepore 1998:191). Its hero was no other than King Philip. In Metamora, Philip's dying words were: "My curses on you white men! May the Great Spirit curse you. . . . May your graves and the graves of your children be in the path the red man shall trace! . . . Spirits of the grave, I come! But the curse of Metamora [Philip] stays with the white man!" On hearing this final speech, Lepore reports, the audience at its first production "rose in wild and reportedly 'raptuous' applause" (1998:191). Once more, it appears, American Indians—certainly King Philip—were back in favor, not as heroes to be emulated but as victims to be honored. The past was being idealized, not the present. And speaking of the present, we might note that within a year of the play's debut, the United States Congress passed the Indian Removal Act—the basis for moving American Indians, such as the Cherokee, west of the Mississippi.

## EXPLAINING THE DIFFERENCE

It is data such as these that make me assert two points. First, Western explorers perceived many places, in many regions, in positive, even paradisaical, terms. Baumer, in writing a foreword to Baudet's *Paradise on Earth,* comments:

During the Middle Ages when Christendom confronted Islam, Europeans canonized *le bon nègre,* believed to be Christian and to inhabit the ancient Christian kingdom of Ethiopia. In the "Atlantic era" the noble savage moved west and changed color. The American Indian displaced the Negro as the paragon. . . . the Indian was clothed with all the attributes which man had supposedly possessed in Paradise before the Fall: natural goodness, innocence, and physical beauty, freedom from the wickedness and suffering of "civilization." There was a further reshuffling of images in the eighteenth century. Now the noble Oriental hove into sight. . . . China, revealed to Europe by the Jesuits, became for many the land of perfect peace, of exquisite taste and ethical wisdom. (1965:vi–vii)

It is easy to believe—since the explorers perceived such a gamut of places in such positive terms—that they brought their paradisaical images with them. Since at least Thomas More's *Utopia,* the way to paradise appeared to lie in voyaging. (We might recall *Gulliver's Travels* in this regard.) In their writings, the voyagers and their interpreters often seemed to be discussing not only what was found but what they wished to find. There were limits to the process, of course. No one, to my knowledge, has ever described Antarctica in paradisaical terms. And there was, in Victor Turner's (1969, 1974) terms, an antistructural element to the descriptions. The travelers and their commentators were interested in a life that was different from the one they lived, the one they already knew. "Utopias," Sargent suggests, "are generally oppositional, reflecting, at the minimum, frustration with things as they are and the desire for a better life" (2000:8). It is important to realize, Bernard Smith adds, "that the ennobling of so-called Pacific savages contained a latent, but valuable, critique of Eurocentric attitudes" (1992:61). What we see in these images, then, is what the Western wanderers and their commentators hoped to see through voyaging—a world better than the one they already knew.

Second, again and again these positive images tended to turn sour with increased contact. It was not contact per se, I would suggest, that caused this but what followed in the wake of that contact: Western entrepreneurs—working within Western mercantile and capitalistic systems—sought resources, products, and markets that would generate wealth for themselves. Where the economic possibilities were comparatively greater, as in the New World and China, the economic conflicts tended to be greater. We see this in the Pacific as well. The Pacific was not without wars. Note, for example, the New Zealand wars of 1845–1872 and the New Caledonia war of 1878–1879. On these islands, there was substantial wealth to be had from a Western perspective, in terms of land and resources. In neither place did Western writers portray the indigenous population in glowing noble terms as they competed with them for valued resources and certainly not when the competition escalated (as it often did) into killing, and being killed by, the indigenous population.

What made the Pacific less susceptible to the above-noted image transformation was what might be viewed, *in comparative terms,* as the region's diminished degree of Western-valued resources, products, and markets. There were, as elsewhere, conflicts. But, speaking of the region as a whole, the perceived wealth was comparatively less and so the pervasiveness, intensity, and duration of the conflicts tended to be less. If they were in search of new markets for Western goods or new resources to transform into Western goods, they would logically turn to China before the Cook Islands. "Following the money" meant heading for Asia, the Americas, or Africa well before they ever turned to the Pacific.

Another way to make this point is to note that the real spur in Pacific Island Studies followed on the heels of World War II. That was when both Pacific History at the Australian National University (see for example Davidson 1966) and the Coordinated Investigation of Micronesian Anthropology, or CIMA (see Kiste and Marshall 1999), were established. It was a time when Australia and the United States had "a need to know" about the Pacific. The former had been threatened by Japanese advances through Melanesia and had trust responsibilities for Papua New Guinea; the latter had assumed trust responsibility for Micronesia (see Kiste and Marshall 1999:17 ff.). Governments were actively concerned, in the war's aftermath, to learn what they could about the region—or perhaps, more precisely phrased, what they needed to know to effectively maintain control. With time, however, this "need to know" softened and economic priorities—related to markets and money—placed the Pacific (comparatively speaking) once again on the margins where it remains today.

I do not want to oversimplify. "Following the money" to Asia, to Latin America, or to Africa does not mean the Pacific is without resources prized by the West. Some islands certainly possess them. Papua New Guinea and New Caledonia, in particular, contain important mineral resources (Lal and Fortune 2000:369–373). And New Zealand, with its relatively large land masses, has become home to millions of settlers and millions more sheep. For some other islands, their location in the midst of the world's largest ocean, between economic powerhouses in Asia and America, make them ideal entrepôt centers. And the fact that particular Pacific islands are fairly far from the Western metropoles that control them and possess comparatively small populations means they are useful for the type of military and atomic testing which would bring heated demonstrations nearer to home. Still, in very general terms, and again speaking comparatively for the region as a whole, there was and is less wealth—defined in Western terms—to compete over. So even with qualifications—and I readily acknowledge them—the real money lies elsewhere, unless one is interested in tourism, and that means, of course, perpetuating the paradisaical image.

Let me also note, in suggesting this economic relationship, that it is not as if the depictions of paradisaical Pacific islands are pure fabrications of philosophers and tourist boards. Many islands are exquisitely beautiful and possess soft, tropical climates. The styles of relating often seem gentler to outsiders: favoring context over absolutes, continuity over disruption. Speaking personally, having lived roughly half my life in Massachusetts and half in Hawai'i, the choice is obvious.

## BROADENING THE FRAME OF REFERENCE

With this foundation, and turning back to the larger picture once more, I want to suggest that we have in this relationship what Braudel refers to as a structure of the *longue durée*. Braudel remarks that "history"

> exists at different levels.... the history of events works itself out in the short term... halfway down, a history of conjunctures follows a broader, slower rhythm... in its developments on the material plane, in economic cycles and intercycles... And over and above [this]... the history of the longue durée, inquires into whole centuries at a time. It functions along the border between the moving and the immobile... if it deteriorates during the long journey, it simply restores itself as it goes along. (1980:74–75)

Such structures involve "both support and hindrance.... Just think of the difficulties of breaking out of certain geographical frameworks, certain biological realities, certain limits of productivity, even particular spiritual constraints: mental frameworks too can form prisons of the longue durée" (1980:31). (In *The Mediterranean,* Braudel refers to structures of the longue durée as "a history in which all change is slow, a history of constant repetition, ever-recurring cycles" [1972:20].)

My point is that limited Western-perceived wealth, pleasant geographical conditions, and Western desires for antistructural (or simply more pleasant) lifestyles have conjoined over the centuries to produce an enduring Pacific/South Sea image. The South Seas are part reality, part fantasy. (We might observe, in this regard, that the region includes archipelagoes well north of the equator.) Still, and this is why I refer to the image as a structure of the longue durée, it has persisted for centuries.

An important part of this structure is a sense of marginality. The Pacific, as noted, is perceived as (a) economically marginal, comparatively speaking, to Western capitalism and as (b) involving lifestyles different from (or, phrased another way, marginal to) the everyday experiences of most Western citizens. Tourism in the Pacific is based on this latter point: Hawai'i and Tahiti are places to "escape" to (not from) for vacations.

Academically, there are two sides to this marginality. On the negative side, this is not where the money and power are. I pointed out, above, that there are comparatively few scholars studying and/or publishing on the region. Equally to the point, few readers buy the books these scholars produce. But at the same time, on the positive side, the region is full of intellectual possibilities, just what one would expect from the margins. Here—as I noted in the chapter's opening paragraphs—is a region full of intellectual excitement: rich in comparative possibilities, the subtleties and complexities of difference, the dynamics of history. Moreover, they are not necessarily framed in forms that reproduce present-day academic arguments. These are the margins—where categories often lack the formal precision of the metropole center, where difference disrupts the easy framing. There are transformative possibilities here waiting to be richly mined.

But let me not wax too poetic. There is a problem: How does one get others to recognize these possibilities? As I indicated early on in this chapter, few people take note of the Pacific's intellectual potential. Academic productions, energy, and money tend to be focused on regions of greater economic power. The noted structure of the longue durée is part and parcel of this process: It fosters a hegemon that dampens intellectual concern with the Pacific's rich possibilities. The region's marginal economic/cultural condition is reproduced, in brief, in the academic sphere. Its intellectual potential remains untapped by academics caught up in the dynamics of other regions.

Hegemony is an overused word meaning many things to many people. Still, let me set down what I am referring to as a way of getting at an important point. The sense of hegemon I am dealing with involves an implicit set of perspectives that frame people's understandings in ways that reinforce and reproduce a set of political-economic-social structures. Gramsci, who is most cited in relation to the term, describes the power of hegemons to shape people's thinking as:

The "spontaneous" consent given by the ... population to the general direction imposed on social life by the dominant fundamental group; this consent is "historically" caused by the prestige (and consequent confidence) which the

dominant group enjoys because of its position and function in the world of production. (1971:12)

Hegemons are rarely nice, neat structures that we can put our arms around, intellectually speaking. They are vaguer, more subtle than this. One needs to be careful of the "big statement" that generalizes in a way that crushes complexities. Once more I want to be careful not to overstate. Let me suggest what I am getting at and, then, you, the reader, decide. What I am referring to is that despite the noted political-economic-intellectual hegemon involving the Pacific, which keeps academic attention focused on other regions, there are exceptions to this general tendency. At times Pacific specialists have transformed the perspectives of those at the centers of academic power. There are ambiguities here, some cases that, at first glance, appear to challenge the hegemon and actually reinforce it; others clearly undermine the hegemon's hold. Let me explain.

The chapter's opening quotes by Crosby, Clifford, and Kirch are a good place to begin. Each of these Pacific-versed scholars is known and respected beyond the Pacific. I would suggest, however, that their reputations are based less on bringing Pacific concerns to the center than on bringing the center's concerns to the Pacific. Each writer frames his Pacific writing in relation to frames of reference that exist beyond the region and uses the Pacific to clarify these broader intellectual frameworks. Crosby's (1986) main foray into the Pacific in book form, for example, is *Ecological Imperialism: The Biological Expansion of Europe 900–1900*. He uses New Zealand as a case study of postulated worldwide ecological trends. The books Clifford is known for, frequently cited by others—*The Predicament of Culture* (1988), *Writing Culture* (1986 with G. Marcus), and *Routes* (1997)—touch on the Pacific mostly in terms of illuminating broader issues, broader questions, that have been defined by and are of concern to people elsewhere. (Clifford's most Pacific-oriented work, *Person and Myth: Maurice Leenhardt in the Melanesian World* (1982), is rarely cited beyond a narrow coterie of specialists.) As the opening quote by Kirch regarding Polynesia's comparative possibilities implies, the same holds true in his case as well. His reputation beyond the Pacific, beyond anthropology, he believes, is based on the ecological and evolutionary implications of his detailed Pacific archeological research for globally significant questions. That is to say, he perceives that his reputation is based less on what his research says about specifically Pacific matters than on what it says about questions others, beyond the region, are concerned with.

Margaret Mead's work fits into this same pattern. She produced two books on Samoa, *Coming of Age in Samoa* (1928) and *The Social Organization of Manu'a* (1930). The former, drawing on Polynesian rearing (and seeming rearing) patterns to critique Western practices, was a huge success, particularly beyond anthropology. But *Coming of Age* gained a large readership because it addressed key questions, key concerns, in America at the time it was published. It was not because of its Pacific focus. *The Social Organization of Manu'a,* an anthropological work on Samoan social organization, barely made a ripple within or beyond anthropology.

The writings of Malinowski and, following him, Firth seem more challenging of the hegemon's hold. Their ethnographies of the Trobriand Islands (Malinowski 1961[1922], 1932, 1935) and Tikopia (Firth 1936, 1939), respectively, formed foundational studies for British functionalism and, more broadly, British social anthropology. We might argue that their approaches were not particularly regarding the Pacific—they could have done their functional studies anywhere. Still, there is no denying they worked in the Pacific and their publications had considerable intellectual import for anthropologists working in other regions.

The last case involves Marshall Sahlins. He has produced four major works on Hawai'i: *Historical Metaphors and Mythical Realities* (1981), *Islands of History* (1985), *Anahulu* (1992), and *How "Natives" Think* (1995). The first two generated much excitement across the discipline, gaining momentum from and giving momentum to efforts that sought to merge historical and anthropological studies during the 1980s. We might note that both included depictions of Captain James Cook—a heroic (even mythical) personage for many around the world (see Robertson 1981; Smith 1992). But it was Sahlins's slant—how he depicted the overlapping of Hawai'ian and English perspectives—that gave these books their power. *How "Natives" Think* again gained momentum from and gave momentum to a more general issue: questions regarding the limitations and possibilities of describing "others" who appear different from "us." We might argue that in all these cases, Sahlins's prior fame drew attention to his Pacific studies; what made people read his work was his already well-established reputation. But even with this reputation, there is no denying that he was deeply grounded in Hawai'ian ethnography and it was this grounding that gave his analyses such power. I would add here, however, that Sahlins's most detailed study, the incisive *Anahulu,* probably the best ethnography Sahlins has written and a winner of the School of American Research's Staley Prize, has barely caused an intellectual ripple in terms of citations within or beyond the Pacific. In contrast to his other work, it is more focused on indigenous Hawai'ian figures.

What I am suggesting then is that while we need to be cautious in our phrasing—the hegemon's hold is far from total—based on the data presented previously regarding the region's limited intellectual significance and the cases discussed here, a *general tendency exists*. For Pacific specialists to gain recognition and renown beyond the Pacific they need to address broader, more general, questions that concern readers in other regions. The critical point is that the frames of reference involved tend to be defined in the frames and phrases of these other region's histories, understandings, and concerns. The Pacific tends to play a supporting role, offering supporting, illuminating data that clarify and deepen these other frames of reference. Readers may perceive something self-evident in this: How can the Pacific, with its limited economic, political, and academic profile, expect to frame the big debates of our times? My point exactly.

This point leads to a set of critical questions for people writing about the Pacific. How non-Pacific must a Pacific article or book be to be relevant to others beyond the region? Is the Pacific destined mainly to contribute data that support (or challenge) non-Pacific framings, non-Pacific questions? And must we have prior status—from works beyond the Pacific—to be noticed by non-Pacific specialists when we dig deeply into the Pacific and come up with transformative insights?

## TWO EXAMPLES

Let me offer two examples to make the discussion less abstract. The first deals with the complex, changing social formations touched on in the chapter's opening paragraphs. The notion of culture—as a set of distinctive traits shared by a distinctive group—tends to be an anthropological "lingua franca" for discussing different groups of people (and their behaviors) around the world (see Borofsky 2000; Borofsky et al. 2001). It offers a way to talk about ethnographic data in terms that other people studying other topics in other regions can comprehend. The formulation, as many note, draws inspiration from European nationalism. "'Culture' of the modern anthropological persuasion," Sahlins writes, "originated in Germany. . . . [it] defined the unity and demarcated the boundaries of a people" (1995:11–12). Kuper adds the German sense that kultur "is bounded in time and space and is coterminous with a national identity" (1999:30; see also page 36).

But as many anthropologists working in Melanesia make clear, the region's dynamics do not fit this neat nationalistic-modeled framework. In discussing the Admiralty Islands (of northern Melanesia), for example, Schwartz focuses on "ethnic groups," based on ecological differentiation. The Manus live over shallow lagoons and sustain themselves through fishing and trading. The Usiai garden in the interior of Great Admiralty and the Matankor dwell on small fringing islands combining gardening, fishing, and trading. They are referred to as ethnic groups, he states, because "they have more

than one language in common (there are roughly twenty-two languages in the area) and are not 'tribal' . . . in the sense of being political or socially solidary." Nor do they constitute "a social grouping vis-à-vis other ethnic groups" (1963:62). More broadly, de Lepervanche reports: "One aspect of social life that is evident in the ethnographies [regarding New Guinea] is that New Guineans are flexible in conceptualizing their social relations" (1973:5). Following Hogbin and Wedgwood, de Lepervanche uses the terms *phyle* for "cultural-linguistic units" and smaller *parishes* for "autonomous local groups" (1973:1–2). She notes it is unusual for there to be "any inclusive idea of social or territorial unity. It is rare for a people to be able to delineate their phyle boundaries. The notion of defined territory usually applies only to [localized] parishes" (1973:30). Strathern casts doubt on the relevance of our Western concept of "society" for understanding such Melanesian dynamics. She writes:

> As I understand Melanesian concepts of sociality, there is no indigenous supposition of a society that lies over or above or is inclusive of individual acts and unique events . . . the imagined problems of social existence are not those of an exteriorized set of norms, values, or rules. (1988:102)

Still, all three distinguished anthropologists return to some sense of the above (nationalistic) cultural framework in their accountings. Schwartz writes: "As for the Admiralty Islands, integration is such that I consider the cultures of the entire archipelago to constitute a single 'areal culture' as distinct from a 'cultural area.' That is . . . the cultures . . . are so interdependent culturally . . . that each must be considered a part-culture" (1963:89). While he began by pointedly using a personal sense of "ethnic groups," Schwartz turns to culture and cultures when he summarizes, for others, his overall themes. De Lepervanche, as she discusses various ethnographic analyses, repeatedly refers back to named cultural-linguistic groups. We read such phrasings as: "among the Kuma," "the people of Tangu believe that," "the Motu use," "unlike Enga and Siane, Melpa have" (1973:9, 15, 17). In drawing on ethnographic examples, she returns to the anthropological framework she is bent on discounting—focusing on cultural-linguistic *phyle* rather than on the parishes (though compare 1973:5). The same holds for Strathern. We read of "Hagen women embody," "the Melanesian personification of objects," and "the two significant axes of Muyuw male-female relations concern brother and sister, husband and wife" (1988:87, 177, 193).

These anthropologists appear "caught," I am suggesting, between describing what they perceive—a fluid, flexible set of social formations—and how they frame these perceptions for others. We might argue that the three are simply following the practices of the ethnographies they are examining. But the very point of their publications is to overturn earlier ethnographers' senses of coherent cultural social formations in which group A has a collective, coherent set of political/economic/social/linguistic traits that easily and effectively distinguish it from the collective, coherent set of political/economic/social/linguistic traits of group B. They seem to be utilizing the traditional anthropological sense of culture, in explaining Melanesia to others, all the while discounting this very notion.

When the cultural frame of reference was challenged in the mid-1980s in anthropology, the Pacific barely played a role. None of the authors in *Writing Culture,* for example, focused on the region (despite both Clifford and Marcus having conducted extensive research in it). Abu-Lughod's famous 1991 article "Writing against Culture" dealt with the Middle East. And Fox's *Lions of the Punjab: Culture in the Making* (1985) centered on India. Similar ideas were presented in the Pacific—sometimes earlier—but they never seemed to capture the attention of readers in other regions.

Let me offer another, more personal, example. What set me to writing this chapter was an interest in—or really confusion regarding—these dynamics. Like many other participants in this volume, I have written books on the region, the latest being *Remembrance of Pacific Pasts: An Invitation to*

*Remake History* (2000). Now that the volume is published, I wonder what I have wrought. Critical commentaries have been positive. Natalie Zemon Davis (of Princeton) writes:

> *Remembrance of Pacific Pasts* is brimming over with new ideas about how history can be found, rethought, understood, and told. The worlds of the Pacific emerge over several centuries in the hands of these talented writers, some celebrated historians and anthropologists, some just making their mark. Whether set in Samoa, Fiji, Hawai'i, Papua New Guinea, or elsewhere, each fascinating essay has resonance for questions being asked by scholars everywhere. Rob Borofsky's edited volume is multi-centered, dialogic history at its best.

Stephen Greenblatt (of Harvard) observes:

> With an impressive array of contributors and a brilliantly innovative format, *Remembrance of Pacific Pasts* makes a crucial invention not only in our attempt to understand the Pacific but also in our attempt to refashion cultural and historical study. This multi-faceted volume is a model for a whole new interpretative practice, a practice based not on monolithic claims but on multiple voices, shifting perspectives, and open-ended critical conversations.

And Benedict Anderson (of Cornell) suggests:

> For many, the image of the Pacific is a foggy, sentimental distillation of Robert Louis Stevenson, Herman Melville, Paul Gauguin, and Marlon Brando's Fletcher Christian. As such it is on the periphery of the academic vision. *Remembrance of Pacific Pasts,* edited ingeniously by Robert Borofsky, blows away this fog and situates the region and its history at the central crossways of contemporary discussions on colonialism and post-coloniality, memory and forgetting, altern and subaltern histories.

With such comments, readers might think I would be "dancing with joy." But is anyone going to read the book? The volume deals with the Pacific in a Pacific-oriented way. Forty percent of the contributions are written by Pacific Islanders. It involves poetry as well as prose. It calls for open-ended conversations among a range of people living in and studying the region. We need only recall that there are many good books dealing with the Pacific that are not read beyond, or even within, the discipline to realize the problem. *The New Yorker* recently reported that, in 1999, 120,000 books were published in the United States, or roughly fourteen per hour (Surowiecki 2001: 67). With such a plethora of publications, how do we get our ideas noticed? Pacific history, the book's overt subject and only natural audience, is a fairly small subfield. The Pacific History Association, as noted, presently numbers 180 members. If that remains its main audience, even in the best of circumstances, the book will never have many readers.

I come back to the same basic question: How does one escape the gravitational pull of the hegemon that encapsulates Pacific studies as an academic study? Most Pacific specialists, it appears, are destined, by the region's political economy and history, to remain intellectually marginal. It is, if you will, the burden that Marx talked of over a century ago: "Material relations are the basis of all . . . relations . . . — the mode of production of material life conditions the social, political, and intellectual life process." Or again:

> Men make their own history [i.e. create their own present and future], but they do not make it just as they please; they . . . make it under circumstances . . . directly encountered, given, and transmitted from the past. The tradition of all the dead generations weighs like a nightmare on the brain of the living. (1973:4–5, 165)

But is it true? Are most Pacific specialists destined—by economics and history—to forever be intellectually marginal despite the region's intellectual possibilities? In a global age of dynamic change and intellectual ferment, *is the Pacific fated to remain intellectually pacific—tranquil and calm?*

## GLOBALIZATION AS OFFERING AN OPPORTUNITY

Perhaps. But then, again, perhaps not. Globalization has not wiped away the dynamics (and resources) that distinguish one region from another, dynamics that I have argued help keep the Pacific marginal (and paradisaical). But it has overlaid, upon these differences, a set of common concerns. It has created a set of shared problems—regarding the environment, development, social stability, and cultural differentiation from the homogenizing whole—that people in Norway, Nigeria, and New Guinea, Suva, San Paulo, and San Francisco all understand. Because of globalization, I am saying, Pacific specialists have an opportunity to escape the economic-historical hegemon and speak to a larger audience about larger problems.

Simple? Well, not quite. There are two problems. The first might be termed, "The Prisoner of Chillon" (after Byron's poem by that name), or as Richard Fariña famously phrased it, "Been Down So Long It Looks Like Up to Me." Scholars of the Pacific have become so accustomed to their marginal position—and the conditions that perpetuate it—that many may feel little urge to change. Down, as Fariña phrased it, feels like up. What globalization offers is not a new appreciation of Pacific scholarship but, rather, a chance for scholars working in the Pacific to speak to larger, more public, audiences about larger, more public, problems. It offers an opportunity to break free from the hegemon. Still, it remains to be seen to what degree scholars of the Pacific are willing to embrace new frameworks—are willing to "make their own history." (Staying with the same old problems, writing in the same old style, I would suggest, will likely perpetuate the same old hegemon.)

Let me provide a concrete example. One obvious global concern that scholars of the Pacific might address arises out of the interaction of postcolonial and globalizing trends: issues of representation, the inclusion of indigenous voices in larger conversations that involve them. Whether one frames it as pragmatic politics or as enlarging the public sphere (see Habermas 1989), the message is the same. Indigenous voices and indigenous perspectives need to be part of global plans, global actions, global understandings (see, for example, Lewis 2001:3–5).

On the surface the Pacific would seem an ideal place for such discussions. The region's scholars were, once, on the cutting edge of this issue. Almost a century ago, based on his work among the Trobriand Islanders of Papua New Guinea, Malinowski preached grasping "the native's point of view . . . *his* vision of *his* world" (1961[1922]:25). And Davidson emphasized decades ago—before social history and, more critically, indigenous perspectives became the rage—the importance of Pacific history studying "the indigenous forces that . . . contributed to the making of the contemporary Pacific" (1966:21; compare Borofsky 2000:26). Moreover, Honolulu and Auckland are among a few select cities in the world where Western academics live in large numbers alongside indigenous groups, with both of them calling the same small place "home." The academics are not expatriates; the indigenous groups are not migrants. They both share the same physical space, they both claim a right to it, and they both justify this right, in part, by events that took place during the two centuries they have lived together. Their pasts, presents, and futures are entwined, I am suggesting, in a special way.

The problem is that today many Pacific specialists in academia, rather than directly engaging with the indigenous perspectives presented by indigenous writers, prefer to remain, themselves, the interpreters of indigenous perspectives. Again and again, there is much talk about involving indigenous voices—without the filter of Western interpreters—in academic writings on the Pacific. But usually there is little more than talk. The two sets of writers rarely write in the same books, participate in the same public conversations, publish in the same journals. Why? Not untypical is the explanation offered by Denoon in his *The Cambridge History of the Pacific Islanders:*

In an ideal history, indigenous scholars would determine the structure and dominate the writing of the text. One consequence of the region's recent history is that few Islanders enjoy the facilities for this task. Rather than wait another generation, we rely on our own largely expatriate experiences of teaching, research and island living. (1997:xvi)

In fact, a large and ever-expanding corpus of literature—on historical and ethnographic topics—has been produced by indigenous writers that is both published and widely read in the region. (Many allude to topics covered in the Denoon volume.) We need only refer to *The Pacific Islands: An Encyclopedia* to see the wealth of indigenous writers (see Lal and Fortune 2000:530–538). Here is the encyclopedia's sampling: Apelu Aiavao, Arapera Hineira Kaa Blank, Nora Vagi Brash, Alistair Te Ariki Campbell, Marjorie Tuainekore Crocombe, Sir Thomas Davis, Alan Duff, Vincent Serei Eri, Sia Figiel, Florence (Johnny) Frisbie, Patricia Grace, Rowley Habib, Epeli Hau'ofa (see also Hau'ofa 1994), Vilsoni Hereniko, Keri Ann Ruhi Hulme, Witi Ihimaera, Arthur Jawodimbari, Jon Jonassen, Lilikala Kame'eleihiva, John Kasaipwalova, Kauraka Kauraka, Celo Kulagoe, Julian Maka'a, Jully Makini, Sano Malifa, Sir Paulias Matane, Sudesh Mishra, Grace Mera Molisa, Satendra Pratap Nandan, Sampson Ngwele, Rexford Orotaloa, Ruperake Petaia, Raymond Pillai, Roma Potiki, John Pule, John Selwyn Saunana, Russell Soaba, Subramani, Robert Sullivan, Kumalau Tawali, Apirana Taylor, Vianney Kianteata Teabo, Teresia Teaiwa, Francis Tekonnang, Makiuti Tongia, Konaiholeva Helu Thaman, Haunani-Kay Trask, Hone Tuwhare, Joseph C. Veramu, Momoe Malietoa Von Reiche, and Albert Wendt.

What these Pacific Islanders do not do is write in the academic style familiar to academics. They write in more literary forms, approaching ethnographic and historical subjects through novels, poems, plays, memoirs, satire, and just plain storytelling. There is an irony here: Using more literary forms, they are more generally read in the Pacific than academics. As Munro observed, Pacific history "is becoming isolated and marginalised *within* the Pacific . . . the very place where . . . [it] ought to be emphasized" (1996:57; see also Munro 1995:83).

Presumably various dynamics are at work. We must tread gingerly in terms of the complexities and egos involved. But we can, at least, make an inference: Seeking to credentialize their work with academics beyond the Pacific, academic anthropologists and historians write in a way that Pacific Islanders (and many others, for that matter) feel uncomfortable with. It is not that these differing groups do not deal with the same subject. They do. But academics seem more inclined to write for fellow academics beyond the region while Pacific Islanders write in a style that captures a wider audience within the region. As a result, rarely is either side substantially represented in the other's writings. (To be fair, the problem of academic writing is not limited to the Pacific, as a discussion with any university publishing house or any newspaper book review editor will make clear. Academics write in ways that alienate; they engage in exclusive dialogs.)

Here is an opportunity for scholars of the Pacific to take the lead in issues of representation. They need not stay with old styles, perpetuate old patterns, hold on to old hegemons. They can openly converse, in shared publications, with Pacific Islanders. In respect to the second difficulty, we might cite Aristotle's *Nicomachean Ethics* (book 1, chapter 7): "One swallow does not make a summer." As noted, *Remembrance of Pacific Pasts* calls for more inclusive styles of writings, for more inclusive conversations, resonates with people beyond the Pacific. But it is only one publication. With fourteen books published in the United States per hour, many more—many, many more—examples are needed to have an impact. To bring change—to make the Pacific the "cutting global edge" in issues of representation—we need a full flock of publications involving academic and indigenous writers writing side by side, engaging one with another.

So there you have it. The Pacific is caught up in an economic-historical hegemon of the *longue durée*. And yet, as globalization spreads across the world, Pacific specialists may well have a way to step free. But will they take it? Marx need not be right: "The tradition of all the dead generations [need not weigh] . . . like a nightmare on the brain of the living" (1973:165). The globalization of problems could well liberate Pacific specialists. Or, more precisely, Pacific specialists could well liberate themselves through globalization. But will they? We wonder. Stay tuned.

## REFERENCES

Abu-Lughod, Lila. 1991. "Writing against Culture." In *Recapturing Anthropology*. Richard Fox, ed. Pp. 137–162. Santa Fe: School of American Research Press.

Adas, Michael. 1989. *Machines as the Measure of Men: Science, Technology, and Ideologies of Western Dominance.* Ithaca, N.Y.: Cornell University Press.

Baudet, Henri. 1965. *Paradise on Earth: Some Thoughts on European Images of Non-European Man.* New Haven, Conn.: Yale University Press.

Beaglehole, J. C. 1967. *The Voyage of the Resolution and Discovery, 1776–1780: The Journals of Captain James Cook on His Voyages of Discovery.* Parts One and Two. Cambridge: Cambridge University Press.

Borofsky, Robert, ed. 2000. *Remembrance of Pacific Pasts: An Invitation to Remake History.* Honolulu: University of Hawai'i Press.

Borofsky, Robert, Fredrik Barth, Richard Shweder, Lars Rodseth, and Nomi M. Stolzenberg. 2001. "When: A Conversation About Culture." *American Anthropologist* 103(2):432–446.

Bougainville, Louis de. 1772[1967]. *A Voyage Round the World.* Ridgewood, N.J.: Gregg Press.

Braudel, Fernand. 1972. *The Mediterranean and the Mediterranean World in the Age of Philip II.* New York: Harper and Row.

———. 1980. *On History.* Chicago: University of Chicago Press.

Campbell, Mary. 1988. *The Witness and the Other World.* Ithaca, N.Y.: Cornell University Press.

Clifford, James. 1982. *Person and Myth: Maurice Leenhardt in the Melanesian World.* Berkeley: University of California Press.

———. 1988. *The Predicament of Culture: Twentieth Century Ethnography, Literature, and Art.* Cambridge: Harvard University Press.

———. 1997. *Routes: Travel and Translation in the Late Twentieth Century.* Cambridge: Harvard University Press.

———. 2000. "Valuing the Pacific—An Interview with James Clifford." In *Remembrance of Pacific Pasts.* Robert Borofsky, ed. Pp. 92–99. Honolulu: University of Hawai'i Press.

Clifford, James, and George Marcus. 1986. *Writing Culture: The Poetics and Politics of Ethnography.* Berkeley: University of California Press.

Cook, James, and James King. 1784. *A Voyage to the Pacific Ocean Undertaken . . . for Making Discoveries in the Northern Hemisphere* 3 vols. London: W. and A. Strahan.

Crane, Fred Arthur. 1952. "The Noble Savage in America, 1815–1860: Concepts of the Indian, with Special Reference to the Writers of the Northeast." Doctoral dissertation. Department of History, Yale University.

Crosby, Alfred. 1986. *Ecological Imperialism: The Biological Expansion of Europe, 900–1900.* New York: Cambridge University Press.

Davidson, J. W. 1955. The Study of Pacific History: An Inaugural Lecture Delivered at Canberra on November 25, 1954. Canberra: Australian National University, Research School of Pacific Studies.

———. 1966. "Problems of Pacific History." *Journal of Pacific History* 1:5–21.

Davis, J. C. 2000. "Utopia and the New World, 1500–1700." In *Utopia: The Search for the Ideal Society in the Western World.* Roland Schaer, Gregory Claeys, and Lyman Tower Sargent, eds. Pp. 95–118. New York: Oxford University Press.

Daws, Gavan. 1980. *A Dream of Islands: Voyages of Self-Discovery in the South Seas.* New York: Norton.

Dening, Greg. 1992. *Mr. Bligh's Bad Language: Passion, Power and Theatre on the Bounty.* Cambridge: Cambridge University Press.

de Lepervanche, Marie. 1973. "Social Structure." In *Anthropology in Papua New Guinea.* Ian Hogbin, ed. Pp. 1–60. Melbourne: Melbourne University Press.

Denoon, Donald, ed. 1997. *The Cambridge History of the Pacific Islanders.* Melbourne: Cambridge University Press.

Durkheim, Emile, and Marcel Mauss. 1963. *Primitive Classification.* Rodney Needham, ed. and translator from the French. Chicago: University of Chicago Press.

Eggan, Fred. 1955. *Social Anthropology of North American Tribes.* Chicago: University of Chicago Press.

———. 1968. "Kinship." In *International Encyclopedia of the Social Sciences.* David Sills, ed. 8:390–401. New York: Macmillan.

Firth, Raymond. 1936. *We, the Tikopia.* London: George Allen & Unwin.

———. 1939. *Primitive Polynesian Economy.* London: Routledge & Kegan Paul.

Foster, Johann Reinhold. 1996[1778]. *Observations Made During a Voyage Round the World.* Nicholas Thomas, Harriet Guest, and Michael Dettelbach, eds. Honolulu: University of Hawai'i Press.

Fox, Richard. 1985. *Lions of the Punjab: Culture in the Making.* Berkeley: University of California Press.

Goldman, Irving. 1970. *Ancient Polynesian Society.* Chicago: University of Chicago Press.

Gramsci, Antonio. 1971. *Selections from the Prison Notebooks.* New York: International Publishers.

Habermas, Jurgen. 1989. *The Structural Transformation of the Public Sphere.* Cambridge, Mass.: MIT Press.

Hau'ofa, Epeli. 1994. "Our Sea of Islands." *The Contemporary Pacific* 6(1):148–161.

Howe, K. R. 1984. *Where the Waves Fall: A New South Seas Islands History from First Settlement to Colonial Rule.* Honolulu: University of Hawai'i Press.

Kahn, Miriam. 2000. "Tahiti Intertwined: Ancestral Land, Tourist Postcard, and Nuclear Test Site." *American Anthropologist* 102(1):7–26.

Keate, G. 1788[1960]. *An Account of the Pelew Islands.* London: G. Nichol.

Kiki, Albert Maori. 1968. *Ten Thousand Years in a Lifetime.* London: Pall Mall Press.

Kirch, Patrick. 1984. *The Evolution of Polynesian Chiefdoms.* Cambridge: Cambridge University Press.

Kiste, Robert, and Mac Marshall, eds. 1999. *American Anthropology in Micronesia: An Assessment.* Honolulu: University of Hawai'i Press.

Kuper, Adam. 1999. *Culture: The Anthropologists' Account.* Cambridge, Mass.: Harvard University Press.

Lal, Brij, and Kate Fortune, eds. 2000. *The Pacific Islands: An Encyclopedia.* Honolulu: University of Hawai'i Press.

La Pérouse, Jean F. G. de. 1799[1968]. *A Voyage Round the World Performed in the Years 1785, 1786, 1787, 1788 . . . Volume 1.* New York: Da Capo Press.

Lepore, Jill. 1998. *The Name of War: King Philip's War and the Origins of American Identity.* New York: Knopf.

Lewis, I. M. 2001. "Why the Warlords Won: How the United States and the United Nations Misunderstood the Clan Politics of Somalia." *The Times Literary Supplement.* June 8:3–5.

Loti, Pierre. 1976[1880]. *The Marriage of Loti.* Honolulu: University of Hawai'i Press.

Malinowski, Bronislaw. 1961[1922]. *Argonauts of the Western Pacific.* New York: Dutton.

———. 1932. *The Sexual Life of Savages in Northwestern Melanesia,* 3rd ed. London: Routledge & Kegan Paul.

———. 1935. *Coral Gardens and Their Magic.* 2 vols. London: George Allen & Unwin.

Margolis, Susanna. 1995. *Adventuring in the Pacific.* San Francisco: Sierra Club Books.

Marx, Karl. 1973. *Karl Marx: On Society and Social Change.* Neil Smelser, ed. Chicago: University of Chicago Press.

McGregor, Gaile. 1988. *The Noble Savage in the New World Garden: Notes Toward a Syntactics of Place.* Toronto: University of Toronto Press.

Mead, Margaret. 1928. *Coming of Age in Samoa.* New York: Morrow.

———. 1930. *The Social Organization of Manu'a.* Bernice P. Bishop Museum Bulletin, No. 76, 2nd ed. 1969. Honolulu: The Museum.

Montaigne, Michel de. 1943[1588]. *The Complete Essays of Montaigne.* Stanford: Stanford University Press.

Munro, Doug. 1995. "Pacific Islands History in the Vernacular." *New Zealand Journal of History.* 29(1):83–96.

———. 1996. "The Isolation of Pacific History." *Journal of Pacific Studies* 20:45–68.

Murdock, George Peter. 1949. *Social Structure.* New York: Free Press.

Nadel, S. F. 1952. "Witchcraft in Four African Societies." *American Anthropologist* 54:18–29.

Robertson, George. 1973. *An Account of the Discovery of Tahiti.* London: Folio Press.

Robertson, Jillian. 1981. *The Captain Cook Myth.* London: Angus & Robertson.

Sahlins, Marshall. 1958. *Social Stratification in Polynesia.* Seattle: University of Washington Press.

———. 1981. *Historical Metaphors and Mythical Realities: Structure in the Early History of the Sandwich Island Kingdom.* Ann Arbor: University of Michigan Press.

———. 1985. *Islands of History.* Chicago: University of Chicago Press.

———. 1992. *Anahulu, the Anthropology of History in the Kingdom of Hawaii: Historical Ethnography* (vol. 1). With the Assistance of Dorothy Barrère. Chicago: University of Chicago Press.

———. 1995. *How "Natives" Think: About Captain Cook, for Example.* Chicago: University of Chicago Press.

Sargent, Lyman Tower. 2000. "Utopia Traditions: Themes and Variations." In *Utopia: The Search for the Ideal Society in the Western World.* Roland Schaer, Gregory Claeys, and Lyman Tower Sargent, eds. Pp. 8–17. New York: Oxford University Press.

Schwartz, Theodore. 1963. "Systems of Areal Integration: Some Considerations Based on the Admiralty Islands of Northern Melanesia." *Anthropological Forum* 1:56–97.

Smith, Bernard. 1960. *European Vision and the South Pacific, 1768–1850.* New York: Oxford University Press.

———. 1992. *Imagining the Pacific in the Wake of the Cook Voyages.* New Haven: Yale University Press.

Spier, Leslie. 1921. "The Sun Dance of the Plains Indians: Its Development and Diffusion." Anthropological Papers, American Museum of Natural History. Vol. 16, Part 7:451–527.

Strathern, Marilyn. 1988. *The Gender of the Gift.* Berkeley: University of California Press.

Surowiecki, James. 2001. "The Power of the Prize." *The New Yorker,* June 18 and 25:67.

Turner, Victor. 1969. *The Ritual Process: Structure and Anti-Structure.* Chicago: Aldine.

———. 1974. *Dramas, Fields, and Metaphors: Symbolic Action in Human Society.* Ithaca, N.Y.: Cornell University Press.

Twain, Mark. 1975[1866]. *Mark Twain's Letters from Hawaii.* Reprinted, edited by A. Grove Day. Honolulu: University of Hawai'i Press.

Wolf, Eric. 1957. "Closed Corporate Peasant Communities in Mesoamerica and Central Java." *Southwestern Journal of Anthropology* 13:1–18.

———. 1982. *Europe and the People Without History.* Berkeley: University of California Press.

# 3

# Crime and "Tribal" Warfare in Contemporary Papua New Guinea

**Paul Roscoe**

*University of Maine*

In recent years, the focus of Melanesian anthropology has shifted from the study of contact-era society to an analysis of the engagement of Melanesian peoples with the West (Carrier 1992; Errington and Gewertz 1995; Foster 1995, 1996; Gewertz and Errington 1999). This "New Melanesian History and Anthropology" (see Foster 1995:1–21) has focused primarily on the economic, political, symbolic, and social dimensions of this engagement, but the perspective is also useful for framing a more neglected issue: the manner in which the encounter with the West has affected the way Melanesians conceptualize, deploy, and manage violence.

In contemporary Papua New Guinea (PNG), no forms of violence attract more concern than a recent rise in violent crime nationally and the reemergence of so-called "tribal warfare" or "tribal fighting" in the country's highlands. Although these trends are linked by the violence common to their commission, PNG policy and politics has treated them as essentially separate and distinct issues. They are conceptualized as different phenomena; they are subject to different legal codes; and governmental attempts to suppress them invoke quite different political, social, and legal policies. In this chapter, I describe and examine how Melanesian agents have deployed and managed these modern forms of violence. My aim is to show that, in traditional PNG terms, what nowadays is labeled war and crime is, in fact, one and the same thing: the deployment of violence or its threat for instrumental purposes. The only difference is superficial: In the lowlands, this violence takes the form of small-scale, surprise ambush while in the highlands it also takes the form of large-scale, open fighting.

That current PNG policy and law differentiates this violence into "crime" and "tribal warfare" (or "tribal fighting"), treating it as though it comprises two qualitatively different social phenomena, is a legacy of the country's Western colonial history. In Western semantic frameworks, large-scale, open, organized violence between large sovereign units (such as nation states) is typically conceptualized as "war" and differentiated from the small-scale, clandestine use of violence within these sovereign units, which is categorized as "crime." Accordingly, under the Western legal codes that PNG inherited when it became an independent nation state in 1975, the form that violence characteristically takes in the Highlands has become "tribal war" or "tribal fighting," while the form it typically takes in the Lowlands has been dubbed "crime."

## CRIME IN CONTEMPORARY PAPUA NEW GUINEA

The perpetrators of the crime wave that began in the mid-1970s and has since spread throughout the country are known in PNG as *raskols,* a Tok-Pisin term meaning "criminal." As Harris (1988) notes in his examination of raskolism in the country's capital, Port Moresby, the term *raskol* first emerged in the mid-1960s to describe young male migrants to urban centers who were given to spontaneous, high-spirited acts of petty crime. Though the term's English overtones of youthful scampery are still applicable to some modern raskols, nowadays it captures a more unfortunate reality, referring to a member of a predatory gang given to organized thieving, rape, and murder (Morauta 1986; Hart Nibbrig and Hart Nibbrig 1991). Today, raskols constitute a major topic of gossip among national and expatriate populations alike. The country's two daily newspapers are seldom without a graphic account of their latest atrocities, and beyond the nation's shores, sensational accounts on the international wires have conspired to present a picture of black savagery run amok.

Beyond the graphic headlines, it is difficult to assess accurately just how serious crime has become in PNG. Police statistics are unreliable for all but the most serious offenses and have not been publicly released since 1990. A recent survey by the United Nations Interregional Crime and Justice Research Institute, however, permits some comparison between PNG's urban centers and a number of cities in Latin America, Africa, and Asia (Levantis 2000). Figures for the mid-1990s indicate that PNG had the highest incidence of sexual assault in any of these cities, with

nearly 12 percent of women over sixteen years falling victim at least once in the preceding year, one in four of them being raped. This statistic slightly exceeded that for Dar-es-Salaam and Cairo and was more than double that of Costa Rica and Jakarta, five times that of Johannesburg, six times that of Rio de Janeiro, and ten times that of Manila. Ten percent of the population had fallen victim to common assault and robbery in the preceding year, a figure slightly higher than that for Rio de Janeiro, close to double that for Tunis, four times that for Manila, and about twenty times that for Beijing and Bombay (Levantis 2000).

These figures must be treated with caution, but they capture a state of affairs that can be both hideous and hair-raising. In August 1998, eighteen female students at Okapa High School in the Eastern Highlands were raped by about thirteen masked men who had broken into their dormitory armed with a rifle and knives (*Post-Courier* 1998). Perhaps the most spectacular incident of raskolism to date took place in 2000 in Port Moresby. According to press reports, a raskol gang member hijacked a helicopter from Jackson's Airport and forced the pilot to land in a city suburb, where the rest of his heavily armed band boarded the aircraft. The gang then helicoptered into downtown Moresby, landed on the roof of the Central Bank, and began to shoot its way down toward the vaults. Acting on a tip-off, armed plainclothes police were already stationed in the building and engaged the gang in a gun battle, forcing them back to the roof of the building and the idling helicopter. There, they reboarded the craft and ordered the pilot to take off, but, as he did so, police stationed outside the building shot them out of the sky. The helicopter crashed into the street below, and after a brief gun battle all but the pilot were dead.

There are no reliable figures for crime in rural areas, but news reports and anecdotal evidence suggest the situation is equally insecure (Reay 1982; Kulick 1991; Roscoe 1992). In 1991, to take Yangoru District of the East Sepik Province (the area of my own field research) as an example, the vehicles traveling the East Sepik highway had something like a one in fifty to one in hundred chance of being held up en route to Wewak, the provincial capital (Roscoe 1999:172). Villagers walking the tracks and feeder roads to the highway were at considerable risk of being waylaid if raskols believed they were carrying money. Occasionally, raskols had even attacked isolated settlements.

The economic cost of these crimes is huge. In 1995, Levantis (2000) estimates, the total value of goods stolen in urban areas alone amounted to K115 million (at that time, about U.S.$100 million) or 1.8 percent of gross domestic product. This sum is dwarfed, however, by indirect losses. The negative impact on international tourism alone likely ran into billions of kina (Levantis 2000), and the costs in terms of terror and injury inflicted on victims are literally incalculable.

## TRIBAL FIGHTING IN CONTEMPORARY PAPUA NEW GUINEA

In contrast to raskolism, which afflicts all parts of the nation, contemporary warfare is confined almost exclusively to the great intermontane valleys of the Highlands. Outbreaks vary considerably in scale and duration, but the largest confrontations typically involve whole tribes or alliances of tribes on each side. They can last for months and are characterized by periodic ambushes, skirmishes, and the occasional massive raid, which may result in massacre, destruction, and large-scale flight (Strathern 1977, 1992; Gordon 1983; Podolefsky 1984; Westermark 1984; Wormsley 1986). Meggitt (1977:174–177) reconstructed the sequence of events of a 1971 war among the Enga of the Wabag region. The senior *kiap*—the Tok-Pisin term for Australian patrol officer—had decided a land dispute between two clans (referred to as A and T to protect their identity) in favor of clan A. Clan T was upset by the decision. It

> armed and swept in force over the border, felling trees and burning houses of clan A. The men of A mobilized and sent many of their families and pigs to shelter with relatives; but, having

won the arbitration, they were still reluctant to retaliate with violence. When, however, the police and kiaps arrived, alerted by the smoke, clan T refused to withdraw and continued its destructive rampage. By then dozens of trees were down, gardens torn up, and 14 houses in flames. Clan A could stand no more. Attacking vigorously, they pushed back clan T, and, outflanking the enemy, crossed the border and put 15 of its houses to the torch. The police fired tear gas and shots in the air to no avail. The fighting went on furiously until dusk, when both sides withdrew to safe positions. Many men had been wounded with arrows, including allies from clans nearby. Clan A already had at least a dozen casualties among its own 60 or 70 warriors. . . .

During the night, an ally of clan T died of an arrow wound in the groin. Incensed, his comrades returned to the battle at dawn and struck deep into clan A's territory. Soon the men of T sent up the victory shout as they cut down and dismembered a wounded ally of clan A. . . . Heavy fighting went on all day as allies streamed in to aid each side. At least 18 men of clan A and its allies were wounded that day, some several times. One, an ally, died of his wounds about four months later. By now riot police and officers from Mount Hagen had joined the local kiaps and police but were unable to contain the combat, which raged until darkness fell. . . .

Fighting resumed at dawn on the third day and before long clan A was getting the better of it, pressing its enemies back to the border and threatening the territory of clan T. . . .

The 500 or so warriors entered the fray again on the fourth day. Although the tempo of the fighting was slowing as tired men felt the effects of their wounds, the police were still unable to halt them. In the morning a party from clan A buried in a safe place the ally . . . who had been killed on the second day. Inflamed by the funeral oratory, the forces of A counterattacked savagely and before long cut off a detachment of the enemy, several of whom they wounded and one, an ally of clan T, they slew. The killers dismembered and mutilated the victim, cutting off his penis and fixing it in his mouth . . . before throwing the remains to the police for disposal. . . .

On the fifth morning, as the weary combatants once more moved into action, the officers judged that the time was right for a strenuous effort to break up the groups of warriors. When the police charged the lines in force, the men of clan A, exhausted and suffering many casualties, were ready to call a halt. (Meggitt 1977:174–77)

As Meggitt (1977) goes on to explain, Clan T was not inclined to reciprocate since they had failed to revenge the entirety of the losses in their ranks and to hold the territory they had taken. The riot police came down swiftly on them, however, and by the end of the day twenty-nine had been arrested and the remainder had dispersed.

Burton is one of a number of anthropologists to witness a confrontation, this one part of a prolonged war in the Wahgi valley (see also Muke 1992:229–262):

The date: 11 December 1989. The place: Minj Station and District Office, inside Konumbka territory. The occasion: a Kondika war party descends from an overlooking ridge and swoops down on an unarmed crowd, firing guns on the run. Two hundred people flee for their lives. Some are forced to dive full length to avoid shotgun pellets. One old man falls into a ditch and the Kondika front line warriors jump over his outstretched body. The police, out-gunned and out-numbered, withdraw in their blue vehicles. For ten minutes the station area is at the mercy of the attackers, who circle round shooting in the vague direction of the Konumbka heartland across the old airstrip, but on this occasion they don't have the numbers to hold the position. The Konumbka are surprisingly slow to react, but finally group together in sufficient numbers to run the Kondika off the station and back into their own territory.

Perhaps twenty gunshots have been fired. . . . It is just fifteen minutes since the raid began. (Burton 1990:226–227)

As with raskolism, the costs of these wars are difficult to calculate but are clearly enormous. In addition to the loss of life, there is often widespread property destruction. In April 2000, a five-month conflict within the Jika tribe outside Mt. Hagen is said to have cost just one of the tribal sections involved K500,000 (about U.S.$150,000) in destroyed houses, household items, vehicles, and cash crops (*National Online* 2001). Bridges that may have taken years to construct are destroyed in minutes or hours, and children are prevented from attending school and the sick from reaching medical centers, sometimes for more than a year.

## THE EMERGENCE OF "CRIME" AND "TRIBAL FIGHTING"

Contact-era New Guinea was rife with what today would be termed crime and tribal fighting. Warfare was endemic, and murder, rape, and theft were common. Most of these acts were perpetrated against other polities classed as enemies, though some also occurred within a polity among kin and allies. In the wake of colonial contact, however, the scale of this violence—both war and crime—diminished significantly. "Pacification" by German and Australian patrol officers quickly suppressed warfare, albeit in a manner that was often equally brutal. Prior to the Second World War, administrative officers occasionally razed entire villages suspected of armed activity, and they sometimes massacred hostile natives when they were threatened, and from time to time they hanged groups of warriors found guilty of war killings (Hides 1936:120–123, compare Townsend 1926:3, 1934, entry for May 21; Sillitoe 1991:154–167; see also Rodman and Cooper 1983). In the wake of World War II, pacification became a more sophisticated process and significantly less violent.

Crime, whether within native communities or against Europeans, was also suppressed under the colonial powers. Less serious offenses like petty theft, adultery, and brawling were dealt with at the local level, if not by traditional conflict management procedures, then by visiting patrol officers and, in later years, by village courts (Scaglion 1985, 1987). More serious crimes—rape, murder, the occasional armed robbery—were dealt with by administrative courts and punished with jail, often with hard labor and, in earlier years, with flogging or hanging. (Though effective in suppressing crimes perpetrated by natives, these measures were used to strikingly less effect against the often hideous crimes that Europeans—most notably labor recruiters, gold prospectors, and even patrol officers—perpetrated.)

These successes in suppressing both crime and tribal fighting proved to be temporary. The rise of today's criminal activity can be traced to PNG's urban centers and in particular the capital. Harris (1988:3–34) pinpoints the late 1960s as the time when the first "true" raskol gangs emerged in Port Moresby. Between 1968 and 1975, they began to organize and focus their activities, and between 1975 and the late 1980s, they became more institutionalized, broadening their activities from breaking and entering to include vehicle theft and drug-related activity. By the late 1970s, they had spread to the city outskirts and, by about 1985, they had consolidated into perhaps a dozen powerful gangs. Their impact on the city is illustrated by estimates of the number of cases of breaking and entering, which rose from 4,200 in 1975, to 7,080 in 1980, 8,800 in 1983, and 11,250 in 1984 (Harris 1988:21). Levantis (2000) tracks a similar explosion in PNG urban crime generally, beginning in the early to mid-1970s and increasing at an annual rate of 20 percent until the mid-1980s. Thereafter, growth appears to have slowed—to 11 percent between 1985 and 1990 and 6 percent between 1990 and 1995—possibly because opportunities for criminal activity were approaching saturation levels.

As crime was blossoming in the country at large, tribal fighting was reemerging in the highlands. The causes of this resurgence are many and this is partly a function of modern developments. In areas such as the Southern Highlands, fighting has occasionally broken out around traditional ownership of, and the distribution of royalties from, oil and gas fields. Elsewhere, similar issues have precipitated wars over ownership of land alienated for tea and coffee plantations. In yet other areas, the run-up to, or outcome of, political elections has led to serious fighting.

In many instances, though, today's reemergent tribal warfare breaks out for much the same reasons as in earlier days. The trajectory of events among the Enga seems typical of the more densely populated areas of the Highlands. Prior to contact, Enga territorial boundaries routinely shifted as the fortunes of war favored first one group and then another. Around 1950, however, pacification had finally taken effect and, in so doing, had frozen these boundaries, solidifying imbalances in the distribution of population over land. To deal with the inevitable land disputes and to circumvent violence, the Australian administration introduced Courts for Native Affairs (replaced in 1962 by the Land Titles Commission). Initially, the Enga took to these new theaters, referring to their legal suits as "fighting in the courts" rather than on the battlefield. Unfortunately, these ill-equipped and undermanned venues rarely succeeded in resolving disputes to the satisfaction of all parties. Meanwhile, population was growing apace—around 2 to 2.5 percent per annum between the late 1950s and early 1970s—increasing the demand for land and intensifying pressures for military rather than civil action. By the early 1960s, sporadic brawls and riotous behavior were being reported, and by the late 1960s serious outbreaks of war were once again a feature of the Enga landscape (Meggitt 1977:156–181).

These resurgent wars differed little from those of precontact days, except that administrative intervention usually brought them to a halt after a few days rather than many weeks or months. Weaponry was still largely traditional. Steel rather than stone axes might be used in close fighting, and in 1986, in the middle Wahgi, Burton (1990:226–227) observed a few men carrying metal spears and one wearing a motorcycle crash helmet. Around this time, however, firearms made their first appearance in the ranks, apparently in a war among the Jika outside Mt. Hagen. The first guns were homemade: an iron pipe for the barrel and a nail, a strip of rubber, and an umbrella catch for the firing mechanism. Twelve-gauge shotgun cartridges served as ammunition. In later years, spring-loaded firing pins and safety catches were added and, by the late 1980s, factory-made SLRs, 303s, and even M16/AR15s were also reaching the battlefields, many of them clandestinely purloined from defense-force armories (Burton 1990:233–236). Ten years later, some combatant groups were even hiring mercenaries. In late 2000, police in the Asaro region of the Eastern Highlands stopped a twenty-five-seater bus and arrested fourteen men from the Kainantu and Henganofi areas armed with a .22, an M16 assault rifle, and an SLR. The men had been hired to help in a fight between the Kofena and Lindima/Kanosa tribes, which by that time had already claimed over twenty lives.

It is widely recognized that this contemporary warfare is but the warfare of old, modernized to a degree by the deployment of Western weaponry, military strategy, and modes of transport. In the old days, Highland fighting took three main forms: the ambush, the open (or "ritual") battle, and the large-scale raid.[1] Ambushes occurred everywhere in New Guinea and usually comprised small-scale, surprise attacks on residences, gardens, or travelers in lonely parts of the countryside. The open battle and large-scale raid, however, were more characteristic of the Highlands than the Lowlands. Open battles were daytime, set-piece confrontations. They might involve hundreds of warriors, and, as several early observers and commentators noted, they often seemed like sporting occasions (Schäfer 1938; Vial 1942; Draper 1952:16; Gardner and Heider 1968:138–146; Meggitt 1977:16–21; Larson 1987:245–261). Though their superficial causes could be serious, they were just as likely to be trivial—a verbal insult, a ceremonial slight, or perhaps even, as Meggitt (1977:18) observed, nothing more than a passion to fight. The time and place of the contest were arranged in advance, and the confrontation itself usually followed codes of what might be called "chivalrous" conduct. Noncombatants were often off-limits to attack (in some places, for example, women and children gathered as spectators on a nearby rise), and the fighting was commonly confined to a traditional arena or delimited

area. After a bout at close quarters, enemy champions among the Enga went so far as to congratulate one another in the center of the field, even embracing and exchanging decorations or weapons as souvenirs of the occasion. Although many warriors might be wounded before a parity of kills could be struck and a truce declared, mortality was often light, and, among many groups, neither side would attempt to follow up an advantage by invading enemy territory, destroying property, or massacring inhabitants.

Like the open battle, the large-scale raid also could mobilize hundreds of warriors, but there the similarities ended. Proximate causes were seldom as trivial as an insult; rather, raids were precipitated by disputes over land, property, or women, or by killings that needed to be revenged. Rather than arrange a time and place for battle, the goal commonly was to launch a surprise invasion of enemy territory, though given the number of warriors mobilized, defenders were often forewarned and able to rally, meet, and resist the attack at their border. The aim and end result, moreover, was not to achieve a parity in kills as in open battle but rather to invade and devastate the enemy. In the worst outcomes, one side would succeed in pushing deep into enemy territory, massacring the inhabitants, raping fleeing women, firing the houses, killing pigs, and destroying crops (Fortune 1936:2t, 90[a], 95–96; Glasse 1959: 273–289; Strathern 1971:67; Meggitt 1977: 21–46, 86–87; Larson 1987:245, 271–276; Strathern and Stewart 2000).

Sheila Draper, an early Lutheran missionary among the Dani in the Pyramid region of the Grand Valley, observed several such raids:

> The clans seemed to be always at war: every few days the cockatoo-like screech that heralded an attack (often a dawn raid) would sound in the early morning, and there would be fleeing lines of women, children and pigs, and then smoke from a burning village somewhere. The latter was usually the work of allied groups who moved in separately from the main battle (1998, personal communication).

Traveling to the north of Mt. Hagen, Michael Leahy (1934) recorded in his diary:

> Hell of a big war on over the Wahgi and houses are going up in smoke at frequent intervals, and an occasional roar from that direction I suppose indicates an advance by the attackers. [T]he track leading up to and on top of the range behind the village is full of the women and kids driving their pigs and carrying their most valued possessions away on their backs every now and again turning around to see whose home is going up in flames. They are having a whale of a time (entry for October 12–13).

## THE RETURN OF THE AMBUSH

The similarities between this traditional warfare and modern Highlands fighting hardly need laboring. What is less obvious, though, is that the same is true of raskolism. Scholarly attempts to understand the rise of violent crime in PNG identify a range of causative factors. Levantis (2000) attributes it in significant part to the 1962 lifting of the prohibition on native consumption of alcohol. Others (for example, May n.d.) suggest it is a function of the widespread failure of economic development initiatives to provide the wherewithal to realize growing consumer aspirations, a theme commonly echoed in the PNG press. Certainly, in the Yangoru District, young people are confronted with an ever-expanding range of material goods and are becoming ever more deeply enmeshed in Western materialist and individualist cultural schemas via schooling, advertising, the cinema, and videos. No longer are peer-group pressures limited to possession of shorts, shirt, meri-blouse, metal tools, tinned meat, and rice, as they were forty or fifty years ago. Today, on the margins of, or beyond, financial reach, Pepsi, alcohol, cigarettes, perfumes, designer clothes and shoes, tape recorders, radios, VCRs, motorbikes, and cars are on display to be coveted on the pages of the nation's newspapers and in the stores and emporia of Yangoru and Wewak. While aspirations have risen, however, economic development has declined. Most cash-cropping endeavors have failed, and over the last fifteen to twenty years job opportunities in urban centers have declined precipitously. By 1990, the chances that young people—even those with some education—had of obtaining a job had dwindled almost to nothing.

A further cause for the rise of raskolism, often touted in the PNG media, is a decline in the potency of traditional cultural sanctions. In traditional Yangoru, crimes such as theft, rape, and other acts of violence were deterred by a variety of means. They include magical and nonmagical booby traps (for example, bamboo splinters planted in gloomy spots near a house or along a garden path to lacerate the feet of a thief; spells placed on door lintels, trees, and garden stiles), physical violence, social opprobrium, and sorcery. Without doubt, the efficacy of these sanctions has declined with modernization. The Yangoru Health Centre, though lately starved of funds and personnel, is available to treat booby-trap injuries. Raskols are said to care little about social opinion; with their ill-gotten gains, they can alleviate the threat of retaliatory sorcery by buying off sorcerers and, though physical reprisals against raskols do occur, they are risky because of the raskols' ability to organize retaliatory violence. The efficacy of traditional sanctions such as social opprobrium, violence, and sorcery, moreover, is predicated on the presence of the malefactor (sorcery requires that the victim's exuviae first be procured). Today, however, with urban environments just a PMV ride away, criminals can escape the consequences of their actions at home by heading off to town until memories have faded and tempers cooled.

In many parts of PNG, though, the most potent factor in the rise of crime seems to be a growing recognition among young criminals of the manifold weaknesses in the structures of state control. Some of these weaknesses are an emergent function of the deteriorating effectiveness of PNG law enforcement agencies. Most, though, seem to have existed unacknowledged for decades, and only recently have young men begun to recognize them, learn how to exploit them, and spread this knowledge to their colleagues. The most important factor explaining the sudden rise of crime in rural Yangoru in the late 1980s was "training" in criminal gangs in towns such as Lae and Rabaul. Some of Yangoru's male migrants to town had joined urban raskol gangs and, in that company, had learned the basic weaknesses in the system and the techniques for exploiting them in breaking and entering, car theft, highway robbery, and mugging. After several years, they then returned to Yangoru, where they put their new-found knowledge and abilities to work (Roscoe 1998).

Whatever its cause, the issue I wish to emphasize is that raskolism is not so much the *emergence* of violent crime from PNG's engagement with Western economies and political structures but rather the *reemergence* of a particular type of warfare that had existed at contact. As noted already, ambush was a universal feature of New Guinea warfare. Everywhere, people had to be ready to defend themselves against surprise attacks on their residences, on the paths to and from their daily rounds, and in their gardens or groves. Among the Yangoru Boiken, for example, the typical ambush against a settlement occurred under cover of darkness. Attackers would infiltrate an enemy village and, with the gray light of dawn, "rise like the morning mist" to surprise their target. But it was a risky undertaking. Those under attack would usually barricade themselves in their houses and quickly raise the alarm. In an attempt to force them out for slaughter, the attackers customarily tried to fire the houses, but with armed warriors from other hamlets rallying to the defense, time was short and killings usually few (Roscoe 1996).

Not surprisingly, perhaps, ambushes against hamlets seem to have been rare, at least in comparison to attacks on people working in the gardens or traveling along isolated bush tracks. Just as darkness favored the surprise ambush against settlements at night, so the extraordinary density of Yangoru's vegetation and the broken nature of its terrain favored a surprise attack on garden parties during the day. If assailants knew or could guess their targets' movements, they would hide along a path or creep up unseen on a garden and fall upon their unwitting victims. Sometime in the early 1900s, for example, several members of the Sima clan of Sima village took revenge on an Ambukanja man, Worumbukia, the leader of a party that had attacked the Sima clan in its gardens, killing an elderly man and woman. Kworabre villagers had seen Worumbukia at work harvesting tubers from a garden near their border. They alerted their allies in Sima village, and an ambush party crept up on the garden and fell on Worumbukia as he was climbing a stile in the fence. Despite multiple spear-wounds, Worumbukia managed to crawl away in the confusion and hide in a nearby pig shelter. He was discovered a few minutes later and repeatedly speared before being dispatched with a black-palm war-sword. His killers paused momentarily to sing the *warantchangile,* the "song of the dogs," which celebrated triumph in battle, and then fled back to the safety of their own territory.

In another incident, apparently dating to the mid-to-late-1800s, a Sima clan member killed a brother-in-law by ambushing him as he walked along a path. The victim, a member of the enemy village of Ambukanja, had married the lone sister of four Sima-clan brothers. It is sometimes said that second sons are resentful and troublesome individuals. However that may be, the second-born of the brothers felt slighted by his portion of a gift of yams that the Ambukanja man had sent to his brothers-in-law. Accordingly, he recruited several enemies of Ambukanja and arranged an ambush. First, he yodeled across the ridge-tops to his sister in Ambukanja, inviting her and her husband to visit him the following day. Early next morning, he and his allies then crept up to the Ambukanja border and lay in wait along the path. When the couple appeared, the party sprang out, cutting the couple off front and rear, and speared the Ambukanja man to death.

In contemporary PNG, it is commonly thought that such ambushes are a thing of the past, but they are not. Their principal elements survive today in raskol activity. The typical robbery of people walking the tracks of Yangoru or of PMVs cruising the East Sepik highway, for example, is essentially the strategy of surprise and encirclement used to waylay enemies en route to their gardens or their relatives. On the highway, the common *modus operandi* is to set an ambush around a sharp bend in the road or at the beginning of a steep grade. At these points, vehicles are necessarily traveling slowly and are easy to hold up. To discourage an adventurous driver from trying to run the ambush, a balk of timber may be laid across the road. Advance guards, sometimes equipped with binoculars, are posted at forward points overlooking the highway to alert their confederates when a promising target appears. As the vehicle nears the point of ambush, one or two masked members step out into the road and train shotguns on the driver, while the others, also masked and armed usually with knives, approach from the rear to execute the robbery. Occasionally, young women passengers are raped, and the gang then vanishes with its spoils into the dense bush at the roadside.

As did ambushers in days gone by, raskols also occasionally attack a hamlet under cover of night. Following the *Pax Australiana,* a number of Yangoru villagers moved away from their traditional ridge-top hamlets to establish homes closer to their gardens, water, and bush. Some of these new hamlets were quite isolated and, with the sudden rise of raskolism, their inhabitants found themselves vulnerable to attack. Early in 1991, an isolated, one-family hamlet on the outskirts of Ambukanja village was held up at midnight by a gang from a village on the Sepik highway. Its members had learned—either from informants within Ambukanja or by observing his cocoa-selling trips along the highway—that the husband was gathering bridewealth for his son's forthcoming marriage. The gang attacked while the husband was away, bound his wife and children, and stole his savings and an expensive radio (see also Kulick 1991, for a particularly tragic, eyewitness account of an ambush on Gapun village in the Lower Sepik region).

The motives for raskol attacks have shifted from those of earlier days. Ambushes were commonly launched to revenge a theft, seduction, rape, murder, or other social delict or offense; to preempt a military threat; and/or to demonstrate bravery and prowess in the field. Other culturally more variable motives included pillage, headhunting, cannibalism, favor with the ancestor spirits, and the conquest of land. Nowadays raskol ambushes are launched primarily to procure Western material goods and cash and only to a lesser extent to rape, revenge a killing, or gain prestige. Headhunting and cannibalism, moreover, are long gone. The fact remains, however, that raskol attacks represent the same sudden and surprise deployment of violence for instrumental purposes as did the ambushes of old. Raskolism, in other words, represents the return of the ambush, as much a form of "tribal fighting" as are the pitched battles currently being fought in the Highlands.

## RECONSIDERING CRIME AND TRIBAL WAR

If raskolism is but the return of the ambush, then the puzzle is why neither in the West nor in PNG is it recognized as war but instead is categorized and talked about as "crime." Or, to put this another way: Why is tribal conflict in the Highlands usually recognized and talked of as "war," "fighting," or "social unrest" but rarely ever as "crime"? The answer lies surprisingly close to home, in the rather arbitrary way that we in the West conceptualize the different forms of violence exemplified in New Guinea. As enculturated members of a nation state, we inherit cultural categories that are adapted to the conditions and properties of life in that nation state. We tend not to acknowledge this consciously, however, because these categories are largely transparent. Rather than recognizing them as constructions by and within our minds, we perceive them as properties of a "natural" order "out there."

Consider, for example, the way in which we conceptualize violence. As anthropologists have pointed out for years (for example, Fried 1967:230; Service 1975:83–90), one of the distinctive features of a state is its monopoly on the use of physical force. The deployment of violence by one member of a state against another is deplored and, in most cases, defined and prohibited as "crime." We accept violence as legitimately exercised within the state only if it is sanctioned and controlled by the state—for example, if it is deployed by state agents such as the police in the interests of enforcing the state's monopoly on force. By contrast, violence deployed outside the state against those the state defines as enemies is considered legitimate and defined as "war," thus, dictionary definitions of war as hostile activity carried on between "nations or states."[2] Because nation states are large, moreover—even the smallest of the earth's early states approached populations of a million, and some of today's nation states number a billion—we conceptualize war as the large-scale deployment of violence.

In sum, to Western minds enculturated into the exigencies of life in a nation state, the deployment of violence within the state by individuals or small gangs is conceptualized and defined as crime and is separated from the large-scale deployment of violence between states, which is defined as war. (The exception proving this rule is hostile activity carried on by *large* social units—ethnic blocs or political factions—*within* the "nation or state." Although it represents the deployment of violence within the state, it is defined not as crime but as war—as civil, revolutionary, or secessionist war—because, first, it is large-scale violence and, second, when it breaks out, the state's existence is actually in doubt. During the Civil War, for example, America was as much two separate states at war as it was a single united state divided by war.)

Modern PNG inherited these Western conceptions as part of the nation-state apparatus imposed on it by its former colonial masters—Germany, Britain, and Australia. Under this heritage, the large-scale violence prosecuted between sovereign tribes in the Highlands[3]—the open battles and large-scale raiding—fits

neatly into Western definitions of war, and the principal goal of the burgeoning PNG state has been to suppress it by armed force or by intervening to negotiate a peace. Only rarely are warriors tried in the courts, and even then charges are usually brought against just a few ringleaders. By contrast, the small-scale ambushes that constituted most contact-era warfare in the Lowlands became legally defined as crime—raskolism—even though it is no less a manifestation of "tribal warfare" than the open battles and invasions of the Highlands. In contrast to its attitude towards tribal fighting, the PNG state's principal goal towards raskolism is to detect, judge, and jail its perpetrators.

## CRIME AND WAR

The people of PNG find themselves at one of the more invidious points of human history. It is now a cliché to observe that, even today, there are individuals in PNG who were born into an age of stone tools but will die having traveled in jet planes constructed and guided by computers. To the Western lay public, this circumstance is a wonder of the modern world. But the Western public does not have to grapple with the extraordinarily accelerated rate of organizational and technological change that this represents. To the people who must live this change, it is a challenging experience. The Western cultural schema that colonialism imposed on PNG sit uneasily on indigenous Melanesian categories and social organization, creating fluid, confusing, even schizophrenic cultural worlds. People are forced to negotiate parallel, often disjunctive sets of cultural schema: those of the Melanesian society into which they were born and those of the Western world they have inherited.

One of the many contradictions between these parallel schema concerns the deployment of violence. As members of a nation state, the people of PNG are supposed to have replaced the thousands of sovereign worlds and identities that divided their land at contact with a single national identity. What once comprised thousands of "us's" and "thems" is, with the wave of a colonial wand, supposed to have become a single, united "us": Papua New Guinea. In practice, sovereign worlds and identities cannot so easily be erased.

What is war and crime in a Western nation state was not always war and crime in traditional Melanesian society. In traditional days, to be sure, theft from or murder of a member of a person's own sovereign world—be it clan, village, or tribe—was considered illegitimate. But perpetrated against a neighboring sovereignty—a neighboring clan, village, or tribe—as ambush, open battle, or invasion, the same undertaking was considered an act of war, of courage and glory. In considerable degree, this remains true today. Under traditional schema, raskolism is warfare just as much as are the pitched battles of the Highlands; just as do contemporary Highland warriors, raskols usually target victims beyond their clan or village, people who, under traditional schema, constitute legitimate enemies.

Under the Western legal codes and practices that PNG inherited, however, raskolism has been singled out and condemned morally and legally as crime and its perpetrators are subject to incarceration, whereas Highland fighting is designated as tribal warfare or fighting, not crime. Although routinely condemned, tribal warfare occupies a more ambiguous moral and legal space, characterized by the kind of ambivalence that the West feels toward civil war. To the Western world, civil war is certainly deplored, but it is lamented more as a rupture of social relations than as a moral offense and a legal crime. Rather than morally condemning and criminalizing the protagonists and throwing them in jail, the aim is to "heal" the breach, to negotiate a peace. And this is what happens in PNG today. Raskols are arrested, tried, and jailed, but warriors—engaged in precisely the same acts according to traditional schema—are not, or much more rarely so. Rather, they are impressed by armed police or political negotiators into a ceasefire and an eventual peace through ceremonial acts and compensation payments of cash, pigs, and even women (on

the latter, see, for example, Gewertz and Errington 1999).

In this light, PNG social and legal policy perhaps merits reconsideration. To avert outbreaks of tribal fighting, it may help to consider this activity as more than just "eccentric behavior in the modern state" (Clifford et al. 1984:100) to be managed with Western models of social control. If raskolism is to be criminalized, then, to be consistent, tribal fighting should be approached under the same policy.[4] It might be more helpful, though, to reconsider raskolism. Raskols are not simply deviants challenging the state's monopoly of violence as Western schema would have it; under traditional schema, they are also warriors deploying violence as a legitimate tool against enemies. This is not to claim that raskols are courageous but misunderstood young men: Like many eminent warriors of old, they are often brutal and ruthless individuals (Watson 1971). But it does suggest that, to control raskolism, PNG policy may need to do more than simply import and execute Western models of crime.

## ACKNOWLEDGMENTS

For access to the papers and/or diaries of Reo Fortune, Michael Leahy, and G. W. L. Townsend, I am deeply grateful to Ann MacLain, Jeanette Leahy, and Laurie Bragge, respectively.

## NOTES

1. Fragmentary evidence indicates that open battles and large-scale raids occurred as naval engagements in some areas of lowland New Guinea.

2. Unfortunately, this definition has been imported into anthropological definitions of war. Thus, war is the use of "organized force" between "groups," "societies," and/or some kind of politically independent "unit," "group," or "community" (Berndt 1962:232; Narroll 1964:286; Otterbein 1973:923; Malinowski 1974[1937]: 141; Ferguson 1990:26). This application to nonstate societies of categories derived from the nature of Western states is unfortunate in that it arbitrarily drives an analytical wedge between different forms of what is all essentially violence.

3. Few sources specify with any precision the numbers of warriors involved in open battles and large-scale

raiding. "Tribes" and "clans" numbering from a hundred or so to a few thousand people are commonly reported as mobilizing for war, suggesting that battles could have involved several hundred warriors on each side. Referring to Mae Enga warfare, Meggitt (1962:397) notes that the "ordinary sort of fighting" involved "a few score men on each side," though occasionally about 2,000 armed men might take the field.

4. It seems to me highly probable that, behind the edifice of Western law and policy they have inherited, Papua New Guinean policy makers are well aware of these points. My argument is addressed rather to Western governmental, NGO, and aid agencies that influence PNG policy.

## REFERENCES

Berndt, Ronald M. 1962. *Excess and Restraint: Social Control Among a New Guinea Mountain People.* Chicago: University of Chicago Press.

Burton, John. 1990. "Tribal Fighting: The Scandal of Inaction." *Catalyst* 20:226–244.

Carrier, James, ed. 1992. *History and Tradition in Melanesian Anthropology.* Berkeley: University of California.

Clifford, W., L. Morauta, and B. Stuart. 1984. *Law and Order in Papua New Guinea.* Port Moresby: Institute of National Affairs.

Draper, S. 1952. *Outline of the Culture of Some of the Enga People, N.G.* Unpublished manuscript. Adelaide: Draper Archive, South Australia Museum.

Errington, Frederick K., and Deborah B. Gewertz. 1995. *Articulating Change in the "Last Unknown."* Boulder, Colo.: Westview Press.

Ferguson, R. Brian. 1990. "Explaining War." In *The Anthropology of War.* Jonathan Haas, ed. Pp. 26–55. Cambridge: Cambridge University Press.

Fortune, Reo. 1936. Men of Purari. Unpublished manuscript. Wellington, N.Z.: Fortune Collection, Turnbull Library.

Foster, Robert J. 1995. *Social Reproduction and History in Melanesia.* Cambridge: Cambridge University Press.

Foster, Robert J., ed. 1996. *Nation Making: Emergent Identities in Postcolonial Melanesia.* Ann Arbor: University of Michigan Press.

Fried, Morton H. 1967. *The Evolution of Political Society: An Essay in Political Anthropology.* New York: Random House.

Gardner, Robert, and Karl G. Heider. 1968. *Gardens of War: Life and Death in the New Guinea Stone Age.* New York: Random House.

Gewertz, Deborah B., and Frederick K. Errington. 1999. *Emerging Class in Papua New Guinea: The Telling of Difference.* Cambridge: Cambridge University Press.

Glasse, Robert M. 1959. "Revenge and Redress Among the Huli: A Preliminary Account." *Mankind* 5:273–289.

Gordon, Robert. 1983. "The Decline of the Kiapdom and the Resurgence of 'Tribal Fighting' in Enga." *Oceania* 53:205–223.

Harris, Bruce. 1988. "The Rise of Rascalism: Action and Reaction in the Evolution of Rascal Gangs." Discussion Paper No. 54. Port Moresby: Institute of APp.lied Social and Economic Research.

Hart Nibbrig, N., and E. Hart Nibbrig. 1991. "Rascals in Paradise: Urban Gangs in Papua New Guinea." *Pacific Studies* 15(3):115–134.

Hides, J. G. 1936. *Papuan Wonderland.* London: Blackie.

Kulick, Don. 1991. "Law and Order in Papua New Guinea." *Anthropology Today* 7:21–22.

Larson, Gordon Frederick. 1987. "The Structure and Demography of the Cycle of Warfare among the Ilaga Dani of Irian Jaya." Unpublished Ph.D. dissertation. Ann Arbor: University of Michigan.

Leahy, Michael. 1934. *Diary.* Canberra: National Library of Australia.

Levantis, Theodore. 2000. "Crime Catastrophe—Reviewing Papua New Guinea's Most Serious Social and Economic Problem." *Pacific Economic Bulletin* 15.

Malinowski, Bronislaw. 1974[1937]. "Culture as a Determinant of Behavior." In *Factors Determining Human Behavior.* Harvard Tercentenary Publications. Pp. 133–168. New York: Arno Press.

May, Ron J. n.d. *The East Sepik Province.* Unpublished manuscript.

Meggitt, M. J. 1962. [Discussion]. In *Administration of the Territory of Papua and New Guinea and UNESCO Science Co-Operation Office for South East Asia.* Symposium on the Impact of Man on Humid Tropics Vegetation. Anonymous ed. Pp. 397–398. Canberra: Commonwealth Government Printer.

Meggitt, Mervyn. 1977. *Blood Is Their Argument: Warfare Among the Mae Enga Tribesmen of the New Guinea Highlands.* Palo Alto: Mayfield.

Morauta, Louise, ed. 1986. *Perspectives on Law and Order.* Canberra: Australian National University.

Muke, John D. 1992. "The Wahgi *Opo Kumbo:* An Account of Warfare in the Central Highlands of New Guinea." Ph.D. thesis. Cambridge: University of Cambridge.

Narroll, Raoul. 1964. "On Ethnic Unit Classification." *Current Anthropology* 5:283–312.

National Online. 2001. "Highlands Tribes End Feud with Compo Payment." *The National Online,* April 20. Port Moresby: The National.

Otterbein, Keith. 1973. "The Anthropology of War." In *Handbook of Social and Cultural Anthropology.* J. Honigmann, ed. Pp. 923–958. Chicago: Rand McNally.

Podolefsky, Aaron. 1984. "Contemporary Warfare in the New Guinea Highlands." *Ethnology* 23:73–87.

Post-Courier. 1998. 18 School Girls Raped. Post-Courier Online, August 9. Port Moresby: *Post-Courier.*

Reay, Marie. 1982. "Lawlessness in the Papua New Guinea Highlands." In *Melanesia: Beyond Diversity.* R. J.

May and Hank Nelson, eds. Pp. 623–637. Canberra: Australian National University.

Rodman, Margaret, and Matthew Cooper, eds. 1983. *The Pacification of Melanesia*. New York: University Press of America.

Roscoe, Jim (Paul). 1992. "Rascalism in Papua New Guinea (Letter to the Editor)." *Anthropology Today* 8(1):26.

Roscoe, Paul B. 1996. "War and Society in Sepik New Guinea." *Journal of the Royal Anthropological Institute (N.S.)* 2:645–666.

———. 1999. "The Return of the Ambush: '*Raskolism*' in Rural Yangoru, East Sepik Province." *Oceania* 69:171–183.

Scaglion, Richard. 1985. "Kiaps as Kings: Abelam Legal Change in Historical Perspective." In *History and Ethnohistory in Papua New Guinea*. Deborah Gewertz and Edward Schieffelin, eds. Pp. 77–99. Sydney: University of Sydney.

Scaglion, Richard, ed. 1987. "Customary Law and Legal Development in Papua New Guinea." *Journal of Anthropology*. Special issue. 6(1–2). DeKalb: Department of Anthropology, Northern Illinois University.

Schäfer, Alfons. 1938. "'Kriegsidyll' aus unserer Südseemission." *Steyler Missionsbote* 65:180–181.

Service, Elman R. 1975. *Origins of the State and Civilization: The Process of Cultural Evolution*. New York and London: Norton.

Sillitoe, Paul. 1991. "From the Waga Furari to the Wen." In *Like People You See in a Dream: First Contact in Six Papuan Societies*. Edward L. Schieffelin and Robert Crittenden, eds. Pp. 147–167. Stanford: Stanford University Press.

Strathern, Andrew. 1971. *The Rope of Moka: Big-Men and Ceremonial Exchange in Mount Hagen, New Guinea*. Cambridge: Cambridge University Press.

———. 1977. "Contemporary Warfare in the New Guinea Highlands—Revival or Breakdown?" *Yagl-Ambu* 4:135–146.

———. 1992. "Let the Bow Go Down." In *War in the Tribal Zone: Expanding States and Indigenous Warfare*. R. Brian Ferguson and Neil L. Whitehead, eds. Pp. 229–250. Santa Fe, N.M.: School of American Research Press.

Strathern, Andrew, and Pamela J. Stewart. 2000. *Collaboration & Conflicts: A Leader Through Time*. Fort Worth, TX: Harcourt.

Townsend, G. W. L. 1926. *Report of a Patrol by A/D.O. Townsend to Kambrindo on the Lower River (with several divergences)*. Ambunti Patrol Report 5–26/27. MS 3661. Canberra: National Library of Australia.

———. 1934. *Diary*. Koetong, Va., Australia: Bragge Archive.

Vial, Leigh G. 1942. "They Fight for Fun." *Walkabout* 9(1):5–9.

Watson, James B. 1971. "Tairora: The Politics of Despotism in a Small Society." In *Politics in New Guinea: Traditional and in the Context of Change: Some Anthropological Perspectives*. Ronald M. Berndt and Peter Lawrence, eds. Pp. 224–275. Nedlands and Seattle: University of Western Australia Press and University of Washington Press.

Westermark, George D. 1984. "'Ol I Skulim Mipela': Contemporary Warfare in the Papua New Guinea Eastern Highlands." *Anthropological Quarterly* 57: 114–124.

Wormsley, William E. 1986. "Courts, Custom, and Tribal Warfare in Enga." In *Customary Law and Legal Development in Papua New Guinea*. Richard Scaglion, ed. Pp. 55–107. DeKalb, Ill.: Northern Illinois University.

# 4

# Fiji's Coups: The Politics of Representation and the Representation of Politics

**Martha Kaplan**

*Vassar College*

Fiji became independent in 1970 and has had coups in 1987 and 2000. As this chapter is written, an appeals court decision to reinstate the 1997 constitution guaranteeing political rights to Fiji's multiethnic citizenry has challenged the governmental plans of the Great Council of Chiefs (backed by an ethnic Fijian military) to promote the political paramountcy of ethnic Fijians over all others in this multiethnic nation. Today, the population of Fiji is about one-half people of indigenous Pacific Islander descent and one-half people of Indian descent. Once again, Fiji citizens debate, with words and force, control over the nation, and the very nature of authority in the islands. Is Fiji to be a nation in which a core of colonial chiefly rulers and one ethnic group have special rights, or a multiethnic democracy?

What do people consider to be a good system of political representation? What kinds of political contests are legitimate, or even desirable? This chapter will discuss the politics of representation and the representation of politics in Fiji. The politics of the postcolonial nation of Fiji since 1970 (including constitutions, elections, and coups) provides a window into just how complicated democracy and self-determination can be in the era of the nation state since World War II. The history of the politics of representation in Fiji includes many competing efforts of citizens, parties, and groups to fashion the institutions of Fiji's government, conflicts over the electoral process itself, and the institutionalization in a national context of such unique authorities as the Great Council of Chiefs. These competing efforts have always involved global contexts, first colonial and more recently postcolonial. To consider the representation of politics, this chapter reviews some recent arguments by Fiji citizens about what Fiji's government is, should be, has to be, and cannot be. These include flat condemnations of any system that could lead to Indo-Fijians predominating or even sharing equally in national leadership, to arguments that Fiji must—or must not—enact United Nations rights requirements. Fiji's history is one of complex local projects and complex global entanglements, first within the structures of nineteenth-century colonial empires and then within the structures of twentieth-century nation states as organized by the United Nations system in the era of decolonization. In conclusion the chapter will ask: When and how does the representation of politics shape the politics of representation? How does discourse about political forms—from overseas and arising within Fiji and in the complex articulations between the global and local—shape the constitutions, the governmental institutions, and the possibilities for Fijian politics? Although it is imagined to be the vehicle of self-determination, the nation state itself as a form for government sets limits and engenders dilemmas for the politics of representation. Fiji provides examples of some of the dilemmas the nation state can engender.

Different from most other Pacific nations whose colonial history is primarily the story of encounters between Pacific indigenes and colonizing Westerners, Fiji's is a story of a three-way encounter. Thus any understanding of Fiji's current politics involves both the rights of postcolonial indigenes and the rights of labor diasporic peoples. In addition to the descendants of Pacific Islanders, Fiji is home to the Indo-Fijians, descendants of South Asian indentured laborers who came to Fiji beginning in the 1870s. Throughout the twentieth century, there have been close to equal numbers of ethnic Fijians and Indo-Fijians in the islands, Indo-Fijians slightly outnumbering ethnic Fijians at independence, ethnic Fijians slightly outnumbering Indo-Fijians more recently. These shifts have had less impact on democracy in Fiji than we might suspect, for reasons that we will explore in this chapter.

The colonial British ruled Fiji through a paternalist system of indirect rule based on their chiefly system, and preserved Fijian land ownership so that ethnic Fijian kin groups currently own 83 percent of the nation's land, inalienably. Indeed, the aristocratic British colonial rulers of Fiji formed a bureaucratic alliance with Fijian high chiefs.

At independence in 1970, Fijian chiefs were Fiji's highest national leaders, and Fiji's first, and succeeding, constitutions have all been written to ensure various degrees of ethnic Fijian political paramountcy and landholding rights. Ethnic Fijians have predominated in civil service and in Fiji's military, but many still gain their livelihood partly from subsistence economic activities on communally owned land.

In contrast, the Indo-Fijians came to colonial Fiji as indentured laborers, in the era of colonial capitalist plantations. Exploited in Fiji's sugar plantation system, they served as the economic backbone of the colony and nation. They also resisted European domination in Fiji, and, joining with the nationalists in India, sought political and economic parity with colonial whites and a path to self-determination. Farming on leased land, and entering diverse fields of professional and wage work, Indo-Fijians have predominated in many areas of business and wage labor, while ethnic Fijians have predominated in government.

Politically, the Indo-Fijians, with their deep anticolonial history, were intended by colonial plans to be the perpetual opposition party within a Fijian-dominated national parliament. From independence in 1970 to 1987, Fiji's parliamentary government was headed by the Alliance Party, a chiefly-led, predominantly ethnic Fijian party. The National Federation Party (NFP), a party with primarily Indo-Fijian support and with historical roots in cane farmers' unions, was the opposition party. But in 1984, a new, multiethnic Fiji Labour party challenged the colonially derived communal politics. In coalition with the NFP, Labour formed a government, headed by an ethnic Fijian commoner as prime minister. This newly elected government was overthrown in a series of military coups led by an ethnic Fijian army colonel who claimed to act on behalf of the paramountcy and political interests of ethnic Fijians. In 1990, Fijian high chiefs approved a constitution that denied Indo-Fijians representation proportionate to their percentage in the population of Fiji and reserved high national offices for ethnic Fijians alone. In 1997, internal disputes and global scrutiny led to a new constitution, still weighted in crucial ways toward ethnic Fijian interests, but with far greater provision for internationally agreed-upon standards of civil and political rights. Under this new constitution, free elections in 1999 resulted in an outright Labour Party majority and the formation of a Labour coalition government, headed by Fiji's first Indo-Fijian prime minister. This government fell to a coup in 2000.

What are the local and global contexts of the coups of 1987 and 2000? What are the chances for a self-determining nation of Fiji in which civil rights of a multiethnic citizenry and provision for special indigenous rights can coexist? In the decades after World War II, many political leaders and social scientists around the world believed that development and decolonization would lead unproblematically to modernization and new nations. Modernization theory is now discredited for its incorrect assumption that everyone everywhere would move, via development, from some condition of "traditional" to an equally poorly specified "modernity." And political leaders and scholars are far more aware today of the ongoing impact of colonial structures—especially of race—that persist in both the former colonizing powers and the decolonized nations. Most recently, scholars have begun to problematize as well the very form of the nation-state finding, as this chapter will show, both strictures and resources in the nation-state form that the decolonization era mandates.

Consequently, this paper focuses on representation as it considers Fiji's political history, engaging the question of representation via two of the word's meanings: (1) in the sense of speaking for (as when someone is elected to represent people in a parliament), and (2) in the sense of speaking about (as when claims are made in a speech about the meaning of past or present political events). The two senses of representation have always been intertwined (see Kelly and Kaplan 2001). In this chapter I will seek to show how the history of recent crises has its roots in two competing versions of the national order of Fiji. One view, as expressed by proponents of ethnic Fijian paramountcy, claims ownership of Fiji on the basis of indigenous priority, and seeks a chiefly-led, Christian polity, in which the nation is literally represented as, and by, Fijian chiefs. The contrasting view, of the twice-overthrown Labour coalition governments, envisions a multiethnic, democratic system, stressing common interests of ethnic Fijian and Indo-Fijian workers in which the nation belongs to those who labored to build it. In this view, representation must involve coalition, electoral politics, and all of Fiji's citizens should have a voice. These different views of Fiji were formed in a complex and unequal British colonial history, in which "racial" divisions were established by colonial rulers and have been fostered and manipulated to the advantage of ruling elites into the present. Fiji citizens today have made different choices in relation to the challenge of decolonization, and in relation to the global system of which Fiji is a part.

Competing visions for Fiji's political order are not a simple matter of some essential Fijian versus Indian political stances, although such simplistic divisions were proposed in colonial rhetoric and are a feature of the rhetoric of a broad spectrum of ethnic Fijian politicians. Neither group is monolithic and both groups are cross-cut by ties of class, region, religion, and, sometimes, pragmatic alliance. Among ethnic Fijians, divisions between chiefly confederacies and regions (sometimes longstanding, sometimes quite recent) and also differing visions of what chiefship and Christianity are about motivate political conflict and can engender alliances. Indo-Fijian divisions arise from religious, economic, and historical differences. Uneven articulations with global economic forces have their impact as well. Equally important have been articulations with global expectations and frameworks for the nation state.

To interpret the coups in Fiji's past two decades, and to analyze the forces that now shape Fiji's future, this chapter begins with a historical overview of the shaping of Fiji as a colony and the contrasting relations of British colonizers with Pacific islander Fijians (ethnic Fijians), on the one hand, and Fiji Indians

(Indo-Fijians) on the other. Then I turn to examine a debate at a watershed moment, the "Deed of Cession" debate following World War II, and then the politics of representation at independence in 1970 and at the founding of the Republic of Fiji in 1987. In conclusion, I examine the possibilities and crises of 2000.

## HISTORICAL OVERVIEW: COLONIALLY CONSTITUTED RELATIONSHIPS

Imperial global transgressions have left legacies of boundaries, and of contradictions to those boundaries. In Fiji, when the British brought over indentured laborers from India they created a contradiction. They wanted to efficiently rule the Fijians, to protect them and extend to them the "benefits of civilization." But colonial imperatives required the exploitation of someone's labor, and therefore, following the pattern that Tinker (1974) has identified as "a new system of slavery," the Indians were contracted to work. In the words of one colonial governor, they were "a working population and nothing more" (Scarr 1980:88), and were exploited in the Fijian's stead. These contradictory British goals of civilizing and exploiting—and the ways in which Fijians and Indo-Fijians accommodated or resisted them—set the framework for the different colonial histories.

### The British and the Fijians

What would become Fiji's "national" boundaries were fixed in the colonial encounter when in 1874 a group of high chiefs ceded the islands to Queen Victoria. Indigenously, there had been no single, united Kingdom of Fiji. Instead a number of expanding chiefly-led kingdoms or confederacies on the two largest islands of Viti Levu and Vanua Levu and in the eastern Lau group (the latter with close ties to Tonga) competed with one another within the island group. In Fiji as in other places in the Pacific, European incursion began with ships engaged in whaling and the China trade and then came to include missionaries, planters, and colonial administrators. Critical in the changing social field were the Wesleyan Methodist missionaries who came to the islands in the 1830s. Following high chiefs, especially Cakobau of Bau, the vast majority of Fijians were converted by 1854. Resistance to Wesleyanism persisted largely in northern, interior, and western Viti Levu, where Cakobau's paramountcy had never been acknowledged. Increasing European settlement by cotton planters in the 1860s engendered conflicts. These and other conflicts brought Fiji to the attention of Great Britain. In 1874, Cakobau and twelve other high chiefs (recognized by Europeans, but not by all Fijians, as Fiji's rulers) ceded the islands to Queen Victoria.

"Cession" is a founding myth in Fiji, interpreted and reinterpreted throughout the past century to serve as a charter for different British and ethnic Fijian projects and political stances. Here I concentrate on the ways in which it was interpreted by Fiji's first colonial government and the way it articulated with indigenous Fijian understandings of the relationship between ruler and ruled.

Like the imperial British more generally, Fiji's founding colonial governor, Sir Arthur Gordon (1879), viewed the relation of British and Fijians within a nineteenth-century social evolutionary racial framework (see France 1969), a hierarchy in which the British conceived themselves to be the historical and racial pinnacle. Paternalistically concerned about the survival of the Fijians, whose population and birth rate had dropped significantly because of European-introduced diseases, Gordon was also impressed by Fijian Christian conversion, and most especially by Fijian chiefs. He found them worth saving and civilizing.

Under Gordon, the native administration created a Fijian polity within the polity, of the sort that later in British colonies in Africa would be called "indirect rule." The native administration built a political structure of administration on the foundation of earlier Fijian regions and chiefly confederacies. Fijian officials headed this polity within a polity, from the Great Council of Chiefs, a group of high chiefs established by Gordon as an advisory body, to the high chiefly heads of provinces, to Fijian heads of districts and villages. Fijians had their own set of courts and a special set of laws. Perhaps most consequentially for Fiji's future politics, Gordon decided that Fijians needed to be protected from the exploitation as plantation laborers planned by resident white planters. He therefore set in motion a highly unusual land policy, reserving 83 percent of Fiji's land inalienably for indigenous Fijians. The land was and is owned by patrilineal kin groups (see France 1969; Clammer 1973; Macnaught 1982; Kaplan 1989a, 1989b; Lawson 1990; Lal 1992).

This colonial structure articulated fortunately with the plans and projects of certain high chiefly and eastern coastal Fijians, and with a Fijian perspective on the relationship of people and their rulers more generally. Successive generations of Fijians have portrayed cession as establishing a relationship between foreign rulers and indigenous people of the land. In the nineteenth century Fijian ritual-political system, chiefs (*turaga*) were symbolically conceived of as foreigners. People of the land (*itaukei*) ritually installed these powerful foreigners as "divine kings" (see Hocart 1969[1927]; Sahlins 1985: 75–111). The relationship of chiefs and people is hierarchical but based on mutual and reciprocal responsibilities and obligations. Chiefs held the *lewa* (rule) while people of the land owned the land, installed the chiefs, and supported them in their ritual and political endeavors.

Over time, the Fijian cultural logic of the relation of chiefs and people has oriented solidary Fijian polities, in which chiefs have exercised prerogatives that some have celebrated as enduring tradition (Ravuvu 1983). Others, however, have described them as syncretic and neotraditional (Macnaught 1982), and some critics from within Fiji have seen them as tyrannical, corrupt, and in the present-day nation state, highly antidemocratic. (For a history of anticolonial and antichiefly Fijian movements, see Kaplan 1995.) Within the colonial polity, nineteenth-century Fijian chiefly politics, notably struggles between the three major kingdoms or confederacies

of Bau, Rewa, and Lau, and struggles over chiefly succession within kingdoms, were given a new forum. Districting and office holding became new forms for chiefly and regional political contests.

## The British and the Indo-Fijians

In contrast to intense British interest in ruling through Fijian chiefs, Fiji Indians were treated as "labor units," their social systems denigrated, their leaders marginalized and denied any substantive forum in the colonial polity. Ironically, the first Governor Gordon brought with him a reputation as a supporter of indentured laborers versus white planters, from his days as governor of Mauritius. But he also brought the plan for temporary indentured laborers from South Asia to grow sugar cane, to form the basis of the colony's economy. The initial view of Indians as temporary in the colony meshed with the colonial government's assignment of organizational responsibilities for the work and lives of Indians on the sugar plantations to the Colonial Sugar Refining Corporation, enabling a brutal plantation regime.

Thus, Indo-Fijians had a strikingly different colonial experience from that of the Pacific Islander-Fijians. Where Fijian institutions, leaders, land ownership, and traditions were paternalistically preserved and shielded from the market, Indo-Fijians were treated as free individuals, without ties or tradition, who could be freely exploited in the market. When they began to organize their anticolonial "challenge to European dominance" (Gillion 1977) (linked to anticolonial nationalism in India itself), they became particularly dangerous figures in the eyes of the British in colonial Fiji.

From 1878 to 1919 over sixty thousand Indians came to Fiji as *girmityas* (the people of the *girmit*, from the English "agreement" referring to the indenture contract). About two-thirds stayed on when their contracts expired. The Fiji Indians came from a range of castes and locales in India; many were seeking work, on pilgrimage, or already separated from rural roots and families (Lal 1983). They were recruited individually and sent on to Fiji through depots in Calcutta and Madras.

The Indo-Fijian colonial experience was one of oppression and resistance to oppression. Both during indenture days, and in later recollections, narratives by *girmityas* told of being tricked by deceitful recruiters and by the oppressive colonial system more generally. In the depots and in the "lines" (plantation living quarters), they were stripped of individual control and of caste markers and identity, forced to eat and live across caste lines. Thus polluted, many found themselves unable to return to India or unwelcome when their indenture contracts expired. Historically, Fiji Indians have narrated their indenture experience as parallel to the "sorrowful story of Ram," a Hindu god and king forced by an evil demon into poverty and exile (Lal 1984; Kelly 1991; Sanadhya 1991[1914]).

Politically, while the British organized Fijian representation via chiefs at village, district, and province level and created the Great Council of Chiefs for colonywide deliberations, they saw the Indians not as a community but as a temporary population of "labor units." Since caste practices were denigrated, Indian forms of decision making and hierarchy were denigrated as well. The colonial government instituted no system of indirect rule among the Indo-Fijians. Initially, plantation discipline and punitive courts regulated Indo-Fijian life on the plantations. Political organization among Fiji Indians was discouraged and labeled "agitation." When the Fiji Indians began to organize themselves in indenture years, they sought "communal uplift" through religion, and rights via strikes against the Colonial Sugar Refining Corporation and other European employers (Gillion 1977; Moynaugh 1981; Kelly 1991; Lal 1992).

Fiji Indians contributed to the end of the indenture system, and also to India's wider anticolonial struggle. Gandhi and others argued that as long as Indians were slaves anywhere in the British Empire, India itself could not be free (Tinker 1974). With the end of indenture, Fiji Indians became small-scale independent sugar cane growers on land leased from Fijians or moved to the cities where they went into various forms of salaried and wage work. From 1920 on in colonial Fiji, Fiji Indians organized to fight for fair payments for the cane they grew, and then increasingly for political representation in the colony. They went on strike to achieve economic goals and struggled to achieve the vote, but they never gained substantive power in Fiji's colonial legislative council. In contrast, their cane growers unions succeeded in changing the terms and relations of cane growing to the growers' interest, finally resulting in the Colonial Sugar Refining Corporation leaving Fiji altogether in 1973 when the sugar industry was nationalized. Such victories would prove hollow in independence days, however, as the world market for sugar decreased, and as ethnic Fijians became less willing to rent their land to their fellow citizens.

Indo-Fijians also looked to India's independence struggle for models of rights and representation, founding a short-lived Fiji Indian National Congress in the 1920s. In some ways, the relationship between Fiji Indians and the British was a colonial backwater version of the political, economic, and devotional struggle of nationalists in India. As in India, some political leaders were also religious leaders, especially leaders of early cane growers' strikes. Several of the Fiji Indian leaders were actually sent to Fiji by Gandhi (see Lal 1996); others came up from the ranks of the cane growers unions and the political parties. As in India, though of course on a smaller scale, Fiji Indians were diverse and groups had sometimes divergent interests. (There were Hindus and Muslims, north and south Indians, Hindu adherents to different religious traditions, and even some free emigrants, especially merchants from Gujerat and farmers from Punjab as well as girmit-descended people.)

Unlike the nationalists in India, and unlike Pacific Islander Fijians, the Fiji Indians were not "indigenes." Thus they did not have the powerful political and rhetorical tool of a colonially defined and idealized common "indigenous identity" as a bond of union. Nor did they have a colonially elaborated system of customary leadership and tradition. Instead, Indo-Fijians most successfully organized their social movements within Fiji as "economic" struggles against European exploitation and as communal uplift projects focused on religious devotionalism. Communal uplift, typified in India by Gandhi's *sarvodaya* (literally "communal uplift" or "welfare for all"), stressed the simultaneously moral, educational, economic, and social goals of anticolonial struggle (see Fox 1989; Kelly 1991). In Fiji, Fiji Indians have long linked religious practice and social organization, initially in the rural Ramayan Mandalis (groups meeting weekly to read the Hindu text the *Ramayan*), and later in the broadly organized and anticolonial organizations for communal uplift. The latter brought in Hindu and Muslim missionaries, teachers, and political leaders from India. The Indo-Fijians have viewed their economic successes as a part of this wider project of moral, social, and religious uplift, begun in the anticolonial struggle. In postcolonial years, however, Indo-Fijians had to develop a new political rhetoric, their political stance no longer could be framed as opposition to British colonial exploitation, and their economic successes were viewed as suspect by Fijians (Kelly 1988).

As many observers have noted, ethnic Fijian and Indo-Fijian colonial history was largely constituted in relation to the British, not to each other. Separated spatially and occupationally and governed differently, the ethnic Fijian and Fiji Indian colonial experiences were separate and unequal. Intermarriage between ethnic Fijians and Fiji Indians has been uncommon and the two groups retained separate religious and cultural practices throughout the twentieth century. It was not until World War II that ethnic Fijians and Indo-Fijians faced each other in political debate, with strikingly different visions of rights and representation. Sweeping global changes following World War II would transform Fiji, resulting in a decolonized, independent nation state in 1970.

## FIJI AND WORLD DECOLONIZATION

World War II saw the end of the British imperial era and the beginning of the U.N. era of nation states. As Dower (1986) has argued, the war exposed the contradictions of Western imperial racial ideologies throughout the world. In Fiji, the war brought into sharp focus the differing colonial pasts and different visions of the future of ethnic Fijians and Indo-Fijians. Fijians envisioned a postwar world run along similar lines to the imperial politics of colonial Fiji. Indo-Fijians, like the Indian nationalists, were more attuned to impending decolonization. Ethnic Fijians fought eagerly on behalf of the British during the war. The Indo-Fijians in contrast offered to serve in the army and auxiliary services on the condition that they have equal status and pay as those of white British citizens. Denied parity, they followed Gandhi in refusing to fight for an imperial system that classed them as inferior. Faced with the Indian challenge, British political rhetoric forged an ever-stronger alliance with ethnic Fijians drawing upon ethnic Fijian fears of Indo-Fijian population growth, and denigrated Indian and Indo-Fijian anticolonial resistance.

In 1946, European, Fijian, and Indo-Fijian representatives sat on Fiji's legislative council, a board advisory to the governor. The majority of representatives was European and was appointed by the governor. The colony's European residents also had three elected representatives. The Indo-Fijians elected three representatives, and three Fijian representatives were appointed (Norton 1977:8).

At the so-called Deed of Cession debate in the legislative council in 1946, European members argued that the original deed of cession "giving" Fiji to Queen Victoria and her heirs in 1874 provided that the British would preserve and protect Fijian interests. These arguments were clearly directed at quelling Indo-Fijian initiatives for greater legislative representation. Fiji Indian legislative council member A. D. Patel pointed out the irony of colonial claims to protect Fijians against foreigners, and made powerful humanistic and political economic arguments against the colonial position. He said:

> It should be well understood and well appreciated that we came here to play our part in turning this country into a paradise. Indians came here and worked here for those people who

gobbled up half a million acres of free-hold land from the Fijian owners. We came and worked, under a semi-servile state, and thank God, saved the Fijian race from the infamy of coming under the same system. As a matter of fact, if anything the coming of my people to this country gave the Fijians their honor, their prestige, nay indeed their very soul. Otherwise I have no hesitation in saying that the Fijians of this Colony would have met with the same fate that some other indigenous races in parts of Africa met with. (Legislative Council of Fiji 1946:48)

At issue was the nature of representation in Fiji. In the colonial era, it had been assumed that different populations or "communities" had different natures and roles to play in the colonial polity, and would each be represented separately in the governing bodies of the colony. At this key moment in world history, with the impetus to world decolonization taking shape, Fiji's colonial Europeans and Fijians sought to enhance the colonial Fijian "polity within the polity," and to secure special Fijian paramountcy. Patel's arguments on behalf of the Indian contribution to Fiji failed to reshape colonial-Fijian chiefly position (see also Lal 1996). Even more crucially, as Fiji moved slowly toward independence, a model of representation based on "communal" rather than "common" electoral rolls dominated Fiji's politics, with fundamental implications for the future of Fiji as a nation.

Common roll electoral systems regard all citizens as equal, with one person one vote, within a particular electoral district. Communal roll systems, on the other hand, require people to register themselves as members of particular communities, and to choose representatives of those communities. They are found primarily in former colonies that relied on "racial" categories for political and economic structuring of the colony. (South Africa's recently dismantled apartheid system is another inheritor of British colonial communal political divisions.) Thus, in every constitution in independent Fiji, citizens have also had to identify themselves as "Indians," "Fijians," or "General Electors" as they carried

out the task of electing representatives and shaping the nation.

Throughout this debate over rights, representation, and the nature of peoples in Fiji, interesting things have happened to terms like "democracy," "demographics," "population," and "representation" in Fiji. They have come to be associated with either an antiracist, anticolonial stance (in the Indo-Fijian historical construction) or as a foreign discourse that denies cultural self-determination to an endangered yet ultimately superior minority (the ethnic Fijians). Given this discourse, Fiji's independence was a contested matter. On the one hand, Indo-Fijians had long sought equality with the colonial British and equivalent forms of political representation. They argued for a democracy with a common electoral roll. Fijians and colonial whites wished to preserve their own special rights, through separate voting rolls, constitutionally mandated proportions of representation and, especially, nominated representation by the Great Council of Chiefs.

In the decades that followed World War II, and in the new frameworks established in the United Nations, world insistence on decolonization propelled Indo-Fijians seeking independence, and ethnic Fijians resisting it, toward independence for Fiji. Decolonization was part of the American plan for the post-World War II world, involving on the one hand a commitment to greater political self-determination for the world's peoples, and on the other hand a commitment to dismantling the unilateral system of trade and currency regulations that had powerfully undergirded the British empire. Colonial officials, Indo-Fijians, and ethnic Fijians made different assessments of the global plans and institutions that were to break up empires and make decolonization a mandate. Certainly Fiji's two major political parties were shaped by the world imperative toward decolonization, and simultaneously in local political histories and colonial experiences, as well as in the negotiations leading to independence. The largely Indo-Fijian National Federation Party was founded by leaders of cane growers' unions and other unions in 1964, with a history of engagement with nationalist politics. The largely ethnic Fijian Alliance Party aspired to be a multiracial party ideal (these aspirations attenuated by the 1980s), under the leadership of a colonially groomed high Fijian chief, Ratu Sir Kamisese Mara. It can be seen as a continuation of the colonial-Fijian partnership of the era of indirect rule.

Because of constitutional requirements, each party had mixed "racial" membership and fielded candidates of all three electoral categories ("Fijian," "Indian," and "General Elector"). (General electors are currently fewer than 8 percent of the population, a category combining self-defined "Europeans," "Part-Europeans," and Fiji citizens of Chinese descent and of other Pacific Islander descent.) Each at times espoused more or less pluralistic ideals. However, a major initial and continuing difference concerning the constitution of independent Fiji separated the two parties. The National Federation Party supported a common roll democracy that would have no racial subdivisions of the electoral rolls. Instead, the colonial and chiefly plan, a constitution based on "racially" defined communal representation (defining voters by race and reserving percentages of parliamentary seats for each community), prevailed in independent Fiji's 1970 constitution.

## REPRESENTATION IN INDEPENDENT FIJI

### The 1970 Constitution

At independence in 1970 the nation of Fiji was to be represented, electorally and meaningfully, through a carefully developed constitution set in place by the departing British administration. The 1970 constitution reproduced the unequal political relations formed in the colonial era in favor of ethnic Fijians, and it reinforced and further reified "race" as a category in Fijian social and political life.

In 1970, Fiji's national government (at independence the Commonwealth Dominion of Fiji) followed the so-called Westminster model, with a governor general representing the queen and a bicameral legislature of appointed senators and elected members of the House of Representatives. Electorally, the majority party's (or coalition's) leader became the prime minister. Most of the seats in the House of Representatives were "communal" with three voters' rolls: Fijians, Indians, and General Electors. There were also seats on a so-called "national roll" on which all voters were listed.

Under the 1970 constitution, the House of Representatives had fifty-two members. Twenty-two members were Fijians, twelve elected by Fijians and ten elected by all of the voters (on the national roll) in particular districts. Twenty-two members were Indians, twelve similarly elected by Indians and ten by all of the voters in their districts. Eight were general electors, three elected by general electors and five by all the voters in the districts. (Note that at the time the numbers were not proportionate.) In 1980 figures, Fijians who were 44 percent of the population elected 42 percent of the elected representatives. Indians who were 50 percent of the population also elected 42 percent of the representatives, while General Electors at 6 percent of the population had 15 percent of the seats (Lal 1986:76). The "overrepresentation" of General Electors (as some would see it) worked largely to ethnic Fijian advantage, since General Electors tended to form coalitions with the predominantly ethnic Fijian party. The second house, the Senate, had appointed members, eight named by the Fijian Great Council of Chiefs, seven named by the prime minister (head of the party in power), six named by the opposition party, and one representing people from the island of Rotuma.

In 1984, a new Fiji Labour Party formed, to combat the "racial" parties. Labour won the 1987 election, forming a coalition government with the National Federation Party, a party primarily supported by Fiji Indians. Within a month, Sitiveni Rabuka, an ethnic Fijian army colonel, led a military coup, claiming to represent ethnic Fijian interests. After criticism of the coup from other member nations of the British Commonwealth, he declared Fiji a republic, withdrawing from the Commonwealth. He first reinstated the Fijian chiefly leaders of the party that lost the election, then Colonel Rabuka (later brigadier general) himself became Fiji's prime minister, under elections held under the new constitution he sponsored.

## The 1990 Constitution

The 1990 constitution written under the auspices of the coup leader and authorized by the Great Council of Chiefs simultaneously simplified and amplified principles already at work in Fiji's constitution at independence in 1970. Like the 1970 constitution, the 1990 constitution sought to ensure that ethnic Fijians would always dominate government, irrespective of demographics. It was simply more direct about it. The office of prime minister was to be filled by a Fijian. It created a single house, of seventy representatives. Ethnic Fijians elected thirty-seven of the members of the house, Indo-Fijians twenty-seven members. Written under the influence of Rabuka and authorized by the Great Council of Chiefs, it insisted on a Fijian, Christian nation. The new constitution also created a thirty-four-seat senate (twenty-four Fijians, nine others, one Rotuman). Ethnic Fijians held all the cards, and the constitutions they debated and the one they promulgated reflected that sensibility. Not only were the "races" out of both balance and demographic proportion, but major offices were reserved for Fijians. Taking upon itself the power to ratify this new constitution, the Great Council of Chiefs institutionalized its role as the central voice of Fijian authority. Indeed the Great Council institutionalized its claim to national political authority. It promulgated the 1990 constitution and it was subject to no popular referendum.

Following the imposition of this constitution, however, political contests among ethnic Fijians reemerged. A long period of contestation ensued, centered especially on struggles between politicians from three historically dominant ethnic Fijian chiefly confederacies (Bau, Rewa, and Lau), and arguments for the creation and representation of a fourth ethnic Fijian confederacy, representing the west of Viti Levu island. Urban Fijians also argued for representation. Competing new ethnic Fijian political parties were formed. Public discourse about the fate of the nation was largely about the ethnic Fijian polity within the polity (see Rutz 1995).

But the debates and fragmentation of ethnic Fijian solidarity created opportunities for multiethnic, nonexclusively ethnic Fijian parties as partners. On the one hand, the leaders of the National Federation Party sought coalition with Rabuka and his SVT party. On the other hand, many voters turned to a variety of other parties. While the multiethnic Labour Party gained some urban ethnic Fijian support, as well as Indo-Fijian support, many Indo-Fijians voted for NFP candidates, and the NFP and the Labour Party split the "Indian" seats. Other ethnic Fijian voters formed diverse regionally and religiously oriented parties, contravening hopes for ethnic Fijian paramountcy through solidarity of the architects of the 1990 constitution. Even more important, concerns driven by a wider, global set of engagements, described below, led to the formation of the Fiji Constitution Review Commission of 1996 (see Lal and Vakatora 1997a, 1997b) that led to the new constitution of 1997.

## The 1997 Constitution

The Fiji Constitution Review Commission's three members were New Zealand jurist Sir Paul Reeves (a Maori), Fiji historian and Australian National University professor Brij V. Lal (an Indo-Fijian), and Fijian longtime parliamentarian Tomasi Vakatora (an ethnic Fijian). In their 1996 report they considered submissions from an enormous number of sources, within and outside of Fiji, from constitutional experts to interested organizations to ordinary citizens (see Lal and Vakatora 1997a, 1997b). Submissions from within Fiji ranged across political and historical positions. Some proposed reenvisioning Fiji and all Fiji citizens in a Pacific Islander tradition; for example, Geraghty (in Lal and Vakatora 1997a) suggested that Fijian become the national language. Others made proposals for affirmative action programs to engage ethnic Fijians in business, emphasizing not traditional development programs for small businesses but rather Fijians as groups of stockholding investors (Narube in Lal and Vakatora 1997a). Others outlined the rights and needs of minority (and majority) populations and groups in the islands (for example, submissions on part-Europeans, Rotumans, other Pacific islanders, and on women in Fiji), with an eye to ensuring representation of diversity.

Key submissions noted the pending crisis of agricultural land leases. The Agricultural Landlord and Tenant Act had been negotiated during the move toward independence in the late 1960s. Thirty-year leases of Fijian-owned land were made available to Indo-Fijian farmers to assure the continuity of the sugar industry, seen as crucial to the soon-to-be-independent nation state. Yet this meant that the vast majority of Fiji's Indo-Fijian cane farmers' leases expired in 1997. Ethnic Fijian interest in using the land, or more commonly in raising rents, created a fearful situation for many Indo-Fijians, and an unstable economic outlook.

Others addressed the problem of increasing poverty in Fiji, especially among urban and periurban residents. Strikingly, both the submissions from constitution experts and many of those from citizen groups brought new questions to Fiji's political process by engaging global cases, models and structures from beyond Fiji. First of all, models for national governance and citizens rights drew on formulations from United Nations organizations, and from a range of international NGOs. Constitution experts from all over the world provided comparative studies and citizen groups used a variety of international declarations and conventions to support their positions. Thus, for example, those arguing for ethnic Fijian paramountcy cited the International Labour Organization (ILO) Convention 169 on Indigenous and Tribal Peoples along with the Bible and Fijian tradition as their authorities. Supporters of common roll voting appealed to documents such as the U.N. Universal Declaration of Human Rights. Secondly, the global financial situation loomed in the background of every report on Fiji's economy. On the one hand, dependence on sugar as a major crop seemed increasingly impossible, given world markets. On the other hand, the booming stock market of the 1990s encouraged visions of outside investment in such fields as tourism, spring water, and other luxuries, and fueled landowners' sense of the potential for high rents on lands.

The Review Commission led to the drafting and adoption of a new constitution in 1997, again promulgated by the Great Council of Chiefs, and supported by coup leader and then prime minister Rabuka. While it continued the 1990 constitution's variety of concessions to Fijian custom and chiefly power (the Great Council of Chiefs appoint the president and vice president, the largely ceremonial head of state), it altered the "racial" composition of representation in important ways. The House of Representatives had seventy-one members, elected from five electoral rolls (twenty-three by Fijians, nineteen by Indians, one by Rotumans, three by others, and twenty-five by all voters on an "open roll"). The prime minister must invite into his (or her) cabinet members from other parties that obtain 10 percent of the seats or more in the House of Representatives, in numbers corresponding to total percentage of members in the House. Again, crucially for future issues of power and authority in Fiji, this constitution was ratified by the Great Council of Chiefs, rather than by popular referendum. The chiefs' agreement seems to have been gained via the assurance of Prime Minister Rabuka that it contained clauses that would ensure ethnic Fijian paramountcy, notably in the reservation of the presidency for ethnic Fijians.

In a crucial expression of the voice of Fiji's citizenry, the first election under this new constitution in May of 1999 did not lead to the electoral return of coup leader Rabuka. Nor did the National Federation Party win any seats, not even its leader Jai Ram Reddy who had become famous for his efforts to work together with coup leader Rabuka. Rather, to the surprise of many, the Labour Party, led by Mahendra Chaudhry, won an absolute majority and formed a new government in coalition with several ethnic Fijian parties. The voice of the people supported the multiethnic democracy envisioned in 1987 in the first Labour victory.

But one year following the election, a complicated aggregation of agents led and solidified a coup against Chaudhry's Labour Coalition government. First, George Speight, a failed businessman, led a group of military personnel and took Prime Minister Chaudhry and coalition parliamentarians hostage. Speight claimed to act on behalf of indigenous Fijian rights. Outside analysts have noted that Speight, past head of the Fiji Hardwood and Fiji Pine commissions in the Rabuka government, had seen his carefully laid plans to sell Fiji's mahogany reserves (planted by colonial planners in the 1950s) to a U.S. buyer overturned by the newly elected Labour coalition government. Speight had incited and championed the ethnic Fijian landowners on whose rented land the mahogany was growing to back his plans for its sale (Kahn 2000). On May 19, 2000, Speight got the jump on other potential coup leaders and led a group of armed soldiers into parliament and began the coup against Chaudhry's Labour Coalition government.

Speight's coup was overtaken and solidified, from the top down, by ethnic Fijian stalwarts, including high chiefs and the military. The president, Ratu Sir Kamisese Mara, resigned and handed power to the military, who installed ethnic Fijian bureaucrat Laisenia Qarase as interim prime minister, with the support of Fiji's military forces, under commander Frank Bainimarama. As head of the interim government, Qarase began to announce and implement a range of programs to solidify ethnic Fijian paramountcy in the nation.

In the wake of the takeover of the nation in May and following months, there were many local takeovers of roads, power stations, tourist resorts, and factories by ethnic Fijians asserting (as in the national takeovers) their rights as landowners and indigenes to define the nation as a whole. The interim government presented its role as returning Fiji to peace, order, and "normality." Their interim budget and blueprint for Fiji sought to reconcile diverse ethnic Fijian claims and projects, once again rendering invisible the rights and contributions of Indo-Fijians to the nation.

In May of 2000, an Indo-Fijian farmer, dispossessed of his rented land and livelihood, and in fear for his and his family's lives, filed suit in Fiji's court, arguing that his civil rights had been violated by the abrogation of the 1997 constitution. Justice Gates of the Lautoka court found for this plaintiff. In March 2001, Fiji's appeal court upheld his suit. The interim government had announced that, in its version of compliance with the court's ruling, Prime Minister Chaudhry would not be reinstated, but elections would be held in August 2001, under the electoral rules of the 1997 constitution.

This moment cuts to the core of the issue of representation in Fiji: whether it is to be a democracy with an impartial court upholding constitutionally mandated civil rights, or whether the ethnic Fijian Great Council of Chiefs and ethnic Fijian military will direct and orchestrate Fiji's national future. In every system of representation in Fiji, from independence in 1970 to the 1997 constitution and beyond, two points have recurred. First, to one degree or another, individuals have been required to register themselves as belonging to one or another "racial"/political group. The electoral system has persistently concretized and perpetuated a system of categorization of persons developed in the colonial era. In essence, it enshrined constitutionally the claim that Fiji's people are to be separate, bounded races, with different natures, interests, political, and property rights. Second, however, in each election in which the popular will has been expressed, voters have increasingly turned to multiethnic alternatives.

## REPRESENTING FIJI, LOCALLY AND GLOBALLY

Over the past century, residents of Fiji have struggled to create a satisfactory system of political representation, with competing visions of what self-determination might mean. Fiji's history has been global for two centuries now.

It has been profoundly shaped by the articulation of local history making with the imperial expansion of the West. From 1800 on, vessels engaged in the China trade, missionaries bringing salvation, planters of cotton and sugar all engaged Fijian chiefs and people, and articulated with the expanding polities and projects of high chiefs such as Cakobau of the kingdom of Bau. Fully seized by the British empire via cession in 1874, Fiji became a node in the history of diaspora of Asian peoples in the era of plantation indenture. So too Fiji was a node in the global history of decolonization, in its relationships to Gandhi's nationalist successes in India, World War II, and the rise of the United Nations.

One of the ironies of Fiji's history has been the use of internal and external sources of power in the politics of representation. The struggle of ethnic Fijians to represent themselves, to control their place in the colonial polity, and now to control the nation state, used and depended on a foreign, global resource: the power and logic of the British empire. Indo-Fijians came to Fiji as part of a worldwide labor diaspora and they articulated their politics with the struggle for *swaraj* in India, the most successful anticolonial nationalist movement of the twentieth century.

In the postcolonial era, what kinds of political contests have been seen as legitimate, or even desirable? We might also ask, when and how does the representation of politics shape the politics of representation? Since independence Fiji has had three different constitutions. The framers of each version each seek a way to establish electoral representation and to represent rights in the nation. They are firmly grounded in the local and colonial history of Fiji, yet these visions of Fiji and that local and colonial history are deeply entwined with global realities. Most recently, the constitution framers show interesting new relations to the global system of nation states and its institutions, especially the United Nations, begun following World War II.

In the work of the 1997 Constitution Review Commission, major narratives and possibilities took shape for representation within Fiji as a nation state. One we might call

the representation of indigenous rights, and the other we might call the representation of universal human rights. The first, derived from efforts of the commission to take heed of various international conventions on the rights of indigenous people (for example, the ILO Convention 169 on Indigenous and Tribal Peoples, and the draft Declaration on the Rights of Indigenous Peoples). It clearly intersected with the history of ethnic Fijian polity within the polity emerging from the colonial era into the present. In contrast, the narrative of universal human rights (derived from such documents as the Universal Declaration of Human Rights, the International Covenant on Civil and Political Rights, the Convention on the Elimination of All Forms of Racial Discrimination) conjoined far more smoothly with Indo-Fijian narratives of struggle for equality and democracy, and with Labour Party rhetorical strategies of multiracial inclusiveness. 1997 could have been the end of the ethnic Fijian nationalist era of the 1980s and a turn to new representational possibilities for the citizens of the nation. The 2000 coups, and the Fiji Appeals Court's reversal of them, make it clear that this contest is on-going.

I will avoid the temptation of prediction and will conclude instead with an analytic point about changes in Fiji over the past thirty years, as the colony has moved to independence. While the competing rhetorical strategies for the 1997 new constitution engage deeper positions within Fijian history, there may also be a real difference in the sources of authority for the nation. Rather than looking to a past font of tradition located in either Fiji or in the colonial relationship (that is, chiefs, people of the land, Christian God, the Queen, the Deed of Cession, empire or Commonwealth), the makers of the new constitution and the new political order invoked a world of other nations and other national and international bodies to serve as examples and precedents. They also invoked a world audience, an international community with whose standards Fiji must engage if Fiji is to establish itself as a legitimate player in a United Nations world, or as an appropriately stable and "transparent" site for international investment. Simultaneously, the principles of national self-determination, formed in opposition to the colonial past, also make it crucially difficult for nations to intervene, at times of military coups, even via economic sanctions. The imperatives to self-determination of the nation-state form, in tension with the realities of a global system of nation states, offer no clear-cut solutions, but many possibilities for the people of Fiji as they continue to make their history.

## REFERENCES

Clammer, John. 1973. "Colonialism and the Perception of Tradition in Fiji." In *Anthropology and the Colonial Encounter.* Talal Asad, ed. Pp. 199–222. London: Ithaca Press.

Dower, John. 1986. *War Without Mercy: Race and Power in the Pacific War.* New York: Pantheon.

Fox, Richard. 1989. *Gandhian Utopia: Experiments in Culture.* Boston: Beacon Press.

France, Peter. 1969. *The Charter of the Land.* Melbourne: Oxford University Press.

Gillion, K. L. 1977. *The Fiji Indians: Challenge to European Dominance, 1920–1946.* Canberra: Australian National University Press.

Gordon, Sir Arthur. 1879. Paper on the System of Taxation in Force in Fiji: Read Before the Royal Colonial Institute, March 18, 1879. London: Harrison and Sons.

Hocart, A. M. 1969[1927]. *Kingship.* Oxford: Oxford University Press.

Kahn, Joseph. 2000. "The Mahogany King's Brief Reign." *New York Times,* September 14, 2000:C1, C8.

Kaplan, Martha. 1989a. "The 'Dangerous and Disaffected Native' in Fiji." *Social Analysis* 26:20–43.

———. 1989b. "Luveniwai as the British Saw It: Constructions of Custom and Disorder in Colonial Fiji." *Ethnohistory* 36(4):349–371.

———. 1995. *Neither Cargo nor Cult: Ritual Politics and the Colonial Imagination in Fiji.* Durham: Duke University Press.

Kelly, John D. 1988. "Fiji Indians and Political Discourse in Fiji: From the Pacific Romance to the Coups." *Journal of Historical Sociology* 1:399–422.

———. 1991. *A Politics of Virtue: Hinduism, Sexuality and Countercolonial Discourse in Fiji.* Chicago: University of Chicago Press.

Kelly, John D., and Martha Kaplan. 2001. *Represented Communities: Fiji and World Decolonization.* Chicago: University of Chicago Press.

Lal, Brij V. 1983. *Girmityas: The Origins of the Fiji Indians.* Canberra: Journal of Pacific History.

———. 1984. "Kunti's Cry: Indentured Women on Fiji's Plantations." *The Indian Economic and Social History Review* 22(1):55–71.

Lal, Brij V., ed. 1986. *Politics in Fiji: Studies in Contemporary History.* Honolulu: The Institute for Polynesian Studies.

———. 1992. *Broken Waves: A History of Fiji in the Twentieth Century.* Honolulu: University of Hawai'i Press.

———. 1996. *A Vision for Change: A. D. Patel and the Politics of Fiji.* Canberra: National Centre for Development Studies, Australian National University.

Lal, Brij V., and Tomasi Vakatora, eds. 1997a. *Fiji Constitution Review Committee Research Papers.* Vol. I. *Fiji in Transition.* Suva: School of Social and Economic Development, University of the South Pacific.

———. 1997b. *Fiji Constitution Review Committee Research Papers.* Vol. II. *Fiji and the World.* Suva: School of Social and Economic Development, University of the South Pacific.

Lawson, Stephanie. 1990. "The Myth of Cultural Homogeneity and Its Implications for Chiefly Power and Politics in Fiji." *Comparative Studies in Society and History* 32(4):795–821.

Legislative Council of Fiji. 1946. Extracts from Debates of the July Session, 1946. Suva, Fiji: Government Press.

Macnaught, Timothy. 1982. "The Fijian Colonial Experience." Pacific Research Monograph No. 7. Canberra: Australian National University.

Moynaugh, Michael. 1981. "Brown or White? A History of the Fiji Sugar Industry, 1873–1971." Pacific Research Monograph No. 5. Canberra: Australian National University.

Norton, Robert. 1977. *Race and Politics in Fiji.* New York: St. Martin's Press.

Ravuvu, Asesela. 1983. "Vaka i Taukei: The Fijian Way of Life." Suva: Institute of Pacific Studies, University of the South Pacific.

Rutz, Henry. 1995. "Occupying the Headwaters of Tradition: Rhetorical Strategies of Nation-Making in Fijian Nation-Making." In *Emergent Identities in Postcolonial Melanesia.* Robert Foster, ed. Pp. 71–93. Ann Arbor: University of Michigan Press.

Sahlins, Marshall. 1985. *Islands of History.* Chicago: University of Chicago Press.

Sanadhya, Totaram, and Benarsidas Chaturvedi. 1991[1914]. *My Twenty-One Years in the Fiji Islands.* John D. Kelly and Uttra Kumari Singh, translators. Suva: Fiji Museum.

Scarr, Deryck. 1980. "Viceroy of the Pacific: The Majesty of Colour, a Life of Sir John Bates Thurston." Pacific Research Monograph No. 4. Canberra: Australian National University.

Tinker, Hugh. 1974. *A New System of Slavery: The Export of Indian Labour Overseas, 1830–1920.* London: Oxford University Press.

# 5

# Legal Pluralism in Pacific Island Societies

**Richard Scaglion**

*University of Pittsburgh*

Chapter 5 explores legal pluralism in the Pacific. Legal pluralism is the simultaneous existence of different types of legal systems within a single setting. All Pacific Island nations and territories had at least one, and sometimes many, customary legal systems before contact with Europeans. However, there were no indigenous states in the Pacific: No countries or even significant parts of countries had a centralized government. Local communities were fairly autonomous, managing themselves through a combination of customary practices and the exhortations of local leaders. After contact with Europeans, all of the Pacific Islands came under the influence of one European power or another. Centralized colonial governments, which superimposed a layer of transplanted Western law over local legal systems, were established in most places.

In some ways, a large-scale blending of legal systems in the Pacific was inevitable, even if there had not been a colonial history. Customary legal practices often operate quite well in the small face-to-face contexts in which they developed, but they prove to be inadequate for coping with the demands of modern nation states in a globalizing world. Pacific nations must manage diasporas of their citizens living abroad, oversee remittance economies, and supervise international trade and banking. They must regulate the activities of multinational corporations, promulgate or enforce laws of the sea, protect intellectual property, enforce contracts, and otherwise deal with a host of issues that are a result of contemporary conditions. One way or another, Pacific nations would have had to draw upon new legal models, in some cases those derived from countries with centralized governments, in order to solve the problems of contemporary national and international conditions. Reconciling customary law (called *kastom* law in many places) with new legal orders is therefore a central problem or issue for all Pacific Island nations as they struggle to create unified and equitable national legal systems. This chapter explores that struggle.

## THEORETICAL BACKGROUND

Unfortunately, anthropologists and lawyers do not talk to each other as much as they should. When studying and writing about legal systems, lawyers tend to focus on the written law and on the state system, an approach that has been called "legal centralism." They do not know much about how dispute management actually takes place "on the ground"—out in the villages and small communities that anthropologists have traditionally studied—and many of them do not care, believing that local-level conflict processing is outside the formal law, and thus outside their concern. On the other hand, anthropologists, who are familiar with how customary law works, understand relatively little about the formal law and how it operates, and thus view it as outside of *their* concern. Some anthropologists are even antagonistic toward legal centralism, adopting a position that Tamanaha (1993:11) has styled as a "'folk law good,' 'state law bad' posture."

Legal scholars have recognized and labeled these contrasting foci, distinguishing between *substantive law* (rules for normative behavior, infractions of which are negatively sanctioned) and *procedural law* (mechanisms through which legal issues are actually managed). Leopold Pospisil (1971:2), an anthropologist/lawyer, pointed out that the English term "law" really consists of two separate concepts that are distinguished in many other languages. In Latin, for instance, *lex* is an abstract rule usually made explicit in a legal code, whereas *ius* refers to the underlying principles implied in actual case decisions. Whereas lawyers are often preoccupied with *leges* (plural of *lex*, the statutory rules), anthropologists tend to be more interested in the procedures by which disputes actually get settled, and with the underlying principles of fairness implied in such settlements. Thus the "rules" have become the domain of lawyers, and the "procedures" that of the anthropologists. Because of these bifurcated interests, there is much less literature aimed squarely at issues of legal pluralism than might be expected.

Even within this literature on legal pluralism, there are two camps. Scholars approaching the problem from the purely legal or substantive law perspective tend to focus on attempts to incorporate aspects of customary law into state legal systems. The state system is taken as a given, and studied as it reaches out to assimilate customary law. On the other hand, social researchers, taking a procedural law perspective, have historically explored the continuing viability of customary systems of law outside of the state system, touching only marginally, if at all, on the interface with state law. They describe how customary law is alive and well out there in the hinterlands, and how it exists alongside (and often in opposition to) the state system. These two positions have been called "weak" legal pluralism and "strong" legal pluralism respectively (see Griffiths 1986).

The increasing importance of reflexive anthropology demands that researchers reveal their own positions and biases, and this seems like an appropriate time for me to explore mine. I conducted my Ph.D. research in anthropology in Papua New Guinea, living for fifteen months in an Abelam village in the foothills of the Prince Alexander mountains. I studied Abelam customary law, which operated outside the state system, and my thesis (Scaglion 1976) is distinctly in the "strong" legal pluralism camp. However, from 1979 to 1983 I was Director of Customary Law for the Law Reform Commission of Papua New Guinea (see, for example, Scaglion 1987; Scaglion n.d.). Working as a legal officer in state legal development, I was by definition in the "weak" legal pluralism camp. My job was to gather and analyze data on customary law, identify areas where state law did not seem appropriate to the circumstances of the country, and help create draft legislation designed to ameliorate problems.

These two experiences have conditioned my perspective. My heart is certainly in the strong legal pluralism camp. I respect customary legal systems and have worked hard to protect them from the increasing encroachments of state law that would eliminate or fossilize them. On the other hand, I realize that migration, international travel, and the processes of globalization require state systems and even international systems that transcend these local structures. My hope is that local, national, and international systems can all be reconciled. In this regard, I agree with the Honourable Sir Buri Kidu, chief justice of Papua New Guinea, who wrote:

> For most of us in the South Pacific, it has been relatively few years since we achieved independence and, with that, the opportunity to develop our own legal systems. . . . legal thought in the South Pacific has gathered its own momentum and is driven by two basic principles. The first principle is the rule of law, the continuing importance of which is symbolized by the homegrown constitutions adopted by most of the island countries. To safeguard the freedoms and rights enshrined in these constitutions, the constitutions have been made the supreme law of the land, and the courts have been empowered to uphold the supremacy of the constitution. The second principle is the creation of a legal system and a common law (or an underlying law, as we call it in Papua New Guinea) that is attuned to the circumstances of our countries and their peoples. (1993:xiii)

The great challenge in legal reform for Pacific peoples lies in reconciling these principles and also in trying to preserve what is good about customary law and to merge it with introduced law. It also lies in developing legal systems that meet both the demands of the modern state in a contemporary world and the needs of ordinary people increasingly affected by global processes. Unfortunately, this has not proven to be easy. In this chapter, I attempt to view the problem from the standpoint of customary law, state law, and the international community. I first turn to a consideration of traditional systems of law.

## INDIGENOUS SYSTEMS: AUSTRONESIANS AND NON-AUSTRONESIANS, CHIEFS AND BIG MEN

Interestingly, the indigenous peoples of the South Pacific are bifurcated along lines that further play into the substantive law versus procedural law dimensions outlined above.

Some societies have fairly complicated normative orders and are rule governed, whereas others have eschewed formal rules, solving disputes on a case-by-case basis as they emerge. Some societies were politically organized as centralized chiefdoms with relatively powerful chiefs who were able to make rules and to enforce them. Others were fundamentally egalitarian groups whose leaders could cajole and exhort followers but enjoyed little formal authority.

Understanding these two types of social orders requires brief consideration of the peopling and prehistory of the Pacific. It is generally agreed that there were two major migrations, or series of migrations, into what is now the Pacific Islands. The indigenous peoples of Australia and New Guinea are closely related biologically, and are believed to have moved into the area between 50,000 and 35,000 years ago from what is now Indonesia (dates are hotly contested and may be even earlier). In contrast, a much later (post-3000 B.C.) migration of seafaring people from Asia discovered and settled in the rest of the Pacific Islands, including all of Micronesia and Polynesia and much of island Melanesia.

The differences between descendants of these two waves of immigrants are significant today. Due to over 35,000 years of isolation, migration, and mixing, the earlier migrants developed a staggering diversity of languages and cultures that continues to challenge anthropologists and linguists just to describe them all. Papua New Guinea, which is only half of the island of New Guinea together with neighboring islands, today contains some 850 ethnolinguistic groups alone. On the other hand, the later migrants, whose descendants today speak languages belonging to the Austronesian language family, display relatively similar languages and cultures due to their presumably common origins and rapid dispersal throughout the islands. The earlier group of migrants is often called simply "non-Austronesians" to distinguish them from the later group. In some literature, the non-Austronesians are called Papuans, but to me this suggests some similarity that they do not share.

What is critical for understanding legal development in the Pacific is that the Austronesians, who probably developed social complexity in Asia before migrating, tend to have hierarchically organized social structures. Non-Austronesians, on the other hand, almost uniformly lack social hierarchies, instead enjoying relatively egalitarian social organizations based on reciprocal relationships. The result is widely different types of customary political and legal organizations (Scaglion 1996). In 1963, Marshall Sahlins wrote an influential article distinguishing between Polynesian chiefs and Melanesian big men as contrasting models of Pacific leadership. While the political types he described at that time have proven to be elusive to define precisely, and are not exhaustive of the types of Pacific leadership, they do nicely illustrate an important distinction between the social orders of Austronesians and non-Austronesians. The former generally has strong normative orders and leaders with more authority than the latter, a fact that has molded the history of Pacific legal development.

The concept of authority held by Pacific chiefs is crucial to an understanding of how different societies organize customary law. Authority is defined simply as power that is recognized as legitimate by society. While organized crime bosses may have power, judges have authority. Hierarchical societies, which usually have an elite group of rulers (like chiefs), normally have very well-developed notions of authority. People tend to believe that chiefs have certain rights and privileges. In socially stratified cultures, then, legal authorities can use their legitimate power to force compliance with rules or laws. Hopefully (but certainly not always), these laws reflect local notions of right and wrong and have been constructed for the greater good of society. But whether or not this is the case, legal systems in hierarchical societies give considerable "weight" to rules of behavior, thus privileging formalized laws and norms. But in the relatively egalitarian, decentralized non-Austronesian tribal societies found in many parts of Melanesia, there are no formal legal authorities, and formal rules are much less important. Disputes between people are handled on a case-by-case basis, sometimes through consensus solutions based on notions of fairness or "equity," and sometimes by various sorts of political maneuverings.

The lack of formal rules in non-Austronesian societies seems rather odd to Westerners, who of course live in rule-dominated cultures. Koch (1974), who studied customary law among the non-Austronesian Jalé of New Guinea, put it this way:

> Jalé society lacks not only forensic institutions like courts and offices whose incumbents exercise a delegated judicial authority, but even more rudimentary institutions such as forums convened to discuss a dispute. Nor do the Jalé have positions of political leadership that empower their incumbents to exercise control over a local community and to adjudicate disputes among its members.
>
> Furthermore, although my own observations of behavior and informants' descriptions of customary modes of conduct could be collated in a catalog of rules, the Jalé themselves do not formulate any legal norms. Rather, they speak of their behavior either as "what we do," which describes a right and approved course of action, or as "what is not done," which refers to wrong and reprehensible conduct. (Koch 1974:31)
>
> Every social group must cope with conflicts among its members and between itself and other social groups. Rather than being something pathological, enmity and disputes are a normal part of social life. A conflict arises when a person or group suffers or believes it has suffered an infringement of a right. Whether or not a right constitutes a legal claim or a customary expectation may be an interesting problem in jurisprudence; for the Jalé such a distinction is meaningless. (Koch 1974:26)

I found a similar lack of interest in "rules" in my study of the customary law system of the non-Austronesian Abelam:

> Most informants not only showed a distinct lack of interest in my attempts to formulate any general statements about traditional conflicts, but also displayed a frustrating refusal to make any definite statements about cases in the

abstract. "Someone might do it that way," "someone would do that if he felt like it," were common responses to abstract hypothetical cases. Thus even abstract hypothetical cases had to be described using specific individuals and situations: "What if X's pig ruined six yams from Y's garden?" (Scaglion 1981:30)

The difference between what we might call the rule-governed versus situation-specific approaches to law is significant. In the situation-specific model, there are no "blind scales of justice." People are never equal before the law. What happens in a case depends very much on the relationship between the parties to a dispute. People never pay much attention to "precedents," since they have no bearing on the case at hand. Furthermore, people in these societies often have fiercely egalitarian perspectives, frequently refusing to "follow orders." So there are no real "decisions" by legal authorities but rather settlements that take the form of negotiations, mediations, and compromises.

Colonial powers were quick to sense the differences between these models of law, and had very different reactions to each. Since Europeans understood the rule-oriented model of law that they shared with many Austronesian peoples, they often made efforts to coopt, complement, or build upon existing legal authority in their colonizing projects. In many parts of Polynesia and Micronesia, introduced legal and political structures reflected, or worked in concert with, traditional forms of authority in some fashion or another. Though power was often contested (because traditional and introduced structures were based on similar hierarchical models), similar sets of expectations applied. Someone was to be "in charge." In parts of Melanesia, however, where societies lacked any forms of centralized authority recognizable to colonial governments, people were considered to be "primitive" or "undeveloped," and efforts were made to supercede indigenous legal systems with hierarchical models of law. Consequently, contemporary national law in these countries has tended to fit less comfortably with traditional forms

than in contexts where indigenous Pacific peoples shared hierarchical models with their colonizers.

A few examples are illustrative. Perhaps the least "colonized" of all the Pacific nations is Tonga, which today is a hereditary monarchy (see Lee and Leslie, chapters 8 and 23, in this volume). Before European contact, Tonga was one of the most centralized and highly stratified societies in the Pacific. Religious authority supported the aristocratic chiefs, since high-ranked birth signified proximity to the gods. Chiefs commanded both land and the people on it. But rivalries amongst competing dynasties prevented consolidation into a kingdom until 1845 when Taufa'ahau, a newly converted Protestant leader of a powerful regional chiefdom, supported by missionaries, coalesced power and became the first modern monarch. As King George Tupou I, he promptly signed treaties with France, Germany, Great Britain, and the United States, all of whom recognized his sovereignty. He gathered about him advisors mostly from Britain, Australia and New Zealand, and, together with the missionaries who had supported him, constructed the Constitution of Tonga in 1875. This is now one of the world's oldest extant constitutions. It gave him absolute power, relegating all rival chiefs to a secondary status. It also established a parliamentary model of government, resembling the English system, with hereditary nobles in charge. Today the sources of Tonga's legal system are the constitution, statutes, and subsidiary legislation of Tonga and English common law and (where necessary) English statutes. But a prodemocracy movement has been growing in recent years (see Lawson 2000), assuring further legal change.

Samoa's early history with Westerners was similar (see chapters 22 and 10 by Shankman and MacPherson in this volume). Consuls of Germany, Great Britain, and the United States tried to manipulate local politics while at the same time being manipulated by Samoan high chiefs. Samoa's short-lived first constitution, adopted by chiefs in 1873, owed much to American influence. After the Samoan archipelago was partitioned in 1900, the German administration in the West continued attempts to coopt and modify traditional structures. In 1903 they introduced a Land and Titles Court, probably the most influential court in Western Samoa today. Comprised of Samoan judges (chiefs appointed for three-year terms) and assessors (senior chiefs appointed from a panel), the chief justice or a judge of the supreme court acts as president of the court and provides guidance on legal and procedural matters. Unwritten Samoan custom and usage are followed exclusively. The court holds three almost continuous and concurrent sittings: two on Upolu and one on Savai'i. They have exclusive jurisdiction over matters involving *matai* (chiefly) titles and land matters. There is no provision for review. No decision can be challenged in any other court, nor can any other court hear matters of chiefly titles or land (Anesi and Enari 1988). Today in contemporary Samoa, Samoan customary law and English common law are both important sources of law. The constitution determines which matters are governed by which and sets priorities among various sources of law.

In both of the above examples, Westerners and chiefly elites were playing by the same rules. The result was a direct blending of introduced and customary law from the very beginning. But the German colonial government had a very different experience in New Guinea. Hempenstall describes it this way:

German Samoa was a compact, homogeneous hierarchical society of 40,000 people, with a few hundred German settlers, as well as small numbers of British, New Zealanders and Australians. The 10 years of Governor Wilhelm SOLF's rule can be read as a continuing contest between his attempts to insert German legal and bureaucratic structures into Samoan society, altering them towards more rationalist, organized ends, and the Samoans' proto-nationalist struggle to retain their decentralized political structure. . . .

German New Guinea with over 1,000,000 people and hundreds of pockets of autonomous, linguistically fragmented and mutually hostile local populations was a more complex proposition for Governor Albert Hahl. . . . Hahl acted like a particularly aggressive warlord to conquer New Guinean communities in the islands and on the mainland. Stations were extended by using mobile police columns to pacify local districts. (2000:229)

The Germans really never came to grips with the fact that no one was "in charge" in decentralized societies. At one point they attempted to establish local authorities by setting up introduced titles of leadership (*luluai* and *tultul*) in village contexts. Not surprisingly, the authority of these "leaders" was generally not recognized by local people. After World War I, Australia, having assumed custody of the former German colony, had its problems in New Guinea as well. The status of custom in the courts remained uncertain until 1963, when the Native Customs (Recognition) Act provided for the recognition and application of indigenous custom. But it was not until 1975 that the first village courts, designed to apply local customary law, were finally established. Some three-quarters of a century later than in Samoa, there were finally courts in which customary law was applied by indigenous adjudicators.

This, then, is the bifurcated legal legacy of traditional systems that underlies Pacific law today. I turn now to consideration of the state systems that were imposed on these traditional structures.

## STATE SYSTEMS: EXPORTED WESTERN LAW

The interesting thing for anthropologists concerned with Pacific national legal development is not so much how the laws have been shaped at the national level to meet global conditions, but rather how these developing systems can be reconciled with the contemporary lives of Pacific Islanders. National law in the Pacific Islands is very much lawyer's law. Catalogs of the laws of most nations are very similar to Western law and have been written by Western lawyers. Any lawyer could easily master the law in any of these countries just by reading the constitution and legal codes, which would all seem quite familiar. Indigenous Pacific logic, even that of hierarchically ordered societies, has had relatively little effect on contemporary state law. Nevertheless, in order to understand what it is that needs to be blended with customary law, we need to consider the categories of Western law.

What lawyers would call constituent laws are laws that constitute or establish the legal framework of government of a state. All of the countries in the Pacific except for Tokelau have written constitutions that provide most of these constituent laws. What they have created, for better or worse, are systems that closely mirror those of former (or present) colonial powers. Ntumy (1993) and his fellow editors use this fact as a basis for organizing their volume *South Pacific Islands Legal Systems*. The first and largest of their organizational groups consists mostly of former colonies and protectorates of the British Commonwealth whose constitutional arrangements approximate a Westminster concept of cabinet government. Following such a "parliamentary model" are the Cook Islands, Fiji Islands, Kiribati, the Republic of the Marshall Islands, Nauru, Niue, Norfolk Island, Papua New Guinea, Pitcairn Island, Samoa, the Solomon Islands, Tokelau, Tonga, Tuvalu, and Vanuatu. Countries and territories whose constitutional systems are closer to the American "presidential model," with its emphasis on separation of governmental functions and powers, are American Samoa, the Federated States of Micronesia, Guam, the Commonwealth of the Northern Mariana Islands, and the Republic of Palau (some might add Hawai'i). Finally, the French territories of New Caledonia, Wallis and Futuna, and French Polynesia are subject to the laws of France and obviously have systems closely modeled on that of the French Republic. It is significant that none of the constitutions in the region establishes and regulates subordinate courts such as island courts, magistrates' courts, local courts, or village courts. These must be established by legislation.

The word "tort" is not heard often in commonly spoken English, but it is a very important concept in the law. Derived from the French for "wrong," torts are certain kinds of civil wrongs. Civil wrongs are wrongs that have been committed against an individual, and may give rise to liability to compensate that individual. They are distinguished from criminal wrongs, which are wrongs so serious that the community or state intervenes to sanction the offender. The overwhelming majority of conflict cases arising in most Pacific villages today would be categorized as civil wrongs. It is relatively rare for individuals in small, face-to-face contexts to commit criminal wrongs. Custom is a powerful force operating to keep people in line, and it is very hard to "get away with" anything in a milieu in which everyone knows everyone else's business. Furthermore, because non-Austronesian societies traditionally lacked central governments, very few of their traditional conflicts would have fallen under Western definitions of criminal law.

Torts law does not cover all of civil law, however. Some civil wrongs involve breaches of contracts, and some arise from breach of a trust or other fiduciary relationship. Contract law is a separate branch of law based on common law. A contract is a legally binding agreement made between two people who intend it to have legal effect. So, as lawyers would say, two elements are necessary for a contract: an agreement and legal enforceability. Because lawyers do not always believe that non-Austronesian societies even had "law," and certainly not law in a Western sense, they question whether customary agreements can be considered contracts. Thus contract law in the Pacific has remained very much Western law. It may cover many new situations in which Pacific Islanders find themselves, but customary agreements and notions will not apply.

In contrast is land law: a body of law that establishes the kinds of interests that people can acquire in land, and how such interests can be transferred, modified, and terminated. Land law is very interesting (and contentious) in the Pacific. It is one area in which customary principles are generally upheld in relationship to land that is owned in accordance with custom. Except for Tonga, the written law in all independent countries makes express provision for custom to be used as the basis for determining rights to customary land. This is important because, in situations where national or international companies negotiate with indigenous peoples for rights to use or settle on customary land, the usages governing the transaction are usually the customs of the people, not the laws of the outsiders.

This has normally worked to protect indigenous rights. In the Pacific, people who are not formal landowners may nevertheless have certain usufructory rights. By custom, people may be permitted to reside on land that they do not own, or use it for gardens, or pass across it, harvest coconuts they have planted on it, cut trees and leaves to make traditional houses, and so on. If a local village leases land to a tuna canning plant, for example, they may retain rights to harvest coconuts, and the plant then may not be able to fence their grounds to prevent trespass of people holding these rights. But new conditions give rise to new situations, and people can attempt to apply these customary arrangements in ways that certainly violate the spirit of the custom when usufructory rights assume commercial value. In the Solomon Islands, the Forest Resources and Timber Utilization Act allows logging companies to make agreements with persons having rights over timber. But when people with usufructory and not ownership rights make these agreements, serious problems can ensue. An example comes from the judgment of the high court of Solomons in *Touva* v. *Meki:*

Mr. Tegavota, on behalf of the applicants (that is, land owners), has argued, with some force, that . . . timber rights and land ownership are not always the same. . . . These secondary rights, when they were granted or acquired, gave rights to things such as harvesting and gathering food and cutting wood to make custom houses. To suggest that these secondary rights may now allow people who do not own the land to enter into agreements with logging companies to extract the most valuable commodity on the land, take the royalties for themselves and leave the landowners with a wasteland, is really taking the

matter too far. I could not be more in agreement with him, but, unfortunately, that is not the way the law is written. (*Solomon Islands Law Reports* [1988–1989]74:76; cited in Care, Newton, and Patterson 1999:246–247)

I return to a further analysis of this case below.

## BLENDING CUSTOMARY AND INTRODUCED LAW

We have already considered the thesis (the traditional systems) and the antithesis (the introduced law, especially for the non-Austronesians). Now for the synthesis. From the viewpoint of lawyers, there are three fundamental ways in which customary and introduced law can be integrated: (1) Customary norms and laws can be codified; (2) customs can be formulated and applied in a manner analogous to what was done with the common law; and (3) new tribunals, based on customary procedural law and comprising indigenous people, can be established.

One of the strengths of customary law, and particularly among the non-Austronesians, has been its ability to adapt to changing circumstances. Since cases are decided fresh each time, without having to pay attention to how things were done before, new circumstances can be easily and quickly considered using basic notions of equity. Given the rapid changes that have accompanied globalization throughout the Pacific, this is particularly important now. By contrast, Western nations, with their more rigid legal structures, often struggle when the law does not fit new circumstances, when legal change lags behind social change. We can all think of glaring examples in women's suffrage, civil rights, and so on.

The excerpt from the judgment given above in *Touva* v. *Meki* provides an example of what happens when customary law is codified. It loses its natural ability to adapt. When custom is written, it becomes frozen at a quickly outdated moment in time and loses the flexibility that made it what it was. A procedural law advocate would say that it ceases to be customary law at all. Customary "rules," where they exist at all, tend to be much less formal and ordered than are written statutes. A tribunal of local dispute settlers following customary law would likely have agreed with the high court that the sale of timber to a logging company by those having only usufructory rights was an improper extension of customary privileges. And thus they could have found for the applicants without worrying about whether it was contrary to written law. But now, the Forestry Resources and Timber Utilization Act and/or written custom will have to be repealed, modified, or rewritten in some fashion to keep pace with social change. For this reason, attempts to codify customary law have not been particularly successful in law reform in the Pacific.

The second strategy for law reform outlined earlier involves an attempt to integrate more of the spirit than the letter of customary law. The common law in England is a body of principles of equity that form the core of the English legal system. It has developed in decisions of the courts over a very long period of time and embodies basic principles of fairness. The vast majority of independent countries of the Pacific, including all of those that were under control of Britain, Australia, or New Zealand, have adopted principles of English common law and equity subject to certain conditions. There has also been an intention to develop an "underlying law" that would be more appropriate to the circumstances of the country by making references to principles of customary law and letting a unique common law develop. In some countries, judges must look first to custom, and only secondarily to English common law. In others, English common law is to be considered except when it is inappropriate to the circumstances of the country. In both of these situations, wide latitude is given to judges to consider contemporary conditions and to integrate customary principles into a uniquely national law.

This direction seems more promising, but in fact very little has been accomplished. As a general rule, judges are loathe to consider custom, and prosecutors and defense attorneys are hesitant to introduce it. Perhaps it is

because, as lawyers, they know much less about custom than they know about law. Because of the practical and intellectual bifurcations explored earlier, there is little interaction between the domains of the anthropologists and the lawyers. While judges often seem to uphold the principle of the development of a national jurisprudence, it just does not seem to happen.

A few examples will illustrate my point. The case of *Waiwo* v. *Waiwo and Banga* in Vanuatu (discussed in Care 1998 and Care, Newton, and Paterson 1999) involved a case of adultery. A provision in the Matrimonial Causes Act of 1986 authorized wronged parties to be awarded "damages." The question was whether "damages" should be interpreted to mean merely compensatory damages (as it does in English law) or could also include punitive damages (as it does according to custom). Recognizing that the awarding of punitive damages in adultery cases was in accordance with widespread custom in Vanuatu, Senior Magistrate Lunabeck held in magistrates' court that the provision should be interpreted as allowing for punitive damage awards.

This seemed promising. Customary law had been recognized and a customary principle upheld. It would seem that customary law was being integrated into the national law. However, the decision was reversed on appeal to the Supreme Court. Oddly, both judges involved upheld the principle that customary law should be integrated into national law, even though the decision of the Supreme Court reinforced the English interpretation and prevented that from happening in this case.

Another judicial decision that acted to impede the true integration of customary and introduced law occurred on Yap. Two similar cases, straightforward from a customary law point of view, became very complicated legally. Two men, in separate incidents occurring a week apart, each committed rape. Soon afterwards, each of them was severely beaten by the families of their respective victims. Everyone involved agreed that these retaliatory beatings were customary and appropriate. In one of the cases, the victim's family agreed that, before a traditional tribunal, the case would be dismissed on the grounds that justice had already been achieved by the beating, which had been severe enough to hospitalize the rapist. However, because rape is a serious crime under introduced law, criminal cases were filed in FSM (Federated States of Micronesia) court.

At the sentencing hearing, the defendants, who had admitted their guilt, asked the judge to take the customary acts of retaliation into account as a mitigation in the sentence. The judge expressed regret that he could not count the beatings to lessen the sentence. He did not want people to get the idea that they could "take the law into their own hands," and believed that if he reduced the punishment he would legitimize the beatings. He sentenced both defendants to two years in jail.

On appeal, the Supreme Court held that the judge should have credited the beatings to mitigate the sentence. Tamanaha (1993: 69–72) discusses the opinion issued by the appellate division of the FSM Supreme Court at some length. On the surface, the Supreme Court's decision would seem to be a victory for customary law. As Tamanaha puts it (1993:70), "It was the very first time that custom had an impact in changing the received law." But there were complications, anticipated by the trial judge. The Supreme Court decision stated in part:

> Lest we be misunderstood, and interpreted as holding that this court and other governmental officials must affirm and support custom in all of its manifestations, we are compelled to point out that the judicial guidance clause requires that our decisons be consistent not only with customs and traditions but with the balance of the Constitution as well.
>
> Measured against that mandate, the kinds of beatings inflicted upon Messrs. Tammed and Tamangrow raise profound and fundamental issues about law enforcement in the Federated States of Micronesia.
>
> . . . if upon remand the trial court is asked to give special mitigative effect to these beatings to reflect their customary nature, the court must

first consider whether these customary activities have become so imbued with official state action that the actions of the assailants must be viewed as actions of the state itself. If that is so, the punishments must be tested by the same standards that would be applied if state officials themselves were to carry out these punishments directly. (*Tammed* v. *FSM*, *Tamangrow* v. *FSM*, App. No. Y1–1998)

The legal implications here are profound. Essentially, in upholding the customary beatings, the state removed them from the realm of custom. The assailants became agents of the state, since the state has a monopoly on the legitimate use of force. This opens the door to the rapists to sue the state on the grounds that the beatings were governmental actions that violated their civil rights. While the decision appears to support custom, it actually undermines it. In the future, taking almost any customary actions into account in FSM courts will also legitimize them (thereby changing their very nature), and will also expose the state to legal action.

## CUSTOMARY TRIBUNALS: PAPUA NEW GUINEA'S VILLAGE COURTS

The first two strategies for law reform mentioned above, codifying customary rules and arguing custom in court, have consequently had very limited impact. What of the third strategy, establishing new tribunals? Perhaps if custom could be asked to integrate introduced law, rather than the other way around, more progress could be made.

Papua New Guinea has been one of the more progressive of the Pacific nations in pursuing law reform. As Care, Newton, and Paterson put it, "It is probably in the neighbouring Melanesian Country of Papua New Guinea that there has been the most concerted pressure for the development of a national jurisprudence" (1999:7). Yet PNG has also had problems with the first two strategies. Apart from the monumental efforts that would be required to codify some 850 different customary legal systems, the overall strategy of codifying custom has not proven to be workable for the reasons outlined above. Nor has custom been argued frequently in court. However, the third strategy has held much promise for legal development in PNG.

Village courts were established in Papua New Guinea by the Village Courts Act 1973 (No. 12 of 1974). As described in section 18, the primary function of a village court is "to ensure peace and harmony in the area for which it is established by mediating in and endeavouring to obtain just and amicable settlements of disputes" by applying relevant native custom. Previous to the establishment of village courts, the lowest officially recognized judicial body was the local court, which is based on Western principles and employs introduced law. However, local peoples generally avoided these courts in pursuing their grievances, because they were unfamiliar with Western law and legal procedures. Village courts were intended to employ the customary dispute resolution practices that were actually used in the villages. But solutions would be accorded the weight of law by empowering traditional leaders to act as local court magistrates. This would allow people to litigate according to custom but still be operating within the boundaries of a national legal system. In actuality, it involves approaching the problem of law reform from the vantage point of procedural law, outlined above, instead of substantive law.

Village courts began operating to mixed reviews. Many of the lawyers and legal sociologists who first observed them became concerned that they appeared too formal, merely mimicking the local courts. Paliwala observed that they brought about "greater involvement and control by the state and a degree of authoritarianism on the part of court officials. The result is relatively alienated dispute settlement with little scope for community involvement and party consensus" (1982:191). But in a restudy (Scaglion 1979) of the area in which I had conducted my Ph.D. research, I found that the newly established village courts were operating at informal as well as more formal levels. The formal operations that Paliwala observed seemed to take place only after the informal system had already failed. But in fact, many cases were being successfully negotiated at this informal level.

Soon other testaments to the success of village courts began to surface from anthropologists who knew the local situations well. Andrew Strathern showed how courts in the Highlands were integrating customary and introduced law:

> When we say that Village Courts reflect the capitalist economic system, this does not exclude the fact that they are also influenced by customary ideas and that the actual decisions they make reflect cultural conceptions about the person, shame, responsibility, and so on. Emphatically, they do reflect these ideas, but it is still significant that these courts have ordered fines to be paid as well as, or instead of, compensation to injured or aggrieved parties, as already mentioned. This indicates that the magistrates quite self-consciously realize they are operating an introduced, state-based institution and not just deciding disputes by "customary law." (1984:64)

George Westermark (1978, 1981) presented similar evidence. He viewed village courts as part of a wider arena of conflict management options, demonstrating how litigants had choices in pursuing their options, and how they often chose village courts. He saw how village court magistrates creatively used mediation techniques to settle disputes as envisioned in the original Village Courts Act. Anthropologists Robert Gordon and Mervyn Meggitt cited the testimony of an Engan man: "The Village Courts here are doing an excellent job. Most of the decisions are a compromise with the new government laws and the traditional laws. Other courts give less consideration to the customs and practices of the people, so today more court cases are heard by the Village Courts than by the Local Court in Laiagam" (1985:221). Gordon and Meggitt concluded that "village courts have greater potential for dealing with the law-and-order problem [in Enga Province] than any of the other options considered" (1985:15–16).

It also became clear that the village courts were successfully managing a wide variety of nontraditional conflict situations. In a ten-year retrospective study (Scaglion 1990) of the village court I had previously researched, I observed numerous cases in which social changes had caused new and unfamiliar situations in village life, and where the resultant problems were being negotiated in the village courts. I witnessed discussions over misman-agement of funds held in trust for new coop-erative economic development associations (including gold mining, cattle raising, and cash cropping ventures), prosecutions for failure to perform government-mandated council work, issues resulting from drunken behavior (a relatively new problem), clashes with tourists and visitors from other local cultures, disputes pitting new Christian pre-scriptions of monogamy with traditional polygynous practices, and a host of other novel confrontations.

It also appears that village courts have brought about legal change at a very broad level. One of the problems in Papua New Guinea has been the achievement of equal rights for women. Meggitt (1964:220–221) de-scribed Mae Enga women's traditional legal status as that of "jural minors" who had no title to valuable property, rarely participated in public affairs, and were little more than the legal wards of males. This situation was not uncommon in many parts of Papua New Guinea where male kinsmen generally liti-gated on behalf of women. Due in part to this traditional situation, contemporary women plaintiffs have not been satisfied with the out-comes of grievances that they raise in the vil-lages. But in a nationwide study of some 481 extended cases of all types gathered by the Law Reform Commission, we found that many women plaintiffs' disputes were success-fully mediated in village courts:

> this research suggests the nature of changes which are taking place in women's access to jus-tice in Papua New Guinea. . . . On the basis of proportions of disputes submitted to village agencies and the success rates of these forums for dispute management . . . women still do not seem to be receiving equal legal treatment in the villages.

Without doubt, the most dramatic changes have come about as a direct result of the intro-duction of village courts. . . . Village court juris-diction in family law cases is quite extensive. Courts have unlimited mediatory jurisdiction, so that consensus settlements can be recorded and enforced as orders of the court (sections 16–18). Adjudicatory jurisdiction is unlimited in matters of custody of children and bride-price, and courts may hear family cases of all types.

The women in our study made good use of this forum, which settled over 35 percent of all their resolved complaints. Local government council officers, who serve a parallel function in areas which do not have village courts, ac-counted for another 22.7 percent. As previously noted, village courts had an extremely high suc-cess rate in settling family cases, to the apparent satisfaction of female plaintiffs.

By removing their grievances from the vil-lage, which traditionally is a male-dominated political milieu, and submitting them in other arenas which recognise local customs, women in Papua New Guinea appear to be achieving some measure of legal equality. However, evidence suggests that women still have problems in pur-suing their grievances at higher levels. Local and district courts are rarely used by women and even when these agents are utilised, their suc-cess rate is not high. Thus, women seem to be truly caught "in between," unable to obtain jus-tice at both lower and higher levels. For the mo-ment, the village courts appear to be their most favourable forum for dispute management. (Scaglion and Whittingham 1985:132)

Still other studies have noted differences between village courts and either *kastom* law or state law that appear promising. In an in-teresting comparison of "law talk" between village courts and traditional moots in pre-marital sex cases among the Huli, Laurence Goldman noted that "perhaps the Village Court provides a new arena in which the in-tersex drama can be played out" (1988:157). He found that "the type of interrogative processes which characterise [the Village Court case] represent a new way of fostering culturally rooted behavioural goals." Other recent analyses of village courts, whether favorable or unfavorable, underline further distinctions between village courts on the one hand and customary practices and introduced law on the other that are suggestive of a blending of legal systems. Zorn (1990) describes considerable flexibility in matters of evidence and decision making in urban village courts, also noted later by Goddard (1996). Zorn suggests that this mixing of elements of "compromise" and "court" models furthers the aims of dynamic customary law (1990:306). Westermark (1991), in a comparative study of rural village courts, found that court effectiveness is highest where a close correspondence between court jurisdictions and local sociopolitical units exists. And Brison (1999) showed how Kwanga magistrates, while employing a rhetoric that contrasted tradition with "new law," in practice blended together both systems. In so doing, they "made use of state institutions in ways that ultimately contributed to their sense of being a meaningful part of a national polity" (Brison 1999:74).

## INTERNATIONAL ISSUES

It would seem, then, that the creation of customary tribunals holds some promise for the struggles of Pacific Island nations in their attempts to blend customary and introduced legal structures at the state level. But there is yet another level to be considered: the international forums in which global issues are also being negotiated. While international "laws" can but rarely be constructed, multilateral attempts to resolve global problems are very much the purview of legal anthropologists. And ironically, international negotiations resemble in some particulars the conflict management efforts of decentralized societies. Sally Merry (2000) has argued for examining such situations via a new type of ethnography that she calls "deterritorialized ethnography." This is "similar to what others have called multi-sited ethnography, but insofar as it is focused on information flows, the Internet, and global conferences, it is not restricted to sites" (Merry 2000:130). Thus we must temporarily shift our gaze from the local and national situations we have concentrated on thus far and consider regional and even global arenas for the contestation of global issues.

There are many themes that we could explore. One broad sphere of activities involves the natural resources of the Pacific, which have always proved attractive to outside interests. I have touched on some of the implications of timber extraction earlier in this chapter. A related topic involves global efforts to regulate the fishing industry, particularly as it involves attempts to end the overfishing and fishing with nonsustainable techniques that have decimated fish stocks and associated wildlife in many parts of the world. Clearly, local legal systems are powerless to protect migratory fish or to regulate the exploitation of international waters, but local people can be dramatically impacted by the loss of marine resources. The only answer to these sorts of problems is through international cooperation. An important step toward multilateral agreements was made with the signing of the United Nations Convention on the Law of the Sea in 1982, which took effect in 1994. The convention "provides for international institutions such as the International Sea-Bed Authority (for management of deep-sea resources extending beyond national borders), and the International Tribunal for the Law of the Sea, established as a means of compulsory dispute-settlement" (Van Dyke 2000:316). International agreements to monitor and control fishing have led to licensing agreements and substantial payments to Pacific nations by the national and international organizations that would exploit Pacific marine resources. Recently, the Forum Fisheries Agency has tackled the problem of environmentally unsound, long driftnet fishing by Japan, South Korea, and Taiwan. An international Convention for the Prohibition of Fishing with Long Driftnets in the South Pacific, signed in 1989, helped to eliminate the problem.

There are many other examples of how Pacific nations, working together or separately, have managed to sway international opinion and affect the behavior of First World nations. One prominent case is the South Pacific Nuclear Free Zone Treaty which prohibited the manufacture, stationing, or testing of any nuclear explosive device, and the dumping of nuclear waste at sea within the treaty area. Aided by the Nuclear Free and Independent Pacific movement, a loose coalition of activist groups, members of the South Pacific forum persuaded first the Soviet Union and People's Republic of China and then later, Britain, the United States, and France to sign the protocols of the treaty by 1996.

Such bargaining and negotiating strategies have worked in not only one direction, however. Foreign aid has been of extreme importance within the region, comprising some 20 percent of GDP in many countries. Apart from bilateral aid, international donors such as the Asian Development Bank, European Development Fund, and various United Nation agencies contribute heavily to Pacific Island nations, but this largess comes at a cost. In return for aid, donors attempt to influence the policies, procedures, and legal structure of recipient nations, which causes considerable tension. In 1996, the World Bank, concerned about the slow pace of domestic reform in Papua New Guinea and the failure of the PNG government to uphold agreements reached with the bank and other donors, suspended a $U.S.210 million structural adjustment loan. In 1995, Australia suspended forestry aid to the Solomon Islands because of the government's logging policies, explored above. The European Union also froze aid to the Solomon Islands because of problems regarding its use. But there are also many successful ventures, in which international organizations, NGOs, and government agencies hammer out mutually satisfactory aid arrangements that provide culturally appropriate assistance.

## CONCLUSION

What I find most interesting in these international attempts to regulate global resources and influence global problems and social issues is a return to the types of conflict-management strategies that originally characterized many Pacific Island societies' customary legal systems. In the international arena, there is no centralized power or authority to make decisions and compel settlement; rather there are the bargaining, compromise, and consensus solutions that have always marked *kastom* law, particularly in non-Austronesian cultures. Thus we are beginning to see an about-face in which industrialized nations are learning to apply the conflict-management techniques that have worked well in small-scale societies. In an influential article on legal pluralism, Sally Merry (1988) distinguishes between what she calls "classic legal pluralism," which analyzes intersections between indigenous and European law, and "the new legal pluralism," which applies the concept of legal pluralism to First World situations. This is yet another way of moving away from the concept of legal centralism that lawyers favor. It focuses attention on other forms of ordering, such as international organizations, agreements, and treaties, and their relationship with state law, and promises to be an increasingly important sphere of legal pluralism research.

If we return our attention to the local places with which we began, it is obvious that social changes have caused a great deal of tension in island life. There are on-going conflicts between local leaders and regional and national authorities, between customary ideas and Christian teachings, between customary and Western practices. Pacific Islanders must cope with changing economic patterns in which subsistence practices are increasingly replaced by a cash economy. Families are increasingly dispersed, and remittances form an important part of their continuing relationships. But there are also exciting new opportunities: Anthropologists Alan Howard and Jan Rensel have created an Internet Web site facilitating expatriate Rotumans' connections with their home island, for example. Clearly, the Pacific region is facing important new challenges.

Legal pluralism can provide the means for reconciling traditional and global life, but much work remains. There are on-going clashes between traditional notions of group-based or corporate responsibility and introduced concepts of individual legal responsibility and rights. There are also clashes between customary approaches, in which disputes cannot be isolated from the broader social context, and introduced legal systems in which courts attempt to deal with offenses as discrete occurrences. So there continue to be competing models of law, authority, and morality that must be reconciled. Paul Roscoe's chapter in this volume (chapter 3) provides a vivid depiction of differing perspectives on "tribal fighting" and "crime." In the contemporary Pacific, the very content of "custom" and "law" are being negotiated on a day-to-day basis. As Pacific people work toward a reconciliation of introduced and customary law and continue to operate in international spheres, legal pluralism provides a shifting ground upon which contemporary political issues are being continually contested and redefined.

## ACKNOWLEDGMENTS

As always, I am grateful to the government of Papua New Guinea for permission to conduct research there, and to the Abelam people for their exceptional hospitality, generosity, and continuing tolerance of me and my work throughout the years. This chapter has been improved through discussions with colleagues who work in the Pacific, many of whom are acknowledged herein through citations to their work. The manuscript was written while I was a visiting colleague at the Center for Pacific Islands Studies, University of Hawai'i. I would like to offer special thanks to the faculty and staff of the center, who have greatly assisted my research activities during two sabbatical leaves. The writing was also supported by grants from the University Center for International Studies and Asian Studies Program of the University of Pittsburgh.

## REFERENCES

Anesi, Taulapapa, and Auelua F. Enari. 1988. "The Land and Chiefly Titles Court of Western Samoa." In *Pacific Courts and Legal Systems*. G. Powles and M. Pulea, eds. Pp. 107–111. Suva: University of the South Pacific.

Brison, Karen J. 1999. "Imagining a Nation in Kwanga Village Courts, East Sepik Province, Papua New Guinea." *Anthropological Quarterly* 72:74–85.

Care, Jennifer Corrin. 1998. Abrogation of the Rights of Customary Land Owners by the Forest Resources and Timber Utilisation Act (1992). QUTLJ 8:131.

Care, Jennifer Corrin, T. Newton, and D. Paterson. 1999. *Introduction to South Pacific Law*. London: Cavendish.

Goddard, Michael. 1996. "The Snake Bone Case: Law, Custom and Justice in a Papua New Guinea Village Court." *Oceania* 67:50–63.

Goldman, L. R. 1988. "Premarital Sex Cases among the Huli: A Comparison Between Traditional and Village Court Styles." Oceania Monograph No. 34. Sydney: University of Sydney.

Gordon, Robert, and Mervyn J. Meggitt. 1985. *Law and Order in the New Guinea Highlands: Encounters with Enga*. New Hanover, N.H.: University Press of New England.

Griffiths, John. 1986. "What Is Legal Pluralism?" *Journal of Legal Pluralism* 24:2–13.

Hempenstall, Peter. 2000. "Colonial Rule: Administrative Styles and Practices." In *The Pacific Islands: An Encyclopedia*. B. V. Lal and K. Fortune, eds. Pp. 229–231. Honolulu: University of Hawai'i Press.

Kidu, Buri. 1993. "Foreword." In *South Pacific Islands Legal Systems*. M. A. Ntumy, ed. P. xiii. Honolulu: University of Hawai'i Press.

Koch, Klaus-Friedrich. 1974. *War and Peace in Jalémó: The Management of Conflict in Highland New Guinea*. Cambridge: Harvard University Press.

Lawson, Stephanie. 2000. "Pro-Democracy Movement in Tonga." In *The Pacific Islands: An Encyclopedia*. B. V. Lal and K. Fortune, eds. P. 307. Honolulu: University of Hawai'i Press.

Meggitt, Mervyn. 1964. "Male-Female Relationships in the Highlands of Australian New Guinea." *American Anthropologist* 66:204–224.

Merry, Sally Engle. 1988. "Legal Pluralism." *Law & Society Review* 22:869–896.

———. 2000. "Crossing Boundaries: Ethnography in the Twenty-First Century." *Political and Legal Anthropology Review* 23:127–133.

Ntumy, Michael A., ed. 1993. *South Pacific Islands Legal Systems*. Honolulu: University of Hawai'i Press.

Paliwala, Abdul. 1982. "Law and Order in the Village: The Village Courts." In *Law and Social Change in Papua New Guinea*. D. Weisbrot, A. Paliwala, and A. Sawyer, eds. Pp. 191–217. Sydney: Butterworths.

Pospisil, Leopold. 1971. *Anthropology of Law: A Comparative Theory*. New York: Harper and Row.

Sahlins, Marshall. 1963. "Poor Man, Rich Man, Big-Man, Chief: Political Types in Melanesia and Polynesia." *Comparative Studies in Society and History* 5:285–303.

Scaglion, Richard. 1976. "Seasonal Patterns in Western Abelam Conflict Management Practices." Ph.D. thesis. University of Pittsburgh.

———. 1979. "Formal and Informal Operations of a Village Court in Maprik." *Melanesian Law Journal* 7:116–129.

———. 1981. "Samukundi Abelam Conflict Management: Implications for Legal Planning in Papua New Guinea." *Oceania* 52:28–38.

———. 1987. "Customary Law Development in Papua New Guinea." In *Anthropological Praxis: Translating Knowledge into Action.* R. M. Wulff and S. Fiske, eds. Pp. 98–108. Boulder, Colo.: Westview Press.

———. 1990. "Legal Adaptation in a Papua New Guinea Village Court." *Ethnology* 29:17–33.

———. 1996. "Chiefly Models in Papua New Guinea." *The Contemporary Pacific* 8:1–31.

———. n.d. "From Anthropologist to Government Officer and Back Again." *Social Analysis* (in press).

Scaglion, Richard, and Rose Whittingham. 1985. "Female Plaintiffs and Sex-Related Disputes in Rural Papua New Guinea." In *Domestic Violence in Papua New Guinea.* S. Toft, ed. Pp. 120–133. Port Moresby: Law Reform Commission Monograph No. 3.

Strathern, Andrew J. 1984. *A Line of Power.* New York: Tavistock.

Tamanaha, Brian Z. 1993. "Understanding Law in Micronesia: An Interpretive APp.roach to Transplanted Law." *Studies in Human Society.* Vol. 7. Leiden: E. J. Brill.

Van Dyke, Jon. 2000. "International Law and the Pacific Ocean." In *The Pacific Islands: An Encyclopedia.* B. V. Lal and K. Fortune, eds. Pp. 316–317. Honolulu: University of Hawai'i Press.

Westermark, George D. 1978. "Village Courts in Question: The Nature of Court Procedure." *Melanesian Law Journal* 6:79–96.

———. 1981. "Legal Pluralism and Village Courts in Agarabi." Ph.D. thesis. University of Washington.

———. 1991. "Village Courts in Papua New Guinea: A Comparative Perspective." *Law & Anthropology: Internationales Jahrbuch für Rechtsanthropologie* 6:67–79.

Zorn, Jean G. 1990. "Customary Law in the Papua New Guinea Village Courts." *The Contemporary Pacific* 2:279–312.

# 6

# Stepping-Stones
# to National Consciousness:
# The Solomon Islands Case

**Christine Jourdan**

*Concordia University*

## INTRODUCTION: THREE STEPPING-STONES

Nationalism is the "in" word in the South Pacific. The sun-drenched island countries with the swaying palm trees of our occidental dream have started to shed the romantic image they have inherited from the colonial era. More pressing images are at stake here, and one of the more important is that of countries sufficiently stable politically and strong economically to attract foreign investment and trust. Political stability would be the proof that decolonization was not only successful but also worthwhile, for in those newly decolonized countries, the ghosts of the colonial powers are still present, looming over the shaky futures of the tiny islands.[1]

The hope a decade ago was that economic strength would in the end allow these countries to discard foreign aid and be truly independent, a dream that was very much part of the ideology of political independence. Yet rising populations, collapsed commodity prices, dwindling forest and marine resources, and the long-range prospect of rising sea levels are pushing Pacific countries into impoverishment and inescapable dependency. Are these countries nations?

Nations are made; they do not exist naturally. The case of the Solomon Islands I present here illustrates the forces at play in the development of nationhood. The postcolonial state must develop the needed ideological and institutional infrastructure. There are three crucial means by which the ideology of nationhood can be fostered: (1) schooling, inculcating a national consciousness and creating a common frame of reference for the young generations; (2) community of language, providing a medium for the spread of the nationalist ideology; and (3) the development of popular culture, redefining old symbols and creating new ones that cut across ethnic and religious boundaries. I will treat these three means as "stepping-stones to national consciousness."

During the fifteen years that have elapsed since they became independent from Britain in 1978, the Solomon Islands have been busy building and consolidating the state apparatus. However, it has been only over the last five years or so that I have observed the development of emotional associations with the idea that the country may be more than the artificial lumping together of different islands and ethnic and linguistic groups, as well as efforts sustained by the central government to foster in the population the concept of a Solomon Islands nation. Emotional attachment to the idea of "the nation" is more obvious in urban circles than it is in the rural areas, for reasons that will become clearer. This attachment is illustrated and fostered by various public celebrations, such as the celebrations of Independence Day (Feinberg 1990; LiPuma and Meltzoff 1990); by the creation of national sports teams representing the country in international competitions (a Solomon Islands team participated in the 1992 Olympic Games in Barcelona); and by the development of a local body of literature and popular songs focusing on the values, habits, culture, and expectations identified by their authors as being national concerns. All play important roles in nation making. Symbolic displays induce people to watch, enjoy, participate, and, in the end, enlist their identification with a national community. All these symbolic displays are discourses that tell members of the society not only what they are, but, more important, what they could be: an image of themselves projected into the future. These collective public displays are surface-level representations of a hidden, more secretive, more intimate, and more individual feeling of belonging in the group.

However, it seems to me that additional elements are crucial in conveying to citizens of the Solomon Islands a sense of shared values and expectations, out of which a sense of common purpose in the future is developing. They are the three "stepping-stones" toward a national consciousness: (1) the education system; (2) Pijin as a common language; and (3) popular culture. These focal areas will be essential sites in the emergence of a new discourse, with which people will identify to some degree and which they will help shape. This new discourse will be sufficiently different from earlier discourses predicated on cultural diversity to serve as the binding agent of new identities, yet it must be sufficiently reminiscent of them not to be too threatening and to be meaningful and symbolically potent. It must therefore seize old symbols and concepts and deploy them for new purposes. Two of these stepping-stones are provided by the state apparatuses and are rooted in the idea that community of language and community of culture (effected through a homogenizing education) will ensure some common ground to a highly diverse population. This is a conception of nationhood very much inherited from the former colonial power. The third stepping-stone, popular culture, develops more or less independent of the influence of the state apparatuses, beyond their control, even though the state may have given the impetus and discreet encouragement that are necessary for its rapid spread.

## NATIONALISM, OTHERNESS, AND INDEPENDENCE

Before examining these stepping-stones in detail, and exploring the Solomon Islands case further, I want to pause to reflect on the special character of postcolonial nationalism in the Pacific. There has been an outpouring of writing on nationalism in Europe, its historical development, and its explosive contemporary manifestations. I do not want to add to this flood of words regarding ideologies of roots, blood, land, shared history, and primordial origins, other than to reflect on the role in all this of concepts of Otherness. I will suggest that there lies one of the crucial contrasts between classical, ethnically framed Eastern European nationalism and the incipient nationalism of the postcolonial Pacific.

An ethnic minority, whether in an imperial state such as the Austro-Hungarian Empire or in a twentieth-century former conglomerate state such as Yugoslavia, Czechoslovakia, or the Soviet Union, defines its identity oppositionally, vis-à-vis the dominant Other. Nationalist ideology in these classic European forms represents resistance against domination, engulfment, hegemony, and the threat of cultural and linguistic oblivion. Myths of a common past, shared blood, or patrimony are cast oppositionally in relation to the Other that dominates. Whether claims to nationhood succeed or not, identity emerges in relation to the Other, through the dialectic of domination and resistance, incorporation and liberation, denial and realization, in which images held on both sides of the encounter are generated through reciprocal self-definition. The result is an image of Self that makes sense only through the presence of an Other.

For colonized peoples, domination took very different forms. The dominant Other was the colonial master; and nationalist liberation entailed struggle against racially based caste systems, drastic resource extraction, labor exploitation in mines and plantations, land alienation, and imposition of alien institutions and laws. Decolonization was a fight to regain a humanness stripped away by the colonial masters. But in the Pacific, the colonial masters were not the Other fought against in Indochina, or Kenya, or Algeria. Independence was in most places handed on a platter to culturally diverse colonial subjects not at all sure whether they wanted it. Who, then, was the Other in relation to which identity could be defined and nationalism forged?

The first Other is nearby: It is the other ethnic group, on the other side of the river, or in the next valley, or on another island, with whom trade and exchange regularly took place, or against whom wars were fought (see as well LiPuma 1995). It is the existence of that Other and the need to assert one's identity vis-à-vis a constructed Other, and not predominantly geographical isolation from one another, that have shaped cultural particularism and the high degree of language diversity in Melanesia, for instance.

The second Other is further removed: It is the world of the colonial or former colonial masters. This colonial world not only brought social chaos but also required of the groups that came under colonial domination a redefinition of their identity and conception of

Self, for colonial domination brought a new form of identity, that of colonial subject: a second or third-class citizen relegated to the newly acquired and pejorative status of "native." It is therefore within the framework of this newly established native citizenship that nationalist movements will emerge. Curiously enough, nationalist movements will seek a redefinition of that citizenship on their own terms, rather than challenging the concept of citizenship itself. The semiotics of the fight will be directly borrowed from the political system that the nationalist movements seek to topple. Interestingly and ironically, most nationalist movements in the Pacific (and in Africa and Southeast Asia as well) have not challenged the artificial creation of new geopolitical entities by colonial powers, beyond the rhetorics that are necessary to create nationalist sentiments. In fact, they may use colonial boundaries as pretexts for imperial expansion, as in the case of Indonesia's seizure of Irian Jaya/West Papua. When independence comes, the one geopolitical entity that will be considered as legitimate, and for which the new excolonial state will fight, is the one created by the former colonial power. In subsequent years, internal ethnic tensions may resurface and lead ethnic-based or island-based groups to seek secession from the newly independent country. Bougainville is a case in point (see Ogan 1991).

When we talk of nationalism in the Pacific, and elsewhere for that matter, we have in mind quite often the political format of the nation state. We thus forget that the nation state is only one avenue to statehood, and that successful countries need not be made of one nation.[2] As Rutz (1995) reminds us, many versions of nationness exist within the same group of people. Nation making, as we understand it, involves the identification of the majority of citizens with the values of "the nation," and relies essentially on the emotional attachment of the citizens to "the nation." How else could we explain the force of chauvinism, the attachment of many people to the symbols representing their country, and the sacredness attached to such symbols? Witness the hoopla that usually follows flag burnings in times of peace or the scorn that is addressed to conscientious objectors in times of war. This emotional attachment is fostered by the very discourses that people create about themselves as a group and is instilled in the population by the ideologies developed by state institutions. Witness the statement made by John Major, British prime minister, concerning the resistance of various European countries to the Maastricht treaty: "Defenses of national culture are instincts rooted deep in the blood. They are not to be swept away by rhetoric about growth or slogans about unity" (Walsh 1992). As the vast literature on that topic has suggested, nationalism is a narrative of a particular kind, giving to people the sense that they may have something to do together within the political confine of the state.[3]

None of this, however, means that nationalist ideologies need to equate unification of the people with their homogenization: Within one geopolitical entity, national consciousness can take many forms and be the result of many versions and interpretations of the same historical events and the same myths. On the other hand, the building of the state implies the establishment of government apparatuses, with or without concomitant legitimacy. The question I am asking is: Do processes of state building in the Pacific entail this identification that would go beyond the simple recognition of the legitimacy of the state? Even though symbols of nationhood, such as flags or national anthems, are being used by new Pacific Island countries, do we need, in our analyses of these political entities, to associate the process of the building of the state and the process of the building of "the nation"?

It seems to me useful to draw a distinction between the creation of "the nation" and the creation of the state. The two processes rest on different principles and could, in theory, exist quite independently of one another. In practice, the history of the Western world and its capitalist system has shown that in order to survive, the state will seek to legitimize its position by infusing in its citizens the ideology of nationalism (Althusser 1971). What we are

witnessing at the moment in most of the recently independent countries of the Pacific, more than blatant nationalism, are efforts by various states to develop and stabilize themselves, even though states are definitely using to this end the ideology of nationalism.

Another distinction should be established between countries that have had to fight for their independence (Vanuatu) or are fighting for it (New Caledonia) and countries that have had their independence handed to them on a silver platter (Papua New Guinea, the Solomon Islands, Kiribati, Tuvalu).

In the first case, the nationalist feeling crystallizes around the possibility of independence: The Other is the colonial power, and even though individuals may still identify themselves first and foremost with reference to the ethnic group, a broader frame of identity momentarily overcomes the barriers of ethnicity. New labels appear as people's conception of their identity broadens to encapsulate new symbols that reflect these new levels of identity. These labels may refer to harmonious conceptions of local history and place, to shared expectations, or to a special relationship to the land; and they may be expressed vernacularly. Recall Walter Lim's Vanuaaku Pati (*vanua* being Eastern Oceanic for "place" and *aku* meaning "my"), the name of Vanuatu taken by the newly independent country and the name taken by the citizens of that country, Ni-Vanuatu (*ni* meaning "those of"). Or the labels may refer to traumatic elements of colonial history; the term *kanak*, by which Melanesians in New Caledonia call themselves, is a case in point. Borrowed from the sociolinguistic history of the labor trade to Queensland, the word *kanak*, then pronounced *kanaka* (Moore 1986) and borrowed from the Hawai'ian *kanaka*, meaning "man" (Clark 1977), was used by Europeans in nineteenth-century Queensland to refer to Melanesians, men and women, who had been indentured to work the sugar cane fields. This term was incorporated into Pacific pidgin as an extremely derogatory term of reference and address and into Pacific French in the form *canaque*.[4] As Bensa (1990) and Winslow (1991) show, the symbolic and semantic value of the word has been reversed in the current usage by the nationalist movement of New Caledonia and stresses nationalist pride. In the case of nationalist struggle, identity is not only relational but also oppositional. This opposition catalyzes the crystallization and the binding of nationalist sentiment and conveys legitimation to "the nation."

In the second case, nationalist sentiment is not present at the time of independence. Not having had to think about themselves as a people, citizens of a new country whose independence was handed to them still define their identity very much locally—in terms of their village, their island of origin, or their language group—at the time the country first becomes independent. First and foremost, allegiance will be to a person's home place or ethnic group. The former colonial state often will become the oppositional Other, with the result that allegiance to the state will be secondary and often nonexistent. This lack of identification with the state is precisely what undermines the unity and eventual survival of the country. Nationalist sentiments that will spring up in those circumstances will be directed against the former colonial state and will be divisive for the country. Bougainville's struggle for independence from Papua New Guinea illustrates the point. So does the alienation from and opposition toward the independent government by traditionalists such as the Kwaio in the Solomon Islands (Keesing 1992).

We need to stop at this point and reflect on the concept of identity, ethnic or national, because it appears as a *leitmotiv* of nationalist struggle. The growing literature on the invention of tradition has stressed how much manipulation of history was essential to nationalist claims, in most cases ethnically based. However, focusing on history as shaping the present obscures the fact that history is reshaped because of interests in the present, and not for the sake of the past itself.[5] Often, what is really at stake in the redefinition of history is possible control over the future. In most of the new countries of the Pacific, nationalist sentiments cannot be built on the basis of a common history people have

shared: Different ethnic groups have been lumped together within the geopolitical boundaries of a country. If anything, ethnic tensions and rivalries surface regularly within the political confine of independent nations and remind us of the arbitrariness of many geopolitical frontiers.[6] Thus, it seems more useful to see nationalist sentiment in such circumstances as being fostered, consciously or not, on the basis of a common future built on a sense of common purpose. Identity is thus defined in terms of a common future, rather than a common history.

I argue that it is a vision of Self projected in the future that often explains the manipulation of history and the shapes history is given. The strength of history in legitimating the present lies precisely in the fact that it is both objective (a series of facts and events) and subjective (a series of interpretations of the same facts and events). While in their interaction with history, people seem to have a closer relationship with its subjective side, the pseudoscientific nature of its objective side is what gives history its political legitimacy. History thus becomes an essential element of nationalist struggles. However, just as a vision of the past can be constructed, a vision of a common future can be constructed as well. But this imagined community, created not so differently from the ones Anderson (1983) describes, is nevertheless perceived as potentially real. The reality of the imaginary, forcefully argued by Castoriadis (1987), is what gives its force to a projection of identity in the future.

This is what is happening in the Solomon Islands, where an urban-based elite in government and administrative circles is trying to promote a nationalist sentiment in the country.[7] This projection of identity creates tensions between the so-called nation builders—those who want to promote the ideology of the nation—and the nation buildees—those who will be caught up in the nation-building process, willingly or not, but whose participation in, acceptance of, and, ideally, identification with the values of the budding nation will be essential to the legitimacy of the national enterprise. This tension should remind us that nation building is not necessarily the result of a consensus (even though some degree of consensus on what the discourse of the nation should be is needed) and is usually the result of the instilling of the national ideology by those institutions and individuals who have the means and the interests to do so. In that light, in the Pacific, just as everywhere else, it may be more useful to think of nationalism as a class-based ideology rather than as an ethnic-based ideology. But we cannot dismiss the role played by ethnic-based ideologies in the legitimation of the national enterprise. We shall keep in mind, however, that towns and cities play a key role in the dissemination of nationalist ideologies: They are cultural marketplaces, multiethnic and multilingual social worlds, where new ideologies have relatively free rein to develop away from the pervasive control of "custom" (*kastom*), and where the state apparatuses and political elite are well represented.

## BACK TO STEPPING-STONES

### Schooling

The first stepping-stone to national consciousness is the school, which has proven to be the crucial mechanism for fostering national consciousness in such ethnically complex postcolonial countries as Indonesia and Malaysia. Not surprisingly, we find the same process in the younger countries of the Pacific, such as the Solomons. Through schooling, ideally mandatory so as to reach out to everybody, new ideologies will be instilled in the future generation of citizens; values, expectations, and attitudes will be diffused in standardized forms. Transmitted by such an official vehicle as the school, these values will be endowed with legitimacy. Children learn that systems of knowledge exist that are fundamentally different from the ones their ancestors have relied on, and they are led to believe that control over those systems of knowledge guarantees progression up the socioeconomic ladder. In the mind of the administrators, the school program will perform another function: It will create a common frame of reference for the children, across ethnic and religious boundaries, thus giving some degree of homogeneity to a diverse population.[8]

The school derives its power from two main points. The first is that it transmits social values that are generally upheld by the majority of the adult population and serve the interest of the state: peacefulness, order, discipline, respect for elders, respect for social order—all elements that control both the body and the mind of the child. The second is the transmission of skills through which, it is hoped by parents, an improvement of the social condition of the child (and collectively of the citizenry and the workforce) will result. Both points are seductive to parents and explain why schooling is generally popular in the country, even where it is not mandatory; parents will make dire financial sacrifices to send their children to school. School fees represent an important part of the family finances, particularly in areas where absence of cash crops and employment makes money difficult to come by. We often forget that what is being taught in school, the content of the education program, and the manner in which knowledge is transmitted are the result of a philosophy of education, whether explicitly developed as such or not. This philosophy of education will be applied indiscriminately to all children of the country, thus unifying as one, single clientele (it is hoped by the school planners) children with very different sociogeographic backgrounds, different lifestyles, and different means.[9]

Those who have looked closely at school systems know that the goal of homogenization planned in ministries of education is not always reached; there is a great discrepancy between what curriculum planners aim at and what the children actually retain from it. Children distort what is being taught to them or simply resist the facts presented to them.[10] Moreover, regional resistance, sheer incompetencies of teachers and staff in some instances, cultural insensitivities, linguistic barriers, and inadequacies or irrelevance of the curriculum in some peripheral areas blur the homogenizing school curriculum. Again it is important to stress that the ideological success of schooling is greater in urban centers than in rural areas. However, beyond the fact that education ensures the reproduction of the servants of the state, and thus the reproduction of the state (Bourdieu and Passeron 1973), as well as the development of a skilled labor force, schooling ensures that children will be exposed to the social values upheld by the state and to a common body of history, literature, and other subjects that will represent a common frame of reference for their future life together. It allows as well for a national sentiment to be fostered in a great majority of children.

The Solomon Islands are no exception. The Solomons inherited from the colonial era an education system that was mostly run by the various religious denominations present in the country. In the earlier years of the protectorate, each congregation had its own curriculum, chose its own language of education, and used its own books. In the later years, the colonial government implemented an education system that was relatively uniform in all the parts of the British Empire. The primers from which children learned to read told the story of Dick and Jane, two young English children growing up in the manicured English countryside and undergoing social experiences that were totally irrelevant to the realities of the local children. The history books taught the history of Britain. Values were those of colonial powers. Those who did well in that system were sent abroad, to England or New Zealand or Australia, to further their education, and they usually came back immersed in the values of the "motherland." It was this first elite generation, well educated, brought up in the British tradition and imbued with British values, which was given the reins of the country upon independence. This process, by then well established in Africa, ensured political continuity of the new country within the confine of the commonwealth.

As independence was nearing, the content of the school curriculum progressively changed to make more room for local issues. Solomon Islanders started to question the education system. A committee appointed to make a review of educational policy produced a report in 1973 titled "Education for What?"; it analyzed the difficulties of making schooling accessible to all and challenged the relevance and the organization of the education system. It voiced the grievances of parents who found a lack of relevance of education to life in the village: "The present system of education is a foreign one, which does not meet the needs of Solomon Islanders," "Education should aim to make children good men and women in the village," and "The people expect the school leaver to come back and help to improve the village" (British Solomon Islands Protectorate 1973:31). The recommendations made by the review committee addressed parents' grievances but also went beyond them and reinforced the idea that education should serve the nation. The committee summarized the aims of education in the protectorate as follows:

**a.** To enable each Solomon Islander to understand his environment and the place of the Solomon Islands in the rest of the world.

**b.** To enable the Solomon Islander to think and develop his reasoning power so that he may face up to and overcome the every day problems with which he is faced.

**c.** To enable Solomon Islanders to become sound citizens of the Protectorate with an understanding and sympathy of the needs of others.

**d.** To enable each Solomon Islander to understand his own customs and the customs of others.

**e.** To promote racial harmony and unity in the country.

**f.** To improve the quality of life in the Solomons.

**g.** To offer skills which will enable each Solomon Islander to play his part in the development of his community and country according to his ability and aptitudes. (British Solomon Islands Protectorate 1973)

As a result, not only have Dick and Jane disappeared from the classrooms, but they have been replaced by two little Papua New Guineans living in physical and social environments similar to the ones experienced by young Solomon Islanders. History, this ever-important developer of national identification (locally called social studies), brings the heroes closer to home: Maasina Rule, the World War II battle of Guadalcanal, Sir Jacob Vouza, independence, the first prime minister of the independent Solomons. All these events and people capture the imagination of the children and adolescents. In the evenings, I witnessed the children in my Honiara neighborhood play "war," with the Solomon Islands Labour Corps, temporarily redefined as an army, playing a glorious role alongside the American GIs against the Japanese. Through geography, pupils and students learn about "our Solomon Islands": the names of the various islands and provinces of the archipelago, the beauty of the land, the wealth of the waters, the pride of a people. At the time of homework, in the evening, young children are drilled by their parents into knowing basic facts about their country. Every school day starts with a prayer asking God to protect "our Solomon Islands." Every official occasion at school will be sanctioned with the singing of the national anthem, which the children have learned at school. Localization of the education program has been paralleled by localization of the teaching and administrative responsibilities in the higher circles of education: Expatriates' contracts are not renewed.

In education, as in other realms of socio-economic life, Solomon Islanders assert themselves. Through schooling, many children, and particularly the urban children, grow up and mature with the comforting certitude that they have a country, unified and glorified. They are very attached to this idea, the urban children even more so because they often do not have first-hand knowledge of their parents' culture as rural children usually do. When people develop emotional attachments toward their country, then the seeds of nationalism that have been sown are bearing fruit. I have observed a great discrepancy in that attachment as manifested by urban children and by their rural counterparts. In rural areas, the relevance of the school curriculum to the everyday life of the children is perceived by parents and children alike as remote. Parents would like to see their children learn more about their immediate environment and lifestyle and not so much about wider concerns of the town and the world.[11] This perception causes many children to drop out of school in the early years of schooling, and many simply never attend. But the marketing value of a school education does not escape some parents. I witnessed quite a few bride-price negotiations in some rural areas of the Solomons where fathers were claiming a higher bride-wealth from the kin of their future sons-in-law on the grounds that their daughters had reached year six of primary education.

The impact of the school system on the country as a whole is not immediate, however, and is more obvious in urban areas than in rural areas. Only about fifteen years have elapsed since independence, and it is much too early to assess the unifying role of the school system in the country. At the same time, the precarious economic situation of the country and the saturation of the public service are such that school leavers and graduates find it difficult to obtain the well-paid job that they were told they would get if they went to school and to which they feel they have a right. This employment crisis may very well jeopardize the unifying mandate that curriculum planners and politicians have given the school.

## Pijin

The second stepping-stone toward a Solomon Islands nation is Pijin, the lingua franca of the archipelago. It is the communication cement that holds together this rich linguistic conglomerate. As with the other Melanesian countries, the Solomon Islands are characterized by high ethnic and linguistic diversity. Some sixty-four languages are spoken: even though some are closely related, most are not mutually intelligible (Tryon and Hackman 1983). In precolonial times, people overcame the linguistic diversity by being multilingual: They spoke the language of the neighboring ethnic groups or at least had a passive competency. Multilingualism was the rule more than the exception. With the establishment of the British Solomon Islands Protectorate in 1893 came a more widespread usage of the pidgin that indentured laborers from the east of the archipelago had brought back from Queensland. This pidgin, locally called Pijin, and sometimes Pisin, was used primarily to facilitate communication among plantation workers and between British administration officers or plantation overseers and the local population. Progressively, the pidgin became the lingua franca of the plantations, allowing workers from various islands to communicate with one another. By the 1950s, Pijin had become the lingua franca of the male segment of the archipelago. Women, however, because they had no access to the social settings in which the language was used, had no opportunities to learn Pijin. It was used widely as a second language by a male population whose daily social life and main activities were conducted in the much more valorized vernaculars: Pijin was everyone's language, but no one's language.

In the subsequent years, four factors were instrumental in strengthening the status of Pijin as the de facto national language of the country: (1) the increase in interisland trade and travel, putting people in contact with one another on a much larger scale than had been the case before; (2) schooling, which exposed pupils to Pijin in multiethnic schools; (3) young women learning the language and using it on a regular basis in bigger marketplaces or during their visits to town; and (4) urbanization, through the expansion of Honiara, the capital city of the Solomon Islands. With all sixty-four vernaculars represented in town, Pijin ceased to be a male prerogative and became the "natural" language of the urban world, superseding the vernaculars. In Honiara today, one needs Pijin if one wants to have a social life that goes beyond the limits of the ethnic group. As more and more children from increasingly numerous biethnic marriages are being brought up in Pijin, the command of vernaculars among the young generation in town is diminishing. For an increasing number of children, Pijin is the mother tongue, the only linguistic tool they have at their disposal, apart from the minimal English they acquire at school. Pijin has become the language of the cultural life of the town, with popular songs, cartoons, radio programs, and advertising being produced in this lingua franca.

These developments have contributed to giving Pijin some form of legitimacy (Jourdan 1988) within the urban population and a social prestige that reaches out into the provinces, even though some may object to the ever-growing influence of Pijin in the life of the country. This newly acquired social legitimacy puts Pijin in a better position vis-à-vis English, the socially prestigious language inherited from the colonial era and the official language of the country. Pijin had been considered by the British, and by some members of the Solomon Islands elite (who nevertheless used it in most realms of their private and social life), a bastardized language doomed to disappear. It had no place in the education system, no formal and official status, no support system such as standardization and literature. This attitude represents a striking contrast from the way Papua New Guinea and Vanuatu politicians and government treated their local varieties of pidgin, Tok Pisin and Bislama, respectively. In Vanuatu, Bislama became the language of New Hebridean politics as a way to allow the political message of independence to reach out in the provinces (see Facey 1995). In Papua New Guinea, Tok Pisin was given the status of a national language and is now used in all realms of social life, even if, in some areas, people resent having to use it.[12]

In the Solomons, the same process has been slower to appear: With the encroachment of Pijin in the social life of the country, the language has begun to be viewed by politicians and administrators as the panacea for the heterogeneity of the country. Its potential as a unifying tool is threefold: (1) It prevents any ethnic rivalry that could stem from one vernacular becoming too visible and important in the country; (2) it is a local alternative to English in a country trying to shake free from its colonial heritage; and (3) being closely mapped onto vernaculars, it is learned quickly by Solomon Islanders, even those (and they are few nowadays) who have not had contact with it from an early age (see Jourdan 1985; Keesing 1988; Crowley 1990). Its usefulness as a language through which political messages can be conveyed to the whole country has not escaped the shrewd eyes of the politicians. As a result, more attention is being paid to Pijin: Research relating to its scope, sociolinguistic usages, structure, phonology, and lexicon is now being encouraged by the Ministry of Education and Training. Rumors of a national language policy giving Pijin an official status in the country have been circulating.[13]

Nevertheless, the emergence of Pijin as the de facto national language of the country should not obscure the ever-important role played by English in many domains of socioeconomic life: official language of education (even if, in practice, Pijin is very often the de facto language of education [Jourdan 1988]), language of international trade and communication, language of the written media of communication. More and more Solomon Islanders are learning to speak English fluently: To do so opens important economic opportunities, vis-à-vis investors and logging companies and tourists from overseas as well as paid employment. Pijin and English are playing complementary roles in the life of the Solomon Islands, and the ever-increasing encroachment of Pijin in the country is not concomitant with the disappearance of English.

## Popular Culture

It is in Honiara particularly that one finds the last of the three stepping-stones I have identified: Popular culture as generated locally or imported from Western or other Pacific countries. The spread of popular culture is new to the Solomon Islands, but it quickly has caught the imagination of the young urbanites. Soccer matches and rock concerts, T-shirts and videos, marches and banners, dress and hair fashion, new words and new body language, all these contribute to make the cultural world of the town increasingly complex.

Gifted musicians have started local string and reggae bands, creating songs that appeal greatly to the public and are being sung in every corner of the archipelago. Interestingly, some of the most successful songs depict the difficulties of making a living in town, an ever-recurrent theme in the life of the country. From "Wakabaot long Chinatown," dating from 1969, to "Mama Karae" and "Masta Liu," dating from 1989, these songs express the love for and fear of an urban lifestyle which many find both exciting and threatening. Not surprisingly, Pijin is the medium of popular culture.

Living in town is new to Solomon Islanders. As people who have no traditional model of an urban lifestyle, they are continuously creating a culture in which they are immersed. They are both agents and recipients in this process, as marginal participants in a worldwide capitalist consumerism and as cultural creators. In this case, one can confidently argue that this urban culture in the making is being created by urbanites as they live it, although the creative possibilities of urban lifestyles are constrained by town structures, the types of socioeconomic activities of urbanites, and the type of social relationships they establish in an urban setting. In that sense, town dwellers are not creating a new cultural world out of a cultural vacuum. For one thing, town life is still connected to life in the villages, through a two-way flow of information that may take the shape of a young thug, sporting sunglasses and a Walkman, going back to the bush, or the shape of a father going to town to collect the bride-price for his daughter. Urban culture in the Solomons is also shaped directly by the influences of the cultural and economic world system. But Solomon Islanders are by no means passive consumers of imported multinational capitalist culture in prepackaged forms; they impose their own creative stamp on the Western phenomena with which they are bombarded.

An interesting example is associated with the movie character Rambo. The film genre in which this character is portrayed as a hero is extremely popular in the Solomon Islands among the male segment of the population.[14] They love the brashness of the character, his strength, his bravado, and his flouting of the authorities if their beliefs and choices go against his own. Christine Ward Gailey (1989) has suggested for Tonga that the admiration manifested for Rambo by the Tongans is best understood as a form of resistance by proxy to neocolonialism. This is possibly the case in the Solomons, but not quite in the same way, as Rambo resonates more with ramo, the traditional warrior of the Melanesian Troika (Keesing 1985) of Big Man, Priest, and Killer than with any form of cultural resistance to imperialism. In traditional lore, a ramo is endowed with the qualities and flaws displayed by Rambo in the movies. In town, naughty little boys and brash young men are often called ramo, and parents are both afraid and proud of the unruliness of such children. The phonetic analogy of the two words is itself tantalizing: It certainly reinforces the assimilation that Solomon Islanders, and Malaitans in particular, establish between the two heroes.

This set of readings of new and old cultural texts by urbanites in Honiara, individually and collectively, gives its shape to the sociocultural world of the town. People in rural areas are aware that the new urban milieu of the Solomons is extremely different from theirs. Old values—both those of the precolonial era and those of village Christianity—are flouted in town. Villagers object to the changes of behavior they observe, to the laxity in respecting "custom," to the lack of respect for the elders manifested by the young people, to increases in the cost and changes in the content of bride-price, to the escalation of food prices, to sexual laxity and prostitution. Yet they will take in stride most of the facets of popular culture surfacing in town and most of the urban lifestyles. This is an interesting paradox. Why object to some aspects of the new cultural world and accept others?

I argue that in Honiara, people will object to social phenomena that threaten them, or impinge directly on and connect directly to valued ways of village life, and will accept, bear with, or ignore those that do not. Popular culture is relatively nonthreatening to

Solomon Islands villagers because it is not produced in their social world—a world they know and feel they can control—but in an alien world, already different and out of their control. Not being of the same scale as their own productions, not being ontologically of the same kind, most elements of urban popular culture (its material representations particularly) are perceived by villagers as nonthreatening. They are culturally neutral, not belonging to anyone, but borrowed. It is this seeming neutrality that gives urban popular culture its cultural binding power and allows its innocuous spread in the country. Not being anyone's culture that can be associated with an ethnic group, but being a type of generic culture (Philibert 1990), it overcomes ethnic boundaries. It allows for new shared meanings, symbols, and representations to reach out on a wider scale.[15]

## CONCLUSION: URBAN CULTURE, NATIONAL CULTURE

Nation making in the Solomon Islands is not a *chose faite*. People keep on defining themselves locally, with kinship remaining the most important pole of identification. Even in town, kinship still occupies a primary function in the organization of social relationships. However, we increasingly perceive new moods, orientations, perceptions, interpretations, and affinities which, linked to increasing changes in poles of identification, contribute to give national sentiment a stronger base. This gradual transformation is due to the cumulative effect of the three stepping-stones I have analyzed here, and to urbanization.

Towns, as wider cultural marketplaces, allow for new negotiations of meaning to take place while at the same time allowing for wider circulation of new symbols and modes of identification. Nationalism is one of them, negotiated publicly and privately by urbanites who have to shape a future for themselves away from custom and tradition (*kastom*). It might make sense to think of nationalism as the *kastom* of the urban folk, the ideology that guides definition of Self in the urban setting. Truly, some urbanites are Solomon Islanders before being from Kwara'ae, from Ranongga, or from Makira—particularly among the younger population born and raised in town. Away from the established discourse of "tradition," urbanites create an image of themselves that is reinforced by education and popular culture; it is from this new cultural center and its productions, tolerated with bemusement or admired by rural Solomon Islanders, that the nationalist ideology now emerging in the Solomons is spreading.

Honiara is a cultural center without a past. Barely forty years old, and developed on the remains of the American army base on Guadalcanal, it cannot use its past as a flag of identity; the best it can offer is a new lifestyle, recognized as the way of the future. It is around this vision of a common future on which they can act that Honiarans develop an original urban culture. It is not surprising that nationalism has more chances to crystallize in that setting. Increasing sharedness of ideas and new poles of identification are possible precisely because of multivocality and multiplexity, those ever more complex, fluid, and situational sets of relationships individuals and social groups create vis-à-vis each other. The cultural creolization that takes place between locally produced and imported foreign elements and ideologies ensures some continuity with ways of contemporary village life, yet it ensures as well the independence of urban lifestyles from the control of the village.

In the Solomons, as in many other emergent nations of the Pacific, nationalism is not ethnic based, and it is encouraged by the state apparatuses for a pragmatic reason—to hold the country together—not to situate Solomon Islanders vis-à-vis an external Other or Others. There is too much internal diversity, with Bellonese and Gilbertese and Kwara'ae and Choiseulese, for an ethnically monolithic Solomon Islands Self to be opposed to an external Other. In the absence of a homogenizing *kastom,* the role of the state will be to create one out of

a compound of cultural traits deemed capable of expressing national identity or unity. As state ideology, the discourse on *kastom* attempts to give

credence to a fictive construction: that of an *imaginary mono-ethnism.* (Babadzan 1988:216)

Insofar as it succeeds, this ideology can, in creating an ethnic Self, create an external Other that will allow the young nation to define itself.

## ACKNOWLEDGMENTS

This chapter was originally published in *Nation-Making: Emergent Identities in Postcolonial Melanesia* (© 1995), Robert Foster, editor. Pp. 127–149. Ann Arbor: University of Michigan Press. Reprinted with permission. I wish to thank the Social Sciences and Humanities Research Council of Canada for providing a research grant allowing me to spend six months in the Solomon Islands over the summers of 1989 and 1990, researching the relationships between Pijin and the development of an urban culture in Honiara. I am grateful to James Carrier, Ellen Facey, Robert Foster, Michael Jacobsen, Roger Keesing, and John Kelly for the comments they made on the initial version of this chapter.

## NOTES

1. I leave aside for the moment the residual French colonial presence in the Pacific.

2. Colonial states and imperial states such as those of Rome, Ottoman Turkey, and Austria-Hungary are good examples. It is a double irony, then, that countries such as Indonesia, created as colonial empires, must try to reconstitute themselves as nations as well as states.

3. Take, for example, the ideological "war" that is being fought in Canada at the moment between the federal government and the Quebec provincial government. As Quebec prepares itself for yet another referendum on sovereignty, the federal government is bombarding the population of the country with songs, video clips, and advertising glorifying the country as a whole, celebrating the indispensable participation of all provinces in the nation, and reminding citizens of the historical contribution of their province to the building of the country. This ideological blitz, using emotions to revive nationalism, is aimed at both Quebec and the rest of Canada, trying to convince each party that they do belong together.

4. Interestingly enough, *kanaka* is still being used in the Solomon Islands and in Papua New Guinea to refer to unsophisticated bush people from remote rural areas. In town, the word is used as a derisive term equivalent

to *lokol* ("yokel") and stresses the social ineptness or lack of sophistication of new urbanites.

5. Take, for instance, Mexico's recent decision to write a new official history better adapted to the newly established free trade agreement with the United States and Canada, stressing a *libre-echangiste* attitude after one century of protectionism. This new official history, which also transforms former dictator Porfirio Díaz into a hero of the modernization of Mexico, will appear in the free and mandatory textbook distributed to ten- and eleven-year-old children in all primary schools of the country (Sberro 1992).

6. The dismantling of the Soviet empire, the dismemberment of Yugoslavia under nationalist pressures, and the recent vote for autonomy taken by the Slovak government remind us precisely of the arbitrariness of colonial borders.

7. The role of the elite as cultural and political buffer is crucial to the postindependence consciousness. Being urban based, the elite in the Solomon Islands is comfortable with many levels of identities and meaning. For more detail, see Jourdan 1990.

8. To homogenize a population, school is a wonderful tool. The French revolutionaries were quick to perceive its power. Within the first years of the Revolution, they had ordered a survey of the state of education in France and had created the basis of a universal system of mandatory education (implemented only eighty years later) for all children beyond the age of seven.

9. Equality of access to schooling does not necessarily mean equality of success for the children, but this is not our purpose here.

10. Recall, for instance, that more than fifty years after the introduction of the Russian language in schools by the Soviet government, a comparatively small percentage of the population of the Soviet republics and countries of the former Soviet bloc actually speaks the language, or acknowledges speaking it.

11. Michael Jacobsen (personal communication, April 24, 1992) has made the same observation: "In my own study of a community school and its relationship to the surrounding local communities among the Dom people of Simbu Province, Papua New Guinea, I found that communication between school and community is not good. . . . This results in an annual student dropout rate of about 40 percent. Furthermore, the school manages to get into contact with only about 45 percent of the potential mass of students in the area I was working. . . . I think this situation has come about because the educational system the school represents, and the skills it instills in the children, do not have anything to do with the reality the students and their families are living in. The school and the local communities represent two completely different worlds, and there are seemingly no means of bridging them."

12. As is often the case for Motu speakers.

13. In this realm, the Solomon Islands are trailing behind Papua New Guinea and Vanuatu, both of which have given the status of official language to Tok Pisin and Bislama, the local pidgins, along with English (and French as well, in Vanuatu). At a time when the three Melanesian countries are setting the bases of an economic, cultural, and political alliance (the Melanesian Spearhead), the varieties of pidgin spoken in these countries, all mutually intelligible, may prove instrumental in bringing about some linguistic unity in the region. Pidginophony could prove an important tool.

14. Women are not seen in movie theaters and movie arcades in the Solomon Islands, except for a few Chinese or Polynesian women who are escorted there by their kinsmen. These women usually go to see romantic movies but keep away from those that their menfolk relish: Rambo movies, martial arts movies (preferably the old ones with Bruce Lee as the lead), and any other type of film showing war, fights, and other violence. Many of these films are commercial failures in the West and find a second life in the Third World. They come to the country on videocassettes and are usually seen on medium-size screens in small movie arcades where, for an entrance fee of one Solomon Islands dollar, men, young and not so young, pile up in an overcrowded and stuffy room to watch. No harm would come to a woman who ventured alone into these movie houses, but she would be frowned upon by the men and would most likely be driven away.

15. Some resistance appears when the foundations of moral personhood are challenged by urban mores (Jourdan 1991).

## REFERENCES

Althusser, Louis. 1971. *Lenin and Philosophy, and Other Essays.* Ben Brewster, translator. London: New Left Books.

Anderson, Benedict. 1983. *Imagined Communities: Reflections on the Origin and Spread of Nationalism.* London: Verso.

Babadzan, Alain. 1988. "Kastom and Nation Building in the South Pacific." In *Ethnicities and Nations: Processes of Interethnic Relations in Latin America, Southeast Asia, and the Pacific.* R. Guidieri, F. Pellizzi, and S. J. Tambiah, eds. Pp. 199–228. Austin: University of Texas Press.

Bensa, Alban. 1990. *Nouvelle-Caledonie: Un Paradis dans la Tourmente.* Paris: Gallimard.

Bourdieu, Pierre, and Jean-Claude Passeron. 1973. *La Reproduction.* Paris: Editions de Minuit.

British Solomon Islands Protectorate. 1973. *Education for What? Education Policy Review Committee Report 1973.* Honiara: Government Printer.

Castoriadis, Cornelius. 1987. *The Imaginary Institution of Society.* Cambridge: Polity Press.

Clark, Ross. 1977. "In Search of Beach-La-Mar: Historical Relations Among Pacific Pidgins and Creoles."

Working Papers in Anthropology, Archaeology, Linguistics, Maori Studies 48. Auckland: University of Auckland.

Crowley, Terry. 1990. *Beach-La-Mar to Bislama: The Emergence of a Natural Language in Vanuatu.* Oxford: Clarendon Press.

Facey, Ellen. 1995. "Kastom and Nation Making: The Politicization of Tradition on Nguna, Vanuatu." In *Nation Making: Emergent Identities in Postcolonial Melanesia.* Robert Foster, ed. Pp. 207–226. Ann Arbor: University of Michigan Press.

Feinberg, Richard. 1990. "The Solomon Islands' Tenth Anniversary of Independence: Problems of National Symbolism and National Integration." *Pacific Studies* 13:19–40.

Gailey, Christine Ward. 1989. "'RAMBO' in Tonga: Video Films and Cultural Resistance in the Tongan Islands (South Pacific)." *Culture* 9:21–32.

Jourdan, Christine. 1985. "*Sapos iumi mitim iumi:* Urbanization and Creolization of Solomon Islands Pijin." Ph.D. dissertation. Research School of Pacific Studies, Australian National University, Canberra.

———. 1988. "Pidgin's Legitimacy." Paper presented at the meeting of the Association for Social Anthropology in Oceania, February 19, Savannah, Georgia.

———. 1990. "No One's Culture, Everybody's Culture: Urbanization in the Solomon Islands." Paper presented at the meeting of the Association for Social Anthropology in Oceania, March 24, Kauai, Hawai'i.

———. 1991. "Where Have All the Cultures Gone?" Paper presented at the Conference on the New Pacific, October 18–19, University of Lund, Sweden.

Kapferer, Bruce. 1988. *Legends of People, Myths of State: Violence, Intolerance and Political Culture in Sri Lanka and Australia.* Washington, D.C.: Smithsonian Institution Press.

Keesing, Roger M. 1985. "Killers, Big Men and Priests on Malaita: Reflections on a Melanesian Troika System." *Ethnology* 24:237–252.

———. 1988. *Melanesian Pidgin and the Oceanic Substrate.* Stanford: Stanford University Press.

———. 1992. *Custom and Confrontation: The Kwaio Struggle for Cultural Autonomy.* Chicago: University of Chicago Press.

LiPuma, Edward. 1995. "The Formation of Nation-States and National Cultures in Oceania." In *Nation Making: Emergent Identities in Postcolonial Melanesia.* Robert Foster, ed. Pp. 33–68. Ann Arbor: University of Michigan Press.

LiPuma, Edward, and Sarah K. Meltzoff. 1990. "Ceremonies of Independence and Public Culture in the Solomon Islands." *Public Culture* 3:77–92.

Moore, Clive. 1986. *Kanaka: A History of Melanesian Mackay.* Port Moresby: Institute of Papua New Guinea Studies and University of Papua New Guinea Press.

Ogan, Eugene. 1991. "The Cultural Background of the Bougainville Crisis." *Journal de la Société des Océanistes* 1 and 2:61–67.

Philibert, Jean-Marc. 1990[1986]. "The Politics of Tradition: Toward a Generic Culture in Vanuatu." In *Customs in Conflict: The Anthropology of a Changing World.* Frank Manning and Jean-Marc Philibert, eds. Pp. 251–273. Peterborough, Ontario: Broadview Press.

Rutz, Henry. 1995. "Occupying the Headwaters of Tradition: Rhetorical Strategies of Nation Making in Fiji." In *Nation Making: Emergent Identities in Postcolonial Melanesia.* Robert Foster, ed. Pp. 71–93. Ann Arbor: University of Michigan Press.

Sberro, S. 1992. "Le Mexique Adapte Son Histoire à Ses Nouvelles Relations avec les Etats-Unis." *La Presse,* September 28, p. A20.

Tryon, D., and B. Hackman. 1983. *Solomon Islands Languages: An Internal Classification.* Pacific Linguistics C-72. Canberra: Australian National University.

Walsh, J. 1992. "Europe's Puzzling Stars." *Time* 140 (No. 12), September 21:26–30.

Winslow, Donna. 1991. "Custom and Independence in New Caledonia." Paper presented at the meeting of the Association for Social Anthropology in Oceania, March 28, Victoria, British Columbia.

# 7

# Print Advertisements and Nation Making in Metropolitan Papua New Guinea

**Robert J. Foster**

*University of Rochester*

In May 1985, the national parliament of Papua New Guinea passed the Commercial Advertising Act, initiated by Ted Diro.[1] According to this act, all commercial advertising in Papua New Guinea must be locally produced by local agencies employing local talent—designers, artists, models, and so forth. Infractions are to be treated as criminal rather than civil offenses.

Letters to the weekly *Times of Papua New Guinea* (hereinafter *TPNG*) by two critics of the act, both expatriate advertising managers, provoked responses from Moale Rivu, then executive officer for Diro.[2] In a *TPNG* article on April 12, 1986, Rivu defended the act as a deliberate effort by the government to promote "nationalism" and "nation building." He asked:

> Is it any wonder that we still find it difficult to be self sufficient in such basic foodstuff as rice and peanut butter? When the Markham factory was in operation it had to compete against imported peanut butter whose agents on numerous occasions used ready-made ads from overseas to promote their products. That, in essence, is the bottom line in this debate on the Advertising Act.

Rivu's nationalism was motivated mainly by economic concerns, the famous "bottom line." It is hardly contentious, however, to maintain that advertising and mass consumption in general are inevitably deeply cultural matters. This is not only a question of cultural imperialism, of resisting "Coca-Colonization"—the flow of images and objects emanating from various dominant regional centers. It is equally a question of the instrumental effects of mass consumption practices in nation making, that is, a question of the potential for advertisements to present constructs of "the nation" and perforce to define the terms of membership in "the nation."

I address this broad question through a consideration of print advertisements taken from several sources: two newspapers, a billboard, and an in-flight magazine. How do these ads construct "Papua New Guinea" and "Papua New Guineaness"? How do these ads and the consumption practices that they publicize enable (if not exhort) the steadily growing population of school-educated, urban-dwelling, wage-earning citizens to imagine themselves as "Papua New Guineans"? To what extent is an emergent urban consumer culture implicated in the processes of nation making in Papua New Guinea (see Jourdan, chapter 6)?

## ADVERTISING AND "THE NATION"

I use two complementary approaches in considering the relationships between advertisements and "the nation"—"the nation" understood here as an imaginative construct. The first approach emphasizes the sociocultural linkages brought about by the spread of mass consumption practices. Social historians have long observed, for example, that the formation of an imagined national community in the United States during the late nineteenth century was coeval with the birth of modern consumerism (Boorstin 1973; Ewen and Ewen 1982; Fox and Lears 1983; Bronner 1989). Department stores assembled within their palatial confines thousands of big-city dwellers; chain stores replicated these gatherings on a smaller scale in towns across the country; and mail-order catalogs functioned to connect the most remote farmer's family to this expansive network of consumers. The proliferation of images and objects of mass consumption brought the most diverse audiences, including newly arrived immigrants, into not only a developing marketplace but also an emergent set of shared understandings, memories, tastes, and habits.

The growth of an advertising industry figured largely in this process, inasmuch as advertisements mediated the anonymous encounter between buyers and sellers. Advertisements became important vehicles for the imagination of a community of consumers whose shared consumption practices and ideals put them in experiential unison with each other. Orvar Löfgren made this point in

reviewing a history of American advertising in the 1920s and 1930s:

> Reading the same ads, listening to the same radio personalities, or watching the same movies created a shared frame of reference for those growing up during the interwar years, in the same ways as it does for those growing up today. (1989a:373)

Circulated through the mass media of newspapers, radio, television, and videos, advertisements continue to expose large numbers of Americans from a cross section of social categories to images of a supralocal world. Put otherwise, shared mass-consumption practices still provide Americans with the means not only for making, remembering, and contesting a common experience, but also for anchoring an imagined national community in ordinary, everyday practice.[3] Benedict Anderson's arresting description of the "mass ceremony" of newspaper reading comes to mind:

> At the same time, the newspaper reader, observing exact replicas of his own paper being consumed by his subway, barbershop, or residential neighbors, is continually assured that the imagined world is visibly rooted in everyday life. (1983:39)

From this perspective, then, it is possible to regard nations as imagined communities of consumption, "large-scale, non-intimate collectivities unified by the ritualized fantasies of collective expenditure," to borrow Arjun Appadurai's (n.d.) words. Such fantasies circulate at high velocity through the mass media, most familiarly in the form of advertisements.[4] The second approach, by contrast, does not focus on the specific content of ads—on the "frames of reference" or "ritualized fantasies" that ads exhibit. Instead, it focuses on what might be called the "ad form." I argue that the general form of advertisements, however different their specific content, communicates a particular conception of both "the nation" and its constituent "nationals." Accordingly, I approach advertising as "a discourse about and through objects which bonds together images of persons, products and well being" (Leiss, Kline, and

Jhally 1990). But I am especially concerned with the general structure of social relations that such a discourse presupposes and naturalizes, a structure of social relations characteristic of commodity consumption in capitalist societies.

More precisely, I am concerned with demonstrating how the ad form at once reflects and constitutes both a definite kind of relationship between subjects and objects (consumers and commodities) and a coordinate relationship between subjects and other subjects (consumers and other consumers) (see Miller 1987). That is, the social relations of commodity consumption implied by ads entail particular definitions of personhood, on the one hand, and of community on the other. It is my argument that these definitions of personhood and community potentially supplement, if not displace, definitions of personhood and community grounded in social relations of kinship and locality (LiPuma 1995). More important, it is my argument that these definitions of personhood and community mesh with a conception of "the nation" as a community of individuals fundamentally similar in their status as "proprietors" or "owners" of a distinctive reification: "their" national culture (Handler 1985). In this conception, everyone who belongs to a nation is everyone to whom the nation belongs.

My approach, then, follows Anderson (1983) in emphasizing that the generic imaginative construct called "the nation" is specifiably distinctive *in form*. "The nation," whatever its particular characteristics, implies a community that is unambiguously bounded, temporally as well as spatially, and inhabited by people whose manifest diversity belies a latent sameness (Handler 1988:6). This sort of imaginative construct derives from and gives rise to a variety of processes of objectification in which "the nation" takes on a thinglike form, external to the individual (see Keesing 1989; Linnekin 1990). Such objective forms—flags, costumes, dances, foods, monuments, languages—are "possessed" in common by the individuals constituting the nation as markers of their shared subjective identity as "owners" (Handler 1988:6). That is, the

proprietors of these forms regard them as elements of a "national culture," as material evidence of an essential national cultural identity. National culture, in other words, emerges as a collection of collectively held things, the discrete, bounded objectivity of which tangibly replicates the conceptual form of the nation itself.

Here I want to consider advertisements as textual vehicles of such objectification. I am not concerned with the intentions of the advertisers themselves—with whether advertisers attempt to enlist nationalist sentiment in the service of selling toothpaste—nor am I concerned with the putative effects of ads on individual purchasing decisions. My primary concern is not with the particular messages of particular ads, but rather with the rhetorical form common to all ads.[5] By rhetoric, I mean two things: (1) the way in which ads transfer meaning to the commodities that they publicize so as to endow these commodities with a set of "objectively" given qualities (Williamson 1978), and (2) the way in which ads involve consumers as participants in constructing the ad's meaning.

The ads that I examine, I argue, qualify commodities as somehow Papua New Guinean, as embodiments and/or possessions of "the nation." They imply, furthermore, that to consume these commodities is to appropriate the quality of Papua New Guineaness as an attribute of a person. The consumption of national commodities, then, nationalizes the person. At the same time, each ad implicitly construes the nation as a community of consumption, a collectivity of nonintimate people whose shared consumption practices and fantasies express and constitute their nationality. Membership or citizenship in this community is acquired through acts of consumption so qualified, by participation in the lifestyle represented in the ad.

When taken together, however, these ads leave open the possibility for consumer-citizens to differentiate themselves from each other on the basis of *unshared* consumption practices. Diversity is (re)construed as differential participation within a single universe of consumer activity. Thus, the national community of consumption is neither mechanically solidary nor even organically cohesive; indeed, differentiation of consumer-citizens constantly threatens to expose and create new cleavages (such as class and status divisions) within the community.

I begin the discussion by demonstrating the semiotic logic by which ads impute qualities or attributes to various commodities (Williamson 1978). The particular quality at issue here is nationality, or Papua New Guineaness, a detachable attribute capable of being attached to embodiments as manifestly diverse as sugar and airplanes.[6] This imputation is complemented by a second, namely, the attribution of Papua New Guineaness to the consumer of commodities qualified with nationality. I concentrate in this regard on how ads define the relationship between commodity and consumer as one of "possession" or "having," and I explicate the presuppositions this definition makes about the nature of persons and objects.

The transfer of Papua New Guineaness from commodity to consumer is completed by a third imputation. Consumers are implicitly put into relation with other consumers on the basis of shared *and* unshared consumption practices. Most inclusively, this scheme of social relations defines the nation as a community of fellow consumer-citizens. However, distinctions among consumers are made with reference to a shared understanding of unevenly distributed consumption practices. That is, consumers of specific commodities are constituted as less-inclusive totemic groups or "kinds" of people (Williamson 1978; compare Comaroff 1987). This totemism thereby allows for a diversity of consumer groups within the larger national community of national commodity consumers.

## NATIONALIZING COMMODITIES, NATIONALIZING PERSONS

The process of nationalizing commodities in advertising works in more or less subtle ways. Ads for state-owned businesses often render the process explicit. Consider an ad (Figure 7.1) for Air Niugini, the state-owned

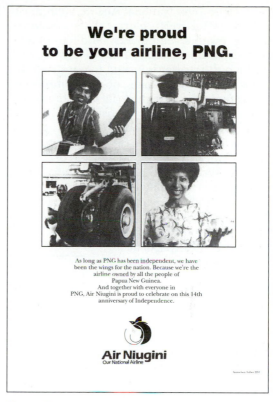

**Figure 7.1**  Newspaper advertisement for Papua New Guinea's state-owned airline

airline, that appeared a few years ago in a special independence anniversary issue of the *Papua New Guinea Post Courier* (hereinafter *PC*), a nationally distributed newspaper with a circulation of 30,000 in 1985.[7] The top of the page announces: "We're proud to be your airline, PNG." Beneath this caption are four photographs, each of which pictures an Air Niugini employee (two women, two men) holding or touching some piece of airline equipment—a ticket, a cockpit control switch, a tire on the landing gear, a coffee cup. These employees are not only apparently Papua New Guineans but also "owners" of Air Niugini. The text continues: "As long as PNG has been independent, we have been the wings for the nation. Because we're the airline owned by all the people of Papua New Guinea." Indeed, the airline's claim to be "*Our* National Airline" (emphasis added) effectively blurs all distinctions among owners, employees, and customers. The ad sets up a closed circuit of signification in which the reader is invited to construct the Papua New Guineaness of the employees with reference to the material objectifications of the airline, and to transfer this quality from these objectifications to the "owners" of the airline, the "people of Papua New Guinea" who purchase the services of the airline. In short, "the people of Papua New Guinea" are assimilated to the ambiguously inclusive "Us" implied in the slogan, "Our National Airline."

A similar discourse of collective national ownership is found in ads for Ramu sugar, product of an industry protected by the state against foreign competition. The text of one such ad (Figure 7.2) proclaims: "From the canefields of Papua New Guinea comes nature's own energy food. . . . The goodness of Papua New Guinea's natural cane sugar can be enjoyed by everyone." Consumption of Ramu sugar thus promises "everyone" (every individual consumer) access to one of Papua New Guinea's natural goods. In a related sense, consumption of Ramu sugar implies consumption of Papua New Guinea itself in the form of one of the land's "natural" products.

**Figure 7.2** Newspaper ad for the state-protected sugar industry

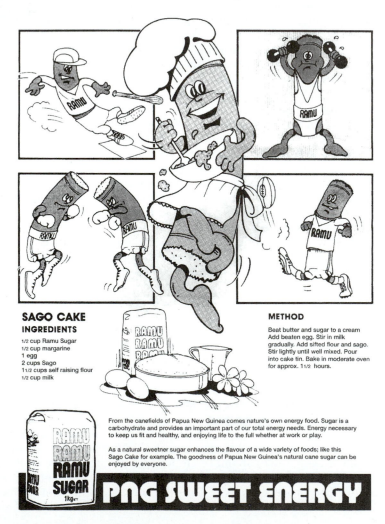

**Figure 7.3**   Newspaper ad for the PNG Credit Corporation

Finally, we have two advertisements that apply the argument of national ownership to the one commodity that seems by its abstract nature impossible to nationalize, yet it operates as perhaps the most potent and mundane symbol of any national community: money. At the top of an ad for the Papua New Guinea Credit Corporation (Figure 7.3) runs the heading KEEP OUR MONEY IN OUR COUNTRY. Beneath this advice is a picture of the national flag and a logo of the Credit Corporation. The text reads:

> Credit Corporation is a 100% Nationally owned company. Invest with us—keep our money in our country and help yourself to interest up to 14.50%.

Likewise, an ad for the Papua New Guinea Banking Corporation (Figure 7.4) appeared with the slogan, "Our country, our bank, celebrating together." At the center of the ad is a photograph of a female bank employee, proffering money in a gesture that extends beyond the border of the picture. The reader is implicitly positioned as the recipient of this gift, just as the ad for Air Niugini positions the reader as the recipient of the ticket and the cup of coffee.[8]

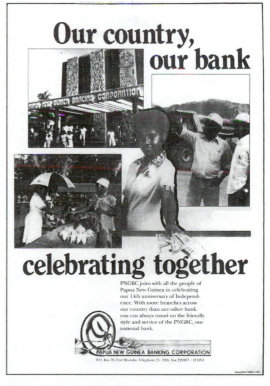

**Figure 7.4**   Newspaper ad for PNG Banking Corporation

Currency, the means of consumption, not only objectifies "the nation," whether in the iconographic forms of pigs and pearl shells or of Michael Somare and the parliament house—the 50-*kina* note depicted in the PNG Banking Corporation (PNGBC) ad. Currency also symbolizes the nation state as one entity in a system of such entities. It is entirely appropriate that the notes proffered by the woman in the PNGBC ad include samples of U.S. and Japanese money, and that the same ad could appear in the in-flight magazine of Air Niugini (*Paradise,* January 1992), captioned "The First Bank You See in PNG," as information for visitors seeking to convert currency. The use of currency, then, practically affirms the existence of a bounded community of consumers, the borders of which are defined by the extent to which the territorial state authorizes the currency as legal tender.

I would suggest that many Papua New Guineans sense these borders despite never having physically crossed them. Their intuition takes the often-reported form of stories about the unease people felt at the time of independence when it became necessary to convert Australian dollars into PNG *kina*. Similarly, I have heard village men in New Ireland recount the history of colonialism and political independence in terms of currency transitions: First we had marks, then pounds, then dollars, now *kina*. These same villagers would also make sense of inflation in terms of the transition from Australian dollars to PNG *kina,* accounting for the relatively weak purchasing power of their money to a perceived weakness of the independent government of PNG relative to Australia. Often they would ask me if there were a different kind of money in America, or comment ironically when I informed them that PNG currency and coinage are produced abroad.

It is important to recognize, nonetheless, that the nationalization of commodities is by no means monopolized by the state. The rhetoric of national ownership also appears in an advertisement for Word Publishing Company (Figure 7.5) that gives an interesting twist to Anderson's observation about the mass ceremony of newspaper reading. The

**Figure 7.5**    Newspaper ad for the paper's publisher

caption asserts: OUR OWNERS. Underneath are eight snapshots of men and women in urban and rural settings, some dressed in blouses and shorts, others in grass skirts and feathers. The ad claims that Word Publishing is "Proud to be the publisher of Papua New Guinea's first nationally owned newspapers" (the *TPNG* and *Wantok*) and informs the reader that Word Publishing is "fully owned by Papua New Guinea's four largest churches: Catholic (750,000 members); Lutheran (550,000 members); United (300,000 members); and Anglican (220,000 members)." It concludes that "Six Out of Every Ten Papua New Guineans Have a Stake in the Company's Future."

What this ad does, semiotically speaking, is to reconcile its own depicted diversity of Christian denominations and of traditional rural and modern urban dwellers through an appeal to joint ownership of the newspapers. That is, at the level of collective ownership, the enumerated members of each church are not Catholics or Lutherans but, rather, Papua New Guineans, all of whom have a stake in the company. Thus, reading these particular newspapers does indeed constitute a mass national ceremony, as Anderson observed, but not merely because it is a shared act of consumption. Here, the newspaper itself is presented as the quintessential national commodity.

## GENERIC INDIVIDUALS, SPECIFIC CONSUMERS

The rhetoric of national ownership makes certain presuppositions about the nature of objects and persons, presuppositions revealed in the following meta-advertisement (Figure 7.6). Placed by Word Publishing in its *Times of Papua New Guinea*, the ad attempts to persuade other advertisers to buy space in Word's Pidgin-language newspaper, the weekly *Wantok*. At the top in large letters: "He likes to eat RICE and TINFISH." On the left, a large caricature of a man dressed in "traditional" style (grass skirt, feather headdress, and a bone through his nose), carrying a bulging briefcase with several *kina* notes carelessly sticking out. To the right of this, a text:

> OH! and he . . .
> SHOPS at major department stores, buys different FOODS, likes SOFT DRINKS, enjoys smoking CIGARETTES, has a family to feed and CLOTHE, sends his kids to SCHOOL, he owns a CAR, has his own HOME, has money invested in a BANK and in his spare time he likes to play SPORT and listen to MUSIC
> OH! . . .
> and one other thing that advertisers tend to forget—he speaks Pidgin, 90% of the time, as his natural language—unlike English!
>
> Make sure you advertise cost effectively!
> There are 2,000,000 Others like him in Papua New Guinea!

Alongside the name *Wantok* at the bottom of the ad are the concluding words, "The

**Figure 7.6**   Newspaper ad in English-language paper for PNG's only Pidgin-language paper

only Pidgin newspaper in PNG[.] Ridiculous isn't it?"

Here is a succinct definition of the prototypic consumer-citizen or, somewhat differently, the essential consumer-citizen (apparently male) who underlies the celebrated manifest diversity of PNG's population. At this level of description, the consumer-citizen is generic and virtual, a potential waiting to be realized in the specific forms of specific consumption practices and fantasies. That is, at this level, all consumer-citizens are identical, potential participants in a national marketplace. I would argue that this conception of a generic individual is similar to the conception of a generic human being, endowed with certain inalienable rights, that is promoted by the state in a variety of other contexts, such as state-sponsored campaigns of civil education, trials, and elections (Foster 1992; LiPuma 1995).

Furthermore, the ad implies that generic individuals distinguish themselves from each other through the work of consuming or appropriating particular objects (Miller 1988; Carrier 1990a, 1991). Such work incorporates these objects into the consumer's definition of his or her social self or personhood. But this implication, in turn, implies a world of anonymous or "neutral" objects, that is, objects "which could be owned by anybody and identified with anybody" (Gell 1986:113)—in short, a world of personless objects. Of course, this world is no more than the necessary complement of a world of objectless persons, the generic and virtual individuals awaiting specification and realization through acts of consumption that attach objects and persons to each other. "Ownership" or "having" is the means for attaching specific qualities to an otherwise generic persona.

Here I would argue that this view of persons and objects, a view communicated by the rhetorical argument of all ads, directly challenges conventional Melanesian views of objects and persons (Hirsch 1995). On the one hand, the Melanesian person is relational, the precipitate (or node) of numerous and particular social relations (Strathern 1988). This particularity is irreducible, so that the concept of generically identical persons is ordinarily unimaginable.

On the other hand, since the 1925 publication of *The Gift,* anthropologists have been aware of the way in which, for Melanesians, persons and objects generally implicate each other. This is a matter of neither mysticism nor animism. Rather, it is a correlate of social practices—most notably, gift exchange—that embed objects in definite social relations (see Carrier 1990b). That is, there are no unattached or "neutral" objects, objects that could be identified or owned by "anybody."

## NATION AND CULTURE AS COMMODITY

One of the effects of the logic of persons and objects operating in ads is to open up the possibility of rendering the nation as a "neutral" object awaiting attachment via consumption to a "neutral" or generic consumer (see Jourdan, chapter 6, on the "neutrality" of popular culture). An ad for Nestlé products, also in the special 1989 Independence Day issue of the *Post Courier,* illustrates this possibility (Figure 7.7). Although part of a transnational corporation, Food Specialties (PNG) Pty Ltd. employs the rhetorical strategy of collective ownership and presents itself as a Papua New Guinea manufacturer. The ad features a drawing of Nescafé Niugini Blend instant coffee, the label of which promises the consumer a beverage made of "100% PNG Coffee." The implication of the ad is that just as the producer and the product are qualified as "100% PNG," likewise will the consumer be qualified.

Perhaps this implication was all the more obvious to an audience already familiar with previously circulated ads that promoted the slogan "PNG Coffee—For PNG People!" Among the ads in this campaign to sell coffee beans grown in the Highlands there appeared

**Figure 7.7**  Newspaper ad for Nestlé products

As a sponsor we are glad to help . . .

As a Papua New Guinea manufacturer we are proud to be involved in ...

**THE HIRIMOALE FESTIVAL**

Food Specialties (PNG) Pty Ltd

**Figure 7.8** Newspaper ad promoting consumption of PNG coffee

one (Figure 7.8), framed by coffee beans, that illustrated in nine steps "How PNG People Make & Enjoy PNG Coffee." The ad functioned as an instruction manual for making a cup of coffee from scratch, depicting in step-by-step fashion a consumption practice ascribed to PNG people in general. By contrast, another ad in the campaign publicized "PNG's Magnificent 5," five different named brands of PNG coffee (No. 1, Goroka, Namasu, Okka, and Koroma) available for PNG people to consume. Uniformity and similarity are thus portrayed with respect to the generic practice of coffee consumption, while singularity and difference are offered through the consumption of particular brands.

Let us return, however, to the Food Specialties ad (Figure 7.7). It identifies Food Specialties as a sponsor of the Hiri Moale Festival, an independence weekend event in which the Boera villagers of Port Moresby staged songs and dances for themselves and visitors. The *Post Courier* of September 14, 1989 described these songs and dances as "some of the oldest . . . in Boera history," and one old Boera man is quoted as saying, "We do not want to see any exaggerated or made-up dances that do not reflect our culture." The juxtaposition of commodity and "culture" in this context valorizes the advertised products as national commodities by associating them with "authentic" native traditions. This valorization occurs despite the fact that the "authentic" tradition in question is not Papua New Guinean, but Boera, for the definition of the national culture implied in the ad is one of a repertoire of diverse "traditions." That is, each tradition is construed as a variable item in the total inventory of traditions—a brand of tradition. Put otherwise, tradition is itself given the form of the commodity with which it is juxtaposed: discrete, objectified, and valuable on account of its intrinsic properties (see Babadzan 1988; Facey 1995).

There could be no clearer demonstration of the commodification of tradition than an ad campaign for Benson and Hedges cigarettes from the early 1970s, on the eve of formal political independence in 1975. In one set of ads, artsy pictures of various locally made artifacts (such as Sepik carvings) were juxtaposed with a picture of a pack of B&H cigarettes. The caption of the ad announced: "From the Benson and Hedges collection." At the bottom of the ad ran the rhetorical question: "When only the best will do . . . and isn't that all of the time?" The symbolic equation of carving with cigarette pack effects a semantic transfer in which the presumably "traditional" carvings are evaluated as "modern" commodities ("the best") and thereby rendered as a thing to be possessed or collected.[9] Reciprocally, the pack of cigarettes is domesticated and rendered indigenous, an element of local culture.

Precisely this process of metaphorical equation making surfaced in the overdetermined symbolism of a parallel set of ads for a cigarette called Paradise Gold. Two of these ads appeared in December 1974. The first ad is captioned in large block letters: "I AM PAPUA NEW GUINEA." Beneath this is a picture of the Rabaul harbor and, further below to the left, a picture of the product: a pack of cigarettes in a gold box, stamped with a bird of paradise logo. To the right of the product is the following text:

> I am the rugged mountain range
> I am the field of waving grass
> I am the mighty river that flows to the sea
> I am the towns and the people of this proud land
> And my cigarette is Paradise Gold

Here, the nation, in a soliloquy that equates natural features of the land and human occupants of the same land, discloses its preference for Paradise Gold. That is, the nation itself discloses its preference to smoke, because Paradise Gold is nothing so much as a material embodiment of the nation.

Another ad for Paradise Gold, which appeared in the December 11, 1974 PC, sounded these same themes in a slightly different key. The ad "contains" snapshot scenes from a variety of broadly identifiable locales: Rabaul, the Highlands, Port Moresby, Madang, and Lae.[10] Its caption is an invitation, or perhaps a command: "Discover the quality and value of this cigarette made specially for the people of Papua New Guinea." The text continues: "A fine taste of selected high quality tobaccos, presented in a superb personal gold pack. A cigarette to be proud of—a true symbol of Papua New Guinea today." At the bottom of the ad runs the predictable conclusion: "Paradise Gold belongs to Papua New Guinea."

The semiotic form of this particular ad accomplishes what I am arguing that mass consumption practices have the potential to accomplish more generally: a reconstitution of social geography. A diversity of disjunct locales (communities) are brought into relationship with each other through their shared relationship to some single object of consumption.[11] The "people of Papua New Guinea" emerge as a collectivity—a nation—only in relation to the cigarette made for their consumption. That is, the nation takes the form of a collection of people united by the commodities they jointly possess and consume in common. What are the implications of this definition of collective identity for the definition of personal identity and interpersonal relations? How does a national community of consumption define relations among its citizens?

## TOTEMISM: NATIONALIZING THE COMMODITY

To some extent, the answer to these questions follows inevitably from defining the nation as a community of consumption; for when such consumption occurs within the context of a capitalist mode of production, the nation comprises a collectivity of commodity buyers. To advertise a fish-flavored biscuit—perhaps the paradigmatic Papua New Guinean product—as "Number 1 in PNG" or "New to PNG" is to define PNG as, above all, a delimited marketplace. The citizens of PNG, in turn, are defined as consumers, people who affirm their membership in the nation through commodity consumption.

Commodity consumption, as I have argued, attaches specific qualities to generic individuals. It also predicates relations among such individuals by categorizing them as either fellow consumers, and thus alike, or as consumers with unshared consumption practices, and thus different. These alternatives are not exclusive; consumers who share consumption practices with regard to one commodity (say, coffee) might differ with regard to the brand of coffee they consume (Goroka versus Namasu). Likewise, consumers of a common brand of coffee might differ in their consumption of other commodities (such as tobacco). The possibilities of similarity and difference with other consumers are potentially infinite, and it is this infinite potential that makes it possible for consumers to create for themselves a specific individuality. By attaching to one's person, in a continuous act of consumerist bricolage, a unique ensemble of qualities, one can aspire to distinction.

Three ads illustrate how commodity consumption introduces new criteria for differentiating and individualizing persons—how commodity consumption can provide the means for producing simultaneously both a national consumption community *and* subcommunities of consumption.

The first ad (Figure 7.9) appeared as a billboard on the side of a small shack not far from the government office buildings in Waigani, next to a path that connected these buildings to a Public Motor Vehicle (PMV) stop on Waigani Drive. Various workers from the surrounding offices, as well as people seeking government services, frequented the shack to buy soft drinks, snacks, and cigarettes. The ad is for a coarse-cut tobacco

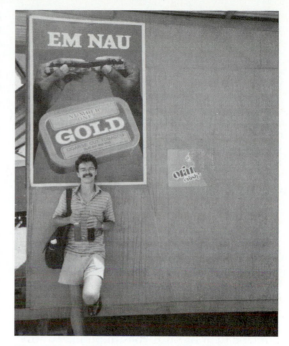

**Figure 7.9**   Billboard in Waigani advertising coarse-cut tobacco sold in Papua New Guinea

called Gold. It pictures two hands, apparently a man's, rolling up some tobacco in a piece of newspaper—perhaps a piece of the classifieds from the *Sydney Morning Herald,* available in many rural trade stores. The caption reads EM NAU, a multivalent Tok Pisin (pidgin) phrase that here expresses an interjection of satisfaction and a recognition of appropriateness on the order of "That's it" or "Perfect."

This cigarette is a popular item of both urban and bush consumption. The ad thus depicts a consumption fantasy with extremely wide geographical distribution. It is accessible primarily to readers of Tok Pisin, but perhaps to nonliterate viewers as well. Moreover, its elliptical form evokes almost entirely through connotation a shared bodily experience, an element of the habitus characteristic of the community of consumption defined by the ad (see Löfgren 1989b). This community is a community of shared tastes and smells. By articulating these otherwise unobjectified sensations, the ad represents to people a particular routine—rolling tobacco in a patch of newspaper—as typical of the collective praxis of Tok Pisin speakers. By associating this routine with Gold tobacco, a commodity produced and distributed in Papua New Guinea, the ad makes the boundaries of its implicit community of consumption coterminous with the product's market.

The second ad illustrating our purpose and presented earlier (Figure 7.2), for Ramu sugar, publicizes a commodity widely, if not universally, available—indeed, the only brand of sugar available in PNG. Ramu Sugar is thus a paradigmatic national commodity ("PNG Sweet Energy"), the consumption of which "can be enjoyed by everyone" and the enjoyment of which constitutes participation in the PNG community of consumption.[12] But notice the recipe for sago cake that appears in the ad. Certain ingredients of the cake—milk and margarine—presume access to a supermarket; it is unlikely that sago cake will be a popular item of bush consumption. To what extent, then, is this recipe an index of an emergent set of urban, middle-class consumption practices? Is this image of the collective expenditures that unite middle-class urban dwellers into a single community of consumption (Jourdan, chapter 6)? Apparently, the same commodity consumed nationwide provides the means for defining a less-inclusive community of consumption. This "subcommunity" would be characterized by relatively different habitus, a differently routinized set of tastes and associations.

That such middle-class consumption practices have taken a discernible enough shape to be parodied is evidenced by a humorous calendar illustration by Bob Browne, originator of a celebrated comic strip portraying the adventures of an unsophisticated urban PNG-everyman, Grass Roots. The illustration depicts: "What All the Young Village Kids Are Getting Educated to Become: The Yuppies." These yuppies synthesize in their consumption practices elements of both a global or transnational marketplace—Walkmans, running shoes, American television programs, instant noodles—and objects with a more local reference—tinned meat and designer-label

*laplaps* (sarongs). Likewise, the sago cake is identifiably local but at the same time unattributable to any particular local cuisine (say, Baktaman or Iatmul). Is the sago cake one homely item in an evolving national cuisine, that is, an element in a consumer lifestyle that is neither wholly local nor wholly imported? The question points to one of the tensions inherent in the relationship between mass consumption and national culture: the massive introduction of objects and images produced abroad (Indo-Mie Noodles, Nike jogging shoes, American TV shows) generates a shared experience that transcends local particularity, but which also potentially effaces national particularity. The national community imagined through mass consumption is thus inherently unstable, always threatening either to fragment into subcommunities of consumption or to melt imperceptibly into the transnational flow of commercial images and objects (see Foster 1991).

The third and final ad in our illustration (Figure 7.10) similarly presents a consumption fantasy with extremely restricted distribution. The ad appeared in *Paradise*, the in-flight magazine of Air Niugini. It is for POSH (Protocol & Overseas Service Hospitality), an agency that provides, among other things, a personalized service for VIPs, executives, overseas visitors, and business travelers; hotel and air travel bookings; and air-conditioned, chauffeured cars for city and country trips. Presumably, this ad is intended as much, if not more so, for overseas visitors to PNG as for the small number of local business executives who might purchase the service for their clients. Its caption reads: "When you need to arrive in style . . ." and despite the association with the National Parliament Building (see Rosi 1991) promotes a rather undemocratic, exclusionary sentiment. Style is available to all who have the means to purchase it, but presumably if this were everyone, then style would no longer be style.

Clearly, the advertisement for POSH reiterates that consumption practices and fantasies furnish people with the means for distinguishing themselves from other people as well as for establishing an imagined similarity or

# When you need to arrive in style...

- A personalized service for VIPs, executives, overseas visitors and businessmen
- Programme of meetings and visits arranged
- Hotel and air travel bookings made
- Met on arrival and assisted through formalities by arrangement
- Trips to other parts of the country arranged
- Airconditioned chauffeured cars available for city and country trips

FOR THIS SERVICE WE DO RECOMMEND AN ADVANCE BOOKING

*"We are proud to be the leaders in this-type of service and we are confident that you will not be disappointed..."*

  Protocol & Overseas Service Hospitality
Gordons, Port Moresby, Papua New Guinea.
P.O. Box 7500, Boroko, Tel:251886 Telex:23301 POSH.

**Figure 7.10**    Magazine ad for travel service agency

commonality. "The yuppies" likewise distinguish themselves from village consumer-citizens in their personal dislikes, items stereotypically consumed by villagers: *kaukau* (sweet potato) and tinned fish. Yet, this sort of differentiation is no more than the complement of the kind of assimilation represented in ads such as the one for Paradise Gold, ads that subsume different locales under the unifying image of a single commodity. If in one case similarity is achieved through shared consumption practices (see note 10), in the other case diversity is achieved through the

consumption of different commodities. In both instances—and this is my point—personal identity and interpersonal relations are effectively defined in and through relationship to consumer commodities. Otherwise generic consumer-citizens take on various individualized identities through the various consumer commodities possessed or owned. A new mode for constituting personal identities thus accompanies the establishment of a collective national identity in the form of a community of consumption.

## CONCLUDING QUESTIONS

Linnekin and Poyer (1990) have made the case that "ethnicity" should be understood to connote a specific ethnotheory of cultural identity rather than some universal feature of social life. This ethnotheory, they explain, rests upon a distinctive ontogeny, or perhaps even ontology—a set of presuppositions about what constitutes a person and what determines collective identities. Its most salient characteristic, in their view, is the privilege given to the "biological inheritance of substance as the determinant of identity" (1990:7). This presupposition can be broadly contrasted with ethnotheories of identity that privilege environment, behavior, and situational flexibility—ethnotheories that Linnekin and Poyer claim underwrite Pacific conceptions of personhood and community.

For my purposes, the more relevant feature of the ethnotheory of ethnicity is its preoccupation with discrete, bounded individuals (persons or groups), the identity of whom derives from putatively innate and essential characteristics. Louis Dumont has long identified this preoccupation as indicative of modern egalitarian individualism, an ideology that renders as "given" the existence of bounded, unitary, categorical individuals. Recently, Richard Handler (1988) has extended Dumont's observations by noting the logical congruence between nationalism and (possessive) individualism; both define integrated, autonomous units as primordial entities.

My questions, then, are these: Are such ontological presuppositions being communicated as an aspect of nation making in the new Melanesian states? If so, how?

I leave aside here the question of whether presuppositions about bounded, categorical personal and collective identities are a necessary feature of all versions of "the nation" (Kapferer 1988; Kelly 1995). Instead, I want to suggest that such presuppositions are indeed being communicated in Papua New Guinea, at least, and communicated in a number of ways. Perhaps the most visible of these ways is the undertaking of the state to expose people through formal schooling and periodic public campaigns to a moral ideal of citizenship based on the inalienable human rights of all individuals (Foster 1992). But perhaps the most effective of these communications is one that is more subtle.

I refer here to the way in which the ontological presuppositions of capitalism and nationalism interpenetrate and reinforce each other. As LiPuma points out, "the association of the nation with commodities—explicitly rendered in some advertisements—"objectifies the nation in such a way as to imbue it with the properties of capitalist commodities": discrete, bounded, intrinsically valuable, a reality apart from and independent of its creators (1995). He continues:

> When linked and likened to a commodity, the nation appears to be "objective" rather than socially constituted; it appears as primordial rather than historical; it appears as "necessary" rather than contingent; and it appears as a unified, autonomous reality. (1995:41)

In this sense, then, participation in mass commodity consumption potentially functions as a practical training ground for the development of a national style of consciousness (as defined in note 6), for such participation conditions us to the presuppositions of categorical identity that define what a nation is and what a national citizen is. Not only is the world of commodities a world of bounded, external objects, but it also is a world in which subjects are related to such objects only externally, by "having" them. We "belong to" a nation or "possess" a national culture much as we have or possess commodities. When such "having" (or "not having") becomes the dominant, taken-for-granted mode in which we relate to the object world, the idea of being a national citizen who "has" and/or "needs" a national culture follows unproblematically.

## ACKNOWLEDGMENTS

This chapter was originally published in *Nation Making: Emergent Identities in Postcolonial Melanesia* (© 1995), Robert Foster, editor. Pp. 151–181. Ann Arbor: University of Michigan Press. Reprinted with permission. I thank the following institutions for supporting my research on nationalism and national culture in Papua New Guinea: the Center for International Studies, University of Chicago; the National Endowment for the Humanities; the American Council of Learned Societies; and the Australian-American Educational Foundation. This chapter has benefited from the comments of James Carrier and of audiences at seminar presentations at the University of Sydney, the University of Adelaide, Australian National University, and Curtin University.

## NOTES

1. Diro, then a backbench member of Parliament (MP) from Central Province, was both deputy prime minister and head of the People's Action Party until a scandal over corruption forced his resignation in 1991.

2. Government delayed enforcement of the Commercial Advertising Act as the result of requests presented by local business executives to Karl Stack, then minister for industrial development, at a public meeting organized by the Chamber of Commerce in July 1985 (*Papua New Guinea Post Courier*, July 29, 1985). A grace period of 540 days, into 1987, was subsequently approved by Parliament (*Post Courier*, November 19, 1985). In 1990, then communications minister Brown Sinamoi announced that he would use the provisions of the act to stop the overseas production of company and annual reports (*Pacific Islands Monthly*, February 1990).

3. Thus, for example, the inclusion of a picture of a jar of Vegemite in the video that introduces visitors to the mission of the National Museum of Australia in Canberra, and the postcard reproduction of a Sunlight soap advertisement from the 1920s on sale at the souvenir stand.

4. This approach converges at points with that taken by Karl Deutsch in his *Nationalism and Social Communica-*

*tion* (1966[1953]). Deutsch argues that the ability to communicate effectively defines membership in a *people* or *nation* (terms that are not synonymous for Deutsch). He stresses, moreover, that such communicative efficiency does *not* require a shared language. Alternative "facilities," including, I suggest, primarily visual advertisements and shared consumption practices, equally enable social communication—mutual understanding of memories, associations, habits, and preferences. I emphasize, however, that shared "language" for communication does not imply social solidarity; shared languages facilitate arguments and disagreements as well as consensus.

5. If consumers do not recognize this by no means self-evident rhetoric, then they will not be able to decode the message of an ad, that is, to recognize the ad *as an ad*. While this might seem a moot point in, say, the contemporary United States, it is particularly germane in contemporary Papua New Guinea, especially rural Papua New Guinea. However, note that consumers who contest, reject, or obviate the message of an ad nonetheless respond to the ad's rhetorical devices.

6. Consider in this regard Deutsch's (1966[1953]:172) definition of national consciousness: "National consciousness . . . is the attachment of secondary symbols of nationality to primary items of information moving through channels of social communication. Not wit, but "French wit"; not thoroughness, but "German thoroughness"; not ingenuity, but "American ingenuity."

7. See Filer (1985) for some informed speculation on the identity of the readership of the *PC*. I would emphasize that although the newspaper reaches only 3 to 4 percent of the total population, its main constituency includes the urban-dwelling politicians, bureaucrats, and business people with most access to the financial and technical means for nation making in Papua New Guinea (see, for example, Figure 7.6; compare Anderson's remarks about the "reading classes" of nineteenth-century Europe [1983:73 ff.]). Put differently, its main constituency is the emerging middle class of urban Papua New Guinea—the population of main concern in this chapter.

8. Both ads seem to have been produced by the same firm, Samuelson Talbot.

9. The tradition-versus-modernity contrast appeared more explicitly in other cigarette ads from the same period that juxtaposed pictures of Highlands-style round houses with the Port Moresby skyline.

10. This motif was used more recently in Toyota's "Wheels for the Nation" campaign, in which ads picture different types of Toyota trucks in various locales.

11. In this regard, it is possible to compare the pilgrimages of colonial administrators (from province X to capital to province Y) that Anderson (1983) interprets as a potent force in first making a national community imaginable to the journey of Jumbo, the elephant sponsored by South Pacific beer. Jumbo traveled from Lae to the Mount Hagen show, stopping at various towns along the way, in a procession that linked communities through reference to the beer. Jumbo's movements were regularly reported in the *Post Courier,* thus linking newspaper readers throughout the country to the elephant's progress (*PC,* July 31, 1973, August 1, 1973).

12. The anthropologist James Carrier reminded me that the introduction of Ramu raw mill sugar and the disappearance of CSR (Australian-made) refined sugar were not greeted happily by many Papua New Guineans, who thought the more expensive domestic product compared unfavorably with its foreign predecessor. These consumers might well reject the message about enjoyment communicated in the ad. But—and this is my point more generally—to reject the message about enjoyment is not necessarily to reject the implicit message about Ramu sugar being a commodity owned by the nation. Indeed, it could be because a consumer has accepted the implicit message that the person is aggravated by the claims of the explicit message, that is, Ramu sugar might be perceived as an inferior national commodity and hence a poor reflection on "the nation." This perception of Ramu as a national commodity was in any case evinced in some of the letters to the *Post Courier* that expressed support for the product.

## *REFERENCES*

Anderson, Benedict. 1983. *Imagined Communities: Reflections on the Origin and Spread of Nationalism.* London: Verso.

Appadurai, Arjun. n.d. Communities of Consumption: Public Life in Contemporary India. Typescript.

Babadzan, Alain. 1988. "*Kastom* and Nation Building in the South Pacific." In *Ethnicities and Nations: Processes of Interethnic Relations in Latin America, Southeast Asia, and the Pacific.* R. Guidieri, F. Pellizi, and S. J. Tambiah, eds. Pp. 199–228. Austin: University of Texas Press.

Boorstin, Danie. 1973. *The Americans: The Democratic Experience.* New York: Random House.

Bronner, Simon J., ed. 1989. *Consuming Visions: Accumulation and Display of Goods in America, 1880–1920.* New York: W. W. Norton.

Carrier, James. 1990a. "The Symbolism of Possession in Commodity Advertising." *Man,* n.s., 25:693–706.

———. 1990b. "Reconciling Commodities and Personal Relations in Industrial Society." *Theory and Society* 19:579–598.

———. 1991. "Gifts, Commodities, and Social Relations: A Maussian View of Exchange." *Sociological Forum* 6:119–136.

Comaroff, John. 1987. "Of Totemism and Ethnicity: Consciousness, Practice, and the Signs of Inequality." *Ethnos* 52:301–323.

Deutsch, Karl. 1966[1953]. *Nationalism and Social Communication: An Enquiry into the Foundations of Nationality.* Cambridge: MIT Press.

Ewen, Stuart, and Elizabeth Ewen. 1982. *Channels of Desire: Mass Images and the Shaping of American Consciousness.* New York: McGraw-Hill.

Facey, Ellen. 1995. "Kastom and Nation Making: The Politicization of Tradition on Nguna, Vanuatu." In *Nation Making; Emergent Identities in Postcolonial Melanesia.* Robert Foster, ed. Pp. 207–226. Ann Arbor: University of Michigan Press.

Filer, Colin. 1985. "What Is This Thing Called "Brideprice"?" In *Recent Studies in the Political Economy of Papua New Guinea.* D. Gardner and N. Modjeska, eds. Special issue. *Mankind* 15:163–183.

Foster, Robert J. 1991. "Making National Cultures in the Global Ecumene." *Annual Review of Anthropology* 20:235–260.

———. 1992. "Take Care of Public Telephones: Moral Education and Nation-State Formation in Papua New Guinea." *Public Culture* 4:31–45.

Fox, Richard Wightman, and T. J. Jackson Lears, eds. 1983. *The Culture of Consumption: Critical Essays in American History, 1880–1980.* New York: Pantheon Books.

Gell, Alfred. 1986. "Newcomers to the World of Goods: Consumption Among the Muria Gonds." In *The Social Life of Things.* Arjun Appadurai, ed. Pp. 110–138. Cambridge: Cambridge University Press.

Handler, Richard. 1985. "On Having a Culture: Nationalism and the Preservation of Quebec's *Patrimoine.*" In *Objects and Others: Essays on Museums and Material Culture.* G. W. Stocking, Jr., ed. Pp. 192–217. Madison: University of Wisconsin Press.

———. 1988. *Nationalism and the Politics of Culture in Quebec.* Madison: University of Wisconsin Press.

Hirsch, Eric. 1995. "Local Persons, Metropolitan Names: Contending Forms of Simultaneity Among the Fuyuge, Papua New Guinea." In *Nation Making: Emergent Identities in Postcolonial Melanesia.* Robert Foster, ed. Pp. 185–206. Ann Arbor: University of Michigan Press.

Kapferer, Bruce. 1988. *Legends of People, Myths of State: Violence, Intolerance, and Political Culture in Sri Lanka and Australia.* Washington: Smithsonian Institution Press.

Keesing, Roger M. 1989. "Custom and Identity in the Contemporary Pacific." *Contemporary Pacific* 1:19–42.

Kelly, John D. 1995. "The Privileges of Citizenship: Nations, States, Markets, and Narratives." In *Nation Making: Emergent Identities in Postcolonial Melanesia.* Robert Foster, ed. Pp. 253–273. Ann Arbor: University of Michigan Press.

Leiss, William, Stephen Kline, and Sur Jhally. 1990. *Social Communication in Advertising: Persons, Products, and Images of Well Being.* New York: Routledge.

Linnekin, Jocelyn. 1990. "The Politics of Culture in the Pacific." In *Cultural Identity and Ethnicity in the Pacific.* Jocelyn Linnekin and Lin Poyer, eds. Pp. 149–173. Honolulu: University of Hawai'i Press.

Linnekin, Jocelyn, and Lin Poyer. 1990. "Introduction." In *Cultural Identity and Ethnicity in the Pacific.* Jocelyn Linnekin and Lin Poyer, eds. Pp. 1–16. Honolulu: University of Hawai'i Press.

LiPuma, Edward. 1995. "The Formation of Nation-States and National Cultures in Oceania." In *Nation Making: Emergent Identities in Postcolonial Melanesia.* Robert Foster, ed. Pp. 33–68. Ann Arbor: University of Michigan Press.

Löfgren, Orvar. 1989a. "Anthropologizing America" (review essay). *American Ethnologist* 16:366–374.

———. 1989b. "The Nationalization of Culture." *Ethnologia Europaea* 19:5–24.

Miller, Daniel. 1987. *Material Culture and Mass Consumption.* Oxford: Basil Blackwell.

———. 1988. "Appropriating the State on the Council Estate." *Man* (n.s.) 23:353–372.

Rosi, Pamela. 1991. "Papua New Guinea's New Parliament House: A Contested National Symbol." *The Contemporary Pacific* 3:289–324.

Strathern, Marilyn. 1988. *The Gender of the Gift: Problems with Women and Problems with Society in Melanesia.* Berkeley: University of California Press.

Williamson, Judith. 1978. *Decoding Advertisements: Ideology and Meaning in Advertisements.* New York: Marion Boyars.

# 8

# All Tongans Are Connected: Tongan Transnationalism

**Helen Morton Lee**

*La Trobe University*

Early in 1999, genealogy was a particularly popular topic on the Tongan History Association Internet discussion forum (http://www.pacificforum.com/kavabowl/tongahistory). Participants in the forum are primarily diasporic Tongans who have grown up overseas, and many of their discussions center around issues of identity. One young man, in particular, was enthusiastically posting detailed genealogical information he had been collecting, and in one post expressed his hope that if enough records could be collected, they would reveal the kinship ties that link all Tongans together. Another participant responded, "I do share your dream and I'm sure that somehow all Tongans are connected."

Whether or not their dreams of charting these links will be realized, the fact that all Tongans *are* genealogically related creates a sense of connection with one another, wherever they may be in the world, and however remote those links may be. The term *komiunitī Tongā*, while most often used to refer to localized populations of Tongan migrants, is sometimes invoked to describe the worldwide Tongan "community." When the connections between Tongans are examined, it becomes apparent that kinship is the primary thread linking Tongans throughout the world. Interwoven with kinship are a range of other ties—through exstudents' associations, churches, businesses, and so on—which create a complex network between migrants in different parts of the world as well as between these migrants and their "homeland" in the Pacific. My aim is to consider these links in relation to recent work concerned with transnationalism, both as a global phenomenon and more specifically as a characteristic of Tongan and other Pacific Islander migrants. I argue that while these transnational ties remain important, they are dwindling over time, as well as shifting from primarily being between migrants and their kin in Tonga to involving links across the diaspora.

## TONGAN MIGRATION

Tongan migration is part of a Pacific-wide phenomenon in which large numbers of people, relative to their island populations, have settled overseas, primarily since the end of World War II.[1] In some cases, such as Niue, there are now more island-born living overseas than remaining in the islands. By the late 1980s, as Connell observed, "it is the new diaspora that extraordinarily rapidly has come to characterize the contemporary South Pacific" (1987:399). The main destinations of Tongans and other Islanders are the United States, New Zealand, and Australia, but Islanders have also settled in many other nations of the world. To give some indication of the number of Pacific Islanders living in the main host nations, the 1990 U.S. census recorded 365,024, with Tongans accounting for 5 percent of this total (U.S. Department of Commerce 1993), and the 1996 New Zealand census recorded 202,236, of whom 15 percent were Tongan (Statistics New Zealand 1998).[2]

Numerous estimates have been made of the number of Tongans now living overseas, and there are no accurate figures available. My estimate is that there are now at least as many Tongans overseas as in Tonga, where the 1996 census recorded nearly 98,000 people (and see Marcus 1993:27). There are relatively large populations of Tongans in some cities in the United States, New Zealand, and Australia, and Tongans are also scattered throughout these nations and in many other parts of the world.[3] Temporary migration of members of the royal and elite families for educational purposes began in the late nineteenth century, but it was not until the 1970s that large-scale international migration took place. Initially much of this wave of migration was temporary; however, many who travelled overseas seeking education and employment decided to settle more permanently. These early migrants initiated chains of migration, bringing siblings, parents, and other family members to join them, who in turn facilitated the migration of still more kin. There are now some large extended families with most members residing overseas, some scattered

across different nations and others clustered in particular cities.

Their island "home" in western Polynesia is an archipelago of coral atolls and volcanic islands which, while never formally colonized, was a British protectorate from 1900 to 1970. Approximately 80 percent of Tonga's population lives on the main island of Tongatapu, and the capital, Nuku'alofa, is becoming increasingly overcrowded. Squatter settlements have developed on the outskirts of Nuku'alofa, and the town suffers from the problems of poor infrastructure and service delivery found in urban areas across the Pacific (Connell and Lea 1995). The Tongan economy is based on agriculture, with products such as squash and vanilla grown for export, but relies heavily on overseas aid and remittances from Tongans overseas. In 1989 and 1990, the officially recorded remittances to Tonga totaled 59.6 percent of Tonga's GDP, and this figure represents only a fraction of actual remittances, given the many forms of "unofficial" remittances (Appleyard and Stahl 1995:33; Brown and Foster 1995).

Tonga is a strongly hierarchical society, with the most important social divisions being the king and the royal family, the nobility, and the commoners, the latter making up the bulk of the population. Family is highly valued by Tongans, and while an increasing number of households comprise nuclear families, the extended family (*kāinga*) remains important. Within the hierarchically structured *kāinga* there is a complex system of rights and obligations, supported by values such as *faka'apa'apa* (respect) and *'ofa* (love, concern, generosity) (Morton 1996). This hierarchical ordering and associated values can influence decisions to migrate and underlie the practice of sending remittances back to Tonga, as discussed below.

The decision to migrate is usually made by the individuals involved, often spurred by the urging of family members in Tonga or those already settled overseas. In some cases family members exert considerable pressure on their members to migrate, particularly migrants exhorting younger kinsfolk to join them. These decisions are sometimes carefully planned, but in many instances migrants admit, "it just happens." In their narratives of migration experiences, most people describe taking opportunities to migrate as they arose, without much forethought, and, as already noted, many of the longer-term migrants initially intended only to undertake some form of education or short-term work overseas and later decided to stay more permanently.

Migration is seen as a way of improving the life chances of those who migrate and of their kin in Tonga. Migrants speak both of "helping the family" and "seeking opportunities" such as employment and education "for our future." Given that wages in Tonga are low and there are limited avenues for paid employment, even unskilled work overseas is seen to offer a better future than is possible in the islands. Agricultural work has been devalued in Tonga, but those who do wish to farm often find it difficult to access land. Access to loans to establish businesses can also be limited, so that overall, there are few opportunities for socioeconomic advancement in Tonga and migration is perceived by many as the only solution.

Of course, there is tremendous variation in the extent to which people's images of the opportunities beckoning overseas are realized, and while some migrants find considerable success overseas others struggle in conditions of poverty. Women and men alike migrate either alone, with their partners, or as nuclear family units. Often one partner stays in Tonga while the other, usually the husband, ideally finds work overseas and sends most of his earnings home, or uses his wages to purchase goods to take back to Tonga. Unfortunately it is not uncommon for men to establish new lives overseas and gradually lose contact with their wives and children in Tonga.

Today, migration from Tonga continues but at a slower rate than in the 1970s, as most of the receiving nations have tightened their immigration policies. The majority of Tongan migration now occurs under family reunification schemes, which are often quite restrictive and even expensive for the family already overseas. "Overstaying," or illegal immigra-

tion, occurs at a high rate, and in Australia Tongans have had the highest rate of overstaying of any group (Connell and McCall 1989:10; Finney 1999:121). However, while the *rate* of overstaying is high, the actual *number* of Tongan overstayers is small relative to many other groups.

While migration slows, the overseas-born Tongan population is increasing, and in the United States and New Zealand Tongans are the fastest-growing group of Pacific Islanders (U.S. Department of Commerce 1993; Krishnan et al. 1994:30). This cohort of overseas-born Tongans is now proportionally larger than the Tongan-born in most receiving nations; for example, they made up 52 percent of the Tongan population in New Zealand in 1996 (Statistics New Zealand 1998:13). Similarly, in a sample of 100 Tongan households in Melbourne, Australia, of the 430 people of Tongan descent, 52.3 percent were born overseas.[4]

## DEFINING TRANSNATIONALISM

The term transnationalism, first employed as early as 1916 (Mahler 1998:16), has been the subject of renewed interest in recent years as part of increasing concern with the issue of globalization (see Kearney 1995). The term is generally taken to refer to the multiple ties migrants (now often called "transmigrants") create and maintain with their home society, while still forging new links with the host society. In her valuable interrogation of the concept of transnationalism, Mahler (1998) has emphasized the importance of recognizing the different forms these transnational ties can take, and their varying significance at both individual and societal levels. It is also critical to acknowledge that not all migrants form these ties; in fact, some distance themselves from their homeland emotionally and socially, as well as geographically. However, as is the case with Tongans, even those who choose not to form transnational ties (or are unable to do so) are often indirectly involved in the multiple links that others form.

Crucial to the concept of transnationalism is the idea that migrants continue to feel "at home" in their nation of origin, while at the same time establishing a new "home" elsewhere. This can make it difficult at times for them to know where they really belong (Basch et al. 1994:5). As they explain, "Transmigrants take actions, make decisions, and develop subjectivities and identities embedded in networks of relationships that connect them simultaneously to two or more nation-states" (1994:7). These relationships mean that they are involved with the "nation-building processes" of the different nation states (1994:22; see also Glick Schiller et al. 1992). Therefore, the emphasis in the literature on transnationalism is on the broader relationship between migrants and the nation states with which they are involved, even when more personal relationships, such as kinship ties, are described.

This creates a difficulty when factoring in the ties that form *across* the diaspora; for example, between Tongans in the United States, New Zealand, and Australia. Tongans in Australia may not feel "at home" in the United States, nor are they involved in the processes of nation building there. Nevertheless, their maintenance of ties to kin and other Tongan social groups in that country are important in their own right as well as for their impact on relationships to Tonga. In the literature on Pacific Islander migration, "transnationalism" has encompassed these kinds of ties, although in another way it is a narrower definition, being almost entirely focused on economic ties.

## TONGANS AS "TRANSMIGRANTS"

In 1974, when the rate of Tongan migration overseas was at one of its highest points, George Marcus identified "the relations among adult siblings who have scattered from their domestic group of origin" as a "hidden dimension" of Tongan family life (1974:87).[5] This migration, as well as internal population movement, was beginning to result in "dispersed family estates," which he described as "a major feature of modern Tonga social structure" (1974:92). Although Marcus's paper did not use the term *transnational,* the

continuing economic links between the dispersed sibling sets were an important element in the creation of the extensive transnational networks that now exist. However, his focus on the economic activities of the family networks led him to deal only briefly with other forms of ties that are created transnationally, and to discuss only those families that were successful in utilizing their overseas links to maintain and enhance their economic position and social status in Tonga (and see Marcus 1981).

Marcus introduced the term *corporate* into his discussion, arguing that relationships among the sets of kin he identified as "family estates" had "a readily observable corporate quality" (1974:94). This was seen primarily in members' sense of responsibility for one another. His argument was later echoed in the work of Bertram and Watters, who described Polynesians' "transnational corporations of kin," and thereby generated considerable discussion about the usefulness of this concept (Bertram and Watters 1985; Bertram 1986; Connell and McCall 1989; Bertram 1999).[6] One of the primary criticisms was that it portrayed families as unified and in agreement about their economic aims and functions, neglecting the conflicts and tensions that also existed within them. Bertram recently argued that the concept is still useful when used in the sense of a "family firm," looking at both consumption and investment by members in different geographical locations (1999:127).

As "corporations of kin" indicates, the focus is on the transnational nature of *groups.* James has argued that this is an "increasingly inappropriate" term for Tongans because of the growing tendency for individuals to act independently (1993:360). She found that in the village she studied in Vava'u, remittances "are highly individual, and many are concerned with capital accumulation" (1993:361). Within the Tongan population of Melbourne, some people operate as members of "corporations of kin" while others maintain their connections with Tongans elsewhere as individuals or nuclear family units. Not surprisingly, this was influenced by how many members of their extended families (*kāinga*) resided in Melbourne. Some of the larger families, comprising a number of separate households, could draw on considerable economic and social resources when needed. These families still maintained ties to kin living elsewhere, although in some cases they had few direct links with Tonga, as so many of their members had migrated.

Mahler has pointed out that much of the literature on transnationalism assumes the movement of people between nations, and she suggests that "the flows of *things*" also need to be taken into account (1998:77, emphasis in original). In the literature on Tongan migration the focus has been primarily on the flow of remittances, both monetary and in-kind, into Tonga. Ideally, remittances are a tangible expression of the moral obligations between kin; they are seen as a demonstration of values such as love and respect. However, as James (1993) observes, in reality remittances often benefit only certain kin, or in the long term the remitters themselves, rather than being distributed among the extended family. Studies of Tongan remittances have shown that over time there has been a movement toward in-kind rather than monetary remittances, including items for sale at Tonga's second-hand goods markets (Brown and Connell 1993), or direct payments of airline tickets, insurance premiums, and so on. Also important are the "contraflows" (James 1997) of goods from Tonga, particularly Tongan foodstuffs and ceremonial wealth (*koloa*), which are to some extent viewed as reciprocating the "gifts" sent to Tonga by migrants.

As remittances are an important element of the transnational connections between Tongans, as well as being crucial to the Tongan economy, their sustainability over the long term is a crucial question. Studies of remittance patterns over time have produced conflicting results, with some claiming a high level of on-going remitting (Brown and Foster 1995; Brown and Walker 1995; Brown 1998) while others revealed a significant decline over time (Connell and Brown 1995). Very few of the Tongans in my study who were under the age of thirty sent money or goods directly to Tonga, and older migrants said

they sent money and goods only infrequently and irregularly. Few migrants were sending regular remittances, with most preferring to wait until they received requests for money or goods for particular purposes (see Lafitani 1992). In many cases people stated that they had no family left in Tonga to whom they felt they should send remittances, and in these cases other forms of transnational ties had also declined or had been redirected to kin in other locations outside Tonga.

Tongan remittance practices underline the need to recognize that the maintenance of transnational ties often occurs through demands from "home" at least as much as from the initiative of those overseas. Marcus has observed that in Tonga "the capacity to call on international resources, continually or on important occasions, has become a crucial factor in influencing a family's local economic conditions" (1993:29). Transnational ties can thus be sustained through sets of obligations (to kin, church, former school, and so on). The changing situation in the homeland can also influence these ties. Particular events, such as major celebrations, natural disasters, and family crises can all create a sudden flurry of activity in which people, information, goods, and money flow to or from Tonga for short periods of time. Likewise, changing circumstances for migrants and the country in which they are living can cause fluctuations in the level of transnational ties.

A hidden aspect of remittances is the significant flow of money reaching Tonga through fundraising activities in the diaspora. Even migrants who do not send money or goods directly to kin in Tonga tend to contribute at fundraising events. These are held when groups representing churches, schools, youth groups, brass bands, and so on travel to one or more locations to raise money for varied purposes, for example, building projects, new uniforms, band instruments, or educational resources. Fundraising events are also organized by groups located overseas, such as ex-students' associations, and the different forms of fundraising and the frequency of these events can constitute a significant drain on migrant families' incomes, especially as they are also called upon to give money for local projects. Thus, even if direct remittances decline, fundraising activities may ensure that migrants continue to contribute to the Tongan economy and the broader processes of "nation building" (Basch et al. 1994:22). However, these activities do not accord with the model of "transnational corporations of kin" as they are clearly not part of any kin-based strategies for economic success, and indeed can be a factor in subverting such strategies.

People sometimes get so carried away by their emotions and competitiveness at fundraising events that they deplete their savings. I was told several stories of people rushing from an event to find the nearest automatic teller machine in order to withdraw more money to donate. Lavish spending at fundraising events was criticized by many of the young people I spoke with, and was frequently attacked on the Kava Bowl discussion forum. These criticisms extended more generally to the *kavenga* (obligations) which drain families' incomes, such as remittances, donations to churches, and gifting at ceremonial events. Two young men posting a joint critique on the Kava Bowl claimed that money is often given "in amounts that are way beyond a family's ability to be self-sustaining." In short, you must help yourself before you can help others. Take it easy on the *kavenga* if you can't afford it. These criticisms are not shared by all young Tongans, but they are shared widely enough to suggest that fundamental changes are occurring in attitudes toward financial matters and notions of *kavenga,* which could have far-reaching implications for the future of the worldwide Tongan "community."

The work by Marcus and others that focuses on the "corporate" behavior of kin groups tends to assume that they are involved in conscious decision-making processes about their economic situations. More recent work by Poirine shares this assumption, arguing that family members engage in "a continually repeated optimization exercise over time" (see Bertram 1999:126). Poirine describes the "informal family credit market," which he sees as an efficient means of achieving

"the highest returns on human capital investments" (1998:75), clearly implying purposeful planning and shared goals within kin groups. Yet decision making, at least in the Tongan case, is often far more ad hoc and much less future-oriented than the economists' models would imply, and to a great extent this is because so many other factors are involved that are not straightforwardly economic and certainly not always economically "rational." This is not to say that there are no deliberate decisions made within kin groups about their economic futures, but even where such decision making occurs it is often subverted by circumstances, as I have shown is the case with fundraising. Other circumstances, such as life crisis events that require a significant contribution of money or goods, can interfere with the most carefully laid plans. In addition, decision making at the level of "kin group" is occurring less frequently, with more individuals preferring to make economic decisions at the level of their immediate family.

## BEYOND ECONOMICS

The model of transnationalism that has been employed in the literature on Pacific migration has centered on economic ties. My aim in this section is to discuss some of the other forms of ties that exist between Tonga and the diaspora, and while some undoubtedly have economic elements, it important to recognize that they are *perceived* primarily as emotional and social ties. There is considerable variation in the extent to which individuals and family groups maintain these ties, and even within a single household, members often have very different levels of engagement with kin and others in Tonga.

### Communicating with Kin

In my interviews with Tongans in the diaspora it was common for people to joke about their enormous telephone bills, as the telephone is by far the most popular means of keeping in contact with dispersed kin. Letters are less common, but technology such as facsimile machines and even e-mail is becoming popular. However, the use of any of these forms of communication ranges from frequent (and expensive) contacts to none at all, the latter being the case for many young people born overseas.

Another form of technology used to facilitate contact between kin is the video camera, and videos of events such as weddings, national celebrations, sporting events, and so on are often circulated among extended family members in Tonga and overseas. Hammond examined Tongan videography in Utah, and found that videos tend to emphasize Tongan "cultural heritage," featuring "social events that, in many ways, highlight their culture and its foundations" (1988:396). For the migrants and their children these videos reinforce their Tongan identity, and Hammond suggests that they will be used to give future generations "a greater sense of knowing who they are by knowing more of their past" (1988:397). Videos sent to and from Tonga can enhance people's familiarity with kin and their lives in different locations, encouraging a greater sense of connectedness between them.

The extent to which this actually occurs is difficult to ascertain, but my interviews with diasporic Tongans led me to believe that videos play a less significant role than Hammond's paper suggests. Certainly, there were some people who avidly watched any video they could access from Tonga or from kin in other locations overseas, but many others expressed a lack of interest, often because videos tend to be long and are perceived as "boring."[7] If the language spoken on the video is Tongan, many young people who have poor language skills lose interest, although some still watch for curiosity value. One young woman told me she loves to watch such videos, mainly to see "what the hell they do down there [in Tonga], especially my age group."

Young people also tended to express a lack of interest in the various Tongan newspapers, which report news from Tonga and the diaspora, particularly those in the Tongan language. Some, like *The Tonga Chronicle* and some church newspapers, are published in Tonga, while others are published overseas, such as the New Zealand-based *Taimi 'o Tonga* (*Times of Tonga*). Interest in these publications is being renewed, however, by Internet sites which contain either online versions of the newspapers or summaries of their main news items. This also provides more immediate coverage of events, whereas mailed copies of the *Chronicle,* for example, sometimes take weeks to reach people.

The Internet more generally has become a new form of transnational connection, and elsewhere I have discussed Tongans' involvement with computer-mediated communication, particularly in relation to its role in constructing and reconstructing cultural identities (Morton 1999, 2001). There are now numerous Tongan-oriented sites on the Internet, many of which allow for discussions between participants and the exchange of news and other information. One of the most popular of these sites, the Kava Bowl, attracted mainly younger Tongans who had been brought up overseas, who were eager to communicate with one another and share their experiences and opinions.[8] Some sites have offered "live" coverage of events in Tonga such as the annual Heilala festival held at the time of the king's birthday,[9] and Tonga's millennium celebrations, offering up-to-the-minute images and information.

Some overseas Tongans in their twenties and thirties told me they had not followed Tongan news and events until discovering the Tongan-oriented Internet sites, and that this sparked a deeper interest in Tonga than they had felt before. Joe, for example, who spent his teenage years in New Zealand and had lost any sense of "bonds" with Tonga, commented in an interview conducted via e-mail: "Actually discovering the kavabowl on the internet has brought the biggest 'piece of something Tongan' back into my life." He said he had been contacting his parents and siblings in Tonga only once or twice a month, but "soon they'll be on the [Inter]net as well so we'll probably talk every day." Joe, and many other diasporic Tongans, are making connections via his computer with other Tongans around the world and increasingly in Tonga itself. For example, in my study of the Kava Bowl, over

40 percent of initial posts were greetings and personal messages, many of which involved people seeking contact with relatives (1999:242).[10]

Within Tonga, access to computers is slowly growing, and fundraising activities for schools in recent years have focused on purchasing computers and establishing Internet connections. Many Tongans have never used a computer in their lives, but the younger generations, particularly those on the main island of Tongatapu, are rapidly becoming familiar with this technology. The use of computer-mediated communication (CMC) is strongly supported by Tonga's crown prince, who has argued that it offers the potential for Tonga to operate on a par with more powerful nations: "It's not as if developed countries have an exclusive on computer training. It's such a new thing in the world that actually we can all start off at the same level" (Fonua 1998). The crown prince's vision, shared by other members of the royal family and the government, is that CMC can end the tyranny of distance and isolation, and the lack of profitable natural resources, that have impeded Tonga's economic growth, opening up new opportunities for businesses, education, tourism, and so on.

The extent to which ties established and maintained via CMC constitute "transnational" links needs to be considered carefully. Such ties can foster an ease of communication, may facilitate links between extended family members, may encourage participants from the diaspora to identify more strongly with Tonga, and may even make them more inclined to visit Tonga. On the other hand, it could also be argued that CMC enables migrants to strengthen their ties with one another, creating a greater sense of being part of a migrant "community," and distancing them even further from Tonga. It is difficult at this early stage to know whether these new forms of communication can actually be part of any "nation-building" processes, although that potential is certainly there.

The ties formed through CMC primarily (although not exclusively) involve younger Tongans, which is in stark contrast to the predominance of older people in other forms of transnational ties. Many of these older Tongans move between households and nations surprisingly frequently, as they actively work to maintain the ties between their dispersed family members. Their airfares are usually paid by younger family members who are much less likely to travel in this manner themselves. Many young people told me they had no contact with family members in Tonga, and the few who did had intentions of returning to Tonga at some point, or of establishing businesses in partnership with kin in Tonga. As I have shown, it is also older people (the first-generation migrants) who are most likely to send remittances, telephone or write to relatives, organize gifts for life crisis events, and so on.

## Children as Transnational Ties

One form of transnational movement of Tongans that is organized by adults but directly involves children and adolescents is the practice of fostering. This is the informal and often temporary "adoption" of children, almost always by kin, and most frequently by grandparents and father's sisters. This is a common occurrence within Tonga; in my study of a village on Tongatapu in 1988–1989 I found that 18.6 percent of the children were currently being fostered (*pusiaki*), and most households had been involved in fostering at some point (Morton 1996:56–60). Fostering occurs for a range of reasons, such as emotional attachment to a particular child, taking in an illegitimate child, or wanting household help. It can happen at the instigation of either the natural parents or the new caregivers, but the children themselves seldom have a say in this process. Nowadays migration is one of the most common reasons for fostering. Parents may decide to leave one or more of their children in Tonga while they go overseas to work or, if they are already overseas, may send the children back to Tonga while they are young. Sometimes parents later rejoin their children in Tonga, but more often they send for the children after some time or simply leave them to grow up with kin in Tonga.

Adolescents are also sent back to Tonga, where their parents hope they will learn *anga fakatonga* (the Tongan way) and the Tongan language.[11] Often there is a more specific aim of removing them from negative influences overseas, and the practice is explicitly perceived as a means of disciplining rebellious teenagers. Young people sent to live with relatives in Tonga often find themselves living in poor households or boarding schools with few of the material possessions and amenities they have come to take for granted. Often, they are expected to contribute their labor to the household or school and to adopt Tongan standards of dress and behavior, and they are strictly supervised and punished for any misbehavior. As with fostering more generally, young people occasionally have a say in whether or not they go to Tonga for a period of time during their adolescence, but usually they are given no choice.

As the migrant population has expanded, the practice of sending children back to Tonga has been partially replaced by moving them around the diaspora. Learning the Tongan way and language are less important in these cases, and the primary motivation is discipline, with rebellious teens sent to live with other relatives away from friends who are thought to be adversely influencing them. However, it can also occur for other reasons, such as giving the child access to a particular educational institution, giving the foster family additional home help, or even because the child is a particular favorite of the relatives concerned.

Much of the literature on transnationalism is concerned with documenting the actual movements of people, goods, and ideas between host and home societies, while neglecting the impact of such movements on individuals. The case of Tongan children being sent between kin in different locations reminds us that there can be adverse effects of transnationalism and that it does not always occur voluntarily. While transnational fostering may have benefits for some of the adults concerned, it can also place a considerable burden on the foster caregivers (see James 1991), and the children themselves are often

confused, angry, and unhappy with these arrangements. Children fostered at a young age may also experience difficulties in their relationships with their own parents if they are reunited at a later stage.

James has noted the instability of some of these fostering arrangements, with children moving more than once between different segments of their extended families (1993). In her study of fostering in households in a Vava'u village, she found:

> [s]ome relationships [between children and kin] appeared to be so highly subject to change and so peripatetic that I came to wonder where the loyalties of these young will ultimately lie, and whether the children will feel called upon to support either set of parents. Thus, while children are sent to ensure social security for themselves, through confirming kinship bonds and also possibly to become effective "second-generation remitters" because of these bonds, I doubt in many cases that the Tongan notion of *'ofa* ("love, generosity") will be successfully instilled into the younger generation born of migrant parents. Instead, they are likely to get more clearly the message of economic individualism, which seemingly dominates the actions of their parents and other relatives, which may mean that they will cut themselves off from wider kinship ties. (James 1991:17)

The emotional impact on children who are moved between families should not be underestimated. For example, 'Ofa (aged twenty-two) told me she had been born in Australia and taken to Tonga with her parents as an infant. On a family visit to Melbourne when she was six years old, her parents left her with relatives when they returned home, so she could attend school in Australia, and she stayed with that family until she was thirteen. She then joined her parents and siblings, who meanwhile had migrated to the United States. At seventeen, when she began to rebel against her parents, she was sent to live with relatives in Australia again, where she has remained. Reflecting on her experiences, she described being left behind at the age of six as "cruel" and admitted that even on her last move, for the "first year I cried every night and then the next year I calmed down for a little while. Then now I don't mind it so much." Although she tried to frame her experiences in a positive way, for example, valuing the opportunity she'd had to form a close relationship with her grandmother in Melbourne, 'Ofa was obviously unhappy and quite embittered, sighing at one point, "I think my whole life is a problem."

Whether or not a young person who is moved between Tonga and the diaspora maintains ongoing ties to Tonga is highly dependent on his or her particular experiences. Some who are sent to Tonga appreciate the knowledge they acquire and the time they spend with relatives, but others have damaging experiences and on their return overseas are disinclined to have any further contact with kin in Tonga. The circumstances of their lives on their return will also impact the likelihood of continuing interactions, and even those who return overseas fully immersed in *anga fakatonga* (the Tongan way) often revert to their "foreign" ways and gradually lose contact with Tonga. The aim of disciplining adolescents may not be met in any case. A Tongan youth (aged nineteen) in Melbourne told me seven of his friends had been sent back to Tonga at different times and, he added, "they've been sent over there to be disciplined, but they've just come back not having changed, just basically gotten worse."

Rebellious teenagers who do not respond positively to Tongan discipline are increasingly seen as a liability to their families in Tonga, and I have heard of several cases in which young people were sent back overseas when their relatives could not control their behavior. There is a growing belief that young people coming from overseas are having a negative influence on the youth of Tonga, particularly those who have been sent because of their involvement with gangs and drugs overseas. This may make people in Tonga more reluctant to take in the children of relatives who have migrated, and in any case it seems that many parents in the diaspora are becoming disinclined to take this option. Although some spoke of the benefits of children being exposed to Tongan cul-

ture, others—even those who could be described as more "traditional"—were adamant that they would not send their children alone to Tonga. One parent exclaimed: "*Never!* I will never, ever do that. Put it this way, Helen, if I can't solve [my children's] problems, who else will solve them?" The young people who spoke positively about the idea of eventually sending their own children to Tonga for a time did not perceive it in terms of discipline. Instead, they thought of it as a way of learning about being Tongan, and these were usually the youth who regretted missing out on that during their own childhoods. More often, young people said they would prefer to visit Tonga *with* their children rather than sending them on their own.

## Visiting "Home"

This option of taking children to Tonga for holidays is a popular one for families that can afford such a trip, and these holidays often are more positive experiences for children than longer stays unaccompanied by their parents. If they go only for a holiday they do not have to attend school in Tonga and may be treated as special guests by their relatives. Numerous posts on the Kava Bowl enthusiastically described visits to Tonga by young people who had grown up overseas, during which they were able to meet extended family members, learn about "Tongan culture," and develop a sense of pride in their identities. As with children sent alone, however, their experiences are mixed and some report a range of difficulties, such as not understanding much of what happens and feeling "trapped" by behavioral restrictions. Young people used to an active social life may find the relatives they stay with disapprove of them going out unchaperoned, and they may encounter for the first time the relationship of avoidance and respect between brothers and sisters (which extends to cousins).

Families returning to Tonga for holidays make up part of the approximately 5,000 expatriates visiting Tonga each year (*Eva* 1998).

According to the Tonga Visitor's Bureau, most migrants taking holidays in Tonga stay with family, but a growing number are choosing to stay at holiday resorts, particularly when they are accompanied by non-Tongan partners (*Eva* 1998). Other reasons for visiting Tonga include special events, such as the Heilala Festival; family celebrations such as the birth of a grandchild; important birthdays, graduations, or weddings, funerals, and events such as church conferences. Tongans who have been particularly successful overseas, in areas such as sports and entertainment, are given celebrity status when they visit Tonga, and play a role in keeping alive the dream of the "opportunities" to be had overseas.

Unfortunately, migrants attempting to revive their ties with Tonga by visiting (often at great expense) may find that they are not unequivocally welcomed. They may be perceived as bringing negative foreign influences, or accused of ostentatiously displaying their "success," and can find themselves being derided as *fie pālangi* (trying to be Euro-American), or *pālangi loi* (fake Euro-Americans). This can be particularly devastating for young overseas-raised Tongans and part-Tongans visiting Tonga for the first time and hoping to explore their cultural identities. Such experiences can be distressing and confusing for the visitors and do not seem likely to promote continuing transnational interactions.

Overall, there seems to be an increasingly ambivalent relationship between Tongans at home and in the diaspora, and a major source of this ambivalence is the role of migrants as remitters. Small has discussed the tensions that can arise when migrants express concern about how their money is being spent in Tonga (1997:197), and although remitting is perceived in terms of family obligations there can be an undercurrent of resentment for both remitters and receivers. The whole issue of whether to meet familial and other obligations through remittances and fundraising is a highly contentious one, and an increasing number of migrants are opting to prioritize the needs of their immediate families, as discussed above.

## THE FUTURE OF TONGAN TRANSNATIONALISM

The phenomenon of transnationalism requires a reconsideration of the idea of the nation state, given that many members of nation states such as Tonga now live beyond their geographic borders. Transmigrants become part of the nation state in which they now reside yet retain their ties to their home country as well (Basch et al. 1994). The process of "deterritorialized nation-state building" can involve both migrants and political leaders from their country of origin constructing an ideology in which the migrants are "loyal citizens of their ancestral nation-state" (1994:3). What this ideology conceals, according to Basch et al., is the migrants' incorporation into the host society, despite the fact that it is this very incorporation that maintains the migrants' significance to their home society.

In the Tongan case, the importance of incorporation into the host society *is* acknowledged by the migrants themselves and the Tongan monarchy and government. The frequent short- and long-term visits by members of the royal and noble families to cities with populations of Tongans does assist in the process of maintaining migrants' affective and other ties to Tonga. But the reliance of the Tongan economy on migrants' remittances also necessitates recognition of their ties to their new homes. Again, it is primarily the older, or more recent, migrants who could be described as retaining membership (real or imagined) in the Tongan nation state. Taking out citizenship of another country immediately invalidates their Tongan citizenship, so those who have any intention of moving "home" in the future are reluctant to change their status. In my Melbourne sample, slightly less than 30 percent of Tongan-born individuals had Australian citizenship.[12]

Younger Tongans, particularly those born overseas with citizenship of their country of birth, are more likely to perceive Tonga as an imagined homeland than as their real home. While some older migrants still hold cherished dreams of retiring to Tonga, I found that very few of their children envisaged moving to

Tonga. Migrants who do hope to return to Tonga to live often put these plans aside once they are settled overseas or because they are loathe to move away from their adult children. In other cases families do attempt to return to Tonga, only to remigrate when they are unable to manage the lower living standard or when they encounter other difficulties.

The ambivalence some people remaining in Tonga feel toward migrants is also found at the level of government. As Basch et al. found for migrants from the Caribbean, a home government in the process of building a "deterritorialized nation" generally welcomes remittances and migrants' home visits, but it may not be so welcoming if they want to return home permanently and bring their new ideas about issues such as class, gender, and power with them (1994). For example, with the rise of the Pro-Democracy Movement (PDM) in Tonga in the 1980s, the government became more wary of returning migrants (in some cases even as visitors), as it could not be sure of their level of support for the PDM or what influence they might have on Tongans at home.

Despite the emergence of the democracy movement, Tongan politics remain comparatively stable, making it highly unlikely that migrant Tongans would form groups to lobby foreign governments to intervene in Tongan affairs, particularly given the overarching Tongan pride in independence, if not always in the monarchy. On the other hand, there has also been no need for the Tongan government to call on immigrant Tongans to support its own policies, or to lobby other governments, as was the case, for example, when Filipinos in America lobbied the U.S. government on behalf of Cory Aquino. For the most part, the organizations formed by Tongans overseas have had links with Tonga only on the basis of fundraising and other support, and have not attempted to involve themselves directly in Tongan politics.[13]

Overseas Tongans are unable to vote in Tongan elections, although the issue was raised with the prime minister's office in 1999 and it is possible arrangements may be in place for the 2002 elections (Fonua 1999). If the overseas Tongans who have retained Tongan citizenship—cautiously estimated as 25,000—were allowed to vote it would make a significant difference to the outcome of elections, since in 1996 only 27,948 votes were made in Tonga (56 percent of potential votes). This issue of voting rights raises wider concerns about the rights of overseas Tongans. Land, in particular, is already a contentious issue and the question of whether long-term migrants should retain rights to land has been raised for some time without resolution. Ward has said of the Pacific more generally, "Those who live overseas and seek to hold to their emotional, social and potential economic links with the homeland, are likely to argue for continued recognition of rights. The whole question has the potential to create great rifts between the homeland and expatriate communities. In matters of rank and status it is possible that similar tensions might arise" (1997:192).

Basch et al. have argued that when "deterritorialized nation-state building" occurs, "there is no longer a diaspora because wherever its people go, their state goes too" (1994:269). The issues of voting and other rights indicate that this process has only been partial in Tonga's case, and even if voting rights are granted to migrants the ability of the Tongan state to exert its influence in the diaspora is unlikely to significantly increase. In 1981, Marcus offered a "futurist scenario" in which Tonga could lose its political and economic importance to migrants. He noted: "Tonga might remain merely a struggling nation-state in the face of flourishing overseas concentrations in places such as Hawaii and California, residents of which would continue to affect the overall conditions of Tongans at home by their selective participation and contributions in persisting family networks" (1981:60). In this, and a later paper, Marcus argued that the king's attempts to find ways to ensure Tonga's economic development should be seen as ways to prevent this scenario from unfolding and ensuring that Tonga remained "*both* the economic and symbolic center of an internationalizing culture" (1981:61, emphasis in original; 1993).

These attempts to find the key to Tonga's prosperity have continued, with ventures as varied as the production of squash for export (van der Grijp 1997) and the establishment of the Friendly Islands Satellite Communications company (known as Tongasat) in the late 1980s (Morton 1999). None, however, has met the underlying aim of achieving prosperity. The latest scheme is the Tongan government's deal with an Australian biotechnology company, Autogen, to have a DNA database established in Tonga, with Tonga ideally benefiting from royalties from any discoveries commercialized by the company (Smith 2000; *ABC News Online* 2000). In addition, the crown prince's enthusiastic embracing of computer-mediated communication effectively continues the pattern that Marcus describes.

The scenario proposed by Marcus thus seems more likely to unfold than that of a deterritorialized nation state, which raises the question of whether transnational ties between Tongans at home and abroad will diminish over time. I believe they will, for a variety of reasons. They include those already discussed, such as the decline in knowledge of the Tongan language and culture within the overseas population, the increasingly ambivalent relationship between migrants and those at "home," the high cost of travelling to Tonga, and the critical stance of many younger Tongans overseas toward expenditures on remittances, including fundraising. A further crucial factor may be the high rate of intermarriage, with a significant proportion of Tongans overseas marrying non-Tongans. Of 113 marriages and former marriages in my Melbourne sample, just less than half (47.8 percent) involved intermarriage, and in her study of Tongans in Canberra, Finney (1999) found over half (52 percent) of the one hundred couples had intermarried. Although the extent to which "mixed" couples follow the Tongan way varies enormously, overall they are less likely to send remittances to Tonga and to maintain other forms of transnational ties. I found that intermarried couples are more likely to purchase their own homes and are more concerned with saving money than

exclusively Tongan couples. Most intermarried couples live a predominantly Western lifestyle, often choose to partially or fully disengage from other Tongans, and are less likely to send their children back to Tonga to live with relatives.

If we define transnationalism broadly to include ties between different migrant populations, a different story emerges in which interactions are increasing. As migrant numbers grow, formal associations and other organizations begin to emerge, fostering a sense of community and tying diasporic Tongans together at local, national, and even international levels. This sense of community can be enhanced by shared experiences and problems, such as the widely shared concerns about the problems of migrant youth, and some of these associations are being established by young people themselves, such as the Tongan Youth Council in Sydney, Australia.

Within the diaspora ties are also forming that can be described as "pan-ethnic," in which people identify as "Pacific Islander" or "Polynesian." The process that has been described in the United States for groups such as Chicanos (Keefe and Padilla 1987), Asian-Americans (Espiritu 1992), and Latinos (Oboler 1995) is now occurring for Pacific Islanders. Externally imposed categorizations encourage the groups they encompass to work together in order to access resources, draw attention to their needs, and so on. In Melbourne, for example, the Department of Immigration and Multicultural Affairs directs funding only to associations that cover the category of "Pacific Islanders," and not to specific Island groups.

Often, pan-ethnic groupings are particularly attractive to young people, partly because it gives them a sense of solidarity with a larger group but also because they feel lacking in the language and cultural knowledge specific to their ethnic group. Even without such knowledge they can find the basis for a secure identity in the pan-ethnic group. In some cases, mixed parentage is a further incentive to adopt the broader identification. Among young Tongans throughout the diaspora there is considerable anxiety about whether or not they can be considered "real" Tongans (Morton 1998), and identification as an Islander or a "Poly" (Polynesian) helps to overcome this.

Espiritu (1992) argues that, over time, there can be a lessening of differences between the subgroups within a pan-ethnic group as they begin to borrow ideas and practices from one another, intermarry, and generally develop not only a shared identity and a shared culture but also a sense of a shared history of disempowerment and discrimination. Thus, while a pan-ethnic identity does not preclude continued identification with a specific ethnic group, over time it can shift primary identification to the larger group. This process may impinge on continued transnational ties between host and home nations, as migrants turn more to one another (within the pan-ethnic group) than to kin and social institutions in the islands.

## CONCLUSION

Marcus's prediction, made two decades ago, has proved accurate: Tonga is still "a struggling nation-state" and the overseas population continues to exert some influence through their family networks (1981:60). Although I have argued here that these family networks are diminishing, as are other networks formed through schools, churches, and so on, it is highly unlikely that Tongans' transnational ties will disappear altogether, even if we use the narrower definition of transnationalism which neglects ties across the diaspora. In each generation there will be some overseas Tongans who continue to maintain an array of links with Tonga, including some who operate as part of "transnational corporations of kin." As the ratio of overseas-born to Tongan-born continues to increase, there is a strong likelihood that the proportion of those maintaining these links will decline. Processes of globalization notwithstanding, the social and cultural gap between Tongans at home and abroad is widening, straining transnational ties and leaving many migrants and their descendants with little sense of Tonga as "home."

## ACKNOWLEDGMENTS

The research on which this paper is based was conducted from early 1995 to mid-1999, with financial support from a University of Melbourne Postdoctoral Fellowship and an Australian Research Council Postdoctoral Fellowship held at La Trobe University. The project focused on Tongan migration, particularly the impact of migration on constructions of cultural identity, and my thanks go to the many Tongans who participated in the research and gave so generously of their time.

## NOTES

1. To some extent Pacific migration has been facilitated by ties between Pacific nations and their former colonizers; for example, American Samoans and Guamanians can move freely to the United States, New Zealand had concessionary migration policies for Samoans, and Cook Islanders, Niueans, and Tokelauans are New Zealand citizens. Labor migration programs to New Zealand also attracted many Islanders, particularly in the 1970s, but today receiving nations have tightened their immigration policies and people rely mainly on family reunification schemes.

2. Due to the categories used in the Australian census and other statistical collection, it is difficult to obtain figures for Pacific Islanders in Australia. A rough estimate based on figures from 1996 and 1998 is that there are 164,000 Pacific-Islands-born people in Australia, of whom approximately 7,000 are from Tonga (Maori and Pacific Islander Community Based Services 2000; statistics supplied by the Department of Immigration and Multicultural Affairs).

3. Often Tongans are grouped for statistical purposes with other Pacific Islanders, or in the category of "Oceania," which also includes New Zealand, or even, in the United States, in the "Asian and Pacific Islander" ethnic category, making it impossible to obtain accurate migration figures. Further complicating this are different definitions of "Tongan," with the overseas-born and/or those with a non-Tongan father often excluded.

4. This survey of 100 Tongan households located across the metropolitan area of Melbourne was part of a broader research project focusing on Tongan migration, particularly the impact of migration on constructions of cultural identity (Lee, forthcoming). The research was conducted from early 1995 to mid-1999, with financial support from a University of Melbourne Postdoctoral Fellowship and an Australian Research Council Postdoctoral Fellowship held at La Trobe University. In addition to the household surveys, detailed interviews were conducted with Tongans and non-Tongan partners in Melbourne and

(via e-mail) across the diaspora. The research also included a study of Tongan participation in Internet discussion fora such as the Kava Bowl (http://www.pacificforum.com/kavabowl/), a site established by Taholo Kami, a U.S.-based Tongan.

5. In a later paper Marcus points out that the earliest families to create these networks were members of the elite, and that their international family networks helped them to maintain their elite status within Tonga (1981).

6. In their original model of MIRAB economies (those based on migration, remittances, aid, and bureaucracy), Bertram and Watters were concerned only with Pacific states with close ties to New Zealand, but their model was quickly applied by other researchers to many other parts of the Pacific (Bertram 1999:114).

7. Hammond states that most videos are at least two hours in length and records an example of a twenty-six-hour video recording of a funeral and postfuneral events (1988:388).

8. I have used the past tense in relation to the Kava Bowl forum as the site has, at the time of writing, been "down" for some time.

9. The Heilala Festival includes a street parade with decorated floats, the Miss Heilala beauty pageant, canoe races, and many other events.

10. This study involved a content analysis of the 1,670 initial posts between March 1996 and March 1997, and the 105 initial posts from April 6 to 12, 1998. The popularity of the Kava Bowl increased rapidly, and by early 1998 it was receiving around half a million "hits" per month.

11. *Anga fakatonga,* or the Tongan way, is a concept that encompasses all aspects of the values, beliefs, and behavior associated with Tongan culture and tradition. While often perceived as unchanging and timeless, it is actually broad and flexible enough to allow for considerable leeway in interpretation and is undergoing a process of transformation in both Tonga and the diaspora.

12. Of the Tongan-born who had been in Australia for over ten years, 36.3 percent had taken out Australian citizenship; for all migrants in Australia, the 1991 census showed that after four to five years 50 percent take out citizenship and 73.1 percent after twenty years (Goldlust 1996:25).

13. Some migrants are attempting to play a more direct role in the affairs of their homeland; the first president of the Tonga-USA Business Council, formed in 2000, described the council and its members as "nation builders" (*Matangi Tonga* 2000).

## REFERENCES

ABC News Online. 2000. "Businessman Secures Rights to Tonga's Gene Pool." Wednesday, November 22. http://www.abc.net.au/news/newslink/weekly/newsnat-22nov2000-25.htm

Appleyard, R. T., and Charles Stahl. 1995. *South Pacific Migration: New Zealand Experience and Implications for Australia.* Canberra: AUSAID.

Basch, L., N. Glick Schiller, and C. Szanton Blanc. 1994. *Nations Unbound: Transnational Projects, Postcolonial Predicaments, and Deterritorialized Nation-States.* Newark, N.J.: Gordon and Breach.

Bertram, Geoff. 1999. "The MIRAB Model Twelve Years On." *The Contemporary Pacific* 11(1):105–138.

Bertram, I. G. 1986. "'Sustainable Development' in Pacific Micro-Economies." *World Development* 14(7): 809–822.

Bertram, I. G., and R. F. Watters. 1985. "The MIRAB Economy in South Pacific Microstates." *Pacific Viewpoint* 26(3):497–519.

Brown, Richard. 1998. "Do Migrants' Remittances Decline over Time? Evidence from Tongans and Western Samoans in Australia." *The Contemporary Pacific* 10(1): 107–151.

Brown, Richard, and John Connell. 1993. "The Global Flea Market: Migration, Remittances and the Informal Economy in Tonga." *Development and Change* 24:611–647.

Brown, Richard, and John Foster. 1995. "Some Common Fallacies About Migrants' Remittances in the South Pacific: Lessons from Tongan and Western Research." *Pacific Viewpoint* 36(1):29–45.

Brown, Richard, and Adrian Walker. 1995. "Migrants and Their Remittances: Results of a Household Survey of Tongans and Western Samoans in Sydney." Pacific Studies Monograph No. 17. Sydney: University of New South Wales.

Connell, John. 1987. "Paradise Left? Pacific Island Voyagers in the Modern World." In *Pacific Bridges: The New Immigration from Asia and the Pacific Islands.* James Fawcett and Benjamin Cariño, eds. Pp. 375–404. New York: Center for Migration Studies.

Connell, John, and Richard Brown. 1995. "Migration and Remittances in the South Pacific: Towards New Perspectives." *Asian and Pacific Migration Journal* 4(1):1–34.

Connell, John, and John Lea. 1995. *Pacific 2010: Urbanisation in Polynesia.* Canberra: National Centre for Development Studies.

Connell, John, and Grant McCall. 1989. "South Pacific Islanders in Australia." Research Institute for Asia and the Pacific. Occasional Paper No. 9. Sydney: University of Sydney.

Espiritu, Yen Le. 1992. *Asian American Panethnicity: Bridging Institutions and Identities.* Philadelphia: Temple University Press.

*Eva.* 1998. "Homecoming Holidays." 40:4–5.

Finney, Frances. 1999. "'I Thought It Would Be Heaven': Migration, Gender, and Community Amongst Overseas Tongans." M.A. dissertation. Australian National University.

Fonua, Pesi. 1998. "It's a Bit Too Late to Be Married, Says Tonga's Bachelor Crown Prince." '*Eva* 41:6–11.

———. 1999. "Too Late for Overseas Tongans to Vote." *Matangi Tonga* 14(1):3–4.

Glick Schiller, N., L. Basch, and C. Szanton-Blanc, eds. 1992. *Towards a Transnational Perspective on Migration: Race, Class, Ethnicity and Nationalism Reconsidered.* New York: New York Academy of Science.

Goldlust, John. 1996. *Understanding Citizenship in Australia.* Bureau of Immigration, Multicultural and Population Research. Canberra: Australian Government Publishing Service.

Hammond, Joyce. 1988. "Visualizing Themselves: Tongan Videography in Utah." *Visual Anthropology* 1(4):379–400.

James, Kerry. 1991. "Migration and Remittances: A Tongan Village Perspective." *Pacific Viewpoint* 32(1):1–23.

———. 1993. "Cash and Kin. Aspects of Migration and Remittance from the Perspective of a Fishing Village in Vava'u, Tonga." In *A World Perspective on Pacific Islander Migration: Australia, New Zealand and the USA.* Grant McCall and John Connell, eds. Pp. 359–373. Sydney: Centre for South Pacific Studies, University of New South Wales.

———. 1997. "Reading the Leaves: The Role of Women's Traditional Wealth and Other 'Contraflows' in the Process of Modern Migration and Remittance." *Pacific Studies* 20(1):1–27.

Kearney, M. 1995. "The Local and the Global: The Anthropology of Globalization and Transnationalism." *Annual Review of Anthropology* 24:547–565.

Keefe, Susan, and Amado Padilla. 1987. *Chicano Ethnicity.* Albuquerque: University of New Mexico Press.

Krishnan, V., P. Schoeffel, and J. Warren. 1994. *The Challenge of Change: Pacific Islanders Communities in New Zealand, 1986–1993.* Wellington: New Zealand Institute for Social Research and Development.

Lafitani, Siosiua. 1992. "Tongan Diaspora: Perceptions, Values and Behaviour of Tongans in Canberra." M. Letters dissertation. Australian National University.

Mahler, Sarah. 1998. "Theoretical and Empirical Contributions toward a Research Agenda for Transnationalism." In *Transnationalism from Below.* M. P. Smith and L. E. Guarnizo, eds. Pp. 64–100. New Brunswick: Transaction Publishers.

Maori and Pacific Islander Community Based Services. 2000. Report on the Maori and Pacific Islander Community of Victoria.

Marcus, George. 1974. "A Hidden Dimension of Family Development in the Modern Kingdom of Tonga." *Journal of Comparative Family Studies* 5(1):87–102.

———. 1981. "Power on the Extreme Periphery: The Perspective of Tongan Elites in the Modern World System." *Pacific Viewpoint* 22(1):48–64.

———. 1993. "Tonga's Contemporary Globalizing Strategies: Trading on Sovereignty Amidst International Migration." In *Contemporary Pacific Societies.* V. Lockwood, T. Harding, and B. Wallace, eds. Pp. 21–33. Englewood Cliffs, N.J.: Prentice Hall.

*Matangi Tonga.* 2000. "Flag of Nation Builders." 15(3):3.

Morton, Helen. 1996. *Becoming Tongan: An Ethnography of Childhood.* Honolulu: University of Hawai'i Press.

———. 1998. "How Tongan Is a Tongan?" In *Echoes of Pacific War.* Deryck Scarr, Niel Gunson, and Jennifer Terrell, eds. Pp. 149–166. Canberra: Target Oceania.

———. 1999. "Islanders in Space: Tongans Online." In *Small Worlds, Global Lives: Islands and Migration.* Russell King and John Connell, eds. Pp. 235–253. London: Pinter.

———. 2001. "'I' Is for Identity: What's in a Name?" In *Computer-Mediated Communication in Australian Anthropology and Sociology.* Theme issue. *Social Analysis* 45(1):67–80.

———. 2002. *Between Two Shores: Tongans Overseas.* Honolulu: University of Hawai'i Press.

Oboler, Suzanne. 1995. *Ethnic Labels, Latino Lives: Identity and the Politics of (Re)presentation in the United States.* Minneapolis: University of Minnesota Press.

Poirine, Bernard. 1998. "Should We Hate or Love MIRAB?" *The Contemporary Pacific* 10(1):65–105.

Small, Cathy. 1997. *Voyages: From Tongan Villages to American Suburbs.* Ithaca, N.Y.: Cornell University Press.

Smith, Deborah. 2000. "Tongans Sell Right to DNA Data." *Sydney Morning Herald,* November 23.

Statistics New Zealand. 1998. "Tongan People in New Zealand: Pacific Islands Profiles." Auckland: Government of New Zealand.

Tongan History Association Forum. http://www.pacificforum.com/kavabowl/tongahistory

U.S. Department of Commerce. 1993. *We the Americans: Pacific Islanders.* Washington, D.C.: Bureau of the Census, Economics and Statistics Administration.

Van der Grijp, Paul. 1997. "Leaders in Squash Export: Entrepreneurship and the Introduction of a New Cash Crop in Tonga." *Pacific Studies* 20(1):29–62.

Ward, Gerald. 1997. "Worlds of Oceania: Implications of Migration." In *Contemporary Migration to Oceania: Diaspora and Network.* Ken'ichi Sudo and Shuji Yoshida, eds. Pp. 179–196. JCAS Symposium Series 3. Osaka: Japan Center for Area Studies, National Museum of Ethnology.

# 9

# Global Imperatives and Local Desires: Competing Economic and Environmental Interests in Melanesian Communities

**Martha Macintyre**

*University of Melbourne*

**Simon Foale**

*The Australian National University*

Since the 1970s, people in Melanesian countries have been beguiled by the prospect of economic development that would enable them to participate in a world market economic system and so allow them to progress, to improve their standards of living, and to take their places as independent nations in a modern world. The forms of participation available to them and those encouraged by international capital entailed the extraction of natural resources—minerals, timber, and fish. In these enterprises, the developers provided the capital and the Melanesians provided the resources and sometimes the cheap labor. These projects were also viewed as ways of supporting emergent independent national governments through equity agreements, taxes, and royalties. "Development" referred to both the economic and the political processes facilitated by resource extraction by multinational corporations.

Globalization, like "development," is a loose term that describes or theorizes the processes whereby economic activities in these small islands are constituted within a broad financial and political landscape that is shaped by the distant, developed nations and their linked corporations. It encompasses the financial, economic, and political policies and practices of this imagined entity—the "global economy"—and incorporates the communication made possible through electronic media. But globalization also includes the emergence of global culture and the dissemination of knowledge, ideas, and desires. As with the economic imperatives, the cultural forces originate predominantly in advanced industrial societies and they include ideas that attempt to subvert the environmental destruction that has so often accompanied development. As Camilleri (1997:13) suggests, the flow of information and networking has also led to the emergence of an ideal "global civil society" focused on reconstructing and imagining world politics, and covering such issues as the environment, human rights, and the rights of indigenous minorities. So we here explore the idea of globalization as an economic phenomenon that includes the promotion of consumerism and as the influence of environmentalism as a cultural ideology.

The term "development" still has currency throughout these Pacific nations, and for those who live in remote rural communities, it retains its promise of material wealth, improved services, and links to the world beyond. Working in Papua New Guinea and the Solomon Islands, we constantly encounter villagers who want development and reproach their governments for failure to deliver its promised bounty. For them, development originates in the world beyond and comes when white men arrive to negotiate access to their land, their fishing grounds, their forests, and their minerals. Our discussion is based on our work in village communities in Papua New Guinea and the Solomon Islands over the period from 1995 to 2001.

In this chapter we examine the ways that people in the Melanesian communities where we have worked[1] engage with global issues in their desire for economic development. The agents of change are multinational companies whose interests are concentrated on the extraction of primary resources: minerals and timber. They are located in a global economy, and the values of their products are established in world markets for primary products. Their interests and aims are contested by international environmentalists who, like the shareholders, live in countries remote from those Melanesian communities whose resources are exploited in the interest of economic development. We therefore examine the responses to, and utilization of, environmentalist concepts by the Melanesians with whom we have worked. These are the Lihirian people from New Ireland Province in Papua New Guinea, where a large mining project

is located, and people from the Western Province of the Solomon Islands where the World Wide Fund for Nature (WWF) has operated a community resource conservation and development project for the last five years.

## HOW "GLOBALIZED" IS MELANESIA?

The economies of Papua New Guinea (PNG) and the Solomon Islands are mostly spoken of as being "in crisis." The countries are relatively rich in natural resources that are valued by industrialized nations: minerals, forests, and fish. Exploitation of these resources has depended on foreign investors: Australian, Southeast Asian, and multinational companies; and foreign aid projects, mainly from Australia and the World Bank (World Bank 1995). The problems of economic and environmental sustainability hang over all major economic activities in the region (Hunt 1997). The forces of globalization at present appear to be mainly negative—forests are destroyed, minerals are extracted, and fish stocks are depleted—with local people and the system of government not advancing in the ways they envisaged. The nominally democratic governments are unstable, dominated by self-interested and often corrupt politicians. Accountability, transparency, and assertion of the rule of law have been lacking in the governance of both nations.

The prolonged civil war in Bougainville in PNG during the 1980s and 1990s (May and Spriggs 1990) and the ethnic tensions between people from Malaita and Guadalcanal in the Solomons during 2000 have taken heavy tolls, economically, socially, and with respect to national stability. These conflicts must be seen as symptomatic of the uneven distribution of wealth, the failure of governments to protect the economic interests of their constituents, and the fragility of institutions that protect the rights of citizens. Both countries face problems of rising crime that discourage investment from outside and engender fear and disunity within the countries (see Roscoe, chapter 3).

While the gold, timber, and tuna gleaned from Melanesia do indeed find their way onto world markets, the flow of goods, ideas, and investments is not multidirectional. The impact of international money markets has been devastating on local currencies and, at the local level, this is experienced as constantly rising prices for basic items such as rice, fuel, and even soap. News of events in these countries filters into worldview occasionally, but mostly when there is a natural disaster such as the Aitape tsunami (see Welsch, chapter 13) or a social disaster such as the fighting and looting in Honiara. The eating and drinking habits of industrialized nations have enormous and visible impact on the daily lives of Melanesians: Beer brewing is by far the most profitable local industry (see Marshall, chapter 12), Coca-Cola is sold from roadside carts, and instant noodles can now be purchased in village trade-stores. Popular music reflects the influence of American culture, and even the disc jockeys affect the accents of Australians imitating Americans. In Melanesia, the claims of global "exchange" sound thin as the situation on the ground looks and sounds much the same as old-fashioned cultural imperialism.

## IS MELANESIA ON THE GLOBAL NETWORK?

The cultural dimensions of globalization are based on technological as well as economic foundations. One of the more notable benefits of globalization commonly lauded by its exponents is the increased interconnectedness of the planet by modern telecommunications wizardry, and the enormously increased access to information that this brings. E-mail and the Internet are probably the most conspicuous positive achievements of the globalization phenomenon. But, in common with most of the developing world, Melanesia has been excluded from the benefits of these advances in telecommunications. While it is possible, when working as a consultant to a mining company, or as a manager of an environmental NGO project, to be in regular e-mail and telephone contact with people all over the world, this access is unavailable to most Melanesian people. In remote areas,

only those who work for foreign companies or NGOs are likely to have a telephone. The crises that have beset the governments of Papua New Guinea and the Solomon Islands over the past decade mean that often government departments are unable to pay telephone bills and so have services disconnected. Maintenance of telecommunication systems is erratic. Repeater stations (in some areas the only concrete, visible, government service) in remote locations have been subjected to damage by vandalism by disgruntled landowners or rural people who resent being excluded from the benefits of these technologies. Cyclones, volcanic eruptions, and other natural disasters wreak havoc that is costly to repair. In short, telecommunication is expensive and unreliable in Melanesia.

Computer technology is similarly subject to problems that are not easy to fix quickly. There is a shortage of trained personnel to sort out technical problems, electricity supplies are not constant, and maintenance often requires sending machines to Australia or New Zealand or waiting for spare parts to be air-freighted at considerable cost. While the wonders of computer technology and the "shrinking of the globe" are touted in advanced industrial societies, in Melanesia communications remain a major problem. As Ward has demonstrated, the world is not shrinking evenly (Ward 1999). The cost of a three-minute telephone call from Australia or New Zealand to Europe or the United States in 2000 is a fraction of the amount charged in 1990, whereas the cost to Melanesian countries has hardly been reduced. The distances between the rich Pacific Rim countries may have "shrunk" but in many ways Melanesians have become more remote and dependent on the foreigners who are there "developing" the economy or providing aid. In the Solomon Islands by May 2001, the only government departments accessible by telephone were those funded by Australian aid projects.

Many expatriate employers and government departments bemoan the abuse of telecommunications by local employees. They claim often that disconnections occur because phone bills are impossible to budget for because people use them for personal calls. One of the main reasons for this is that ordinary people cannot afford the cost of a telephone connection at home, so that keeping in touch with kin is managed by those who are employed phoning each other at their place of employment. Working in places where phones and e-mails are available, it is clear that Melanesians embrace new technologies enthusiastically and would welcome the opportunities to be part of a smaller world, but at present the technology is too expensive.

The large companies selling equipment are all based in advanced industrial nations, and the profits made from computerization go back to these economies. Computers might give the illusion of "breaking down boundaries," but they are in fact more indicative of the gulf between the rich nations (where middle-class people have them as personal possessions at home) and the poor (where the majority of people do not even have reticulated electricity).

There is a dearth of qualified Melanesian people who can operate, service, and manage computer systems and inadequate educational facilities to provide them. Most are trained in the context of employment by foreign companies, NGOs, and aid-funded training within government departments. Telecommunication in Melanesia remains the province of expatriates. It is an area of dependency on foreign funding that is in some ways hidden. Enthusiasm for the possibilities of computer-based education, commerce, and communication in underdeveloped nations rests almost exclusively on the capacities of the technology and barely takes account of the economic incapacity of those nations (Goldstein and O'Connor n.d.; Toland n.d.). The government education departments cannot ensure primary education for all children, much less the tertiary education of the computer-literate. The infrastructure costs of telecommunication and computerization are immense in countries where all stock has to be imported, where communities are spread out over hundreds of islands, and where installation and maintenance present far greater practical difficulties than in advanced industrial nations. The fantasy of

computer technology and telecommunications as a democratizing force in undeveloped countries rests on ignorance of the extent to which all current telecommunication facilities, training, and use are dependent on foreign funding.

## Travel and Transport

Air travel, freight services, and other forms of communication are beyond the means of the majority of Melanesians. Those who travel internationally are usually people who are employed by foreign companies, who are funded by aid or other nongovernment organizations, or who are politicians. Internal travel is expensive and wages are low[2] so that even people who are employed in towns find it hard to make their annual trip home to their villages. A most telling effect of the high cost of air travel within Papua New Guinea is the fact that rural people increasingly find themselves unable to pay the cost of freighting a body home for burial when a relative dies in town. In 2000 there were pleas from the Port Moresby Hospital mortuary for relatives to remove their dead, as over two hundred bodies were awaiting collection. In most instances the village relatives had requested that the hospital allow them time to find the money, but they had then been unable to do so. All Melanesian cultures emphasize the burial of kin on clan land, and many people fear the consequences of not performing proper mortuary rites for the dead. Being unable to pay for a body to be sent home is perhaps the most poignant symbol of the relative poverty of rural people, in a country where the urban drift of employment seekers keeps rising.

## THE DESIRE FOR DEVELOPMENT

When gold was initially discovered on Lihir in Papua New Guinea in the 1980s, the local people were satisfied that it would prove the means whereby they would at last have development. Lihir is a relatively isolated island group to the north of New Ireland, and, apart from a coconut plantation on the main island run by an expatriate family, had experienced very little economic development prior to the gold mine. The pre-mining population of around 6,000 people mostly subsisted upon yams grown by swidden farming, and pigs, and did a small amount of fishing. Social life for most Lihirians was (and still is) very much focused around the traditional funerary feast cycle, or *Karot*. People typically spent a large proportion of their time preparing for and participating in these feasts, which were also a venue for competitive land transactions. Access to education, modern medicines, and transport was very limited on Lihir prior to the mining project. Although the island was accessible by air, it had no road, and very few locally owned motor vessels capable of interisland travel. The incidence of malaria was high, many women were chronically anemic, and a large proportion of them died in childbirth.

In spite of their enthusiasm for the mining project, the Lihirians drove a hard bargain and the landowners did not allow the project to begin until 1995. By that time they had negotiated an Integrated Benefits Package (IBP) that gave them 50 percent of a 2 percent royalty rate (far higher than any previous landowner group had received) and 30 percent of the national Special Support Grant to the provincial authority. The IBP also provided funds for a village development scheme to be managed by local-level government which provides one million kina (one kina = US$0.39 at the time of writing) each year for the construction of water supplies, houses, and other amenities in villages. The Lihir leasing agreement is significantly more responsive to local desires for direct benefit than those in other areas:

> It features a more holistic approach to compensation issues than precedents established at large mines. There are a mix of on-off and continuing payments for a wide range of issues, a significant equity share, the bulk of the royalties paid, and a range of infrastructure developments. The Lihir regime is now the benchmark within Papua New Guinea for such arrangements. (Banks 1998:62)

However, these agreements were forged with relatively little input from the national government, and the lack of state control over such negotiations warrants some comment here. Critics of globalization have interpreted the move to a global system as a progression from the economic development policies of the immediate post–World War II period during which international agreements were made covering trade and investment backed by the International Monetary Fund. This provided the "vehicle for the institutional stabilization under U.S. hegemony of the world capitalist economy" (McMichael 1998:100). McMichael argues that capitalist development encouraged and supported nation building so that national economic growth could be managed via macroeconomic policy. Globalization then represents the subsumption of national autonomy and an undermining of the capacities of nations to direct their own financial affairs. Large institutions such as the World Bank and the International Monetary Fund or foreign aid donor nations determine policies that were formerly national. It assumes that the period from 1945 onward was marked by a gradual strengthening of the state and the advancement of economic and human development through bureaucratically defined policies and controls.

While this might hold for some nation states, in practice the situation in Melanesian states has been marked by the weakness of the nation state (Dauvergne 1997a) and, in recent years, its failure to implement structural adjustments (see, for example, with respect to forestry, Dubash and Filer 2000) or to comply with the conditions imposed by these global institutions. Nonetheless, they have had to float their currencies, and the prices that are set for commodities in the world market affect every aspect of their economies.

The power of the landowner communities in resource development negotiations in Papua New Guinea illustrates the way that in Melanesia the process of globalization can in fact be one where the state has a relatively impotent role. But the Lihirian landowners' demands are not made in respect to their understandings of the value of gold or their nation's economy. In a survey of 120 major landowners in the special mining lease area undertaken in 1998, during which time there were demands for dividends and increased equity, only two could define these concepts and most simply said that they wanted more benefits from the mine. Some understood that the low price of gold would affect profitability, but they viewed the fact that the mine continued to pay wages as an indication that it "must be making money."

The understanding of the global economy that Lihirians (and many other Melanesians) have is partial. In meetings concerning their perceptions about the lack of anticipated cash benefits, some men explained that they wanted large sums of money in order to invest it in businesses. The ideas of capital and investment are understood only in broad terms. But they perceive the difference between themselves and foreigners in terms of a structural disadvantage that is explained in a variety of ways. For some, the wealth of expatriate businessmen and their capacity to invest in Papua New Guinea is attributed to "secret knowledge" that historically has been denied them on racial grounds. These views form part of so-called "cargo cults" and have been written about by many anthropologists (Lawrence 1964; Worsley 1968; Trompf 1991). There was a cargo cult on Lihir in the 1970s and some older people remain convinced that the mine is effectively the fulfillment of their prophesies. But most young people are skeptical of cargo cults while still adhering to what is called (usually disparagingly, and by white expatriates) a cargo cult mentality. This is used to imply that Melanesians expect "something for nothing" from foreign investors. In some instances it is the expectation that capital (especially in the form of equipment, see below on the portable saw-milling) will be provided by a foreign donor without any conditions and will become personal property. Sometimes it is simply a vague idea that any white person has privileged access to money and so might be persuaded to give some of it away.

Loans from foreign governments and various forms of infrastructural aid feed into a range of misconceptions about capital and investment. In 1999 and 2000, when a series of pyramid schemes were set up, hundreds of Papua New Guineans and Solomon Islanders lost millions of kina in schemes that promised returns of up to 100 percent in the first few months. Even the ombudsman (the government officer appointed to investigate individual complaints against public authorities), several members of parliament, and highly educated businessmen were apparently convinced that their money would multiply. It is hardly surprising, then, that some of the Lihirian villagers who had been given several thousand kina as compensation "invested" it in one such scheme, *U-Vistrac,* and were baffled when they lost everything. Interviews with them revealed that they believed that the money literally multiplied by magically reproducing itself in bank vaults. Arguments about free trade and global market forces are not only inaccessible to the majority of Melanesians but are also concerned with abstractions that would have little meaning to them anyway. This is a reflection of both the lack of secondary education and the lack of business opportunities available to local people.

In the case of the Lihir gold-mining project, the constant demands by landowners for compensation are based on two understandings of their rights. First, they assert that the resource is theirs and they are not being adequately paid for it. Second, they argue that the initial agreements for the mining lease merely gave access to the minerals, establishing a relationship with the mining company that is renegotiable at any point. Given the misunderstandings that prevail about the gold price and the apparent belief that the company has access to inexhaustible supplies of cash that it is withholding from Lihirians, it is difficult to see them as equally informed participants in any aspect of a globalized economic system. In view of the fact that Melanesians do not generally understand the mechanisms whereby their economy is drawn into the global sphere, much less have any control over its direction, it is hardly surprising that "the wealthiest countries and powerful transnational corporations have disproportionately captured the benefits of globalisation" (Australian Council for Overseas Aid 2001:116).

Lihirians do not believe that the PNG state owns minerals (see Ballard 1997). Many local people consider that they own the gold and that is why they can threaten to close the mine. The relationship that they see themselves in is one where the mining company pays what is effectively "rent" for the pit and for all land affected by the presence of the mine: the housing for expatriate employees, the camp site, the plant site, the roads, and the township built on formerly alienated land. The term "compensation" covers all payments received and incorporates in the Integrated Benefits Package such things as electrification, water supplies, the hospital, and the houses constructed as part of the village development scheme.

Environmental issues played a part in landowner demands, but the inspiration at this early stage did not come from Western environmentalism. Rather, people were acquainted with the impacts of pollution at the Bougainville and Ok Tedi mines and knew that the claims for environmental damage or destruction were another means of gaining compensation. During the first five years, all claims around environmental issues were directed at extracting payments of compensation. The regular payments for inconvenience and discomfort caused by dust, noise, and disturbance constituted a form of income. The main interest was in increasing the amounts of money paid or finding new forms of environmental degradation that might become the subject of compensation. Even the few Lihirians who have a more scientific understanding of the potential dangers of pollution and environmental destruction have concentrated on recompense rather than conservation or rehabilitation.

The lack of concern has been made clear in the context of several compensation claims presented by people from the relocated villages close to the mine. In the initial agreements, the mine agreed to revegetate the cleared area around the plant site so as to provide a buffer zone, shielding the village from dust, noise, and light emanating from the plant. At the end of the construction phase, when claims were made to increase and extend the payments for these forms of pollution, some of the villagers pointed out that the trees had not yet been planted. The company agreed to fulfill its obligations and to pay compensation until the trees were mature—by which time the roads would be tar-sealed and dust would be minimized. The villagers then argued against revegetation as they did not want to lose the source of income. That some of the leaders acted in bad faith on this matter is undeniable, as the demands for compensation for "light pollution" (which took the form of a lighter night sky) were accompanied by insistence on the provision of street lighting.

Much of Lihirian education on environmental issues has come from the mining company, as there has been no environmentalist NGO presence on Lihir. The mining company produced a video showing the system of tailings disposal that was shown in villages. A local woman provided narration in Tok Pisin and members of the environmental and community relations staff answered questions. Villagers observe the regular monitoring of sediment in rivers and off-shore and they are acutely aware of increased silt run-off into streams, associated with clearing. The mining company and the local government officers from the Office of Environment and Conservation conduct regular information meetings in villages, during which people are given information and the opportunity to air their concerns. But even in this context peoples' interest appears to be stimulated primarily by the prospect of compensation, so that when sessions are purely educative there is less interest.

## LOCAL AND GLOBAL UNDERSTANDINGS OF ENVIRONMENTAL IMPACT

The environmental destruction from the mining projects in Bougainville and Ok Tedi has been extensive, and the costs of reparation have proven very expensive for the companies involved. Mining companies have paid millions of dollars in compensation for damage caused by tailings disposal into the rivers and sea. The ecological damage in both places means that real rehabilitation of the affected areas is unlikely; Ordinary human exploitation of riverine resources is now unsustainable and the traditional uses of some areas are no longer possible. Many Papua New Guineans, especially those in mining areas, are aware of the potential for environmental damage and familiar with the large sums of compensation money paid to people whose rivers have been polluted. Their knowledge of other forms of pollution and environmental degradation derives mainly from radio and newspaper reports. In areas where people have some cash income, radios are a prestigious consumer item and people listen to news broadcasts. One effect of globalization is that the international news reports, which are delivered in minute "bites," do not explain or elaborate, but they attach names to phenomena so that people become broadly familiar with terms such as "pollution" and "acid rain." Many people interviewed during the drought of 1997 named the "El Niño effect" as a cause. Only those few who were employed in the mining company's environmental department were able to explain these concepts; the others who attempted often held bizarre views as to their meaning. But they were all aware of the monetary values of legal claims and of amounts paid.

In Papua New Guinea and other Melanesian countries, unlike industrialized countries in the globalized community, there are few public libraries and those that exist have few books that can be consulted on environmental issues. The only bookshops that deal in scientific books are located in universities in urban areas. Imported books are exorbitantly expensive. The national university libraries are underresourced. Ordinary people cannot surf the Web for information about pollution or acid rain, and even if they could, they usually lack the educational background to grasp scientific explanations. It is far easier to obtain fundamentalist Christian booklets that

decry evolutionary theory than it is to find out the meaning of biodiversity.

Villagers see compensation for environmental destruction as the main means of increasing their claims for compensation. This attitude compromises attempts to explain ecological processes or to develop a consciousness of environmental destruction as something that should be avoided. Five years after the opening of the mine, villagers seek and value knowledge of environmental issues mainly as part of a strategy for gaining more income from the mine. As the government Office of Environment and Conservation is inadequately funded, the officer on Lihir is unable to implement the education programs that could enable people to make informed decisions about environmental problems. The mining company environment and community relations sections are then left with the tasks of educating and informing people—an unsatisfactory situation which allows Lihirian suspicions to flourish.

The situation on Lihir is complicated and paradoxical. While the external, international pressures on the mining industry (from the globalized environmental movement) have ensured that large international companies monitor and attempt to contain environmental impact, the internal, national pressures are virtually nonexistent, and even when they exist, they are ineffectual. Lihirans, and indeed rural people throughout Melanesia, are as suspicious of environmentalists as they are of industrialists, but for different reasons.

All of the environmental organizations within Melanesia are dependent on international organizations for funding. Their aims, and the conceptualizations that they work with, are derived from Western European scientific understandings of the environment. Most oppose mining projects and favor small-scale forms of economic development. Lihirian people dismiss these ideas of sustainable development as part of a conspiracy to deny them access to the wealth they desire. They are well aware that a multinational company mining gold makes many times more money than a locally organized agricultural project. They recognize that having a mine enables them to establish links with the world beyond and provides services and infrastructure that would not be supplied by their government. They see their interests as best served by supporting mining and attempting to increase the benefits by demanding a greater proportion of the profits. Claims for environmental damage are one of their main levers in the struggle for an increased share. There have been a number of instances in recent years where these contradictory elements have come into play. An illustrative case is the infestation of the island by Giant African Snails (GAS).

Giant African Snails are an introduced, extremely destructive pest in Papua New Guinea. Before the mining project there were no Giant African Snails on Lihir, although they were endemic on the large neighboring island of New Ireland. Outbreaks occurred in three places on Lihir in 1998 associated with the development of local trade with New Ireland. Some came on local boats with vegetables that were brought across by villagers. Another infestation occurred in a village when some timber was brought over and a third in the area around the mining camp mess, probably brought in on imported vegetables.

At first, because the infestations were localized, the environmental section of the mining company responded with a concerted (and extremely expensive) attack. Chemical baits (in areas near the mining camp where they posed no danger to pigs or dogs), collection of all snails, and the clearing and burning of vegetation (to create breaks so that the snails were confined for easier detection) were employed successfully. Months passed without any further outbreak. At the same time an information campaign was waged involving the government agricultural officers and the conservation and environment department scientist, as well as company employees. They distributed brochures produced by the environment section and conducted information sessions with men and women in every village. Colored posters and warnings in Tok Pisin and Lihirian were displayed in all villages.

The government scientist produced a paper for the local-level government councillors informing them of the dangers in the following terms:

> The snail can act as a vector of human disease such as *eosinophilic* meningitis which is caused by the rat lungworm parasite, *Angiostrongylus cantonensis*. However, this creature can cause major socio-economic and environmental related problems within communities [as it causes] defoliation and stress on plants. Because of the GAS aggressive attack on vegetables such as "Aibika," corn, sweet potatoes, nutrition uptake by the local communities will be severely affected. Malnutrition may occur if there is a reduction in the nutrient uptake within communities. And this, as mentioned would pose tremendous socio-economic impact on the Lihir community. The snail if crushed and left out in the open can have a very unpleasant odour which is not acceptable to humans. (Giant African Snail (GAS) Infestation Management Plan for Lihir Group. January 1999, S. Keu)

The government scientist designed a quarantine and inspection program and requested funds for continued publicity to ensure that local people were diligent in detecting and ensuring the destruction of snails. No funds were designated. In this campaign, as in other areas, people, especially politicians, decided that the issue was one that could be dealt with by the mining company.

The responses of villagers provide an interesting case study of the ways that Lihirians think about environmental hazards. From interviews conducted as part of the independent social monitoring program later in 1999, it was clear that the information campaign had been successful. People were well informed. Of over 100 people interviewed, 90 percent recognized the picture of the snail and could explain its dangers to food crops. All were familiar with its voracious eating habits and over 80 percent mentioned two features that had been emphasized: that it multiplied very quickly and that to ensure that it was destroyed all snails and eggs should be burned and breaks in vegetation should be made to prevent the spread. About twenty people mentioned that they had seen the destruction caused by snails on New Ireland.

In spite of the high levels of awareness, villagers inside the special mining lease area said that they would not carry out any of the proposed measures as they were "too much work" and that they wanted compensation from the mine. Many of the villagers outside the mining lease area conceded that they would have to do the clearing and searching themselves, but most considered that the alarm was exaggerated. About 75 percent believed that the mine should eradicate the snails and compensate people if garden crops were affected. Although most admitted that the snails were unwittingly brought in by Lihirians themselves (or islanders bringing vegetables to sell on Lihir), they reasoned that "before the mine we did not get vegetables from other places," and as the trade in vegetables occurred in the context of the new economic situation, the mining company should be responsible.

The prevention and quarantine measures necessary to eradicate the pest and prevent further outbreaks were the province of government. The mining company has no authority over agricultural officers and has no rights to inspect or cordon land or set up quarantine inspections. No funds were allotted. The government conservation and environment officer, who was alarmed at the infestations, decided that the only way he could have any effect was to work with the members of the mining company environmental section. Over the two years following there have been further infestations in different villages. In some places local people deal with them in the ways that they learned from the information campaigns, but responses are erratic or desultory and the snails are gaining ground.

The reactions to the Giant African Snail outbreaks reveal much about local understandings of environmental damage. Many people are resigned to the fact that the snails will eventually be endemic on Lihir as they are elsewhere. Some even contend: "It doesn't matter now because we have the mine and we can buy our food." There is certainly no collective alarm or view of the problem as a potential disaster for the community. The outrage and distress that is invoked in environmentalist discourse, reflected in the government scientist's reports and requests to government, are born of a different view of the dangers and possible preventative measures. He is a Papua New Guinean with a university degree in environmental science. Lihirians are skeptical of scientific forecasts and disinclined to engage in activities that they consider futile.

But the fact that the presence of the pest might constitute grounds for monetary compensation should not be underestimated. The only Lihirians to become vehement about the risks the snail posed to sustainable subsistence gardening were those who were demanding compensation. The willingness of people to consign all eradication activities to the company cannot be viewed only as an expression of their cynicism about the government. It exposes a willingness to relinquish responsibility because they believe that the mining company has an obligation to Lihirians that encompasses many of the roles of the state. It is also a pragmatic reaction based on their observation that the mining company does work to rehabilitate environmental damage. As one Lihirian man expressed it: "The mine has money to do these things and we do not. If I work hard finding snails all I get is tired. They have the money to pay people to do this work. They should pay."

The view of environmental damage as primarily a means of getting money is expressed in a variety of ways (see Macintyre and Foale n.d.). For example, when several pigs died mysteriously in a village close to the mine, the government veterinary surgeon was called to do an autopsy. All villagers were invited to attend and those who were seeking compensation did so eagerly. As he dissected and examined internal organs, providing explanation of their condition to his audience, it became clear that the pigs had died from malnutrition, probably associated with parasite infestation. There were no signs of toxicity or disease. The people concerned were disappointed with these results and uninterested in dealing with the causes of the parasite problem. Many left before the autopsy was finished.

## HOW GREEN?

Lihirians, like many other Melanesians desirous of development, are phlegmatic about much of the environmental degradation entailed. Perhaps this can be attributed to the fact that for centuries they lived in a fairly unstable environment where environmental destruction from cyclones, droughts, and other natural disasters occurred, but things grew back again. The population densities of the islands were very low. Clearing for gardens was confined to lower areas and fallow periods were over ten years. As many other anthropologists have observed, most people in Melanesia do not think of their resources as finite (Van Helden 1998:242). But the rapidly expanding population of Lihir, even without a mine, presents a threat to subsistence sustainability employing traditional agricultural methods. Soil degradation associated with shortened fallows is recognized, but as with the pig deaths, such recognition would obviate the possibility of compensation claims and require that people change their system of agriculture. With low population densities, swidden systems were not destructive and ideas of conservation were unnecessary. Now, as gardens are cleared at higher levels, on steeper gradients, erosion occurs, faunal habitats are vanishing, and the lack of a conservational ethos is becoming perilous.

The large number of motor vehicles on the island means that rubber from discarded tires can be used to make sling shots. Whereas before rubber was scarce, the abundance now allows every boy to make a sling shot for killing birds (see Figure 9.1). Already the number of birds around the villages is diminishing. While some villagers observe this depletion, none who were interviewed considered this to be a problem, and some men were hostile at the suggestion that boys should be discouraged from wanton killing. They regarded the activity as traditional. Killing small animals with sling shots was a way that Lihirian men learned to hunt. People are aware that

**Figure 9.1**    Boys killing birds with sling-shots

hunting with more efficient, modern weapons has already obliterated some species of birds and marsupials on Lihir. Several old men reported that tree kangaroos were hunted to extinction when men acquired guns during the 1950s. Others observed that two varieties of cuscus (*Phalanger* species) that had been plentiful in their youth were no longer found on the island. While people did express regret at the loss of these animals from their diet, none appealed to any idea approximating a concern about maintaining biodiversity.

On Lihir, there is ample additional evidence that people comprehend the nature of environmental degradation, but, as we have discussed earlier, they see this as their main lever for obtaining further cash from the mining company in the form of monetary compensation. Spokespersons from the affected communities even begin negotiations by claiming damages and a continuing payment for inconvenience rather than a cessation of the degradation or pollution. They do not make claims against businesses that they see as lacking the capacity or will to pay. Thus, when businesses owned by local people dispose of oil and other dangerous wastes into streams, killing fish and plants, villagers do not demand compensation from them, nor do they insist that the companies clean up. Rather they argue that as such adverse effects are indirectly caused by the presence of the mine, then the mining company should both compensate and restore the damage. Even when they appear angry about an environmental problem, they demand money rather than rehabilitation.

## TIMBER EXTRACTION IN THE SOLOMON ISLANDS

For people who are living on small islands, where development opportunities are negligible, selling off their timber often appears to be a golden opportunity. The idea of becoming instantly rich is far more attractive than the alternatives of gradual, minimalist, and self-managed projects. Blandishments and promises of roads or school buildings that logging companies offer along with the immediate cash payments mean that voices of dissent—from those who foresee the long-term disadvantages and unsustainability of resource extraction—are silenced.

The weakness of the state sector in regulating the developers and the eagerness for instant cash, regardless of the long-term environmental implications, mean that the main restraints are those that are self-imposed by the large multinational corporations who are sensitive to the arguments of environmentalists based in the industrialized nations. As Colin Filer has observed, in these circumstances

> we should be less inclined to represent the multinational companies as unscrupulous and dirty beasts, and think of them instead as tame elephants performing in a circus without a ringmaster or wild elephants consuming the resources of a national park whose gamekeepers are all ivory hunters in disguise. (1998:174)

But if multinational mining companies are constrained now by environmental lobbying in their countries of origin, logging companies are not, and the environmental impact of logging in the Solomon Islands is already devastating.

## Local Responses to Overharvesting of Timber

At least half of the Solomon Islands national government's export revenue currently comes from logging. However, for most of the 1990s, timber has been harvested at rates well beyond what anyone regards as sustainable. AUSAID[3] forestry experts predicted in early 2000 that the average rate of timber extraction in the Solomon Islands is such that the commercially available timber resource would be exhausted in approximately ten years. In the Western Province the remaining resource will be exhausted in just four years.

The AUSAID forestry policy reform project that calculated these predictions was suspended as a result of the militia coup in June 2000. Despite the impending economic disaster predicted by the governor of the Central Bank, and the departure or bankruptcy of many businesses in the Solomon Islands as a result of the breakdown of law and order since the coup, logging appears to be continuing unabated. Log ships are still a common sight around the port of Gizo in the Western Province and at log ponds in many rural areas, and the number of new logging proposals reported each month remains high. Despite a drastic drop in tourism since June 2000, the Gizo Hotel has been able to stay in business primarily on sales of beer, a significant proportion of which is to landowners spending logging royalties.

While many people recognize the implications of such predictions, logging contracts continue to be signed, and timber continues to be harvested at unsustainable rates. Subversion of government-level attempts to rein in the number of operations and the harvesting rate of industrial logging appears to have been the norm in both PNG and the Solomon Islands (Forests Monitor 1996; Dauvergne

1997a, 1997b). A recent enquiry to the finance department of the central government revealed that the logging export revenue records for the Western Province since September last year (2000) have "disappeared." Despite widespread local acknowledgment of the plausibility of the gloomy predictions made by forestry experts, the pressure to log areas that are still forested is intense, and increasing. Landowners still seem to be desperate for a taste of consumerism, in any of its multitudinous forms, and appear to be willing to gamble their resources, and in some cases food security (Oliver 2001) to get it. Oliver describes in some detail the case of Viru Harbour on southeastern New Georgia Island (in the Western Province), where severe social and economic consequences have accompanied environmental impacts in the aftermath of logging. Viru Harbour has the dubious honor of being one of the first places in the Solomon Islands where food security has also been compromised by logging, with people having to pay for vehicular transport to get access to gardens they previously could walk to. This has placed significant handicaps on a subsistence workforce (mostly women) that has little or no access to the cash generated by the logging projects.

There is some evidence that women, as a group, are more critical of environmental destruction and actually oppose logging developments, but they are not included in negotiations and their opinions are rarely canvassed. Their opposition rests mostly on the fact that they are rarely beneficiaries of payments and that the flush of money is usually spent on beer and items that men consider prestigious, such as boat engines, trucks, or ostentatious clothing. Their subsistence work is also increased as men gain employment and disparage agricultural labor as "backward."

Convincing people to forego "free money" for a sustainable alternative (such as eco-forestry) that involves considerable labor, and often some risk, for a lower return is a difficult case to argue, as Filer points out for PNG:

> The basic problem here, which is both a political and an economic problem, is to persuade villagers to forsake a form of "economic dependency," in which they receive a substantial economic windfall without having to lift a finger, and opt instead for a form of "self-reliance" which will eventually yield to them a higher income in return for substantial labour input. Fighting loggers on this terrain is not an easy business. (1997:75)

Frustration at the lack of sustainable yet lucrative (and easy) alternatives to logging is not infrequently directed at NGOs charged with finding community-based solutions to this dilemma. The frustration is compounded by the fact that the environmental rationale for seeking an alternative to logging is based on logic which both is long term and draws on complex ecological arguments. Moreover, it is expounded by foreigners who, in the eyes of villagers, are not only already fabulously wealthy but typically come from countries that have already logged most of their forests. In this context, schemes for ecotourism which cater to the needs of foreign travelers, who want only to walk around in an "untouched tropical paradise" and appreciate its biodiversity, are viewed with some suspicion. The simplicity of village life that attracts jaded Europeans (see Silverman, chapter 20 in this volume) is precisely what drives discontented Melanesian youth into towns in search of work, money, and the excitement of urban existence.

The most common complaint about the Solomon Islands WWF Community Resource Conservation and Development (CRCD) Project from the landowners with whom it has worked (referred to as "partner communities") was that the project officers spent too much time and effort on "awareness" work, and not enough on assisting with alternative, income-generating developments. People are not interested in the conservation message if it is not accompanied by the real promise of an alternative development, preferably one that provides similar levels of cash to those offered by large companies, in the short term. The government also regularly makes this demand when engaging in debates with NGOs over the sustainability of large-scale resource extraction projects. The urgency that people feel for immediate cash frequently overrides all arguments about sustainability and long-term profitability.

Many of the strategies employed by both partner communities and the project's field officers (who are often members of those communities) comprise a form of "playing along" with the conservation agenda, which in the case of the WWF project comprised a set of stages, including "awareness," "resource planning," and "development." This sequence of activities was most often effectively interpreted as a series of hoops through which one had to jump in order to get at the reward, the development. When the "game" failed to deliver the final stage, or "pay-off," of the sequence, which was usually anticipated to be a boat, sawmill, sewing machines, house, or other such expensive capital assets to the community, its members inevitably voiced their annoyance very clearly to the project managers.

So despite the appearance, often supported by very colorful and convincing rhetoric, of landowners "buying" the conservation agenda, in reality they very rarely do. The experience of the WWF CRCD Project indicates quite clearly that most of their engagements with conservation NGOs are based on attempts to sequester some kind of substantial material or financial benefit from the relationship. This point is made nowhere more clearly than in meetings with WWF staff in which landowners have attempted to extort the project into delivering the "cargo" (sawmill, boat, whatever) by threatening to invite the loggers in if they don't (the so-called "gate-keeping" strategy that Filer [1996] writes about for PNG).

Similarly, when the project recently expressed interest in assisting landowners to improve fishery management in a chain of islands that are claimed by a number of different clans, the initiative only sparked arguments over ownership, and will probably have to be abandoned. Since the proposed work for the area only involved strategies to conserve turtles and improve fishery management, and thus yields, of artisanal invertebrate and fish stocks—something that would ultimately benefit existing users of the area (through long-term sustained income from fishing, as opposed to an immediate cash windfall)—the response is perplexing. This case further highlights the ambivalence landowners have toward concepts of environmental sustainability and husbanding of resources. It is possible that the landowners assumed that the work would culminate in the development of a tourist resort (WWF previously assisted with development of an ecoresort in the same area), ownership of which would obviously spark conflict.

Whether or not Melanesian landowners understand or believe the environmental rationale for eschewing logging, many are still driven by short-term economic goals. These are underpinned by the desire to participate in the global economy: to consume imported goods, to improve their standard of living, and to enjoy the way of life that they observe only foreign developers, aid advisors, and expatriates working for NGOs can maintain. Sadly, this is indeed a recipe for disaster in the medium to long term, as the environmental costs of logging and poor resource management accumulate and the majority of local income is rapidly used up on consumer goods imported or manufactured by foreign companies.

## CONCLUSION

Economic globalization is manifest in Melanesia in the processes whereby the natural resources of these independent nations are exploited by foreign, multinational companies whose primary commitment is to their shareholders. The commitment to development and the payments to governments and local people are part of the "trickle down" effect that world capitalism is supposed to generate. For the outsiders, that commitment rests on the need for timber, minerals, and fish, not on any altruistic desire for global economic equity. But as many of the opponents of economic globalization have pointed out, the fundamental asymmetries remain and the wealth accumulates in the industrialized nations while the people in undeveloped nations remain poor. At the same time, the global culture communicates and stimulates desires for consumer goods and ways of life that can only be fulfilled if people have the incomes of those who live in technologically advanced, urban industrialized societies.

From the perspective of Melanesia, the cultural values of environmentalism must be seen also as foreign and introduced rather than shared and global. They are in part the legacy of centuries of environmental destruction in Europe and America, which has generated the wealth that enables urban middle-class people to build and furnish their homes with rainforest timbers, dine on imported fish, manufacture their machines and adorn their persons with the minerals from developing countries. But just as these people became aware of the environmental impacts of industrialization long after their forests were gone and their waters polluted, so the desires of Melanesians for the goods that money can buy take precedence over the concerns for the natural environment that may be destroyed in the process of gaining them. It is unlikely, however, that in Melanesia the same level of resource overexploitation, with its accompanying ecological damage and loss of biodiversity, will bring about the affluence and equality to which Melanesian people presently aspire.

## NOTES

1. The authors have both worked in Lihir, Papua New Guinea as consultants, monitoring the social impact of the gold mining project there over a period of five years beginning in 1996. Simon Foale has worked in the Western Province, the Solomons Islands, as senior technical advisor, WWF Solomon Islands Community Resource Conservation and Development Project, and Martha Macintyre has evaluated a social impact study for a logging/oil palm project in that province.

2. In the Solomon Islands a tertiary-educated technical specialist working for a well-funded NGO can expect to earn around US$6,000 per annum. Government wages for the same qualifications and experience are considerably lower than this. Rural people rarely earn more than US$600 per annum, unless they are receiving logging or mining royalties.

3. AUSAID is the Australian Federal Government's international development assistance agency.

## REFERENCES

Australian Council for Overseas Aid. 2001. *Report from the Australian Council for Overseas Aid.* Canberra: Australian Council for Overseas Aid.

Ballard, Chris. 1997. "It's the Land, Stupid! The Moral Economy of Resource Ownership in Papua New Guinea." In *The Governance of Common Property in the Pacific Region.* Peter Larmour, ed. Pp. 47–65. Pacific Policy Paper No. 19. Canberra: National Centre for Development Studies and Resource Management in Asia-Pacific Project.

Banks, Glenn. 1998. "Compensation for Communities Affected by Mining and Oil Developments in Melanesia." *The Malaysian Journal of Tropical Geography* 29(1):53–67.

Camilleri, Joseph. 1997. "Making Sense of Globalisation." In *Alternatives to Globalisation.* J. Wiseman, ed. Pp. 6–14. Melbourne: Community Aid Abroad.

Dauvergne, Peter. 1996/7. Department of International Relations, RSPAS, ANU, Canberra.

———. 1997a. "Weak States and the Environment in Indonesia and the Solomon Islands." Paper presented at a workshop on Weak and Strong States in Southeast Asia and Melanesia. Australian National University, August 1997.

———. 1997b. "Corporate Power in the Forests of the Solomon Islands." Working Paper No. 1997/6. Department of International Relations, Research School of Pacific and Asian Studies, Australian National University, Canberra.

Dubash, Navroz K., and Colin Filer. 2000. "Papua New Guinea." In *The Right Conditions: The World Bank, Structural Adjustment, and Forest Policy Reform.* Frances J. Seymour and Navroz K. Dubash, eds. Pp. 29–58. Washington, D.C.: World Resources Institute.

Filer, Colin. 1996. "Compensation, Rent and Power in Papua New Guinea." In *Compensation for Resource Development in Papua New Guinea.* Susan Toft, ed. Pp. 156–189. Boroko: Law Reform Commission of PNG (Monograph No. 6). Pacific Policy Paper No. 24. Canberra: Australian National University, National Centre for Development Studies.

———. 1997. "Logging and Resource Dependency in Papua New Guinea: A Response to Henderson." In *Environment and Development in the Pacific Islands.* Ben Burt and Christian Clerk, eds. Pp. 69–77. Pacific Policy Paper No. 25. National Centre for Development Studies, Australia, and University of Papua New Guinea Press.

———. 1998. "The Melanesian Way of Menacing the Mining Industry." In *Modern Papua New Guinea.* Laura Zimmer-Tamakoshi, ed. Pp. 147–178. Kirksville, Mo.: Thomas Jefferson University Press.

Forests Monitor. 1996. Kumpulan Emas Berhad and Its Involvement in the Solomon Islands. Draft briefing document, April 22, 1996. London: Forests Monitor.

Goldstein, Andrea, and David O'Connor. n.d. "E-Commerce for Development: Prospects and Policy Issues." Paper presented at the International Symposium on Information Technology and Development Assistance, Tokyo, July 3–4, 2000.

Hunt, Colin. 1997. *Pacific Development Sustained: Policy for Pacific Environments*. National Centre for Development Studies, Australian National University. Canberra: Asia Pacific Press.

Lawrence, Peter. 1964. *Road Belong Cargo*. Carlton: Melbourne University Press.

Macintyre, Martha, and Simon Foale. n.d. "Transformations of Values: Land, Resources and Social Responsibilities in the Context of Development." In *Post-Colonial Virtue: Worth, Morality, and Modern Success in the Western Pacific*. Bruce Knauft and Martha Macintyre, eds. forthcoming.

May, Ron, and Mathew Spriggs. 1990. *The Bougainville Crisis*. Bathurst: Crawford House Press.

McMichael, Philip. 1998. "Development and Structural Adjustment." In *Virtualism: A New Political Economy*. James G. Carrier and Daniel Miller, eds. Pp. 95–116. New York: Berg.

Oliver, Pam. 2001. Caught Between Two Worlds: A Social Impact Study of Large and Small Scale Development in Marovo Lagoon, Solomon Islands. Greenpeace Pacific.

Toland, Janet. n.d. "Information and Communications Technology in the South Pacific." Paper presented at Brisbane Dialogue: South Pacific Futures, November 23–24, 2000.

Trompf, Gary W. 1991. *Melanesian Religion*. Cambridge: Cambridge University Press.

Van Helden, Flip. 1998. *Between Cash and Conviction: The Social Context of the Bismarck-Ramu Integrated Conservation and Development Project*. Port Moresby: National Research Institute.

Ward, R. Gerard. 1999. "Widening World, Shrinking Worlds? The Reshaping of Oceania." 1999 Pacific Lecture, Australian National University. Cited in *A History of Australia, New Zealand and the Pacific*. D. Denoon, P. Mein-Smith, and M. Wyndham, eds. Oxford: Blackwell.

World Bank. 1995. *Pacific Island Economies: Building a Resilient Economic Base for the Twenty-First Century*. Washington, D.C.: World Bank.

Worsley, Peter. 1968. *The Trumpet Shall Sound*. London: Paladin.

# 10

# Transnationalism and Transformation in Samoan Society

**Cluny Macpherson**

*University of Auckland*

## IN THE BEGINNING . . .

Some 3,000 years ago, ocean voyagers brought a proto-Polynesian language, culture, and society from Southeast Asia across the Pacific to the Samoan archipelago.[1] In that group, over some 3,000 years of continuous residence, a unique and distinctive culture, language, and society evolved. These differed in important respects from those from which they had evolved and those to which they later gave birth.[2] For many centuries, Samoan society, culture, and language were found only in the Samoan archipelago where they had developed, largely unchallenged by external agencies, until the eighteenth century when explorers, missionaries, and later commercial interests began to arrive in Samoa. There, culture, language, and society emerged into what has become known as *fa'asamoa:* the Samoan way. Specifically, the *fa'asamoa* embodied a worldview, lifestyle, and language.

The *fa'asamoa* was, however, for the Samoans, more than a culture: It was a sacred trust and the basis of the Samoan claim to autochthony within the islands and, indeed, within the Pacific (Turner 1983). Samoan history explained how a god named Tagaloa a Lagi arose in Samoa and moved across the Pacific, creating and colonizing islands as he went. The *fa'asamoa,* articulated, managed, mediated by its guardians, explained and justified social relations within that archipelago and became the authorized version of Samoan reality, albeit with some minor regional variations. It was so widely embraced within the group that early missionary, and later secular, ethnographers were able to speak with confidence about Samoan society as if it were a homogeneous social entity (Turner 1983; Kramer 1994).

## PRIESTS AND PROFITEERS

A form of Christianity was introduced into this relatively homogeneous society initially by a single agency, the London Missionary Society (LMS), and only later was this authorized version of religion augmented by those of the

**165**

Wesleyans and Roman Catholics. The impact of incorporation of the Christian religion into Samoan society, which occurred very rapidly between 1830 and 1850 under the joint oversight of the missionaries of the LMS and the *matai*, or leaders of Samoan society, appears to have been relatively uniform throughout the archipelago (Gilson 1970; Gunson 1976). Many families appear to have converted en masse and at the direction of their *matai* as the latter became convinced of the benefits that might flow from acceptance of the new doctrines (Macpherson 1997a). The result was that the postconversion Samoan society appears to have displayed a similar homogeneity, albeit one which now embodied a significant external cultural element.

Colonization too had an impact on Samoan society. Commercial interests followed the missionaries into Samoa in steadily growing numbers in search of cheap land and labor with which to produce such commodities as cotton and copra. The presence of colonists created personal, political, and commercial linkages with other parts of the world system, which in turn created markets for land, labor, and commodities that had previously only been exchanged and then only within matrices of relations defined by kinship (Macpherson 1999). Observation of the activities of colonial entrepreneurs raised the possibility of the individual accumulation of capital, its use to acquire control of factors of production, and the use of this control to expropriate surplus value for individual use. Even the impact of these activities was, however, relatively uniform. Traders and colonists settled throughout the archipelago and intermarried and traded with the Samoans around them (see Shankman, chapter 22) so that their activities, and the social and financial possibilities that they raised, were visible to all Samoans who were interested.

Colonization had an impact on the organization of Samoan society, but this was limited (Gilson 1970). Samoans remained the dominant population in Samoa and resisted external challenges to their autonomy and attempts to transform their society by successive colonial powers. The Samoans were able

to do this because the colonial powers and their representatives in Samoa at the time—Germany, Britain, and the United States—were divided among themselves and the Samoans were able to exploit these divisions. Only at the turn of the twentieth century when, through a treaty, the Germans gained sole control of the western part of the archipelago and the Americans gained sole control of the eastern part of the archipelago, did the Samoans confront united colonial powers. From there on the story focuses on the events in the larger, more populous western part of Samoa, which came under German control through the Treaty of Berlin. Even then, German attempts to restrict the power and influence of the Samoan dynasties between 1900 and 1914 met with only limited success, as did later New Zealand attempts between 1918 and 1961 (Boyd 1969a, 1969b).

From early on, Samoans insisted on their right to self-government and pursued that objective until they won independence in 1962. Ironically, while actively adopting the colonial powers' religious models and traditions, Samoans equally actively resisted their models of government where these threatened to encroach on Samoan political autonomy. The history of the *Mau a Pule* movement, which developed to resist first German and then New Zealand administrations' attempts to limit Samoan autonomy, reflects an on-going belief in the right and the capacity of Samoans to govern themselves by Samoan styles of government (Field 1984). Even on the eve of independence, the ever-civil Samoans were still protesting that "good government was no substitute for self-government."

On the eve of their independence, Samoans controlled 87 percent of the land area[3] of Western Samoa. Their distinctive language and worldview were enacted and reflected in their social, economic, and political organization and were taught formally in the nation's schools. The Samoan acceptance of, and commitment to, the *fa'asamoa* was apparent to the architects of Samoa's independence (Davidson 1967). The constitutional conventions, required under United Nations decolonization procedures, were preceded by consultations in each of Samoa's villages. They revealed a clear consensus for embodying central elements of tradition into the Constitution of the State of Western Samoa[4] (University of the South Pacific 1988) alongside elements of the "modern state," such as representative democracy and a permanent public service (Boyd 1969a, 1969b; Davidson 1967). On the eve of Western Samoan[5] independence, there was little doubt that Samoa remained both the cradle and the home of the *fa'asamoa*. The diaspora that was to follow independence would, however, have a profound impact on that certainty.

## A CENTER AND ITS NODES

The quickening pace of economic growth in larger states around the Pacific Rim soon began to have an impact on the states within it. As the New Zealand economy was transformed from primarily agricultural to one based primarily on industry, it faced shortages of domestic labor. The New Zealand government turned to her former metropole Britain for skilled labor and to her former territories in the Pacific for semi- and unskilled labor. In Samoa's case, the pull of the New Zealand economy, combined with rapid population growth, crop diseases, a decline in the prices of primary products such as cocoa and copra, and a cyclone in 1966, produced a steadily growing interest in out-migration.

The movement from Samoa to New Zealand began in the 1950s and gathered momentum until the early 1980s, when labor market demand declined (Bedford 1993, 1994). Around the same time, the demand for labor in the United States led to movements from American Samoa to Hawai'i and the west coast of the United States. Samoans with kin ties to American Samoa could use these to gain access to the United States and did so in steadily increasing numbers (Ahlburg and Levin 1990). Later on, Samoans who had settled in New Zealand discovered opportunities in Australia and were able to move relatively easily into that country (Va'a 1995), where they formed enclaves in Melbourne, Sydney, and then in Brisbane. Smaller Samoan communities

developed in Suva in Fiji where former students of the University of the South Pacific found work and spouses and settled, and in Noumea in New Caledonia where employees and former employees of the South Pacific Commission found work and later settled.

## ENCLAVE FORMATION

The result of this period of out-migration was the growth of significant Samoan populations beyond Samoa (Ahlburg 1991). Enclaves grew in cities in New Zealand, Australia, and the United States where opportunities for unskilled and semiskilled work were available. The process of transnationalization of kin groups and of Samoan culture had commenced. Kin corporations, formerly concentrated in a single village, were now effectively transnationalized, with "centers" in the village of origin and "nodes" in one or more overseas enclaves. During this period, the term "transnational kin corporation" was coined for these entities which, as we will see below, acted like commercial transnational corporations. Much of the subsequent migration involved people moving down the migration chains, which linked more and more Samoan villages (centers) to enclaves (nodes) that were forming in these metropolitan sites.

Many of those who moved, or were sent, to the enclaves abroad initially were younger, often single, people who would contribute to the family by remitting a part of their earnings to their families in the islands (Macpherson 1997b). In this respect, families who arranged for their young abroad were acting rationally. Recent crises in the Samoan economy had made Samoans acutely aware of the risks of concentrating all of the families' resources in one place. This was particularly true since wages were low, commodity prices were falling, plant diseases such as bunchytop struck the banana crop, insect pests such as the rhinoceros beetle had reduced coconut production, and periodic natural hazards such as cyclones could hit families' earnings without warning and disrupt their plans. Having young wage earners abroad diversified families' earning streams and reduced their dependence on high-risk activities. Having family members in *several* locations abroad diversified earning sources and reduced risk levels still further.

Families, using intelligence from migrants abroad, periodically surveyed risks and returns in various enclaves and encouraged others already abroad to relocate in places in which returns were found to be higher and risks lower. This risk evaluation process often involved a pioneer who moved to a new location or to a new area of employment in which higher wages and better conditions of work existed. The pioneers established themselves and then publicized the new opportunities. Families and parents encouraged, and in some cases directed, new migrants and other migrants to these sites there to take advantage of newly discovered and more profitable opportunities (Pitt and Macpherson 1974; Macpherson 1978).

For example, within families in American Samoa, young men and women were encouraged to join the U.S. military because job tenure was assured, wages were higher, uniform and board were provided, education could be obtained without loss of earnings, and military training in certain areas was portable. In another, from what was then Western Samoa, young male migrants in New Zealand were encouraged to join the construction crews that were building hydroelectric dams in rural areas. Because crews worked long hours, wages were high, isolation allowances were paid, and accommodation and food were provided free, there were few distractions on which to spend wages, and continuity of employment was more or less assured. Within a third family, young migrant women in New Zealand were encouraged to shift from Auckland to work in fish-processing factories in the provincial cities where higher wages could be earned because of the piece work and bonus payment schemes, and housing costs were lower than in the cities. In encouraging young people to move to better employment, these transnational kin corporations were doing what any prudent transnational corporation does, which is to make sure that, within certain constraints, its human and physical resources are employed as effectively and as profitably as possible.

If this analysis depicts Samoans as calculative and instrumental, it is because, in relation to risk and return, they are necessarily so. The material aspirations of individuals and the demands of Samoan custom are infinite and the sources of capital to meet these are not. The author, who had visited many of the enclaves, was, throughout the 1960s and 1970s, party to many discussions in which the risks and returns available in various places were formally canvassed and modeled by families. They became the basis of decisions to send people and advice to people already abroad.

It was always assumed that this strategy would ensure a stream of remittances from these expatriate nodes to the center, which was, of course, the village of origin in which the family's landholdings, its chiefly title, and the core of its members resided. The deployment of the center's resources was at first intended to generate funds and resources to permit the center to engage more effectively in social, economic, and political affairs in the island setting within which the family was centered and in which it derived its status and identity. The movement of people to the nodes was a means to an end and that end was, for many *matai* and families, the aggrandizement of the family and title and, indirectly, the village with which these were connected. As people left the islands, families held farewell celebrations for departing migrants at which the emigrant, and indeed all those present, were reminded publicly of the nature of the relationships which connected the migrating individual and his or her family and village.

Migrants were reminded that they were privileged to be able to serve, or *tautua,* the family, the village, and the church. They were reminded that from day of birth they had "eaten the sweat" (*'ai le afu*) of those members of the family who had labored in various ways to provide the family with an identity of which it could be proud, and from which the migrants derived personal identity, pride, and the benefits of association. People were reminded that the village had provided a home, schooling, an identity, and the benefits of association with a place and a history. They were reminded that they had derived spiritual guidance from the church and educational benefits from the pastor's school. The message in all of this was clear.

A person who had derived all of these benefits from the family, village, and church had an opportunity, and indeed an obligation, to recognize and to repay his or her debt to them. This request was not considered remarkable. In the families' eyes, those who went abroad remained part of the family and were bound to serve the family and the title. In the eyes of the *fono a matai,* or village council, expatriate villagers remained part of either the *'aumaga,* or men's association, or the *'aualuma,* or women's association, which together provided the *malosi o le nu'u,* or strength of the village. Those who remained in Samoa repaid their debt to the family, village, and church through service in the village and the plantation. Those who went abroad simply served the family, village, and church from workplaces in another location. Service was, for many, the primary reason for going abroad.

To ensure that this commitment was maintained, new migrants were sent to the households of older migrants with established records of service to the family and village. There they resided with established migrants on whom they depended for social capital, and with younger, more recent migrants who were committed to support those whose sweat they had eaten. In many cases, they worked and worshiped with people who shared similar histories and biographies and were similarly oriented (Macpherson 1997b). In these circumstances, it is hardly surprising that within these enclaves, *fa'asamoa* became the operating culture in the private sphere and in some places in the work sphere (Macpherson 1997b; Ngan Woo 1983).

This commitment to the center lay behind the steadily growing volumes of remittances in cash and kind that flowed from the nodes to the center throughout the 1960s, 1970s, and 1980s. The migrants served their families by building and furnishing new, larger homes from permanent materials, establishing stores and providing the goods to stock them, and by buying them vehicles, boats, and outboard motors and agricultural equipment (Macpherson 1992). They invested in their families' human assets by paying for school fees and additional musical and sporting instruction for kin, and by supporting others who were chosen to continue their education in New Zealand. They also contributed to parents' and families' attempts to enhance their status within the village by supporting their bids to obtain chiefly titles and parliamentary seats (So'o 1998).

They remained attached to their villages of origin, and their remittances supported villages' programs to build new facilities and to rebuild older facilities. Expatriate villagers' remittances built and rebuilt schools, dispensaries, and women's committee houses and provided such assets as fish traps, access roads, and electricity generating plants. They did this through periodic direct levies for specific projects, by underwriting the costs of visits by villages' visiting fundraising groups and then supporting them, and by organizing fundraising activities. Expatriate villagers also rebuilt village facilities after the cyclones that periodically devastated them.[6] Expatriate villagers also supported churches in their villages directly, by building, maintaining, and, in some cases, rebuilding the churches and pastors' houses, providing new organs, pews, and decorations, and, indirectly, by supplying remittances which were used by parents and families to recruit and support their religious leaders.

The center continued to dominate the nodes. Migrants continued to look to the center for direction in a range of matters and for organizational models. Migrants continued to return to the island to be married and buried, to seek chiefly titles and health treatment for illnesses that did not appear to respond to Western medicine. Throughout this period it was not unusual for wedding parties of twenty to thirty people to return to Samoa to hold weddings in villages where the majority of their families still resided. Similarly, it was not at all unusual for parties of migrants to return to Samoa with the body of a person who had died abroad to hold the funeral and associated ceremonies in Samoa and to bury the person in their family cemetery in their village of origin.

When, for various reasons, it was not possible to return to Samoa, key people from the center were transported to expatriate enclaves to plan and manage a range of ceremonies. Thus, it was not unusual to attend weddings in Auckland to which large numbers of the bride's and groom's families from Samoa (often including the families' *matai*) had traveled to plan, organize, and attend. This ensured that the conduct of formal events in the enclaves met the expectations of those at the center, whose approval in these matters the migrants considered all-important.

The volume of remittances grew steadily as more young, often single, migrants continued to return significant parts of their earnings to repay those whose sweat they had eaten. In this way they participated vicariously in the society into which they had been born, within which they had spent their formative years, and from which their personal and collective identities were derived (Ahlburg 1991). But this could not continue forever.

## FROM NODES TO CENTERS

As the populations in the nodes grew and matured in the late 1960s and early 1970s, new dynamics came into play. It became increasingly clear that these were no longer temporary settlements of people who would eventually return to Samoa. As goods and cash from abroad fueled competition between families and villages in Samoa, the demands for support from family and village escalated and more and more migrants were sent abroad to meet them. The opportunities presented by life in enclaves exerted their own pull and many who had planned to return to Samoa postponed, and eventually abandoned, their plans. Many chose instead to make periodic visits home for short vacations and family celebrations of various sorts. Many of those

who did return to settle permanently found that transition more difficult than they had anticipated and returned to New Zealand, Australia, or the United States after only a few years abroad. Albert Wendt's novels provide some delightful insights into the sorts of challenge that these transitions presented (Wendt 1973). It was beginning to be clear that the migrant enclaves were becoming permanent, or at least semipermanent, expatriate settlements.

As young migrants married, bought homes, and formed families their interests changed. As critical masses were reached in these enclaves, the earlier ad hoc forms of social organization, which depended heavily on direction and leadership of people from Samoa, were simply inadequate for the new setting. It was no longer possible, or practical, to depend on the center for leadership of the increasing numbers of activities and life crises, *fa'alavelave*, which were occurring in the steadily growing enclaves. Many Samoan settlers felt somewhat excluded and alienated from the institutions of the predominantly European host communities, which were, at best, indifferent to them and, at worst, overtly racist (Trlin 1972). They began to replicate the Samoan social institutions to which they remained committed in a new community to which they were becoming increasingly committed (Ngan Woo 1983; Pitt and Macpherson 1974). They built their own churches, and established parallel family and village organizations abroad. In the cases of village and family structures, this involved increasing the autonomy that these expatriate branches enjoyed over planning and decision making. These would, however, differ in various ways from those on which they were modeled.

While the principles that underpinned these replications remained similar, the ways in which they were managed and enacted were modified to varying degrees.[7] The beginnings of this process of transformation were becoming apparent in enclaves as far apart as Auckland (Macpherson 1974), California (Ablon 1971; Rolff 1978), Hawai'i (Franco 1990), and Washington state

(Kotchek 1978) by the mid-1970s. The transformations reflected the new social and economic realities that confronted Samoan migrants in different places. So, while all Samoan enclave communities were beginning to change, not all were changing in the same direction or at the same speed and there were clear differences in the ways communities were organized, as a study of three such enclaves showed (Fitzgerald and Howard 1990).

While the term *fa'asamoa,* or Samoan language, custom, and practice, was retained to describe these emerging variants, Samoans were able to, and did, characterize the differences between practices in Samoa and in the various Samoan nodes that they had visited. Auckland-based Samoans who returned from visits with Samoan relatives in Los Angeles would comment on the differences in the *fa'asamoa* they had seen in the United States and vice versa. Samoans from Carson in California would, in turn, comment on the difference between their practices and those of Samoan communities that had formed around military communities in Seattle. Samoans in the community that had formed around the Pearl Harbor naval base in Hawai'i (Forster 1954) would discuss the differences between their *fa'asamoa* and that of their nearby neighbors at Laie who had formed a community near the temple of the Church of Jesus Christ of Latter Day Saints (Stanton 1978). Some would even speculate on possible causes of the observed divergence.

It seems likely that a set of generic factors influenced changes in all of the enclaves, but that individual factors assumed different significance in various places. From this point on, the chapter concentrates on the process as it occurred in the largest of these nodes to illustrate the processes that were at work. Some of these factors, observed in the New Zealand enclave, are set out below. While it is not possible to say with certainty that all of these factors are present in all Samoan migrant enclaves, it seems highly probable that they will be, because they are byproducts of a common set of structural factors and dynamics.

## SAMOANS IN NEW ZEALAND

The migrants who began to assume leadership roles in the enclaves had, in many cases, left the island as adolescents and young adults. While many had lived in rural villages and were familiar with the principles of *fa'asamoa,* not all were conversant with the detail that comes from exposure to, and direct personal participation in, the full range of activities and processes over an extended period of time. Some more commonly enacted institutions, such as weddings, *fa'aipoipoga,* and funerals, *oti,* had clear and relatively fixed forms and requirements which were well understood and could be relatively easily replicated. The language, forms, and requirements of less commonly enacted ones, such as chiefly title installations, *saofa'i,* and ceremonial apologies, *ifoga,* were not always as readily available and a certain amount of improvisation was called for as young migrants sought to replicate all of the institutions without all of the knowledge necessary. In discussions on these occasions, aspiring leaders canvassed a range of possibilities in search of the correct one. This often included long, and expensive, telephone calls to Samoa to locate people who could provide clues, and the appropriate content and structure of speeches which were considered necessary for the occasions. In the absence of a clearly correct option, they would assemble a composite. In other cases, where key people or props were not available, elements would either be modified or omitted.[8]

Some degree of variation was possible because many of the migrants who would attend, and judge, these events shared similar backgrounds and were themselves uncertain about the correct language, structure, and forms of the ceremonies. If those who had left the village as adolescents were uncertain, their New Zealand–born children were even more so. The latter's confidence and competence in the Samoan language, in which linkages between the actors and elements of the processes and institutions were linked, was often limited and they had not been exposed to the activities as frequently as their parents had.

Some institutional transformations were the consequence of the increasing amounts of resources which were available and which circulated in these expatriate communities (Macpherson and Macpherson 1999). These led in some cases to the expansion and variation of a form until it was qualitatively different from that from which it had sprung. For instance, between death and the formal funeral service of chiefs in Samoa, there was a period during which women of the village visited the chief's family and sang songs and hymns to comfort the deceased and his or her family. This practice was known as the *osilagi* and those who performed it were known as the *'au osilagi*.

In New Zealand, this simple and informal ceremony has been transformed over time into an event known as the family service. At the family service, which is now usually held in a church, choirs from congregations to which members of the deceased's family belong, groups of associates, and coworkers of the deceased sing hymns, outline the deceased's life, and give eulogies and testimonials. The number of choirs and ministers who attend these occasions, and the status of those who address the family service, reflects on both the deceased and the family, and well-attended ceremonies reflect significant social prestige on the sponsoring family. All those who appear at a family service must be thanked appropriately for their contributions to the dignity of the occasion, which requires a considerable pool of food, cash, and fine mats, *'ie toga,* which are the traditional currency of formal Samoan ceremonies (Schoeffel 1999). These items are distributed to representatives of those groups who appear and who, in turn, redistribute them amongst the groups' members. Such expensive ceremonies are only possible because the migrant families can afford to underwrite such occasions. Thus the *osilagi,* a ceremony once reserved for chiefs, has been almost entirely eclipsed by the family service that is now routinely held at the death of many adults and even some children. The original *osilagi* has been displaced by a ceremony intended primarily for the family's social and political benefit.

A certain amount of organizational variation was necessary to incorporate the increasing numbers of non-Samoans who started to attend family and village activities. These people were usually spouses of Samoans who wanted, or were encouraged by partners, to become involved in and to attend the activities of their family and village. Some of the willingness to accommodate these non-Samoans was born out of Samoan sensitivity to their guests. In Auckland, for instance, a family would go out of its way in choosing a venue, providing extra comforts and an often intrusive translation of a ceremony for the European spouse and elderly parents-in-law of a man who was about to receive a family title. At the *'ava* ceremony[9] which followed, the ceremonial order was varied to allow the father-in-law and brother-in-law to participate in the ceremony. These accommodations were made out of respect for both the new titleholder's spouse, who supported his commitment to the family, and her parents who were entitled to consideration because of their age.

In other cases, the variations were born out of a purely pragmatic need to retain the non-Samoans' valuable support and to gain access to their human capital and disposable income. For instance, families replaced their long-standing Samoan language bingo games with bilingual games to allow family members' European and Maori workmates and partners to play, to increase the returns from the bingo evenings which they held to raise funds for family and, occasionally, village projects.

In still other cases, the variation was necessary to accommodate both the new circumstances and the increasing numbers of family members who did not speak Samoan fluently and could not otherwise actively participate in the activity comfortably. For instance, one family became concerned that its New Zealand–born children were unaware of the kinship linkages between branches of the extended family and were at risk of forming romantic attachments with relatives with whom relationships would have been inappropriate. This family decided to hold annual family reunions at which members of the kin group met one another, entertained each other, and ate together and during which family rolls were called so that people recognized the names and faces of people to whom they were related. The family also decided that if the events were to serve the purpose for which they were intended, significant parts of the ceremony would have to be performed in English if they were to be clear to and were to engage their growing New Zealand–born cohort. This, in turn, meant that the discourses that had previously given meaning and justification to the symbols and forms were augmented by others that had not traditionally been part of them. Such events were unnecessary in Samoa because continuous coresidence, the sociopolitical significance of kinship in everyday life, and sporadic meetings of the entire family, *aiga potopoto*, ensured that members of a family in Samoa typically recognized more of their kin and knew a great deal more about kinship.

Perhaps the greatest force for transformation was the increasing number of people who wished to take part in formal activities and had the resources to claim the right to do so. More and more people had access to *'ie toga* or fine mats[10] and cash which they would not have had in Samoa. People who, in Samoa, would have been represented by their family's *matai* were, in New Zealand, able to attend in their own right. New categories of people, including workmates, fellow worshipers, sports team members, and drinking companions had to be accommodated, entertained, and given presentations on all sorts of occasions from baptisms through funerals. Families organizing these events were caught between the need to gain access to these peoples' resources to supplement their own, and the need to recognize, feed, and return gifts to these people.

The *matai* who officiated at ceremonial activities in New Zealand found themselves confronted with larger numbers of people, many of whom had no traditional right to be formally recognized and acknowledged on occasions such as funerals. The families found themselves in a dilemma. While the presence of large numbers of these new guests reflected well on the deceased and the family and increased their stock of fine mats and cash, their presence also increased the costs of hospitality, the complexity of the ceremony, and the amount of time required to complete the ceremony. After three days of officiating at a funeral in New Zealand, one older *matai* observed that in Samoa, he knew exactly who would come to a funeral, the bases of their claims to be present, and the appropriate honorifics and treatment for them. He compared that situation, somewhat caustically, with the New Zealand one in which, he observed, all sorts of people, including untitled nobodies, turned up with fine mats they had no right to, making speeches and claiming treatment to which they were not entitled. He objected to the fact that these people had to be treated with respect, fed, and given gifts.

A certain amount of the increasing variation arose out of the need to extend *fa'asamoa* to incorporate events which were not typically commemorated in Samoa. In the absence of an established formulae for these events, some experimentation was possible but over time certain formulae became accepted as convention and the variation was replaced by elaboration of the chosen form. When, for instance, students began to graduate from universities in the mid-1970s, no formulae were available within *fa'asamoa* for those graduates' families who wished to commemorate these occasions. Families sought to incorporate a range of elements including the sharing of food, a service of thanksgiving, a recounting of the graduates' life history, testimonies from teachers and other key figures in graduates' lives, speeches of thanks to family and friends by graduates, reaffirmation of their commitment to their family and culture, and presentation of gifts of fine mats and food to those who had contributed in various ways to the success.

Initially, there was considerable variety in the ways in which these various elements were combined in graduation ceremonies. The elements and the order in which they were combined varied from graduation to graduation. A lot of discussion between those who attended graduations, and discreet inquiries of non-Samoan guests during and after the ceremonies, resulted over time in a move toward a particular format and the amount of variation declined. Over time one could be increasingly confident that a graduation done according to *fa'asamoa* would contain certain key elements in a certain order by key people.

New events were created in the name of celebration of the practices of *fa'asamoa*. In Samoa both men and women were tattooed. Men typically received an extensive tattoo, which covered the area from lower back to the knees, and was known as a *pe'a* in late adolescence. Women similarly received a series of tattoo markings on the front and rear of their thighs and knees (Marquardt 1899). The tattoos were designed to make their wearers more attractive and were, because of the pain involved in the process, also symbols of individual courage. In Samoa, these tattoos were apparent to people as they went about their work in the village and during dances and celebrations where they were routinely exposed. In New Zealand, the combination of a cooler climate and different forms of dress mean that those who have undergone the pain have fewer and fewer opportunities to display their tattoos than they would have had in Samoa. Now, in New Zealand, there are formal showings and competitions at which Samoan men and women discuss and display their tattoos at a public gathering in a nightclub at which judges reflect and comment on the tattoos.

Tattooing has also been transformed in other ways. At one time, some women received a traditional tattoo, applied with traditional hammer and bone combs, around their wrist or on one hand. At some time, however, a male U.S. Peace Corps volunteer wanted a tattoo to recall his stay in Samoa but wanted it where it could be covered at certain times. He was given a tattooed band around his upper bicep that became known as a *taulima*. Unlike others whose tattoos symbolized family connections, this peace corpsman had no Samoan kin and apparently chose a pattern for its aesthetic properties. This new tattoo form has, however, become an increasingly common symbol of ethnic, as opposed to family, identity among young Samoan men and

women living overseas. These forms are now chosen, often for their aesthetic properties, from a range supplied and applied by commercial tattoo artists using a modern machine tattooing technology. Those who bear them, however, regard them as a Samoan art form and an overt display of their Samoan identity.

## TRANSITION

Those who had migrated from Samoa were generally disposed to support *fa'asamoa,* albeit to different levels and in different ways (Macpherson 1994). On occasions, disaffected migrants would withdraw their support, and indeed some withdrew completely (Macpherson 1984), but most were conscious that their actions also reflected on their families. They were conscious that their disengagement would reflect badly on their parents and immediate kin and participated, even when they were personally uncomfortable or angry, out of concern for the social honor and prestige of the collectivity to which they belonged.

If one thing characterizes the transformations described above, and others, it is that they represented attempts to ensure that *fa'asamoa* not only survived in the new milieu, but that it was adapted to ensure that it remained relevant to life in that enclave. Thus, for instance, the number of speakers who spoke at funerals was reduced because of fear that elderly *matai* who were required to speak at the graveside in the cold wet weather of New Zealand would become ill. The number of speakers at the *lau'ava* or wake which followed was also reduced because the halls in which they were held were owned by churches or companies and were hired for finite periods of time. The time allocated for various parts of the funerary rites was shortened simply because those who were centrally involved were generally employed in the wage economy and the amount of time that they could take off work was limited.[11] Without these modifications, the funerary rites might have lost support among the people. With them, Samoan funerary rites survive, albeit in different ways shaped by different constraints.

## THE GROWTH OF A CRITICAL MASS IN THE NODES

As the New Zealand labor market shrank and the numbers of Samoan in-migrants declined, internal population growth accounted for most of the increasing Samoan population (Cook et al. 2001). By 1996, for instance, New Zealand–born Samoans comprised nearly 60 percent of the Samoan descent population of 101,000 in New Zealand and this trend is set to continue.

The Samoan migrant population can be divided into New Zealand–born and overseas-born components (see Table 10.1). Such simple dichotomies, however, do not present the full picture. Significant numbers of overseas-born Samoans have been resident in New Zealand for relatively long periods of time: 33 percent had been present for more than twenty years and a further 26 percent had been present for between ten and nineteen years. Demographic trends suggest that over time the influence of New Zealand–born and educated will continue to increase. The New Zealand–born component of the Samoan population became an increasingly significant influence on the form that *fa'asamoa* would take in the 1990s and beyond. The growing number and significance of Samoan migrants' New Zealand–born children changed the equation by creating a critical mass: a group that is increasingly influential because of its size and economic significance and one that is increasingly critical of elements of the culture of their parents' generation. The influence of these New Zealand–born Samoans derives not simply from their numerical size and wealth but from their upbringing and education, which has freed, and some would say encouraged, them to reflect on and criticize elements of *fa'asamoa*. I wish to deal with each of these elements separately.

Many New Zealand–born and educated Samoans differ in significant ways from their parents. Ninety percent of Samoan-born people aged 5 and over living in New Zealand reported that they could speak Samoan;[12] that compares with only 46 percent of New Zealand–born Samoans (Statistics New Zealand 1998). On the other hand, the New Zealand–born typically possess more social capital as a consequence of their formal education and familiarity with the language and culture of New Zealand society. New Zealand–born Samoans are more likely to have higher formal qualifications (Macpherson et al. 2000), to have some form of postschool education (Statistics New Zealand 1998), to be employed (Statistics New Zealand 1998), and to be earning higher incomes (Macpherson et al. 2000).

**Table 10.1**  New Zealand and Overseas-Born Components of Samoan Population Resident in New Zealand in 1996

| Age Gp (Yrs) | NZ–Born (%) | Overseas-Born (%) | Total(%) |
|---|---|---|---|
| 0–4 | 26 | 2 | 15 |
| 5–9 | 21 | 3 | 13 |
| 10–14 | 14 | 6 | 11 |
| 15–24 | 23 | 14 | 19 |
| 25–34 | 11 | 23 | 16 |
| 35–44 | 4 | 22 | 12 |
| 45–54 | 1 | 16 | 7 |
| 55–64 | 0 | 8 | 4 |
| 65+ | 0 | 6 | 3 |
| Total | 100 | 100 | 100 |

*Note:* The overseas category includes all people of Samoan descent born outside of New Zealand. Most of those will have been born in Samoa, but increasing numbers have been born in Samoan enclaves in Australia and elsewhere.

*Source:* Statistics New Zealand 1998.

**Table 10.2**    Ethnicity of the Samoan Population Resident in New Zealand

| Reported Ethnicity | Numbers | Percentage |
|---|---|---|
| One response only | | |
| Samoan only | 64,395 | 63 |
| Two responses only | | |
| Samoan and other (nec)[a] | 9,312 | 9 |
| Samoan and NZ European | 7,987 | 8 |
| Samoan and other Pacific Island | 5,032 | 5 |
| Samoan and NZ Maori | 4,235 | 4 |
| Three responses | | |
| Samoan/NZ European/Maori | 2,574 | 3 |
| Samoan/NZ Maori/Other | 2,500 | 3 |
| Samoan/NZ European/Other | 2,063 | 2 |
| Samoan/Other Pacific/Other | 1,696 | 2 |
| Samoan/NZ Maori/Other Pacific | 1,350 | 1 |
| Samoan/NZ European/Other Pacific | 701 | 1 |
| Total | 101,754 | 100 |

[a]not elsewhere classified

*Source:* Statistics New Zealand 1998.

Perhaps more significantly, they are more likely to have mixed ancestry as a consequence of the relatively high rates of intermarriage which have characterized Samoan marriage patterns in New Zealand since the 1960s (Macpherson 1972; Trlin 1975). The extent of intermarriage was revealed in the 1996 census, as Table 10.2 shows. People of Samoan descent who are born into, and grow up in, mixed families do not get an uncontested Samoan worldview. Instead, they find themselves with several, often competing, available worldviews. In these circumstances, Samoan worldviews compete with others and may become one of a number of sets of values which become incorporated into syncretized multicultures. Similarly, Samoan lifestyles in these mixed families become one of a number which become incorporated into syncretized lifestyles. The ways in which a Samoan worldview and life ways are reflected in these mixed families, and the extent to which they shape the lives of those living in them, vary significantly (Macpherson 1984, 1991). In short, these people no longer necessarily consider themselves unambiguously Samoan.

Furthermore, some of these families have moved and lived away from centers of Samoan population and have few opportunities to watch or to participate in the cycles of Samoan activity which occur in places such as Auckland, Wellington, and Christchurch where the bulk of the population resides. These isolates have limited contact with their Samoan kin and with the cycles of kinship activity, with Samoan churches and cycles of religious cum social activity in which the *fa'asamoa* assumes its most concrete form and meaning. Some of those who have moved back to the centers in adolescence have variously described their experience as "culture shock" and "freaky" as they come to grips with the differences between their "Samoanness" and that of their "full-on Samoan cousins."

These New Zealand–born children, and those who arrived from Samoa as children, had different histories and biographies from their parents, as Anae (Anae 1998) and Tiatia (Tiatia 1998) have shown. These differences become in many cases a source of tension. These children had also been exposed to a Western educational tradition that encouraged questioning and critical analysis. The willingness of young people to question and criticize the culture and conduct of older people, in a gerontocratic Samoan society, created its own tensions, as Utumapu showed in her study of Samoan families' attitudes to education in New Zealand (Utumapu 1992).

Furthermore, young New Zealand–born Samoans' increasing willingness to criticize aspects of Samoan social organization could not be easily controlled or curtailed by those who had traditionally exercised these powers because they were no longer dependent on their families for access to a livelihood. This fact, and New Zealand law, made it difficult for elders to exercise the same types of discipline. The rights of women and children were explicitly protected in New Zealand law, and this provided a degree of security for those who wished to criticize elements of the Samoan worldview and lifestyle. Parents and elders could not isolate their children from the influences of non-Samoan education, mass media, and peers, which led children to reflect on and to criticize aspects of culture and practice. Their children's social networks invariably included many more non-Samoans than did their own (Maingay 1995) and these more cosmopolitan groups became increasingly influential as both peer and reference groups. Parents could no longer demand their children's allegiance to Samoan values and norms and so those who wished to exert influence had to employ different strategies such as appeals to Christian values, Samoan values of respect and love for parents, and the desirability of protecting family honor. They did this with varying degrees of success.

There were, however, Samoans who were prepared for a range of reasons to write critically, and satirically, about aspects of their society. Albert Wendt (Wendt 1973) was the first to draw attention to the sources of tensions between generations within families. He was followed by writers and novelists such as Sia Figiel (Figiel 1996a, 1996b, 1999) who went on to write very critically about a range of aspects of Samoan society. Issues such as the treatment of groups such as women, children, and gay people, parental discipline, spouse abuse, the conduct of Samoan clergy, incest, pressure on children to achieve unrealistic parental aspirations, and adolescent suicide were among the issues raised by Samoan writers.

As increasing numbers of Samoans entered the creative arts, the criticism found its way into drama and comedy in the works of David Fane and Oscar Kightley (performed by such groups as Pacific Underground), into the comedy of solo performers such as Eteuati Ete, and into duos such as the Brownies. As the work of these writers became better known, their critical and satirical commentary found its way out of theaters and onto national television (Pearson 1999) in such satirical shows as *Milburn Place.* Serious, critical discussion of some Samoan social issues found its way into local soap operas such as *Shortland Street,* short films such as the *Tala Pasifika* series, and longer television dramas, such as *O Matou Uma,* and the *Overstayers* (Macpherson 2001). Talk-back radio, particularly on Samoan language radio stations, provided another social space in which these social issues could be aired openly and without any one set of interests being able to prevail. But these limited the participation of those children who wanted to discuss issues but who did not speak Samoan. This group was able to take part in these debates when the leading Pacific radio station provided opportunities to participate in English-language talk-back for a younger New Zealand–born audience.

The newspapers and magazines provided another social space in which people could discuss issues about Samoa, the Samoan worldview and lifestyle. As younger, New Zealand–educated and trained Samoan journalists started to take their places in the ranks of New Zealand journalism, the quality of reporting on Samoan affairs improved dramatically. But these journalists were also able to, and did, expose Samoan life to critical gaze. Journalists spotlighted the moral and ethical shortcomings of their pastors, elders, and titleholders revealed in criminal and civil court cases and then delved into the background of these events to reveal the ways in which various institutions were open to abuse by those with power. While these exposés ostensibly focused on the activities of particular individuals, they invariably led to widespread public discussion of the abuse of positions and offices in ways which might not have been possible, and by people who would not have been able to take part, in Samoa. There, public commentary on, and judgment of, the conduct of the social élite was restricted to their peers.

The criticism revealed commonalities in the experience of New Zealand–born Samoans and a growing awareness of what they had in common, and how this was related to the realities of their parents. This led to the formation of an identity which was counterposed, not to that of the dominant *Papalagi* or European ethnic group, but rather to that of their parents: a New Zealand–born Samoan identity (Anae 1998, 2001). This emerged in what Anae called an identity journey, which, for many, took some time but which eventually provided a secure identity from which to acknowledge difference between their Samoanness and that of their parents, and to criticize some elements of their Samoan origins.

This is not to say that all those of Samoan descent resident in New Zealand suddenly turned to open criticism of Samoan institutions and practices. This is not the case. It is only to show that this criticism was now possible and that those who wished to do so were free to do so with fewer constraints and to a larger audience. Creative and performing arts policy and agencies ironically assisted this process because their policies of encouraging minority writers and performers tended to result in support for younger writers and performers who were more likely to, and did, write about sensitive issues.

In this respect, the Samoan enclave which, under an earlier immigrant leadership, sought to protect and preserve a distinctly Samoan worldview and lifestyle is now a site in which accelerated transformation can and does occur. This pressure comes not only from the enclave in New Zealand, or indeed enclaves elsewhere. It occurs in hyperreality in the Samoan chat rooms on the Internet where young people from Samoan enclaves all over the world, including some in Samoa, "gather" to discuss their feelings about the culture and practices of their parents' societies (see Helen Morton Lee, chapter 8, for

the Tongan case). Not all discussion is critical: Much stresses the importance of holding fast to those values, practices, and institutions that are considered central to "being Samoan." There is, however, an apparent willingness to criticize others and particularly the abuse of power in the name of *fa'asamoa*.

## CONCLUSION

The transnationalization of Samoan society has had a significant effect on society in Samoa. It has resulted in a steadily expanding network of relatively strong linkages[13] between the island homes and the rim-based communities (Bedford 1997). It is the strength of these linkages which has ensured that developments in the enclaves quickly move back to center. The existence of a series of large and relatively wealthy enclaves, in which such open debates can occur, freely places pressure on the center. The declining costs of travel and communication and the inexpensive and ubiquitous videotape have meant that the images and experiences of the enclaves have an almost immediate impact in the core. The standards and practices of the enclaves are no longer something which occur beyond the view of Samoans at home.

People in Samoa watch the New Zealand television news nightly, New Zealand soap operas, and televised weekly magazine programs such as *Tagata Pasifika* in which the activities of overseas Samoans are reported. They watch videotapes of the baptisms, weddings, funerals, graduations, title-bestowing ceremonies, church openings, family gatherings, church picnics, fishing trips, and just about anything else that the ubiquitous video camera can capture. The enclaves are closer and more visible than they have ever been and their attractions more difficult to resist.

In the past, many migrants sought to replicate the worldview and practices to which they were committed by their upbringing wherever they went. Their "reference society" was that in which they had been born and educated—Samoa. They were influenced primarily by the views of those they regarded as the arbiters and judges of their activities.

Their overseas-born and educated children have a different reference society which they seek to replicate but it is not wholly Samoan and is, in some cases, critical of areas of Samoan society.

These changes in the enclaves are not of purely academic interest. Significant amounts of money flow into Samoa from these enclaves and this places a certain amount of power in the hands of these expatriates who are free to choose to support activities and causes selectively and, in so doing, to influence the course of local and national politics and legislation. It is possible that, over time, the nodes have become the centers and that the standards of the enclaves have become those to which those in the homeland aspire.

In 1997, in an attempt to summarize what seemed to be happening, I noted that

> Ideas and practices move so freely between Samoan societies in various parts of the world that what is forming at the intersections of all this movement is some meta Samoan society and culture which draws freely on what passes for Samoan culture and practice in various localities. From this inventory of knowledge communities 'draw down' those elements which are needed at different times to make conduct and practice seem intelligible and reasonable. (Macpherson 1997b:96)

In the period since then, the pace of this process, and the excitement inherent in it, have increased as people of Samoan descent find ever-more-creative ways of reconstituting Samoan culture and practice. The enclaves have simply provided sites in which this process can proceed more quickly and beyond the constraints that are inherent in the social structure within Samoa. In the process, the nodes have become centers and Samoan culture has become a global one.

## NOTES

1. The archipelago lies between 169 and 172 degrees west longitude and 13 and 15 degrees south latitude and comprises the independent nation of Samoa and the unincorporated territory of American Samoa.
2. Samoa was a staging point in the eastward migration into and settlement of the Pacific. Descendants of the early Samoans later explored and settled eastern Polynesia before moving on to the Hawai'ian group and south into Aotearoa.
3. At independence a large proportion of the remaining land, which had been confiscated by New Zealand during the First World War and operated as the Western Samoa Trust Estate Corporation (WSTEC), was returned to the Samoan government. This transfer effectively increased the amount of land that remained in some form of Samoan control.
4. Thus, the joint heads of state were drawn from Samoa's royal families. Only *matai*, who represented traditional districts, could stand for parliament, and voting was confined to other *matai*. Customary land, the control of which is vested in *matai*, cannot be alienated, which ensures the continued significance of the traditional chieftaincy.
5. In 1997, fifteen years after independence, the parliament of Western Samoa changed the name of the state from Western Samoa, Samoa I Sisifo, to Samoa.
6. Because cyclones struck different parts of the archipelago different villages were involved in rebuilding at different periods of time. Because much of the fundraising activity in migrant communities depended on involving people from villages that had not suffered damage in a particular event, the impression that such commitment was the norm was widespread.
7. This is not to suggest that the practices remained stable and/or unchanging in Samoa. There were variations within Samoa, which was recognized in the widely used proverb, *'ua tofu le nu'u ma lona aganu'u'*, to each village its own custom. Pressures for continuous change had always been present in Samoa. Migration created forces that exerted further pressures for change in Samoa (see Gold 1988; Macpherson 1990).
8. A young man and his sister had to choose between inviting a young and inexperienced *matai* to perform part of a ceremony for them or to omit it entirely. They eventually decided to omit it on the grounds that to have it mishandled would expose the entire family to ridicule from more-experienced observers.
9. Better known as the "kava ceremony," in which the new titleholder's membership in the council of chiefs is acknowledged for the first time.
10. In Samoa, fine mats are generally accumulated by chiefs for use on behalf of the family. In New Zealand, the choirs which competed for prizes of fine mats at church openings and cultural competitions often distributed the fine mats among their members so that untitled people could acquire significant numbers of these items of ceremonial currency which they could hold and use in their own right.
11. This has become more and more the case since 1990 when the power of the labor unions, which had protected the relatively generous conditions of work of their members, was reduced by a significant change in labor legislation which was intended to deregulate the labor market.

12. The census question asks respondents to name languages in which they can conduct an everyday conversation, and the basis of individuals' judgments may vary significantly.

13. The strength of these is reflected in the continuing and relatively high value of remittances and in the amount of regular travel and other forms of communication between rim-based and the home communities.

# REFERENCES

Ablon, J. 1971. "The Social Organization of an Urban Samoan Community." *Southwest Journal of Anthropology* 27(1):75–96.

Ahlburg, Dennis A. 1991. *Remittances and Their Impact. A Study of Tonga and Western Samoa.* Canberra: National Centre for Development Studies, RSPS, Australian National University.

Ahlburg, Dennis A., and Michael J. Levin. 1990. *The North East Passage. A Study of Pacific Islander Migration to American Samoa and the United States.* Vol. 28. Canberra: National Centre for Development Studies, Australian National University.

Anae, Melani. 1998. "Fofoa i vaoese: Identity Journeys of New Zealand-Born Samoans." Ph.D. dissertation, Anthropology. University of Auckland.

———. 2001. "The New 'Vikings of the Sunrise': New Zealand–Borns in the Information Age." In *Tangata o te Moana Nui: The Evolving Identities of Pacific Peoples in Aotearoa/New Zealand.* C. Macpherson, P. Spoonley, and M. Anae, eds. Pp. 101–121. Palmerston North: Dunmore Press.

Bedford, Richard D. 1993. "Migration and Restructuring: Reflections on New Zealand in the 1980s." *New Zealand Population Review* 19(1 and 2):1–14.

———. 1994. "Pacific Islanders in New Zealand." *Espaces, Populations, Sociétés* 2:187–200.

———. 1997. "Migration in Oceania: Reflections on Contemporary Theoretical Debates." *New Zealand Population Review* 23:45–64.

Boyd, Mary. 1969a. "The Record in Western Samoa to 1945." In *New Zealand's Record in the Pacific Islands in the Twentieth Century.* A. Ross, ed. Pp. 115–188. Auckland: Longman Paul.

———. 1969b. "The Record in Western Samoa Since 1945." In *New Zealand's Record in the Pacific Islands in the Twentieth Century.* A. Ross, ed. Pp. 189–270. Auckland: Longman Paul.

Cook, Len, Robert Didham, and Mansoor Kawaja. 2001. "The Shape of the Future: The Demography of Pacific Peoples." In *Tangata o te Moana Nui: The Evolving Identities of Pacific People in Aotearoa/New Zealand.* C. Macpherson, P. Spoonley, and M. Anae, eds. Pp. 44–65. Palmerston North: Dunmore Press.

Davidson, J. W. 1967. *Samoa mo Samoa: The Emergence of the Independent State of Western Samoa.* London: Oxford University Press.

Field, Michael J. 1984. *Mau. Samoa's Struggle against New Zealand Oppression.* Wellington: A. H. and A. W. Reed.

Figiel, Sia. 1996a. *Girl in the Moon Circle.* Suva: Mana Publications.

———. 1996b. *Where We Once Belonged.* Auckland: Pasifika Press.

———. 1999. *They Who Do Not Grieve.* Auckland: Vintage.

Fitzgerald, M., and Alan Howard. 1990. "Aspects of Social Organization in Three Samoan Communities." *Pacific Studies* 14(1):31–54.

Forster, John. 1954. "The Assimilation of Samoan Migrants in the Naval Housing Area, Pearl Harbor, Hawai'i." M.A. thesis. University of Hawai'i, Manoa.

Franco, Robert. 1990. "Samoans in Hawaii. Enclaves Without Entrepreneurship." In *Migration and Development.* Pacific Research Monographs No. 28. J. Connell, ed. Pp. 170–181. Canberra: National Centre for Development Studies, Australian National University.

Gilson, Richard P. 1970. *Samoa 1830–1900. The Politics of a Multi-Cultural Community.* Melbourne: Oxford University Press.

Gold, Jerry. 1988. "Modern Human Migration and the Emergence of a Class System in American Samoa." Ph.D. dissertation. University of Washington.

Gunson, W. N. 1976. *Messengers of Grace.* Melbourne: Oxford University Press.

Kotchek, L. 1978. "Samoans in Seattle." In *New Neighbors: Islanders in Adaptation.* B. Shore, C. Macpherson, and R. Franco, eds. Pp. 19–26, 286–294. Santa Cruz: Center for Pacific Studies, University of California, Santa Cruz.

Kramer, Augustin. 1994. *The Samoa Islands.* 2 vols. T. Verhaaren, translator. Vol. 1. Auckland: Polynesian Press.

Macpherson, Cluny. 1972. "Intermarriage in the Samoan Migrant Community in New Zealand." M.A. thesis. University of Auckland.

———. 1974. "Toward an Explanation of the Persistence of Extended Kinship Among Samoan Migrants in Urban New Zealand." Ph.D. thesis, Sociology. University of Waikato.

———. 1978. "The Polynesian Migrant Family: A Samoan Case Study." In *Families in New Zealand Society.* P. Koopman-Boyden, ed. Pp. 120–137. Wellington: Methuen.

———. 1984. "Samoan Ethnicity." In *Tauiwi: Racism and Ethnicity in Aotearoa/New Zealand.* P. Spoonley, C. Macpherson, D. Pearson, and C. Sedgwick, eds. Pp. 107–127. Palmerston North: Dunmore Press.

———. 1990. "Stolen Dreams: Some Consequences of Dependency for Western Samoan Youth." In *Migration and Development.* Pacific Research Monographs, No. 28. J. Connell, ed. Pp. 107–119. Canberra: National Centre for Development Studies, Australian National University.

———. 1991. "The Changing Contours of Samoan Ethnicity." In Nga Take. *Ethnic Relations and Racism in Aotearoa/New Zealand.* P. Spoonley, D. Pearson, and

C. Macpherson, eds. Pp. 67–86. Palmerston North: Dunmore Press.

———. 1992. "Economic and Political Restructuring and the Sustainability of Migrant Remittances: The Case of Western Samoa." *The Contemporary Pacific* 4(1): 109–135.

———. 1994. "Changing Patterns of Commitment to Island Homelands: A Case Study of Western Samoa." *Pacific Studies* 17(3):83–116.

———. 1997a. "The Persistence of Chiefly Authority in Western Samoa." In *Chiefs Today: Traditional Pacific Leadership and the Postcolonial State.* G. M. White and L. Lindstrom, eds. Pp. 19–49. Stanford, Calif.: Stanford University Press.

———. 1997b. "The Polynesian Diaspora: New Communities and New Questions." In *Contemporary Migration in Oceania: Diaspora and Network.* JCAS Symposium Series, Vol. JCAS Symposium Series 3. K. Sudo and S. Yoshida, eds. Pp. 77–100. Osaka: Japan Centre for Area Studies, National Museum of Ethnology.

———. 1999. "Changing Contours of Kinship: The Impacts of Social and Economic Development on Kinship Organization in the South Pacific." *Pacific Studies* 22(2):71–96.

———. 2001. "One Trunk Sends Out Many Branches." In *Tangata o te Moana Nui: The Evolving Identities of Pacific Peoples in Aotearoa New Zealand.* C. Macpherson, P. Spoonley, and M. Anae, eds. Pp. 66–80. Palmerston North: Dunmore Press.

Macpherson, Cluny, Richard Bedford, and Paul Spoonley. 2000. "Fact or Fable? The Consequences of Migration for Educational Achievement and Labour Market Participation." *The Contemporary Pacific* 12(1):57–82.

Macpherson, Cluny, and La'avasa Macpherson. 1999. "The Changing Contours of Migrant Samoan Kinship." In *Small Worlds, Global Lives: Islands and Migration.* R. King and J. Connell, eds. Pp. 277–291. London: Pinter.

Maingay, Samantha. 1995. "The Social Mobility, Identity and Community Networks of Second Generation Pacific Islanders in Auckland." M.A. thesis. University of Auckland.

Marquardt, Carl. 1899. *Die Tatowirung Beider Geschlechter in Samoa.* S. Ferner, translator. Berlin: Verlag Von Dietrich Reimer.

Ngan Woo, Feleti. 1983. *Fa'asamoa: The World of the Samoans.* Auckland: Race Relations Conciliator's Office.

Pearson, Sarina. 1999. "Subversion and Ambivalence: Pacific Islanders on New Zealand Prime Time." *The Contemporary Pacific* 11(2):361–388.

Pitt, David, and Cluny Macpherson. 1974. *Emerging Pluralism: The Samoan Community in New Zealand.* Auckland: Longman Paul.

Rolff, K. 1978. "Fa'a Samoa: Tradition in Transition." Ph.D. dissertation. University of California, Santa Barbara.

Schoeffel, Penelope. 1999. "Samoan Exchange and 'Fine Mats': An Historical Reconsideration." *Journal of the Polynesian Society* 108(2):117–148.

So'o, Asofou. 1998. "The Price of Election Campaigning in Samoa." In *Governance and Reform in the South Pacific.* Pacific Policy Papers No. 23. P. Larmour, ed. Pp. 289–304. Canberra: National Centre for Development Studies, Australian National University.

Stanton, Max. 1978. "Mormons, Matais and Modernization: Stress and Change Among Samoans in Laie, Hawai'i." In *New Neighbors: Islanders in Adaptation.* B. Shore, C. Macpherson, and R. Franco, eds. Pp. 272–285. Santa Cruz: Center for Pacific Studies, University of California, Santa Cruz.

Statistics New Zealand. 1998. *Samoa People in New Zealand.* Wellington: Statistics New Zealand.

Tiatia, Jemaima. 1998. *Caught Between Cultures: A New Zealand–Born Pacific Island Perspective.* Auckland: Christian Research Association.

Trlin, Andrew D. 1972. "Attitudes Toward West Samoan Immigrants in Auckland, New Zealand." *The Australia Quarterly* 44(3):179–196.

———. 1975. "Western Samoan Marriage Patterns in Auckland." *Journal of the Polynesian Society* 84(2): 153–175.

Turner, George. 1983. *Samoa a Hundred Years Ago and Long Before.* Papakura: R. McMillan.

University of the South Pacific. 1988. *Pacific Constitutions,* 2 volumes. Vol. 1, *Polynesia.* Suva: University of the South Pacific.

Utumapu, Tafili. 1992. *Finau i Mea Sili: Attitudes of Samoan Families in New Zealand to Education.* Auckland: University of Auckland.

Va'a, Unasa Felise. 1995. "Fa'a Samoa: Continuity and Change: A Study of Samoan Migration in Australia." Ph.D. dissertation. Australian National University.

Wendt, Albert. 1973. *Sons for the Return Home.* Auckland: Longman Paul.

# 11

# Wave and Reflection: Charting Marshallese Participation in Globalizing Processes

**Jim Hess**

*University of California, Irvine*

A child's first birthday is an important event in many Pacific Islander communities, ritually marking the end of a liminal period in the baby's life. The family formally presents the child to the community with a celebration, *keemem* in Marshallese. Demonstrating the strength of the lineage, it is densely packed with cultural symbols. As Marshallese have traveled abroad and built communities overseas since the 1970s, the *keemem* has traveled with them, and I first attended a *keemem* in Southern California in 1991.

A typical first-birthday *keemem* is held in a community center or church hall. On arriving, the guest will find that the walls have been decorated with colorful cloth items, often T-shirts and pillowcases, and the tables are covered with printed fabrics. A table near the front is reserved for community leaders and other honored guests. Balloons are spread around the hall, and a band is playing Marshallese music on electric keyboards and guitars to entertain arrivals. Families seat themselves near friends, and groups of adolescent boys and girls congregate separately, boys on the fringes of the gathering, girls among the tables filled with families. The women of the extended family are busy in the kitchen, preparing to assemble plates of food from dishes prepared in institutional quantities by men and women over several days.

Formal events are coordinated by a man acting as master of ceremonies and open with a prayer by the pastor of one of the Marshallese congregations. Following the prayer, plates of food are distributed by the adolescent girls while the band plays. Plates are piled high with rice, potato salad, lettuce salad, spaghetti or oriental noodle dishes, and Marshallese-style donuts and dinner rolls. There will be marinated beef and barbecued chicken. There might be a pig roasted in an earth oven. There will be distinctively islands foods, brought by visiting relatives for the occasion: fresh or preserved breadfruit, coconut soup, puddings of pumpkin or banana with coconut milk, and fresh reef fish barbecued or deep-fried. Rarely is all the food eaten; it is served in Styrofoam carryout trays for convenience in taking home for consumption the next day and sharing with family members who might not be able to attend. Following a period for eating, one or more youth dance groups of both boys and girls will perform traditional and new Marshallese dances or various forms of hula borrowed from Pacific Island neighbors. Women then dance through the audience, distributing gifts of cloth: T-shirts, towels, children's clothing, men's shirts. The distribution is accompanied by much humor and clowning; a woman might pull a shirt over someone's head or offer a child's shorts to a grown woman or wrap a towel around a man's neck while wiggling her hips at him. Other gifts include Marshallese handicrafts, particularly pandanus-leaf mats, possibly hats and handbags. A family member makes a speech to thank guests for coming and contributors for their help.

Then it is time for the introduction of the one-year-old to the community. The child is held by one of the females of her lineage, sometimes her mother but often by her mother's mother or an auntie, sitting on a mat at the front of the room. While the band sings happy birthday to the child, the guests form a line and file past the child, shaking her hand or pinching her cheek, and deposit a gift of a dollar bill, sometimes a larger denomination, in a paper bag or box. More entertainment follows, and a large cake is brought out. While the little children swarm around, the cake is cut and distributed. There may be more entertainment or a formal closing prayer; the *keemem* ends as families gradually drift away.

The *keemem* illustrates some of the processes commonly associated with globalization, such as the substitution of industrial commodities for locally produced goods, the mix of cultures and symbols, and the economic and symbolic power of the dollar. In the account above, I have noted the substitution of nonindigenous purchased foods acquired through waged labor for the products of family labor on the land. As gifts, mass-produced fabrics are distributed in greater quantities than women's hand-produced leaf-fiber goods such as mats and handicrafts. Even some of the handicraft forms are introduced by commercial agents looking to expand a small market for their sale to foreigners. The prayers opening and closing the *keemem* are given by a Christian minister usually affiliated with either the United Church of Christ or the Assemblies of God, denominations centered in the United States. The instruments the musicians play were introduced from the United States but are manufactured in Japan. Some of the dances performed were originally inspired by the marches of Japanese soldiers and policemen once present in the Marshalls; others are the result of more recent exposure to Polynesian forms. The latest dance innovations have drawn on music videos and hip-hop. Dollar bills, given to the baby, are the opening of gift exchanges, the sharing expected of all Marshallese persons, establishing the first direct relationship that makes this child a social person. The ceremony is capped by a birthday cake that would be utterly familiar to most of us—a white sheet cake coated with white frosting and decorated in colored icing.

There are, however, several differences between my account and the usual accounts of globalization. In the standard accounts, globalization is a phenomenon of the recent past, and I have included cultural incorporations that began a century ago. Many accounts further regard globalization as a process of homogenization, the creation of a "McWorld" (Barber 1992) or, going further, Americanization (Rodriguez 2000). According to this perspective, it is the result of large multinational corporations and economic elite actions, supported by powerful international organizations such as the World Trade Organization and the International Monetary Fund, forced on local communities, a form of neocolonialism. While I agree with some of this version, I hope my account adds a layer of complexity to the issue of who are the agents and who are the victims. This typical *keemem* takes place not in the Marshall Islands, but in Costa Mesa, a middle-class city in southern California. Who is colonizing whom, whose culture is spreading or declining? How can the experiences of the people of the Marshall Islands, a small population of only about 60,000 people, help us understand better the powerful forces transforming our world?

## IMAGING GLOBAL SPACE

I wish to make one basic point: Marshallese are active participants and agents in processes contributing to the phenomenon we call globalization. In order to arrive at this destination, however, I will first have to pass by some way-marks, establishing an alternative cartography to allow Marshallese action to become visible. I compare and contrast European and Marshallese representations of space and place, using their respective material artifacts, maps and stick charts, and trace some of the voyages of Marshallese navigators in these waters. My choice of the metaphors of voyaging and navigation is compatible with Marshallese conceptions of life, with traditional tattoos symbolically marking the body as a canoe making its way between ocean and the heavens, with terms from the domain of voyaging used to describe a person's life-course (Carucci 1995).

"Globalization" has become popular in the past decade to refer to processes leading to increasing economic interconnections as well as international transmissions of media images and popular culture. Some analysts have noted similarities with the late nineteenth century (Lee and Foster 1997; Massey 2000), identifying globalization with economic liberalization, the international lowering of barriers to trade and increased global circulation of capital, commodities, and migrants. Stewart Firth applied this model to the Pacific region, seeking lessons for the present in the past (2000). He concludes that in both cases, globalization means incorporation into the global economy on terms that mostly benefit outsiders: foreign firms, colonial powers, financial markets, aid donors. The outcome is determined from outside, and few islanders benefit. Typical of much writing on the topic, Firth's perspective is consistent with Western sociogeographic imagination as laid out in maps. Unfortunately, it fails to acknowledge the extent to which islanders incorporated outsiders into their own political and social projects. It breaks the long history of globalization up into discrete, unconnected periods, separating economy from society and

trade from war. Concerned with challenges for governments operating within state borders, it misses opportunities for nations and families in wider spaces.

This spatial imagination is made explicit by Ferdinand Braudel, tracing the emergence of world economies in the third volume of his acclaimed history, *The Perspective of the World* (1984). A world economy is established by an urban center with a dominant form of capitalism, a hierarchy of economies, and boundaries,[1] "the line that defines it gives it an identity. . . ." (Braudel 1984:25). Border lines are dominant features on maps, setting off land from sea, marking presumed political boundaries, establishing limits and identities. It is this imaginative division of the world into individualized, autonomous nation states that disempowers Oceanic countries and peoples.

Stick charts used by Marshallese navigators present an alternate view that emphasizes not borders but fields of interacting forces and the ways in which they reinforce and interfere with each other. Maps are framed by borders, fixing the extent of their reference. Stick charts are framed by lines projecting outward, suggesting not limits but extensions, showing not *border lines* but *boundary processes*. In general, the narrow, curved sticks represent ocean swells while the wider sticks may serve both as structural supports for the chart and as representations of swell directions and nodes. Cowrie shells represent islands or atolls. Main swells roll in across thousands of ocean miles from multiple directions, energized by distant trade winds. The islands and coral reefs absorb some of their energy, but also refract them as they pass and reflect them back along the path of their origin. Navigators learned to locate their position by the interference patterns, guiding their craft on paths connecting place to place across seaways that extended as far as Wake to the north, west to Pohnpei, south to Kiribati, and possibly to Hawai'i in the east (Spennemann 2000). "Wave and reflection" in the title of this chapter is both a reference to the dominant feature of stick charts and my metaphoric image for the balance of forces in Marshallese globalization processes. While the swells of globalization arise in the geographically distant centers of industrial and postindustrial capitalism, Marshallese people absorb and transform these forces according to their own indigenous epistemologies and models of development (Gegeo 1998). They then reflect them back in smaller but persistent waves of people, goods, symbols, and ideas that carry all the way back to the original sources.

Westerners tend to divide not only space into discrete and bounded areas, but also time, breaking continuity into discrete, countable periods (Whorf 1967). There are advantages and disadvantages to this cognitive orientation; while counting days we may neglect the nights. High tides and swell crests are necessarily followed by low tides and swell troughs. The periods of trade liberalization usually identified with globalization provoked reactions through redistribution of rents, wages, and wealth and opened new arenas of international conflict (Polanyi 1957; Williamson 1998), including contests among European powers and between the United States and Japan. Liberalization was followed by rising trade barriers and arms build-ups, a period that included two world wars and a depression, but globalization rolled on. The Cold War contested whose economic and political institutions would control the future of globalization.

A full account of globalization would include a historical essay on how the Marshalls were connected to the world economy in the first phase of liberalization, incorporated in the German world economy as a protectorate in 1885, and taken from Germany by Japan in World War I. As part of Japan's expanding world economy, the Marshall Islands and the rest of Micronesia experienced a dramatic intensification of globalization even as liberalization waned (Hezel 1983, 1995; Peattie 1988; Hiery 1995). The economic tide receded somewhat in the backwash of U.S. conquest in World War II (Mason 1947; see Poyer et al., chapter 18, and Carucci, chapter 24) as military engagement endured. On the periphery of empire, the Marshalls became a center of global contests where boundary processes were visible not only in battle but also in the testing and development of nuclear weapons at Bikini and Enewetok and missile systems at Kwajalein (Mason 1954; Tobin 1954, 1967; Kiste 1974; Teaiwa 1994; Carucci 1997), and in studies of the effects of radiation (Barker 1997). Later, as imperialism waned, economic liberalization waxed, and the United States pressed its Cold War advantage against the U.S.S.R., the Marshalls gained self-government and a form of independence under the Compact of Free Association with the United States implemented in 1986 (Meller 1985; Mason 1989; Kiste 1993).

How did the Marshalls absorb and transform these impinging waves? What benefits did they extract; what routes did navigators open? The opening to globalization was an invitation by *iroijlaplap* (paramount chief) Kabua to missionaries of the American Board for the Commission of Foreign Missions, who came to Ebon in 1857 (Hezel 1983). Adopting a world religion, Marshallese gained access to education, literacy, and new medicines. Christianity moderated the power of chiefs, opened new paths to moral claims on fellow Christians, and, for members of the *kajur* (worker) class, access to status positions as ministers and deacons. Yet Christianity itself was transformed in the process, as demonstrated by the *Kurijmoj* ritual in which Christmas becomes a months-long cycle of ritual performances directed toward renewing exchange relations with God which sustain the fertility of people, land, and sea (Carucci 1993, 1997).

Commerce followed quickly in the wake of religion, with the first permanent trading station established on Ebon the year following arrival of the missionaries. Marshallese acquired access to a wide range of new goods—tools, food, clothing, luxuries—and new subsistence options, as many came to prefer growing coconuts, cutting copra, and buying rice to working in mucky taro pits and processing the crop for food. The Marshalls produced more copra than other islands of Micronesia. Production and trade were mostly organized not through the European plantation system but through the relations of redistribution existing between chiefs and the people. Some chiefs were more successful at accumulating wealth than the traders (Hezel 1983). Other Marshallese traveled abroad as sailors or earned wages as workers on plantations at home and abroad. The first urban centers appeared in Jaluit and Majuro on the economic base established by commerce and administration. Later the island of Ebeye became one of the most densely populated places in the world on the basis of rents and wages from the Kwajalein antimissile defense test base built by the United States.

Another way of benefiting from globalization was by absorbing the people who landed on Marshallese shores. Marshallese families incorporated foreigners through marriage, acquiring their knowledge, skills, and wealth for economic and social advantages. Today their descendants occupy many important positions in government, education and social services, and business. If some areas of Marshallese culture were abandoned, others were elaborated. The marches of the Japanese were transformed into new dance forms, and some Marshallese believe that the trickster-god *Letao* traveled on new journeys, helping the United States win World War II but later fomenting trouble in the Persian Gulf (Carucci 1989; Hess Fieldnotes 1993).

During this time anthropology also came to the Marshalls in the service of colonial administrations, including the Coordinated Investigation of Micronesian Anthropology in 1946, one of the largest anthropological projects ever (Kiste and Marshall 1999). This founded the intellectual lineage that adopted me as I traveled from Iowa to California and introduced me to the Marshallese community of Costa Mesa. Deciding to write my dissertation on economic development, I booked passage from Los Angeles via Honolulu, another arrival on the latest tide of globalization.

## CONNECTIONS AND TRANSFORMATIONS

Flying into Majuro on my first trip to the Republic of the Marshall Islands (RMI) in 1992, my plane banks left to line up the north-south runway after the long west-southwest leg from Honolulu by way of Johnston Atoll. As the wing on the port side drops, I see the runway, a strip of concrete on a narrow strip of land, barely twice the width of the runway itself: water to the left, water to the right. The land rises barely two meters above the water. What would happen if a big wave came along, I wonder? How fragile, how remote, are these islands here in the middle of the Pacific. The Marshall Islands sit just north of the equator, just west of the International Date Line, diametrically opposite the Greenwich Meridian, the center from which all longitude is measured. The Marshalls are in the middle of the Pacific Basin; 7,800 kilometers from Los Angeles, where I began my flight west; 4,500 kilometers southeast of Tokyo; 6,500 kilometers east of Beijing; and 5,300 kilometers north-northeast of Canberra. For most people in the world, they are not only remote geographically, but also perceptually; few people are aware that they exist. Increased attention to the Pacific in the last decades mostly focuses on the Pacific Rim, not the nations and states of Oceania. When Pacific Basin peoples arrive in the United States, they are appended as an afterthought to the peoples of Asia: Countless official documents refer to Asian Pacific Islanders, but effectively address Asians alone.

Despite my doubts, the plane touches down on the runway and lands successfully. We passengers exit the plane down the stairs and walk across the tarmac to the small terminal building, which is open to the warm and humid tropical air. First stop is the customs room, where we wait for the ground crew to roll over our luggage. One by one we present our bags and suitcases and boxes to the customs officers for inspection. I hope they won't decide my new laptop computer is for resale and ask me to pay a duty on it. We crossed the borders of the RMI miles ago as we entered the airspace over the RMI exclusive economic zone, but here in this little room is the actual boundary. The borders are lines on a map; boundaries are the processes of inclusion and exclusion and exchange through which living systems relate to their environment. The relationship of borders to boundaries is extremely complex,[2] but vital to understanding the history and organization of the society and the life of Marshallese peoples.

If I ever desired to visit a remote corner of the world untouched by industrial civilization, here I realized that such a desire would never be fulfilled. Immediately upon exiting the terminal, I am confronted by the physical evidence in the form of a parking lot full of Toyotas and Nissans, cars and pickups and vans mostly of Japanese manufacture. The material environment is decidedly unlike those images of thatched huts and grass skirts that romantic tales set in the Pacific bring to mind. Buildings are predominately concrete or plywood and tin. Women usually dress in the long, loose dresses in printed fabrics called "mother hubbards" introduced by Christian missionaries in the last century. Men generally wear dark-colored slacks and short-sleeved shirts. Unless on official business, both wear zories, plastic sandals held on by a strap across the toes. Sunglasses are "in." I look across the lagoon in vain for signs of the slender and swift Marshallese canoes. Instead, I see small outboard motor boats, rusty fishing boats from Taiwan or other Asian fleets, and a few sailing sloops and cabin cruisers such as I would expect to find along the coast of California.

Having found a ride from the airport, located on the western side of Majuro Atoll, toward the urban center fifteen miles away on the eastern side, I pass houses, stores, restaurants, fields of grass and coconut palms, areas of bush, and the occasional church marked by a steeple or cross. There is the white and gleaming two-story U.S. ambassador's residence and embassy compound, surrounded by a fence. Here the road swerves from lagoon side to ocean side; an intransigent landowner didn't want it to run by his house. On the left I see the rusting remains of a freighter in the lagoon, later the generators of the Marshalls Energy Company. Most buildings are one or two stories; a few taller ones stand out. One is five stories of white concrete; it houses an FM stereo transmitter on the top floor, the antenna sprouting from the roof. Next to it is a construction largely of exposed steel beams and rebar, the relic of an ambitious undertaking by a Korean entrepreneur that failed while still under construction. A bit farther on I encounter a building that would not look out of place in Los Angeles, covered by panes of silvery reflecting glass. It is the new capitol building. The dedication will be held next week, and a group of Marshallese musicians and dancers known as the Navigators have flown out from Orange County, California to join in the celebrations, taking their place among performing groups from each of the atolls and islands. But which group should greet the arriving dignitaries from other Pacific countries at the airport? If the capitol building represents the importation of global metropolitan architecture, the Navigators, dancing in the airport reception area, represent the export of Pacific culture to the metropoles.

In the neighborhood of the capitol are other signs of connections. Just down the road is Gibson's department store, extension of a company based in the U.S. territory of Guam. Here I buy groceries, kitchen utensils, computer supplies, and hardware. I pay with a Mastercard, manage my funds through the Bank of Hawai'i office which shares the building, and eat hamburgers and salads with 1,000 Island dressing in the cafe around the side. Toward the ocean from the capitol, across the baseball field, is the hospital, staffed by doctors from the Philippines, where I will get my teeth fixed by a dentist who spent the previous decade working on U.S. Indian reservations. Across the road is the twenty-foot-high concrete tower of the meteorological station maintained by the U.S. National Weather Service. Beyond the station is the blue tiled exterior of a resort hotel, still unfinished after ten years, begun by the island nation of Nauru with capital from payments for the phosphate mined there by the British. Down the road a bit are the radio dishes of the national telephone service, pointed at geosynchronous satellites, connecting to the United States through operators in Hawai'i.

Also standing out above the houses, shops, schools, and occasional palm trees are water towers, classic white cylinders with conical roofs, components in one of several water systems drawing on rain, wells, and the ocean. Maintaining an urban population on a coral atoll takes a complex technological infrastructure. I pass churches and their schools—there on the lagoon the Assemblies of God, with a small basketball court out in front. Down the road, on the right, the Catholic church and school, run by American Jesuits, successors to German and Spanish predecessors. Next to it, the buildings of the College of the Marshall Islands, which has several hundred students in vocational-technical and liberal arts programs. Across the road from the college and the church is a house of white-washed concrete, a heavy wire mesh over the windows to protect against the predations of juvenile delinquents, which I will share for a few months with an Australian overseas volunteer. Like the Japanese volunteers who whiz by on their motor-scooters, he's taking time off in mid-career to spend a couple of years overseas. A professional archivist, he works with the government and historic preservation office to develop policies and facilities for storing documents and artifacts. Many of the Japanese are trained health assistants or nurses and work at the hospital. The Peace Corps volunteers, usually just out of college, who have their office a few hundred meters down the road, are sent off Majuro to work in the rural schools as instructors.

Down the road another few hundred meters, the Mobil Oil tank farm sits behind a wire-mesh fence on the lagoon side. Then on the right, construction is beginning on a bowling alley. After it, an open lot in the middle of the island, unusual in this part of Majuro where there are usually two or three rows of houses packed into the fifty meters between road and beach. Then there are the buildings of the courthouse and the museum, raised a story in the air by concrete pillars, protecting them from the waves that roll over the island every dozen years and providing pedestrians welcome shade from the intense sun overhead. In the museum, only a few people walk through the room holding pictures and artifacts from the past exhibited as in Western museums. But there are always people at the tables below, watching the TV which endlessly plays videos of local dance and music, performance being the way islanders have preserved the past in an environment where artifacts rarely last. It is an orientation that bedevils my roommate the archivist.

Past a church and a motel, there's the Kitco restaurant, an operation of the Kwajalein Islands Trading Company established back in the fifties. In later months I will stop by for broccoli-beef stir fry whenever I come in from a month in the outer islands with a craving for the vegetables, red meat, and fats missing from the usual diet of rice and fish. Next to it there's Charlie's Pub, which serves a good pizza. Another restaurant, then a department store in one room with items running from thread and fancy underwear to sacks of concrete mix. Here's the post office, zip code 96960, where you rent a box and collect your mail, when it is not held up in Honolulu waiting for cargo space on a flight out. Here's Reimers' store, looking like a U.S. supermarket except perhaps for the chest freezer's bins of turkey tails and sheep flaps. Gibson's, partly owned by president and *iroijlaplap* Amata Kabua, represents the economic success of the chiefs, based on capital initially accumulated through the copra trade and land rents. Reimers' is the most conspicuous emblem of a new elite rising from the *kajur* through commercial success, tapping not only the copra trade but the market in goods and services generated by money flowing into the Marshalls from U.S. payments and international development funds. Across the road on the lagoon side are other components of the Reimers' organization, including an Ace Hardware store, franchisee of the U.S. chain. Above it, the Tide Table restaurant, run by a Chinese Hawai'ian, and a favorite hangout of the expatriots. It shares the second floor with some of the rooms of Reimers' hotel, which go for $75 per night and up. Other groups have had commercial success in the Marshalls. Behind the post office on the oceanside is the Marshall Islands Club, where I can listen to a local band and drink American and Australian beers while playing pool. It's owned by an Irish-American who came out as a Peace Corps volunteer and married a Marshallese woman, and with his Marshallese partner he also publishes the weekly dual-language newspaper. A bit down the road, there's the cable TV station, feeding subscribers week-old programs shipped in from a San Francisco cable operator.

## HINTERLANDS

But this is Majuro, one of the urban centers, connected to the world by an international airport and port facilities as well as communications satellites and a constant flow of officials and businesspeople coming and going. What of the rural communities, where anthropologists used to go in search of authentic culture, escaping the presumptively inauthentic hybrid forms of the cities? My research follows a fisheries development project that straddles the urban-rural boundary, buying from fishers in nearby Arno Atoll and selling to consumers in urban Majuro. It gives me the opportunity to do something Marshallese government officials rarely find time for, traveling frequently between rural and urban places. Technology in Arno reminds me of summer scout camp. Food is often cooked over a fire of coconut shells in a separate little shelter to the side of the main house, although others use simple one-burner kerosene stoves. Water for washing dishes is heated by leaving it in the sun, the sink for washing and rinsing the split half-spheres of a float from a deep sea fishing net that drifted up on the beach. A few houses have solar panels or a gasoline generator; most use kerosene lanterns. A couple have washing machines, a treasured luxury where most women spend hours every week carefully washing clothes by hand, but drying is always sun and wind powered. Houses are usually made of plywood with a tin roof; the floor is a cement slab or a spread of soft coral gravel. Windows are unscreened; a wood shutter closes against wind, rain, or night, and lifts to form an awning against sun or light showers.

My census of households takes me to all the inhabited islets of Arno but one, which we miss because of distance and time and my assistants' assurance that the inhabitants are one small family from Kiribati, the next country to the south, who are only taking care of the land for the absentee owner. Here in the islands boundaries and borders are still configured in complex ways. Kiribati people are even assigned a fictive clan of their own, the *Ri-Bit.* Later a week-long survey and other activities provide the opportunity for a longer stay in each of the four *bukon* or districts of Arno. I learn that there is a geographic gradient to economics even across this atoll. In Kibjeltok, the *bukon* closest to Majuro, stores are readily restocked as a small boat can usually make the passage, and there is even one man who commutes to his job in Majuro during the week and returns to Arno and his family on the weekends. On the far side in Reaarlaplap, stores must await the arrival of the *bumbum,* named after the sound of its diesel engine, and supplies of rice, sugar, flour, tea, ramen, soap, kerosene, matches, and cigarettes often run low. The gradient is also reflected in representations. In Majuro, some people warn me to watch out for sorcerers in Arno. In Kibjeltok they warn me that the dangerous magic is over in Reaarlaplap.

Social and economic relations are less monetarized in Arno than Majuro. One health aide puts it more concretely: "In Arno, if you put a $20 bill in your pocket at the end of the month it's still there. In Majuro, by the end of the day there's nothing left" (Hess Fieldnotes 1994). The health aide has one of the few salaried jobs in Arno; there are also the school teachers and cooks, several employees of the fisheries project, and a couple of agricultural extension agents who are more successful at agriculture than extension. The local government pays the mayor a salary and quarterly stipends of a few hundred dollars to councilmen and a few very part-time police. Ministers receive donations from their congregations, which they supplement with their own work. Copra is still the major cash producer, followed by the fisheries project. Women make handicrafts, weaving fibers from pandanus and coconut fronds into mats, baskets, hats, wall hangings, and so on. Some sell them to a buyer in Majuro; in one islet they pay the tuitions of students at the Catholic elementary school run by Maryknoll sisters. Quite a few families try to make a little money from retail stores in their homes, some located in a separate room with a counter opening onto the road, some a pile of sacks and boxes in one corner of a room. A village of 30 families, about 250 people, might have three or four of these.

Majuro is a crossroads of people on commercial and official business, people just passing through, outsiders who have settled down. Most people speak or at least understand English. Arno is a little quieter. Less than a quarter of the people can communicate with me in English. Besides the Maryknoll sisters and I, there are five other Americans here out of a population of 1,700 residents. Four of them are young women here as volunteer teachers—one Peace Corps and three at an Assemblies of God school, opened not in the community where they have the biggest congregation but in the "capital" where the *iroijlaplap* lives. Here, I conjecture, they hope to make headway against the well-established Protestant church affiliated with United Church of Christ, the modern descendent of the New England Congregationalists who sent the first missionaries a century and a half ago. The other American might be a character out of a Joseph Conrad novel. Over eighty years old, he came to the Marshalls sailing his boat after his first marriage broke up in the 1960s, married a Marshallese woman and flew a seaplane for years. Now suffering from Alzheimers, he lives here in this small village and spends hours every day sitting on the lagoon beach, watching to see if any ships go by, cared for by his wife, his pension the boxes of food his children in Majuro send him. There is one Japanese resident, who came with a construction crew in the 1970s, married and stayed behind. Now he operates a successful store, owns more boats that anyone else on the atoll, and is building a small hotel he hopes will attract businessmen from Japan looking for a secluded resort for business retreats.

More than foreign residents, changing transport and communications are means and sign of Arno's connection to the international economy. The elegant canoes have been replaced by fiberglass and aluminum, or local boats made of imported marine plywood which does not demand the specialist skills of a canoe builder. These boats are powered by Yamaha, Johnston, or Honda. The seaplane is needed no longer; there are landing strips on the east and west sides of the atoll, visited weekly by the small turboprops of Air Marshall Islands, unloading packages and pickup truck loads of boxes and coolers, goods sent by relatives in Majuro. The pickups are found wherever there is a road more than five miles long, symbols of wealth, but most owners happily subsidize their cost by running taxi services; it is prestigious to ride (Carucci 1995). There are as well a few motorbikes and several dozen bicycles. Communications also tie the islets of Arno to each other and to the Marshallese nation. You can pick up AM broadcasts on the national station, providing music, news, and announcements. For two-way communications there are numerous CB radios weaving a web around Arno and extending it to Majuro and other locations in the Marshalls. Enthusiasts put antennas atop tall trees and add powerful booster amplifiers, contacting Guam or Hawai'i or Australia.

The connections that bring goods, information, and people from distant metropolitan countries to Arno also draw people out of Arno, facilitating their movements into an increasingly global space. For most rural residents of the Marshalls, the pathway has been education. Rural schools only provide an elementary education. While some children leave school after the primary grades, others go on to secondary schools that are found in only four locations in the Marshalls: Jaluit, the urban center under German and Japanese administrations; the current urban centers of Majuro and Ebeye; and Wotje, a developing center of the northern Ratak (eastern) chain of atolls. Students who go on taste the excitement of the centers, and gain skills for jobs that do not exist in the rural islands. If they go on to college, Majuro is the only possible destination in the Marshalls. Other opportunities take students beyond the borders of the RMI, to schools elsewhere in Micronesia and beyond, including the University of the South Pacific in Fiji, the University of Guam, the University of Hawai'i, or two- and four-year colleges spread throughout the mainland United States. Special programs and training courses may also take students to New Zealand, Australia, and Japan. As detailed below, some of these students remain abroad and form the nucleus of new Marshallese communities (Hess, Nero, and Burton 2001; Allen 1997).

There are other factors influencing the distribution of Marshallese people. Jobs are more plentiful in urban areas, but with the monetarized economy the cost of living is more expensive and many jobs pay little, making it hard to feed and clothe everyone, and requiring several full or part-time incomes. Families respond by locating working-age adults in the urban centers and children and elders in the rural areas where they can be partially supported by the productivity of the land. At later stages in the process, a successful family may decide to reunite all members in the urban centers. By the 1988 census, two-thirds of all Marshallese enumerated lived in Majuro and Ebeye.

## REFLECTED WAVES

The geographical extension of families now includes urban areas of the United States as well, through the students who remained abroad. With the access granted in the compact, the circuits traveled by kin encompass these overseas households and, as in the Marshalls, movements are initiated by diverse motivations. Education continues to be important, but now younger Marshallese have joined the stream. Analyzing the problems students faced in the United States, many families decided the solution was to send them earlier, now that they had siblings or aunties or cousins abroad who could house them. This would give them a chance to learn the language and culture and catch up academically in junior high and high school. Elders join overseas children to play the same important roles they play in households in the islands— directing family affairs, caring for children,

applying their medical skills. Others travel for medical care themselves, seeking treatments not available in the Marshalls. A few people specifically looking for work began showing up in the United States after the compact was implemented; after government restructuring and decreased compact funding began to take effect in the mid-1990s, labor migration greatly increased. In a couple of years, a Marshallese community in Arkansas grew from a few families to the largest in the United States, several thousand residents, with the help of a new poultry processing plant that provided jobs and a low cost of living.

Family communications are maintained by letter and telephone and circulating videotapes which carry images of events such as *keemems* and funerals to close relatives in distant places, maintaining social proximity across geographic distance. The Marshall Islands newspaper carries occasional stories and pictures of overseas Marshallese, and is sold in one of the neighborhood convenience stores in Costa Mesa. Attending a celebration of a Marshall Islands holiday in Costa Mesa, I once saw an announcer giving a play-by-play commentary on a baseball game through a cell phone. He was connected, I was told, to the studios of V7AB, the national radio station in Majuro, which was broadcasting the game! The latest technologies are used to connect dispersed Marshallese; the Bikini Atoll Web site both tells the story of the weapons testing and their relocation and promotes scuba diving adventures among the sunken ships in the lagoon. Of the official and unofficial Web sites, Yokwe Online is the most vital with topical message boards and chat rooms recreating community in virtual space. Some adult Marshallese thought of computers as school aids for their children before Yokwe Online; after discovering its chat rooms they connect practically every night. The Minister of Education hailed its creator "for being a great captain and creating this Yokwe Yuk Web page for our new sailors surfing the high waves of the world wide web" (deBrum 1998).

In other ways, people think of places in the United States as part of Marshallese space and their practices as continuations of Marshallese *manit,* or tradition. It is signaled by assigned names such as "Enid Atoll" for the Oklahoma community (Allen 1997) and "Marshalls Town" and "Our Place" for neighborhoods in Costa Mesa, and claims in each community that they are the true keepers of custom while Marshallese at home are changing.

Communications and connections are also maintained by the constant circulation of people conducting family, church, government, or personal business. Communities located around the United States often send sports teams for inter-Marshallese community competitions on almost any holiday that provides a three-day weekend: Hawai'i and Oregon to California, California to Arizona, California and Oregon to Oklahoma. Official delegations of RMI government officials on the way back from meetings in Washington D.C. or at the United Nations in New York make visits to these communities, sometimes holding hearings on important matters. Politicians make appearances before national elections and recruit local campaign managers, and predictably a few overseas Marshallese throw their hats in the ring as candidates for office. Government officials as well as family members express wishes that overseas Marshallese would return home to assist in development projects (M. Madison, personal communication, 1993); both levels use them nevertheless as resources and consider them to be full members of family and society. Their continuing membership was enacted recently when the Marshallese minister of transportation, having arranged the purchase of several used landing craft through a San Diego broker, arranged for the culturally important dedication ceremonies conducted for vessels (Carucci 1995) to be held there also, drawing on the communities of southern California.

Marshallese in the United States are also connecting to the larger communities in which they live, while demonstrating their own approach. Like larger immigrant communities, they socialize and attend church with other Marshallese, creating a distinctive social space. Where possible, they tend to settle in the same neighborhood. They do not have the numbers, however, to establish a relatively exclusive Little Italy, Chinatown, or Little Saigon. In Costa Mesa they share blue collar neighborhoods with other immigrants, primarily Mexican and Vietnamese, with whom relations are cordial but distant. Just as the *weto* (lands) of a *bwij* (approximately a matrilineage) are dispersed among others' holdings spread around an atoll, their residences are similarly interleaved with apartments of other ethnic groups. Marshallese seek not an exclusive place, a "hood," but a social space with easy access to other Marshallese selves.

Work and school are two other contexts of contact. In multiethnic southern California these encounters are routine. In the schools, Marshallese numbers are small relative to other groups, and remediation programs designed to address the particular challenges of ethnic groups have mostly left them out. Recently parents have formed alliances with sympathetic administrators to educate both schools and parents and develop strategies to improve outcomes. Sports as well as classes offer contact with others, and some teenagers date non-Marshallese. On the job, Marshallese make acquaintances and friends among coworkers. Given limited awareness of the Marshall Islands, however, explaining who you are, where you are from, and how Marshallese are different from Hawai'ians or Samoans can be a challenge, a challenge that Marshallese meet through culture. Coworkers and friends are invited to *keemems,* where culture and community are on display. The Navigators perform at various public and private occasions. One in particular, the annual Pacific Islanders Festival held every May in a park near Long Beach, has connected them to larger and more-established Islander communities, enabling Marshallese to draw on their social and political experience. Churches are also links to community through denominational affiliations; the Protestant congregation of Costa Mesa meets in the picturesque church of the United Church of Christ in the seaside community of Corona del Mar, whose congregation is helping the Marshallese acquire their own church.

## REMITTANCES

Globalization presumably homogenizes places, incorporating them into a universal space created by international processes. The tale I have presented here could, with modified details, apply to many Pacific locales: trade, missions, colonial incorporation, culture change, war, migration, national independence. Local differences grounded in history persist, however. With the implementation of the compact, citizens have open access to the United States, and compact payments and services have given Marshallese a higher per capita income than most people of the economic periphery. The result has been an unusual configuration of flows of people and capital in the form of migration and remittances. In many Pacific Island societies people travel abroad to work overseas in metropolitan countries with more-developed economies and more opportunities for wage labor. Many of these overseas residents send portions of their income home to their families, and in some cases these remittances contribute a substantial proportion of a country's income. Among Marshallese, the pattern is reversed: More money is sent from the Marshalls to relatives in the United States than in the other direction.

The basis for this pattern is U.S. payments and the importance of education in the migration process. Parents of students, who often have above average incomes, send money to support their children's school and living expenses. When overseas students graduate, they usually return to the Marshalls, where they have job opportunities that bring more social status than the positions available to them in the United States. Marcus (1993) discusses a similar process in Tonga that he calls bootstrapping; children are prepared for positions that will improve the status of the whole family. Students who fall short of their goals are likely to stay abroad but do not remit for a variety of reasons. In the highly competitive labor markets in the United States, people without degrees find their wages limited, and in Costa Mesa expensive real estate makes rents very high. Marshallese households in the United States also often carry the expenses of visiting relatives, including new students and parents who have joined them abroad. Flows from the United States to the islands usually take the form of goods sent as gifts to parents, grandparents, and siblings.

Academics have joined a spirited debate on why people remit, whether remittances form a stable base for a country's economy, whether or not remittances contribute to economic development. One point has concerned whether remittances are used for investment, increasing the fund of capital available for economic development, or whether remittances are dissipated through consumption. Economists have often equated household spending with consumption, rather than seeing it as investment in the reproduction of people and the labor power necessary to maintain an economy. The study of overseas communities show Marshallese making investments in education and job skills, sometimes called human capital. The distinctive Marshallese pattern[3] is an important test case for theories about migration and remittances.

## DISTRIBUTING PEOPLE IN MARSHALLESE SOCIAL SPACE

World systems theory is an earlier perspective on the integration of regions in an international economy, emphasizing the geographical distribution of economic opportunities across a global political economy. The world system is composed of a wealthy industrialized core exporting finished goods and capital, a poor periphery exporting people and raw materials or primary products of agriculture and mining, and an intermediate semiperiphery with characteristics of both. Educational opportunities correlate with economic level. Comparing Marshallese communities positioned differently within the world system reveals this distribution of opportunities. The Costa Mesa community is closely tied to Los Angeles, a "global city" center of media, technology, finance, and shipping, while Majuro is a peripheral node of transport, information, and distribution, and Arno is a terminus of the system. The percentages of students and workers increase as we move from rural periphery to urban periphery to the core. The concentration is summarized by the dependency ratios for each locale. This is the ratio of people under fifteen and people over sixty-five (presumed to be economically inactive) to people between fifteen and sixty-five. The ratio for the rural Marshall Islands is 1.50; for Majuro it is 0.99; for Orange County it is 0.63. Overall, the data show that educational and employment patterns within Orange County are extensions of patterns that also pertain within the Marshall Islands. This can be viewed as the rational allocation of family members to different settings within a single transnational system. On the surface the effect looks like the work of the "invisible hand" of the market. Looking at the unequal participation of different families and the mechanisms for this redistribution of members, I see not autonomous market transactions but the distribution of people, information, and money through very personal channels, paths of kinship, alliance, and history.

## THE MARSHALLESE STATE

Statehood gave the Republic of the Marshall Islands its own border and its own identity, which finally gained international recognition on admission to membership in the United Nations in 1991. In a capitalist world, with identity come rights to market the identity. The RMI issues stamps and commemorative coins, established a ship registry, and for a time sold passports. These projects, like navigational stick charts, imply extensions and the nonlocality of Marshallese space, in particular the association with the United States. Images on commemorative stamps and coins, issued through a company located in Wyoming, draw on events and artifacts of U.S. history or ahistorical Marshallese culture (see Wolf 1982). The ship registry markets First World standards at discount prices (International Registries, Inc. 2001). The attraction of a Marshallese passport was the right of free access to the United States. The United States pressured the RMI to end the sales and imposed a requirement for a five-year residence in the RMI before allowing access to its shores. The result was the sudden appearance of a sizable number of Chinese in Majuro. Many Chinese went into business, opening stores, restaurants, and car rental and taxi services, putting strong pressure on small Marshallese enterprises. The legislature recently moved to make these kinds of operations out-of-bounds (as are voting rights) to holders of these second-class passports, which allow holders access to Marshallese territory but not Marshallese social space.

The government of the Marshall Islands is a hybrid, a synchretic form, demonstrating partiality in the reflection and absorption of impinging currents by local forms. Like the United States, the head of government, called the president, is simultaneously head of state. But like the Westminster parliamentary model, the executive and legislative functions are both based in one body, blurring a border important to their last colonial mentor, the United States. Members of the legislative body are called senators; the legislative body is called the *Nitijela,* the pit of knowledge, taking its name from the group that advised powerful *iroij* (chiefs). The president is elected by the *Nitijela* from among its members and selects his cabinet from the same group. There is also a second body, the *House of Iroij,* which does not legislate but has the power of advice and consent over matters touching on important traditional areas of their authority such as land.

Representation follows a distinctly Marshallese logic: Senators are elected to represent an island or atoll; in a sense, the senators represent the landed estates. The people with rights to vote because of their endowment of land do not all reside on those lands but are scattered around the islands and overseas territories. Further, as most people have rights in several locations, they may choose which affiliation to activate in an election. A senator is competing not only for votes against opponents but also for voter affiliations with his allies. Politicking requires many acts, current and promised, demonstrating a candidate's willingness and ability to care for his constituents. Constituent commitments, political alliances, and personal interests create complex interference patterns and chaotic evolutions in practice, and make *Nitijela* watching one of the great recreations in the Marshalls. A standing wave forms and the waters are predictable for several years, until an issue like gambling comes along, waves begin to diverge, to pound against each other, producing spume and swelling peaks (Walsh 1999, 2001). The pattern dissolves and reappears in a radically changed form, old faces and alliances lost, new ones in their place.

Globalization is not just about economics but also about governance, as demonstrated in the "Free Association" status of several former U.N. trust territories in the Pacific. For the RMI, this means that the nominal autonomy of the nation state within its own borders is undercut by a myriad of associations with U.S. governmental agencies and legal regimes. Mail service is tied to the U.S. Post Office, and the Marshalls have a zip code and area code. The Federal Emergency Management Agency responds to severe typhoons and tidal waves. Cultural preservation activities are funded by the Historic Preservation Office of the National Parks Service. The Federal Aviation Agency certifies the airports. Headstart and the Job Training Partnership Act have programs in the Marshalls. The police are required by the compact to cooperate with the U.S. Drug Enforcement Agency. Currency is the U.S. dollar. Yet the RMI makes its own foreign policy within the security constraints set by the compacts, for instance deciding to grant formal diplomatic recognition to Taiwan, whereas the United States recognizes only Beijing. The RMI also joined the Lome convention, an organization of former colonies of European countries, a strategy of spreading ties as broadly as possible in seeking economic assistance.[4]

Globalization is but one of the currents challenging the somewhat compromised state in the Marshall Islands. The Pacific is still a frontier region, where institutional arrangements are tentative, novel, and shifting, as witnessed by current (as I write) crises of state and nation in Fiji (see Kaplan, chapter 4), the Solomon Islands, Papua New Guinea (see

Roscoe, chapter 3), or Niue. Frontiers attract adventurers and carpetbaggers looking for quick profits, whether they are renegade capitalists looking to protect profits through offshore banks, trawlers poaching on someone's fishing grounds, or entrepreneurs promoting virtual states based in some small island through the Internet. It takes a master navigator to find the way through troubled waters. A master navigator can find the precise angle to the wind and trim of the sail to lift the outrigger out of the water, reducing drag, balancing it on a knife edge, and send it skimming on its way.

Amata Kabua, first president of the RMI, appeared to have these skills. On several occasions someone had come along with a plan to generate new land and new income in the Marshalls, charging industrial countries a fee for disposing of their waste in a distant lagoon. Kabua entertained these plans, to the distress of environmentally minded members of the opposition. With the cabinet as the canoe and the opposition the outrigger, he would catch the passing wind by taking money to fund a pilot study, lift the outrigger, send the vessel on its way until he thought the wind tapped out, ease out a line, and let the outrigger's weight drop it back into the sea, stabilizing and slowing the canoe. At the time of his death in 1996, he was promoting a plan to store spent nuclear fuel from electricity-generating reactors in the Marshalls, making way against opposition from both the United States and Pacific Islands neighbors. He had pointed out that several sites already contained radioactive wastes from U.S. weapons tests presumably sealed off for eternity. As the United States was not providing adequate compensation to pay for the costs of those tests and had failed to develop the Marshalls economy adequately during its administration, the income was needed and the project justified. After Amata's death, his successors were unable to maintain his course against the winds of opposition from Washington.

With the shifting emphasis from security to business at the peak of this cycle of globalization, the relationship between the United States and the Marshalls is changing. As the renegotiations of financial provisions of the Compacts of Free Association with the RMI and the Federated States of Micronesia opened, congressional committee chairs directed the General Accounting Office to conduct an audit of operations financed by compact monies. The GAO reported that use of the funds was not effective, efficient, or suitably legible. The House Subcommittee on Asia and the Pacific seemed to regard the matter not as negotiation of rent payments between nations but as misuse of funds. Only one congressman took the stance that the United States was paying for security, not development (U.S. Congress 2000). As international security is regarded as less problematic, cost considerations become more salient.[5] With the national government in Washington reluctant to provide funding for the social services used by compact immigrants, there are proposals to screen prospective travelers and exclude those affected by diseases of poverty such as tuberculosis (Farmer 1999) or leprosy, as well as those tagged with a criminal record. With new concerns, boundaries change and borders become selective. Globalization is likely to proceed the same way. Rather than joining in a global village without boundaries, we will observe a proliferation of pathways with restricted access.

The nation state emerged as a form of governance and identity fairly recently in history, and its proliferation has been even more recent, the years of decolonization following World War II. Bennett (1988) has argued that this proliferation was a method of enforcing accountability for territories and populations. It should be no surprise that, as the spaces in which global elites travel change and they seek to discipline new places and practices, the nation state itself should be challenged. Will the RMI state weather this change? No one knows. New Zealand has called for a reassessment of the self-governing status of Niue, a Pacific Islands state in free association with New Zealand (Pacific Islands Report 2001). Looking to the nation, however, I see signs of successful coping. There are now more Marshallese than ever before, spreading over a wider portion of the globe, preserving,

adapting, and sharing with others significant cultural practices, playing a greater range of roles in the international division of labor. Marshallese are clearly subjects, not just objects, of globalizing processes.

## THE POLITICAL ECONOMY OF BORDERS AND BOUNDARIES

Phil Goff, the foreign minister of New Zealand, recently diagnosed the economic problems of Niue. There were not enough people and not enough jobs, he said (Pacific Islands Report 2000). I experienced a moment of cognitive dissonance: How can you need jobs for workers who are not there, or workers to fill jobs that do not exist? The source of New Zealand's discomfort is that the Niueans are working in New Zealand (where they have citizenship), so they are not paying enough taxes to Niue's government to support its operations and social services programs, which are financed by New Zealand aid. Goff expressed no awareness that perhaps Niuean workers were supporting social services for their relatives by working in a more advanced economy where they generated more value and paid more in taxes than they could in Niue. There are two states, as identified by their borders, but one economy, where boundaries direct flows of labor in one direction and goods and services in another.

This is how political and economic space is imagined in such a way as to turn Pacific islands into places of devalued dependency (Nero 1997; Hau'ofa 1994, 1998).[6] The assumptions of economic development programs are that the nation will be developed in the territory commanded by the state; that physical place and economic space are the same (Redfield 1996). In one of my analyses of the fisheries development project on Arno and Majuro atolls, I suggested that the revenues of the fishers over the first five years could have been generated in one year if the money had been conservatively invested in overseas financial markets (Hess 1999).[7] Based on an imagined space and history of economic development in industrialized nations,[8] development relies on a theory of "comparative advantage" that mostly ignores the role of politics and corporations in establishing the unequal distribution of economic opportunities, that struggles against the inertia of history. Poor people cannot afford fictions; hence they cross imagined borders and struggle against very real boundaries (physical barriers, immigration police, exploitation, uncertainty, culture, language) to maintain livelihood and advance their prospects, in spite of desires to stay in place with their families and communities.[9] A few Pacific Island states such as Kiribati, Nauru, Tuvalu, and Palau have adapted to such economic realities by investing monies earned from metropolitan exploitation of their resources (phosphates for most, but also their position adjacent vital shipping lines in East Asia for Palau) in overseas markets to fund on-going government operations. This was reducing their dependency on aid. When borders are boundaries only for the movement of labor but not capital and commodities, people have fewer opportunities than financiers and industrialists and hence less bargaining power in the market. Maps and stick charts have different political intent.

## CONCLUSION

On my first trip to the Marshalls, I arranged a trip from Majuro to Arno on the small ten-meter fisheries project boat. It was my first venture on the open sea. I sat in this thin shell of fiberglass as swells higher than the boat rolled by, first lifting us up, then dropping us into a trough from which no signs of land were visible. The ocean surrounding me exceeded my attempts to fathom it in my imagination, to grasp its depth and extent. I thought, if the vast energies contained in these waters should turn violent, how could we survive? Navigators could not oppose those forces; rather they learned to trace their path by negotiating a way between wind and current and wave, riding the swells and taking advantage of the opportunities they offered with the best of their science and technology, while asking higher powers for their protection. Ancient Marshallese navigators established and

traversed a cultural space encompassing a diversity of environmental zones and political regimes, physical journeys following paths established by relations of land and family as well as chance and ambition.

Modern Marshallese navigators have done, and are doing, no less. The waves of globalization are no less real and little more responsive to individual action than the waves of the ocean. Building on the accomplishments and traditions of their ancestors, adopting or adapting the new when they find it useful or desirable, they have moved into new resource zones, diversified their opportunities, and struggled to provide their children with new opportunities suited to the changing world they inhabit. The heat exhaust of the industrial engines of globalization may raise sea levels (see Connell, chapter 15), washing their home islands from the face of the globe and cartographers' maps, but Marshallese people have tracked the rising tide to a new landfall.

## ACKNOWLEDGMENTS

Some of the data and conclusions presented in this chapter were originally published in the author's dissertation: "Institutions of Change: Development and Migration in the Political Economy of the Marshall Islanders," University of California, Irvine, 2001.

## NOTES

1. I argue below for a conceptual distinction between boundaries and border; from Braudel's reference to *lines* it seems that he is thinking in terms of borders.

2. Consider for example the extraterritorial status of foreign embassies, or the extension of USDA regulations into Mexico (Alvarez 2001).

3. A similar pattern holds for the Federated States of Micronesia (Levin 1999) and probably Palau, the other Micronesian countries in free association with the United States.

4. Other countries experience different reconfigurations. In some, various government functions are dispersed among globally networked nongovernmental organizations. Some have contracted out "security" operations to commercial armies. In Palestine, the national territory itself is not defined by a continuous border but fragmented by roads and settlements over which Israel maintains sovereignty. Are these harbingers of future changes in the form of nation states?

5. The events of and following September 11, 2001, intervening between drafting and printing of this chapter, have changed assessments of national security and brought calls for renewed attention to Pacific states as possible channels for attacks on the United States.

6. Like my Marshallese friends in Costa Mesa, I am an immigrant to California. Like them, I came from an urban center of a rural area (Iowa) that exports people, the most educated among them. In both cases, our mutual destination was as much the result of California's booming economy as personal choice. Internal and international migration are constituted by different discourses whose boundary process keeps the topics separate.

7. This was one of several analyses I generated with purposefully contradictory conclusions to make a larger point; in particular it ignores long-term investment in research and treats important social benefits as externalities, but also associated costs to the fishers and depletion of the fish stocks.

8. See Rostow 1960 for the paradigmatic (if now outdated) version, and Levantis (2000) for a current example.

9. Social critic and playwright George Bernard Shaw's Alfred Doolittle comments on morals in *Pygmalion,* "Can't afford them, Governor. Neither could you if you was as poor as me." What are international borders if not moral claims?

## *REFERENCES*

Allen, Linda. 1997. "Enid 'Atoll': A Marshallese Migrant Community in the Midwestern United States." Ph.D. dissertation. Department of Anthropology, University of Iowa.

Alvarez, Robert R. 2001. "Beyond the Border: Nation-State Encroachment, NAFTA, and Offshore Control in the U.S.-Mexican Mango Industry." *Human Organization* 60(2):121–127.

Barber, Benjamin R. 1992. "Jihad vs. McWorld." *The Atlantic Monthly.* 269(3):53–65.

Barker, Holly M. 1997. "Fighting Back: Justice, the Marshall Islands, and Neglected Radiation Communities." In *Life and Death Matters: Human Rights and the Environment at the End of the Millennium.* Barbara Rose Johnston, ed. Pp. 290–306. Walnut Creek, Calif.: AltaMira Press.

Bennett, John W. 1988. "Anthropology and Development: The Ambiguous Engagement." In *Production and Autonomy: Anthropological Studies and Critiques of Development.* John W. Bennett and John R. Bowen, eds. Pp. 1–29. Society for Economic Anthropology Monograph No. 5. Lanham, Mass.: University Press of America.

Braudel, Ferdinand. 1984. *The Perspective of the World.* New York: Harper and Row.

Carucci, Lawrence. 1989. "The Source of the Force in Marshallese Cosmology." In *The Pacific Theater.*

Geoffrey M. White and L. Lindstrom, eds. Pp. 73–96. Honolulu: University of Hawai'i Press.

———. 1993. "Christmas in Ujelang." In *Contemporary Pacific Societies.* Victoria Lockwood, Thomas G. Harding, and Ben Wallace, eds. Pp. 304–320. Englewood Cliffs, N.J.: Prentice Hall.

———. 1995. "Symbolic Imagery of Enewetak Sailing Canoes." In *Seafaring in the Contemporary Pacific Islands.* Richard Feinberg, ed. Pp. 16–33. DeKalb: Northern Illinois University Press.

———. 1997. *Nuclear Nativity: Rituals of Renewal and Empowerment in the Marshall Islands.* DeKalb: Northern Illinois University Press.

deBrum, Justin. 1998. Message posted in the education forum of Yokwe Online. http://www.yokwe.net (last accessed February 27, 2001).

Farmer, Paul. 1999. *Infections and Inequalities: The Modern Plagues.* Berkeley: University of California Press.

Firth, Stewart. 2000. "The Pacific Islands and the Globalization Agenda." *The Contemporary Pacific* 12(1):178–192.

Gegeo, David W. 1998. "Indigenous Knowledge and Empowerment: Rural Development Examined from Within." *The Contemporary Pacific* 10(2):289–315.

Hau'ofa, Epeli. 1994. "Our Sea of Islands." In *A New Oceania: Rediscovering Our Sea of Islands.* E. Waddell, Vijay Naidu, and Epeli Hau'ofa, eds. Reprinted in *The Contemporary Pacific* 6(1):147–161.

———. 1998. "The Ocean in Us." *The Contemporary Pacific* 10(2):391–410.

Hess, Jim. 1999. "Artisanal Coral Reef Fisheries and Sustainable Development: The Arno Atoll Fisheries Association." *Pacific Studies* 22(3/4):109–135.

Hess, Jim, Karen L. Nero, and Michael L. Burton. 2001. "Creating Options: Forming a Marshallese Community in Orange County, California." *The Contemporary Pacific* 13(1):89–121.

Hezel, Francis X. 1983. *The First Taint of Civilization.* Honolulu: University of Hawai'i Press.

———. 1995. *Strangers in Their Own Land.* Honolulu: University of Hawai'i Press.

Hiery, Hermann J. 1995. *The Neglected War: The German South Pacific and the Influence of World War I.* Honolulu: University of Hawai'i Press.

International Registries, Inc. 2001. Homepage for International Registries, Inc. and the Marshall Islands Vessel and Corporate Registry. http://www.register-iri.com/index.cfm (last accessed September 12, 2001).

Kiste, Robert C. 1974. *The Bikinians.* Menlo Park: Cummings.

———. 1993. "New Political Statuses in American Micronesia." In *Contemporary Pacific Societies.* Victoria Lockwood, Thomas Harding, and Ben Wallace, eds. Pp. 67–80. Englewood Cliffs, N.J.: Prentice Hall.

Kiste, Robert C., and Mac Marshall. 1999. *American Anthropology in Micronesia.* Honolulu: University of Hawai'i Press.

Lee, Susan, and Christine Foster. 1997. "The Global Hand." *Forbes Magazine* 159(8):85. http://www.forbes.com/forbes/1997/0421/5908085a.html (accessed April 21, 1997).

Levantis, Theodore. 2000. *Papua New Guinea: Employment, Wages, and Economic Development.* Canberra, Australia: Asia Pacific Press, Australian National University.

Levin, Michael J. 1999. "Micronesian Migrants: Who They Are and Where They Are Going." International Programs Center, Population Division, U.S. Bureau of the Census, Washington, D.C. Paper prepared for Out of Oceania: Diaspora, Community, and Identity, Center for Pacific Islands Studies, October 20, 1999, Honolulu, Hawai'i.

Marcus, George E. 1993. "Tonga's Contemporary Globalizing Strategies: Trading on Sovereignty Amidst International Migration." In *Contemporary Pacific Societies: Studies in Development and Change.* Victoria Lockwood, Thomas Harding, and Ben Wallace, eds. Pp. 21–33. Englewood Cliffs, N.J.: Prentice Hall.

Mason, Leonard. 1947. *The Economic Organization of the Marshall Islanders. U.S. Commercial Company, Economic Survey of Micronesia.* Vol. 9. New Haven, Conn.: Human Relations Area Files.

———. 1954. "Relocation of the Bikini Marshallese: A Study in Group Migration." Ph.D. dissertation. Department of Anthropology, Yale University.

———. 1989. "A Marshallese Nation Emerges from the Political Fragmentation of American Micronesia." *Pacific Studies* 13:1–46.

Massey, Douglas. 2000. "To Study Migration Today, Look to a Parallel Era." *The Chronicle of Higher Education.* August 18, XLVI(50):B4–5.

Meller, Norman. 1985. *Constitutionalism in Micronesia.* Honolulu: Institute for Polynesian Studies, Brigham Young University, Hawai'i Campus.

Nero, Karen L. 1997. "The End of Insularity: Islander Paradigms for the Pacific Century." In *The Cambridge History of the Pacific Islanders.* D. Denoon, S. Firth, J. Linnekin, M. Meleisea, and K. Nero, eds. Pp. 439–467. Cambridge: Cambridge University Press.

Pacific Islands Report. 2000. New Zealander's Goff to Niueans: You Have to Pay More Yourself. December 20. http://166.122.164.43/archive/2000/December/12_20-11.htm (accessed September 12, 2001).

———. 2001. Niue, New Zealand Discuss Niue's Future Status. February 20. http://166.122.164.43/archive/2001/February/02-20-04.htm (accessed September 12, 2001).

Peattie, Mark R. 1988. *Nan'yo: The Rise and Fall of the Japanese in Micronesia, 1885–1945.* Center for Pacific Islands Studies. Honolulu: University of Hawai'i Press.

Polanyi, Karl. 1957. *The Great Transformation.* Boston: Beacon Press.

Redfield, Peter. 1996. "Beneath a Modern Sky: Space Technology and Its Place on the Ground." *Science, Technology, and Human Values* 21(3):251–274.

Rodriguez, Gregory. 2000. "Vicente Fox Blesses the Americanization of Mexico." *Los Angeles Times.* Sunday, December 10, Section M, pp. 1, 6.

Rostow, Walt W. 1960. *The Stages of Economic Growth, a Non-Communist Manifesto.* Cambridge: Cambridge University Press.

Spennemann, Dirk H. R. 2000. The Sea—The Marshallese World, Albury. http:/life.csu.edu.au/marshall/html/culture/SeaNavigation.html (accessed September 12, 2001).

Teaiwa, Teresa. 1994. "Bikini and Other S/pacific N/oceans." *The Contemporary Pacific* 6(1):87–109.

Tobin, Jack A. 1954. *Kili Journal,* August 28 to September 18, 1954. Mimeographed. Majuro, Marshall Islands: Trust Territory of the Pacific Islands.

———. 1967. "The Resettlement of the Enewetak People: A Study of a Displaced Community in the Marshall Islands." Ph.D. dissertation. Department of Anthropology, University of California, Berkeley.

U.S. Congress. 2000. U.S. Assistance to Micronesia and the Marshall Islands: A Question of Accountability. Hearing before the Subcommittee on Asia and the Pacific of the Committee on International Relations, House of Representatives, 106th Congress, second session. Washington, D.C.: U.S. Government Printing Office.

Walsh, Julianne M. 1999. "Micronesia in Review: Issues and Events, 1 July 1998 to 30 June 1999: Marshall Islands." *The Contemporary Pacific* 12(1):204–211.

———. 2001. "Micronesia in Review: Issues and Events, 1 July 1999 to 30 June 2000: Marshall Islands." *The Contemporary Pacific* 13(1):211–216.

Whorf, Benjamin Lee. 1967. *Language, Thought, and Reality: Selected Writings of Benjamin Lee Whorf.* John B. Carroll, ed. Cambridge, Mass.: M.I.T. Press.

Williamson, Jeffrey G. 1998. "Globalization, Labor Markets and Policy Backlash in the Past." *Journal of Economic Perspectives* 12(4):51–72.

Wolf, Eric R. 1982. *Europe and the People Without History.* Berkeley: University of California Press.

# 12

# Market Highs: Alcohol, Drugs, and the Global Economy in Oceania

**Mac Marshall**

*University of Iowa*

During the last three decades the production, distribution, marketing, and consumption of legal and illegal substances has been transformed. The rise and consolidation of huge transnational corporations (TNCs) selling alcoholic beverages and tobacco has been mirrored by the growth of sophisticated international drug cartels moving cocaine, heroin, and marijuana across national borders. At the same time, many traditional substances, like kava, betel, and qat, have been converted into market commodities and sold for money within and among nation states. The ways that all of these substances have entered the global economy and accompanied the ever-more-rapid movement of people and ideas around the world have only begun to be explored by social scientists. This chapter examines these new patterns of substance manufacture, movement, and use for the world region known as Oceania or the Pacific Islands.

The two major substances used by Pacific Islanders when outsiders initially came among them—betel and kava—will be discussed first. Both substances continue to be widely consumed in the islands, both have been incorporated into a market economy, and kava has entered the global economy, albeit in a modest way. The historical encounter of Pacific Islanders with alcoholic beverages will then be sketched as a necessary prelude to a more detailed look at the establishment of beer breweries in the islands, tied to TNCs that have extended their reach even to these far outposts of world trade. What is known of the production, use, and international transshipment of marijuana (cannabis, or pot) in Oceania will be reviewed next, and no effort will be made to discuss other illegal drugs such as cocaine, heroin, and methamphetamines. Final comments will concentrate on the economic and public health impacts of the marketing of kava, betel, beer, and pot on the lifestyles and well-being of Pacific peoples. Due to space limitations and because the topic has been explored in depth elsewhere (for example, Marshall 1981, 1987, 1991, 1997) the production and marketing of tobacco products in the islands will not be examined here.

# GOING NUTS OVER ROOTS: BETEL AND KAVA

Betel-chewers masticate three separate ingredients: the endosperm of the *Areca catechu* palm seed (often mistakenly called "betel nut"), the leaf or inflorescence of the *Piper betle* vine, and slaked lime usually made from ground coral or seashells. The first two of these are pharmacologically active; the third can be caustic, especially when commercially manufactured lime is substituted, as is often done today. Melanesians generally do not add tobacco to the betel quid, although this is now commonly done in such areas of Micronesia as Yap and Palau. Leaving tobacco aside, the active ingredients in the betel quid are central nervous system stimulants that enhance arousal and produce mild euphoria and a general sense of well-being. Chewing betel also reduces thirst and hunger. Beginners may experience dizziness, nausea, and diarrhea, and even experienced chewers may sweat and salivate profusely.

Made from the chewed, pounded, or ground root of *Piper methysticum,* a shrub related to *Piper betle,* kava is drunk as an infusion made by soaking the prepared roots in water and straining the resultant mixture through coconut bast or cloth (for details see Lebot, Merlin, and Lindstrom 1992). Kava contains several potent alkaloids and taken in the traditional island manner, kava-drinking produces a range of physical effects, notably analgesia and muscle relaxation, and it leads to a sense of sociability and tranquility. While the drinker's physical coordination may be impaired after several cups, the mental faculties are left clear, and kava induces a quiet, contemplative camaraderie.

Betel and kava have limited distribution in Oceania, although in recent years consumption of both substances has expanded among people who formerly did not use them. Betel is chewed primarily in western Melanesia (Papua New Guinea [PNG] and the Solomon Islands) and in western Micronesia (Yap, Palau, and the Marianas), and is absent from the Polynesian Triangle. Kava is found in most major Polynesian islands, in Fiji and Vanuatu, in scattered coastal and island locations of PNG and west Papua, and on the island of Pohnpei (and formerly also Kosrae) in Micronesia. Betel-chewing also is common through mainland and island Southeast Asia, in Sri Lanka and the Indian subcontinent, and as far east as the Zanzibar area of east Africa. Unlike betel-chewing, kava-drinking remains a peculiarly Pacific Islander pastime and, except among migrant communities, it is not practiced elsewhere in the world.[1]

Betel-chewing occupies a social position similar to coffee or tea drinking in the West—it stimulates social activity, suppresses boredom, enhances work, increases personal enjoyment, and symbolizes friendly, peaceful social relations. Nearly all adults and many children in betel-chewing societies partake regularly. As with tobacco users, betel-chewers carry the necessary ingredients on their person so that they can prepare a quid several times a day. Once again, kava is different. Rather than a mundane, widely shared substance like betel, kava had sacred overtones, its use typically was restricted to adult men, and its preparation and consumption often were surrounded by elaborate ceremony. Over the past quarter century, however, patterns of kava use have changed markedly in much of the Pacific. Young and untitled men now drink it with impunity, as do growing numbers of women, particularly in urban areas. While in certain contexts it retains its sacred connotations, kava has become secularized as it has entered the market economy. In its patterns of sale and distribution, although not in the behavioral outcomes that follow its consumption, kava increasingly resembles alcoholic beverages, being sold by the drink in special "kava bars" where substantial quantities are prepared on a daily basis for customers' pleasure.

These transformations in the distribution and cultural positions of betel and kava reflect the forces of both tradition and modernity operating on Pacific societies. Hirsch has argued that the growth of towns, urban centers, and a monetary economy during the colonial period in PNG (but especially following national independence in 1975) led to the breakdown of old regional trade networks and to the emergence of newly valued resources—including betel—that are now sold in commercial markets. Calling betel "the quintessential PNG commodity" (1990:26), he makes a case that its prominence is "related to types of life-style and status symbols which adhere to the personal and social identities" that are associated with "a formative PNG national culture" (1990:19). Among the legal substances available to most PNG nationals, betel is the only one that "is grown, marketed and consumed solely by Papua New Guineans. It has no association with the norms or values introduced by Europeans" (1990:25). As such, Hirsch sees betel as a perfect commodity for the creation of a nascent, national culture.

A similar point has been made concerning kava as a neotraditional symbol in Vanuatu (Philibert 1986), where "kava-drinking has become an established part of the emerging national, as against local or regional, identity, as a kind of 'neo-tradition'" (Crowley 1995:13). Kava bars, called *nakamal* in Vanuatu, have outstripped alcohol bars in popularity in Port Vila, where by 1995 their numbers had increased to around 140 since the first one was opened in 1979, a year before the country's independence. Kava bars also exist today in the urban centers of Fiji, Guam, Hawai'i, New Caledonia, and Pohnpei, and a number of Pacific polities besides Vanuatu have used kava to symbolize their new political fabric.[2] This is true of Fiji, Tonga, and Samoa, and also of Pohnpei in the Federated States of Micronesia (FSM), where the kava-drinking shell is depicted on the state's flag.

For the most part, betel circulates *within* national economies, and it has made relatively small inroads into international trade. The development of towns and markets, as noted by Hirsch (1990), has facilitated the spread of betel-chewing into areas of PNG where it did not exist until perhaps the 1960s, notably the Highlands. Lutkehaus (1981) adds an increase in air travel and the job mobility of PNG's educated elite as other factors accounting for the contemporary diffusion of betel-chewing. Certain coastal, island, and lowland peoples, such as the Mekeo, the Manam Islanders, the Kaliai, and the Biwat, have profited from having plentiful *Areca catechu* nuts to transport and sell for cash in towns and cities such as Angoram, Kimbe, Mt. Hagen, and Port Moresby. Indeed, as urban markets have developed throughout PNG's nineteen provinces, betel-chewing ingredients have become staple items offered for sale (Figure 12.1).

The monetary incentives to participate in the betel trade are considerable. Counts

**Figure 12.1**  Betel for sale in PNG market

(1981) records that in the mid-1970s a Kaliai could earn one and one-half times as much money for about one-quarter the effort by selling betel in the Kimbe market instead of making copra. Watson (1987) reports that the first long-distance Biwat trading trip to Mt. Hagen in 1979 netted 1,400 kina (about US$2,100 in 1979) from *Areca* nuts and *Piper betle* sales in just three days. Lutkehaus (1981) observed that people from Manam would prepare 25-kg. bags of *Areca* nuts, haul them by boat from the island to the government station at Bogia on the New Guinea coast (a trip of anywhere from two to six hours), carry them by truck from Bogia to the provincial capital of Madang (another six-hour journey), and then put them on an Air Niugini flight to Mt. Hagen. A Manam relative or *wantok* resident in Mt. Hagen would receive the shipment, take it to the public market, and sell single nuts for 10 to 20 *toea* each (the price of ten or twelve nuts on the coast). *Areca* nuts even have begun to affect inflation rates in PNG. For example, reporting on a close to 22 percent surge in annual inflation in PNG during 1998, Nick Suvulo of the National Statistical Office said: "one of the main contributing factors to the huge increase in the level of inflation was the price hikes for betel nuts nationwide" (PNG *Post-Courier*, February 18, 1999). While it is clear that betel has become a significant economic commodity within the country, betel-chewing ingredients are not exported from PNG. Elsewhere in the Pacific, however, in Micronesia, they *do* cross national borders.

Just as betel-chewing has spread into new areas such as the Highlands of PNG, so has betel-chewing expanded into new islands in Micronesia. The timing and reasons for this expansion are somewhat different than in the PNG case. The people of Yap, Palau, and the Marianas all chewed betel aboriginally, and all continue to do so with gusto. As Guam has developed into a major regional urban center, especially since the early-to-mid-1980s, islanders from all of the new Micronesian countries (FSM, the Republic of Palau, and the Republic of the Marshall Islands) have migrated there in substantial numbers for employment and educational opportunities. Guam also has a large Filipino population, many of whom also chew betel. As in PNG, one consequence of Guam's regional ascendance has been that islanders from formerly nonbetel-chewing areas (for example, Chuuk and Pohnpei) have experimented with betel in the urban area and some have adopted the habit.

More important for betel's eastward spread in Micronesia, though, was the establishment of FSM's capital on Pohnpei. The FSM national government employs citizens from all four states (Chuuk, Kosrae, Pohnpei, and Yap), and the Yapese who moved to Pohnpei created a market for betel there. Yapese chewers led others to try their habit, and by 1995 betel was prominently for sale in stores on Pohnpei and Chuuk (Figure 12.2). While some of this was locally grown, much was imported on Air Micronesia flights from Palau and Yap to Guam, and thence to Chuuk and Pohnpei. By 1993 betel-chewing had become so thoroughly integrated into life in the FSM national center on Pohnpei that when then-President Bailey Olter signed a policy statement establishing a drug-free workplace, betel (and *sakau*—Pohnpeian kava) was specifically excluded (Ashby 1993). Based upon a 1992 survey of over 6,000 youths ages twelve to eighteen in all four states of the FSM, nearly a third of the respondents from Chuuk and Kosrae, and over half from Pohnpei, had chewed betel in the preceding month (Reed 1993:68). So the substance clearly had taken hold in the Eastern Carolines.

Even back in the mid-1980s betel contributed importantly to Yap's economy. Local retail stores sold an estimated 50,000 Zip-Loc bags (called "a plastic") containing fifteen to eighteen *Areca* nuts and some *Piper betle* leaves for US$1.25 each in 1986, and boxes of *Areca* nuts were sold to transiting Palauans at the airport for US$5 each. Beyond that, "huge boxes of nuts . . . are exported wholesale by Joe Tamag Enterprises and other companies [to Guam]" (Bird and Ruan 1986). By 1999, Yap's betel business had shown sufficient potential that with help from the Pacific Business Center at the University of Hawai'i, a local entrepreneur, Francis Reg, was developing plans for an

**Figure 12.2** "Mi uor pu"

*Areca* nut plantation so as "to sell his product throughout Micronesia" (Pacific Business Center News 1999). Many retail stores on Palau sold single chews (called *elaus*), each consisting of half an *Areca* nut, a piece of *Piper betle* leaf, some lime, and half a cigarette "all wrapped together in aluminum foil" (Ysaol, Chilton, and Callaghan 1996: 252). The market value of an *elaus* varied between US$0.10 and US$0.20 depending upon the time of year. Not including exports, these researchers estimated the annual market value of betel-chewing ingredients consumed in Palau in 1995 as in excess of US$9.2 million. This expenditure was "for a nation with a 1993 estimated gross domestic product of $75.8 million" (Ysaol, Chilton, and Callaghan 1996:253).

Although to some extent betel is involved in international trade, when compared to kava this pales in significance. Even more than a century ago kava was exported from Hawai'i to Germany for medicinal use (Gatty 1956). In the 1970s kava figured in trade between island countries; for instance, Tonga began shipping kava to Fiji in 1973 and sent six tons in November 1974 (*Micronesian Independent,* January 10, 1975, p. 4). Such intra-Pacific trade crossed regional boundaries, too, with packages of powdered kava from Samoa on sale in Pohnpei in early 1989

(Ashby 1989; this product was still being sold during my visits to Pohnpei in 1993 and 1995). It was during the decade of the 1990s, however, that kava boomed as an export crop.

As far back as 1984, when Vanuatu began to look at kava as a possible export to other kava-drinking island countries like Fiji and Tonga, they also began to communicate with the European pharmaceutical industry. By the mid-1990s this had clearly paid off for Vanuatu and other island nations as kava became "the focus of interest from a growing number of pharmaceutical companies from Germany, the United States, Japan, and France" (Decloitre 1995:44). At that time Fiji was the leading kava exporter in the region, earning on average about US$3.5 million a year, Vanuatu's domestic market was worth approximately US$900,000, and the production and sale of kava provided income for some 6,000 ni-Vanuatu growers (Decloitre 1995). By 1997, domestic kava consumption in Fiji exceeded domestic beer sales in value at US$11 million (Islands Business 1998). Vanuatu's kava exports were worth US$6.83 million in 1997—almost one-fourth of all the country's commodity exports—and US$7.4 million in 1998, while the value of Fiji's kava exports in 1998 reached US$7.7 million (Guille 1999; Islands Business 1999c).

In the mid-1980s before this economic bonanza began, it appeared that the huge U.S. market might be closed to kava products when the Food and Drug Administration (FDA) prohibited kava imports under the U.S. Food and Additive Amendment of 1958.[3] The ban was specifically on kava as a food or food additive, and did not affect its import for use in pharmaceuticals. By late 1986, however, U.S. officials reclassified the substance as a "dietary supplement," which meant it no longer fell under FDA scrutiny, and the ban on kava as a beverage (food) was lifted. This paved the way for the 1990s market expansion. Between 1988 and 1994, Vanuatu "increased its export income from *kava* by six-fold . . . earning US$520,000 in 1994" (Seneviratne 1997:48). By 1996 the huge German pharmaceutical firm, Schwabe, was "making big money by selling a tranquiliser drug made with extracts from the kava plant" (Keith-Reid 1996:30). A year later, Kava Kompany, locally registered in Vanuatu, introduced ten new products to the U.S. market, among them a drink called Mellow Out sold at US$90 per liter, Kavatrol sold in thirty-capsule packets for under US$9, Liquid Kalm (an after-dinner stress-relief syrup), and Erotikava, "a 200-ml bottle of *kava* syrup recommended to be taken after dinner preferably in a candlelit room with soft music" (Seneviratne 1997:48).

In April 1997, a Noumea-based company, the Richard Group, planned to invest in a kava-processing plant in Vanuatu, after research it had done "enabled it to develop *kava* chewing gum, *kava* juice, *kava* lolly and instant *kava*," all of which they apparently had patented (Seneviratne 1997:49). Instant kava is the fine grey powder containing kava's active ingredients that "those in the know refer to . . . as *neskava*," an "amusing play on words with *neskafe*, which in Bislama is a generic term for 'instant coffee' [Nescafe]" (Crowley 1995:18). To further mix categories (if not drugs), a U.S. company has marketed a brand of instant coffee called Kava for many years. When questioned, this company's consumer service representative wrote that they "have no information on how the Kava name came about" (Lois Jacobs, personal communication); it probably derives from the

**Figure 12.3**  Kava brand coffee

"K" sound in coffee, combined with the -ava ending from Java, a common American English slang name for coffee (Figure 12.3).

A new US$3 million factory in Port Vila was scheduled to "begin producing kava paste for export to overseas extraction companies" by March 1999 (Johnston 1998:27). Named Botanical Extracts Limited, this company was owned 40 percent by a ni-Vanuatu shareholding group, with the other 60 percent comprising independent investors of various nationalities, many of them also ni-Vanuatu. According to the company's chief executive, the then-current world price for a kilogram of 30 percent kavalactone paste was around US$200.

But as often happens with a good thing, what began as an export primarily from Fiji and Vanuatu soon spread. The Hawai'i Kava Growers Association had been organized by 1998 and farmers were planting kava, especially on the Big Island, "as an ideal high value substitute for lost sugar cane and pineapple income" (Islands Business 1998:38). Heavy international demand had driven the kava price up to between US$5 and US$10 per pound, depending on quality, and in 1996 international sales of kava capsules alone "were a record US$14 million" (Islands Business 1998:38). U.S. consumers spent US$30 million on kava products in 1997 (Grady 1998), and over US$35 million in 1998 (MacDonald 1999). During this same period the wholesale price of a kilogram of dried root nearly doubled, several popular books were published about kava, and it was sold on numerous Web sites. Accompanying this run on kava-related products—comprising a whole range of antianxiety, depression, and tension pills and tonics—a Pacific Kava Council was set up in the hope of invoking intellectual property rights and protecting it as a special Pacific crop that is a part of the islanders' cultural heritage. But this was wishful thinking.

By the end of 1998, according to the editor of *Nutrition Business Journal,* a San Diego-based trade publication, kava had become one of the top ten or twelve herbal supplement products sold in the United States (MacDonald 1999). And by then major corporations like the L'Oreal cosmetic company and the German pharmaceutical firm, Schwabe, had taken out U.S. patents on their kava products. Natrol, which launched Kavatrol in 1996, also had patented its particular kava mixture, and net global sales of Kavatrol for the first nine months of 1998 were US$48.9 million, up nearly 66 percent over the same period the year before (MacDonald 1999). Despite this rapid growth, recent reports suggest that the kava boom may be over. "Demand, prices and exports collapsed" at the beginning of 1999 and Vanuatu's exports in the first seven months of 1999 were only equivalent to sales in October 1998 alone—and at a price of "only US$15 a kilo compared to US$20–US$25 six months ago" (Guille 1999:36). An even larger threat to continued profits for Pacific Islands countries from the sale of kava were reported plans for large-scale kava plantations in Australia and Mexico, which would seriously undercut the international market price and be much closer to major international markets.

## CREEPING MODERNITY: BEER WASHES OVER THE PACIFIC

Western-focused histories of the explorations by Europeans and others of the Pacific Islands routinely document the wondrous new peoples, plants, and places that were "discovered." Typically left out of such histories is much discussion of the simultaneous discoveries being made by islanders as they, too, encountered new people and new things. One major new thing that often formed part of these early encounters was beverage alcohol. Unlike betel and kava, beverage alcohol did not exist in the Pacific Islands before foreigners arrived beginning in the sixteenth century. Europeans offered it to islanders in at least some of their early encounters, but such contacts were too sporadic for this to have much impact until the nineteenth century. By then the number and frequency of voyages by outsiders increased, previously uncontacted islands were visited, and beach communities sprang up in some of the nascent port towns frequented by whalers. Beachcombers and whalers often taught the islanders how to ferment coconut toddy or *ti* root into alcohol drinks, and provided rather intemperate models for how to behave when drunk. With missionization and the beginning of commercial enterprises during the first half of the nineteenth century, Protestant missionaries, reflecting changing attitudes toward alcohol in their mother countries, spoke out against "Demon Rum." This set the stage for colonially imposed prohibition laws as foreigners claimed control over different island areas by the end of the nineteenth century. While many islanders tasted alcoholic beverages and learned how to ferment their own home brew before the establishment of colonial governments, some were not exposed to beverage alcohol until after World War II. Stay-at-home PNG Highlanders had no experience with such drinks until prohibition was ended in 1962, and in some of that country's more remote areas alcohol remained unavailable as late as the 1980s. For most Pacific Islanders, then, alcohol was an alien substance that most of them first encountered sometime in the nineteenth century.

Beer is Pacific Islanders' favorite alcoholic beverage today, although this has not always been so. When alcohol first made its appearance in the Pacific it was in the form of distilled drinks such as brandy or rum carried aboard European sailing vessels. A common first reaction by islanders when offered a taste was to spit it out in disgust. Its bitterness, akin to the bitterness of kava, led many islanders to dub these distilled beverages "European kava." The coconut toddy and mashed fruits that islanders learned to ferment had approximately the alcohol content of beer, but toddy sometimes was distilled to make a more potent drink. Distilled drinks of this general sort were being made in Hawai'i as early as 1802. Since those early days of Western contact, the beverage preferences of Pacific Islanders have changed considerably. For at least the past forty years beer has been the drink of choice everywhere in Oceania, once it became legal for islanders to drink.

What appears to have been the first commercial brewery anywhere in the Pacific Islands opened in Honolulu in April 1854 under ownership of J. J. Bischoff and Co. (Schmitt 1997). This venture failed by January 1857, and in March 1865 another brewery was launched in Honolulu, producing "Hawaiian Beer" in casks, kegs, and bottles. Its two partners split after just a few months, with one retaining the Hawaiian Brewery and the other starting the O'ahu Brewery. Within a year both operations folded, and the owner of the latter opened the Honolulu Distillery instead. Local beer manufacture in Hawai'i then languished until 1888 when the National Brewing Company began, although it, too, lasted only a short while. Finally, early in the twentieth century, a brewery opened in Hawai'i that survived more than a few years. Honolulu Brewing and Malting Company, Ltd. began offering Primo Lager in February 1901, and this company prospered until the advent of Prohibition in 1918 (Schmitt 1997).

Soon after the fourteen-year dry spell during national Prohibition, two breweries opened in Honolulu in 1934: the American Brewing Company (offering Pale Ambrew)

and the Hawai'i Brewing Corporation (offering Primo). Ambrew was replaced by Royal, a new brand, in 1937, which survived until 1962 when the American Brewing Company ceased production. After becoming, in 1958, the first U.S. brewery to sell beer in aluminum cans, Primo fell on hard times during the 1960s. The Hawai'i Brewing Corporation had been acquired by Beatrice Foods of Chicago, and at the end of 1963 the Jos. Schlitz Brewing Company purchased the brewery from Beatrice Foods. From then until May 1979 both Primo and Schlitz beers were brewed in a new facility near Pearl Harbor, but "on 15 May 1979, Schlitz shipped the last cases of Hawai'i-brewed Primo and transferred production to its Los Angeles plant" (Schmitt 1997:148).

Next to the beers brewed in Hawai'i, the oldest Pacific brewery outside of the European-dominated societies of Australia and New Zealand was Brasserie de Tahiti. It began making Aora'i brand beer in 1914, a name that referred both to Tahiti's second-highest mountain and to a god's or king's palace. Instead of Prohibition, which destroyed the Honolulu Brewing and Malting Company, German warships literally blew up the original Tahiti brewery in 1917 during a World War I bombardment (Islands Business[Pacific] 1991). Purchased by an American company in 1922, Brasserie de Tahiti once again came under local ownership in 1937. While Keith-Reid (1997) dates the production of Tahiti's popular Hinano brand beer to 1982, it apparently was inaugurated in 1955 (Hinano 2000). French colonists also established a brewery in New Caledonia in 1920 (see Table 12.1).

The year 1955 was a momentous one for brewing in Oceania because it marked the initial penetration of this industry by large TNCs from elsewhere in the world. South Pacific Brewery Limited (SP) began producing beer at its Port Moresby plant in November 1952. Three years later the controlling interest in the brewery was sold to a Singapore-based company, Malayan Breweries Ltd. (MBL, now called Asia Pacific Breweries), which had been formed in 1931 by the merger of Fraser and Neave Ltd. of Singapore (a soft-drink

**Table 12.1**    Pacific Islands Breweries in the Year 2000

| Country (Island) | Brewery Name | Year Established[a] | Name(s) of Top Brands | Ownership and Operation |
|---|---|---|---|---|
| Papua New Guinea (PNG) | South Pacific Brewery | 1952 | South Pacific Lager ("SP") | Owned 80% by Asia Pacific (Malayan) Breweries of Singapore, which is owned 42% by Heineken of the Netherlands and 20% by PNG government and local interests; also brews San Miguel on license (since 1983). |
| French Polynesia (Tahiti) | La Brasserie de Tahiti | 1955 | Hinano[b] | Owned by Heineken of the Netherlands. |
| | | | Hei-Lager | Local interests; also brews Heineken on license (since 1976). |
| Fiji | Carlton Brewery (Fiji) | 1958 | Fiji Bitter; Fiji Light; Fiji Stout; Fiji Draught; Fiji Gold | Owned 63% by Carlton and United Breweries of Australia, the major production arm of Fosters Brewing Group, and 30% by the Fijian Holdings, Ltd. and 7% by other local interests. |
| New Caledonia | Grande Brasserie de Nouvelle Caledonie | 1974 | Number One | Owned 87.1% by Heineken Brewery of the Netherlands.[c] |
| Samoa | Samoa Breweries | 1978 | Vailima[d] | Owned 68.3% by Carlton Brewery of Fiji, in turn part of the Fosters Brewing Group of Australia; remaining shares held by the Samoan government (15%), the Nauruan government (10%), and the remainder by small shareholders; also brewed San Miguel on license from 1982–1990; also brews EKU Bavaria beer under license to Erste Kulmbacher Actienbrauerei AG.[e] |
| Tonga | Royal Beer Company | 1987 | Royal; Ikale[f] | Owned 50% by Pripps Brewery of Sweden (which is owned by ORKLA, a Norwegian food company that has merged Pripps with Ringnes, a Norwegian brewery) and 50% by a wholly owned Tongan firm, CFTL.[g] |
| Cook Islands | Rarotonga Breweries | 1987 | Cooks Lager | The major current owner is Richard Barton; formerly owned 94% by George and Metua Ellis (local business people). |

*(table continues on page 209)*

manufacturer) and Heineken Brewery of the Netherlands (Heineken 2000). SP's subsequent success is owed in no small measure to "the huge resources of the Heineken Group and MBL" (Sinclair 1983:32).

In mid-1958, a local competitor, Guinea Brewery, began selling beer from its new Lae facility, and this plus the pressure of imported beer from Australia severely stressed SP. Fortunately for the company's future well-being, in November 1962 Papua New Guineans won the right to drink. From that point on the

quantity of annual beer imports declined and SP's production soared—to over one million gallons in 1965–1966 and three million gallons in 1968–1969. In the process, SP took over Guinea Brewery in 1965. Not long thereafter, in 1971, another new brewery was established in Port Moresby—Territory United Brewery Ltd. (TUB), with technical assistance from Asahi Breweries of Japan. Marketing TUB brand beer, the new brewery opened to considerable fanfare, but its product never really took hold with PNG's drinkers and it

| Country (Island) | Brewery Name | Year Established[a] | Name(s) of Top Brands | Ownership and Operation |
|---|---|---|---|---|
| Vanuatu | National Breweries | 1990 | Tusker; Vanuatu Bitter | Owned 50% by Pripps Brewery of Sweden (which is owned by ORKLA, a Norwegian food company that has merged Pripps with Ringnes, a Norwegian brewery), 25% by the Vanuatu National Provident Fund, and 25% by the Vanuatu Development Bank; also brews Pripps on license.[h] |
| Samoa | Apia Bottling Company | 1991 | Manuia[i] | Owned by Dick Carpenter, the American managing director of a diversified miniconglomerate in Apia. |
| Solomon Islands | Solomon Breweries | 1993 | Solbrew | Owned 72% by the government of Nauru, with remaining shares held by Brauhaase International of Germany, and two smaller German shareholders; also brews EKU Bavaria beer under license to Erste Kulmbacher Actienbrauerei AG.[j] |
| Niue | M.K. Viviani Brewery | early 1990s | Fiafia Lager[k] | Brewed by Onehunga Spring Brewery in Auckland, New Zealand for the Niue market. |

[a]This is the year that the brewery's beer first went on public sale, not the year of the company's incorporation.
[b]Hinano refers to the pandanus blossom; hei means a flower garland (cf. Hawaiian lei).
[c]Grande Brasserie de Nouvelle Caledonie (GBNC) was created by the 1974 merger of two breweries: Le Grande Brasserie Caledonienne (GBC) and La Grande Brasserie de Noumea (GBN). Soon thereafter, Heineken bought in and by 1980 had acquired a 76.5% interest. The Grande Brasserie de Caledonie began in 1920, became La Glaciere in 1953 (producing "La Marybet," the first locally brewed beer in New Caledonia), and then in 1966 again changed its name to La Grande Brasserie Caledonienne, brewing a beer named "L' Ancre Pils." In 1969 a second brewery (GBN) began producing "La Number One" beer, and that has remained the merged company's primary product. Heineken increased its share of GBNC from 28% to 76.5% in 1980, and later to the current 87.1% (Heineken 2000).
[d]Named after Robert Louis Stevenson's residence and burial place in Samoa.
[e]Sources: Ah Mu (1999), *Islands Business [Pacific]* (1999a, 1999b), *Pacific Islands Monthly* (1999), and Hugh Ragg, Vice President for Pacific Operations, Foster's Brewing International (personal communication).
[f]This is the Tongan spelling of "eagle" and the brand depicts a sea eagle on its label.
[g]Sources: *Pacific Islands Monthly* (1987) and Tu'itahi (1987).
[h]Sources: Douglas (1994), Douglas and Douglas (1991, 1992), Grynberg (1993), and Sharma (1990).
[i]Manuia means "health, healthy, in good health" in Samoan and is used as a toast. Apia Bottling Co. "produces a range of fruit juices, soft drinks, and ice creams, and employs about 70 workers," although the Manuia brewery only had three full-time employees in 1992 (Robinson 1992:51). Manuia beer is sold in two-liter plastic Coca-Cola bottles (Douglass Drodzow-St. Christian, personal communication).
[j]Sources: Grynberg (1994) and *Islands Business [Pacific]* (1993).
[k]Fiafia means "happy" in Niuean (Vili Nosa, personal communication).

closed in March 1972 (Sinclair 1983). By February 1973, TUB accepted a take-over offer from the San Miguel Corporation of the Philippines (itself a giant TNC) and the Swan Brewery Group of Perth, Australia, who together formed Papua New Guinea Brewery Pty. Ltd. and began to sell both San Miguel and Swan beers brewed in PNG. Swan soon dropped out of this joint venture, and by the beginning of 1977 the new brewery was simply known in PNG as "San Mig."

In June 1975, a few months before national independence, SP had over 92 percent of the PNG market, but by the beginning of 1977 San Mig had captured nearly 15 percent of the domestic market. As the competition between these two breweries intensified, SP had the decided advantages of priority in PNG and breweries in both Port Moresby and Lae, the latter of which gave it easy access to the large market in the Highlands. Finally, in February 1983, SP successfully took over San Mig in PNG (Sinclair 1983).

Except for the breweries in Hawai'i, Tahiti, New Caledonia, and Papua New Guinea, all other Pacific breweries in 2001 postdate the end of colonially imposed prohibition in the islands. The oldest of these, Carlton Brewery (Fiji), dates to 1958, the year that prohibition was lifted there. The Pacific's eight other commercial breweries[4] all began between 1974 and 1993 and most of these operations are now controlled by large TNCs (see Table 12.1). Periodically, items appear in regional magazines about plans for new breweries, but most such plans fail to materialize. For many new nations around the world, having a brewery seems to take on some of the same status connotations as having their own national airline, although this rush to have a "national brewery" usually is done in the name of import substitution.

As if to make this very point, after PNG's national independence SP Lager was marketed as "bia bilong yumi; bia bilong PNG" ("our beer; PNG's beer"), and the Export Lager label featured the same Raggiana bird-of-paradise that appears on the country's flag (Figure 12.4). When the Royal Brewing Company opened in Tonga, Tongans were "asked to show their loyalty to the kingdom by switching to the new beer" (Pacific Islands Monthly 1987:33). Apparently Tongans took this seriously. Tuita reports that "with the establishment of a locally brewed beer (Royal Beer) in 1987, consumption of beer increased tremendously because it was widely available and cheap" (1999:151) (Figure 12.5). Other Pacific breweries also have made ready use of important cultural or national symbols of identity to market their products. For example, the label on Samoa's Vailima beer used to depict a traditional multilegged kava bowl and cup with a talking chief's fly wisk draped over the bowl's edge (Figure 12.6). Likewise, Vanuatu's Tusker beer takes its name from the curved boar's tusk that is symbolic of traditional value and authority in that country, and the brewery was opened on the country's tenth anniver-

**Figure 12.4**    South Pacific Lager

**Figure 12.5**    Friendly Islands Own Beer

**Figure 12.6** Vailima Beer

mous engraving of Captain James Cook (c. 1779) on its label. All of these advertising ploys illustrate that Pacific brews are among the "specific, tailor-made products" characteristic of the flexible economy of the late twentieth century (Martin 1994:93).

Four major TNCs are involved with Pacific breweries in 2001: Heineken of the Netherlands (PNG, Tahiti, New Caledonia), Foster's Brewing Group of Australia (Fiji, Samoa), ORKLA of Norway (Tonga, Vanuatu), and Brauhasse International Management (BIM) of Germany (the Solomon Islands, and until October 1999, Samoa). Globally, Heineken had the second-highest market share in the transnational brewing business in 1995, and Foster's ranked ninth (Jernigan 1997).

The power and reach of these major alcohol TNCs is enormous. The Heineken Company dates back to the establishment of a brewery in an Amsterdam shed in 1592. The company's international expansion began in 1931 with the joint venture in Singapore that resulted in what is today called Asia Pacific Breweries, and by 1960 Heineken owned or had an interest in twenty-four breweries outside the Netherlands (Heineken 2000). Today, Heineken supervises more than 110 breweries spread around the world in some fifty different countries, and Heineken brands are sold in 170 countries.

sary of national independence (Figure 12.7). When National Breweries introduced Vanuatu Bitter in July 1993, it was "in a can that used the national colours of the Vanuatu flag" (Grynberg 1993:23), and Solomon Breweries manufactures "Solbrew," a play on nationalism akin to SP's "bia bilong PNG" (Figure 12.8). Finally, appropriately enough, Cooks Lager, produced by Rarotonga Breweries in the Cook Islands features Nathaniel Dance Holland's fa-

**Figure 12.7** Tusker Beer

**Figure 12.8**    Solbrew Beer

**Figure 12.9**    Bounty Brand Rum

Foster's Brewing Group, whose beer and leisure arm is Carlton and United Breweries (CUB), employs more than 14,000 people, generates more than $3 billion in total annual sales, and runs breweries in six different countries, including India, China, Vietnam, Australia, Fiji, and Samoa (Foster's Brewing Group Limited 2000).[5] In addition to the breweries in Fiji and Samoa,[6] CUB acquired an 81 percent share of South Pacific Distilleries Ltd. from the Fiji Sugar Corporation in Lautoka, Fiji in 1998 (Hugh Ragg, personal communication). The distillery was established in 1980 to produce rum and other drinks from byproducts generated from the Fiji Sugar Corporation mills (Figure 12.9). The only other current manufacturer of distilled beverages in Oceania outside of Hawai'i, New Zealand, and Australia is Fairdeal Liquors of PNG, makers of Gold Cup products and backed by Malaysian capital (Marshall 1999) (Figure 12.10).

As of October 2000 ORKLA, a Norwegian food company that bought and merged

Pripps Brewery of Sweden with Ringnes Brewery of Norway, was negotiating with the Danish Carlsberg Group. The goal was to merge Pripps-Ringnes with Carlsberg Breweries (ranked eighth internationally in 1995; Jernigan 1997), but approval had not yet been granted by the Office of Fair Trading of the European Union (Bjorn Trolldal, personal communication).

Brauhasse International Management (BIM) developed originally out of a family-run German brewery founded in 1858. Haase Brauerei (Haase Brewery) at Kulmbach became Erste Kulmbacher Aktienbrauerei (First Kulmbach Shareholding Brewery), with EKU (from E[rste] + KU[lmbacher]) as their major export beer. Beginning in the mid-1960s, Haase Brauerei made overseas niche markets its major focus, always selling EKU along with local brews (as with Solbrew and Vailima), and in 1989 the company was renamed Brauhasse International Management. BIM is an interna-

**Figure 12.10**  Fairdeal Liquors Plant of PNG

tional consortium with shareholders all over the world and with brewery projects in twenty different countries, including the Solomon Islands, and until October 1999, Samoa (Peter Mesenholler, personal communication). Today BIM and Kulmbach Brewery have no formal corporate connection, although the former continues to produce and market EKU beer in various locations around the world.

In the relatively small economies of most Pacific Islands countries, a brewery can become an important revenue earner. For example, in 1988 "Western Samoa Breweries Limited [was] . . . the single largest revenue earner in the country, with a turnover of 12 million tala ($A8.5 million) and a workforce of 130" (Strachan 1988:38). Even so, the Pacific Islands breweries produce primarily for their domestic markets, which they typically dominate. However, Hinano is sent abroad to New Zealand, Europe, and the United States, Vailima is exported to many other Pacific Islands countries, Australia, and the United States, PNG's SP export lager is available in Australia and the United States, and Fiji's beers are exported to Canada, the United States, Australia, New Zealand, and other Pacific Islands countries. Even Solbrew is exported, in this case to Australia, Fiji, Nauru, and Vanuatu. Thus economically, island-brewed beer operates in a similar fashion to the ways betel and kava function: It circulates both within and among Pacific Island countries, and it also enters into the global marketplace.

In spite of the economic significance of beer exports—for example, Samoa sent US$850,000 worth of Vailima to American Samoa in 1992 (Pacific Magazine 1993)—imported beer continues to be important in many parts of Oceania, especially in those areas like Micronesia that do not have breweries of their own. San Miguel beer was brewed on Guam beginning in November 1971, but the brewery closed in March 1975, perhaps due to an economic recession on the island at that time (Donald H. Rubinstein, personal communication). During the 1990s the Republic of the Marshall Islands had a succession of a small brewery (Majuro Brewery) and two microbreweries on Majuro, none of which survived in November 2000 (Giff Johnson, personal communication). Thus in 2001 the market in the FSM, the Republic of the Marshall Islands, and the Republic of Palau is dominated by Budweiser, the main brand produced by Anheuser-Busch of the U.S.A., itself the global market share leader in beer in 1995 (Jernigan 1997). Even so, imports from Australia, Japan, and New Zealand are readily available in these island areas, as are other U.S.

brews and even European beers. And while Budweiser also is the market leader on Guam and in the Commonwealth of the Northern Marianas Islands (CNMI), heavy reliance on Asian tourism has meant that these islands' markets have been penetrated by beers from Japan, South Korea, and the Philippines as well. Beer imports comprise a very significant dollar amount of all imported products in such island areas. For example, one-third of Palau's US$38 million in imports in 1992 was for beer (Keith-Reid 1994), and beer was the third-ranking import category in dollar amount for the FSM in 1992, after vehicles and rice (Marshall 1993). When combined with cigarette imports (the fourth-ranking category), these two substances vaulted into the number one import position at US$5.4 million (Marshall 1993).

Elsewhere around the Pacific imports often continue to provide stiff competition for the local breweries, notably imported brands from Australia and New Zealand such as Victoria Bitter, Castlemaine XXXX, Foster's, Lion Red, and Steinlager. Finally, as is true the world over, the Pacific Islands breweries typically are licensed to bottle and sell major brands of soft drinks (for example, Coca-Cola and Pepsi products), fruit juices, and mineral water, and these products contribute significantly to their profitability.

## GOING TO POT

Marijuana (cannabis, or "pot") is far and away the most common and widespread illegal drug in Oceania today. Back in the 1970s *pakalolo,* as marijuana is called in Hawai'ian, reportedly had become the largest cash-producing crop in Hawai'i, worth hundreds of millions of dollars annually, before determined efforts by the government to eradicate gardens and cripple or eliminate marketing of the drug began. A sense of the scale of *pakalolo* growing just on the Big Island of Hawai'i alone can be gained from the following quotation:

> If the Big Island's $94-million sugar industry died, the economy would teeter. If the island suddenly lost its $250-million visitor industry, the economy would collapse. So, the question

naturally arises, what effect has the $500-million-plus loss so far this year [as of November 1985] suffered by the marijuana industry, thanks to intensified law enforcement actions, had on the Big Island economy? (*Hawaii Business* 1985:88)

The magazine writers' initial answer to their own question was "a lot," but then they noted that even though about 250 growers already had been arrested in 1985 and that it had become much more difficult to move marijuana off the island, the island's economy was "feeling no pain" because there was "another $4.5 billion worth of marijuana out there that the police know of" (*Hawaii Business* 1985:89). Despite such government efforts, Hawai'i was still the nation's top producer of illegal marijuana in the mid-1980s, and the police continued to engage in major drug busts. For example, agents confiscated a "record 607,960 marijuana plants in '86 worth $608 million," double what they had seized in 1984 (*USA Today,* September 22, 1986, p. 8A).

On the other side of the Pacific during the 1980s Palauans also grew substantial amounts of marijuana which they sought to sell in the lucrative tourist-rich markets of Guam and Saipan, smuggling it in ice chests of frozen fish before the use of drug-sniffing dogs by customs agents began. The U.S. Drug Enforcement Agency crackdown on this trade, as in Hawai'i, substantially slowed but did not stop the flow altogether. As evidence of this, two stories in the Saipan newspaper in 1993 made it clear that efforts to export marijuana from Palau continued (*Saipan Tribune,* April 2, 1993, p. 8; May 14, 1993, p. 1). And on January 12, 2001, police seized nearly half a million dollars worth of marijuana after raiding a plantation on Angaur Island, Palau (*Pacific Islands Report* 2001), so the supply side of this trade appears to be thriving.

Elsewhere in Micronesia marijuana is grown, in most cases for personal consumption or local sales, and smoked widely. Likewise, there are scattered reports of small-time marijuana growing, use, and arrests from Tonga, Fiji, Solomon Islands, Vanuatu, and both Samoas. But far and away the current "hot spot" in the Pacific for the commercial production and international marketing of marijuana is PNG. Although cannabis proba- bly reached coastal and island areas of PNG during the colonial era following World War II, there is no mention of this in the liter- ature and the drug was not adopted by Papua New Guineans at that time. By the mid-to-late- 1970s, however, pot had reached areas of the Highlands such as Simbu (Sterly 1979), and since then its planting and use has spread quickly throughout this region.

The PNG press reported as early as 1980 that cannabis was being cultivated "in remote areas" of the country for sale overseas (PNG *Post-Courier,* November 13, 1980, p. 3), but only during the mid-1980s did marijuana really seem to take hold in the highlands. People in both Simbu and Eastern Highlands Provinces were said to smoke (and even drink) it at vil- lage socials, and it had acquired the Tok Pisin names of "Maria" and "*spak brus*" "intoxicating tobacco" (PNG *Post-Courier,* March 13, 1984, p. 2; Koroma 1984). By 1988 reports claimed that PNG was "experiencing a big increase in drug trafficking—mostly cannabis," and that marijuana from the Highlands had "become recognised internationally as being of ex- tremely good quality" (Pacific Islands Monthly 1988). This increase in marijuana gardening no doubt had to do with the substantial profits to be made, but it may have been prompted initially by a huge downturn in the world mar- ket price for coffee—another major cash crop grown in the Highlands. Destined for south- ern Australian cities, "PNG Gold" was being grown in the Highlands and smuggled across Torres Strait in boats or flown in small planes to North Queensland by international drug rings, one of which was exposed in January 1992. That ring reportedly "bought" the mari- juana in exchange for firearms.

In more recent years, this arms-for-drugs trade has expanded. An estimated 92,000 to 130,000 people in Simbu, Eastern Highlands, Western Highlands, and Madang Provinces were cultivating cannabis for sale in 1991. And the crop had an average annual value of about 39 million kina for farmers in Simbu and Western Highlands alone (Iamo et al. 1991, cited in Chen et al. 1999). Grown mostly in remote villages, "PNG Gold" was turning up not only in Australia, but also as

far away as Hawai'i and New York, to which it was transshipped from Australia. In a 1996 report, the marijuana trade was said to have expanded to include Western and San- daun [West Sepik] Provinces, and the "drugs- for-guns" exchanges continued (Vulum 1996). At that time most guns appeared to be shotguns, handguns, and 22-caliber rifles, with relatively few military-type weapons, but by September 2000, matters took a decidedly more ominous turn:

> A large number of automatic weapons from Australia and Indonesia, including M-16 and AK-47 assault rifles, are being smuggled into Papua New Guinea in trade for high quality marijuana, according to local and regional reports. While the arms are currently going to criminals in the cities and feuding highland tribes, there are historical links between the arms-for-drugs trade and the Indonesian sepa- ratist Free Papua Movement (OPM) based in neighboring West Papua. Given the instability in Indonesia, the growing weapons trade repre- sents a threat to cross-border stability and po- tentially to the Papua New Guinea government itself (<http://www.stratfor.com>, September 13, 2000, posted on ASAOnet).

Even though the international drug cartels have become involved in the smuggling of marijuana out of PNG, it is important to note that, as with betel and kava, pot is grown lo- cally by village cultivators, most of whom are paid by buyers for their crop in cash, not guns. (The guns enter the trade when the buyers later sell to representatives of the in- ternational drug rings.) Given the limited cash-earning options in places like the PNG highlands, marijuana becomes an extremely attractive crop to grow because there is a strong international demand for it.

## CONCLUSION: THE ECONOMIC AND PUBLIC HEALTH IMPACT OF BETEL, KAVA, BEER, AND POT

Over the years a number of concerns have been expressed about the negative effects of betel-chewing on human health. For example, the spitting often associated with the heavy salivation betel-chewing produces (the world of chewers is divided into spitters and swallowers), or the sharing of a lime spatula, may provide avenues for the spread of infectious diseases such as tuberculosis (Talonu 1989). Another concern, although the finding is preliminary, is that chewing betel may provoke and aggravate asthmatic attacks (Kiyingi 1991). But far and away the biggest concern is that chewing betel may contribute to precancerous conditions and oral cancer. This has been widely discussed in the clinical and epidemiological literature for years, but clear evidence for this remains somewhat elusive. The primary reason is that when betel-chewers add tobacco to quid, it is as likely that the tobacco rather than the *Areca* nut or the *Piper betle* is the culprit that causes cancer. Equally confounding to researchers are the common circumstances in which betel-chewers also smoke cigarettes (although not at the same time!), or where chewers are also alcohol drinkers. In such cases it is impossible to determine whether it was the betel, the tobacco, the alcohol, or an interactive effect among them that induces oral cancer. And last but not least, there is some evidence to suggest that it is the lime—especially commercially manufactured lime—that may be the problem ingredient in betel-chewing. What this shows is that psychoactive substances often are taken together, or in sequence, making a clear causal connection between the use of any one substance and a subsequent disease extremely difficult to pin down. On balance, chewing betel without adding tobacco to the quid and using traditionally manufactured lime, in the absence of smoking or drinking, has not been shown to be a serious health risk.

In fact, there is evidence for several positive and protective effects of betel-chewing on human health. It reduces tooth decay, has anti-helminthic and purgative properties that may lead to a lower frequency of maternal anemia in malarious communities, and an extract from *Piper betle* leaves has been demonstrated to inhibit both mutagenesis and carcinogenesis in laboratory mice. Moreover, a Danish firm has developed an epilepsy drug based on a substance isolated from *Areca* nuts, and the symptomatology of schizophrenia has recently been shown to be milder among betel-chewers than among nonchewers in Palau; this suggests that the powerful alkaloids in the *Areca* nut may have therapeutic consequences for schizophrenics (Sullivan et al. 2000).

From an economic perspective betel is a cash crop for people in some areas of the Pacific, notably in Yap and PNG, but for most growers it is not a huge revenue earner. Nor is it a source of money for government since betel and kava are not taxed in Pacific Island countries, as are alcoholic beverages and tobacco products. Perhaps betel's greatest economic impact lies at the household level where the costs of ingredients consumed regularly by several household members—particularly in those places where people cannot grow their own—may comprise a significant portion of total household expenditures.

Fewer health concerns have been raised about kava than about betel, but there are some nonetheless. Perhaps the most notable of these is that heavy kava consumption leads to a scaly skin, a condition that reverses if the person stops drinking kava. A study on Pohnpei showed a relationship between kava-drinking and severe gastritis (Ngirasowei and Malani 1998), and investigations among members of an Aboriginal community in Australia who drank very heavy amounts of kava suggested possible liver and kidney damage and malnutrition to be among the consequences (Mathews et al. 1988). Kava has not been shown to impair cognitive functioning, although other functioning may be impaired. Heavy doses of kava supposedly "deflate" the male sex drive (Verebalavu 1998, citing Dr. Jude Ohaeri at a meeting of the Fiji Medical Association), and police have arrested drivers ostensibly intoxicated by kava in California and New Zealand. When these "drunk" drivers have come to trial, however, they have in every case been acquitted.

Other concerns that have been raised about kava bear on the larger socioeconomic scene. In Fiji it is claimed that because kava is a lucrative crop farmers often plant it instead of food crops, presenting problems for some families. Related to this is the claim that excessive kava-drinking leads men to neglect their gardening and other responsibilities to their families. On Pohnpei kava farming has raised an important environmental issue: as people have began to destroy the upland forests illegally to plant more kava they have threatened the island's watershed and contributed to a substantial reduction in forest land over the past fifteen years.

Even allowing for these socioeconomic and health problems, though, kava has been a huge economic success for the Pacific Islands over the past twenty years. If the market for kava holds in the West, and if megaplantations of kava are not established in places like Mexico, using rootstock taken from the islands, then "the Pacific drug" has great promise as a continued money winner for island peoples.

One possible health issue surrounding kava not addressed above concerns polydrug use. Traditionally, kava, and kava alone, was drunk, but today kava-drinkers often take other substances at the same time or subsequently. Kava is followed by beer or other alcohol chasers in Fiji, Pohnpei, and Vanuatu, and doubtless elsewhere as well. The physiological consequences of this have not yet been studied, but Foo and Lemon's (1997) research suggests that kava may serve to potentiate alcohol-induced impairment. Also, cigarette smoking is strongly identified with kava-drinking in Fiji, with some drinkers smoking up to two packs during a single kava session (Meo et al. 1996). Regardless of the possible synergistic effects between kava and tobacco (which also remain uninvestigated), we know that this level of smoking presents serious health risks.

Of all the substances discussed above, alcohol is the one that has been most demonized. There is no question that over time excessive alcohol consumption can contribute to numerous serious physical and mental health problems for the drinker. But what often gets ignored in such a focus are the ways that alcohol abuse relates to various kinds of injuries, notably those resulting from drinking-driving crashes. Although systematic data on such traffic crashes are not available for most Pacific Island countries, Barker (1993, 1999) has pro-

vided a detailed and well-contextualized study from Niue. Her work shows that deaths and injuries resulting from road accidents exact a very substantial economic toll (not to mention the personal and personnel loss) in Pacific countries, and that many of these crashes are alcohol-related (about half on Niue).

Other alcohol-related injuries also show up with numbing regularity in clinics and hospitals throughout the islands. For example, in a two-year period during 1996–1998, 88/100 injuries treated at Yap State Hospital were alcohol-related. Of these, 59 were cases of assault, 14 resulted from drinking-driving crashes, 9 were instances of domestic violence, 4 were from falls, and 2 were rapes. Five cases that had to be referred off-island, all related to alcohol, cost Yap State a sum of $50,686 during the two-year period, "money that could have been used to buy medicines and supplies that the hospital needs" (Ravia 1999:56). Drunkenness also is strongly correlated with domestic violence in Palau (Nero 1990) and Guam (Pinhey et al. 1997), and this kind of injury is common in other parts of the Pacific as well. Alcohol-related injuries or deaths also figure prominently as factors that engender outbreaks of tribal fighting in the PNG Highlands (Dernbach and Marshall 2001).

Heavy drinkers are often heavy cigarette smokers, and Pacific Islanders are no exception. The point is pertinent here because "alcohol and tobacco appear to have a synergistic carcinogenic effect" (Lichter and Rothman 1999:68), and because noncommunicable diseases like cancer have become the major causes of death in much of Oceania in the twenty-first century. Indeed, Johnson (1999:11) emphasizes that globally "excessive consumption of alcohol is the second most important risk factor [for oral cancer]." Heavy alcohol use also is one of several contributing factors to other chronic diseases now common in Oceania such as ischaemic heart disease and NIDDM (Non-Insulin Dependent Diabetes Mellitus).

Of course, when alcohol is used responsibly it can aid sociability and contribute positively to people's lives. In addition to its use as a social lubricant, an item of exchange, and a marker of social status, alcohol also is a significant source of revenue for island governments, and the breweries and their distributors are important employers as well. To the extent that beer (and to a much lesser extent distilled beverages) are exported from the islands, it aids national balance of payments in what are mostly rather fragile economies. In a few cases, remunerative uses have been found for brewery byproducts. Recently in Tonga waste yeast from the local brewery was converted into a protein bait to help control fruit fly infestations on fruits and vegetables, and Vanuatu and Fiji are now investigating the possibility of establishing similar facilities (Hoerder 2000).

Like betel and kava, cannabis produces mild euphoria, relaxation, and sociability. None of these drugs leads people to act aggressively. Pot smoking heightens sensory perception and increases the appetite. In some people, however, marijuana produces depersonalization, loss of a time sense, confusion, and anxiety. There is growing evidence that regular marijuana use for long periods of time may negatively affect memory, and it has been known for years that smoking it impairs psychomotor skills such as those necessary for driving. Marijuana smoke contains numerous carcinogens, and hence—like cigarettes—"joints" are a risk factor for lung cancer and other respiratory diseases if indulged to excess.

Selling marijuana resembles the marketing of kava and betel by small-scale growers, or the marketing of coca by peasant farmers in South America (see Leons and Sanabria 1997). Because it is illegal everywhere in the Pacific, marijuana forms a part of the hidden economy and it is difficult to determine just how much it might contribute to people's incomes. Its illegality also means that it is untaxed, so governments reap no financial benefit from this now widespread crop. Indeed, pot's very illegality is ironic in Oceania, since the idea that it is a "bad" drug was imposed on islanders along with many other colonialist prejudices. As just about everywhere else in the Pacific, except perhaps Hawai'i, much of the cannabis cultivated in PNG is consumed locally, and in this respect it is also like both betel and kava.

Betel, kava, and cannabis are all locally grown. Nearly all of the betel stays within the Pacific, mostly within the country or island where it was planted. Until perhaps a quarter of a century ago this was also true of most of the kava grown in Oceania, but then kava "caught on" as both a dietary supplement and a pharmaceutical, and the rise of a sizable international export market along with continued strong domestic consumption led to an economic boom in the 1990s. Marijuana mimics kava in this regard: much, probably most, cannabis grown in Oceania is consumed locally, but an increasing amount finds its way into international trade. The difference is that its illegality means that cannabis circulates in the shadow economy through international drug rings and cartels, adding value at each step along the way.

Alcohol—especially in the form of beer—is clearly in the Pacific to stay and has become woven into people's lives in many ways. But while beer is brewed locally in a number of island countries, the financial capital, the equipment, the ingredients, and the technical know-how to make it all come from abroad and are not locally controlled. The same is true of tobacco products, most of which are imported to the Pacific region. The result is that the major profits from these drugs *leave* the islands and line the pockets of stockholders in the major TNCs that control their manufacture and distribution. But that is, after all, the nature of market highs in a global capitalist economy.

### ACKNOWLEDGMENTS

The following persons have kindly assisted me in gathering information for this chapter, although none of them bears responsibility for what I have written: over thirty participants on ASAOnet (concerning kava bars), David Akin, Kalissa Alexeyeff, Philippe Arvers, Douglass Drodzow-St. Christian, F. Allan Hanson, Nick Henry, David Jernigan, Giff Johnson, Dorothy Levy, Robert Levy, Victoria Lockwood, Jacob Love, Peter Mesenholler, Vili Nosa, Hugh Ragg, Robin Room, Donald H. Rubinstein, Bjorn Trolldal, Stan Ulrich, and Richard Wilsnack.

## NOTES

1. One exception to this statement was the introduction of kava by Fijian missionaries to Australian Aborigines in the Northern Territory during the 1980s in a failed effort to reduce alcohol-related problems there.

2. As a public house for the commercial sale of kava by the drink, a kava bar also is to be found in Canberra, ACT, Australia, although it is only open on Friday nights (Ian Fraser, personal communication). In Tonga, Samoa, and New Zealand kava bars do not exist, although these countries have numerous informal kava clubs that meet frequently.

3. Also known as the Delaney Clause, this legislation was repealed by Congress in 1998 (Lichter and Rothman 1999).

4. Commercial breweries are defined here as those that produce their product in bottles or cans for a national and/or export market, and microbreweries that brew only draft beer for a local market are not included.

5. Founded in 1905, CUB produces well over half of Australia's beer. In 1996, Foster's bought Mildara Blass, a premium Australian wine producer that controls 10 percent of the global share of the wine club market and is one of the top three profit earners in the global wine industry. Another arm of the Foster's Group is the Continental Spirits Company, formed via a strategic alliance between CUB and the Seagram Company Ltd. (Foster's Brewing Group Limited 2000). This involved the purchase of Seagram assets in Australia and New Zealand and distribution rights in those countries of selected international Seagrams brands (in 1995 Seagrams had the fourth-largest global market share in the distilled beverages business; Jernigan 1997).

6. Foster's (via its Carlton Brewery [Fiji]) only acquired a majority share in Samoa Breweries in 1999. By August of that year it had a 51 percent share purchased from the Samoan government under a privatization policy (*Islands Business [Pacific]* 1999a), and in October 1999 Carlton bought another 12.8 percent of shares from Brauhasse International Management of Germany and 4.5 percent from Grove International (Ah Mu 1999). When Samoa Breweries originally was established, 75 percent of the shares were held by the national government, 17 percent by German interests (the German Development Bank, a trading firm, Breckwoldt & Co., and a German brewery, Haase Brauerei, that managed the Samoa venture; Casswell 1985). Other shareholders along the way have included Neptunia Corporation of Hong Kong (the holding company for San Miguel Brewery), and the government of Nauru. Carlton Brewery (Fiji) Ltd. was established in 1958, and in 1973 New Zealand Breweries Ltd. (now Lion Nathan Ltd., in which the Kirin Brewing Company of Japan has held a 45 percent interest since 1998; Lion Nathan 2000) opened a brewery at Lautoka, Fiji called South Seas Brewing Company. The latter venture failed, was bought by Carlton (Fiji) in 1977, and reopened in 1978 producing Fiji Bitter (Hugh Ragg, personal communication).

## REFERENCES

Ah Mu, Alan. 1999. "Ragg Predicts Riches in Brewery Trade." *Pacific Islands Monthly* 69(11):17–18.

Ashby, Gene. 1989. "Western Samoa Kava Dragging in Pohnpei." *Pacific Magazine* 14(1):14.

———. 1993. "New Drug Policy Carefully Excludes Betelnuts, Kava." *Pacific Magazine* 18(3):43.

Barker, Judith C. 1993. "On the Road to Health? Road Traffic Accidents in Pacific Societies: The Case of Niue Island, Western Polynesia." *American Journal of Human Biology* 5:61–73.

———. 1999. "Road Warriors: Driving Behaviors on a Polynesian Island." In *Anthropology in Public Health: Bridging Differences in Culture and Society*. Robert A. Hahn, ed. Pp. 211–234. Oxford: Oxford University Press.

Bird, Dave, and Ben Ruan. 1986. "Big Betelnut Business Helping Yap Economy." *Pacific Magazine* 11(1):27.

Casswell, Sally. 1985. "The Alcohol Industry in Developing Economies of Oceania." In *The World Alcohol Industry with Special Reference to Australia, New Zealand and the Pacific Islands*. John Cavanagh, Frederick Clairmonte, and Robin Room. Pp. 219–231. Sydney: Transnational Corporations Research Project, University of Sydney.

Chen, Paul C. Y., Felix Y. A. Johnson, and Tukutau Taufa. 1999. "Societal and Health Aspects of Psychoactive Drug Abuse in Papua New Guinea." *Pacific Health Dialog* 6(1):93–100.

Counts, David R. 1981. "Taming the Tiger: Change and Exchange in West New Britain." In *Persistence and Exchange*. Roland Force and Brenda Bishop, eds. Pp. 51–59. Honolulu: Pacific Science Association/ Bishop Museum Press.

Crowley, Terry. 1995. "The National Drink and the National Language in Vanuatu." *Journal of the Polynesian Society* 104(1):7–22.

Decloitre, Patrick. 1995. "Kava—The Next Boom Industry?" *Pacific Islands Monthly* 65(4):44–45.

Dernbach, Katherine Boris, and Mac Marshall. 2001. "Pouring Beer on Troubled Waters: Alcohol and Violence in the Papua New Guinea Highlands." *Contemporary Drug Problems*, forthcoming.

Douglas, Norman. 1994. "Business Briefs. Vanuatu." *Pacific Magazine* 19(4):28.

Douglas, Norman, and Ngaire Douglas. 1991. "Vanuatu Joins Beer Producers of South Pacific." *Pacific Magazine* 16(3):52.

———. 1992. "Business Briefs. Vanuatu." *Pacific Magazine* 17(4):24.

Foo, H., and J. Lemon. 1997. "Acute Effects of Kava, Alone or in Combination with Alcohol, on Subjective Measures of Impairment and Intoxication and on Cognitive Performance." *Drug and Alcohol Review* 16:147–155.

Foster's Brewing Group Limited. 2000. http://www.fosters.com.au

Gatty, Ronald. 1956. "Kava—Polynesian Beverage Shrub." *Economic Botany* 10:241–249.

Grady, Denise. 1998. "Kava May Soothe Jagged Nerves, But Is It Safe?" *The New York Times,* October 13, 1998, P. D8.

Grynberg, Roman. 1993. "Tusker Finds Its Taste Buds." *Pacific Islands Monthly* 63(9):23.

———. 1994. "Solbrew Sets Up Niche in Solomons." *Pacific Islands Monthly* 64(2):13.

Guille, Daniel. 1999. "The Growing Battle over Kava Exports." *Islands Business* 25(9):36–37.

Hawaii Business. 1985. "Up in Smoke: Has the Crackdown on the Marijuana Industry Hurt the Hilo Economy?" *Hawaii Business* 31(5):88–89.

Heineken. 2000. http://www.wvb.com/pre-calc/quickview/01189EN.htm and http://www.heinekencorp.nl

Hinano. 2000. http://www.hinano.com

Hirsch, Eric. 1990. "From Bones to Betelnuts: Processes of Ritual Transformation and the Development of 'National Culture' in Papua New Guinea." *Man* [n.s.] 25(1):18–34.

Hoerder, Donna. 2000. "Brewery Waste Helps Pests Drop Like Flies." *Pacific Islands Monthly* 70(5):27.

Islands Business [Pacific]. 1991. "Tahiti Finds Its Beer's a Winner. Hinano Hits Export Road." *Islands Business [Pacific]* 17(7):38.

———. 1993. "A New Brewery That's Got a Hope. Solbrew Provides an Incentive for Many Happy Returns." *Islands Business [Pacific]* 19(4):49–50.

———. 1998. "Hawai'i Farmers Plant Kava. Vanuatu and Fiji Should Worry." *Islands Business [Pacific]* 24(2):38.

———. 1999a. "Business Briefings. Samoa." *Islands Business [Pacific]* 25(9):31.

———. 1999b. "Business Briefings. Samoa." *Islands Business [Pacific]* 25(7):45.

———. 1999c. "Whispers. Kava Boom." *Islands Business [Pacific]* 25(7):13.

Jernigan, David H. 1997. *Thirsting for Markets: The Global Impact of Corporate Alcohol.* San Rafael, Calif.: Marin Institute for the Prevention of Alcohol and Other Drug Problems.

Johnson, N. W. 1999. *Oral Cancer.* London: FDI World Dental Press Ltd.

Johnston, Ranadi. 1998. "Botanical Extracts Brings Kava Growers a Choice." *Islands Business [Pacific]* 24(12):27.

Keith-Reid, Robert. 1994. "Signs of Testing Times." *Islands Business [Pacific]* 20(10):39–41.

———. 1996. "The New Drug Trade That Is Ripping Off the Islands." *Islands Business [Pacific]* 22(3):30–31.

———. 1997. "Cracking the Can Market." *Islands Business [Pacific]* 23(12):42–44.

Kiyingi, Kikuttobudde S. 1991. "Betel-Nut Chewing May Aggravate Asthma." *Papua New Guinea Medical Journal* 34(2):117–121.

Koroma, Joe. 1984. "The Village Drug Dens." *The Times of Papua New Guinea,* March 8, 1984, P. 1.

Lebot, Vincent, Mark Merlin, and Lamont Lindstrom. 1992. *Kava: The Pacific Drug.* New Haven, Conn.: Yale University Press.

Leons, Madeline Barbara, and Harry Sanabria, eds. 1997. *Coca, Cocaine, and the Bolivian Reality.* Albany: State University of New York Press.

Lichter, S. Robert, and Stanley Rothman. 1999. *Environmental Cancer—Political Disease?* New Haven, Conn.: Yale University Press.

Lion Nathan. 2000. http://www.lionnathan.co.nz/ir_prfl_overview_9.cfm

Lutkehaus, Nancy. 1981. Diffusionist Questions Reconsidered: Or, Who Are the Betel People? Unpublished manuscript.

MacDonald, Christine. 1999. "US Interest in Kava Fuels Multi-Million Dollar Sales." *Pacific Islands Monthly* 68(13):22–23.

Marshall, Mac. 1981. "Tobacco Use and Abuse in Micronesia: A Preliminary Discussion." *Journal of Studies on Alcohol* 42(9):885–893.

———. 1987. "An Overview of Drugs in Oceania." In *Drugs in Western Pacific Societies: Relations of Substance.* Lamont Lindstrom, ed. Pp. 13–49. ASAO Monograph No. 11. Lanham, Md.: University Press of America.

———. 1991. "The Second Fatal Impact: Cigarette Smoking, Chronic Disease, and the Epidemiological Transition in Oceania." *Social Science & Medicine* 33(12):1327–1342.

———. 1993. Prevention and Control of Alcohol and Drug Abuse. FSM/WHO Joint Conference on Alcohol and Drug-Related Problems in Micronesia. World Health Organization Regional Office for the Western Pacific, Manila (ICP/ADA/001).

———. 1997. "Tobacco Prevention in the Federated States of Micronesia." *Drug and Alcohol Review* 16(4):411–419.

———. 1999. "Country Profile on Alcohol in Papua New Guinea." In *Alcohol and Public Health in 8 Developing Countries.* Leanne Riley and Mac Marshall, eds. Pp. 115–133. Geneva: Substance Abuse Department, Social Change and Mental Health, World Health Organization.

Martin, Emily. 1994. *Flexible Bodies: The Role of Immunity in American Culture from the Days of Polio to the Age of AIDS.* Boston: Beacon Press.

Mathews, John D., Malcolm D. Riley, Lorna Fejo, Estrella Munoz, Nicholas R. Milns, Ian D. Gardner, Jennifer R. Powers, Elizabeth Ganygulpa, and Bilin J. Gununuwawuy. 1988. "Effects of the Heavy Usage of Kava on Physical Health: Summary of a Pilot Survey in an Aboriginal Community." *Medical Journal of Australia* 148:548–555.

Meo, Litea, David Phillips, and Richard Brough. 1996. "Smoking in Viti Levu, Fiji." *Pacific Health Dialog* 3(1):41–42.

Nero, Karen L. 1990. "The Hidden Pain: Drunkenness and Domestic Violence in Palau." *Pacific Studies* 13(3):63–92.

Ngirasowei, Janice, and Joji Malani. 1998. "The Relationship Between Sakau (Kava) and Gastritis." *Pacific Health Dialog* 5(2):266–268.

*Pacific Business Center News.* 1999. "Yap Planning Betel Nut Plantation." *Pacific Islands Report.* http://pidp. ewc.hawaii.edu/pireport/1999/February/02-22-11.html

*Pacific Islands Monthly.* 1987. "New Beer for Tonga." *Pacific Islands Monthly* 58(8):33.

———. 1988. "PNG Drug Scare." *Pacific Islands Monthly* 59(5):28.

———.1999. "Vailima Waits Out the Bidding Process." *Pacific Islands Monthly* 69(8):19.

*Pacific Islands Report.* 2001. "Palau Police Seize Huge Haul of Marijuana." http://PIDP.EWC.Hawaii.edu/pireport/2001/January/01-12.html

*Pacific Magazine.* 1993. "Western Samoa." *Pacific Magazine* 18(5):25.

Philibert, Jean-Marc. 1986. "The Politics of Tradition: Toward a Generic Culture in Vanuatu." *Mankind* 16(1):1–12.

Pinhey, Thomas K., Daniel A. Lennon, and Nicholas A. Pinhey. 1997. "Consumer Debt, Alcohol Use, and Domestic Violence in Guam." *Pacific Studies* 20(3):51–60.

Ravia, Ayesha Adelbai. 1999. "Alcohol Related Injuries in Yap." *Pacific Health Dialog* 6(1):52–56.

Reed, James. 1993. "Behavioral Risk Factor Assessment Among Youth of the Federated States of Micronesia." In *Report FSM/WHO Joint Conference on Alcohol and Drug-Related Problems in Micronesia.* Pp. 65–69. Palikir, Pohnpei, FSM.

Robinson, Martin. 1992. "Beer Fight in Bars of Apia. Prices Tumble as Manuia Takes On the Strength of Vailima." *Islands Business [Pacific]* 18(4):1–52.

Schmitt, Robert C. 1997. "Hawai'i's Beers and Brewers." *The Hawaiian Journal of History* 31:143–150.

Seneviratne, Kalinga. 1997. "Kava Set to Calm Western Nerves." *Pacific Islands Monthly* 67(4):48–49.

Sharma, Davendra. 1990. "Turning on the Tusker." *Islands Business [Pacific]* 16(9):48–50.

Sinclair, James. 1983. *South Pacific Brewery: The First Thirty Years.* Bathurst, N.S.W.: Robert Brown & Associates.

Sterly, Joachim. 1979. "Cannabis am Oberen Chimbu, Papua New Guinea." *Ethnomedizin* 5:175–178.

Strachan, Laurie. 1988. "Here's to a New Islands Brew. Western Samoa's Vailima Beer Is a Foaming Success." *Pacific Islands Monthly* 59(6):38.

Sullivan, Roger J., John S. Allen, Caleb Otto, Josepha Tiobech, and Karen Nero. 2000. "Effects of Chewing Betel Nut (Areca catechu) on the Symptoms of People with Schizophrenia in Palau, Micronesia." *British Journal of Psychiatry* 177:174–178.

Talonu, N. T. 1989. "Observations on Betel-Nut Use, Habituation, Addiction and Carcinogenesis in Papua New Guineans." *Papua New Guinea Medical Journal* 32:195–197.

Tuita, H. R. H. Princess Salote Mafile'o Pilolevu. 1999. "Social Context of Alcohol in Tonga." *Pacific Health Dialog* 6(2):149–152.

Tu'itahi, Sione. 1987. "Local Tonga Brewery to Cut Down Imports." *Pacific Magazine* 12(5):18.

Verebalavu, Filimone. 1998. "Men's Kava Drinking Has Women Looking Elsewhere." *Pacific Magazine* 23(1):44.

Vulum, Sam. 1996. "PNG's Guns-for-Drugs Trade Gains Momentum." *Pacific Islands Monthly* 66(11):17–18.

Watson, Pamela. 1987. "Drugs in Trade." In *Drugs in Western Pacific Societies: Relations of Substance.* ASAO Monograph No. 11. Lamont Lindstrom, ed. Pp. 119–134. Lanham, Md.: University Press of America.

Ysaol, Joseph, Joseph I. Chilton, and Paul Callaghan. 1996. "A Survey of Betel Nut Chewing in Palau." *ISLA: a Journal of Micronesian Studies* 4(1):244–255.

# 13

# Recovering and Rebuilding after the Tsunami in Papua New Guinea: International Aid and Village Aspirations

**Robert L. Welsch**

*Dartmouth College*

On the evening of July 17, 1998, an earthquake struck fifteen kilometers off the north coast of Papua New Guinea (PNG) creating a tsunami or tidal wave, whose forty-five-foot waves completely destroyed four communities along the coast west of Aitape in the West Sepik province. Revised estimates suggest the tsunami killed 2,200 of the area's 12,000 inhabitants. Government, mission, and international organizations reacted quickly to rescue thousands of survivors, many of whom were seriously injured when the wave washed them into the large lagoon and mangroves that lay behind their villages. The national and international response to this emergency was extraordinary. Dozens of international and local nongovernmental organizations (NGOs), including religious groups and secular aid organizations, quickly sent emergency aid. Survivors were moved into temporary "care centers" at inland sites away from the coast. For three months care center residents received emergency rations, water, tents, cooking pots, tools, and second-hand clothing.

After three months the emergency phase of the disaster had ended. Deliveries of rations ceased as the care centers were closed and villagers moved into their new settlements, well inland away from further threat of another tidal wave. The Catholic mission formed a Diocesan Rehabilitation Committee charged with rebuilding schools, teachers' houses, and village-based medical facilities. But the Catholics were not the only ones involved in the rehabilitation effort as several Protestant NGOs insisted on providing aid on their own. Government officers at the district office in Aitape had also attempted to organize their rehabilitation committee but found their efforts thwarted by the central government in Port Moresby who failed to send them funds for any meaningful rehabilitation work, particularly road building. These officers also found themselves confronted with an energetic Catholic mission, whose expatriate priests were more than eager to pick up the slack where the government was either unable or unwilling to help local people. Thus, during two years of rehabilitation there was competition between mission and government to control the rehabilitation process, matched by a similar but uneven competition between the well-established Catholic church and Protestant groups, who wanted to expand into the Aitape region.

Local people did not sit idle during the rehabilitation phase but were vocal in their criticisms of the entire rehabilitation process. Their complaints were directed primarily at the Diocesan Rehabilitation Committee and the Catholic mission, but a certain amount of criticism was also aimed at both the provincial and national governments. It took the Rehab Committee a full two years to complete all of the classrooms, teachers' houses, aid posts, and health center upgrades in the four affected communities. By the second anniversary all of the schools had been opened with great fanfare and elaborate parties. Every one of the fifty or so teachers in the four affected villages is now housed in a modern structure made of permanent materials with water tanks that make them completely self-sufficient for drinking water, quite unlike most village people. Ironically, although the Rehab Committee was successful in all the projects they had taken on and had even completed some projects that other sectarian NGOs had left unfinished, village people in all four of the devastated communities remained unsatisfied and viewed the rehabilitation effort as a failure. The situation in Aitape, which is still unfolding, raises three questions: (1) Why is nearly everyone directly involved—villager and missionary alike—dissatisfied with the course of the rehabilitation process? (2) Is the miscommunication that has characterized the rehabilitation and rebuilding process an inevitable consequence of natural disasters of this sort? and (3) What part did the presence of large international NGOs and religious organizations play in the confusion and contention that accompanied the process?

## WHAT GENERATED THESE TENSIONS?

Tension between aid providers and local people frequently arises in postdisaster settings (see, for example, Barton 1969; Erikson 1976; Oliver-Smith 1986; Benthall 1993; Neumann 1997). But the Aitape tsunami was so localized and humanitarian aid arrived from overseas so quickly that conditions were very different from most other disasters that affect broad regions, large numbers of people, and have relief efforts that are fundamentally undersubscribed by international donors. For example, Hurricane Mitch, which caused considerable damage to most of Honduras a few months after the Aitape tsunami, killed several times as many people and caused billions of dollars of damage, leaving most people without power or drinking water. International aid was swift and generous in Honduras, too, but per capita donor aid was far below what was pledged to help the tsunami victims. Both donor groups and reporters like dealing with small localized disasters better than with broad catastrophes because they are so much easier to comprehend and deal with.

In Aitape, it should have been relatively easy to help tsunami victims get back on their feet. But the area is remote, the facilities for providing aid are limited, and rebuilding was far more difficult than most observers might have imagined. Villagers knew that a large number of international donor groups had pledged what they perceived as an enormous amount of aid for rehabilitation. It appears that many of the problems that arose during the rehabilitation period emerged because different parties had very different expectations about what should be accomplished. Each party had its own perceived interests at stake. But while donors and villagers should, in principle, have been working toward the same ends, they often seem to have been working against one another.

The Catholic Diocesan Rehabilitation Committee tried to coordinate their efforts with those of various other donor groups, but often other groups had different approaches and sometimes different goals. Both the central and provincial governments wanted to control donor funds as well as rebuilding efforts. But their competing interests helped to undercut the role of government in the process and often put them in conflict with the

Rehab Committee. The people who lived in the four devastated villages were in competition with one another for Rehab Committee attention. And all four communities found themselves in competition with other Aitape District people who were affected by the disaster even though few of these people's homes were washed away by the tidal wave. During the rehabilitation phase, an evolving pattern emerged in which various parties seem not to have understood how different their perceptions and understandings of the situation were from those of other parties. These differences in perception were both situational and cultural; they illustrate the kinds of intercultural processes that emerge when global forces provide needed aid in remote communities.

## THE DISASTER: THE RAW POWER OF THE TSUNAMI

Sometime before the sun had set around 6:30 on the evening of July 17, 1998, families in villages all along the Aitape coast were finishing up afternoon chores and greeting relatives and friends home for the beginning of a four-day weekend. Public servants were home from town for the holiday, as were most students in the two boarding high schools at Aitape. Young people from all along the coast were preparing for an all-night party. As mothers were cooking the evening meal, an earthquake struck about fifteen kilometers off the coast north of the villages of Warapu and Arop, both situated on narrow sand spits at the mouth of Sissano Lagoon. Earthquakes are not uncommon in this part of PNG and people who felt it in other villages did not think much about it. But people in Warapu and Arop who were closest to the epicenter knew it was a big one, although every adult would have previously felt larger quakes.

This earthquake was different from any tremor people had ever experienced before. At Arop it caused cracks in the sand and water spouted up from some of these. All across the coast, the sky got very dark as if a moonless midnight had suddenly descended on the shore. Everyone in the area, including people living ten kilometers inland, heard the sea

roar loudly, although most people did not recognize the noise as coming from the ocean because it sounded like a jumbo jet or a very large helicopter. The sound grew louder as the fast, spinning waves from the sea floor rolled unimpeded toward the shore. Within about fifteen minutes the wave approached the shallow coastline. The shore pushed the waves up, reaching between ten and fifteen meters. The wave broke at the beach and came crashing down along the avenues that ran through the center of Warapu and Arop. Both of these communities were densely packed settlements, long and skinny, situated on 100- to 200-meter sand spits that separated the sixty-square-kilometer lagoon from the sea. No one had much more than a minute or two to react after they had seen the wall of water approaching. For most it was not enough time to launch their dugout canoes into the lagoon.

With tremendous force, the wave broke onshore and washed nearly all of the 7,000 people in these two settlements into and across the lagoon. Minutes later hundreds found themselves five or six kilometers away at the back of the lagoon, surrounded by floating debris, pitch blackness all around them. These were the lucky ones; hundreds of others from Arop found themselves washed into the dense mangrove swamp a kilometer or less behind the eastern end of the settlement. Most of these people found themselves skewered like pieces of kabob on the gnarled, hardwood mangrove branches. Others were struck by coconuts, house timbers, sheets of corrugated roofing iron, canoes, walls, and sections of roofs. Perhaps as many as 600 people were washed out to sea as the wave receded, most of them never to be seen again. When calm returned, thick debris from more than a thousand houses covered the entire surface of the lagoon. Cries of pain, calls for help, and muffled whimpers hovered over the dark surface of the water like the debris. The wave had been so powerful that it washed the clothes off the bodies of most of the people.

Every house in Arop and Warapu was washed away. When people returned several days or weeks later, few could find more than a bit of a house post broken off at ground level, or a coconut palm they had planted near the house. Nothing remained of the villages, which had been swept clean and then covered with sand. But, of course, in the early hours of that particular evening, nobody was worried about their houses; they were only worried about survival, finding family members who had been washed in all different directions, and getting medical assistance for injured friends and relatives. It was a moonless night, but it was much darker than usual even after fifteen or twenty minutes, when the second and third tidal waves had receded. Even now it is still not entirely clear what was causing the intense darkness, but it was probably the effect of sea mist stirred up by the tremendous speed of the waves. Within fifteen or twenty minutes, the tsunami had come, had killed and injured thousands, and had grown calm as if nothing had happened. But it left terrified, injured, dead, and dying people all around the lagoon and up and down the coast for a stretch of sixty kilometers.

In Malol and Sissano, to the east and west of Arop and Warapu respectively, the devastation was severe, but not as complete as along the narrow sand spits. Only Nimas, one of four villages that make up the Sissano community, was destroyed, and only two of some thirty houses remained. Nearly all of Sissano's 300 dead were from Nimas, while the other three villages lost only a few people and suffered minor damage to houses. Later, people would learn that the wave had washed away the concrete-block priest's house and the church built by German priests in the 1920s. When the government quarantined the lagoon for health reasons, people were forced to settle in temporary camps. Only in one village (Maindroin) were houses salvaged and inhabited once more after the quarantine was lifted.

At Malol, the damage was mostly limited to two areas. The three villages known collectively as "Big Malol" suffered considerable damage to more than half of their houses and here Malol experienced most of its injuries and fatalities, which numbered somewhat more than 200 dead. At Tellis, further east

along the coast toward Aitape, most people lost their houses, although most had time to gather their children and run into the forest behind the village where they were generally safe from the worst of the wave. Here, fatalities numbered about eight or ten small children and babies, but the destruction to the settlement was nearly as complete as at Warapu or Arop. Quite a number of the Malol dead were young men who were walking along the beach toward the party at Arop when the earthquake and tsunami struck. Even further east along the shore at the Tumleo settlement of Yakoi a number of families lost children, houses, and personal possessions, but nowhere were devastation, injuries, or fatalities as severe as in Warapu, Arop, Sissano, and Malol.

Many news reports in the international press from Aitape made it seem like people from the lagoon villages had run away into the bush in terror and were lost and hiding in the vast rainforest behind the lagoon. People were certainly terrified by the horror of the sudden devastation of so forceful a wall of water, but for those who could move about, their first strategy was to find their way to the comfort of their bush houses. These were situated on their own family lands where most people planted gardens, harvested sago, and hunted for wild pigs and marsupials. Here they would have access to some food from their gardens and they would be safe from any subsequent wave. Most of the rest of the survivors in Arop and Warapu made their way in small groups of two or three or ten to the neighboring inland villages of Pou and Ramo, respectively, where the majority of families would have had at least one "hereditary friend." As I have written elsewhere, the traditional economy of the Aitape coastal region was centered on exchanges of foodstuffs, local products, and raw materials between friends (Welsch and Terrell 1990, 1998; Welsch 1996, 1999). Men inherited these friends from their fathers or mothers, or even from a wife, an uncle, or a grandparent. These relationships were characterized by generosity and sociality, and through these relationships they could obtain whatever material or social support they needed. Apart from reaching their own bush houses, finding their hereditary friends would naturally have been the first idea that would occur to most of the tsunami victims. And in Arop and Warapu, which were situated no more than two hours by foot from their inland friends, hundreds set off for Pou and Ramo after rounding up what family members they could.

The seriously injured remained in the water or were helped to shore and would have to wait for help from Aitape. By early morning hundreds of battered, bruised, and naked survivors had made it to the inland villages where their friends provided them with clothes, food, water, tobacco, and betel nut and found places inside their houses, under houses, in any available space. During the first and second nights, hereditary friendship was doing exactly what it had always done, supplying whatever friends needed within the spirit of real generosity. Even people without friends in Pou or Ramo found clothes, sustenance, and the luxuries of tobacco and betel nuts. All of this would change within forty-eight hours when emergency rations began to arrive. Pou and Ramo people were more than happy to assist their friends together with the friends of their friends, but they stopped feeling so generous when tons of rations, clothes, utensils, and the like started arriving in the first week. Once the government began bringing a steady supply of emergency aid, the villagers in Pou and Ramo wanted to know where to find their share of this cargo. This shift from reliance on hereditary friendship to reliance on government and international donor aid would have a profound impact on everything that would follow.

## AFTER THE WAVE RETREATED: THE IMPACT OF THE TSUNAMI

Within half an hour of the earthquake it was obvious to everyone in the tsunami's path that life would never be the same. Yet, while the cries of the wounded emanated from all parts of the lagoon, rebuilding was the last thing on anyone's mind; survival was the only issue. No one in Aitape knew about the

disaster or had any sense of the power of the tidal wave west of town. The only government officer in the impact area was patrol officer Pascal Urum, based at Sissano. He and his family had just returned from Aitape when the wave broke, washing away everything at the patrol post, killing his wife and child and breaking Urum's arm. In the pitch black night Urum managed to build a fire and gather some survivors together; by dawn, from several different villagers, he had cobbled together a dinghy, an outboard motor, and sufficient fuel to make it back to Aitape by morning. He was the first to report to the outside world what had happened, triggering the dramatic efforts to rescue survivors and bury the dead that would dominate the next week.

People at Arop and Warapu were essentially on their own until mid-morning on Saturday when the first dinghies from Aitape arrived to assess the damage. When Dr. Minno Swire from the Raihu Health Center and his party arrived, they were so stunned by the extent of the destruction and the number of dead and dying in the lagoon they hardly knew where to begin. Within a few hours, helicopters started arriving to carry the seriously wounded back to the Raihu. Just three hours before the tsunami struck Raihu Health Center had closed its doors and discharged all its inpatients for lack of funds from the central and provincial governments. This closure was an ironic blessing because although the facility had officially closed just hours before the wave struck, all of the staff were still around and the wards were totally empty. As a result the health center could take far more of the severely injured than if it had been operating as usual. Soon after, Dr. Leslie Roberts-Thompson arrived with a team from Vanimo by light aircraft and began moving the injured at Sissano to the hospital in the provincial capital. Within a day, the Australian Defense Force had sent rescue teams and physicians to Vanimo, while the Papua New Guinea Defense Force based its efforts at Aitape. The mining camps at Frieda River offered the use of their helicopters for the rescue effort. And teams of men from around

Aitape assisted the Defense Force rescue parties in the lagoon and helped bury the dead.

Twenty-four survivors required amputations and about 400 required casts for broken bones, skin grafts, or surgery. Hospital wards were quickly filled and hundreds more were moved to temporary quarters on the lawn in Aitape and Vanimo. Rescue helicopters were in the air at sunrise and did not stop for three days. The United States sent a special team of rescue dogs trained to sniff out the injured and dead after earthquakes in collapsed buildings. There was so much debris in the lagoon that it was very hard to recover the bodies floating in the water. But after a few days, even these search teams gave up looking for the dead because of the foul smell of rotting flesh that hung over the lagoon. Citing health concerns for the safety of village people, the government quarantined the lagoon. Some 800 bodies were never recovered and it was assumed that most had sunk to the bottom of the lagoon or had been washed out to sea.

Survivors at Sissano had moved inland away from the coast fearing another tsunami. Some went with the young Catholic priest (Father Oton)—whose house and church were washed away and who barely escaped injury himself—to Olbrum, a series of small hills away from the coast. Others set off for their own lands in three other areas. At Malol, villagers abandoned the beach settlements and moved inland to four temporary settlements. As the first week passed, more and more of the Arop people settled at Pou and gradually all of the Warapu people settled at Ramo. By Monday or Tuesday after the tsunami, the government had sent emergency rations and blue plastic tarpaulins to use as tent flies to all of these temporary camps. The emergency authority at Aitape recognized each of these temporary camps as "care centers." Authorities selected high-ranking public servants as "camp managers" for each center and assigned armed policemen to each. About this time the government banned all fishing for 100 kilometers along the coast for three months, a measure, like the quarantine, ostensibly aimed at preventing the spread of disease. But declaration of a state of emergency and the quarantine on coastal fishing meant that the impact area now extended well beyond the four affected communities. Everyone in Aitape district was directly affected by the disaster, even though relatively few people outside the four communities had suffered damage or loss of life from the tsunami. The impact was far more significant for people on the Aitape islands of Tumleo, Ali, Seleo, and Angel because the ban on fishing deprived them of their subsistence base. These islanders still exchanged their fish with their hereditary friends along the mainland for sago and other garden produce or sold their fish directly in Aitape.

The international (and PNG national) response to the disaster was swift. Within days tons of emergency supplies were pouring into Aitape and Vanimo. Pledges of funds started to flow into bank accounts all over the country. Helicopters that had been needed for the rescue operation were turned to provisioning the survivors in the care centers. They flew back and forth nonstop each day bringing loads of food, clothing, and other supplies to people in the care centers. A combination of government and NGO funds provided new roads to three of the care centers, and international aid for schools and aid posts in the affected communities was pledged soon after the disaster. More than a dozen NGOs, some religious organizations (Catholic, Protestant, Fundamentalist, and Buddhist), others secular (for example, the Red Cross) became involved in the rehabilitation process. The Catholic church has been the most prominent and most active religious organization in the district for more than a century, and it played a key role in coordinating international aid through its Rehabilitation Center. It worked with other religious groups and secular NGOs, but these relations were not always smooth.

Local hospitals were remarkably successful in helping the injured and sick recover from their wounds. But grief and other psychological trauma at the loss of so many relatives and friends was more difficult to treat. For several weeks some survivors were clearly suffering from posttraumatic stress and were nonresponsive. Tears, sadness, and soft whimpers were common in the care centers late at night immediately following the tragedy (O'Callaghan and Hamilton 1998). These overt symptoms of grief had mostly ceased by mid-September 1998, when I first visited the area following the disaster. The Catholic mission trained forty grief counselors to visit people in all of the care centers and hospitals. On-going grief counseling seems to have been highly successful, and within a few months of the disaster most survivors were thinking about rebuilding their houses, gardens, and lives in new villages.

Thus, against this background of trauma, suffering, and total loss, came armies of defense force personnel, helicopter pilots, doctors, nurses, and other care-givers. As the helicopters whirred relentlessly to and from the disaster area and airplanes landed to off-load needed cargos, Aitape witnessed a second flood of visitors: journalists, NGO representatives, United Nations Development Program advisors, government officers, and other well-intentioned people. For two or three months there was scarcely a free bed anywhere in Aitape. For several weeks there was hardly a spare seat on any scheduled aircraft into Aitape, so many visitors had to charter their own flights in. The Catholic mission housed as many as they could in their complex of structures all over town. But many priests and brothers working at inland stations in the Torricelli Mountains were brought in to Aitape and had to be housed as well. The old Aitape hotel, which had been purchased by a Malaysian logging firm, was filled to the rafters, though it normally slept only twenty. Most important families in town had visitors sleeping with them. Everyone was busy and the atmosphere resembled some sort of cross between a carnival and a war zone.

Many of the visitors had come to Aitape to assist with some specific aspect of the humanitarian aid needed for tsunami victims, but many others seem to have had their own interests in mind. The prime minister and provincial governor posed for photo-ops during their visits to the disaster area and to the care centers, promising to do all they could. World Vision was able to bring surgeons,

nurses, and physical therapists to the Raihu. The Red Cross, the Salvation Army, and several other NGOs sent representatives to the area to assess how they could help. When I visited the area seven weeks after the disaster, most of the traffic from abroad had thinned out, but one Buddhist NGO group from Taiwan was in town. They numbered fifteen individuals, only two of whom could speak English, and they wanted their entire group to visit care centers that were only occasionally accessible by road. What trucks and other four-wheel-drive vehicles were available to reach the care centers were needed for shipping food, gardening tools, second-hand clothing, and other supplies.

For villagers in the disaster area, of course, and for the wounded and recovering in the Raihu Health Center, life was anything but a carnival. For people living outside the four communities designated as the "affected area" life would also not be the same for many months to come because everyone's attention was focused on helping those in the disaster area. From the first weeks following the disaster, it now seems clear that miscommunication among individuals and groups with different interests and structural positions within the region began almost as soon as the disaster had occurred.

## THE DISASTER WITHIN THE DISASTER: ATTEMPTS TO GET THINGS DONE CAUSED PROBLEMS

By early September 1998, the time of my first visit to the disaster area after the tsunami, much of the chaos of the first few weeks had settled down and many critical decisions had already been made. International donor groups had divided up responsibilities for the four devastated communities. Various donors had agreed to provide specified facilities for a certain care center, such as water from wells or tanks, or had agreed to provide some specific kind of assistance to the whole area. Road contractors, who had already had considerable experience in the district, pushed through new roads to Pou, Ramo, and sites intended as new settlements for Warapu and

Arop. The central government had pledged funds to cover road maintenance, including laying gravel and building culverts or small bridges along some sixty kilometers of roads. The British High Commission promised funds for a new bridge at Waipo River leading to Malol. Many of the sectarian NGO groups had limited resources and personnel and worked with only a few families or a segment of the large community. Some of the larger organizations, such as the Red Cross, provided tanks and corrugated iron catchment roofs to all of the recognized care centers for use by all residents. The Japanese government provided tents for teachers throughout the affected area. The United States government and a number of other countries gave untargeted aid directly to the PNG central government. Private sector donors from all over the world sent tons of supplies of various kinds, including bales of second-hand clothing, axes, spades, and bush knives, while other groups sent or pledged cash. Quantities of donated pharmaceutical supplies sent to hospitals in Aitape and Vanimo were enormous, but personnel on the ground with knowledge of pharmaceuticals was so limited that Stephanie Klappa, an anthropologist working in Vanimo District who happened to have pharmaceutical training, volunteered to sort out the medications at Vanimo Hospital.

Part of the confusion of the first few weeks after the disaster arose because of tensions between the Catholic mission and the government, and these tensions would only build over the following two years. The Catholic Mission and Diocese of Aitape had long been the most well-organized institution in and around Aitape. Having been established in Aitape during German colonial times in 1896—a decade before the government station was established—the mission has played a major role for more than a century. Before independence in 1975 government officers and Catholic priests had worked cooperatively with one another and with local expatriate business interests. But with the devolution of power of the late 1970s and 1980s, which gave authority to provincial governments, local politicians and provincial officers increasingly

came into conflict with mission personnel. Provincial and district public servants mistrusted diocesan motives; misunderstandings arose frequently. The situation was not helped by the fact that until December 1993 no local priests had been ordained in the diocese. Although there were a few priests from other provinces, the Catholic mission was largely an organization run by white Australian priests, mostly Franciscans, who had served in the district since the 1950s or 1960s. For their part, the Franciscans mistrusted provincial and district personnel, who often received little financial or logistical support from the provincial headquarters in Vanimo. Many officers were thought to be inefficient and ineffective in handling projects that better trained staff could easily have completed. The provincial government had been suspended for a time, and many nationals as well as expatriates in Aitape had long believed that Vanimo officials were corrupt and had often withheld funds that were earmarked for Aitape District. While most of these charges were undoubtedly false, the provincial government had, in fact, neglected Aitape District, and the small staff at the district office has never had sufficient funds or personnel to allow it to organize much of what happened in the district. Tension between effective expatriate-run religious organizations and local or provincial governments is by no means unique to Aitape, but here this tension surely contributed to difficulties that would follow.

Just who had both the jurisdiction and the ability to coordinate the rehabilitation process was never formally defined to everyone's satisfaction. Because rehabilitation would focus attention on classrooms, teachers' houses, aid posts, health centers, drinking water, and transport (particularly roads), both government and mission felt themselves qualified and capable. Historically the government provided funds for education, health, and basic infrastructure. But at least in the areas of education and health, the mission had long provided the services, even if the funding came from the government.

The Diocese, for example, ran most of the schools in the district and even had its own diocesan education coordinator. These schools included St. Ignatius High School, which has recently expanded to cover grades seven through twelve, the only grade twelve high school in the province. The Christian Brotherhood Church, a Swiss fundamentalist mission, had opened several community schools in hinterland villages. But only Aitape High School (grades seven to ten) and a handful of community schools (grades one to six) were run more or less directly by the Provincial Department of Education, even though all teacher salaries were paid from provincial funds. The same conditions existed in health care. Raihu Health Center and most of the sub-health centers in the district (at Pes, Sissano, Suain), and a majority of aid posts, were supervised directly by doctors and staff at the Raihu, although funding for staff, supplies, and operations came from the provincial government. Diocesan administrator Father Austin Crapp (now bishop of Aitape) had closed Raihu Health Center on July 17, 1998 because for several months provincial authorities had not sent funds for staff salaries. The diocesan decision to shut the Raihu down was partly a realization that the diocese could not advance salaries indefinitely, but it was also an effort to force the provincial government to provide the funding they were legally obligated to provide.

Soon after the tsunami, the district administrator formed an emergency committee that included high-ranking district personnel as well as representatives from the mission and the private sector. After placing the district under a state of emergency, the administrator held extraordinary powers over everything that happened in the four affected communities. Even two months after the tsunami these emergency powers generated a remarkable amount of activity around the previously sleepy district office at Aitape. With lower- and mid-level clerks and functionaries running in and out of the eight or so rooms that made up the district office block, it was a dramatically different scene from what had been customary in all of my previous visits from 1990 to 1997.

Yet despite the underlying tensions between government officers and missionaries,

the emergency committee seems to have functioned more or less effectively. These tensions increased dramatically when some international donors feared corruption by the central government and were only willing to contribute to rebuilding projects if the diocese controlled donated funds. Paralleling its educational and health care efforts, the diocese formed its own emergency relief committee soon after the disaster. Then, planning to transform this emergency committee into a Diocesan Rehabilitation Committee, the mission asked its former diocesan accountant, Greg Smith, to return to Aitape from Australia and asked Balthasar ("Tas") Maketu, a local politician from Sissano, whose mother had died in the tsunami, to chair the committee in Aitape.

After a few months, central government funding failed to materialize for local officers' accounts with local merchants. Some expenses for roadwork, helicopter rentals, and a variety of other services went unpaid, much as had happened at Raihu Health Center in the months before the disaster. During this period the Diocesan Committee stepped in to take on a growing role in directing the rehabilitation process, and the central government ceased direct involvement. This lack of central government support undermined the role and responsibility of local officers, and it emasculated the district office just when these officers were beginning to assert themselves. Nevertheless, government officers remained key figures for certain functions, such as surveying and alienating lands, but most of these functions were directed from the capital rather than locally.

During the confusion of the emergency period, a time when both government and mission were active participants, many key decisions were made that set in motion much of what would unfold over the following years. The most important decisions concerned where people would rebuild their settlements. The mission had its staff in place coordinating relief supplies and the Rehabilitation Committee developed a similar organizational structure to manage its rehabilitation plan. Central to this plan was building a set number of classrooms, teachers' houses, and health facilities. As these coordinators perceived the situation, only two problems faced them: (1) finding donor funds for each building project, and (2) getting construction underway. By mid-September 1998, the Rehab Committee had already decided how many classrooms, houses, and other structures were to be built and they had ratified a plan that set out where each of these structures was to be constructed.

From the villagers' point of view the situation was more complex. For months after the tsunami nearly everyone in the affected villages was deeply afraid of the sea. In 1998 I heard many people say that they never wanted to return to their old village sites. These fears were not lessened by the frequent tremors in the weeks following the tidal wave. The fact that so many bodies were never recovered from the lagoon led many people to say that they would never eat fish from Sissano Lagoon where so many had perished (Christianthy Menkhaus, personal communication, 1999, describing her experiences in Aitape during October and November 1998). People would, of course, eventually return to their traditional fishing activities in the lagoon, just as a few would later rebuild houses in the direct impact zone. But it appears that the emergency committees and the Diocesan Rehabilitation Committee took villager concerns quite seriously, if at face value and probably too literally.

Six or seven weeks after the tsunami when I visited the disaster area it seemed to me that few people had sufficiently recovered from the tragedy to have any clear sense of what they wanted in the future. They disliked living in crowded conditions under blue tarpaulins in the care centers and nearly everyone was eager to get on with their lives. Conditions in the care centers were clean but often muddy. People were well fed, but everyone longed for sago, the region's primary staple food. And everyone longed for fresh fish. But eager as they were to leave the care centers, tsunami victims were not prepared to make decisions about what would be best for them in the long term, as most people were still suffering from various kinds of posttraumatic stress. The problem was that the Rehab Committee was keen to start rebuilding. They knew that donor groups who had pledged funds would want to spend their allocated monies sooner rather than later. Decisions about where classrooms, teachers' houses, and aid posts would be built had to be made if construction was to begin.

Although villagers in the affected communities needed more time to decide where they really wanted to rebuild their lives, they also wanted to get out of the stifling care centers. When offered an opportunity to start building new houses and planting gardens, people in Arop and Warapu jumped at the chance. They gladly marked off new village sites on lands individuals from each community had previously exploited. In both cases these lands were as far from the sea as one could possibly get before encroaching on land unambiguously belonging to Pou and Ramo people respectively. After three months, people abandoned the care centers, which closed without fanfare.

For the Rehab Committee, these land disputes had a very different impact, partly because, unlike the houses tsunami victims were building for themselves, the classrooms and teachers' houses were to be of permanent materials. Rehab Committee staff needed assurances that land title was clear before they started building. This premise seems prudent on the one hand but underscores the differences between the worldview of the committee and the villagers, who knew that land issues would eventually be resolved. The Rehab Committee also faced a more immediate logistical problem. The easiest care centers to reach were those belonging to Malol people, who chose care center sites easily connected to existing roads. Thus, Malol, the least damaged of the four communities, was the first to receive Rehab attention.

At the time of the first anniversary, only a dozen classrooms and a similar number of teachers' houses had been completed. Ground had not even been broken in Warapu and Sissano and there were constant tensions between villagers and Rehab Committee staff.

As government funds either dried up or failed to materialize, government officers in Aitape had little interest in the rehab activities that were being run by the Catholic mission. Without improvements to the incipient road network, it became harder and harder to get trucks with building materials to the work sites in the new villages. By mid-1999 no one viewed the rehabilitation process as a success. Donor groups were unhappy because facilities were not complete. Villagers were unhappy because they felt that undeserving people in other communities were getting all the committee's attention. And the rehabilitation staff were themselves in shock that villagers did not appreciate any of their hard work. The best intentions of the Rehabilitation Committee had unfolded into a second disaster within the bigger disaster of the tsunami itself.

## "DOING RIGHT BY THE PEOPLE": HOW ATTEMPTS TO BE FAIR CREATED DISPARITIES

One of the key features of the rehabilitation process was the attempt to be "fair" and to provide equitable services to all of the tsunami victims. But there never seemed to have been much serious thought until the process was nearly complete about who in fact was affected, how they were affected, and what could help bring people back to living conditions that resembled the lives people had been living before the disaster. Never had anyone involved with the Rehab Committee intended to replace everything lost in the tsunami, although it seems that this message was never clearly conveyed to the people. The goal of "rehabilitation" was to provide health and educational services, to rebuild the government's patrol post, and to establish a network of roads that would connect local people to Aitape. Rebuilding houses, gardens, and lives or reacquiring the dinghies, outboard motors, and other goods that had been washed away were responsibilities of the people, not of the government or the Rehab Committee.

Many people in the four devastated lagoon villages interpreted the term "rehabilitation" to mean "restoration." As helicopters brought supplies to the care centers in the first weeks, many must have imagined getting back everything they had lost. But this difference in perspective never overtly surfaced during the rehabilitation period, and rehab staff interpreted the people's demands as grasping and overbearing. Claims by several village leaders and other prominent individuals that the mission had been diverting rehab funds to its own uses merely clouded the complex differences in expectation.

Such claims included a widely circulated rumor that unnamed foreigners had detonated a bomb triggering the earthquake and tidal wave, explicitly to get at local people's natural resources. Several men in Aitape were extremely vocal in their charges against the bishop, charging that he had stolen rehab funds for the purchase of several vehicles and for the construction of several new buildings. Both stories resonate with several cargo cult ideologies that have circulated in PNG for a century in which foreigners intercept goods, magically sent by the ancestors, that were intended for villagers (see, for example, Burridge 1960; Lawrence 1964; Eri 1970; Worsley 1970).

What emerged in my conversations with many rehab staff members was the feeling that it was essential for the committee to be fair and equitable in what it provided for one or another community. For example, when a local leader of one of the smaller care centers worked with a Protestant NGO to build its school buildings with a different floor plan and different amenities, Rehab Committee staff objected on the grounds that facilities should be equal throughout the impact area. When one donor pledged K42,000 for the headmaster's house at one community school, the Rehab Committee stuck to its principle of equality among all the residences by building the standard model teacher's house for K30,000 and shifted the difference to other school-related expenses. This decision led the headmaster of that particular school to claim that the committee was stealing money that had been allocated to tsunami victims.

Thus, while the Rehab Committee tried scrupulously to be fair, the committee had a different sense from most villagers of what would constitute a fair distribution. During the emergency, the committee tried their best to give every family the same rations. The problem with this strategy was that families varied in size and some families inevitably got more than others. While this was not so much a problem for rice and tinned fish—the main staples during the emergency—it was much more of a problem with axes, bush knives, buckets, and cookware. Large families generally came away with less than smaller families. Note, however, that families in Malol and Sissano, whose houses were not destroyed by the tidal wave, tended to get the same as everyone else. Such distributions of goods seemed grossly unfair to people who saw co-villagers whose houses were intact getting just as much as those who had lost everything. Moreover, once emergency rations were being distributed on a regular basis, villagers in Pou and Ramo expected a share of the distributions; they were after all paying a high price having three or four times more people living on their land. Traditional "hereditary friendships" or not, the cargo that arrived daily in the care centers was not coming from their friends in Warapu or Arop, but was arriving from foreign donors overseas. Thus, according to the local logic of fairness, all of the affected villages should get a reasonable share. By looking after Warapu and Arop people these villagers' lives were also disrupted.

Note also that this notion of a fair distribution of aid after the tsunami was quite different from the concerns used by the colonial administration to compensate villagers for damages to their houses and gardens during the Second World War. In the late 1940s compensation for damages caused, for example, by Allied bombing of coastal villages was assessed according to how much was lost. Those who lost more received more in compensation. But no one associated with the rehabilitation process seems to have even considered allocating humanitarian or rehabilitation assistance on the basis of how much was lost. The reason for this blind spot likely has to do

with the semantic differences between the terms "compensation," on the one hand, and "assistance" or "humanitarian aid," on the other. Had officials formed a restoration committee or a compensation office, everyone would have thought in terms of a graduated structure of aid. But viewing donor funds as "aid" or "assistance" invoked a very different notion of what would be fair.

On the question of who is an "affected person," the Rehab Committee and most villagers had radically divergent notions. The government, the mission, and most of the international donor groups generally shared the same sense of which groups were affected by the tsunami; to a one, these organizations defined the affected people as encompassing only those four communities that were severely damaged or destroyed by the tsunami. For the most part, neither the Rehab Committee nor the various NGO groups nor even the United Nations Development Program (UNDP 1998) distinguished among these villagers in terms of who was entitled to rehab services—schools, health facilities, surveys, and road access. During the emergency phase the government-led committee made it a policy that only people residing in one of the various care centers were eligible for emergency rations, tent flies, tools, and the like.

As the months passed this sense of who was an affected person—a concept I view as the "four-village model"—became more and more accepted by rehab staff and NGO providers alike. Villagers from the four communities started defining themselves as "tsunami victims" or "tsunami survivors," even to the extent that they carved, painted, or scrawled these words on their dugout canoes, their jeans, T-shirts, and knives. During the first year after the tidal wave, being a tsunami victim became a primary identifier for many people, young and old alike; but it also became an entitlement.

For other people in Aitape District the situation was quite different. For example, two issues affected residents of the Aitape Islands of Ali, Seleo, and Angel. Frequent tremors in the weeks following the tsunami frightened about half of the residents of these islands so much that they fled to the mainland. Some stayed with families in town; others moved in with their hereditary friends on the adjacent mainland. About twenty families from Ali built lean-tos on one of several unused World War II airstrips. These families received next to nothing from any governmental or NGO agency. After the ban on coastal fishing went into effect, nearly everyone on the islands lost their sole means of support for themselves and their families. With no fish, they had no access to sago. These families and several others who stayed on the islands were forced to rely on their hereditary friends for basic subsistence. As with precolonial friendship relations, these families asked their friends for help and were given enough sago to survive. They gathered greens in the brush around the abandoned airfield, but it was a meager existence. Later, after the coastal fishing ban had been lifted, they gave fish to their mainland friends. Because these families were not defined officially as "tsunami victims," they were forced to rely on traditional relationships rather than government, mission, or NGO support. All of the island families I interviewed who fled to the mainland during the tragedy feel strongly that they too were victims of the disaster and were not treated fairly by aid providers.

## "THESE PEOPLE WANT TOO MUCH"

Most villagers in the four lagoon villages expressed their dissatisfaction with the rehabilitation process by complaining directly to the rehab coordinator and to other members of his staff. It was an odd circumstance, but Malol people who had received the most attention from rehab staff and construction crews were the most vocal and raised the most complaints. To rehab staff, this response was incomprehensible since these were the people who had already received the most classrooms and houses. And in addition, because Malol was so accessible to Aitape, nearly every family had relatively easy access to a fresh water supply—either a pump and fresh well or a water tank. There were no serviceable wells in the new Arop or Warapu settlements

and even today there are few water tanks. Why were these people who had received so much so hostile to the rehab staff?

Most rehab staff interpreted Malol people's hostility in terms of traditional cultural stereotypes. From the earliest days of colonial contact in the region, the Malol had been viewed as members of one of the most belligerent communities on the coast (Rodatz 1908, 1909; Höltker 1940/1941:9). They have long had a reputation as a temperamental community that is aggressive and pushy. Even if Malol people have been more difficult to deal with over the last half-century—an interpretation that I do not personally share—I feel this explanation misses the point of what was happening. Malol people were not the only people to complain. During the first year, being so close to town they were the first to realize that the Rehab Committee was only planning to provide communal services. They were the first to understand that the Rehab Committee would not provide what they really wanted.

In other villages, dissatisfaction also took on an overtly hostile form. In August 1999 I was present in Arop when a rehab truck gathered up unused building materials on the school grounds that would not be needed to complete buildings there. Rehab staff were merely moving it to Warapu where these extra timbers and plywood could be used to build the school there. Rehab staff were confronted by an irate village official whom I knew ordinarily to be quite mild mannered. Here in Arop, as in all four of the devastated communities, villagers felt that they had been promised much more than they had received.

At the Mission, as well as at the rehab office, most felt that the people simply wanted too much. Rehab staff had found the logistics more difficult than originally expected, though many of the delays would have been minimized if the government had made good on its promise to maintain all of the new roads. But even with the delays, the Rehab Committee fully expected to complete everything they had originally promised, and by the second anniversary in July 2000 all the projects were complete. Rehab staff disliked the frequent confrontations with angry villagers and village officials both in the villages and at the rehab office. In short, rehab staff felt that people in the affected villages were simply ungrateful for the hard work that was being done on their behalf. As villagers in the affected communities asked for more and more, rehab staff became increasingly frustrated with what they viewed as ingratitude. If the people did not appreciate what they had already been given, why should anyone give them more?

The response from staff of the Rehab Committee was both predictable and in certain respects unavoidable, because neither party really understood the expectations of the other. It was not at all clear to me in 1998 or 1999 (and only gradually became obvious in 2000) that although all of the contention in the two years after the tidal wave focused on various rehab building projects, very few people in the devastated communities were interested in the projects that had consumed all of the rehab staff's time and energy. The people, in fact, were far more interested in how they could get back the things they had lost in the tsunami.

After the carnival-like atmosphere that pervaded the first few months following the disaster, with one NGO and international donor after another offering something in the way of humanitarian aid, what the Rehab Committee ultimately provided seemed like very small potatoes indeed. Nevertheless, by the beginning of 1999 the Rehab Committee was just about the only body providing anything at all to most people in the four lagoon villages. Rehab might not be planning to give them what they wanted, but whatever they offered in the way of buildings and services, affected villagers wanted to get as much of as possible. Then, when a rehab truck started loading excess building materials, tensions rose and anger flared. These villagers who still had so little saw what they had been given taken away by expatriates who have so much themselves, a traditional cargo cult theme (see Burridge 1960, Lawrence 1964).

The tensions between villagers and the Rehab Committee were heightened by the presence of several other smaller NGOs, most of them from Protestant organizations who wanted to expand into the Aitape area. Without local knowledge of the area, none of these sectarian NGOs ever imagined that they could rebuild all the devastated schools and health facilities on their own. Their strategy was to focus their attentions on a single school. In every case these Protestant groups chose to work with one section of a larger village that had chosen to break off from the main part of the community. In one case a Protestant NGO provided funds at Pou for a sub–health center, and naturally they found this village quite receptive.

From 1896 until fairly recent times, Aitape District had been a Roman Catholic stronghold. Apart from some mission work by the Swiss Christian Brotherhood, mostly in inland villages, and a few transient Jehovah's Witnesses and Bahai followers, religious diversity in the area was largely a result of indigenous Papua New Guinea missionaries. They were nearly all local people who had converted to some other faith elsewhere in PNG and brought their new religions with them when they returned to Aitape. The most important of these had been the Assemblies of God and to a lesser extent the Baptists, the New Apostolic Church, and the Revival Church. But the disaster brought new opportunities for sectarian expansion, since these churches could and did offer opportunities not immediately available from the Catholic mission through its Diocesan Rehabilitation Committee.

Nowhere was this process as pronounced as in Arop, which in 2000 had eleven different churches present: Roman Catholics, the Assemblies of God, the Christian Brotherhood Church, the PNG Revival Church, the New Apostolic Church, the New Life Church, the Seventh-Day Adventists, the Baptists, the Lutherans, the South Seas Evangelical Church, and Bahai. Several of these churches are new since the disaster and one, the South Seas Evangelical Church, has only a single extended family as converts, and these primarily won by offering to help in building houses and providing a few basic amenities. Religious sentiments are intense in Arop, but the sectarian competition about spiritual things heightened tensions between these sectarian organizations when they became NGOs providing aid. In Arop and Sissano, villagers actively played one sectarian group against the other.

## "WE WANT OUR OLD LIVES BACK"

By the second anniversary the Diocesan Rehabilitation Committee had completed all of the work they had originally promised. Each of the communities had nice new schools, with two exceptions built to a common set of specification. These were simple structures but far better as school buildings and residences than in any other school in the district. None of these schools had any difficulty attracting a full complement of teachers and nearly all of the teachers were originally from the villages where they now taught. But after the parties to celebrate opening the schools, people were still not happy. This fact became obvious when in August 2000 I visited Barapu, the new settlement for Warapu people. I spoke with all of the teachers as a group and asked how the disaster was affecting their community and its cohesiveness. Although polite and respectful, every one of the seven or eight teachers who spoke had a long list of complaints. They missed the sea; they missed the sand and the easy access to the lagoon. They were now too isolated from Aitape and women could no longer take their sago to the Aitape market to earn a little cash. The road which now linked them to Aitape was still not graveled and only passable with four-wheel drive in dry weather. These teachers went on and on discussing how difficult life was here in the new inland settlement.

If we summarize their comments collectively, they were all in agreement that fundamentally they all wanted their old life back. They longed for their beautiful old beachfront village as it was before the disaster. They did not particularly like the new village site, which was hot, muddy, and full of mosquitoes. The problem was that after complaining for two years about how slow the Rehab Committee had been, rehab had ended and their brand new school was situated on a site that no one really liked. It was the driest inland site that Warapu people could have chosen on lands that they had some legitimate claim to, but it lacked all the charm of the old village nestled on the narrow sand spit between the lagoon and the sea.

In the last analysis, the hostilities and tension that arose during the long rehabilitation period had less to do with the pace of the Rehab Committee's work than it did with the realization that the tsunami had changed everything. Although many people are genuinely afraid of returning to live along the beach, they are not satisfied with life as they currently experience it. In all of the villages people really want to be back in their old villages but realize that they will never be able to go back to the way things were.

Many of the middle-aged leaders of these communities had worked hard as teachers, public servants, businessmen, and in other capacities. During their productive years they had saved and acquired dinghies, outboard motors, generators, furniture, stereos, and the like. They had acquired all of these things when they had some regular income, but now they have lost everything and have no hope of reacquiring any of the things they lost in the tsunami. Physically, the tidal wave caused much pain, injury, and death. Psychologically, the tsunami was a painful experience and it was difficult living in the care centers and moving into new villages. But knowing that it will never be possible to recover what was lost has brought another kind of secondary trauma.

## HOW LOCAL PERCEPTIONS AND EXPECTATIONS WERE SHAPED BY GLOBAL PROCESSES

People's responses to the tsunami were largely those common to the kinds of posttraumatic stress that follows most natural disasters (see, for example, Demarath and Wallace 1957; Erikson 1976; Davis 1986; Oliver-Smith 1986; Neumann 1997). But the difference between this disaster and what is usually observed in other areas is the large number of NGOs that became involved shortly after the tsunami. In many disaster situations ordinary people do not routinely see many NGO aid workers. Rarely do they see representatives of more than one or two aid providers. But in Aitape the carnival-like atmosphere and the constant movement of helicopters bringing emergency supplies to the care centers created an environment in which people expected the cargo would continue to flow.

Such sentiments actually emerge from a variety of cargo cult sentiments that have long circulated around the region. For many during the emergency period the large number of airplanes, helicopters, and foreign aid workers must have suggested that a time of plenty was at hand. Warapu people, for example, discussed a variety of explanations for the tsunami that centered on a secret, underwater cave that contained large quantities of manufactured goods presumably provided by their ancestors. This is a familiar ideology found in New Guinea cargo cults (see Burridge 1960; Lawrence 1964; Worsley 1970) and suggests that "cargo thinking" has shaped local responses to the disaster. More skeptical minds would probably have interpreted all the activity around Aitape as simply a measure of things to come. Dozens of visitors to the area announced millions of *kina* in aid from both international donors and sources within PNG. Moreover, according to some informants before the actual formation of the rehabilitation committee, members of the Emergency Committee had discussed the "restoration" of the disaster area. It is not clear what this committee may have envisioned, but for some local people the shift from "restoration" to "rehabilitation" was merely symptomatic of an effort to divert thousands of kinas' worth of aid to other purposes. What people wanted was money to rebuild their lives into something that approached what they had had before.

But the fickle nature of international donor aid is such that donor groups have rapidly shifting interests. For a month or two a dozen NGO and aid agencies had focused their attentions on Aitape, only to shift a short time later to Honduras and then other troubled areas. The Catholic Mission and Diocese of Aitape were dependent upon these international aid agencies. The Rehab Committee was similarly influenced by the desire of international organizations to spend their funds as quickly as possible. Thus, both the district administrator and mission officials had good reasons to hasten the process of rebuilding. They needed to start the rehabilitation process while international attention was focused on Aitape. Such fiscal concerns are reasonable given the nature of international aid, but they encouraged everyone to make decisions about where new schools would be built before anyone was in a position to make rational decisions. These decisions would, of course, have long-term consequences.

## CONCLUSION

The core problem that played out over the two years of the rehabilitation period was that there were many different interested parties, each with somewhat different expectations about what was to happen during this period. The intensity of activity in Aitape shortly after the disaster combined with the intense psychological stresses tsunami victims were experiencing seemed to raised local people's expectations to extraordinary levels. None of my informants mentioned any of these high expectations either in September 1998 or in August 1999. But as early as September 1998 friends and informants hinted at some ideas about the causes of the disaster that I immediately identified as related to traditional cargo cult ideologies. While these ideas were only hinted at two months after the disaster, they were widely discussed by the first anniversary. By the second anniversary many of these same cargo cult ideas had even taken on a new secrecy.

When the promised international donor aid did not materialize in ways that villagers expected or hoped it would, tensions erupted throughout the district. Never does anyone seem to have been seriously threatened, but anger, small-scale demonstrations, and rage were commonplace. People at the Mission and Diocesan Rehabilitation Center focused on tensions between themselves and angry villagers in the four lagoon communities hardest hit by the tsunami. They also focused on tensions between the Rehab Committee and the government and problems that emerged between themselves and the most active of the Protestant NGOs. These latter organizations were clearly competing with the Catholic missionaries, and it is to the Rehab Committee's credit that they actually helped complete several projects left unfinished by rival organizations.

The Aitape tsunami raises one unmistakable contradiction. While humanitarian aid during the emergency and rehabilitation periods are necessary and essential following natural disasters, international aid can have considerable impact on traditional cultural patterns and local values. The Aitape tsunami of 1998 is probably an extreme case, but it shows how disruptive international aid for disaster relief can be. Necessary as this aid may be, it comes at a significant local cost.

In several respects this case is unique. The disaster was extraordinarily localized, directly affecting a narrow strip of coast only forty miles long. Overall, the region was sparsely populated except for the four communities in the direct path of the tsunami. Tons of emergency rations and supplies started arriving within days, and NGOs and donors began visiting the impact area within a week. Both had remarkable visibility throughout Aitape town and in the care centers. Many representatives of donor organizations made public announcements about their pledged gifts, and many gifts were publicized with dollar or kina amounts attached. These sums seemed enormous to nearly anyone living in the disaster area. Nowhere was the presence of these global forces and the financial power behind them more visible than in the constant movement of goods and people by helicopter for the first two or three months.

Ironically, international donors, reporters, members of the defense force, aid workers, government officers, and even ambassadors lost interest in the tsunami almost as quickly as they had arrived. But by the time they left, people in the impact zone had already formed expectations about what would follow. These expectations could, of course, never be met because international aid could never match what local people felt was necessary to compensate them for the very real pain and suffering they had experienced.

Such a narrow, localized disaster is uncommon in the world at large where entire countries can suffer at the hands of a drought, an earthquake, or a hurricane. Even in PNG most natural disasters are far more widespread than was the tsunami. During the el Niño of 1997, for example, more than a million Papua New Guineans were directly affected by the drought, the fires, and the smoke that clouded the sky and turned the midday sun into a bright red orb. During the periodic frosts that have ruined large expanses of highlands gardens, tens of thousands have been affected (Waddell 1975, 1989; Allen 1989; Clarke 1989; Wohlt 1989). Even the volcanic eruption at Rabaul in 1994 displaced larger numbers of people, although few if any died as a direct result of the disaster (see Neumann 1997). Only one other significant disaster in PNG had been so localized, the eruption of Mt. Lamington in 1950 (Belshaw 1951; Keesing 1952; Schwimmer 1969), and this happened at a time when international attention of the kind seen in Aitape could not have been mustered had anyone desired it.

But as this case study suggests, the more localized the impact and the more visible the global presence, the more complex will be the negative impact of international aid. There is really no villain in this story. Every NGO, every government officer, every aid worker, and everyone working for the Rehab Committee was trying to help the people. Nearly every one of these individuals and the organizations they represented did more or less what they promised. But all of these groups, along with the villagers affected by the power of the tsunami, found themselves on a collision course because each party had its own interests and agendas that were largely opaque to many of the other parties. The fiscal power of the donor groups and the sudden international attention merely heightened the effect and raised the intensity of expectations all around.

The situation in most Pacific Island countries is likely to resemble conditions at Aitape, because most of these island nations have small populations, tiny land areas, and remoteness from the rest of the world. Thus, natural disasters in the Pacific will probably take on many of the characteristics of the Aitape tsunami. The impact of global forces on most Pacific Island countries will likely be as powerful on most of these nations as what I have described here. It is in these settings that the impact of international humanitarian aid will be most profound.

## ACKNOWLEDGMENTS

I wish to gratefully acknowledge the research support for this project received from the Field Museum, the Claire Garber Goodman Fund administered by the Department of Anthropology at Dartmouth College, the National Research Institute (which graciously offered me a visiting professorial fellowship), the National Science Foundation (for Grant No. BCS-0077721), and private donors. My colleague John Edward Terrell and I visited the Aitape District together in 1990, 1993, 1996, and 1997 to conduct research on the peoples of this area and their cultures. Many insights about the region and its people have been shaped by our discussions and collaborations since 1990, and for these I will always be grateful. Wilfred P. Oltomo of the National Museum and Art Gallery also assisted with this research in 1993–1994, 1996, and 2000. John ("Jack") MacDonald, an associate in the Department of Anthropology at the Field Museum accompanied me to Aitape in 1998 and has provided insights and assistance in diverse ways for more than a decade (see Welsch 1999 about this visit). Three of my students from Dartmouth have visited Aitape since the disaster, Christianthy Menkhaus, Aaron Peletier, and Gabriel J. Levy, and each has contributed to my insights in varied but important ways. Joshua A. Bell and Sebastine Haraha also assisted with my field research in 2000. I would also like to thank Bishop Austen Crapp, Father Timothy Elliott, Father Tom Ritchie, and the other Franciscan fathers and brothers who have assisted me in this research. The Diocesan Rehabilitation Committee, Rehabilitation Coordinator Balthasar Maketu and the rest of his staff, the Catholic mission, the staff of the Aitape District Office, Robert and Margaret Parer, and many others in Aitape have been generous with their time and insights. Most of all I wish to thank the people of Aitape District who have so graciously allowed me to share their lives since 1990. Many people patiently sat down to discuss the disaster with me, for which I will always be grateful. In particular, I wish to thank the families of Ferdinand Wakenu and the late Adolph Woichom, who have looked after me and my research team over the years. Their kindness can never be fully repaid.

## REFERENCES

Allen, Bryant. 1989. "Preface to Frost and Drought in the Highlands of New Guinea: A Special Collection of Papers." Bryant Allen, Harold Brookfield, and Yvonne Byron, eds. *Mountain Research and Development* 9(3):199–200.

Barton, Allen H. 1969. *Communities in Disaster: A Sociological Analysis of Collective Stress Situations*. Garden City, N.Y.: Doubleday.

Belshaw, Cyril Shirley. 1951. "Social Consequences of the Mount Lamington Eruption." *Oceania* 21:241–252.

Benthall, Jonathan. 1993. *Disasters, Relief, and the Media*. London: I. B. Tauris.

Burridge, Kenelm. 1960. *Mambu: A Study of Melanesian Cargo Movements and Their Social and Ideological Background*. London: Methuen.

Clarke, W. C. 1989. "The Marient Basin, 1972–1976: Recovery or Adaptation?" *Mountain Research and Development* 9(3):235–247.

Davis, Nancy Yaw. 1986. "Earthquake, Tsunami, Resettlement and Survival in Two North Pacific Alaskan Native Villages." In *Natural Disasters and Cultural Responses*. Anthony Oliver-Smith, ed. Studies in Third World Societies, Publication No. 36. Pp. 123–154. Williamsburg, Va.: Department of Anthropology, College of William and Mary.

Demarath, Nicholas J., and Anthony F. C. Wallace, eds. 1957. "Human Adaptation to Disaster." Special issue. *Human Organization* 16(2):1–40.

Eri, Vincent. 1970. *The Crocodile: A Novel*. Milton, Qld.: Jacaranda Press.

Erikson, Kai T. 1976. *Everything in Its Path: Destruction of Community in the Buffalo Creek Flood*. New York: Simon and Schuster.

Höltker, Georg. 1940/1941. "Verstreute ethnographische Notizen uber Neuguinea. (Eine Art Regestensammlung aud dem "Steyler Missionbote," 1895–1941)." *Anthropos* 35–36:1–67.

Keesing, Felix M. 1952. "The Papuan Orokaiva versus Mt. Lamington: Cultural Shock and Its Aftermath." *Human Organization* 11(1):16–22.

Lawrence, Peter. 1964. *Road Belong Cargo: A Study of the Cargo Movement in the Southern Madang District, New Guinea.* Manchester: Manchester University Press.

Neumann, Karl. 1997. *Rabaul: Yu Swit Moa Yet: Surviving the 1994 Volcanic Eruption.* Oxford: Oxford University Press.

O'Callaghan, Mary Louise, with Patrick Hamilton. 1998. "After the Wave: The Tsunami That Struck the North-West Coast of Papua New Guinea Destroyed Several Thriving Communities. The Survivors Are Struggling to Deal with the Horror of That Terrible Night." *The Australian Magazine* (with *Weekend Australian*) September 19–20:20–25.

Oliver-Smith, Anthony. 1986. *The Martyred City: Death and Rebirth in the Andes.* Albuquerque: University of New Mexico Press.

Rodatz, Hans. 1908. "Aus dem neuen Bezirk Eitape." *Deutsches Kolonialblatt* 19:15–20.

———. 1909. "Eine Expedition im Norden von Kaiser-Wilhelmsland." *Deutsches Kolonialblatt* 20:174–76.

Schwimmer, Eric G. 1969. *Cultural Consequences of a Volcanic Eruption Experienced by the Mount Lamington Orokaiva.* Eugene: Department of Anthropology, University of Oregon.

United Nations Development Program. 1998. *Mission Report (Rev.1) Papua New Guinea: The Aitape Disaster Caused by the Tsunami of 17th Jul 1998. 23rd July–6th August 1998.* Port Moresby: UNDP, Disaster Assessment and Coordination South Pacific Team.

Waddell, Eric. 1975. "How the Enga Cope with Frost: Responses to Climatic Perturbations in the Central Highlands of New Guinea." *Human Ecology* 3(4):249–273.

———. 1989. "Observations on the 1972 Frosts and Subsequent Relief Programme among the Enga of the Western Highlands." *Mountain Research and Development* 9(3):210–223.

Welsch, Robert L. 1996. "Collaborative Regional Anthropology in New Guinea: From the New Guinea Micro-Evolution Project to the A. B. Lewis Project and Beyond." *Pacific Studies* 19(3):143–186.

———. 1999. "Papua New Guinea Begins Rebuilding after Tidal Wave Disaster." In *The Field: The Field Museum's Membership Publication* 70(1):7.

Welsch, Robert L., and John Terrell. 1990. "Continuity and Change in Economic Relations along the Aitape Coast of Papua New Guinea, 1909–1990." *Pacific Studies* 14(4):113–128.

———. 1998. "Material Culture, Social Fields, and Social Boundaries on the Sepik Coast of New Guinea." In *The Archaeology of Social Boundaries.* Miriam Stark, ed. Pp. 50–77. Washington: Smithsonian Institution Press.

Wohlt, Paul. 1989. "Migration from Yumbisa, 1972–1975." *Mountain Research and Development* 9(3):235–247.

Worsley, Peter. 1970. *The Trumpet Shall Sound: A Study of "Cargo" Cults in Melanesia.* 2nd augmented ed. New York: Schocken Books.

# 14

# The Meanings of Work in Contemporary Palau: Policy Implications of Globalization in the Pacific

**Karen L. Nero**

*University of Auckland*

**Fermina Brel Murray**

**Michael L. Burton**

*University of California, Irvine*

> Everywhere we look, we see institutions that appear the same as they used to be from the outside, and carry the same names, but inside have become quite different. We continue to talk of the nation, the family, work, tradition, nature, as if they were all the same as in the past. They are not. The outer shell remains, but inside all is different. (Anthony Giddens, BBC Reith Lectures 1999)

The globalization of labor, technology, capital, communications, and transport challenge ways of understanding contemporary societies and their ways of living in the world. This is especially true for Pacific Island nations, which commonly have one-third or more of their citizens living and working abroad, often counterbalanced by the importation of laborers from other cultures. To many writers, such as Anthony Giddens, the cultural and institutional transformations entailed are sweeping. But are they as deep-seated as they might appear? How can such issues be studied? Clearly research must be ethnographically based, but how are the "field" sites to be determined? (Gupta and Ferguson 1997; Hastrup and Olwig 1997). The Pacific presents special opportunities for the analysis of the transnationalization of households and the labor force (Wallerstein and Smith 1992). Long adapted to interisland linkages as a way of life as well as a survival strategy, Pacific islanders now participate in regional and global economies and cultural practices (Hau'ofa 1993; Nero 1997a:439–451). They also have had to fight for recognition of their primary resources—the sea and its products (Nero 1997b:368–373). Most islanders have retained active systems of food production. However, foreign workers were brought in to fill low-paid positions during most of the twentieth century, while islanders sought or were forced to seek overseas labor. Currently, few island nations are able to absorb their working-age population in wage labor, which has resulted in out-migration. Most now import workers for a range of professional to artisanal positions, and many struggle to maintain numerical superiority in their own homelands.

Palau is strategically located in the western Pacific, close to Southeast Asia and part of Oceania. Palauan involvement in regional trade networks predated European incursions, and linguistically and culturally Palau shares prehistoric links with the peoples of the Philippines and eastern Indonesia. Palau also shares with the Philippines a history of American colonization and continues to use the U.S. dollar as currency. Its varying positions in the networks of international capitalism and colonialism have influenced population flows.

During the early years of the American administration the Palauan economy was stagnant, and Palauans increasingly sought employment and education in the United States and its Pacific territories, thus beginning a process of Palauan out-migration. The current overseas Palauan population is estimated at 7,000, while the resident native population has been stable at around 13,000 since 1973. Natural increase has been counterbalanced by out-migration. There are now second- and third-generation emigrants, especially in Guam, Saipan, and Hawai'i, who have well-established social networks that facilitate education and employment opportunities for the extended families that now spread across Palau, Guam, the Northern Marianas, the United States, Japan, China, and the Philippines. Since the 1960s, Palauan students have had access to U.S. scholarships and loans for college and other tertiary training. The educational level of the overseas Palauans is high, and many hold professional and managerial positions. Palau's 1994 Compact of Free Association with the United States provides overseas Palauans with the right to live and work

in the United States and its territories. As a result, immigrants enjoy access to U.S. social services, and those who hold skilled or semi-skilled positions enjoy pay levels higher than those available in Palau.

After Palau became self-governing in January 1981, successive Palauan administrations sought to provide increased social services and to support economic development. These policies produced considerable growth of Palauan public sector employment, an increase in the wage labor participation rate to 59 percent, high labor force participation by Palauan women, the introduction of many new categories of occupations, a rapid increase in foreign workers, and continued out-migration of young Palauans for education and employment.

Palauans are internationally recognized for the tenacity with which significant numbers successfully opposed proposals for an international superport, for U.S. military use of Palauan lands, and for the fifteen-year struggle by the entire nation to resolve its political status. They now face a more serious threat: apparent prosperity. Palau became independent and joined the United Nations in 1994, and began to receive substantial front-end Compact of Free Association payments from the United States for the development of its infrastructure. In return for fifty years of exclusive strategic association with Palau, the United States granted Palau about $450 million for its first fifteen years of independence, with an undetermined amount to be allocated in the remaining thirty-five years. This influx of new money is producing an even greater increase in foreign workers. In this chapter we discuss the changes in Palauan society resulting from the introduction of many new occupations and the great increase in foreign workers. First we discuss in more detail the economic and demographic changes that have occurred in Palau. Second we describe ethnographic research on the meanings of work in Palau and how these have been affected by contemporary social processes. Finally we consider the results of a series of qualitative and structured cognitive interviews that we conducted with Palauans. We believe these can provide insights into the ways Palauans have incorporated new occupations and values into contemporary conceptualizations of work.

## ECONOMIC AND DEMOGRAPHIC TRANSFORMATIONS

The pre-European (1783) Palauan population has been estimated at 50,000, declining to fewer than 4,000 by the turn of the nineteenth century (Palau National Committee on Population and Children [CoPopChi] 1997:7). The indigenous population then began to recover but was eclipsed by an influx of Japanese and Okinawans during the prewar and World War II periods. During the Japanese period, Koror, the Japanese administrative center, was mainly a Japanese town. Palauan participation in wage labor was limited to lower-level occupations. Japanese and Okinawans were imported to provide labor in farming, fishing, and food processing. Of the 1943 population of 32,000, roughly 7,000 were native Palauans.

During World War II, the significant economic and social infrastructure, which had served Palauans as well as Japanese, was mostly destroyed. After an initial period of reconstruction, the Palauan economy languished during the early years of the U.S. administration. Many of the basic services that are essential to economic development, such as roads and a transportation system, were never completed. Under the early U.S. administration, high-level administrative positions were held mainly by Americans, while Palauans were increasingly drawn into other levels of public sector employment.

As first president of the republic Haruo Remeliik and his advisors pondered the development of the economy, it became apparent that Palauan workers might not be sufficient in number and training to perform all the tasks required. By then the Palauan labor force was dispersed not only throughout the islands of Micronesia but into the United States as well. In many cases Palauans, who were highly educated in comparison to many other islanders and to many U.S. minority populations, had been quite successful in obtaining good positions abroad. The relatively higher earnings available in the United States, and Palauan youths' obligations to pay back student loans, contributed to difficulties that some Palauans encountered when trying to return to Palau. Nevertheless, beginning in 1980, many returned to join the new government and to start private sector businesses.

In 1992, prior to free association, Palau's per capita gross domestic product was more than US$5,000, placing Palau in the upper economic bracket of Pacific Island nations. Palau enjoys high literacy and health standards and ranks among those countries the United Nations classifies as having high levels of human development (UNDP 1995). Palau is blessed with favorable natural resources for fishing and agriculture, and has developed world-class diving attractions. The Bank of Hawaii estimated a 32.3 percent growth in gross domestic product in 1995 and a 2.0–3.4 percent increase in 1996 (1997:12). Will Palau be able to turn its large public sector investments into a strong private sector capable of generating sufficient income to maintain its current high standard of living once U.S. government payments under the compact begin to decline? Agriculture, fishing, and tourism, Palau's three identified development options, all require careful monitoring to ensure that they are environmentally sustainable. More important, however, are labor and population issues and their impact on the social and natural environments.

Labor has been imported at all levels but particularly in the production and service industries. In 1973, just 4 percent of Palau residents were foreigners, but by 1995 that figure was 24 percent. Of the foreign residents, 80 percent were workers, and another 10 percent were dependents of workers (CoPopChi 1997:12). Table 14.1 compares foreign workers in Palau in 1981, the first year of self-government (Knowles 1982), with 1998 figures covering only private sector employees (Palau Office of Administration, May 1998). The table shows the top seven countries of origin of these workers in 1998. In 1981 foreign workers made up 37 percent of the

**Table 14.1**   Foreign and Palauan Workers, 1981 and 1998 by Country of Origin

| Sector | 1981 Workers | | 1998 Private Sector Foreign Workers | | | | | | | |
| | Palau | Foreign | Philipines | China | Bangladesh | Japan | U.S. | Taiwan | Korea | Total Foreign |
|---|---|---|---|---|---|---|---|---|---|---|
| Professional | 34 | 35 | 225 | 31 | 9 | 38 | 31 | 8 | 4 | 365 |
| Managerial | 69 | 39 | 83 | 79 | 2 | 68 | 41 | 35 | 22 | 353 |
| Clerical | 125 | 8 | 179 | 24 | 2 | 4 | 1 | 3 | 0 | 228 |
| Sales | 82 | 0 | 85 | 11 | 0 | 2 | 0 | 1 | 0 | 102 |
| Service | 172 | 18 | 1,157 | 138 | 129 | 12 | 44 | 13 | 14 | 1,533 |
| Production | 592 | 522 | 1,512 | 509 | 171 | 8 | 1 | 16 | 8 | 2,247 |
| Total | 1,074 | 622 | 3,241 | 792 | 313 | 132 | 118 | 76 | 48 | 4,828 |

*Note:* For 1998 only the first seven countries of origin are shown. The seven nations contribute 97.7 percent of all foreign workers. (Column and row figures may not add to totals shown because totals are drawn from the full data.)

*Source:* Figures for 1981 from Knowles 1982; figures for 1998 from Palau Office of Administration.

workforce.[1] To the 1998 private sector workers we add several hundred public sector employees, for a total of over 5,000 foreign workers. Thus, the number of foreign workers expanded eightfold in seventeen years.

The three largest groups of foreign workers, Filipinos, Chinese, and Bangladeshi, have increased even more rapidly and are especially concentrated in the lowest-paid service and production sectors. Filipinos increased eightfold from a few hundred in 1981 to 3,241 just in the private sector in 1998. Filipinos today constitute 67 percent of Palau's resident foreign workers, including some who have been living and working in Palau for three decades. Whereas only eighteen Chinese workers registered in Palau in 1983, there were 792 in the private sector alone in 1998.

The native Palauan workforce has increased less rapidly. Kick (1995) estimated there were 5,000 indigenous Palauan workers in 1995, with 1,800 of them in government employment, and that the indigenous workforce was increasing by 300 persons per year. This would make it about 5,900 in 1998, less than a sixfold increase since 1981. Foreign workers now constitute nearly half the workforce in Palau.

What kinds of jobs do foreign workers hold? In 1983, Antonio counted 418 private sector foreign workers. Of these more than half (220) were fishers. Of the remainder, sixty-three worked in construction, and only

nine were domestic helpers (Antonio 1983). In 1995 Kick found that foreign workers held half or more of the production and construction jobs, and one-third of all service jobs. Foreign workers continued their high concentration in production occupations and greatly increased their representation in the service sector. As most foreign workers would accept lower private sector wages than would Palauans, there was little incentive for Palauans to work in the private sector, especially in comparison to the government sector (Kick 1995)

In the 1998 data summarized in Table 14.1, many foreign workers continue to be employed as carpenters, masons, electricians, or mechanics (19.2 percent of the total), in food production (9.4 percent), and in the food and tourism industries (10.4 percent).

The rising numbers of foreign workers will have not only social and environmental impacts but also substantial cultural impacts, especially on the younger generations. Many private sector foreign workers are employed as domestic helpers. In 1998 low-paid domestic helpers and housekeepers constituted 12.3 percent of all private sector foreign workers. This category of employee increased more than sixtyfold in fifteen years, from 9 to 596.

High-ranking Palauan households historically had servants. Today an estimated one in five households employs a domestic helper.

These workers support the participation of ordinary Palauan adults in the workforce. They care for children and the growing numbers of elders, and often assist with family farms and small businesses. Many children are cared for by women who do not speak Palauan, and who also undertake many of the tasks that were previously children's household work. In the past most domestic servants and ancillary workers were extended family members, or Palauan dependents. If they were hardworking and conformed to Palauan social practices, even foreign dependents could be incorporated into Palauan society, recreating a unified sociality. Many of the households incorporating foreign workers have modeled their interactions on such familial and incorporative models of humanity, which are deeply held in Palau. But others treat their workers poorly, as a separate class of transients hired simply to perform menial labor. Perhaps more important, certain types of work are becoming labeled "domestic helper" work, or, like janitorial work, are often now considered suitable only for foreigners.

Palauan government officials and community members are aware of the dangers of rapid economic growth and high foreign investment, and are concerned about the impact on Palauan society and culture of large numbers of foreign workers. Yet Palau would not have enough people to provide labor for currently planned infrastructure development even if all out-migrants returned. Palauan workers have become a scarce resource.

At present, Palauans still form the majority population, but foreign workers and their dependents make up approximately one-third of the total. These workers have made significant contributions to building the new nation. In addition, the presence of so many foreigners has generated growth in existing businesses and led to the creation of new businesses that provide services for residents and foreign workers. Even if the government could complete infrastructure construction during the next decade, and thereafter reduce the requirement for foreign workers, what would be the impact on businesses and buying power if several thousand people left Palau?

Palauan planners recognize that population management is the key to achieving sustainable development. In 1995 President Kuniwo Nakamura created the Palau National Committee on Population and Children (CoPopChi). This committee's policy recommendations consider three scenarios of Palau's future population growth (CoPopChi 1997). The low growth, sustainable scenario would limit foreign workers to 70 percent of the total workforce. The moderate growth scenario assumes a continuation of existing policies, some internal opposition to development, and a decline in public sector employment. The high-growth scenario assumes unchanged government policies, high economic growth, and an increase in public sector jobs. The projected percentage of Palauans in the total population at the end of the compact funding in 2010 would be 67 percent under low-growth conditions, 49 percent under medium-growth conditions, and 33 percent under high-growth conditions. By 2020 the population dynamics of the three scenarios are even more striking: 60 percent under low-growth, 39 percent under moderate-growth, and 2.5 percent under high-growth conditions (derived from CoPopChi 1997, Table 10, p. 78). Even under the low-growth scenario the participation of foreigners in Palau would remain significant; under middle- and high-growth scenarios foreigners would outnumber locals in Palau, as they do in neighboring Saipan and Guam. This possibility is what Palauans most fear.

Palau's ability to achieve its low-population-growth scenario rests on its ability to cut emigration, attract an average of 150–200 overseas Palauans home each year, and restrict visas for foreign workers (CoPopChi 1997:4). The third recommendation would require careful consideration of policy guidelines and the enactment of enabling legislation. Can the nation's politicians and citizens find the political will to limit the importation of foreign workers, on which economic growth now appears to depend, to levels that are sustainable by the environment and the culture? A related problem is the large public sector, currently supported by U.S. compact payments. High dependency on public sector employment, at "a ratio of three Government employees for each four Palauan households," constrains current public policy choices (POPS 1996:2–11). Many Palauans enjoy the stability of public sector employment, which has provided capital to invest in private sector enterprises, but will such investments support a sufficient number of Palauans to shift to the private sector? National and local governments also employ foreign workers. Can and will Palauans provide services now provided by foreign workers?

## THE INDIGENOUS ECONOMY AND CONCEPTUALIZATION OF WORK

To better understand the cultural impacts of new occupations and foreign workers on Palauan society, we begin with an overview of traditional Palauan work roles. The two-volume study by the Palau Society of Historians, *Rechuodel* (PSH 1995, 1996), is an extraordinary resource; its discussions of the tasks of men and women in Palau in the past set the framework and linguistic understanding on which our study was based.

Underpinning the introduced economy supported by U.S. transfer payments, the Palauan economy continued to exist in the late twentieth century, with its emphasis on food and labor exchanges. It is perhaps in the nexus of the deeper meanings of work that some of the transformations of the past century can best be understood. The indigenous economy of Palau is based on *ongraol* (starch) and *odoim* (protein). The primary starch foods are taro and other root crops, and the most important protein foods are fish and shellfish. As symbols, *ongraol* and *odoim* encompass Palauan society: They stand for the productivity of the land and the sea, and also the responsibilities of women and men within broad divisions of labor. Women as providers of *ongraol* are farmers, and men as providers of *odoim* are fishers. Encompassed in this complementary system, further organized by age and rank, are the myriad specialization and work activities

necessary to maintain the *telungalek* (family), *kebliil* (clan), and *beluu* (village). Even the highly regarded specialists such as master carpenters or fishers participate in a full range of work activities.

Two fundamental Palauan concepts make up Palauan understandings of work: *kerruul,* and *omengereker.* It is difficult to translate these terms into single words in English. We have glossed *kerruul* in terms of the deep responsibilities of providing substance and nurturance to family members. The second concept, *omengereker,* might more directly translate as occupation. Nevertheless, these concepts are highly interconnected and must not be applied simply as dichotomous representations of traditional and introduced occupations. We offer here a brief summary of the ways that these two concepts encompass the meanings of work.

*Kerruul* (from *meruul,* to do or to make) relates primarily to performing family responsibilities. In this matrilineal society, *kerruul* is integrally associated with the woman's economic support of the household and clan, although both men and women have their own areas of responsibility within *kerruul.* The *kerruul* responsibilities of Palauan women and men are basic to the extensive system of exchanges of Palauan food and valuables, which continues today in a restructured form that incorporates the products of wage work—American dollars and purchased foods. In the gendered system of exchange, women are responsible for providing *ongraol* and men for providing *odoim.* Exchanges of food, traditional money, modern money, and goods operate within families, between families, and between larger social units.

*Omengereker* means to provide services or produce something in order to earn something. At the time of the earliest recorded European visit, Palauans had a well-established system of valuables, which included the earning of interest, so this "commodification" is not the result of recent interactions with outsiders. In the past, individuals could earn valuables or land by providing taro and other specialty foods, certain fish, turtles, or a dugong, or sexual or construction services to the male and female chiefs, among others. *Omengereker* literally refers to collecting provisions from the sea. It is therefore more associated with males than females in Palau, but both males and females *omengereker,* just as both men and women collect fish and shellfish from the seas and lagoon areas.

Like *ongraol* and *odoim, kerruul* and *omengereker* are complementary to one another. And, like *ongraol* and *odoim,* these concepts have been broadened to incorporate contemporary substances and activities. Today *kerruul* is interwoven with the workplace as well as the family. As observed ethnographically over the past two decades, the various government agencies have become, to a large extent, like villages to which loyalty, identity, and reputation are tied. People today are commonly referred to by their workplaces, for example, as *chad era ospitar* (hospital people). Traditional functions such as a funeral or a first child ceremony involving work mates invoke monetary contributions (*kerruul*) and representative visits from fellow workers. A person's ability to provide *ongraol* and *odoim* to the family depends not only on his or her skill in production, but also on skills in acting appropriately to bring *ongraol, odoim,* and valuables into the family through *kerruul* and to a lesser extent *omengereker* (see Smith 1983). People can provide well for family needs through a skillful application of *kerruul* and *omengereker,* which today tap both the local food production and monetary sectors of the economy.

It is critical that *kerruul* and *omengereker* are understood as interlinked, each containing both local and introduced work activities and conceptualizations of relationships that transcend any simple dichotomies such as traditional versus modern, or familial versus village. Similarly *kerruul* and *omengereker* do not constitute simply a "traditional" frame of work activity that concerns local food production, but they have incorporated new social relationships and valuables from the monetary economy. Through participation in the spheres of *kerruul* and *omengereker,* overseas Palauans can continue to hold their places in village and community hierarchies.

Similarly, and critically, in this chiefly matrilineal society social status is derived primarily from position in the family, clan, and village hierarchies. In addition, whereas an individual's placement in the system rests to a substantial degree on lineage, that person's actual position is only achieved through the hard work involved in producing and providing the appropriate foods and services for family, clan, and village elders during special occasions as well as on a daily basis. Hard work in the service of the community is a prerequisite of the actual position a person will hold among a range of possibilities provided within the kin system.

In general, individuals are not associated with a single occupation. Rather they are seen as productive members of their household, clan, and village, who are responsible for a number of different tasks. To learn how to fish or to grow taro does not necessarily prepare a person to become a fisher or a farmer. Status is not based on specific career or vocational skills, but rather on learning a combination of life skills that can promote a Palauan way of life. The Palauan system of status and prestige, with its locus primarily in the position of the family, clan, and village rather than in individualized occupations, is the fundamental way in which Palauan and American (and other Western) conceptualizations of work differ. While Palauans have incorporated many new work occupations and ways of thinking from the Japanese and the Americans during the past century of colonial administration, the ways in which they have incorporated new occupations do not necessarily imply a fundamental transformation of their conceptualizations of work and prestige systems.

To further understand how traditional work activities are valued today, we obtained judgments of the importance of twenty-two traditional work activities to the family and to the village community. We asked 118 individuals to select the eight tasks that they would most want family members to be skilled in. We then asked 126 individuals to select the eight tasks that they would want a member of their community to do well. Responses are listed in Table 14.2.

**Table 14.2**   Individual Judgments of the Importance of Traditional Tasks to the Family and to the Community

| Task | Village | Family | Task | Village | Family |
|---|---|---|---|---|---|
| Know clan history | 69 | 87 | Build summerhouse | 35 | 53 |
| Make fishing tools | 64 | 82 | Feast fishing | 41 | 45 |
| Master fisher | 56 | 86 | Chanting | 45 | 32 |
| Know local medicine | 59 | 71 | Mat weaving | 34 | 42 |
| Dancing | 59 | 63 | Make turtle/shell money | 39 | 31 |
| Know community history | 61 | 59 | Make grass skirts | 25 | 29 |
| Prepare feast food | 64 | 49 | Know local massage | 19 | 23 |
| Build community house | 69 | 43 | Carve plates/dishes | 24 | 17 |
| Taro farming | 47 | 64 | Pigeon hunting | 16 | 21 |
| Navigating | 53 | 55 | Jewelry making | 14 | 11 |
| Master farming | 44 | 49 | Stone masonry | 11 | 4 |

*Note:* Responses are listed in decreasing order of total choices across the two contexts. The correlation between judgments regarding the contexts is 0.84.

While 0.84 is a high correlation, there are some notable differences in the relative importance of work activities to the two contexts. For example, master fishing is selected more often in the family context than in the village context, while chanting and building a community house are selected more often in the village context. Figure 14.1 represents the relative importance of these tasks to the two contexts. This figure places the two contexts—village and family—on the same scale as the work activities, which are ordered in terms of their role in discriminating between the two contexts.[2] Activities that are relatively more important to family are at the top of the scale, while activities that are more important to village are at the bottom of the scale. Activities that are equally important to either context are placed near the zero point of the scale.

Tasks that have highest relative importance to the family include building a summerhouse, knowledge of clan histories, and four activities pertaining to food production (master fisher, taro farmer, pigeon hunter, and fishing toolmaker). Tasks that have highest relative importance in the village context include building a community house and four activities associated with public ceremonies—carving plates, chanting, making feast food, and making shell money.

In summary, there are four fundamental aspects of traditional conceptualizations of work and occupations, as shown in the list below:

- *Kerruul* and *omengereker* together comprise the types of work that men and women perform, both to fulfill their customary obligations to their families and communities and to earn income for their families and communities (which is also a family obligation).

- While there is a high correlation between the cultural valuation of tasks in the contexts of family and community, there are also systematic differences between the two contexts.

- Palauan conceptualizations and practices emphasize mastery of a basic area of responsibility that is highly gendered, although both men and women may do particular work tasks within either domain.

- In basic concept and in practice, individuals are expected to perform well a number of different *omengereker,* or occupations, especially over the course of their lifetimes.

We will next demonstrate that these fundamental Palauan conceptualizations of work remain active in the face of change. Many Palauans fulfill new occupations introduced during colonial administrations, and derive much of their sense of personal identity and worth from these occupations. They also continue to fulfill their responsibilities of *kerruul* and *omengereker,* which have become interlinked with the new occupations. Most notably, with the exception of a few highly

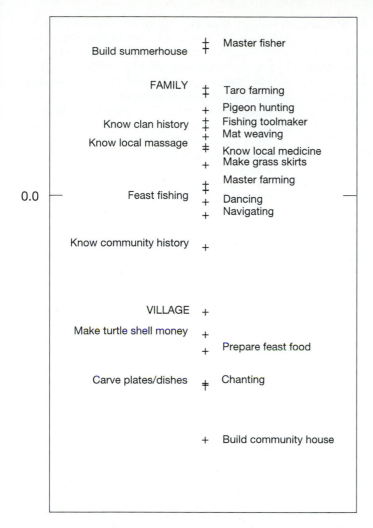

Build summerhouse   ‡   Master fisher

FAMILY   ‡   Taro farming

  +   Pigeon hunting

Know clan history   ‡   Fishing toolmaker

  +   Mat weaving

Know local massage   ‡   Know local medicine

  +   Make grass skirts

  ‡   Master farming

0.0     Feast fishing   +   Dancing

  +   Navigating

Know community history   +

VILLAGE   +

Make turtle shell money   +

  +   Prepare feast food

Carve plates/dishes   ‡   Chanting

  +   Build community house

**Figure 14.1**    Relative importance of work activities to village and family

educated professions such as doctor and nurse, most Palauans continue to traverse a number of occupations.

## PALAUAN PERCEPTIONS OF THE CHANGING MEANINGS OF WORK

The rise of new occupations, the increased prevalence of wage labor, and the influx of foreign workers have had profound effects on Palauan society. To explore how these changes are perceived, we conducted a series of qualitative interviews about Palauans' con-

cerns. We then collected structured cognitive data to examine how Palauans have integrated traditional and modern occupations into a single, uniquely Palauan system.

The Palauans whom we interviewed included government officials and a number of other individuals. Those consulted were highly concerned about the number of foreign workers and their dependents living in Palau and their potentially significant impact on Palauan ways of life. Concerns centered around the numbers of foreign workers and investors involved in the development of tourism, changes in the relative valuation of different kinds of work, and the impact of domestic servants on the socialization of children.

Tourism is one of the most rapidly expanding sectors of the economy. Since the 1970s Palau has been among the top diving destinations in the world. The luxury hotel Palau Pacific Resort has recently expanded, and the new Palasia Hotel opened with 165 rooms. Numerous diving and other tourism-related businesses are currently in operation, under construction, or in the planning stage. Cabinet ministers, community members, and government agencies are concerned that existing plans and policies will be unable to control the tourism industry in Palau, in particular the importation of foreign workers, resulting in a repetition of the experience of the Northern Marianas. The Palau National Committee on Population and Children has investigated these issues and recommended strategies that would balance economic growth with cultural and environmental sustainability. The Palau Visitors Authority (PVA) is equally concerned with proposed tourism developments and has begun strategizing ways to achieve a sustainable tourism development (PVA 1996). As of December 1996 it had published information outlining twenty-six tourism plans then under consideration (see CoPopChi 1997:81–82). Even if only a portion of these were approved, the numbers of foreign workers required for construction, hotel, and restaurant employment would increase significantly. A key concern is that there is no legislated mechanism to limit the absolute number of projects that may be approved. If each plan in turn complies with environmental and planning criteria, must each be approved? What criteria would be used to select among the plans?

A related area of serious concern was the effect of large numbers of foreign workers employed in Palau on the meanings of the various occupations they fill and on work-based inequality. This issue related, in part, to various placements of both Palauan and foreign workers in the larger international economy. Many Palauans can find higher-paid employment overseas, and many foreign workers who hold good jobs in Palau receive higher pay or special allowances (such as for housing) that are not generally available to Palauans. At the other end of the spectrum, some foreign workers will accept very low wages in order to earn U.S. dollars, as they will be able to remit significant sums to support family members at home.

A significant area of impact is in the low-skilled and low-prestige jobs. The occupations of domestic servant, janitor, and even farmer are often held by foreign workers, with the result that many young Palauans refuse to train for or fill these occupations. Similarly, because many of the workers in the construction trades are foreigners, some of these occupations are becoming more segregated by ethnic groups, and fewer Palauans are attracted to them. While many young Palauans would like to find jobs, they do not wish to be seen publicly in low-status jobs, believing that foreigners should fill these instead, and that Palauans should supervise the foreigners. These labor practices have a long history in Palau, going back several hundred years to the time when Palauans liked to hire low-caste Yapese to perform certain tasks. Later in Palauan history the ethnic differentiation was between Japanese and Palauans, then between Americans and Palauans. Today the primary distinction is between Palauans and foreign workers.

This process has led Palauan elders to fear that certain occupations are now becoming racialized, and that Palauan children are coming to consider some categories of foreigners as less than human. In the recent past there was no loss of status if, say, a male elder chose to contribute to society and to earn money through being a janitor. His status depended, after all, on his position within his family, clan, and village, rather than where he worked. And he was a part of the workplace community as an active contributing member. However, the new system of occupations threatens to undermine the community-based system.

At the national government level, we found that all of the Palauan traditional work activities (fishing, farming, weaving, and carving) are now considered parts of the "informal sector of the economy" as stated in the republic's Master Plan. These occupations tend to be marginalized in terms of government policies and support. Only recently, as a result of a United Nations Development Program initiative, have informal sector activities been recognized as part of the gross domestic product and policies considering their integration into the national economy considered. Under the previous international labor categories, as described in the analyses for the 1980 Palau Community Action Agency census, many of these activities were generally practiced by those considered "economically not active" (Nero 1983). Subsistence farming and fishing activities at the household and village level are supported primarily by the Palau Community Action Agency, a nongovernment organization. The Palau Senior Citizens Center and the Belau National Museum carry out preservation of Palau's arts in weaving, carving, dancing, and music.

One of the common themes of the interviews was the fear that Palauan children are losing the traditional values. People, especially elders, complain that the children are not literate in the Palauan language, and that they don't do any household chores or learn family responsibilities because hired Filipino workers are filling those jobs. Further, because most parents carry full-time employment, they no longer have time to teach their children the Palauan values and traditional skills. What happens when these activities are delegated to foreign workers? Dr. Kuartei, one of the speakers at the 1997 Moving Cultures conference in Palau, posed the questions, "What do Palauans give up when they allow foreigners to butcher the pig at the funeral? Are we letting our sacred cultural rites be taken over by foreign labor? The right hand says there are too many foreigners in Palau—it is a big problem—but the left hand hires the foreign workers to do a lot of tasks that perhaps could be done by Palauans."

Palauans remain ambivalent about the foreigners living among them. At one level many fear the presence of so many foreigners. They desire that foreigners come to Palau for a while and then return home. Nevertheless, one of the core Palauan values is hospitality and care for strangers. Foreign workers, especially domestic workers who reside in Palauan households, are generally considered as dependent "children" for whom the household has responsibility. It is difficult not to consider such foreigners in personal, human terms, rather than in the less-personal category of "foreign laborer." While everyone agrees that foreign laborers should not stay too long, once individuals enter a household or a company as employees, they are often treated as family members. Individuals may be in favor of controlling foreign workers, but at the same time they are equally adamant in supporting their "children," not only because of the time they have invested in training them, but also because of the personal relationships they have established.

## How Contemporary Palauans Classify Occupations

To further explore changes in concepts of work, we administered a triads test on a set of nineteen occupation terms. Triads tests are one way to measure similarities and differences in order to map cognitive domains according to the cultural values of the respondents (Weller and Romney 1988). Ideally we would have preferred using pile-sort techniques that would have allowed the inclusion of more occupations. However, Palauan coresearchers and advisors suggested that the additional complexity and time required for administration would make pile sorts of occupations unwieldy. Together we selected and pretested nineteen occupations for the tests.

Important issues identified during qualitative interviews included the increasing designation of certain types of unskilled work as appropriate only for lower-status foreign workers, the fear of replacement of Palauan cultural values with externally based values, and changes in the gender composition of occupations. The triads data collection was designed to address these questions.

We focused primarily on youth between seventeen and twenty-five years of age, drawing the younger respondents primarily from classes at the Palau Community College. This group included college students from other

Micronesian societies (mainly Yap), and a few from the Philippines, Taiwan, and Korea, many of whom had grown up in Palau. Here we have used the more inclusive term "Islander" for our participants, although 90 percent of the sample participants were of Palauan ancestry. Other young respondents were drawn from the National Congress of Youth Leaders, and from youth who had left formal education and were pursuing graduate equivalency diplomas. We obtained smaller samples in the twenty-six to fifty-four, and fifty-five-plus age groups, primarily among the staff at the Palau Community College, a number of private and public sector employees, self-employed researchers, officials, and elders of the community. About equal numbers of men and women were interviewed in each age group. Twenty-five different randomizations of the questionnaire that included fifty-seven triads were administered to 111 participants.

English is an official language of the Republic of Palau, is used for most reading materials, and is often the preferred language for writing. Furthermore, most Palauan occupation names are loan words from either English or Japanese. Thus we decided to conduct the tests in English. Occupations were presented three at a time (hence triads), with respondents asked to select the item that was most different. In each case one of the researchers, or the teacher to whom the tasks had been explained, provided the introduction to the tasks and solicited any questions or clarifications desired by the participants. After the questionnaires were completed, researchers asked individuals to indicate what sorts of criteria they had used in making their selections, any difficulties they encountered, and what they felt about the tasks.

Figure 14.2 presents a spatial analysis of the judged similarity data from the respondents.[3] Identification of the underlying principles represented by the graph was then made by the researchers and members of the community studying the spatial representation.

After completing the triads questionnaire, respondents of all age groups told us that the most important distinction was whether the occupation or work-related task was "Islander" or introduced. We can see this distinction horizontally in the figure. "Islander" occupations (farmer, fisher, carpenter, carver, boat driver, maid, food preparer, and weaver) are on the right and introduced occupations on the left.

Several of the Islander occupations have been reshaped since the colonial period. "Boat driver," for example, is categorized among the Islander occupations. The boat driven today is generally a motorboat, sometimes primarily to take tourists sightseeing. However, it appears that the various work tasks associated with driving the boat (knowledge of the lagoons, navigating safely within and outside the reefs) remain firmly within Islander cognitive frames. Even more significant in meaning is "maid." Historically Palauan families, especially of the high clans, included servants who performed routine household tasks such as caring for children, preparing food, cleaning, and carrying water. The occupation of maid or servant is long-standing in Palau, as is the possibility of a foreigner being in this position. Of the nearly 5,000 foreign workers in Palau at this time, nearly 500 are domestic helpers, and another 100 are houseboys. Yet this occupational category remains within the Islander portion of the occupational grid.

The horizontal dimension has some resemblance to the prestige dimension that is often found in studies of occupations, and Trieman's (1977) occupational prestige scale has a correlation of 0.75 with the left side of the scale. What this means is that people from countries such as the United States would see the introduced occupations on the left of the figure as having greater prestige than the Palauan occupations. However, this is lower than the correlations obtained in comparable studies done in the United States, which are greater than 0.90, and it would not be correct to interpret the scale as meaning "prestige" to Palauans (Burton 1972; Magaña, Burton, and Ferreira-Pinto 1995).

The vertical dimension is slightly more difficult to identify. Partly this is because a third dimension discussed later, that of gender, intervenes within the islander group of

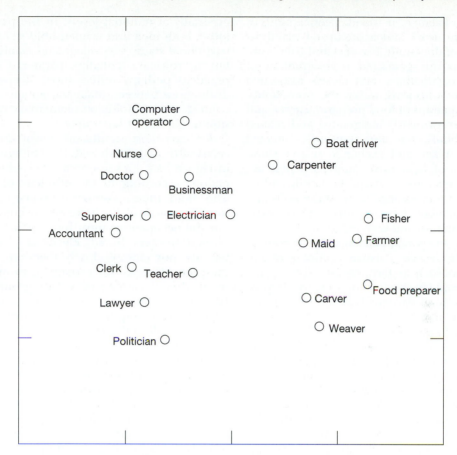

**Figure 14.2**  Multidimensional representation of occupations

occupations but is not present in the introduced group. The main vertical dimension, however, is that of workplace or work domain. Those interviewed also indicated that they considered what clothes would be needed. This dimension supports interview data suggesting that place of work has become a new focus of identity and a basis of social relationships similar to that of village membership. The most telling example is the proximity of doctor and nurse, who both work in the hospital. In representations based on either gender or prestige dimensions, these two occupations would be separated. The importance of workplace can also be seen in the proximity of supervisor and accountant, and of clerk and lawyer, then moving further toward politician,

an occupation sought by many lawyers. There may also be a component of skill source underlying the vertical dimension, with occupations in the upper half of the chart integrating new skills and materials with indigenous knowledge, whereas those in the bottom half retain a larger indigenous component (the law retains a significant cultural component in Palau).

Within the Islander group of occupations, the occupations are further divided by gender. The top three occupations (carpenter, boat driver, and fisher) are predominantly held by males, while four of the lower five occupations (maid, farmer, food preparer, and weaver) are mostly female (carvers are generally male). These occupations are further clustered. As discussed earlier, gendered food production is central to Palauan or Islander conceptions of meaningful work and is organized mainly at the level of the family. Farmers and fishers are central to this gendered representation of Islander occupations, and closely associated with maids who work within the households. The occupations of food preparer, carver, and weaver are primarily indigenous and related to the family, but also outwardly directed through village and exchange relationships. The skills of boat driver and carpenter are generally exercised outside the family and involve the wider society; today these skills also contain a much larger component of introduced materials and knowledge.

One of the young Palauans interviewed reported that within Palauan occupations and work tasks such as farming and fishing, the young people in general conform to accepted gender differentiation. However, in other occupations they feel they can all compete equally for positions regardless of gender. These conceptualizations are confirmed in practice; there are Palauan women doctors and male nurses, women as well as men who are professional administrators. Within Palauan society it appears that new money and wage labor have not significantly damaged women's economic position. While it has been difficult to get good data, there appears to be a high level of equality between Palauan men and women with respect to kinds of wage jobs held, as well as compensation levels. Furthermore, the position of Palauan women in the exchange system assures that men will give them money, goods, and valuables. The de-gendering of work, however, has been mostly within the introduced occupations. Palauans (and other islanders in the sample) continue to gender Islander occupations such as farmer and weaver, as opposed to fisher and carver. In both interviews and in the structured data, Palauans told us that occupations such as doctor, nurse, and lawyer, which may be strongly gendered in the American occupational system from which they were derived, are not gendered in the Palauan model.

The one occupation that continues to be highly male-gendered is that of politician,

especially at national levels. In the past and today, both men and women hold significant traditional statuses as village and clan elders, but the roles are spatially separated. Current practices perhaps reflect more deep-seated distinctions between male and female chiefly councils, which hold complementary responsibilities but meet separately.

Perhaps most significant, given the concerns of those interviewed, the configuration in Figure 14.2 does not seem to classify occupations according to the ethnicity of those who hold them. Foreign workers may be found in most of the nineteen occupations, but the occupations most frequently held by foreign workers (maid, electrician, carpenter) do not cluster closely together. While these occupations are proximate to one another, they do not form a close group. The Islander or introduced and workplace dimensions are more important than considerations of the outsider ethnicity of many of those in the occupation.

The mean consensus among respondents was 0.62, showing a significant degree of sharing of the aggregate pattern, but not so high as to rule out meaningful variability within subgroups of respondents (Romney, Weller, and Batchelder 1986). We examined variability across respondents by ethnicity, gender, and age. To our surprise, there was no significant difference between data produced by ethnic Palauans and data obtained from members of other ethnic groups resident in Palau. Similarly, there were no significant differences by gender of respondent. The only significant differences were between elders and all others. While these seemed interesting, we have too few elders in the sample to generalize about the possible differences.

We might think that Palauans, who were administered by the United States for fifty years, would be greatly influenced by American conceptions of occupations. Although many new occupations have been incorporated into Palauan life, Palauans do not conceptualize them in the same way as do residents of the United States. We compared the Palauan representation of occupations with those derived from respondents in the United

States (Burton 1972; Magaña, Burton, and Ferreira-Pinto 1995) and found the two systems substantially different.

As we have discussed, the first dimension of the U.S. system is based on status, or prestige. In the U.S. model, "computer operator," "electrician," "clerk," and "nurse" would be noticeably lower in prestige than occupations such as "lawyer," "doctor," and "supervisor." In the U.S. model, nurse and physician differ in prestige value, whereas the Palauans put the two close together. This is interesting given the strongly gendered nature of the doctor-nurse relationship in the United States, and given that our Palauan information stressed the gender-free nature of the "modern" occupations in the Palauan setting.

Furthermore, in the U.S. model, the higher status occupations are divided between service occupations (doctor, teacher, lawyer, nurse) and business or bureaucratic occupations (clerk, supervisor, computer operator, businessperson, politician, accountant). This dimension does not replicate in the Palauan structure, where businessperson is next to doctor and nurse, and lawyer and politician are next to teacher.

Finally, the U.S. model has a cluster of skilled craft occupations (carver, carpenter, weaver, and electrician) whereas in the Palauan system these are not together. There is nothing in the U.S. picture comparable to the cluster of weaver, carver, food preparer, maid, farmer, and fisher that we see in the Palauan system. This point is critical, because these are the most traditional Palauan occupations. The cluster is meaningful in the Palauan setting, and would not be meaningful in the U.S. system.

To summarize, we find in English-language structured interviews that Palauans and members of other ethnic groups living in Palau share a Palauan/Islander conceptualization of both traditional and introduced occupations. This shared view among contemporary Palauan residents is a new cultural formation. It is not purely traditional Palauan, nor does it represent the view of modernity represented by the system of occupational cognition found in the most recent colonizer of Palau, the

United States, even though Palauans have long participated in modern Western bureaucratic systems and use International Labor Organization categorizations. What we have seen is a distinctively Palauan system, one that is not restricted to ethnic Palauans but is shared by residents in Palau who appear to participate in the Palauan economic and social system sufficiently to know how it works. While the system includes "traditional" work activities, many of them have been restricted. We see the emergence of a new Palauan system geared to the present era.

## CONCLUSIONS AND A DILEMMA

Our research partly supports Giddens's cautions on the effects of globalization. Whether or not servants existed in Palauan families in the past, the incorporation of so many foreign domestic helpers in child care and family work tasks, along with wage labor and formal education, is transforming the institution of the Palauan family. Parents must now work hard to ensure that core values and relationships retain desired meanings; some succeed, others do not. Yet urbanization and the incorporation of new occupations and workplaces appear to have had less impact and appear to have been integrated into a new Palauan framework. Their inside meanings reflect Palauan values and practices. Islanders treat and rely on social relationships among work mates much as they used to rely on village mates, and work mates are now brought into the realms of *kerruul* and *omengereker,* fulfilling longstanding cultural practices. Thus we cannot assume the inner meanings of apparent outside-based transformations, but must take them as the subject of careful research.

We have discussed new forms of ethnic inequality due to the influx of foreign labor. Perhaps the most striking change in the system of social inequality involves relationships within Palauan families. Wage labor is increasing the levels of inequality within extended families, as some households have access to wages and others do not. Seventy percent of the population resides in Koror, but most urban residents have their primary clan membership and land rights in one of the rural states. In the recent past, urban wage-earning households would give rural members of their family money and consumer goods in exchange for food produced in the rural communities. This allowed urban women to continue their contributions to food exchanges without themselves having to work in the taro gardens, for which they no longer had time. This exchange relationship gave members of unwaged households access to the benefits of wage labor, while supporting their continued participation in systems of local food production.

More recently, members of urban households have begun to use domestic helpers to work in their taro gardens, as well as for commercial farming on lands near Koror. This process undercuts intrafamilial exchange relationships, and deprives members of unwaged households of the benefits of wage labor. Concern about this process was expressed in interviews in the early 1990s.

How do we reconcile the different emphases we found, depending on the style of ethnographic research, on the contemporary meanings of work in Palau in 1997? In the qualitative interviews we heard about fears that occupations are becoming associated with ethnicity. However, the triads judgments did not seem to be based on ethnic identities ascribed to the occupations, nor was there variation in the judgments by ethnicity of respondent. At one level, perhaps no simple reconciliation is either necessary or valuable. The cognitive measures may perhaps reflect more deeply held beliefs or more slowly changing systems, while open-ended interviews elicit current concerns. The differing representations stand for the tensions currently existing as Palauans try to contain the possible deleterious effects of rapid economic growth and incorporation of new cultural groups. Since many of the foreign workers are living and working as domestic helpers in Palauan households, caring for young children and performing many of the tasks previously performed by children and youth, these are very real issues. It is possible that only through this tension and constant vigilance to protect Palauan values from change may negative transformations be avoided.

## They Looked for Labor and Found Human Beings

In the process of bringing together two disparate systems, the internal tensions generated may themselves bring about radical transformations (Sahlins 1981). The differences in perspectives and practices between the systems reflect the very essence of the problem identified by the elders. Palauan government infrastructure and tourism development projects require a large number of short-term laborers. If these foreign laborers are to be contained and controlled, and their impacts minimized, then measures such as recent proposed legislation to control the entry of the laborers' dependents may be necessary. Such measures treat the workers as labor, not as human beings. Palauans can benefit from their relatively strong position in the world economy to bring in less-fortunate people willing to work in service and production jobs at low wages. If, however, as the elders fear, the low status of these workers is allowed to be generalized to the work they perform, then a Palauan's personal status may come to be defined primarily in terms of a job (a relatively ephemeral identity from an Islander perspective) rather than being based on kin and village position. The janitor from our earlier example is in danger of having his work contribution devalued and his status undermined.

Perhaps more important to the elders, however, acceptance of this generic devaluation of a category of persons would itself be a significant transformation of Palauan social thought and practices. While the society is strongly hierarchical, any one individual or family will be positioned differently in the different communities with which they are linked, and few are universally highly ranked. In the past even low-ranking individuals and families could better their positions through hard work and participation in *kerruul* and *omengereker*. Under the ethics of equality and individual action propagated during the American administration through the system of education, such hierarchical rankings have been significantly leveled. The institution of new, ethnically based distinctions could be highly divisive, creating separable categories of personhood and increased racism. If foreign workers do not speak English (at least), and come from cultural systems outside those of the islands, Japan, and the United States (to which Palauans are now accustomed), the possibility of racism is increased.

Cross-cutting these tendencies for increased social differentiation is the Palauan practice of incorporating foreigners as family members and socializing them into understanding and following Palauan norms of behavior—treating foreigners as human, making them into human beings. In the past individuals accepted into a home as foreign worker or visitor gradually became accepted as members of the family. Over time, such individuals might also be accepted into the community and allowed to marry Palauans, with their children accepted as Palauans. Foreigners could thus be incorporated as members of the family and village into which they had been accepted. This practice continues today. Many of the domestic helpers who have been with families for some years are now treated as family members. Their sponsors may support their desire to marry a Palauan, or to bring a child to Palau, even while supporting a general ban on the practice. For this person has become a human being, not a unit of labor.

If foreigners are socialized and humanized, then Palauan values are not abrogated. Perhaps it is a matter of scale: How many people can thus be incorporated into Palauan society? What are the effects of incorporating too many?

One striking conclusion of the cognitive studies we conducted is that, despite the common rhetoric concerning foreign workers, the deep-seated ways in which Palauans and other resident islanders conceptualize work occupations has not radically changed. Occupations held mainly by foreigners are not segregated into a low-prestige category. Equally important, those foreigners who now reside in Palau appear to have learned the same cognitive system concerning occupational domains. Hence, at least in this arena, there is a new, shared cultural competence that transcends ethnic identities.

The greatest area of change is in the gendering of occupations. While the more traditional tasks are still strongly gendered, gender is not a primary consideration of the introduced occupations. The introduced occupations still show few signs of being segregated by status, similar to Western conceptualizations of labor, and they still do not cluster along the lines of ethnic groups. While Palauans have added a whole new domain to their understandings of the meanings of work and occupations, they have not fundamentally altered the ways in which such work is valued. This is highly significant. If Palauans are able to control labor migration, to maintain policies that result in the repatriation of the majority of foreign workers, and to consider high-level importation of foreign workers as a transitory factor, it is possible that the feared deep-seated transformations of social values may be less pervasive than expected. If, however, in the process of controlling the numbers of foreigners such measures succeed in creating a separate, lower-status category of human, the desired mitigation of impact will have failed.

### ACKNOWLEDGMENTS

This article was originally published in *The Contemporary Pacific* 12(2):319–348 (2000). It is reprinted with permission. We wish to thank the Palau Society of Historians, Vicki Kanai, Florencio Gibbons, Sato Remoket of the Palau Community Action Agency, the elders at the Palau Elders' Center, and Lily Nakamura for sharing their wisdom. Katharine Kesolei, Palauan anthropologist, substantially contributed to our understandings of Palauan meanings of work and occupations and assisted in designing the structured questionnaires we used. We would also like to thank the government officials who provided access to reports and government statistics. Vice President Tommy Remengesau, Jr., Minister of Culture and Youth Affairs Alex Mereb, Minister of Education Billy Kuartei, Delegates Umetaro and Meyar and Senator Pierantozzi of the Palau National Congress, and Palau Community

College Board Members Emesiochl and Dengokl provided support and the framework of our work in Palau, while Dr. Steve Kuartei, Bena Sakuma, and Florencio Gibbons provided tbought-provoking challenges to the research team. In particular we thank Minister Mereb (Culture and Youth Affairs), Ginny Nakamura and his other staff members, and members of the Palau National Youth Congress and the general education diploma students; Minister Okada Tecbitong (Commerce and Trade) and Henaro Antonio, Chief of Labor; and the late Joseph I. Ysaol, Director of the Office of Planning and Statistics (OPS), Bena Sakuma, and other OPS staff members for the many hours of assistance they provided. Delegate Alan Seid of the Olbiil era Kelulau and Kaleb Udui, Jr. of the Office of Administration provided insights and statistics. Mary Ann Delemel and Chairman Johnny Isbikawa of the Palau Tourism Office were extremely helpful in providing information and statistics. We cannot sufficiently thank Acting President Mario Katosang and Dean of Instruction Meredith Randall for being our hosts in Palau, and all of the faculty and students at Palau Community College for working with us, in particular Alvina Timarong, Julie Anastacio, Tutii Chilton, Sally Graham, Howard Charles, Joel Miles, Sherman Daniel, Margo Vitarelli, Erich Carlson, and the staff of the development office. We would like to thank Julita Tellei, Maura Gordon, and P. Kempis Mad of the Palau Resource Institute and Faustina Rehuber and Augusta Ramarui of the Belau National Museum for their advice and participation. All these relationships are built upon two decades of work in Palau on these and related topics by the primary researcher, Nero, and a lifetime of relationships for Brel. Finally we would like to thank Ellen Greenberger for her constructive comments on the chapter and Kirsten Wall for her assistance in entering the data.

## NOTES

1. Antonio showed an average of 35 percent foreign workers between 1980 and 1983, ranging from 25.2 percent to 40.7 percent (Antonio 1983).
2. The figure was derived using the correspondence analysis module of Anthropac (Borgatti 1992).
3. This was done using the multidimensional scaling module of Anthropac.

## REFERENCES

Antonio, Henaro. 1983. *Resident and Non-Resident Workers Report.* Palau: Department of Labor. Manuscript in Nero's files.

Bank of Hawaii. 1997. *Republic of Palau Economic Report.* Honolulu: Bank of Hawaii Economics Department.

Borgatti, Steve. 1992. *Anthropak 4.0.* Columbia, S.C.: Analytic Technologies.

Burton, Michael L. 1972. "Semantic Dimensions of Occupation Names." In *Multidimensional Scaling: Theory and Applications in the Behavioral Sciences.* A. K. Romney, R. N. Shepard, and S. B. Nerlove, eds. Pp. 55–71. New York: Seminar Press.

Burton, Michael L., and S. B. Nerlove. 1976. "Balanced Designs for Triads Tests." *Social Science Research* 5:247–267.

CoPopChi, Palau National Committee on Population and Children. 1997. *Population and Development: Toward a Palau National Policy for Sustainable Human Development.* Koror: Office of the President.

Giddens, Anthony. 1999. BBC Reith Lectures 1999. http://news.bbc.co.uk/hi/english/static/events/reith_99

Gupta, Akhil, and James Ferguson. 1997. "Discipline and Practice: 'The Field' as Site, Method, and Location in Anthropology." In *Anthropological Locations: Boundaries and Grounds of a Field Science.* A. Gupta and J. Ferguson, eds. Pp. 1–46. Berkeley: University of California Press.

Hastrup, Kirsten, and Karen Fog Olwig. 1997. "Introduction." In *Siting Culture: The Shifting Anthropological Object.* K. Olwig and K. Hastrup, eds. Pp. 1–14. London: Routledge.

Hau'ofa, Epeli. 1993. "Our Sea of Islands." In *A New Oceania: Rediscovering Our Sea of Islands.* Eric Waddell, Vijay Naidu, and Epeli Hau'ofa, eds. Pp. 2–16. Suva: University of the South Pacific.

Kick, Charles G. III. 1995. *Palau Human Resource Development.* Port Vila: ESCAP. Manuscript in Nero's files.

Knowles, William H. 1982. *Mission to Republic of Belau, 23 January–7 February 1982.* Port Vila: ILO/UNDP Regional Manpower Project for the Pacific. Manuscript in Nero's files.

Magaña, J. Raul, Michael Burton, and Joao Ferreira-Pinto. 1995. "Occupational Cognition in Three Nations." *Journal of Quantitative Anthropology* 5:149–168.

Nero, Karen L. 1997a. "The End of Insularity?" In *The Cambridge History of the Pacific Islanders.* Donald Denoon, Stewart Firth, Jocelyn Linnekin, Malama Meleisea, and Karen Nero, eds. Pp. 439–467. Cambridge: Cambridge University Press.

——— 1997b. "The Material World Remade." In *The Cambridge History of the Pacific Islanders.* Donald Denoon, Stewart Firth, Jocelyn Linnekin, Malama Meleisea, and Karen Nero, eds. Pp. 359–396. Cambridge: Cambridge University Press.

Nero, Karen L., analyst. 1983. *1979–1980 Palau Community Action Agency Census of Palau*. Koror: Palau Community Action Agency, Palau Office of Administration.

Palau Office of Administration. 1998. National Government Statistics of Private Sector Foreign Workers. Supplied by Palau National Planner. May. Copy in Nero's files.

POPS (Palau Office of Planning and Statistics). 1996. Palau National Master Development Plan: Revised Draft Final Report, the Foundation for Development. Koror.

PSH (Palau Society of Historians). 1995. *Rechuodel [Foundations of Palau]*. Vol. 1. Koror: Division of Cultural Affairs, Ministry of Community and Cultural Affairs.

———— 1996. *Rechuodel*. Vol. 2. Koror: Division of Cultural Affairs, Ministry of Community and Cultural Affairs.

PVA (Palau Visitors Authority). 1996. *Sustainable Development Policies and Action Plan*. Koror: Palau Visitors Authority.

Romney, A. Kimball, S. C. Weller, and W. H. Batchelder. 1986. "Culture as Consensus: A Theory of Cultural and Informant Accuracy." *American Anthropologist* 10:489–502.

Sahlins, Marshall. 1981. "Historical Metaphors and Mythical Realities: Structure in the Early History of the Sandwich Islands Kingdom." ASAO Special Publications No. 1. I. Brady, ed. Ann Arbor: University of Michigan Press.

Smith, DeVerne Reed. 1983. *Palauan Social Structure*. New Brunswick, N.J.: Rutgers University Press.

Trieman, D. J. 1977. *Occupational Prestige in Comparative Perspective*. New York: Academic Press.

United Nations Development Program (UNDP). 1995. *Human Development Report, 1995*. New York: UNDP.

Wallerstein, Immanuel, and Joan Smith. 1992. "Introduction: Households as an Institution of the World Economy." In *Creating and Transforming Households: The Constraints of the World Economy*. J. Smith and I. Wallerstein, eds. Pp. 3–23. Cambridge: Cambridge University Press.

Weller, Susan C., and A. Kimball Romney. 1988. *Systematic Data Collection*. Newbury Park, Calif.: Sage.

# 15

# Environmental Change, Economic Development, and Emigration in Tuvalu

**John Connell**

*University of Sydney*

In the past decade, concern has increased over the possible impact of the accelerated greenhouse effect on sea-level rise and thus over the implications of that sea-level rise for countries with substantial areas of land at or close to sea level. Many island states fall into this category, none more so than those where coral atolls predominate, since atolls rarely rise even three meters above sea level. For most coastal dwellers one response to rising sea levels is moving inland to higher ground. For residents on atolls, such a choice is not possible, as high land does not exist. Though all island states face new environmental problems, as many people, all urban centers, and much infrastructure related to tourism, trade, and economic development are concentrated on the coast, the five world states composed solely of atolls—Tuvalu, Tokelau, Kiribati, the Maldives, and the Marshall Islands—are most at risk. It is in these atoll states that the challenges posed by global warming are most severe and where the necessity to respond to the threat of the greenhouse effect is most apparent (Connell and Lea 1992). Small island states also face difficult economic circumstances. They are remote, with economies that are dependent on primary commodity production and increasingly on aid, but the potential "aid fatigue" of metropolitan nations coupled with increasing expectations over standards of living pose new challenges for future socioeconomic development. This chapter examines the recent development trajectory in the very small island state of Tuvalu, the extent to which contemporary problems may be exacerbated by the greenhouse effect, and the possible outcomes.

Tuvalu is one of the smallest independent nations in the world in its population size, land mass, and national economy. In the nineteenth century the island group, then called the Ellice Islands, along with its northern neighbors the Gilbert Islands became separate British protectorates jointly governed in the interest of administrative convenience. This arrangement was formalized in 1915, when the two protectorates merged into the Gilbert and Ellice Islands Colony. In 1975 the Ellice Islands voted to secede (Macdonald 1975), and Tuvalu became an independent state in 1978 (Connell 1980). It is an archipelago consisting of three small reef islands and six coral atolls located on the western margin of Polynesia and some one thousand kilometers north of Fiji. A total land area of only 24.4 square kilometers is spread over 750,000 square kilometers of the central Pacific; the largest island, Vaitupu, has just 4.9 square kilometers. The highest point in the country is no more than five meters above sea level, and most areas are well below that; hence Tuvalu is highly vulnerable to natural hazards. Over a third of the population of ten thousand is concentrated on the main island of Funafuti, which has an area of just 2.4 square kilometers. Tuvalu suffers from most of the conventional disadvantages of small island states, further accentuated by very small size, extreme isolation and fragmentation, and thin and porous coral soils lacking in nutrients. This makes agricultural and most other forms of development exceptionally difficult. There are also severe problems related to administration, transportation and communications, an inadequate social and economic infrastructure, a small entrepreneurial base, limited skilled human resources, and few development projects that can attract external financial support.

Population growth has been rapid in the postwar years and has not been relieved by the safety valve of out-migration, as has occurred in most other parts of Polynesia (especially in New Zealand dependencies). Agricultural and fisheries production has not grown as rapidly as population, and a transition to imported food, especially rice, has followed changing tastes, preferences, and convenience. This transition has been so substantial that in Tuvalu, as in other atoll states, imported foods and drinks now constitute about one-third of all imports by value, a substantial drain on domestic resources. The combination of high postwar rates of population increase, a growing desire for consumer goods, the location of the hospital in the single urban center, and the concentration of formal sector employment there has resulted in urban migration from the islands of the periphery. Rapid urbanization even in a very small state has posed a range of social problems, all of which are complicated by the threat of climatic change.

## THE GREENHOUSE EFFECT

Scientific studies have drawn increasingly consistent conclusions regarding future climatic trends. Although enormous uncertainty remains, especially over chronology, some indication of the impact is possible. That impact is likely to involve rising sea levels, with some low-lying lands inundated and coasts eroded. Erosion is not unusual and was evident in Nanumea and Nukufetau even before recent concerns over accelerated sea-level rise. A gradual rise of mean sea level will progressively lift the zone of flooding and increase the impact of storm waves, eroding areas hitherto considered safe. Human responses will vary depending on the value of the coastal land under attack and the resources available to provide protective measures. In states where resources are very limited and small populations thinly spread, the provision of expensive engineering works will not be a commonly available option.

Coastal erosion will increase as the rise of sea levels accelerates, perhaps beyond the upward growth of corals, and this erosion will probably be accentuated by the greater frequency of storms. Increased temperatures will decrease human comfort in the tropics and may worsen human health. The intertropical convergence zone is likely to shift northward, changing the distribution of zones of upwelling, hence altering the distribution of fish stocks and thus affecting fisheries. Such major climatic changes as the frequency and severity of cyclones and tropical storms may also increase as temperatures increase.

Island ecology, in terms of the capacity to support human habitation, is closely tied to the existence of a permanent groundwater system. Islands above a certain size, about 1.5 hectares, contain a permanent lens of fresh water surrounded by salt water. The volume of the lens is roughly proportional to the surface area of the atoll. Hence a decline in the area of an atoll would have a disproportionate impact on the volume of the lens. During droughts water-table levels fall and the groundwater may become brackish. Environmental stress is manifested by trees losing leaves, not fruiting, and even dying. Yet the most severe threat to permanent water supplies is not from climatic factors directly, but rather from marine processes that cause coastal erosion and increase the frequency of storm overwash.

Increased groundwater salinity will reduce its potability, which for most atolls is currently of considerable significance. It will also reduce the productivity of agriculture, since no plant species will gain from increased salinity. In drought conditions access to groundwater on atolls is crucial, although on some atolls with reasonably high rainfall, construction of better cisterns may enable the use of groundwater to be minimized or even ended. If increased salinity is combined with any long-term decline in rainfall, as is possible in some areas, the results will be even more serious, since the cost of water purification and desalination is extremely high. If groundwater becomes no longer potable, human habitation will be effectively impossible. Fresh water is most scarce after cyclones or tidal waves have swept over an atoll, salting soils and wells, a situation likely to increase under greenhouse conditions (Roy and Connell 1991). Tropical storms are of present concern in Tuvalu. The national submission to the United Nations Framework Convention on Climate Change (UNFCCC) meeting in Kyoto, Japan, in December 1997 stated:

> We are already experiencing increased frequency of cyclones, tornadoes, flooding and tide surges, many of which hit us outside the usual climatic seasons. This year alone, in 1997, Tuvalu was devastated by three tropical cyclones: the first two in March—Gavin and Hina—and more recently Keli. The costs of these effects to us in Tuvalu are enormous. Not only were houses and whole villages damaged, but also vegetation and food crops were completely destroyed. In one recent incident, an entire island community was left homeless and its vegetation damaged so much so that the island is uninhabitable right now. In another incident, one whole islet completely disappeared into thin air. Erosion to coastal areas of our already scarce land is further worsened, and the

increased salinity in underground water is seriously affecting not only vegetation and traditional food crops but also the health and lives of the people. (quoted in *Pacific News Bulletin,* December 1997:7)

Erosion reduces land area, and, where there is minimal elevation, such losses may become severe and increase the swampiness and salinity of areas that remain above sea level. Areas immediately at risk will be those that have previously been reclaimed from the sea, including parts of Funafuti, the main island and urban center, now used for agriculture and roads. Land losses will lead to a decline in agricultural production, increased competition for scarce land, and a related decline in handicraft materials (such as wood and pandanus) and firewood, which is already in extremely short supply in the urban area. Such changes will further threaten the already limited subsistence base and introduce new environmental problems. Erosion of fringing reefs may disturb and reduce the distinctiveness of lagoon ecology as lagoons increasingly become indistinguishable in content from the surrounding ocean. Mangrove habitats may also be damaged. This damage would reduce the artisanal fishing potential of many areas, especially where lagoons currently provide fisheries diversity.

The greenhouse effect is likely therefore to lead to reduced agricultural production, a possible decline in fisheries production, and a loss of vital water, timber, and firewood resources, thus reducing the potential of the few areas in which island states currently demonstrate a degree of self-reliance. These effects will occur alongside continued population growth. An increase in population pressure on diminishing resources will further encourage rural-urban migration from the outer islands in search of wages and salaries, rather than the increasingly unpredictable agricultural and fisheries income.

Much of what is currently known about the impact of the greenhouse effect is derived from conjecture and speculation, since the order of magnitude of future physical events cannot be determined, and there is no real precedent for what is likely to follow. Though the postglacial marine transgression that ended around six thousand years ago must have had a similar effect, it occurred in a vastly different social and economic context, leaving few records of its human impact (and none in then-uninhabited Polynesia). With complex and interrelated causes and with consequences involving changing natural processes and a variety of human adaptations to those changes, the greenhouse effect is effectively an uncontrolled experiment on a global scale. Whatever the outcome, it is apparent that the greenhouse effect offers nothing positive to tropical island states. In atoll states like Tuvalu where all the land is low-lying, problems will be more apparent and quicker to occur.

Island states have consequently sought to discourage greenhouse gas production, most of which occurs in the north, individually and through the Association of Small Island States (AOSIS) in international and regional forums. Island states themselves have done little or nothing to cause changes in atmospheric composition and thus in global climate change, nor can they directly influence mitigation. As the prime minister of Tuvalu, Bikenibeu Paeniu, has said: "We strongly believe that we have done the least to cause this hazardous problem, although we are now faced with the highest possibility of losing the most" (*Pacific Report,* July 10, 1997:5). Collectively the island states have had some success, notably in negotiations leading to the United Nations Framework on Climate Change (signed at Rio de Janeiro in 1992), but subsequent achievements have been fewer. In the Pacific region this downturn was most apparent at the South Pacific Forum meeting in September 1997, when island states were unable to reach consensus on binding targets for greenhouse gas reductions that would include Australia, a situation that was maintained at the UNFCCC meeting in Japan later in that year. Paeniu led the move by Pacific islands to insist that greenhouse gas emissions be reduced to a lower level than Australia was prepared to contemplate. Though it has become widely recog-

nized that global warming constitutes a new and significant problem for small island states (Commonwealth Advisory Group 1997), and a considerable threat to security, the impact of small states on international policy changes on global warming has been slight (Shibuya 1997). Even if an international agreement were reached to stabilize global greenhouse gas production levels, a notion that appears unlikely, there would still be considerable future impact from present greenhouse gas levels. Adaptation to climate change is therefore essential.

Opportunities for adaptation (and for socioeconomic development) are naturally constrained by limited land areas and the simplicity of atoll environments (where natural ecosystems may easily be disrupted). Moreover, uncertainty over the outcome of the greenhouse effect has restricted the ability and willingness, nationally and internationally, to respond to potential problems through policy formation. Indeed, response is least likely in small island states where information is inadequate, planning offices are small and fully stretched to cope with standard recurrent activities, and options are few. Environmental planning remains in its infancy, and the five-year plans that presently exist are usually the extreme limit of long-term planning. Many conventional measures to reduce vulnerability, such as transferring populations, infrastructure, and economic activities to higher land, are impossible in atoll situations. Other conventional measures, such as the construction of dykes, sea walls, and pumping stations, are extremely expensive (especially in developing states, where small populations are spread over a large number of islands). Even defending the urban area would be a complex and costly operation, and would itself be a pointless exercise. Financing for such projects is absent in all small states, and no donor would contemplate aid on the appropriate scale.

However, island states can develop programs to improve environmental conservation and management. Opportunities exist for the increased use of solar energy (rather than expensive, imported greenhouse gas from fossil fuels or local firewood), afforestation (in order both to guard against erosion and storm damage and to produce new and old species of social and economic value), and improved water supplies (especially the construction of rainwater catchments to improve water quality and reduce dependence on underground lenses). Because of increased pressure on resources, especially coastal resources, stemming from rising population and solid waste disposal problems, the necessity for improved coastal zone management is paramount. Although none of these policies will significantly reduce the impact of the greenhouse effect, and atoll states cannot develop such policies themselves, still they would stimulate wise resource use, improve the physical quality of life, and lead to more sustainable development.

## AN ATOLL ECONOMY

In spite of basic difficulties in stimulating development, Tuvalu has experienced limited economic growth in recent years after stagnating in the first half of the 1980s. The GDP per capita has steadily increased to around A$1,500, representing growth in several sectors, including agriculture (especially the subsistence component), manufacturing, and trade. The small and open economy and absence of a national currency restrict the ability of government to manage comprehensive macroeconomic policies. The economy is particularly vulnerable to external influences, including fluctuating aid flows and commodity prices. Tuvalu is heavily dependent on aid for development capital and technical assistance, with most of the budget receiving overseas support. Aid is supported through the now sizable Tuvalu Trust Fund, established in 1987 with substantial contributions from the United Kingdom, New Zealand, and Australia, which provides almost a quarter of total recurrent revenue. Remittances contribute more than 10 percent of national income (substantially more than export earnings) and are mainly derived from nationals working in the phosphate mines on nearby Nauru or on overseas shipping lines.

Economic activity is almost entirely dominated by the public sector, which is responsible for most nonsubsistence activities.

In contrast to many other Pacific island states, agriculture is of limited importance, contributing less than 20 percent of GDP, primarily because of the low potential of coral soils. It is still an important activity, primarily because, outside Funafuti, most of the population is at least partly dependent on it. Commercial production was dominated by copra exports, but they ended in 1993 because of low world prices. There is some limited potential for encouraging the production and local marketing of other crops, but distance from markets and intervening opportunities are major constraints to most commercial production. In view of substantial stocks of tuna, the potential for a larger fishing industry is considerable and offers the best possibilities for future sustainable growth. The industry is currently dominated by small-scale subsistence activities. Fish exports, which were substantial during the 1982–1984 period, ceased in 1985, when the government-owned pole-and-line fishing vessel ended its local operations because of a lack of bait fish (Fairbairn 1993). Tuvalu benefits from licensing fees gained from its share of the multilateral fisheries treaty with the United States, and some infrastructure and other support services have been developed for future fisheries expansion.

Manufacturing contributes less than 10 percent of GDP and is unlikely to develop much further. Other than handicrafts, the sole export-oriented activity is a garments venture sending shirts to Australia. A small number of processing activities—mainly in Funafuti—produce import substitutes for items such as soap and biscuits. Intentions to establish a "mini-industrial zone" on Funafuti have not eventuated. Tourism is similarly of very limited significance because of high transport costs and limited facilities of all kinds. Most visits are related to government activities, and tourism development prospects are poor, though in the 1990s a number of guest houses have complemented the one small hotel on Funafuti.

Most of the workforce in Tuvalu is dependent on rural-based subsistence activities. Formal employment in the wage and salary sector accounted for the small total of just under fourteen hundred people in 1991 and highlights the importance to the country of overseas employment and remittances. Two-thirds of all employment (just over one thousand persons at that time) was in the government sector. Cooperative societies and nongovernment organizations accounted for a further 17 percent of employment, while only 14 percent of all workers, just 130 persons, were employed in the private sector. Working for the government is therefore more dominant in Tuvalu than in almost any other Pacific island state and has grown steadily since independence.

Formal sector employment is concentrated in Funafuti. In 1991 no fewer than 936 people (68 percent) out of the total wage and salary workforce were located there. This proportion has remained much the same since 1979 despite rapid population growth on the island over that time period. Unemployment on Funafuti has grown during the same period and has become a particular problem because of the limited opportunities for some migrants to gain access to subsistence resources. "Anecdotal evidence suggests that only one in four of all school leavers can now find employment and that the subsistence sector is, in fact, becoming less receptive to the unemployed" (Forsyth and Plange 1992:45). The growth of the formal sector workforce has been twice that of employment opportunities since the 1980s.

Achieving economic development in Tuvalu has always been difficult. Future expansion of productive activities depends on developments in agriculture and fisheries, and the prospects for Tuvaluans of employment overseas. External employment currently accounts for as much as 18 percent of the total labor force. Shifting the balance in national development from Funafuti to the outer islands is also crucial to the structure of economic change, as the population has become extremely concentrated on one island, putting enormous pressure on services and land areas with consequent problems of urban environmental management. Because of difficulties in expanding agriculture and fisheries and the numerous obstacles to economic growth in such a small island state, Tuvalu is likely to continue to face adverse economic conditions in the foreseeable future.

## POPULATION GROWTH

Documentary evidence on the population of Tuvalu before 1865 is sketchy, but subsequent data are more readily available. In the last quarter of the nineteenth century, the population increased from under twenty-five hundred in 1876 to just over thirty-five hundred at the end of the century. Population growth was then so marked that, as early as the 1890s, resettlement was being suggested as a solution to what was perceived as an impending overpopulation problem. Nineteenth-century evidence suggests that there was a fine balance between population and resources, and extensive controls included both abortion and infanticide. As early as 1865 it was suggested that the islanders were "genuine Malthusians": "They feared that unless the population was kept down they would not have sufficient food" (cited by Munro and Bedford 1980:3), and the people of Vaitupu were reported to have such a fear of starvation that "there was a rule that only two children should be reared in a family" (Munro and Bedford 1980). While infanticide was common, it was counterbalanced by extensive adoption. However, such traditional forms of population control were effectively abolished by missionaries, leading to more rapid growth of the population in the second half of the nineteenth century.

Between 1901 and 1911 there was a sharp decline in the resident population of Tuvalu, a result of both rising mortality levels and migration to Ocean Island (Banaba), then a phosphate mine (Munro 1990). Concern for the demographic future of Tuvalu became grounds for considerable pessimism. But the period of decline was brief, and from 1910 onward the population of Tuvalu has grown steadily (Table 15.1). Growth became more

**Table 15.1**    Population of Tuvalu

| Year | National Population | Year | National Population |
|------|---------------------|------|---------------------|
| 1876 | 2,497 | 1963 | 5,444 |
| 1887 | 2,902 | 1968 | 5,782 |
| 1901 | 3,543 | 1973 | 5,887 |
| 1911 | 3,080 | 1979 | 7,349 |
| 1921 | 3,429 | 1991 | 9,043 |
| 1931 | 3,994 | 1997 (est.) | 10,900 |
| 1947 | 4,487 | | |

rapid after the Second World War, primarily because of the more effective extension of modern medical services to the country, which was still a remote archipelago in a remote British colony. Growth was fastest during the 1970s (averaging 4.3 percent per annum between 1973 and 1979), as a result of return migration from the new state of Kiribati, but slowed to 1.7 percent between 1979 and 1991. The slower rate of growth was a result of substantial migration away from Tuvalu. Excluding permanent emigrants but including those temporarily overseas (mainly seamen, workers in the Nauru phosphate mining industry, or students), the de jure population of Tuvalu would have been 8,730 in 1979 and 10,114 in 1991. The de jure population is regarded in Tuvalu as the more appropriate total for planning purposes on the assumption that almost all those away from the country will return permanently at some point in the future.

The fertility rate in Tuvalu declined steadily between 1965 and 1979, producing, in 1979, a crude birth rate of 23.7 per thousand. Since independence the fertility rate has risen, but it may have stabilized at around the 1991 level of 29.4. The total fertility rate was then estimated at 3.4 but had declined to 3.1 in 1994. A family planning program began in 1968 and had considerable success until 1973, when there was an apparent decline in the proportion of acceptors, at least until 1979, when the proportion of eligible women practicing family planning was 21.4 percent. The proportion of acceptors has long been twice as high on Funafuti as on the other islands, with an acceptance rate of about 54 percent (in 1990) there and 31 percent on the outer islands. The low acceptance

rate and regional variations have been a consequence of cultural inhibitions, the reluctance of men to participate or allow their wives to participate, lack of knowledge and contraceptive availability, and the desire of households to have substantial numbers of children so that at least one might, through migration, become a successful wage or salary earner and provider of remittances (Chambers 1986). Increasing the extent of contraceptive use on the outer islands will prove difficult.

The fall in the fertility rate in the 1960s and 1970s paralleled a fall in the mortality rate, especially after 1976, when the establishment of an administrative center at Funafuti enabled improved service to the outer islands, and medical services, water supplies, and sanitation were also improved. The crude death rate in 1979 was fifteen per thousand, and the infant mortality rate was forty-two per thousand; the crude death rate has continued to fall, reaching 8.8 in 1991, but the infant mortality rate in 1991 was fifty-six per thousand (Rakaseta et al. 1998:20). The Tuvalu population is youthful, with 35 percent under age fifteen, and has an unbalanced sex structure. There are slightly more females than males because of selective emigration of men as mine workers and seamen; this imbalance is most pronounced in the age group from fifteen to twenty-nine.

If current fertility and mortality rates remain constant, the population of Tuvalu will continue to grow steadily past the end of the century; unlike in other parts of Polynesia, the actual extent of population growth depends more on natural increase than on migration. Tuvalu already experiences considerable threats to national development because of its small area relative to population size (and the distribution of that population over nine small atolls at some distance from other countries). National development plans have recognized these basic constraints and have increasingly acknowledged that both a reduced rate of population growth and greater regional balance in population distribution are necessary in order to avoid a reduction in what is increasingly perceived to be an austere quality of life. A growing consensus has emerged that the rate of population growth must slow if Tuvalu is to achieve a pattern of sustainable development.

Tuvalu has sought to develop a comprehensive population policy, aimed at both fertility reduction and the slowing of rural-urban immigration to Funafuti. The need for such a policy has been expressed by former prime minister Kamuta Latasi:

> Tuvalu's population growth rate of 2.5 per cent is "very alarming for us" Latasi said, and a committee has been established to conduct education tours of the country's eight [sic] islands. "The only way to be successful with family planning is to make people understand. If they don't understand they won't care. It's not a matter of getting on the radio and saying 'if you have five children this is what will happen!' You have to physically visit the island, get the blackboard and illustrate that if you have two metres of cloth it will cover two kids but if you have seven kids it won't." Previous opposition of church groups to family planning has changed, Latasi said, with the realisation of how serious the problem is. (*Pacific Report,* April 4, 1994:7)

A new Population Policy Coordination Committee was established in 1993 to formulate a comprehensive national policy for outer-island development programs, population redistribution, and a means of implementing slower rates of population growth. Implementation is crucial because of the anticipated return migration of workers from Nauru when the phosphate deposits are depleted around the turn of the century, but the task is considerable:

> Although a level of optional population growth is not specified, clearly a rate near replacement level would be in the national interest. This would amount to an average of less than three children per couple. . . . Two children per couple may well be in the national interest, but few couples would find it personally advantageous to have such a small family. The vast majority specifically want two children of each sex not only to give parents support in their old age, but to provide sibling support for the children themselves. (Chambers 1986:324)

There are many other reasons, including the need for strong families and some chance of access to education and employment, for having families with more than two children. Economic conditions at the village level in the outer islands favor larger families because of shared responsibilities. Establishing new directions for population change in Tuvalu will be difficult, and future population growth is likely to be considerable.

## URBANIZATION AND MIGRATION

No country in the Pacific region has experienced more recent or more rapid internal migration and urbanization than Tuvalu. Between 1973 and 1979, the period during which Tuvalu seceded from Kiribati to become an independent state, the population of Funafuti grew from 871 to 2,120 as a result of the closure of the Banaba mine, return migration from Kiribati, and movements from the outer islands. In 1973 three other atolls had populations larger than Funafuti, but by 1979 it was unchallenged as the most important island in the new nation. Only the atoll of Vaitupti had achieved relatively rapid growth in the same time period. During the 1980s that supremacy increased, as Funafuti took on more of the trappings of a national capital and its population grew to 3,839 in 1991. It has now passed 4,000. Its proportion of the national population increased from 29 percent in 1979 to nearly half of the national total by the mid-1990s. Moreover, the population of Funafuti has increasingly become concentrated on just one island, as natural hazards have intensified urbanization. Before 1972 there were about one hundred people living on Fongafala, the southernmost islet of Funafuti, but after Hurricane Bebe struck, most people moved to the center of Funafuti, and by 1976 Fongafala was completely uninhabited, though there has been limited subsequent return migration. Whether on Funafuti or throughout the country, decentralization is a crucial issue in national development.

The urban situation is very different from that of most other Pacific states because of the high proportion of Tuvaluans living in a single place, the very high urban population density, and the consequential difficulties in achieving adequate service provision (especially fresh water) and providing formal employment (Connell and Lea 1995). These problems have long contributed to some tension between the long-established "true owners" of Funafuti atoll and migrants from other atolls. As early as the mid-1970s, "[d]emands for restriction of entry to the capital were being expressed by women's committees and island councils in Tuvalu: the outer islands seeking to retain active young people; Funafuti seeking to retain its separate identity" (Howard 1976:25). Since then these issues and resentments have smoldered on but have not resulted in related policy formation. Migration into Funafuti had also begun to create an "urban elite" of those who have wage jobs and government housing and are unwilling to return to their home islands, and this elite may be self-perpetuating to the detriment of the development of those remaining on the outer islands (Tuvalu 1980: 35). Further migration has accentuated those problems, produced more substantial problems of overcrowding, and reduced the possibilities for developing appropriate urban management policies.

Because it has been both recent and rapid, this urban concentration has created problems. Many of these problems are no different from those of much larger urban centers in other developing countries: overcrowding in poor housing conditions with attendant health risks, pollution from inadequate sewerage and garbage disposal, unemployment (even if disguised by sharing in extended families), the growth of uncontrolled settlements, worsened nutrition (as cash incomes are often inadequate to purchase diets based on imported foods), and some increase in crime and social disorganization. Since migrants are not always successful, they may be unable or unwilling to contribute significantly to the needs of their rural kin. These urban problems are not unique to Tuvalu or to atoll states, but the small size of the land and lagoon areas and the problems of achieving economic growth and hence generating employment or financing service provision accentuate the basic difficulties.

Emigration has long been a way of life in Tuvalu, though the first experience of migration in the mid-nineteenth century was of "blackbirding"—forced labor migration—to South America (Maude 1981). Blackbirding gave way to more controlled movements to the plantations of Tahiti, Fiji, Hawai'i, Samoa, and Queensland. In 1900 migration to the phosphate mines at Banaba began, and there was such enthusiasm for overseas employment that British colonial authorities had to restrict the number of migrants to safeguard population numbers. Subsequently migration diversified to Nauru and elsewhere, and the number of emigrants remained high. Their remittances enabled superior house construction (at least in terms of imported "modern" materials) and changing patterns of food consumption.

By the time of the Second World War, population growth in Tuvalu had already indicated to colonial authorities that resettlement might be necessary. Two proposals to resettle Tuvaluans in the unpopulated Line Islands, two thousand kilometers to the east, and in Tonga were never implemented, the latter because of fears that the Tongan islands might eventually be needed for Tongan resettlement. However, between 1947 and 1963, a substantial number of Vaitupu islanders were resettled on Kioa, a small Fijian island (Koch 1978). Subsequently, as most Pacific island states achieved independence, the prospects for resettlement faded, and migration generally became possible only on a temporary basis.

The extent of emigration further increased after the war, particularly through continued circular labor migration to Nauru and Banaba, to the extent that in the early 1970s more than a third of all Tuvaluans were overseas. However, that proportion had fallen by the 1980s, with both the closure of the Banaba mine and the independence of Kiribati in 1979, resulting in return migration (Connell 1983:22–24). In the 1980s population pressure on resources became critical. By the end of that decade the number of migrants apparently permanently overseas was less than 5 percent of the total population. Nonetheless, in 1991 there were more than twelve hundred Tuvaluans overseas, rather more than 10 percent of the de jure population. The largest number of these, 735, were working on Nauru, where the phosphate mine was slowly contracting, necessitating that almost all those contract workers would ultimately have to return to Tuvalu. The future of other overseas Tuvaluans—as seamen, students, or contract workers in New Zealand—is scarcely more secure. Tuvalu therefore faces the likely and perhaps imminent return of a significant proportion of its population (though short-term migration overseas will continue). Just as in the larger Polynesian countries, that return is likely to place particular pressure on the urban center, where population density and its impact on limited resources is already considerable. Since the skills learned overseas (on ships and in a mine) are of limited local value, especially in the rural sector, return migration often intensifies despondency rather than contributing to development.

Because of limited national development opportunities, those countries where international migration is now extremely important and where dependency on migration has become considerable are not only reluctant to control overseas migration but have become anxious to seek new and better opportunities. Tuvalu as well as Kiribati have not only specifically trained seamen for work overseas (alongside exporting workers to Nauru) but have requested many countries inside the Pacific and beyond to provide new opportunities for migrant labor. Such pressures have continued, despite the increased difficulties of access to metropolitan states, as the prospects for economic development have failed to improve, population density has increased, and environmental problems have become more apparent.

In parallel with Tuvalu's increased interest in international migration, there has long been a growing recognition of the relevance of migration as one solution to development problems. In a paper produced by the South Pacific Commission, an organization for technical cooperation covering all Pacific island states, it was argued, in the case of Kiribati and Tuvalu, that for both temporary and permanent migration, "with the relatively small numbers that will be involved and with the severity of their plight, assistance from other Pacific countries and from Australia and New Zealand may be considered more favourably than is generally thought" (South Pacific Commission 1982:14). Little subsequently changed, though Tuvalu gained access to the New Zealand guest-worker scheme, allowing a small number of migrants access to employment in New Zealand for periods of less than a year. A subsequent review of Australian aid, which attached concern to the impending closure of the Nauru mine, gave particular emphasis to the special needs of the small states in the South Pacific. The executive summary assigned sufficient importance to the problems of Kiribati and Tuvalu to recommend measures denied to all other states except Papua New Guinea:

> Kiribati with a population of 60,000 and Tuvalu with a population of 8,000 have special problems. Their remote and minute land areas are heavily populated. They depend very much on remittances from their emigrants and on foreign aid. Their long-term development prospects are discouraging. In view of structural problems which are beyond their control and beyond the reach of aid, Australia should make available limited opportunities for immigration from Kiribati and Tuvalu. (Australia 1984:8)

The review argued that Australia should "go beyond traditional ideas of aid" to provide a special immigration quota for the two countries, with which Australia hitherto had few ties (Australia 1984:181). As in the case of an Asian Development Bank survey that made similar suggestions involving a range of metropolitan states (Castle 1980:136), external perceptions increasingly recognized the potential role of international migration, from at least the smallest countries in the South Pacific, in contributing to development.

Other than marginally improved access to New Zealand, little changed. Metropolitan states feared that concessional migration access to one or more small states would stimulate pressures from larger states and that international migration would reduce the likelihood of successful self-reliant development initiatives. Island states, except Tuvalu, were reluctant to press for improved access, fearing that other forms of aid might then decline. In 1994 Tuvalu's prime minister stressed that his country was continuing to seek employment opportunities in Australia and that Tuvalu "would not take no for an answer" on the provision of either employment or education opportunities. Regarding those Tuvaluans who have been educated overseas: "We want them to come back, but certainly [we] cannot have everybody, even if they are graduates. There will come a time when we can only take back a portion of our population. The rest—we will have to assist them in obtaining employment overseas and we need to prepare people for when that time comes" (quoted in *Pacific Report,* April 4, 1994:4). Despite being rebuffed, two years later the prime minister was again requesting that Australia accept a small number of Tuvaluans each year as guest-workers to relieve existing overcrowding and enable the country to cope with the return of Nauru migrant workers: "We haven't even got homes for them. These people have been there for 20 years with the Nauru Phosphate Corporation. They have no experience working in the gardens, growing taro, cutting toddy, fishing or building houses. I am sure some of them are really good tradesmen and I am sure that they can be absorbed by companies in Australia" (quoted in *Pacific Report,* August 5, 1996:2). Once again the request was ignored. Since the early 1980s the notion of providing new international migration opportunities for small Pacific island states has been absent from external reviews, primarily a result of the recognition that there was virtually no prospect of any positive response from metropolitan states. Island states were increasingly directed to resolve their own population and development issues.

## TOWARD THE FUTURE

The modern era has increasingly demonstrated the tyrannies of distance that have restricted contemporary development in small island states. Atolls are tiny, resource poor,

often distant from each other, and remote from substantial land masses. Atoll states consequently face a host of development problems, often in a more accentuated form than in other island microstates. Problems include limited skills, a small domestic market size, the high cost of imports and exports, the restricted diversity of exports, and substantial administrative costs. These disadvantages have usually led to large trade deficits, balance of payments problems, and considerable dependence on foreign aid and technical assistance. Only in the Maldives has there been any industrialization or tourism. In the South Pacific, especially in Tuvalu, both types of development are absent. Atoll states have moved rapidly into situations of extreme dependence on the outside world, primarily for aid, concessional trade, and migration opportunities. The absence of international migration opportunities comparable to those in many other island microstates, in turn, has necessitated domestic responses to the problems of achieving economic development, but with few human or natural resources the problems have been increasingly difficult to address.

Concessional trade schemes are of diminished importance in an era of increasingly free world trade, and aid from most donor nations is currently declining; in both spheres greater self-reliance and increased privatization are being thrust upon less-developed states by reluctant donors and international organizations. Where island states, like Tuvalu, are disadvantaged in their geographical location and physical characteristics and, further, have little trade and no strategic location to provide bargaining status, these trends are of concern. There are few prospects for significant economic growth in Tuvalu and none that are likely to be possible without some degree of external support.

Because of limited economic and social development, migration has become a way of life. The government of Tuvalu has encouraged international migration and intermittently sought improved temporary and permanent migration opportunities in metropolitan states. Elsewhere in the Pacific migration has been a common response to difficult economic circumstances, and, where political ties permit migration, flows have been substantial and the populations of some dependent territories have declined (Connell 1987; Aldrich and Connell 1998). Although this migration does constitute a brain and skill drain, the investment in human capital that it constitutes has been an essential element in household survival strategies in the absence of attractive domestic investment opportunities, and Polynesian migrants continue to remit at high levels for periods of more than twenty-five years (Connell and Brown 1995). The provision of migration opportunities thus results in significant income flows to small island states, constituting a valid form of aid in a context where conventional forms of aid have been of minimal value in stimulating economic development. However, most metropolitan states have increasingly restricted migration opportunities, while focusing on skill requirements that are rarely evident in the atoll states. Indeed, the former Australian minister for Development Cooperation and Pacific Island Affairs stressed in 1993 that "it should . . . be remembered that the migration safety valve may no longer be an option in a future, more crowded world" (Gordon Bilney, quoted in Moore and Smith 1995:110). That is also the position in New Zealand and North America.

Environmental change is likely to exacerbate domestic development problems in Tuvalu, and in other atoll states, and increase the demand for emigration. In the coral atolls that constitute the Carteret Islands (Papua New Guinea), where there has been a regional sea-level rise, resettlement has transferred people onto the large island of Bougainville (Connell 1990). In other world regions, environmental problems, whether natural (including drought and volcanic eruption) or anthropogenic, have stimulated emigration (Hugo 1996; Swain 1996), and a worsened environment in Tuvalu is likely to add to existing pressures for new emigration opportunities. More adequate coastal zone management, sustainable development, and a slowing of population growth will delay but not avert this situation. Yet the resettlement of the national population would pose ethical issues, as Tuvalu has enunciated: "There is nowhere else that can substitute for our God-given homeland of Tuvalu. The option of relocation as mooted by some countries therefore is utterly insensitive and irresponsible. . . . Ignoring our pleas will amount to nothing less than denial of our rights to exist as part of the global society and of the human race" (quoted in *Pacific News Bulletin,* December 1997:7).

In the 1890s, when population densities were much lower than they are now, labor migration was perceived to be "the only alternative to starvation" (Macdonald 1982:53). A century later there is a growing possibility that at least some of Tuvalu's population will become environmental refugees at some time in the next century and that metropolitan states on the fringes of the South Pacific will thus have to respond eventually to one of the most profound impacts of the accelerated greenhouse effect: the challenge to human rights.

## ACKNOWLEDGMENTS

This chapter was originally published in *Pacific Studies* 22(1):1–20 (1999) and is reproduced with permission. The author is indebted to Dr. Doug Munro and an anonymous reviewer for comments on an earlier version of this chapter.

## REFERENCES

Aldrich, R., and J. Connell. 1998. *The Last Colonies.* Cambridge: Cambridge University Press, Australia.

Australia. 1984. *Report of the Committee to Review the Australian Overseas Aid Program.* Canberra: Australian Government Publishing Service.

Castle, L. 1980. "The Economic Context." In *South Pacific Agriculture—Choices and Constraints.* R. G. Ward and A. Proctor, eds. Pp. 107–136. Canberra: Australian National University Press.

Chambers, A. 1986. "Reproduction in Namomea: An Ethnography of Fertility and Birth." Auckland. Working papers in anthropology No. 72. University of Auckland.

Commonwealth Advisory Group. 1997. *A Future for Small States—Overcoming Vulnerability.* London: Commonwealth Secretariat.

Connell, John. 1980. "Tuvalu: Independence or Dependence?" *Current Affairs Bulletin* 560 (February):27–31.

———. 1983. *Migration, Employment, and Development in the South Pacific.* Country Report No. 19, Tuvalu. Noumea: South Pacific Commission and International Labour Office.

———. 1987. "Paradise Lost? Pacific Island Voyagers in the Modern World." In *Pacific Bridges: The New Immigration from Asia and the Pacific Islands.* J. Fawcett and B. Carino, eds. Pp. 375–404. New York: Center for Migration Studies.

———. 1990. "The Carteret Islands: Precedents of the Greenhouse Effect." *Geography* 75:152–154.

Connell, John, and B. Brown. 1995. "Migration and Remittances in the South Pacific: Towards New Perspectives." *Asian and Pacific Migration Journal* 4:1–33.

Connell, John, and J. Lea. 1992. "My Country Will Not Be There." *Cities* 9:295–309.

———. 1995. *Urbanisation in Polynesia.* Canberra: National Centre for Development Studies.

Fairbairn, Ian. 1993. *Tuvalu: Economic Situation and Development Prospects.* Canberra: Australian International Development Assistance Bureau.

Forsyth, D., and N. Plange. 1992. *Manpower Needs and Incoming Generating Potential in Tuvalu.* Suva: International Labour Organisation.

Howard, D. 1976. *Problems of Social Deviance in Tuvalu.* London: Overseas Development Administration.

Hugo, G. 1996. "Environmental Concerns and International Migration." *International Migration Review* 30:105–131.

Koch, K.-F. 1978. *Logs in the Current of the Sea.* Canberra: Australian National University Press.

Macdonald, B. 1975. "Secession in the Defence of Identity: The Making of Tuvalu." *Pacific Viewpoint* 16:26–44.

———. 1982. *Cinderellas of the Empire.* Canberra: Australian National University.

Maude, H. E. 1981. *Slavers in Paradise.* Canberra: Australian National University Press.

Moore, E., and J. Smith. 1995. "Climatic Change and Migration from Oceania: Implications for Australia, New Zealand, and the United States of America." *Population and Environment* 17:105–122.

Munro, D. 1990. "Migration and the Shift to Dependence in Tuvalu: A Historical Perspective." In *Migration and Development in the South Pacific.* J. Connell, ed. Pp. 29–41. Canberra: National Centre for Development Studies.

Munro, D., and R. D. Bedford. 1980. "Historical Backgrounds." In *A Report on the Results of a Census of the Population of Tuvalu, 1979.* Pp. 1–13. Funafuti: Government of Tuvalu.

Rakaseta, V., G. Haberkorn, A. Demmke, and C. Lepers. 1998. *Tuvalu Population Profile.* Noumea: Secretariat of the Pacific Community.

Roy, P., and J. Connell. 1991. "Climatic Change and the Future of Atoll States." *Journal of Coastal Research* 7:1057–1075.

Shibuya, E. 1997. "Roaring Mice against the Tide: The South Pacific Islands and Agenda-Building on Global Warming." *Pacific Affairs* 69:541–555.

South Pacific Commission. 1982. "South Pacific Economies: Recent Trends and Future Challenges." Noumea: South Pacific Commission Working Paper No. 12.

Swain, A. 1996. "Environmental Migration and Conflict Dynamics: Focus on Developing Regions." *Third World Quarterly* 17:959–973.

Tuvalu. 1980. *Tuvalu Second Development Plan, 1980–1983.* Funafuti: Government of Tuvalu.

# 16

# Toward an Ethnographically Grounded Study of Modernity in Papua New Guinea

**Deborah Gewertz**

*Amherst College*


**Frederick Errington**

*Trinity College*

To convey with accuracy the place of Papua New Guineans in a global world, we must first address the remarkable persistence in popular magazines, newspapers, and books of a particular view. This view is that Papua New Guineans are peoples whose desires derive from conditions of unchanging remoteness, peoples whose desires befit those living "untouched by the outside world" within the "land that time forgot" (see Shenon 1994; Raffaele 1996; Bruckner 1999; Flannery 1999; Stille 1999). However, the Papua New Guineans we have long known have become very much aware of themselves as engaged in processes of change; correspondingly, they would not, in fact, want to have their current desires represented in such an erroneous and (insultingly) anachronistic fashion.

Significantly, anthropologists themselves have, to some extent, contributed to such a (mis)representation, especially through their use of the stylistic convention that has become known as the "ethnographic present." (This use of the present tense for describing social practices deemed "traditional," whether they last took place many years before or that very day, has served in many ethnographies to portray peoples and practices as out-of-time, as changeless.) We, therefore, stress at the outset of this chapter that cultural anthropologists must, once and for all, abandon this convention and write with the recognition that no societies have ever been truly static in their practices. This means that ethnographic writing must employ a range of tenses to convey accurately when events, including "traditional" ones, have actually occurred.

Moreover, since cultural anthropologists are meant to understand the way people have been living their lives, and these lives have always been led under conditions of change (albeit to varying degrees), anthropologists must pay close attention to these lives as they have been taking shape in their fully contemporary circumstances. In the case of Papua New Guineans, the last thirty years have brought them such interrelated transformations as the following: an end of formal colonialism with political independence from Australia (in 1975); an increasing reliance upon money for ceremonial, subsistence, and commercial purposes; a concomitant focus on cash-cropping, tourism, wage labor, and entrepreneurial activities (ranging from small roadside stalls selling local foods or imported second-hand clothes, to large stores, service stations, and construction companies); a generally irreversible devastation of entire areas through large-scale mining and logging by multinational firms; a rapid increase in population and in urbanization (with about 20 percent of Papua New Guineans living in urban areas); an intensification of the importance of education, literacy, and Christianity (especially charismatic forms); and the accelerating importance of class-based social and economic distinctions.

Finally, and perhaps paradoxically, these contemporary lives should be described so as to indicate that they may have undergone further change since anthropologists were last in the field. Thus, we will use some variant of the past tense throughout this chapter as we focus on what contemporary Papua New Guineans have desired in what has undeniably become a Melanesian modernity. (We should also note that we will usually place quotes around "traditional" but not "modern." This is to provide a reminder that the "traditional" has never been static. Such a reminder is presumably not necessary concerning the modern, as most people assume the fluidity of modernity.)

We are especially interested in two things about this Melanesian modernity: how these modernist changes have affected, and have been affected by, the construction of new sorts of desires and the creation of new sorts of selves; and how these modernist changes, while globally impelled, have been locally configured. By way of illustration, we begin by describing what some Chambri of Papua New Guinea's East Sepik province have stated to us about what they desire to have and to be. First studied by Margaret Mead and Reo Fortune in 1933 (see Mead 1935) and subsequently by us (during seven field trips, beginning in the early 1970s and most recently in 1999), the Chambri—and their desires—have, like others in Papua New Guinea, undergone significant transformations.

When Mead and Fortune visited them, the Chambri lived in three large villages, each having between 300 and 500 individuals. Indingai, Kilimbit, and Wombun were located south of the Sepik River on an island-mountain within Chambri Lake. They caught fish, some of which they bartered for sago produced by non-Chambri; they also participated in an elaborate social and ritual system predicated on patriclan-based totemic prerogatives. (Gewertz 1983 and Errington and Gewertz 1987 discuss this social and ritual organization.)

From the 1930s through the 1950s, relatively few Chambri left their villages to travel to the coastal town of Wewak: These were mostly labor migrants traveling to plantations elsewhere in Papua New Guinea or prospective catechists training for the Catholic mission service. However, by the early 1960s, Chambri began to journey to Wewak in greater numbers for other purposes and for longer periods of time. They came, for example, to supervise their children who, having completed the limited schooling available at Chambri, were attending mission schools in Wewak; or they came to watch out for their kin who were receiving treatment at the Wewak hospital. In order to provide housing for themselves, they eventually rented from indigenous landowners a small area adjacent to one of the main roads. Here they built the makeshift houses that formed the nucleus of what became Chambri Camp.

By the early 1970s, ever more Chambri traveled to Wewak, usually staying with those kin or covillagers already living in Chambri Camp. Many came primarily to earn money to take or send home. But they also came to see what town life was like. Women who came to sell fish might stay several months before returning to Chambri; men who accompanied them, or those who came alone, might look for jobs and stay longer. If no jobs were found, they eked out a living selling "traditional" carvings and baskets to tourists. They built houses or additions to existing structures from whatever was available—bush materials, scavenged pieces of sheet metal, and even cardboard—and squeezed these in as they could. And eventually many living in the camp came to consider town their home.

This is not to say that Chambri living in Wewak and Chambri living in the home villages became entirely disconnected from one another (Carrier and Carrier 1989). Those from the town might visit the home villages to attend such rituals as death ceremonies. And those from the home villages might visit the town to seek medical attention, sell produce or artifacts, make major purchases, or just experience urban life. While it is true that many in the town and in the villages came to view the other as more backward or less grounded, their lives remained both mutually affecting and affected. Their lives were still influencing each other and were still influenced by the same deeply penetrating global forces, primarily those of commodification, Christianity, and class.

But how, more precisely, had these globally driven modernist changes influenced Chambri desires, indeed, Chambri selves? To find out (during the mid-1990s), we asked Chambri—both at the camp and at the home villages—what they wanted for their futures. We give a sample of their responses.

Soli Pasap (we use pseudonyms throughout) was an unmarried twenty-four-year-old unemployed Chambri who lived at Chambri Camp. He neither knew the Chambri language nor the name of the group into which he was supposed to marry, facts which only mildly embarrassed him. At our suggestion and in response to our questions about his future, he wrote (in English):

> I as an individual will be a future leader of my home community, my family and my future life. As Papua New Guinea is a democratic country, I have all the authority over my life. I will choose my own partner who I know would be the right one for my future and the well being of our children and ourselves as parents. In my future life I have always planned to live a simple life. I will have just enough to build a permanent house, buy food and clothes for the family and also school fees for the kids. That I will have. I as an individual don't want to be a person that everyone would look upon as they would a rich person with a lot of money. I've learned much from the past years and proven to myself that people with a lot of money face lots of problems, such as drinking alcohol every day, husbands busting up their wives, going around with other women and many more things.

He also told us that he hoped his music career would flourish because, like many of his peers, he was "very music-minded." He was a keyboard player for the interethnic, pop-gospel group "Shalom"—a group that often played for an American-derived but Papua New Guinea-run Catholic youth organization known as Antioch. (This group was introduced into Papua New Guinea in 1985 [via Australia] so as to win back urban youth from increasingly popular, charismatic, Protestant sects and—as we shall see—to focus these youth on Christ rather than on commodities, perhaps acquired through crime.)

Cleanne Kalap was an unmarried, forty-year-old leper, with missing toes and fingers and a badly eroded nose, who also lived in the Wewak settlement. She reported to our research assistant, in response to his questions about what she wished the future to bring (and we translate): "I want to weave baskets so that I will have some money to buy food and other things I need. And, in addition, I want to pray to God and Jesus to guide me in my life so that I can remain at peace for all time."

Peter Yuman was a married fifty-four-year-old big man living at Indingai Village (again, one of the Chambri home communities) who was at the height of his powers. He had just sponsored a large, expensive, and prestigious ceremony for the construction and naming of a huge motor canoe. He told us that his future would be even better than the present. This was so because his already extensive powers had been recently augmented by Christian power. He was receiving visitations from Jesus, with whom he had first conversed, in the Chambri language, on August 17, 1991 at 3 A.M. Although he would still exercise ancestral prerogatives in the control of natural resources (in particular, he would regulate the water level in Chambri Lake and control the reproduction of several species of fish), he could now do so more effectively. Rather than regulate through the uncertain and often hazardous medium of complicated incantations and manipulations of ritual paraphernalia, he would use the more reliable medium of the Holy Spirit. Commensurate with the augmentation of his powers, he wished to extend his connections abroad. He, therefore, instructed us to send him a photograph of one of Deborah's classrooms. Students were to be shown standing in front of a picture of him projected on a screen. Also to be included in this picture was a table on which were placed a Catholic Bible and a carving he knew we owned of his ancestor. We were to send him this picture, along with the names and the addresses of the female students portrayed. His son could examine the picture and correspond with the students he fancied and then, perhaps, choose from among them for a bride.

August Soway was an unmarried twenty-two-year-old who was the son of the only successful trade-store owner in Indingai Village (and one of the few successful businessmen on Chambri Island). He had been sent to Wewak to replenish his father's stock. While staying in Chambri Camp, a case of beer, a case of canned mackerel, and a case of cooking oil were stolen from him by other Chambri, including a very close relative—his own mother's brother's son. Immediately after the theft—and before compensation was eventually paid—August told us in considerable distress that he intended to live his future as a "white man," as someone beholden to, and trusting of, no one. He also told us, on other less-trying occasions, that he thought his and his father's future—especially as it pertained to their business—would be much brighter if they (and other Chambri) were not obligated to disperse large sums of money on expensive funerals, initiations, marriages, and the like, and if they could own and develop land individually (rather than as members of large kinship groups).

Adam Kendu was a married forty-three-year-old resident of Chambri Camp, who had recently registered as a "mastercrafts person" with the Department of Tourism and Culture. In his application, he described himself as an expert in dancing, carving, and painting, and in telling traditional stories. To implement his plans for the future, he sought funds from various government officials to purchase a 15-horsepower outboard motor, two drums of gasoline, two amplifiers, one generator, three microphones, and a mixer. Together with other members of a Chambri cultural performance group (a group of which he was president), his goal was to travel throughout the Middle Sepik in order (and we translate) "to teach all the young people to learn their traditional dances. They will see how we Chambri perform ours and this will please them and cause them to follow their own traditions." He had become a great supporter of "tok ples" schools, designed to ensure that all Papua New Guinea children achieved literacy in their own native tongues. And he also hoped to continue with his work as a soccer referee and, perhaps, to gain certification to preside over international matches. Finally, he hoped that some corporation, such as Pepsi Cola or Arnott's Biscuits, might sponsor his cultural performance group to represent Papua New Guinea (and the corporation) at international cultural festivals.

Marcus Legu was a sixty-year-old resident of Kilimbit Village on Chambri Island who supervised the building of the Olimbit men's house in the "traditional" manner. It was to him that other villagers went when they needed clarification concerning the techniques of construction and the significance of such structures. He was very optimistic about the future because he believed many tourists would visit Kilimbit to see this men's house, and he hoped that these tourists would not only spend money on admission to Olimbit but would also buy the many artifacts that would be displayed therein. He told us he wanted (and we translate) "tourists to come by plane, by boat and by foot, every day, every hour, every minute."

Roger Bemas was a forty-eight-year-old Chambri who had been among the first B.A. graduates from the University of Papua New Guinea. Serving as a government administrator in the national capital of Port Moresby, he hoped to find time to write a book about the Chambri past and its traditions. In addition, he hoped to implement his vision about the Chambri future and its possibilities. These he described in a proposal he intended to submit to the government for funding. In the (English) draft we saw of this proposal, he portrayed Chambri as "people in bondage" to squalid life in the squatter settlements where they lacked sufficient land, money, and food and were subject to disease, malnourishment, evil influences, and disturbance and attack by drunks and criminals. The solution was to transform life in the village so that people would choose to come home—so that they would no longer be attracted by "bright city lights." There needed to be a well-organized development project to freeze and market the abundant fish in Chambri Lake in order to provide the money for a variety of village amenities: electricity, television sets and receiver dishes, sports programs, social clubs with snooker tables.

Agnes Alatip was an unmarried nineteen-year-old resident of Chambri Camp who had to leave high school after her second year. She told us that she had long worried about why she had been born a woman, about why God had put women on this earth. Recently, however, she had joined the Antioch Catholic youth organization, which had taught her (and we translate) "to be proud that I'm special because God first visualized and then made me. I am the way I am because of God and I thank him for making me that way. I am not a robot woman made of discarded pieces of metal. . . . I have life and I have blood and God gave me this body to do his work." Before she had to leave school, she thought she might want to be a banker, but now she wanted to be a policewoman. In addition, she wanted to continue to take Jesus into her life because he had helped her find equanimity.

Jonna Parep was a married twenty-three-year-old resident of Wombun Village on Chambri Island who devoutly supported the Catholic organization called the "Legion of Mary" (whose members fervently prayed for the sick and troubled). When we asked her about her future, she told us that, once her six children were older, she wanted freedom to travel, perhaps as a member of a cultural performance group. Until then, she hoped that her many overseas friends—those who had visited Chambri as tourists and with whom she corresponded—would send her the presents she had asked for, in return for the baskets she had woven and sent them. From us, according to the note she slipped us as we were leaving Chambri Island, she wanted (and we translate) "a little wrist-watch and a radio cassette. I want both of these things. You can send the wrist-watch airmail. The radio cassette you can bring with you when you come next time. . . . I want a JVC or a National Panasonic. A big radio, I don't want it; I want one of the nice, really small ones."

It is not exclusively because we are still immersed in our data that we have presented them in this "experience-near" form. We have provided these accounts—some might call them scarcely more than field notes—to convey with immediacy important aspects about a contemporary context. Contemporary Chambri *were* caught up in—indeed, *were* preoccupied with—processes of rapid and ongoing change. Moreover, they were responding to these processes of change through a range of desires (sometimes contradictory). These processes and the varied responses they engendered suggest a significant fluidity to contemporary life among the Chambri (and other Papua New Guineans). It is this fluidity—this sense of life under circumstances of transformation and possibility—that anthropologists must deal with lest we ultimately endorse the perspective of the popular articles referred to earlier.

What we as ethnographers of the Chambri must come to terms with, then, in what must (at least in part) be an ethnography of modernity (see, among others, Miller 1994; Friedman and Carrier 1996; LiPuma 1998; Gewertz and Errington 1999) are circumstances in which people were wanting, for instance, big ceremonies; no ceremonies; "traditional" men's houses; endless streams of tourists; Jesus in their lives as a source of personal tranquility; Jesus in their lives as a source of augmented personal power; autonomy in the choice of marriage partners; continued social entailment to avoid becoming white men; private land ownership; increased personal efficacy as women; fulfillment of their place in God's plan; successful individually owned businesses; continuation of the Chambri language and culture; movement back to Chambri from Wewak; international travel; enough food; snooker tables; televisions and receiver dishes; name-brand electronic gear.

Making sense of such circumstances demands a fine-grained ethnographic exploration of the lives of those many Chambri who have been caught up in that complex of sociocultural transformations increasingly significant throughout the contemporary world. Many of these transformations have involved a partial shift from what were experienced as "traditional" identities derived from kinship, occupational, and gender positions to ones frequently constituted (and reconstituted) through (more) subjectively focused forms of self-expression—including those centered on consumption and other displays of personal taste. (And, in such a shift, the nature of the "traditional" itself has become subject to transformation and contestation. See Giddens 2000:54–68 for an interesting discussion of what happens to the idea of the "traditional" under modernity.) Such an ethnographic exploration, thus, must consider what, for instance, the consequences would be for Chambri personhood of "a modernity in which . . . [they would find themselves] with ever more responsibility for self-creation" (Miller 1994:71).

To elucidate these experiences and consequences, we must confront the processes driving the globalization of modernity, both in their local particularities and in their worldwide generalities. This is so not only because "[w]ithout ethnography one can only imagine what is happening to real social actors caught up in macroprocesses" (Marcus and Fischer 1986:82). This is what has been happening, in this case, to the Chambri as they, for instance, have sought corporate sponsorship of cultural performance groups from PepsiCo and Arnott's Biscuits. But it is also so because without ethnography we cannot comprehend the macroprocesses themselves. In other words, unless one knows what actual people have been doing with the "practices, institutions, and discourses" (Foster n.d.) of modernity, one cannot clarify what effects—both immediate and cumulative—these practices, institutions, and discourses have been having and how they have been, in turn, shaped. In this latter respect, we subscribe to Friedman's statement that "global social processes are constituted largely by local strategies" (1992:365), as well as to Miller's claim that, in studying modernity, it is crucial to consider "all those elements of contingency and variability characteristic of humanity" (1994:80). It would, hence, be a mistake to expect global processes ever to be entirely monolithic (see Kelly 1992).

Completing an ethnographically grounded study of modernity among the Chambri of Papua New Guinea would, therefore, involve the presentation and analysis of a substantial range of often on-going, various (indeed, sometimes competing) efforts at self- and social construction (see Battaglia 1995; LiPuma 1998). (In addition, it would involve the consideration of the frequently contradictory characteristics of modernity itself: thus, we would have to consider both increasing bureaucratization and increasing social fragmentation, both increasing personal idiosyncrasy and increasing cultural uniformity throughout the globe [Miller 1994].) To complete this project would, clearly, be a long-term endeavor. But, to sketch out the way we might deal with the construction of contemporary Chambri desires, we offer the following observations followed by a somewhat extended example.

There have been huge shifts in the lives of Chambri (and other Papua New Guineans) since we began working among them in the early 1970s. These have been linked to the changes Friedman documents "in the flows of and accumulations of capital in the world arena and (consequently) . . . in identity construction and cultural production" (Friedman 1992:333). In particular, as can be seen from our accounts, we have found ever more emphasis on various aspects of individualism in important and interrelated areas of life. (This is not to say that individualism takes the same form everywhere.) In economics, increasing numbers have tried to rationalize business activities by separating them from the demands stemming from other, more "traditional," aspects of social life (see Gewertz and Errington 1999). In religion, there have been increasing numbers who have left "mainstream" Christian religions (such as Catholicism and Lutheranism) to find more intensely subjective forms of religious experience and expression as members of charismatic Christian groups (Robbins n.d., 1995). (See Westermark, chapter 26.) (Some Chambri have even prohibited their children from playing with other "non-reborn" kinsmen—those who haven't taken Jesus into their hearts.) In consumption, there have been (and here our data agree with those of Foster 1995, 1997) increasing numbers who have been defining themselves, by virtue of their preferences for often brand-name consumer goods, as members of the "new generation" (to use a phrase from the almost ubiquitous Pepsi Cola commercials of the mid-1990s Papua New Guinea).

As both product and producers of these shifts, Chambri and other Papua New Guineans were, hence, reframing themselves and their desires in modernist terms. Moreover, as modernists—or at least incipient modernists—they were being actively encouraged in their self-creation: they were being actively encouraged (and have been encouraging each other) to adopt new ways of constructing their identities and objectives.

To give one example focusing on these shifts especially as they pertain to self-creation in religion and consumption, many Chambri youth have joined the recently imported, Catholic-sponsored, charismatic, Antioch youth organization. During intense weekend retreats (that were explicitly compared to now generally defunct initiation ceremonies),

young men and women from diverse cultural groups, under the guidance of older Papua New Guineans designated as "mommies" and "daddies," were enjoined to write life histories. These histories were typically cast in the form of testimonies that established disconnections and contrasts between old lives in "traditional"—kin-based—social contexts and new ones in freely and fully entered religious fellowships. Moreover, these particular histories contrasted a worldly modernism, based on the competitive acquisition of consumer goods, with a more spiritual modernism, based on the sharing of religious experience.

Such disconnections and contrasts can be clearly seen in the testimony of Pauline Kamasap. Entitled "Self-Image or God's-Image?," it was delivered at an Antioch retreat we attended and well conveyed the globally derived but locally compelling Antioch rhetoric of modernist self-creation. In its virtual entirety (and in translation):

> God made me special so that I could do special works. I know that I must grow and become better, inside of me. All of us have to concern ourselves with what is special about each of us, with our own special competencies. I am almost ashamed to reveal to you all that I have learned. Once I thought that I was alone with my feelings, that no one else felt the things that I did, that no one else would understand. But we must talk to each other about what kind of men and women we are. God has a plan for my life and he has made me sufficient to fulfill it. I must take care of myself to insure that I am able to fulfill God's plan for me. . . . God is my friend and I want to talk to you today about the ways in which we can all be good friends with each other and with Him. Friends know each other well; they tell each other everything.
>
> There are Prime Ministers; there are Kings, Queens and Presidents. These are important people, but they are worldly people. It is their custom to lie and to trick people. Many have married two or three times. Although they may be able to play a four-string guitar with one finger, although they may be muscle men who have all the women following after them, although they may appear to be needed by

everybody, these people are a long way from God. I have seen them and I know.

God is in competition with worldly things. Who will win? What do I think? I'll tell you. I laugh at the big men. Yet, I have discovered, I still have two sides, a good one and a bad one. Yes, Antiochers, sometimes even now I sit down and think to myself that I would like to be a famous singer like Janet Jackson. I would like to take a big airplane all around the world. I would like to wear long earrings, lipstick and my hair in little snakes. I haven't done any of this. Yet, I still want it all. Sometimes, Antiochers, sometimes I feel that I am insufficient, that I am inadequate. I tell you this because it is not right if I hide my desires. My desires, my wants, are tools I must use to make my life better. I can't fool myself. I can't say that I don't want these things.

My mother and my father struggled to pay my school fees; they wanted me to go to high school. It was their dream that I would finish school, find a job and be able to repay all of their hard work on my behalf. But I ended up with a Standard Six Certificate—with nothing. They were angry with me. And I thought I was rubbish. I couldn't find a job, but, Antiochers, I have come to discover that it is all right. God has a plan for me: I can sew clothes; I can help my parents take care of the house. And I know God loves me.

I began by sewing for myself and for my best friends, but now I sew for many people. They are happy with my work. They let me know that I have wisdom, that I count in God's eyes. There are many of us who wonder what kind of people we are. All of us would like to be admired by others. All of us would like our names on top. Now I know that I have a style and a way of my own. I can help others. . . . When my friends are angry with one another, I can help out. I am like the local radio, laughing and trying to make my friends feel happy. They know I can help them and have come to share their thoughts with me. They appreciate my advice. . .

Let me tell you about a time when I was afraid and when I was courageous. I was angry with my father. I threw a stone at our house. I wanted to fight with him, I was so angry. I thought to myself, "I have bones [strength, for-

titude], not only men have them." A true friend, a member of Antioch, took me to her house and told me that this attitude wasn't good. I took her advice, and now I am a new woman. Now I am peaceful: I smile and chat freely. . . . I have dedicated myself to sewing. I practiced hard. I learned how to use the big machines in the Wirui [Catholic Mission] laundry house. I am happy with what I have accomplished. When I was in school, I always was pleased when I did well and sad when I missed the mark. But now I realize that God doesn't make rubbish things. Everything he created is good; everything he created bears his imprint. . . . He made me because he liked me. I am a good person because God only makes good things. And, I'm the only one like me that he made: My fingerprints are mine alone; my name is mine alone. In Isaiah, verse 49, line 16, it says that God will not forget me, that he thinks about me all the time. In Psalm 139 it says that God knows my feelings and understands me. He may appear to be far away, but he knows my thoughts. He sees me as I work and sleep. He knows everything I do. I cannot run away from God's sight. God knew me before I was born. I can't run away from you, God. I can't hide my feelings from you, God. You know me. You know my feelings. You wrote in your book of life that you wanted me to walk on this ground. I cannot know your thoughts, but I know you think of me. I know you love me.

Yes, Antiochers, I have told you everything. God wants me to be a special person. He put special things inside of me. God knows what is special about me, even if I don't know it myself. I mustn't envy others. I must look inside myself and discover how I can best become the special person I am.

Every Antioch novice to whom we spoke found such testimonies extremely compelling, particularly the revelations about personal experience to which, often to their surprise, they could relate. One young man (in ways echoing Pauline) told us—and, he said, he had told his fellow Antiochers—that he thought he had been alone in his insecurities, but now knew others shared his feelings. Another told us, excitedly, that he hoped someday to be asked to testify. About his misguided former life, he would tell of sharing the booty of a theft his friends had committed: He had not only gratefully accepted some of the music cassettes they had stolen, but had congratulated them for their success.

In this way, Antioch sought to provide a context of self-creation—a context to shape and verify a modernist, a subjectively focused, personhood. Through a process of individual resocialization, based on the model of the Western nuclear family, Antioch youths were transformed in an impressively effective way. Pauline Kamasap's testimony was, by its very nature, an example of such resocialization at work; it conveyed in axiomatic fashion the parameters of an Antioch-constructed and authorized subjectivity. Her account, like those of the others, freely acknowledged the personal shortcomings of her former self-centered, commodity-oriented life: Defiant of legitimate (especially parental) authority and wedded to worldly things, she was unhappy. She was filled with loneliness and a sense of worthlessness. But her life changed when she decided to accept the positive influence of an Antioch friend as well as the influence of Antioch more broadly. Pauline, hence, came to realize that God had a plan for her in particular. From this she gained peace, renewal, respect, many additional friends, and satisfying, useful work. In other words, she learned in the context of the Antioch community (in the context of "God's Great Big Family," to cite an Antioch song) what the special things were that God had put inside her.

Pauline's testimony revealed a subjectivity that elicited responses of empathetic identification. It was, at the same time, a means both of self-discovery and of mutual validation. Antiochers learned, *and rehearsed,* that each of them was a special and valued subjectivity, with a specific place in God's eyes and plan and composed of a distinctive mix of goodness, desire, frustration, longing, self-doubt. Each, thereby, was shown to be both unique and comparable to others.

Antioch, therefore, provided a context in which personal testimony and response were understood as providing convincing evidence, both idiosyncratic in detail and general in purport, about the nature of matters both worldly and spiritual (and, moreover, about the appropriate relationship between them). It was, in so doing, defining and creating a certain variety of subjective self for Antioch participants. In these regards, we would like to suggest, in passing, that the Antioch testimony was somewhat analogous to the early European novel. Without wishing to imply that the processes of modernism (and capitalism) in late-twentieth-century Wewak were precisely replicating those, for instance, in eighteenth-century England (Miller 1994), there may have been in each case a somewhat similar focus on the development of a roughly comparable subjective self in rapidly and profoundly changing socioeconomic circumstances (see also Anderson 1983).

Addressing the often linked experiences of personal isolation and mutual curiosity, both Antioch testimonies and novels purported to provide realistically detailed glimpses of the personal life of others (see Watt 1957; Abercrombie, Lash, and Longhurst 1992). Through these accounts, listeners and readers gained empathetic access to a largely hidden world of domestic details and to the private sensibilities often engendered there. And in gaining access, listeners and readers were able (as "models of" joined with "models for" [see Geertz 1973]) to form, comprehend, and validate their own subjectivities as both comparable to, and distinct from, those of others.

All of this being said, we must stress that—despite continuing personal and social transformations—local, ethnic commitments remained highly significant to many Papua New Guineans. (Recall that contemporary Papua New Guinea was characterized by various and often competing efforts at self-creation, efforts that sometimes blended the "traditional" and the "modern.") Chambri, for instance, universally supported the creation (in accord with national policy) of the Chambri-language elementary schools alluded to earlier. Such schools, they thought, would not only accustom their children to a school setting but, more significantly, would serve to preserve Chambri language and cultural identity. Chambri also continued to participate actively with each other in various forms of reciprocity and compensation; indeed, we often saw Chambri giving other Chambri the consumer goods that they had just purchased or received.

And, in fact, even in response to our persistent questions, we could find no Chambri who could imagine ceasing to be a Chambri. Even one such as Soli Pasap (with whose account we began)—a youth who had spent his entire life in town, spoke no Chambri, was strongly invested (like Agnes Alatip) in new forms of social organization such as Antioch, and was very concerned with self-definition as a new-generation consumer of pop-music and other products—shook his head with horrified amusement at our outlandish questions. "What after all," he said, "would I be if I weren't a Chambri?"

But we must also stress (as the bulk of this chapter has indicated) that what being a Chambri consisted of had become less clear: It had become for many an increasingly diffuse and varied experience. It was as much characterized by stressing the importance of preserving Chambri language as by actually speaking it; it was as much characterized by giving voluntary presents to friends and age mates as obligatory presentations to kin and in-laws.

Finally, we must suggest that this lack of clarity had broader implications. Speaking Chambri with other Chambri was yielding to speaking Pidgin English (the lingua franca of the country) to Chambri and non-Chambri alike, and payment of bride price to in-laws was yielding to giving a cassette to a friend (possibly someone not even a Chambri) who shared a person's musical taste. These signaled a transition in the most general system in which desire was formulated. The increasing importance of non-ethnic alliances and engagements based on consumption corresponded, we think, to a continuing postcolonial transition: one linked to the earlier mentioned "flows of and accumulations of capital in the world arena" (Friedman 1992:333).

Corresponding to these flows and accumulations, Chambri—both collectively and individually—were less affected and preoccupied than before by the absolute and categorical differences of the sort that had characterized a colonial caste system. As this hierarchical and exclusionist (caste) system had played out in Papua New Guinea, blacks and (largely Australian) whites were often sharply distinguished in status and worth by the (allegedly) inherent characteristics of race. In contrast, Chambri of late have become more affected and preoccupied by the still incremental (though nonetheless increasingly extensive) differences of an emerging postcolonial, modernist class system. As this hierarchical though seemingly less exclusionist class system was developing in Papua New Guinea, all, regardless of race, were often importantly distinguished by (allegedly) acquired characteristics of relative wealth and access to economic resources. This class system, moreover, was operating within the orbit of a transnational capitalism that generated what Sklair has described as the "cultural-ideology of consumerism" (1991:129).

The absolute and categorical distinctions of the colonial system had fostered local desires for absolute and categorical transformation, as (perhaps) through cargo cultism. In these cases, people wished to transform abruptly old lives and societies into new ones, so that blacks hoped that they would suddenly become whites, or at least the equivalent of whites. In contrast, the incremental distinctions of the postcolonial system were fostering local desires for incremental personal enhancements as through lifestyle shopping (whether of a material or antimaterial sort). Thus, elite Papua New Guineans (who became the particular focus of our research during 1996) distinguished themselves (and the members of their nuclear or, at least, nucleated families) from others within their cultural and linguistic groups. This was not only in terms of their key economic positions within the country but also in terms of their successful embodiments of a coveted, consumer-focused lifestyle (see Ogan n.d.a., n.d.b.; Hooper n.d.; Ogan and Wesley-Smith 1992; Gewertz and Errington 1999).

Correspondingly, they often associated themselves with others of their class position, regardless of ethnic background.

Zimmer-Tamakoshi vividly illustrates class-based, cross-ethnic commonalities in her depiction of the arrival lounge at Papua New Guinea's principal airport:

> There . . . one sees expatriate children and the children of mixed-race marriages and elite Papua New Guineans arriving home from school in Australia, wearing western fashions. . . . As . . . [they] leave the airport in their parents' air-conditioned cars and head for the comfort of European-style homes, less affluent youths stare openly, their expressionless faces masking whatever feelings they have about the differences between their own and the students' lifestyles. (1998:1–2)

This is not to say that the injuries of caste have been entirely eliminated. (However, the relatively few caste-like encounters that contemporary Papua New Guineans would likely have—as with sometimes disdainful tourists—were more often sources of passing, though perhaps evocative, irritation than abiding and infuriating preoccupation.) It is to say, though, that the injuries of class have been increasingly affecting Papua New Guineans. Indeed, it is to say that the primary factor shaping the construction and possible fulfillment of modernist Papua New Guinean desires would be the future form and trajectory of Papua New Guinea capitalism within a global world.

Many of us, in reflecting on past fieldwork, have rebuked ourselves for having ignored certain of our "informants'" concerns, especially those that did not seem to fall within the purview of our anthropology. Certainly, for a long time (and to our present regret) we were inclined to put down our pencils, as it were, when our Papua New Guinea friends began talking about such topics as Christianity and World War II. Correspondingly, in reflecting on our contemporary research contexts, we need to think about what have been the matters of local concern that we have tended to ignore or downplay in importance. Without here probing the complex of personal and professional considerations for our selective inattentions, we nonetheless suggest the following. Unless we can fully recognize the extent to which our informants have been and, presumably, will continue to be caught up in such world-pervasive preoccupations as brand-name products, popular music, and evangelical religions (and, we might add, sports), we would be repeating the error of the popular articles—that of misplaced anachronism—with which we began.

## REFERENCES

Abercrombie, Nicholas, Scott Lash, and Brian Longhurst. 1992. "Popular Representation: Recasting Realism." In *Modernity and Identity*. Scott Lash and Jonathan Friedman, eds. Pp. 115–140. Oxford: Blackwell.

Anderson, Benedict. 1983. *Imagined Communities*. London: Verso.

Battaglia, Debbora, ed. 1995. *Rhetorics of Self-Making*. Berkeley: University of California Press.

Bruckner, D. J. R. 1999. "There Goes the Neighborhood." *New York Times Book Review*. March 7:13–14.

Carrier, James, and Achsah Carrier. 1989. *Wage, Trade, and Exchange in Melanesia*. Berkeley: University of California Press.

Errington, Frederick, and Deborah Gewertz. 1987. *Cultural Alternatives and a Feminist Anthropology*. Cambridge: Cambridge University Press.

Flannery, Tim. 1999. *Throwim Way Leg*. New York: Atlantic Monthly Press.

Foster, Robert. 1995. "Print Advertisements and Nation Making in Metropolitan Papua New Guinea." In *Nation Making*. Robert Foster, ed. Pp. 151–181. Ann Arbor: University of Michigan Press.

———. 1996/1997. "Commercial Mass Media in Papua New Guinea." *Visual Anthropology Review* 12:1–17.

———. n.d. Bodies, Commodities and the Nation-State in Papua New Guinea. Unpublished manuscript.

Friedman, Jonathan. 1992. "Narcissism, Roots and Postmodernity." In *Modernity and Identity*. Scott Lash and Jonathan Friedman, eds. Pp. 331–366. Oxford: Blackwell.

Friedman, Jonathan, and James Carrier, eds. 1996. *Melanesian Modernities*. Lund: Lund University Press.

Geertz, Clifford. 1973. "Religion as a Cultural System." In *The Interpretation of Cultures*. Clifford Geertz, ed. Pp. 87–125. New York: Basic Books.

Gewertz, Deborah. 1983. *Sepik River Societies*. New Haven: Yale University Press.

Gewertz, Deborah, and Frederick Errington. 1999. *Emerging Class in Papua New Guinea*. Cambridge: Cambridge University Press.

Giddens, Anthony. 2000. *Runaway World*. New York: Routledge.

Hooper, Anthony. n.d. Class in the South Pacific. Unpublished manuscript.

Kelly, John. 1992. "Fiji Indians and 'Commoditization of Labor.'" *American Ethnologist* 19:97–120.

LiPuma, Edward. 1998. "Modernity and Personhood in Melanesia." In *Bodies and Persons*. Michael Lambek and Andrew Strathern, eds. Pp. 53–79. Cambridge: Cambridge University Press.

Marcus, George, and Michael Fischer. 1986. *Anthropology as Cultural Critique*. Chicago: Chicago University Press.

Mead, Margaret. 1935. *Sex and Temperament in Three Primitive Societies*. New York: Morrow.

Miller, Daniel. 1994. *Modernity: An Ethnographic Approach*. London: Berg.

Ogan, Eugene. n.d.a. Culture, Class and the Modern Pacific Island State. Unpublished manuscript.

———. n.d.b. Class and Other Inequalities in Contemporary Papua New Guinea. Unpublished manuscript.

Ogan, Eugene, and Terence Wesley-Smith. 1992. "Papua New Guinea: Changing Relations of Production." In *Social Change in the Pacific Islands*. A. B. Robillard, ed. Pp. 35–64. New York: Kegan Paul International.

Raffaele, Paul. 1996. "The People That Time Forgot." *Reader's Digest*. August:100–107.

Robbins, Joel. 1995. "Dispossessing the Spirits." *Ethnology* 34:211–224.

———. n.d. Missions without Frontiers. Unpublished manuscript.

Shenon, Philip. 1994. "In Isolation, Papua New Guinea Falls Prey to Foreign Bulldozers." *The New York Times*. June 5:1, 14.

Sklair, Leslie. 1991. *Sociology of the Global System*. Baltimore: Johns Hopkins Press.

Stille, Alexander. 1999. "The Man Who Remembers." *New Yorker*. February 15:51–63.

Watt, Ian. 1957. *The Rise of the Novel*. Berkeley: University of California Press.

Zimmer-Tamakoshi, Laura. 1998. "Introduction." In *Modern Papua New Guinea*. Laura Zimmer-Tamakoshi, ed. Pp. 1–16. Kirksville, Mo.: Truman State University Press.

# 17

# Placing Tahitian Identities: Rooted in Land and Enmeshed in Representations

**Miriam Kahn**

*University of Washington*

> The space in which we live, which draws us out of ourselves, in which the erosion of our lives, our time and our history occurs, the space that claws and gnaws at us, is also, in itself, a heterogeneous space . . . we live inside a set of relations. (Michel Foucault 1986:23)

In grappling to understand social life and the formation of social identities, late twentieth-century scholars have begun to give the same kind of intense analytical attention to place and space that nineteenth- and early twentieth-century scholars gave to history and time. In the past, as Michel Foucault (1980[1976]:70) has pointed out, "space was treated as the dead, the fixed, the undialectical, the immobile. Time, on the contrary, was richness, fecundity, life, dialectic." As scholars have reconceptualized the relative positioning of space and time, however, space has emerged as more central than before and, around it, a new body of literature has developed. This may be in part because, in our contemporary world of increasing placelessness, "the anxiety of our era has to do fundamentally with space, no doubt a great deal more than with time" (Foucault 1986:23).

Foucault not only recognized the importance of space but developed new ways of envisioning spatiality, even coining the word "heterotopology" to refer to ways of thinking about space. For him, space is open, inclusive, and relational. Place is merely a point in its movement and has both metaphorical and material resonance. Heterotopology encompasses "a sort of simultaneously mythic and real contestation of the space in which we live" (1986:24). Foucault also understands space as fundamental in any exercise of power.

Henri Lefebvre, likewise, has challenged conventional modes of thinking about space and place. In his powerful treatise on the production of space, he calls for a "science of space" that moves beyond mere description and examines its complex production. He desires to overcome the "abyss

**285**

between the mental sphere on one side and the physical and social spheres on the other" (1991[1974]:6). To embrace space and its multiple intersections, he creates a theoretical unity between fields that are apprehended separately (the physical and the mental), but interact with and influence one another (1991[1974]:14). He arrives at what he calls a "thirdspace" that includes both first (physical, perceived) space and second (mental, conceived) space. It is this thirdspace that he wants to understand. Simultaneously physical and mental, concrete and abstract, it encompasses and emerges from the dialectic of the two. For example, mental space, formulated in the head, is projected onto physical reality, which in turn feeds the imaginary.

This idea of a relational thirdspace, formulated by Foucault and Lefebvre in France in the 1970s, and applied by the geographer Soja (1989, 1996) in the United States in the 1980s and 1990s,[1] has had surprisingly little impact on disciplines like anthropology. Indeed, for much of anthropology's history, place has been neglected. For decades, it was relegated to a static physical backdrop, a kind of stage setting removed from human action and interaction—the mandatory first chapter in every early ethnography. Only in the past decade or so have anthropologists come to grips with the complexities of place, even pleading for a theory of place (Rodman 1992).[2]

Here I apply ideas about thirdspace to explore and understand the "place" of Tahiti and Tahitian identities within this place. In doing so, I move beyond the seemingly contradictory perspectives of Tahiti as either fantasized image or inhabited locale and instead embrace Tahiti as a thirdspace within which identities continually evolve. Tahiti emerges as a complex lived space that is generated within historical and spatial dimensions, both real and imaginary, immediate and mediated. Tahitian identities, likewise, continually unfold within a context that encompasses both local notions of physical land and global projections of mental images. Throughout the following narrative, various notions of place, like ideas about identity, are often at battle

with each other. Yet, they nonetheless intersect and interact with, indeed generate, one another.

## PLACES OF TAHITI

When I began new research on the production of place in 1994, I chose French Polynesia as a field location precisely because, more than most places, Tahiti has a life of its own that dwells in outsiders' imaginations.[3] While conducting my research, I lived in two different villages, both in the Leeward group of the Society Islands (one of the five archipelagoes in French Polynesia).

One village, Fetuna, on the island of Raiatea, is located twenty-five kilometers from Uturoa, the island's main town and the local French administrative center. Raiatea is heavily influenced by its administrative role, which produces a strong French bureaucratic presence. I chose Fetuna because, on Raiatea, it was as far away as one could get from Uturoa. Although some Fetuna residents worked in town, most spent their days in the village. There, houses lined an unpaved, poorly maintained, coastal road made of dirt that had been packed with crushed coral and shell dredged from the sea. One day, the *mara'amu* trade winds blew fiercely and the sea thrashed over the road, leaving behind piles of trash that usually resided unobtrusively on the ocean floor. Rusty tin cans, plastic bottles, disposable diapers, plastic bags, torn clothes, and broken thong sandals littered the road. Several days after the winds had calmed down, government employees responsible for road maintenance arrived. They sat on top of their massive yellow road graders and lethargically but methodically plowed the garbage back into the sea. That same road circled the island and, eventually, wider and paved, led into Uturoa where it was flanked by numerous shops selling food, clothing, pharmaceuticals, stationery goods, fishing gear, and other sundries. Upon entering these stores, shoppers were usually greeted by posters and calendars with pictures of sandy white beaches under stunning blue skies, racks of postcards of coquettish, bare-breasted women, or magazines with glossy photos of multicolored fish darting through sparkling turquoise lagoons.

The other village I lived in was Faie, located on Huahine, an island whose inhabitants have a reputation for being proud and independent. The center of Faie was densely packed with colorful houses nestled among trees. At the southern end of the village, the road crossed a small bridge before it climbed a steep hill to a lookout with a magnificent view over the bay and surrounding peaks. Every Sunday, like clockwork, an air-conditioned van full of tourists passed through the village. They came from the *Windsong,* a cruise ship that sailed the waters of the Society Islands, stopping each day in a different port during a week-long trip. In Faie, their destination was a group of "sacred eels," which guidebooks describe as being the biggest in the world. The eels lived under the bridge, slithering in a stream often littered with debris. The van parked and the tourists, usually wearing designer clothes and clutching cameras, piled out. Tahitian children stopped their playing, shyly clustered nearby, and watched. The guide encouraged the tourists to go into the small store next to the bridge, buy canned mackerel (where, cleverly, the price of mackerel was exceptionally high), and hand-feed the eels. Most tourists stood at the bridge and asked the guide a few questions about the eels or took pictures, while the more adventuresome among them gingerly stepped into the murky water below, dangling pieces of fish from their fingers. Soon thereafter everyone climbed back into the air-conditioned van and left.

Fetuna and Faie are very different from one another, as are the two islands of Raiatea and Huahine on which they are located. Yet, as I lived in each, I was struck less by the difference between them than by a greater, more-powerful contrast. As in many tourist destinations, the disparity was between daily life as lived by the local inhabitants—Tahitians working in their gardens, fishing in the sea, visiting with friends, looking at tourists, repairing broken vehicles, or staying in their houses to clean, cook, or watch television—and the

seductive images offered on calendars and postcards, and in magazines and guide books, that lured tourists to an exotic destination (perhaps only to be disappointed by such a lackluster experience as tossing greasy mackerel to eels in a dirty stream).

As time passed, I continually wondered about these two different "places"—to use Lefebvre's terminology—the physical and perceived, on the one hand, and the mental and conceived, on the other. At first I had thought of daily perceived life as existing in a separate realm from the conceived tourist representations. I assumed that Tahitians, other than those few who worked in the tourist industry, remained unaffected by the seductive images. But suddenly, in September 1995, my thoughts changed. On September 5th, the French government resumed nuclear testing by exploding a bomb on the atoll of Moruroa, 1,200 kilometers from Tahiti. The next day, riots swept the capital city of Papeete on the island of Tahiti and images of protesters, fires, and looting flooded world television sets and newspapers. The French government's response to the dissemination of these negative images was tinged with obvious anxiety. I immediately gained new insight. I awoke to the destructiveness that was not only lodged in the exploding bomb but in the alluring images as well. I began to realize, both through ethnographic research and by studying media representations, how economically motivated, politically manipulated, and consciously constructed the images were and, above all, how deliberately intertwined they were with the French colonial enterprise. Moreover, I understood how intimately they affected Tahitian identities. Indeed, the production and distribution of images of Tahiti as paradise seem to serve colonial interests by allowing those in power—primarily the French and *demi,* who are people of mixed ancestry whose background is both Tahitian and French, or Chinese, German, English, American, and so on—to convince those without power (primarily Tahitians) that the status quo serves Tahitian interests.[4] The thirdspace that gradually emerged from my research and growing understanding was a vastly more complex and political space, and one that profoundly impacted individual lives and identities.

## GLOBAL POLITICS AND LOCAL HABITAT

Lefebvre and Foucault are both mindful of the political aspects of the production of space. Lefebvre's science of space stems from his commitment to understanding political practices. As he states, "the dominant tendency is towards homogeneity, towards the establishment of a dominated space" (Lefebvre 1991[1974]:411). Foucault also emphasizes a political understanding of space. He reminds us that "the military and the administration actually come to inscribe themselves both on a material soil and within forms of discourse" (Foucault 1980[1976]:69). Indeed, he sees the history of spaces as the history of power. "A whole history remains to be written of spaces—which would at the same time be the history of powers . . . from the great strategies of geo-politics to the little tactics of the habitat" (Foucault 1980[1977]:149).

In French Polynesia, locally inhabited space is definitely interlaced by dominant, global politics. In today's largely postcolonial world, French Polynesia remains one of the few colonies still in existence. Lying halfway around the world from France, French Polynesia is administered under France's Ministry of Overseas Departments and Territories. Under the terms of France's 1946 constitution, the colonies in the Atlantic and Indian Oceans (Martinique, Guadeloupe, French Guiana, and Réunion) became *départements d'outre-mer* (DOMs), with a legal structure and administration that is identical to the metropolitan departments. The colonies in the Pacific Ocean (New Caledonia, French Polynesia, the former Franco-British condominium of the New Hebrides, now called Vanuatu, and—after 1961— Wallis and Futuna) were renamed *territoires d'outre-mer* (TOMs). Territories, unlike departments, are administered by a governor or governor-general. The constitution defined the French Union, the new incarnation of the empire, in such a way that "the word 'colony,' like 'Empire,' was thereby banished from French

constitutional usage" (Aldrich 1993:67). The result, however, was that France established a political presence in all the world's major oceans, with a similar colonial configuration in all DOM-TOMs (see Giradet 1972; Bensa 1995; Price 1998). In fact, many administrative personnel rotate between DOM-TOMs during their careers. A decade after the 1946 constitution, the need to maintain a nuclear testing base in French Polynesia, and the desire to link the DOM-TOMs so they formed a chain of French bases encircling the globe, provided the theoretical pillars of France's international policy in the South Pacific (Aldrich 1993:336).

In French Polynesia, the constitution of the Republic of France remains the supreme law of the land. The French parliament legislates laws. The French president appoints the chief administrator and most local officials. Paris retains control of defense, law and order, foreign policy, currency, education, immigration, health care, social services, television, radio broadcasting, and newspapers. The degree of autonomy exercised by the French Polynesian government depends on the goodwill of the *métropole*. When it deems such action necessary, the French state can assume direct and near total control (Aldrich 1993:159). The thousands of French soldiers and civil servants in French Polynesia can vote in local elections the day they arrive in the territory.

This colonial grip manifests itself daily in numerous ways. Tahitian children devote the majority of their school day to learning French language, history, and geography. Postsecondary education, other than at the Centre Universitaire de Polynésie Française on the island of Tahiti, is usually limited to universities in France since French is the only language officially taught to Tahitians. Most television broadcasts are through Radio France Outremer (RFO), which represents "the voice of France," and all their employees are paid directly from France.

This position of domination is not without cost to France, which, in 1995, pumped 625 million French francs (US$1.25 billion) into the economy to maintain it (Benchley 1997:9).[5] Unlike other colonial relationships rooted in economic exploitation, this one, instead, is motivated by economic investment and national pride.[6] The system is also self-perpetuating. The French payments, upon which the economy depends, are filtered through a system that is controlled by a few families, most of whom are French or demi.[7] This well-entrenched privileged class provides built-in assurance that the economic and political system will endure.

## A RECIPROCAL RELATIONSHIP WITH LAND

For Tahitians, as for most Pacific Islanders, a sense of place and identity is deeply rooted in land.[8] Both ancient history and contemporary life are grounded in the relationship between people and land, and all that this relationship encompasses, bestows, and justifies. Islands are believed to be born of deities, and an island's topographical features may represent physical attributes of the gods. From the human offspring of the gods come all living things. Genealogies instruct individuals about their spiritual and familial relationship with the land. Above all, it is a reciprocal relationship. People must care for the land because it, in turn, feeds and provides for them. Land provides people with the means to survive and care for their offspring, as well as with a moral and spiritual feeling of identity and connection.

The importance of land can be seen in numerous ways. For example, as pointed out by Raapoto (1994), the central Tahitian concept of *'utuafare,* or household, hinges on a notion of shared family land, including various houses for sleeping, cooking, and eating, as well as trees and plants. He explains that land is both the mother who nourishes her children and the source and marker of personal identity. As a nurturing mother, land provides food such as taro, yams, and breadfruit. As the place upon which ancestral movements and settlements are imprinted, land connects individuals to their family history through their genealogies.

These beliefs come together most poignantly in the Tahitian custom of a mother burying her child's placenta in the ground (Raapoto 1994). The placenta is called the *pu fenua* (call to the land). The umbilical cord, which is buried next to the placenta, is called *pito o te fenua* (center of the land). Marama, a middle-aged woman on Huahine, who had given birth at home to twenty-four children, explained this practice to me.

> The placenta is always put back in the ground. When the child is in the womb the mother takes care of it, but when it is born the mother calls the land to take care of her child. The land will give life to the person by providing food. Now there are lots of pu fenua here because I had many children, plus my children bring their children's placentas. You can bury it and then move away. It doesn't matter because you are still connected to your family's land. (Marama Teiho, personal communication, 1995)

The placenta can also be placed in the ground on land that one does not own. As a Tahitian woman living in urban Papeete told me, "When I asked the doctor for the placenta he had no trouble giving it to me because everyone does that. I had to stay in the hospital five days, so the placenta was put in a plastic bag and refrigerated. Later I put it in the ground next to the house I rent in Papeete" (Manolita Ly, personal communication, 1994).

Some of the general differences I noticed between life on the island of Raiatea (where people are more cash-dependent and reserved) and Huahine (where people are more self-sufficient and outgoing) were in part the result of different relations between people and land. When I was originally looking for a field site, I was advised against working on Raiatea precisely because its designation as the administrative center of the Leeward Islands meant that many of its inhabitants came from elsewhere and lived on land they did not own (Pierre Sham Koua, personal communication, 1994). On the other hand, I was told that certain islands, such as Huahine or Maupiti, would be more representative of Tahitian values because Tahitians still owned most of the land. People on Huahine, in particular, are known for their combative spirit when their land is at stake, as evident in the following *paripari,* a style of ancient chant.[9]

Huahine, on whose north shore is *marae*
Manunu (the home of the god Tane)
Huahine, which was divided into ten districts
by brothers
The people of Huahine will fight for their
land, their life, their country
They won't stand there and take what they
don't like.

This determination to fight for one's land was illustrated a few years ago when a Japanese group proposed buying the land around Huahine's Fauna Nui Lake, with the intention of developing a Sea World-type of amusement park. Six thousand signatures were quickly collected to halt the project (Chantal Spitz, personal communication, 1995).

Nowhere is the importance of the connection between personal identity, land, history, genealogy, and spirituality more evident than in the many marae that rise majestically from the earth. These are sacred sites of ancient temples that were dedicated to individual deities and served as portals for the deities to descend to earth. Today, usually all that remains of a marae is a rectangular area that is covered with paving stones, often surrounded by low walls, and a large stone altar at one end. Large upright stones in front of the altar, or elsewhere within the walled area, symbolize the genealogies of the marae's creators. Although marae are no longer used for religious ritual as they once were, they are deeply respected as living memorials. They mark the presence of deities in the landscape. They signify the history of the movement of ancestors who established marae as they settled in new locations. Salmon (1904:3) relates how Ta'aroa, the Tahitian god of creation, is permanently imprinted in the landscape, visible in various marae on different islands. "Ta'aroa's marae was Vaiotaha; his upper jaw rested at Ahutaiterai, on Marae Faretai (on Bora Bora); his lower jaw rested on Tahuea i te Turatura, at Marae Mata'ire'a (on Huahine); his throat and belly, Tetumu and Harura, at Marae Vaearai (on Raiatea)." On Huahine, for instance, the names of the first four sons of the village of Maeva are also the names of four of its marae. Maeva, which has

a greater concentration of marae than any other village in Polynesia, is said to be *tu'iro'ohei* (renowned for its deep cultural roots) because it exists on land that has always provided for its inhabitants and is rich in ancestral history. In addition to these large historical marae, there are smaller, family marae located next to people's houses that still serve as burial sites for family members.

As can be seen, land is pivotal in providing Tahitians with a sense of place and identity. Yet, most Tahitians also believe in the spiritual and complementary association between land and sea. "We need both. From the land we get taro, yams, and breadfruit. From the sea we get fish and seafood" (Marereva Tetuanui, personal communication, 1994). Indeed, in ancient times, each island was divided into several wedge-shaped districts, each of which spread from the inland mountains down to the coast. Royal families exercised rights to land for cultivation as well as to coastal areas for fishing (Tetiarahi 1987:48). It is this belief in the complementarity of land and sea that accounts for the Tahitian practice of bringing coral inland to add to the stones at a marae and explains why coral can be found at almost every marae, no matter how far inland it is located (Eric Komori, personal communication, 1995). Yet, Tahitians see the fascination with the sea and the beach, as such, as a trait that is unique to tourists. "Tahitians don't care to live next to the sea or to have a view of water. They see the water all the time. It's nothing special. Tourists are the only ones who crave the water" (Haapa Hautia Dituru, personal communication, 1994). Where, then, does the tourist's desire for a turquoise Tahiti originate?

## RETRACING IMAGES ON EUROPE'S CONFINING WALLS

For more than two hundred years, Europeans, and later Americans, have created a long, continuous line of relatively consistent images in which an idyllic Tahiti is constructed and maintained as its own referent. Like many such narratives that represent stereotypes about the past rather than the past itself, "cultural production has been driven back inside the mind . . . it can no longer look directly out of its eyes at the real world for the referent but must . . . trace its mental images of the world on its confining walls" (Jameson 1983:118).

The earliest images of Tahiti were shaped by European imperialist philosophies and, later, by French colonialist politics. When the French explorer, Louis-Antoine de Bougainville, first arrived in Tahiti in 1768, Jean-Jacques Rousseau had just made the "noble savage" popular in Europe. Upon seeing Tahiti, Bougainville named it "New Cytheria" after the legendary birthplace of Aphrodite, the Goddess of Love, aestheticizing Tahitians through classical reminiscences (Despoix 1996:5). When he returned to Europe with reports of beautiful women with uninhibited manners, visions of sexual abandon swept like wildfire through Paris and London. His French publication of *Voyages* in 1771, followed by the English translation in 1772, provided European men with a vision of earthly paradise and an endless source of dreams. It contained passages such as the following:

> They pressed us to choose a woman, and to come on shore with her; and their gestures . . . denoted in what manner we should form an acquaintance with her. It was difficult . . . to keep at their work four hundred young French sailors, who had seen no women for six months. In spite of all our precautions, a young girl came on board, and placed herself upon the quarter-deck, near one of the hatch-ways, which was open in order to give air to those who were heaving at the capstan below it. The girl carelessly dropped a cloth, which covered her, and appeared to the eyes of all beholders, such as Venus showed herself to the Phrygian Shepherd, having, indeed, the celestial form of that goddess. (Bougainville 1772:218–219)

A comparison of *Voyages* with Bougainville's original journal (Taillemite 1977), however, indicates the extent to which negative first encounters were rewritten in a positive way for later publication, thus providing us with a classic foreshadowing of the politics of representation. In contrast to the journal notes, which include ample descriptions of European frustrations with the Tahitian custom of "stealing," the published narrative was carefully rewritten in order to appeal to European romanticism. Bougainville made changes and additions, such as "references to goddesses, nymphs, noble savages, and the beauty of the landscape" (Claessen 1994:23).

When James Cook visited Tahiti between 1769 and 1777, he took along artists like John Webber, who created intoxicating images that further reinforced European romantic notions. European appropriation of the noble savage was furthered when Cook transported Omai, a Tahitian from the island of Raiatea, back to England, making him the first Polynesian to reside in Europe for any length of time (Baston 1790; Clark 1941; McCormick 1977). Omai became the darling of English society. "Friendly and charming, he was dressed by his benefactors in velvet jackets and other finery. Over the next two years he dined in London's best homes, met the king, learned to shoot and skate and was a favorite with the ladies" (Kay 1997:281). Immediately after Omai's celebrity in England, and the exhibition of Cook's ethnographic collection in London, a Polynesian vogue blossomed in Europe. "Travel literature was popular . . . 'Tahitian' verandas were designed for country houses, 'Polynesian' wallpaper was fashionable, and artificial 'South Seas' lakes were built into landscaped vistas" (Daws 1980:11).

In 1789, the mutiny on the *HMS Bounty*, the most notorious in British naval history, further fixed images of legendary Tahiti in the minds of Europeans. During the mutiny, Fletcher Christian set Captain Bligh out to sea in a small skiff and returned to Tahiti with the *HMS Bounty*. Forever after, the name of the *Bounty* has been associated with male adventure and freedom, with shirking the shackles of oppressive government on the high seas, and with finding sexual pleasures under the palms.

By the turn of the century, a backlash arose to the noble savage images. British Protestant and French Catholic missionaries arrived to subdue a way of life that they interpreted as licentious. They also were opposed to joint ownership of land and tried to convert Tahitians to a land tenure system more in tune with the idea of a Christian nuclear family (Ward and Kingdon 1995). Missionaries slowly became part of a growing colonial presence as English and French vied for possession of new colonies. When two French Catholic priests arrived in Tahiti in 1836, the Tahitian ruler, Queen Pomare IV, immediately expelled them. In response to this perceived insult, a French ship arrived in Papeete in 1838, demanding monetary compensation and a salute to the French flag. At the same time, a French consul, Moerenhout, was appointed to Queen Pomare. In 1842, while she and the English consul were away, Moerenhout organized local chiefs into signing a petition asking to be brought under French protection.

A year later, the Queen's flag was lowered and Tahiti was declared a French protectorate. Tahitian resistance was strong, resulting in three years of guerrilla warfare (1844–1847). During this period, legislators attempted to further dismantle the ancient land system by establishing various laws in the 1840s and 1850s that allowed for real estate transfers. From then on, Tahitians could sell, and thus lose, their land (Tetiarahi 1987:50). In 1880, the queen's son and successor, Pomare V, gave his land to France. The protectorate was given the name of Établissements Français d'Océanie (EFO) and became the French colony it is today.

The arrival of French rule, after a century of romantic images, encouraged European and American writers and artists to make their way to Tahiti to live out, write about, and paint their dreams. Places in literature and art, as Lefebvre (1991[1974]:15) has said, are "enclosed, described, projected, dreamt of, [and] speculated about." Tahiti was no exception. The list of literati who enclosed Tahiti in their minds and projected their images to the world is great—Herman Melville, Robert Louis Stevenson, Pierre Loti, W. Somerset Maugham, Jack London, Victor Segalen, Charles Nordhoff, James Norman Hall, and James Michener, to name the most prominent.

But none played as powerful a role in creating an enduring vision of Tahiti on the world's imagination as did the French painter, Paul Gauguin. Gauguin's interest in Tahiti was first piqued when he viewed exhibits of colonial outposts at the 1889 Exposition Universelle in Paris, and was later reinforced when he read Pierre Loti's *Le Mariage de Loti*. In letters Gauguin wrote to friends, he reported his affairs with women brought from the colonies (Maligne 1949:118) and described his desire to "buy a hut of the kind you saw at the Universal Exhibition . . . this would cost almost nothing" (Maligne 1949:142). Influenced by both colonial and romantic representations, he embarked on a voyage that allowed him to recreate these representations for others. Penniless in Paris, he sailed to Tahiti to live cheaply while advancing his career and fulfilling his dreams, setting canvasses colorfully ablaze with his impressions of Tahiti and Tahitian women. It is important to note that Gauguin's relocation to Tahiti in 1891 was possible primarily because he was a French citizen and Tahiti was a French colony. Although Gauguin's artistic accomplishments in Tahiti were complex expressions of the convergence of European decadence and French colonialism (Perloff 1995), he continues to be regarded as a symbol of the simple rejection of European civilization and the embracing of South Seas primitivism. Ever since Gauguin, European painters have flocked to Tahiti to recreate Gauguin-like images on canvases of their own (Jacques Boullaire, Pierre Heyman, Jean Masson, and Yves de Saint-Font, to name only a few).

These nineteenth-century colonial foundations, depicted romantically in late nineteenth- and early twentieth-century literature and art, solidified and intensified in the twentieth century. At the outbreak of World War I, Europe's flourishing economy caused an increase in the ties between France and Tahiti. The EFO exported local products, such as dried coconut and vanilla, in exchange for European manufactured goods. This rapid economic expansion required an increasingly larger workforce. Lured by images created in the literary and art world, French colonists flocked to Tahiti in great numbers. By 1911, there were 3,500 French residents (Wheeler and Carillet 1997:23) among a Tahitian population of 31,400 (Newbury 1980:272). As colonists moved in, images radiated out. In 1913, the EFO government produced their first postage stamp of Polynesian inspiration—a Tahitian woman with a crown of flowers on her head and a hibiscus blossom behind her ear. With this one stamp, the idea of Tahiti as beautiful, seductive, and feminine, but securely under French control, was circulated to the world at large.

World War II brought 4,500 American soldiers to Bora Bora in the Society Islands, which was one in a chain of refueling stations across the Pacific. Bora Bora, which previously had no vehicles or paved roads, was transformed by bulldozers, trucks, seaplanes, bombs, ammunition, tents, and prefab buildings (Kay 1997:219). When soldiers returned home after the war, their stories about tropical romance kindled imaginations across the United States. Ever since, Bora Bora has been regarded as one of the ultimate American tourist fantasies.

Stirrings of desire for emancipation from France rumbled through Tahiti after the war. Pouvanaa a Oopa, from the island of Huahine, became the leader of the Tahitian independence movement, serving in the Territorial Assembly and denouncing the French for their treatment of Tahitians as second-class citizens. At the peak of his power, however, his voice was silenced. He was convicted of conspiracy in a plot to burn down Papeete and was imprisoned, first in Papeete (1958–1960) and later in France (1960–1961), and banned from returning to Tahiti for eight years.

In 1957, the name of the colony was changed to Polynésie Française. French plans were underway for still greater changes.

## MUSHROOM CLOUDS, TOURISM, AND TECHNICOLOR VISIONS

A major turning point in Tahitian colonial history occurred in the 1960s. Events took place that both deepened France's political entanglement with its colony and broadened the worldwide demand for exotic images of French Polynesia. It was the era in which nuclear testing and tourism came of age side-by-side. Within this political context, France was increasingly able to reap the bounty of two centuries of seductive imagery and to use these representations to its economic advantage.

Prior to 1960, anticipating that Algeria might soon gain independence, France was preparing to transfer its nuclear test site from Algeria to French Polynesia. In 1963, a year after Algeria became independent, President Charles de Gaulle established the Centre d'Expérimentations du Pacifique (CEP) and officially announced that Moruroa and Fangataufa, two uninhabited atolls in the Tuamotu Islands (one of the five archipelagoes in French Polynesia), would be the new test sites. In addition, headquarters and support facilities were later established in Papeete, on the island of Tahiti, where a large area of coral reef was reclaimed for the construction of new docks to shelter and service the numerous ships required to support and monitor the nuclear tests. While preparations were firmly underway for developing the nuclear testing program, another major change was taking place, namely the construction of an international airport at Faa'a, a few kilometers down the road from Papeete, which opened in 1960. The presence of the airport permitted easier access to Tahiti both for the government, which had begun to transfer equipment and personnel in preparation for the nuclear testing program, and for tourists, who were in search of Gauguin's paradise.

The simultaneous arrival of nuclear testing and tourism served to obscure the intensity of the testing preparations from most residents. As nuclear supplies and personnel were channeled through the airport and harbor en route to the outer islands of Moruroa and Fangataufa, tourists began arriving on international flights in record numbers. Whereas only 1,620 tourists had come to Tahiti in 1960, a year later, when the airport was open, 8,700 arrived, a number that continued to grow steadily.[10] Tourism, which is by far the most influential industry in French Polynesia, provides the main avenue through which non-French money is introduced into the territory.[11]

In 1962, a year after the airport was operational, American film crews descended upon Tahiti as well. Hollywood glamorized the events of the mutiny on the *HMS Bounty* in a three-hour color film starring Marlon Brando and Tarita, a Tahitian woman. In contrast to an earlier, 1935, black-and-white version of the story that had been filmed in Hawai'i (implying that "exotic" locations are interchangeable), the 1962 film was shot on location on Tahiti and Bora Bora, bringing Tahiti—in Technicolor—into movie theaters around the world. The film emphasized the natural beauty of the islands and the physical splendor of Tahitians, and thereby continued to feed people's dreams about Tahiti being an earthly paradise of sexual abandon. Technicolor fantasies seemed to slip even closer within reach when, in real life, Marlon Brando married Tarita and purchased Tetiaroa, a picture-perfect atoll forty kilometers north of Tahiti. With the new airport awaiting the arrival of tourists, a newly established Office of Tourism Development luring them to Tahiti, hotels springing up to accommodate them, and Hollywood's spectacle encouraging iridescent dreams, many forces were set in motion. Travelers' fantasies could now be turned into realities with the simple purchase of an airline ticket.

While the world comfortably embraced this alluring image of Tahiti in the mid-60s, French military were occupied differently. They quietly, but collusively, changed the name of Moruroa, which in Tahitian means "big lies," to Mururoa, a word with no special meaning.[12] France began atmospheric explosions on the atoll in 1966, refusing to acquiesce to the 1963 agreement (by the United States, the former Soviet Union, and Britain) to halt atmospheric tests and to shift instead to underground testing. It was not until 1974 that France moved its tests below ground.[13] Moruroa, as its original Tahitian name indicates, truly embodies deep deception. It ap-

pears neither in the French Polynesian phone book nor on airline schedules, and is impossible for nongovernment people to visit. On the one hand, the government claims that the testing poses absolutely no environmental or health dangers. Yet, Tahitians who have worked on Moruroa all recount similar stories of local bans on the consumption of fish from the lagoon and coconuts from the land, and of the death of people following their illegal ingestion of these foods (Peto Firuu, personal communication, 1995; Étienne Piha, personal communication, 1995). It has also been mandatory for individuals to carry Geiger counters and wear special antiradiation suits while there (Constance Cody, personal communication, 1995). In spite of the government's policy of putting a secrecy stamp on all local health statistics (B. Danielsson and M. Danielsson 1986:307), it was discovered that, within a decade after testing began, such typically radiation-induced diseases as leukemia, thyroid cancers, brain tumors, and eye cataracts began to appear in alarming numbers (M. Danielsson 1986:165).

In 1992, French president François Mitterand declared a moratorium on all testing, which was lifted by President Jacques Chirac in 1995. By the time tests were finally stopped in January 1996, France had conducted a total of 45 atmospheric and 134 underground tests in French Polynesia, with bombs up to two hundred kilotons, or more than ten times the size of the bomb that destroyed Hiroshima. Each test cost an average of two billion CFP[14] (US$20 million) (Sancton 1995:23).

The nuclear testing program and all its ramifications totally transformed Tahiti economically and socially. In addition to pumping money into the territory for the testing program, France injected extra funds and goods to encourage local acquiescence, generating a colonial dependency relationship and artificial prosperity.[15] For example, in 1960, military spending in the territory was 4 percent of the gross domestic product, but by 1966 it had increased sharply to almost 80 percent. In the 1950s, returns on exports were 90 percent of the cost of imports, but by the early 1970s had slumped to only

10 percent (Henningham 1992:127–128). Government welfare allocations also began in the 1960s, with the amounts given and the categories of who qualifies steadily increasing over the years. Television, too, arrived in 1966, the same year as the first atmospheric explosion.

Tahiti's importance as the administrative and economic center of French Polynesia caused many people from the outer islands to migrate to Tahiti, attracted by jobs such as building the new harbor, airport, and hotels, and working in the budding tourism industry. Like many towns in the South Pacific, Papeete was transformed from a sleepy colonial port town to a cosmopolitan city, almost doubling its population between 1960 and 1970. Prior to CEP, most of the population had fed itself by subsistence agriculture and fishing. Within a decade the territory was importing most of its food.[16] In the space of a single generation, many Tahitians were transformed into a working-class population that had become almost completely dependent on the money and goods brought into the territory by France. Land, too, slipped increasingly out of Tahitians' control. Some people, particularly those who had been educated in France, took advantage of opportunities to sell their land. The purchasers, often real estate agents, then sold the land to French, Chinese, and other nonindigenous buyers (Tetiarahi 1987:54). One woman described this spiraling descent into dependency and the related loss of land.

> Before CEP, Tahitians lived well. They worked in their gardens. They went fishing. They built their houses. After the first test in 1966 Tahitians became dependent on money. Now they need money in order to live. They buy their food. They buy cement and metal to build their houses. Tahitians buy more and more things and how can they pay for everything? They can't. They go to the bank and get a loan. Then how can they pay the bank back? They can't. After a while the bank comes and takes their land and sells it. Who buys the land? Foreigners. Later where do the Tahitians live? They have no land. No house. They end up living in a tiny shack. Tahitians have gotten lazy. They don't

grow their own food anymore. They buy it in the store. If they want Tahitian food they buy it in the market. I go to the market every Sunday to sell my food. Do you know who buys it? Tahitians. Every week I get sad when I see that. (Kim Tai Piha, personal communication, 1995)

The verbal picture Kim Tai painted of her personal experience with increasing destabilization is in stark contrast to the visual images of permanent splendor that are mass-produced to entice the world at large.

## THE POWER OF A CAMERA

In view of the growing interdependence of France's political agenda, French Polynesia's political economy, and the representation of Tahiti as paradise, it is not surprising that the production of alluring images has become a major industry. Lefebvre has commented on the destructive abilities of illusive imagery. His words apply to the situation in Tahiti.

> Images fragment, they are themselves fragments, cutting things up and rearranging them, découpage and montage, the art of image-making. Illusion resides in the artist's eye and gaze, in the photographer's lens, on the writer's blank page. The visual world plays an integral and integrative, active and passive, part in it. It fetishizes abstraction and imposes it as the norm. The image kills. (Lefebvre 1991[1974]:97)

In French Polynesia, the Office of Tourism is the prime producer of these images that "fragment" and "kill." Their images emphasize scenery—sandy beaches, blue skies, colorful fish, fancy hotels—rather than people.[17] In a 1994 move to gain more control, Gaston Flosse, the president of French Polynesia, wrote a letter to all government agencies requiring them to use only images of French Polynesia that were produced by the government agency Institut de la Communication Audio-Visuelle (ICA) (Paul Auzépy, personal communication, 1995). The Office of Tourism and ICA, however, are not the only agencies to produce and distribute images. It is relatively easy for others to enter the business, as long as they don't sell their images to government agencies.

The individual who monopolizes the nongovernment production of photographic images is Teva Sylvain, a blond, blue-eyed demi, who is the Director of Pacific Promotion Tahiti. His seductive images of women, as well as scenery, adorn postcards, calendars, posters, place mats, coasters, address book covers, rulers, cigarette lighters, books, stationery, and envelopes. Several of his images are reproductions of Gauguin's paintings. He credits his father with having inspired his own outlook.

> De Gaulle sent my father, Adolphe Sylvain, to Indochina to fight, but with a camera not a gun. His job was to educate the French people about Indochina. From there, he was also sent to the South Pacific. Again, he went as a photographer. Soon after he arrived in Tahiti in 1946 he met a Tahitian woman whom he later married. He kept his position as a war correspondent but stayed in Tahiti, documenting his new surroundings in black-and-white. My father became the first journalist to really publicize the island of Tahiti. He photographed for the *Kon Tiki* expedition and for *Life* magazine. By and by he had five children, four daughters and me. He needed to support his family and did so with his photographs. He wanted to show the paradise aspect of Tahitian life. He was conscious of the contrast between the Tahitian images of a peaceful life and the Western atrocities he still carried with him from the war. He photographed only those aspects that portrayed paradise—the childlike, simple, carefree side of life. (Teva Sylvain, personal communication, 1995)

In 1970, Teva, then sixteen years old, followed his father's footsteps, creating images of his own fetishized view of Tahitian life. Postcard production, which he started in 1974, represents the largest part of his business.[18] Every year, one million of his postcards are purchased in French Polynesia, to begin their journey all over the globe. His decisions about image production are guided by sales statistics. As Teva explained to me, "I create images that I think people want to buy. I come up with an idea and then test it on the market. If an image sells well, I produce more. If something doesn't sell, I take it off the market." His computer program tracks sales of every postcard image and arranges them according to their market popularity.

Teva elaborated on the marketing strategies specifically for the postcard images of women.[19] "Most of the women are not fully Tahitian because the men who visit Tahiti want a woman that they have in their head or in their libido," he confided to me. "They want one who looks like women they are used to. They don't want her skin to be too dark, her nose too broad, or her thighs too strong." As a result, the women on the postcards have an assortment of genetic backgrounds. As Teva pulled a few postcards off the top of a stack on his desk, he told me, "For example, #911 is French, #976 is Tahitian, #977 is demi," and so on. "Look at #911. She is one hundred percent French. But I put the crown of leaves on her head and a coconut leaf basket in her hands to give her a Tahitian look. That's all it takes. Other than those props, there is nothing Tahitian about her." He explained, "I simply produce what people want because, like my father, I have to feed my family." Although rationalizing that he was only manipulating the market, he seemed very aware that, in doing so, he was also reconfiguring the very image of Tahiti and Tahitian women. He admits that "the women of one's dreams that one admires in my lascivious poses are not found on every street corner" (Sylvain 1994:64).

The Office of Tourism, as well as entrepreneurs like Teva Sylvain, have enormous capacity and capability to create and disseminate images of Tahiti. The consistency of their intent and the forthrightness with which they discuss their motivation is remarkable. Teva, like his father, wants to help other men find a Tahitian woman, even if she only exists on a postcard or on the pages of a calendar. In perpetuating his father's dream, he encourages others to hold onto their dreams as well. Several times he emphasized how important it is to "keep the myth alive."

For the past two centuries, and until recently, the découpage and montage of images of Tahiti and Tahitians for the world at large has mainly been by the French, Americans, and demi. Although the motives for producing seductive Tahitian imagery have increased in economic and political complexity, the images have remained unimaginatively similar from Bougainville's revised verbal descriptions to Teva's touched-up "Tahitians." What happens, though, when the production of images is removed from this sphere and put, instead, into the hands of Tahitians, themselves also part of the larger entangled dialogue about Tahiti? What happens when the turquoise veil of paradise is lifted and, instead, unexpected, more realistic, and potentially negative images are revealed and disseminated around the world? Examining such a situation sheds further light on just how integral to the colonial agenda these images and image fragments are, and how enmeshed Tahitian identities become in these representations.

## THE EVENTS OF SEPTEMBER 6, 1995

On June 13, 1995, French president Jacques Chirac ended former president François Mitterand's moratorium on nuclear testing by declaring that he would resume testing before the end of the year. The rationale was that additional tests would allow for the perfection of simulation and computer modeling techniques. Within days of President Chirac's announcement, antinuclear protesting began on a scale that was unprecedented in the history of French Polynesia, spreading to all major islands. International media responded swiftly. Journalists, television crews, and radio reporters from all over the world swarmed to Tahiti. Greenpeace's antinuclear ship, the *Rainbow Warrior II* (the original *Rainbow Warrior* had been blown up by French agents in Auckland in July 1985, killing one crew member), left New Zealand for Tahiti with an international crew representing ten different countries.

A record number of protesters (15,000–20,000 by some accounts) took to the streets in Papeete on June 29, demanding a referendum on the resumption of nuclear testing. These particular protests were initiated by Oscar Temaru, who was the mayor of Faa'a as

well as the leader of Tavini Huira'atira, the proindependence party. People, many of whom carried ukuleles, sat down in the streets. Traffic came to a halt. Papeete was paralyzed (Gluckman 1995). Protesters set up a blockade along the main access roads to the city, which lasted until July 2, the twenty-ninth anniversary of the first nuclear test at Moruroa. In the words of one crew member on board the *Rainbow Warrior II*, "The commitment of the people is amazing—sitting all day through 35 degree [centigrade] heat, and then sleeping on hard asphalt all night" (Leney 1995). Protests again erupted on July 14, which coincided with the French holiday of Bastille Day and the height of Tahiti's annual Heiva (a month-long festival that features dancing, singing, and sporting competitions, arts and crafts, beauty contests, feasting, and partying). The protests were so disruptive that they caused the festivities to be postponed by a week.

Because of near universal moral opposition to nuclear testing in the 1990s, as well as the media's aggressive coverage of the situation, the entire world was suddenly listening and responding. People burned croissants and stomped on French bread in the United States, picketed French restaurants in Hong Kong, bombed one French consulate and delivered a truck load of manure to another in Australia, demonstrated in Chile, and held an antinuclear rock concert in Belgium (Gluckman 1995). Even in France, former president Mitterand publicly condemned President Chirac's decision to resume testing. Yet, in spite of local and global protesting, the governments of both France and French Polynesia remained unresponsive.

Instead, President Flosse invited political leaders, including Oscar Temaru (who refused to go), to a "picnic" on Moruroa July 16–18. A few days later, *La Dépêche de Tahiti*, the main newspaper in French Polynesia, printed a two-page spread about Moruroa and Fangataufa with the headline "Fish from the Lagoon Are Delicious." The article included photos of government officials drinking coconuts, catching tuna, and posing in front of fifty barbecued lobsters. Most prominent was a photo of President Flosse taking a relaxing dip in Moruroa's lagoon.

In August, several more, but somewhat smaller, peaceful protest marches took place in Papeete. The largest was organized by the Église Évangélique de Polynésie Française,[20] whose president, Jacques Ihorai, prayed for an end to the testing. As September approached, the month in which the nuclear tests were scheduled to begin, again hundreds of journalists from all over the world arrived in French Polynesia.

At 11:30 on the morning of September 5, 1995, without prior public warning, "operation thetis" was carried out at Moruroa. The explosion was almost as large as that at Hiroshima, generating temperatures of several hundred million degrees and pressures of several million atmospheres. The instruments recording the explosion transmitted data for only a billionth of a second before they were destroyed by the blast (Sancton 1995:27).

That night, on the television news, a crowd of reporters fired questions at the Director of CEP, Admiral Jean Lichère, who appeared in his crisp white naval uniform bedecked with medals. He explained matter-of-factly that at 11:30 he had received orders from Paris to push the button. He said that there had been no noise, just a minor shaking of the ground for three seconds, some slight agitation in the sea with waves and geysers, and then everything was calm and "back to normal." He explained that the test was "for the stability of the world, to insure security for everyone," and declared that "it will have no significant impact on the environment." When asked by the angry reporters why he didn't test the bomb in France, he responded with the standard phrase, "But this is France!" He then deflected further inquiries by claiming, "One can't even call this a bomb. It's nuclear physics."

Although the Moruroa lagoon gradually quieted down, the explosion sent lasting waves of rage and indignation throughout French Polynesia and the world at large. The following day, thirty-six hours of uninterrupted rioting, burning, and looting erupted in Papeete and nearby Faa'a.[21] It started when about thirty Tahitian women began an

antinuclear sit-in on the airport runway and gathered momentum when several hundred Tahitian men joined in (Strokirch 1997:228). When police fired tear gas into the crowd, the confrontation escalated. Protesters drove a bulldozer through the airport, demolishing internal walls and shattering windows, before setting fire to the terminal building, making it unsafe for commercial planes to land or take off for several days. After wrecking the airport, the demonstrators moved into downtown Papeete, torching buildings, smashing store windows, and looting the stores. More than 120 cars were overturned and set afire. Stones, steel barricades, garbage bins, and bottles were thrown at the high commissioner's office. Police tried to surround and arrest the demonstrators, many of whom were thrown in jail. Additional military were brought in from France and New Caledonia. Miraculously, only forty people were injured, although damage was estimated at around four billion CFP (US$40 million).

A phrase that was often used in the media during this explosive period was that the images of the riots had "gone on world tour." And, indeed, they had. For example, the words "Fallout in Paradise" graced the cover of the international edition of *Time* magazine (September 18, 1995). The cover story featured photographs of Tahitian demonstrators kicking and clubbing a French policeman who lay writhing on the ground. The government blamed foreign reporters for the worldwide dissemination of these "ugly" images. Not only was their distribution out of government control, but the images themselves were in complete contrast to what the French government wanted the world to see. News reporters' photos that traveled out into the world—pictures of men throwing rocks, torching buildings, and clubbing policemen—were a far cry from the pictures of paradise that for centuries had been purposefully created and circulated. And, what was striking about them, in contrast to the beautiful, peaceful, feminine images, was that they had greater universal appeal. They were of angry, and completely ordinary, people. Although the government found no need to respond earlier to the relatively peaceful protests and blockades, they responded now with great agitation to these war zone images. Indeed, as this profusion of images spun out of their control, government officials attempted to suppress their production. The senior reporter for RFO (the television station) described the government's deliberate political tactics.

> I was at the airport when it was burning. I and others were evacuated from the scene and taken back to Papeete. When I got there I wanted to take my camera and go into town to film the burning of Papeete for television. Instead, RFO forbid me from going. They decided to shut down the office at 8 PM. This was unprecedented. That decision was one hundred percent political. (Erick Monod, personal communication, 1995)

## MISSILES OF DEATH IN THEIR MOTHER'S WOMB

During the following weeks and months, a battle escalated over the control of image manipulation. Exactly one week after the events of September 6, *La Dépêche de Tahiti* made direct reference to an image problem by featuring, on the front page, a picture of a postcard, jaggedly ripped in two, with the main headline "The Postcard Has Been Torn." Below the picture was a caption that juxtaposed symbols of French wealth against visions of Third World poverty.

> Good-bye calf, cow, pig, and brood [a French idiom for wealth] . . . after the world-wide reporting about the riots, television stations created an image of a shantytown. These images make Tahiti look worse than Rio or Haiti. Visitors obviously canceled their vacations *en masse*. The foreign media's orchestration of the problems and certain journalists' manipulation of the events are complete. (*La Dépêche de Tahiti,* September 13, 1995, front page)

Ironically, a cleverly crafted countermanipulation of the situation by French-controlled media, such as RFO and *La Dépêche de Tahiti,* was just heating up. Whereas the nuclear test on September 5 had received minimal media coverage, the demonstrators' reaction on September 6 launched a media explosion. A special twenty-page supplement in *La Dépêche de Tahiti* appeared with the ominous headline "Black Wednesday in Tahiti". Page after page featured images of charred buildings, shattered glass, dismembered store mannequins lying in the streets, Tahitians hurling rocks, Tahitians lighting fires, and police with weapons. Alongside the photos were captions such as "Airline companies, travel agencies, and hotels are all powerless as tourists shun our destination!" (1995a). The same images that had been "manipulated" by foreign media to show the world the ugly side of paradise were now used by government-controlled media to threaten Tahitians into submission.

Yet, there seemed to be a feeling of empowerment on the part of many Tahitians when projecting their own images and identities out to the world. Unlike previous images produced by outsiders of a romanticized Tahiti, these images were truly of Tahitians as they experienced their world. They allowed a voice that was otherwise silenced to be heard. As one man said, "The riots may not be the best way for us to express ourselves, but when we tried peaceful marches, no one listened. The French express themselves powerfully with their bomb. Now we are speaking and being heard" (Hiti Gooding, personal communication, 1995).

The riots were not the only form of communication. Another, less-visual, Tahitian way of expressing the denunciation of nuclear testing, and of French politics in general, was in the compositions (solely in the Tahitian language) of Tahitian songwriters and singers.[22] Angélo Neuffer Ari'itai, one of the leading singers for the younger generation, released a cassette at this time. The words to one song, "Atomic Poison," juxtapose images of a destructive bomb with those of an otherwise nourishing land.

> The land is poisoned, the people are poisoned, the sea is poisoned,
> As is the language of our leaders, who claim that the bomb is not harmful.

The air is poisoned, the fruits of the land are
poisoned, the children are poisoned,
As is the conscience of those who lie, claiming
that the bomb is not harmful.
Atomic bomb, we don't want you.
You are unwelcome here, on this island, in
this land.
Atomic bomb, we don't want our land to be
polluted.
Atomic bomb, we don't want death here, on
this island, in this land.
Atomic bomb, go away from here, from this
island, from this land.

After the first bomb, there was another
peaceful march, organized once more by the
Église Évangélique de Polynésie Française
and led by its president, Jacques Ihorai. Songs
(such as the one above), prayers, and silences
were used to try and sway the government.
The church became a powerful, unifying
voice of protest against nuclear testing.[23] In
late September, Jacques Ihorai and Ralph
Teinaore, the secretary general of the church,
flew to France to try and convince President
Chirac to cease the testing. Ihorai declared
that France did not have the right to explode
bombs in the nourishing womb of the motherland. Using an image he evoked often, even
when speaking to Tahitian audiences, he explained that Tahitians consider the land to
be their mother who nourishes them and
that the bomb is like a missile of death in
their mother's womb (*La Dépêche de Tahiti*
1995b:21). Even though Tahitians generally
had shown little concern about the mythical,
touristic images of Tahiti, they reacted pas-
sionately when others' behavior violated their
own notion of place. When bombs were
lodged and exploded deep within their land,
it was their sense of place and identity that was
profoundly disturbed. Precisely because land
is seen as nourishing—a place to bury the placenta of a child—the burying of a bomb in
the land seemed a particularly offensive assault. When Ihorai compared the nuclear testing to the lodging of a missile in their
mother's womb, he spoke about a Tahitian
experience of place in a way that postcards
and guidebooks never do.

Soon thereafter, on Sunday, October 1, at
1:30 in the afternoon, the second bomb was
exploded. The detonation had been carefully
timed to coincide with the hour when most
Tahitians would be in church, a subtle attack
on the church's peaceful but powerful antinuclear stance. This time the television coverage
was quick and efficient, surgically and cyni-
cally wedged between two items of minor
interest. There were no riots.[24]

As time went on and more tests occurred,
the numbers of tourists kept dropping,
especially among Japanese and Americans.
By November, hotels that usually had
80–100 percent occupancy had 10–20 percent. The large Nara Hotel on Bora Bora,
which depended on Japanese tourism, was almost empty.[25] Whereas previously there had
been two weekly flights from Tokyo, now
there was one with only a handful of passengers. Tahiti had slipped from turquoise Technicolor to black and gray.

## "EVERYTHING IS ALL RIGHT AGAIN"

As nuclear tests continued on the average of
one a month for five months, the anxiety intensified for those people who were well
entrenched in an economic system that
depended on tourism-generated income.
Tourism suddenly became a rallying cry and
political lever. In an interview about the
decline of tourism, Patrick Robson from the
Office of Tourism said, "The cancellations
are surely due to the riots [not the nuclear
tests].... Step by step, we will launch a campaign to replace our image that was shattered" (*La Dépêche de Tahiti* 1995a:24). The
campaign to manipulate the images was calculated and unabashed.

Gilles Tefaatau, the supervisor of airport
operations and the president of GIE Animation, the branch of the Office of Tourism that
oversees tourist activities within French Polynesia, explained that after the tests were over
in January 1996, there would be a massive
campaign to recapture the market. "The reason tourism is down is because people saw
pictures of rioting and burning. In order to
rid them of these images, we need to replace

these with new, positive images" (Gilles Tefaatau, personal communication, 1995). Suzanne Lau-Chonfont, the supervisor of statistics at the Office of Tourism, focused on the overseas marketing strategies. "Now, because of the riots and nuclear tests, there is a conscious change in marketing. In an attempt to capture those people who canceled their reservations, there will be counter-marketing that will show positive images and will try to communicate the message that everything is all right again ... and that nothing happened" (Suzanne Lau-Chonfont, personal communication, 1995).

At about the same time, a promotional campaign with a budget of 545 million CFP (US$5.45 million) was launched in France to offer tourists "the most beautiful present in the world—Tahiti." A French singer, Antoine, was to "come to the rescue." He was slotted for 250 radio spots, all day long, seven days a week, for several weeks. Through seductive song, he would ask people to join him in Tahiti, emphasizing the legendary Tahitian hospitality, the charm and beauty of the natural environment, and the profusion and quality of tourist activities. Tahiti was to become "the pearl of the Pacific."

President Flosse participated energetically in the campaign. Imagining a Polynesian landscape populated with French personalities, he denounced the protesters as "those who want to fade the colors of Gauguin, extinguish the voice of Jacques Brel, and obliterate the memory of Paul-Émile Victor" (Didier 1995:21). He said, "We want our visitors to know that Polynesia offers itself to them. ... We are proud to have succeeded in uniting the natural attraction of the South Seas with the security of the western world ... the object of the present campaign is to make this better known" (Didier 1995:21). As part of his long-term plan he purchased a new luxury 320-passenger cruise ship to tour the Society Islands, and named it the *MS Paul Gauguin*. It was launched in 1998 and advertised as taking tourists to "worlds so breathtaking even the word paradise seems inadequate" (magazine advertisement by Radisson Seven Seas Cruises, 1998).[26]

Although the French saw tourism and its "new" marketing images as coming to the rescue, the view of tourism is quite different from the perspective of most Tahitians. As with much else, their response to tourism is, and always has been, filtered through their understanding of land. Tourism has taken their land, destroyed their fishing grounds, and tapped into water sources without providing much in return.[27] They express their outrage through the legal system where, in Papeete, for example, one-third of all court cases pertain to land (Tetiarahi 1987:46). They also communicate their frustration and anger in symbolic actions that speak about, and through, land. For example, Tahitians have refused to sell land that provides access routes to hotels, have blocked hotel water sources, and have even burned down hotels. One of the fanciest tourist accommodations on Huahine, built on prime land and along favored fishing grounds, ignored and rebuffed local residents. When the manager wanted to import staff from France, food from Papeete, and souvenir shell necklaces from the Philippines, Tahitians spoke through land, a powerful force that cannot easily be ignored. As tourists were driven in the hotel van to their $500 per night overwater bungalows, they bounced painfully into gaping potholes in a dirt road that provided the only land access to the hotel. The Tahitian owners of the land quietly refused to maintain it. The same hotel forbid Tahitians from walking on the hotel grounds. When one woman and her friend were asked to leave, she responded, "No, this is our land, not yours. We belong here, not you. You're the one who has to leave" (Turia Gooding, personal communication, 1995).

## TAHITIAN IDENTITIES

Foucault, Lefebvre, and Soja have all theorized about space and how spaces combine numerous contradictions and ambiguities that, when understood together, generate a complex thirdspace within which human identities evolve. Here, following their lead, I have explored Tahiti as a place that embraces such ambiguities that underlie human identities. I have examined a wide range of beliefs, representations, and events, as well as ways in which they intersect and interact. The list includes elements as seemingly diverse as ancient chants: postcards; the imprisonment of Pouvanaa a Oopa; colonial changes in a land tenure system; a Hollywood film; peaceful protests; eighteenth- and nineteenth-century European imagery of the South Pacific; rioting, burning, and looting; the lyrics of an antinuclear song; the Office of Tourism's marketing strategies; land claims in court; cruise ships; beliefs about placentas and umbilical cords; Gauguin; potholes; a nuclear testing program; and much more.

Only when eluding the politics of polarity and examining various realms together do the details shed light on a lived, or third, space that is generated from the dialectic, the set of relations in which people live. Indeed, all realms involve, underpin, presuppose, generate, influence, and expand upon one another. Exploring the relationship and tension between local understandings of place and dominant, mass-mediated representations allows for the emergence of a thirdspace that is both real and imaginary, immediate and mediated. Whether quietly coexisting, or violently colliding, local Tahitian perspectives and global political agendas are not separate, independently operating realms. They are in constant, daily, intertwined dialogue. For example, visual representations create a meta-language that, while speaking to the world at large, discourages local inhabitants from participating in the discourse. Yet, local voices have their own powerful modes of communicating and, with access to the media, may even end up as a media centerpiece.

Tahitians, on the whole, do not communicate their feelings and ideas about their place and their identity with images of turquoise lagoons or bare-breasted women on postcards and in guidebooks.[28] Instead, they communicate in nonvisual ways that are rooted in a reciprocal relationship with land. They take pride in ancient chants about the historical importance of land. They think about burying their babies' placentas in the earth to en-

sure their child's well-being. They research their land rights and go to court to file land claims. And when their senses of place and of self are threatened, they speak eloquently. They respond with petition signatures, protest marches, popular songs, purposeful potholes, and, when all else fails, a fire set to a hotel, an airport, or even the capital city. All of these acts communicate unmistakably, as one woman said in words, "This is our land, not yours." Or, this is who *we* (not you) are.

In contrast, the meta-language that speaks to the world at large speaks with a somewhat forked tongue. Idealized representations speak past Tahitians in a language of visual imagery that means little to the local population. But, at the same time, these images speak to, and profoundly impact, Tahitians' daily lives and senses of self. Tahiti as paradise is *not* a benign image. Indeed, the confining walls on which the images are traced and retraced create a claustrophobic enclosure of another sort for Tahitians. Although these images were first created by romantic imaginations to transport Europeans to another world, they soon became willfully employed as a political and economic tool to serve colonial agendas, to attract tourists and their money in order to support the ruling class, and to distract the world from noticing nuclear atrocities. By now they have become an integral and indispensable component of French Polynesia's political economy, and of Tahitian identity as well.

It is clearly the case in French Polynesia that representations of place are enmeshed in politics, and that human identities are ensnared in the politics of representation. One is "never outside representation—or rather outside its politics" (Foster 1983:xv). Images may become weapons of sorts, used to beguile, blind, pacify, incite, injure, or control. While superficially seeming to reveal one place, images may, in fact, serve to conceal a different place. Postcards of bare breasts distract attention from nuclear tests. Guidebook photos of colorful fish darting in crystalline water keep one from noticing government clean-up crews who dispose of trash by shoveling it into the sea.

Tahitians, such as those in Fetuna or Faie, of course, do not live in picturesque ways that match up with touristic representations of Tahiti (see Cizeron and Hienly 1983). Today, only a few years after the events described in this article, people in Fetuna and Faie still go about their daily lives much as before. Garbage is still plowed into the sea in Fetuna. Tourists are still brought to see the eels in Faie. Yet, the thirdspace that emerges at the intersection of global politics, mass media, and local beliefs is where Tahitians, in both Fetuna and Faie, live their social life on a daily basis and gain a sense of who they are. For example, the events of September 1995 allowed Tahitians to be heard more clearly than ever before. Nuclear testing generated antinuclear protesting. Ugly images infiltrated the world. The government panicked and took measures that enraged Tahitians even more. Today, there is an increasing Tahitian involvement in pro-independence politics. As France's international power is challenged and its "empire" shrinks, the remaining cards France holds—including Tahiti—assume heightened importance. The recent *force de frappe* of France as a declining world power in the mid-1990s contrasts sharply with, but at the same time opens a space for, a greater desire for independence in France's dependent territory.

The Tahitian thirdspace that has emerged in this discussion supports the idea that space can no longer be seen as a fixed entity, or even as an entity that is explainable from one or another point of view. Instead, as Lefebvre has concluded, space might better be seen as a medium, a milieu, or an intermediary.

Space has now become something more than the theatre, the disinterested stage or setting, of action. Space can no longer be looked upon as an "essence," as an object distinct from the point of view of "subjects," as answering to a logic of its own. Is space a medium? A milieu? An intermediary? It is doubtless all of these, but its role is less and less neutral, more and more active, both as instrument and as goal, as means and as end. The production of space is a generative process, with variations, pluralities and multiplicities, disparities, disjunctions, imbalances, conflicts and contradictions. (Lefebvre 1991[1974]:410–411)

Tahiti, as we have seen, is all of these. Tahiti comprises overlapping and often contradictory fields of experience, representation, and intervention. It is a complex and interwoven, dynamic and intertwined, historical and spatial process. It is within this space, both rooted in ancestral land and enmeshed in global representations, that Tahitian identities are placed.

## ACKNOWLEDGMENTS

Research in French Polynesia was conducted over a ten-month period during three trips in 1994, 1995, and 1996. I thank the Fulbright Program, the Max and Lotte Heine Philanthropic Fund, and the American Philosophical Society for having made the research financially possible. In French Polynesia many friends facilitated my work, most notably the families of Edouard and Kim Tai Piha, Hiti and Turia Gooding, Peto and Mariette Firuu, and Dorothy Levy. I am also grateful to Teva Sylvain, Erick Monod, Gilles Tefaatau, Suzanne Lau-Chonfont, and Eric Laroche for their assistance. My husband, Richard L. Taylor, not only accompanied me to the field but helped in the gathering of data as well as with the formulation of my ideas. An earlier draft of this chapter benefited greatly from the comments of Oscar Barrera-Nunez, Stevan Harrell, Michael Herzfeld, Jocelyn Linnekin, Elizabeth Notar, Margaret Rodman, Bruno Saura, Maureen Schwarz, Kathleen Stewart, and anonymous reviewers. This chapter is a slight modification of an article that appeared under a different title in the *American Anthropologist*. Reproduced by permission of the American Anthropological Association from *American Anthropologist* 102:1. Not for sale or further reproduction.

## NOTES

1. Other scholars, like bell hooks and Homi Bhabha, also use the term thirdspace but do so in slightly different ways. Bell hooks (1990) chooses a marginal space that is the location of radical possibility, a space one comes to through struggle. Bhabha (1990, 1994) uses the term for spaces of resistance and firmly rooted in the experience of postcolonialism.

2. Some scholars have recently tried to understand places from the perspectives of their inhabitants, noting that places are developed interactively as individuals relate to them, shape them, and create them. They have connected places to social imagination and practice, to dwelling and movement, and to memory and desire (Feld and Basso 1996:8, 11). Focusing on the internally constructed and negotiated nature of place, anthropologists have produced a variety of new descriptive phrases to debunk the old notion of location as static backdrop. These newly perceived spaces are said to be "discursively constructed" (Appadurai 1988), "multilocal" and "multivocal" (Rodman 1992), unconfined "ethnoscapes" (Gupta and Ferguson 1992), and "dynamic multisensual processes" (Hirsch and O'Hanlon 1995).

3. See, for example, Claessen 1994; Daws 1980; Day 1986; Despoix 1996; Margueron 1989; Nicole 1993; Rennie 1995; Ritz 1983; Smith 1960, 1992.

4. The situation in Tahiti is far from a simplified opposition of French versus Tahitian. As Panoff (1989) states, there is extensive genetic and cultural crossbreeding within the population. Whether one refers to oneself as French, demi, Chinese, Tahitian, Ma'ohi (the Tahitian word for a native person), and so on is only loosely related to genetic make-up. Instead, it can be a political statement. The terms "French" or "demi," on the one hand, equate roughly with those who are upper class. The terms "Tahitian" or "Ma'ohi," on the other hand, usually refer to people who are lower class. Politics, not only genetics, can determine one's outlook. It is not uncommon, for example, to find someone whose mother or father is 100 percent French, and who not only refers to himself as Tahitian but even refuses to speak French or eat French food.

5. Other, but less recent, figures have been considerably lower (see Henningham 1992:155; Aldrich 1993:114; and Bresson 1993:27 for figures from the late 1980s).

6. See Chesneaux (1991), who sees France as a mid-sized world power trying to create itself as a major world power. To describe France's deployment as "colonialism," he says, misses the point.

7. According to Spitz (1991), demi are politically more dangerous than the French because, unlike the French, they are there to stay.

8. See Feld (1996) and Kahn (1996) for other Pacific Island examples.

9. Throughout this chapter, all information that I received in Tahitian or French, whether by interviewing individuals or seeing or hearing information in the media, has been translated into English. The translations are my own.

10. In 1966, some 37,300 tourists visited Tahiti and in 1971 there were close to 78,000 (Aldrich 1993:88). Each succeeding year, for the next few years, witnessed dramatic increases in the number of tourists, most of whom were Americans.

11. Recently, tourism has generated 23 billion CFP a year (US$230 million). Tourism has an annual budget of 800 million CFP (US$8 million), of which 500 million CFP is spent on promotion, advertising, and marketing. The remaining 300 million CFP is for personnel. The tourism industry employs 8,000 people, 32 of whom work directly for the Office of Tourism. (Suzanne Lau-Chonfont, personal communication, 1995; Gilles Tefaatau, personal communication, 1995).

12. Most Tahitians, as well as people opposed to the use of the atoll for French nuclear testing, still refer to it as Moruroa.

13. France was not the only nation to test in the Pacific. Americans carried out a massive nuclear testing program on Bikini and Enewetak atolls in the northern Marshall Islands of Micronesia from 1946 to 1958 (see Kiste 1972; Gusterson 1996).

14. CFP stands for "cour franc pacifique," a monetary unit created in 1945, the value of which is fixed to the French franc. 1 FF = 18,1818 CFP.

15. See Lockwood (1993) for a discussion of this form of financial benevolence on the island of Tubuai in French Polynesia.

16. Food imports rose from 37 percent in 1960 to 80 percent in 1989 (Henningham 1992:263).

17. According to French law, previous written permission is needed for commercial production of a picture of a person.

18. Picture postcards, as a form of cheap communication for the masses, first appeared in the 1880s and 1890s. The most popular story of their origin traces their appearance to the 1889 Universal Exhibition in Paris (Staff 1966; Geary and Webb 1998), the same colonial event that fired Gauguin's imagination.

19. Teva employs models, thus circumventing the French law that restricts the Office of Tourism from using images of people.

20. L'Église Évangélique de Polynésie Française, which has been independent since 1963, is the most popular church in French Polynesia, with about two-thirds of Tahitians being members. Its name, in English, is glossed as the Protestant Church, as distinguished from the Catholic Church.

21. Riots had also occurred in late 1983 (triggered by a hotel workers strike) and in October 1987 (resulting from a dock workers strike). The 1987 riots, in particular, left Papeete looking like a war zone and resulted in the declaration of a state of emergency. "Several dozen shops and businesses were damaged or looted, and eight buildings were destroyed by fire, at an estimated cost of several million Australian dollars" (Henningham 1992:154).

22. See Saura (1999) for his interpretation of these popular songs as a uniquely Tahitian discourse that combines political activism with a spiritual quest.

23. The church took an active role in the protest to communicate that, in contrast to Tavini Huira'atira's

political position, the church kept the antinuclear movement separate from the proindependence movement.

24. By this time many of the protesters were in jail. Tahitians often joked that if tourists wanted to see the "real Tahiti" they should visit the jail.

25. The Japanese were particularly outspoken in their opposition to the nuclear testing as they marked the fiftieth anniversary of the bombing of Hiroshima and Nagasaki in September 1995.

26. Tourists on the *MS Paul Gauguin* explain their cruise choice with phrases like, "We came to sample paradise" and "We wanted to share Paul Gauguin's vision" (Costello 2001:10).

27. See Kent (1993) and Trask (1993) for a similar interpretation of tourism in Hawai'i—as an extension of colonialism.

28. Those who are involved in the tourism industry, of course, perpetuate touristic images on a daily basis. Others, who support themselves through the craft industry, create objects such as wooden carvings, decorated pearl shells, and *pareu* (colorful cloths that are worn around the body in various styles) that likewise utilize images tourists crave.

## REFERENCES

Aldrich, Robert. 1993. *France and the South Pacific Since 1940*. Honolulu: University of Hawai'i.

Appadurai, Arjun. 1988. "Introduction: Place and Voice in Anthropological Theory." *Cultural Anthropology* 3(1):16–20.

Baston, Guillaume A. R. 1790. *Narrations d'Omai, Insulaire de la Mer du Sud, Ami et Compagnon de Voyage du Capitaine Cook*. Rouen: Chez Le Boucher Le Jeune.

Benchley, Peter. 1997. "Charting a New Course: French Polynesia." *National Geographic* 191(6):2–29.

Bensa, Alban. 1995. *Chroniques Kanak: L'Ethnologie en Marche*. Paris: Floch.

Bhabha, Homi K. 1990. "The Third Space." In *Identity, Community, Culture, Difference*. J. Rutherford, ed. Pp. 201–207. London: Lawrence and Wishart.

———. 1994. *The Location of Culture*. New York: Routledge.

Bougainville, Louis-Antoine de. 1772[1771]. *A Voyage Round the World*. Johann R. Forster, translator. London: J. Nourse.

Bresson, Louis. 1993. *Tourisme: L'Anti-Crise*. Papeete: Pacific Promotion Tahiti S.A.

Chesneaux, Jean. 1991. "The Function of the Pacific in the French Fifth Republic's 'Grand Design.'" *Journal of Pacific History* 26(2):256–272.

Cizeron, Marc, and Marianne Hienly. 1983. *Tahiti: Côte Montagne*. Papeete: Haere Po No Tahiti.

Claessen, Henri J. M. 1994. "Tahiti and the Early European Visitors." In *European Imagery and Colonial History in the Pacific*. T. van Meijl and P. van der Grijp, eds. Vol. 19. Pp. 14–31. Nijmegen Studies in Development and Cultural Change.

Clark, Thomas Blake. 1941. *Omai, First Polynesian Ambassador to England*. San Francisco: Colt.

Costello, Ann. 2001. "Running Away to Tahiti." *The New York Times*. Section 5. February 4, 2001:10–11.

Danielsson, Bengt, and Marie-Thérèse Danielsson. 1986. *Poisoned Reign: French Nuclear Colonialism in the Pacific*. New York: Penguin.

Danielsson, Marie-Thérèse. 1986. "Pacific: The Nuclear Colonization of the Pacific—Especially French Polynesia." *IWGIA Newsletter*, Copenhagen, No. 45.

Daws, Gavan. 1980. *A Dream of Islands: Voyages of Self-Discovery in the South Seas*. Honolulu: Mutual.

Day, A. Grove, ed. 1986. *The Lure of Tahiti*. Honolulu: Mutual.

Despoix, Philippe. 1996. "Naming and Exchange in the Exploration of the Pacific: On European Representations of Polynesian Culture in Late XVIII Century." In *Multiculturalism and Representation*. J. Rieder and L. E. Smith, eds. Pp. 3–24. Honolulu: University of Hawai'i.

Didier, Chantal. 1995. "Pour Relancer le Tourisme en Polynésie: Promotion de 545 Millions CFP!" *La Dépêche de Tahiti*, November 30, 1995:21.

Feld, Steven. 1996. "Waterfalls of Place: An Acoustemology of Place Resounding in Bosavi, Papua New Guinea." In *Senses of Place*. Steven Feld and Keith Basso, eds. Pp. 91–135. Santa Fe: School of American Research.

Feld, Steven, and Keith Basso, eds. 1996. *Senses of Place*. Santa Fe: School of American Research.

Foster, Hal. 1983. "Postmodernism: A Preface." In *The Anti-Aesthetic: Essays on Postmodern Culture*. Hal Foster, ed. Pp. ix–xvi. Seattle: Bay.

Foucault, Michel. 1980[1976]. "Questions on Geography." In *Power/Knowledge*. Colin Gordon, ed. Pp. 63–77. New York: Pantheon.

———. 1980[1977]. "The Eye of Power." In *Power/Knowledge*. Colin Gordon, ed. Pp. 146–165. New York: Pantheon.

———. 1986. "Of Other Spaces." *Diacritics* 16:22–27.

Geary, Christraud, and Virginia-Lee Webb, eds. 1998. *Delivering Views: Distant Cultures in Early Postcards*. Washington, D.C.: Smithsonian.

Giradet, Raoul. 1972. *L'Idée Coloniale en France, 1871–1962*. Paris: La Table Ronde.

Gluckman, Ron. 1995. "No Boom Boom Here." *Asiaweek*. Vol. 21. August 1995.

Gupta, Akhil, and James Ferguson. 1992. "Beyond 'Culture': Space, Identity, and the Politics of Difference." *Cultural Anthropology* 7(1):6–23.

Gusterson, Hugh. 1996. *Nuclear Rites*. Berkeley: University of California.

Henningham, Stephen. 1992. *France and the South Pacific*. Honolulu: University of Hawai'i.

Hirsch, Eric, and Michael O'Hanlon, eds. 1995. *The An-thropology of Landscape: Perspectives on Space and Place.* Oxford: Clarendon.

hooks, bell. 1990. *Yearning.* Boston: South End Press.

Jameson, Fredric. 1983. "Postmodernism and Consumer Society." In *The Anti-Aesthetic: Essays on Postmodern Culture.* Hal Foster, ed. Pp. 111–125. Seattle: Bay.

Kahn, Miriam. 1996. "Your Place and Mine: Sharing Emotional Landscapes in Wamira, Papua New Guinea." In *Senses of Place.* Steven Feld and Keith Basso, eds. Pp. 167–196. Santa Fe: School of American Research.

———. 2000. "Tahiti Intertwined: Ancestral Land, Tourist Postcard, and Nuclear Test Site." *American Anthropologist* 102(1):7–26.

Kay, Robert. 1997. *Hidden Tahiti.* Berkeley: Ulysses.

Kent, Noel J. 1993. *Hawai'i: Islands Under the Influence.* Honolulu: University of Hawai'i.

Kiste, Robert. 1972. "Relocation and Technological Change in Micronesia." In *Technology and Social Change.* H. Russell Bernard and Pertti Pelto, eds. Pp. 72–107. New York: Macmillan.

*La Dépêche de Tahiti.* 1995a. "Retombées des Émeutes: Le Tourisme Sinistré." *La Dépêche de Tahiti.* September 13, 1995:22–25.

———. 1995b. "Jacques Ihorai Inquiet par l'Argent des Essais." *La Dépêche de Tahiti.* September 27, 1995:21.

Lefebvre, Henri. 1991[1974]. *The Production of Space.* Donald Nicholson-Smith, translator Oxford: Blackwell.

Leney, Alice. 1995. Internet Diary from the Crew of the Rainbow Warrior. June 29, 1995. http://gopher.greenpeace.org

Lockwood, Victoria. 1993. *Tahitian Transformations: Gender and Capitalist Development in a Rural Society.* Boulder, Colo.: Lynne Rienner.

Maligne, Maurice, ed. 1949. *Paul Gauguin: Letters to His Wife and Friends.* Cleveland: World Publishing.

Margueron, Daniel. 1989. *Tahiti Dans Toute Sa Litterature.* Paris: Éditions L'Harmattan.

McCormick, Eric Hall. 1977. *Omai: Pacific Envoy.* Auckland: Auckland University.

Newbury, Colin. 1980. *Tahiti Nui: Change and Survival in French Polynesia, 1767–1945.* Honolulu: University of Hawai'i.

Nicole, Robert. 1993. "Images of Paradise." In *Last Virgin in Paradise.* V. Hereniko and T. Teaiwa, eds. Pp. 59–64. Suva, Fiji: Mana Publications.

Panoff, Michel. 1989. *Tahiti Metisse.* Paris: Éditions Denoël.

Perloff, Nancy. 1995. "Gauguin's French Baggage: Decadence and Colonialism in Tahiti." In *Prehistories of the Future.* E. Barkan and R. Bush, eds. Pp. 226–269. Stanford: Stanford University.

Price, Richard. 1998. *The Convict and the Colonel.* Boston: Beacon Press.

Raapoto, Jean-Marius. 1994. "'Utuafare' et 'Opu': Contradiction ou complémentarité? Les concepts de "utuafare" et "opu" au sein du groupe humain de base de la société traditionnelle ma'ohi: Leurs fonctions réciproques dans la vie du groupe. Questions de Familles: Quels liens possibles avec la tradition en Polynésie?" Papeete: Deuxièmes Journées de Recherche de l'A.P.R.I.F. 15–16 Avril.

Rennie, Neil. 1995. *Far-Fetched Facts: The Literature of Travel and the Idea of the South Seas.* Oxford: Clarendon.

Ritz, Hans. 1983. *Die Sehnsucht Nach der Südsee: Bericht über Einen Europäischer Mythos.* Göttingen: Muriverlag.

Rodman, Margaret. 1992. "Empowering Place: Multilocality and Multivocality." *American Anthropologist* 94:640–656.

Salmon, Tati. 1904. *The History of the Island of Borabora and Genealogy of Our Family from Marae Vaiotaha.* Papeete: Privately printed.

Sancton, Thomas. 1995. "Fallout in Paradise." *Time (International).* September 18, 1995:22–27.

Saura, Bruno. 1999. "The Emergence of an Ethnic Millenarian Thinking, and the Development of Nationalism in Tahiti." *Pacific Studies* 21(3).

Smith, Bernard. 1960. *European Vision of the South Pacific: 1768–1850.* Oxford: Oxford University.

———. 1992. *Imagining the Pacific: In the Wake of the Cook Voyages.* New Haven, Conn.: Yale University.

Soja, Edward M. 1989. *Postmodern Geographies.* London: Verso.

———. 1996. *Thirdspace: Journeys to Los Angeles and Other Real-and-Imagined Places.* Oxford: Blackwell.

Spitz, Chantal. 1991. *L'île des Rêves Écrasés.* Papeete: Éditions de la Plage.

Staff, Frank. 1966. *The Picture Postcard and Its Origins.* New York: Praeger.

Strokirch, Karin von. 1997. "French Polynesia." *The Contemporary Pacific* 9(1):227–233.

Sylvain, Teva. 1994. *La Légende des Filles des Mers du Sud.* Tahiti: Pacific Promotion Tahiti S.A.

Taillemite, Étienne. 1977. *Bougainville et Ses Compagnons Autour du Monde, 1766–1769.* 2 volumes. Paris: Imprimerie Nationale.

Tetiarahi, Gabriel. 1987. "The Society Islands: Squeezing Out the Polynesians." In *Land Tenure in the Pacific.* Ron Crocombe, ed. Pp. 45–58. Suva, Fiji: University of the South Pacific.

Trask, Haunani-Kay. 1993. "Lovely Hula Hands: Corporate Tourism and the Prostitution of Hawaiian Culture." In *From a Native Daughter: Colonialism and Sovereignty in Hawai'i.* Pp. 179–197. Monroe, Maine: Common Courage Press.

Ward, R. Gerard, and Elizabeth Kingdon. 1995. "Land Tenure in the Pacific Islands." In *Land, Custom and Practice in the South Pacific.* R. Gerard Ward and Elizabeth Kingdon, eds. Pp. 36–64. Cambridge: Cambridge University Press.

Wheeler, Tony, and Jean-Bernard Carillet. 1997. *Tahiti and French Polynesia.* Oakland: Lonely Planet.

# 18

# The Impact of the Pacific War
# on Modern Micronesian Identity

**Lin Poyer**

*University of Wyoming*

**Suzanne Falgout**

*University of Hawai'i-West Oahu*

**Laurence M. Carucci**

*Montana State University*

The study of identity, with a long history in the social sciences, has in the past few decades taken on a special urgency and theoretical interest in light of worldwide concerns about diversity, genocide, interethnic warfare, and the construction and fragmentation of nations new and old. Issues of ethnic identity emerge in many ways and are shaped by many pressures and events. Questions about the level of analysis loom large in the study of ethnicity. Should we study how individuals choose and express their identity? How minority communities respond to and resist majority ethnicity? How majority communities impose hegemony? How perceptions of shared ethnicity transcend national boundaries? How global issues are shaped, in part, by perceptions of ethnic relations? Ethnic identity is a topic that can—indeed, it must—be studied at every level, from the individual and local to the global and universal.

In Micronesia, the local and the global came together in the violent and transformative ordeal of World War II. Small kin-based island communities were caught up in the conflict between Japan and the United States, two major world powers. World War II altered the political and economic balance of power in the world and stimulated major changes in many societies. Western readers are most familiar with its impact on Europe, the United States, and East Asian nations. Yet Micronesia was one of the major battlegrounds of the Pacific war, and that era played a significant role in determining the future of the region (Poyer, Falgout, and Carucci 2001).

Ethnohistory has proved to be a fertile field for the study of global and transnational processes, and, in this chapter, we focus on two ways in which the experience of World War II shaped modern Micronesian identity.

First, the war physically transformed Micronesia through the construction of military bases and the damage from air attack and invasion during the years of war. It has taken half a century for Micronesia to recover, physically, from the destruction of the war years (some would say it has not yet recovered). Second, as a result of the war, Micronesia underwent a dramatic shift in colonial rule. Before the war, the islands were a part of the Japanese empire, which sought to integrate the islands into its national polity and economy. After the war, the United States took control of Micronesia—not to integrate it into American society, but to hold it in a special relationship called a "strategic trust," in which the islands were not considered part of the United States but were not independent entities, either. The shift in governance was dramatic, both because it took place as a military conquest and because the two powers had very different aims in governing Micronesia.

As a result of the outcome of war, and the historical memory of suffering, Micronesians today understand their identity in global, as well as local, terms. They are building national communities in the context of postwar military strategy, and maintaining local identities shaped by the interaction of indigenous, Japanese, and American cultural ideas.

## OVERVIEW OF THE WAR IN MICRONESIA

Micronesia,[1] the "little islands," consists of 2,500 islands with a total land area of only 1,000 square miles. Guam, at 209 square miles, is the largest. Micronesia's history has been shaped by the fact that the region offers less in commercial resources than the larger islands of Melanesia or Polynesia. Guam was part of Spain's sea route from the Philippines to Mexico for two centuries. Other Micronesian islands traded in turtleshell, pearlshell, or coconut oil, or provisioned European ships during the eighteenth and early nineteenth centuries. When Great Britain claimed Kiribati phosphate, Spain focused its colonial efforts on missions in the Caroline Islands while Germany developed trade (mostly copra) in the Marshalls, Carolines, and Northern Marianas. Guam became a U.S. possession as a result of the Spanish-American war in 1898. Yet overall, the colonial presence in the region until 1914 was much less intensive than in Polynesia and Melanesia.

Political, economic, and cultural interests led Japan to claim German-held Micronesia at the outbreak of World War I, and Japan was awarded control of the islands as a League of Nations mandate. Japan's goal in Micronesia was to further its own expansion through emigration and economic development of the newly acquired islands. Colonial administration dealt primarily with Japanese immigrants and emphasized agricultural and industrial development on a few key islands, mostly in western Micronesia (Saipan, Tinian, Palau). As a result, Japanese influence on Micronesian life was uneven. Most Islanders continued to live in small, kin-centered, subsistence-based communities, but they nonetheless experienced significant social and economic change. Colonial institutions such as education, health care, labor recruitment, some exposure to state Shinto, and the availability of imported Japanese goods, mass media, and personal contact with Japanese and Okinawan immigrants familiarized Islanders with a wage economy and led them to internalize some Japanese customs and attitudes. Under Japanese rule Micronesia was more integrated with regional and global systems than it had been during Spanish or German colonial regimes. Micronesians visited the region's small cities, read newspapers, listened to radios, saw movies; some visited Japan. At the same time, they were limited in education and job opportunities by a racial hierarchy that ranked them as "tomin"—"third-class people"—behind Japanese, Okinawans, and Koreans (Peattie 1988:111–112; Poyer, Falgout, and Carucci 2001:15–32).

Within a few decades, Micronesia had become a successful part of Japan's expanding empire. In the mid-to-late-1930s, the Japanese military began to prepare infrastructure and offensive bases in the region. The military capitalized on Micronesia's strategic location, launching the early attacks of their Pacific campaign from island bases and using them to ship troops and supplies to fronts to the east and south.

The islands' involvement in the Pacific war began with the Japanese bombings of Pearl Harbor and other targets in December 1941. In the first years of war, Micronesia was behind the front lines. Loss of land to military bases, increased labor demands, patriotic displays, and restrictions on Christianity all affected Islanders, but they responded favorably to Japanese self-confidence and apparent military strength (Poyer, Falgout, and Carucci 2001:8–9, 33–72). But conditions changed rapidly after the Japanese defeat at Midway in June 1942, losses in the Southwest Pacific, and the U.S. war on shipping. In September 1943, Japanese strategy in Micronesia turned from offense to defense (Peattie 1988: 262–265), as the Allies began their push toward Japan in late 1943 and early 1944. Now the islands came under attack, and Micronesians found themselves on the front lines of a global war. This was the worst phase of war, as defensive preparations produced massive troop influxes, confiscation of Islanders' land, repeated relocations, labor drafts, and food shortages (Poyer, Falgout, and Carucci 2001:73–116).

From the Allied perspective Micronesia lay along the "second road to Tokyo" (a central Pacific path to Japan), and American forces intended to move along that road simultaneously with an advance through the Southwest Pacific. The plan was to recapture Kiribati and Nauru, then attack airbases in the Marshalls, and, from there, to extend American control across Micronesia through the Carolines to the Marianas and Palau. From western Micronesia air attacks could be mounted on Japanese-occupied Asia and on Japan itself.

Costly Allied losses in the South Pacific taught the advantage of "leapfrogging" well-defended islands. In this strategy American forces invaded only a few islands, using them as bases to launch the next attacks. As a result most Micronesian islands, including some fortified bases, were bypassed—blockaded to prevent resupply, bombed to neutralize their military capacity, and left to starve until surrender. The strategy meant that Micronesians' experiences differed on islands fully captured by U.S. forces and those blockaded islands that suffered twin dangers of bombing and malnutrition.

Micronesia's war survivors carry memories of profound suffering (see chapter 24 by Carucci). Except on isolated atolls, most Islanders spent the war years working to meet Japanese military needs. Military construction forced many to relocate. Property was confiscated, families disrupted, schools and churches closed. As Allies blocked shipping, food became scarce, clothing, medicine, and luxuries nonexistent. Military rule tightened as the war continued and starvation threatened tens of thousands of troops and civilians. Micronesian affection and admiration for the Japanese turned to resentment as many Islanders suffered from brutal treatment. Near the end of the war, Micronesians suspected that the Japanese planned to exterminate them, a fear that remained only rumors in most cases, though there were mass executions in Guam and in the Marshall Islands (Falgout, Poyer, and Carucci 1995; Poyer, Falgout, and Carucci 2001:9–10, 169–229, 231–234).

Micronesians also suffered at the hands of attacking Americans, from large-scale invasions such as at Kwajalein and Saipan to the constant bombing of blockaded islands; Chuuk, for example, suffered almost daily bombing for one and a half years. Islanders came to doubt Japanese claims of eventual victory as repeated attacks, the loss of planes to defend bases, and the starvation of Japanese troops implied defeat. Japanese propaganda warned Islanders that if the Americans won, they would be executed. This threat proved false; Americans treated most Islanders as friendly neutrals to be liberated. But Micronesians were killed and wounded and their property destroyed, though Japanese commanders often re-moved Islanders from harm's way, and American forces often tried to avoid target-ing them (Poyer, Falgout, and Carucci 2001:117–168).

Kwajalein, Enewetak, Majuro, unfortified Marshall Islands, Saipan and Tinian, Peleliu, Angaur, and Ulithi came under U.S. control through invasion and occupation. But by-passed islands remained in Japanese hands. As a result, Micronesians' initial experiences with Americans took vastly different forms. Micronesians on invaded islands suffered through attack and battle, then encountered U.S. Navy civil affairs units which immediately began to supply the food, health care, and se-curity so desperately needed. But on unin-vaded islands, the war did not end until Japanese surrender, and people suffered ad-ditional months or years of starvation, hard labor, and constant air attack. (Where U.S. forces were nearby, in the Marshalls and Palau, Micronesians on bypassed islands even-tually began to escape to American lines.) Even Japan's official surrender in September 1945 did not bring immediate relief to the by-passed Caroline Islands, as American military obligations prevented them from occupying the area until several months later. Even after the United States established control over central Micronesia, shortages of shipping and personnel restricted relief and reconstruction efforts.

## THE TRANSFORMATION OF MICRONESIA

This brief summary indicates the enormous impact of the Pacific war on Micronesia. When we turn to how the events of the war shaped modern Micronesian identity, we can examine two major effects. One is the simple fact that the physical damage wrought by war has had long-lasting consequences for how Micronesians live. The second is that the Allied victory meant that the islands left the Japanese colonial sphere and came under American control, with a resulting change in the economic, political, and cultural world of Micronesians.

## Physical Impacts of War

Micronesians are in a way like war refugees; they never left home, but their home disap-peared around them.[2] Military action in preparing for and conducting war on a major scale resulted in the destruction and alter-ation of land and resources. In parts of Micronesia, the postwar landscape was unrec-ognizable. John Embree wrote: "The only thing left of prewar Saipan is steady damp op-pressive heat" (1946:2); the island was strewn with pillboxes, bomb shelters, and the aban-doned farmhouses and fields of Okinawan settlers. Spoehr noted:

> The most extensive ruins of all, however, are of American origin and date from the time when Saipan was a great wartime base. These are the rows and rows of abandoned rusty quonsets, and the lines of vacant, gradually rotting ware-houses. Scattered around the island are the sagging remains of officers' clubs, Red Cross libraries, and chapels. . . . In this curious milieu, repeated at many a deserted American base in the Pacific islands, live some five thousand people. (1954:18)

Such ruin of landscape and economy was found throughout the islands. Every urban area was destroyed—if not by bombs, then by postwar American activities. The infrastruc-ture of the Japanese colonial economy was gone—airstrips, shipping, roads, and capital goods such as boats. Subsistence and export crops were devastated. Airbase construction caused major, permanent loss of agricultural land, especially critical on atolls. Throughout the islands, gardens had been concreted for airstrips, land cleared for defense installa-tions, coconut and breadfruit trees felled for lumber, and taro swamps drained and filled in for planting emergency crops; cattle, hogs, and chickens had been destroyed. Fish deple-tion, especially through the use of explosives, and the impact of bombing and mines caused long-term damage to marine resources (Poyer, Falgout, and Carucci 2001:316–320).

The destruction began with the start of war preparations, as Japanese military construc-tion (first in the Marshall Islands, later in the

Marianas and Palau) consumed scarce island land. In the Marshalls, airbases were built at Kwajalein, Mili, Wotje, and Maloelap, with Enewetak developed later in the war; the civilian capital of Jaluij was also fortified.[3] In western Micronesia, Japanese military construction in the Marianas began early in 1941 and included airfields on Saipan and Tinian. Even Pohnpei and Kosrae in the central Carolines, which played little direct role in the Japanese offensive, were altered by defensive preparations, and by the expansion of huge plantations that absorbed the forced labor of Islanders, military workers, civilian and prisoner labor to supply the war effort. In Chuuk, tens of thousands of laborers, including Chuukese, built an airbase and facilities for the Japanese Combined Fleet in Chuuk Lagoon.

The shift to a defensive war in late 1943 and 1944 intensified the destruction of Micronesia's landscape. The Japanese Army arrived in great numbers, with much of its materiel lost to Allied submarines and blockades preventing resupply. Tens of thousands of troops had to be supported from a food base already feeding construction laborers, civilian Japanese, and Islanders (Spector 1985:485–487; Peattie 1988:265). Allied progress and the retreat of the Japanese Combined Fleet from Chuuk to Palau in February 1944 turned the western Carolines into a reinforced defensive line and brought Japanese military control to areas that had been in the backwaters of the war. Puluwat, Woleai, and Satawan (Mortlock Islands) were developed as airbases. In spring of 1944, Japan strengthened its defenses at Palau with some 40,000 troops, which had to be fed and supplied locally. Japan also rushed to strengthen the Marianas, within striking distance of the homeland. When the loss of the Marshalls and neutralization of the eastern and central Carolines put the Marianas on the front line, the effort began in February 1944 to make Saipan an "impregnable fortress" (General Obata's words, in Peattie 1988:282).

As U.S. forces prosecuted their successful offensive, construction of American military bases began a second phase of resource destruction in the region. With the first victories in the Marshall Islands early in 1944, U.S. bases and airstrips were built on Majuro, Kwajalein, and Enewetak. In western Micronesia, Ulithi became a major U.S. Navy fleet base, recreation base, and airstrip. The invasion of Saipan in June-July 1944 was followed by construction of major bases used to attack Japan itself. The island held two huge B-29 fields, additional smaller airfields, a naval base at Tanapag, and extensive support facilities. The first raids on Tokyo flew from Saipan on November 24, 1944. On recaptured Guam, too, Seabees came ashore behind the marines, building airfields, highways, and harbors. Guam became a major U.S. Navy base with a mid-1945 military and civilian population of over 220,000;[4] thousands of native Chamorros were employed as laborers and clerical workers. Wherever they built installations, the U.S. Navy's choice of sites reshaped local geography, society, and economy (Hezel 1995:250–253).

The construction of Japanese bases, the destruction of landmarks through bombardment and land battles, and American military land use all created lasting problems. In addition to the physical destruction, land tenure and subsistence were permanently affected (Poyer, Falgout, and Carucci 2001:320–326). On Saipan, for example:

> Almost all land records were destroyed during the American assault, property markers were obliterated, and normal lines of inheritance were broken. Extensive areas were occupied by the military, native families were displaced from rural and urban holdings. . . . In no cases have the islanders been paid for their land by either rental or purchase. Property exchanges have been made, but titles have not yet been cleared. (Bowers 1950:77)

Even after the war, resolution of land claims was slow. On Saipan, 1,587 land-ownership hearings were held in 1947–1948 but, by the end of 1948, only 19 cases had been settled (Bowers 1950:80–82). Meanwhile, the U.S. military was using private land without compensating owners or confirming local property rights (Spoehr 1954:129–130).

After reoccupation of Guam in July 1944, the United States took much of the island's land for military use. As a result, the "land-title situation on Guam was in extraordinary confusion" and problems "multiplied out of all proportion to the area involved" (Souder 1971:105–106).[5] While many rights became clarified over time, and much land was returned, it took decades for people to feel confident in possession, if indeed they yet do. In the Marianas and the Marshalls, fear of losing land has been pervasive because of U.S. military landholdings extending into the postwar years—in some cases, into the present. Islanders also challenge the right of their own modern state or federal governments to use public lands for infrastructure, since much of what is now "public land" became "public" through illegitimate acquisition by German or Japanese administrations (McGrath and Wilson 1971:187). Land tenure disputes continue to absorb time and energy throughout the islands.

The U.S. Navy also affected land tenure by relocating islanders (although to a much lesser extent than the Japanese military had done). People on Enewetak, Kwajalein, Majuro, Guam, and Saipan moved to make way for American bases; smaller-scale relocations happened in the Northern Marianas and Chuuk. The best-known cases are those of the people of Bikini and Enewetak in the Marshall Islands, removed when their homes became U.S. nuclear testing sites in 1946 and 1947 (see Carucci, chapter 24). The removal of Kwajalein people for military facilities has also led to long negotiations between the U.S. government and the Marshallese.[6]

In thinking about Micronesian identity, we must recognize that current generations of Micronesians live in a physical landscape still shaped by the fight between Japan and the United States. Issues of war reparations continue to reverberate in Asia and Europe, where nations harmed by the conflict press for public recognition of their losses. Micronesians, though they have repeatedly requested consideration of reparations from both Japan and the United States, have received little worldwide acknowledgment of

their losses. When they engage in negotiations with the United States or other entities, they keep in mind that control of their own land and resources is vital to their identity, and that military activities are an on-going threat to that control.

## The Shift in Colonial Rule

Before the war, Micronesia was part of the expanding Japanese political, economic, and cultural sphere. The islands became an outlet for Japanese emigration and a profitable element of the imperial economy. In evaluating Japanese colonial rule, Mark Peattie (1988:81–117) concludes that despite Japan's early commitment to League of Nations guidance for mandated territories, Micronesian interests were eventually overshadowed by Japanese priorities. But although the Japanese colonial order privileged its own citizens above Micronesians, Islanders nonetheless benefited from development projects and infrastructure. By the 1930s, the 50,000 Micronesians were living in a period of economic growth, a stable government, and a restricted but in many ways satisfying way of life (Poyer, Falgout, and Carucci 2001:15–32). As a result, Micronesians began the war as loyal supporters of Japan's imperial aspirations, and some joined the war effort, even volunteering for hazardous missions. But the long years of war and the harsh and punitive conditions they experienced under the Japanese Army eventually caused Islanders to welcome American victory.

When the United States took control of Micronesia, it was not with the goal of integrating Islanders into the American polity and economy but to deny the region to other powers. In July 1947 the United Nations assigned Micronesia to the United States as a "strategic trust" (a designation invented for this case), the United States Trust Territory of the Pacific Islands. The U.S. Navy administered Micronesia for six (in some places, seven) years, before turning it over to the Department of the Interior in July 1951 (Saipan and Tinian returned to Navy control for military reasons in November 1951).

Beginning in 1969, a series of negotiations over the next decades ended the Trust Territory and established new political entities in Micronesia.

The difference in the goals of the two nations that governed Micronesia over the past century has had a great impact on how Micronesians saw themselves. Whereas Japan had used Micronesia as a building block of empire, American interest in the region was strategic, not economic. Japan had identified Islanders as "third-class peoples" but had encouraged them to identify with Japanese identity (through education, religion, and loyalty programs). The United States did play a role in changing Micronesian cultures, but did not pursue a policy of trying to make Micronesians potential citizens (note that Guam's people are American citizens, and the Northern Marianas Islands eventually became a U.S. commonwealth). During the Japanese colonial era, Micronesians were learning a Japanese identity. During American times, although Micronesian culture underwent much "Americanization," Islanders were learning to identify themselves as Micronesians and to explore what that identity might mean in the postwar world.

## Postwar Micronesia

The regions of Micronesia had different postwar experiences, which depended in large part on how their home islands figured into U.S. military plans. In 1944, the United States needed bases in the Marshall Islands and the U.S. Navy worked hard to promote good relations with Islanders on Kwajalein, Enewetak, and Majuro. American attention to the invaded islands, along with the Marshallese people's history of Christian missionary links with the United States, eased their transition to the new order. In contrast, by the time Americans came ashore on bypassed islands of the Carolines, the war was over. The U.S. Navy's new goals were to repatriate Japanese troops and govern the region, with less immediate need to respond to local concerns. The Navy found that its inability to communicate with Caroline Islanders, the lack of up-

to-date information about island cultures, and the decline in financial support for postwar operations made it difficult to work as easily with central and western Micronesians as they had with Marshall Islanders. The Navy had also to wrestle with its lack of experience governing civilians, and with ambiguous policy decisions and little official guidance. The recommendation of a congressional committee encapsulates the paradox that frustrated the region's new rulers: "Teach the American way of life but do not disturb native institutions" (Useem 1946a:9; Kiste and Falgout 1999; Poyer, Falgout, and Carucci 2001:264–266).

Many of the difficulties Islanders and U.S. administrators faced in the first postwar years arose from this change in Micronesia's geopolitical role. Micronesians sought to recover their prewar standard of living, the type of economy that they had known under the Japanese, but found the United States unconcerned with the economic potential of the area (Embree 1946:163). After addressing the immediate needs for basic health care and subsistence, the U.S. Navy military government faced questions about Micronesia's future, including the question of the region's economic future, which could be phrased "restoration or subsistence?" (Poyer, Falgout, and Carucci 2001:289–309). That is, should Micronesia's island economies be restored to prewar levels, when the islands were integrated with Japan's economy? Or should the goal be to establish a small-scale, subsistence local economy?[7]

In parts of Micronesia, the economy—infrastructure, access to cash, wage labor, and imported goods—has never returned to the level Micronesians knew in the 1930s. The weak postwar economy was due to several factors: limited natural resources, security issues, administrators' unfamiliarity with the region, and U.S. sensitivity to charges of exploitation. The war destroyed infrastructure, but it was American policy decisions that determined why Micronesia, unlike Europe or Japan, did not benefit from postwar reconstruction (see Hanlon 1998). The decision to repatriate the thousands of Japanese and Okinawan civilians who had been the managers and merchants of the region, "together with the destruction resulting from the war, caused the Micronesian economy to collapse entirely" (Ballendorf 1984:3).[8]

Americans brought their own ideas about Micronesians to their administrative posts, including racial ideas and ideas about "primitive" Islanders. The first American administrators persistently misperceived Micronesians as primitive peoples who should be content with a subsistence economy, despite the reports of social science researchers who repeatedly urged them to recognize that Micronesians had been accustomed to a high level of services, media, and consumer goods in the Japanese era (Useem 1945:580; Useem 1946b:84–85). But as the months and years passed amid the ruins of war, knowledge of how Islanders had lived under Japanese rule faded from American memory, replaced by an image of subsistence-level, "traditional" life. For U.S. Navy officials, Hanlon writes, "World War II created a zero point from which history was to begin" (1998:65; see also Hanlon 1999:61–71). But Micronesians did not forget how they had lived in the 1920s and the 1930s, and parts of Micronesia retained an identity as urban, managerial, and globally linked.

The stated U.S. Navy goal was to restore "self-sufficiency" to the islands (Richard 1957b:406). On isolated atolls, people were able to restore their local subsistence economy in the years following the war. But larger islands that had seen much economic development during the Japanese colonial era found the idea of "self-sufficiency" inadequate. Saipan and Palau, economic centers in prewar Micronesia, both lost prominence under American rule and struggled throughout the postwar years with American reluctance to revive prewar economies. After the Japanese, Okinawans, and Koreans on Saipan were repatriated in early 1946, the U.S. administration judged that Marianas Islanders lacked the "background and experience" to restore the high prewar standard of living (Bowers 1950:62). Instead, they were encouraged to turn to agriculture, since war and repatriation had left the land unused. But

Saipanese Chamorro identity was not linked with farming (they had worked for the Japanese in towns, or rented their land to immigrant farmers); they saw themselves as participants in an international cash economy, and they consistently disagreed with U.S. Navy plans for their economic futures. Most continued to pursue ways to engage in a wage or commercial economy, for example at U.S. military bases.[9] Chamorros on Saipan and Tinian acculturated quickly to American ways, aided by their familiarity with global capitalism during the Japanese era and by postwar U.S. Navy installations that gave an economic boost to these islands. The people of Saipan were the first of the former Japanese mandate to request American citizenship, and they have consistently represented themselves as more "advanced" (that is, more similar to Japanese and American ways of living) than their Micronesian neighbors (with the exception of Guam). They have, over the decades, chosen political and economic strategies that have separated them from the rest of Micronesia, culminating in their decision to seek U.S. commonwealth status (Poyer, Falgout, and Carucci 2001: 301–305, 349).

Like Chamorros on Saipan, Palauans were accustomed to a wage economy and links with metropole culture because of Palau's role as capital of Japanese Micronesia. Unlike Saipan, however, Palau did not become an American military center during or after the war, and Palauans received no encouragement to revive what had been a thriving prewar economy. Many Palauan men had been office workers for the Japanese government or private firms, or entrepreneurs in their own businesses. Under the new American administration, they "have been encouraged to take up the practice of old crafts such as fish-net construction and old methods of carpentry which do not require the use of manufactured tools" (Vidich 1980:271–272). The Navy urged a simple economy based on "self-sufficiency," which ambitious Palauans interpreted as an attempt to restrict their future. To them, "the American [economic development] efforts seemed not only feeble, but deliberately regressive and counterproductive" (Ballendorf 1988:61; see also Poyer, Falgout, and Carucci 2001: 305–307).[10]

This rapid turnaround in Micronesians' economic prospects after the war caused considerable difficulty for Islanders. Insofar as a people's identity is linked with its economic activity, it caused them to reevaluate their vision of their future. Claiming that it did not want to "exploit" Micronesia, the United States restricted outside investment and limited economic development. Yet the United Nations Trusteeship Council and the 1950 U.N. Visiting Mission to the region reported that Islanders wanted and needed more income, wage labor opportunities, and exports. While older Micronesians selectively remembered what life had been like before the war, during the prewar economic boom, young people learned about the luxuries of American life from magazines, school, and movies. Visitors sometimes criticized Micronesians for wanting to "be like Americans" when they sought the means to purchase imported goods (some American visitors still do this). But in fact, Micronesians have had a long history of access to cash through wage labor or selling goods and have used that cash to purchase imports. World War II and the postwar years were memorable for them because of the extreme scarcity of such goods. After the war, it is true that Micronesians devoted a great deal of effort to finding ways to revive their links with the global economy. But outsiders who saw this as Micronesians "losing their culture" or "abandoning tradition" failed to see the broader historical context.

In the mid-1960s, policy changes in the Kennedy era increased the cash available to Micronesians. But by then, other changes and the maturing of a new generation in a new global context caused a reevaluation of American motives and altered Islanders' ideas of a desirable future. Micronesians coming of age in the 1960s and the 1970s, like their age mates in the United States, developed ideas of tradition and independence that pointed them away from their elders' visions of a comfortable but colonized prewar life. The new American policy introduced economic and social programs designed for the "war on

poverty" being fought on the U.S. mainland into small island cultures (see, for example, Gale 1979). The rapid changes that followed have dramatically reshaped Micronesian culture and society and have caused Islanders themselves to wonder whether their cultural traditions have been endangered by the influx of imports. Imported ideas and government programs have been at least as influential in this as imported goods, if not more so. Today, Micronesians seek a difficult balance between an adequate economy and a strong sense of indigenous culture (Poyer, Falgout, and Carucci 2001:307–309).

## STUDYING IDENTITY

Sociologists' and anthropologists' ideas about identity have developed rapidly over the past half-century, spurred by the changing contexts in which human similarities and differences have been measured and explained. Sorting people into groups, with political and social consequences, is a human habit so widespread that some have argued that it is part of the basic human cognitive trait of classification. Two broad approaches characterized the post–World War II study of what has usually been called "ethnicity." One, the "primordialist" approach, argued that ethnicity is a sort of natural "blood" tie expressed in shared geography, kinship, language, and religion and that people feel and express a sentiment of sameness or kinship with their group as a fundamental part of human social life. The alternative view is "circumstantialist," arguing that ethnic ties are not eternal and fundamental but are responses to specific historical or social contexts (Glazer and Moynihan 1975). In this latter view, we cannot understand an ethnic group by looking at it in isolation; we must consider how each ethnic identity has been shaped by historical, economic, and political circumstances.

As is so often the case in social science theory, the chance to argue these two competing positions during the 1950s to 1970s produced a new approach integrating them. Beginning in the 1980s, anthropologists began to construct a theory that explains how social circumstances and cultural beliefs shape identity in such a way as to make it seem "natural" to sort people into categories. In other words, members of ethnic groups often do think that their identity is eternal, fundamental, and "in the blood." But if we examine the historical, cultural, and social context, we can see how this identity has been created and shaped by specific circumstances (see Linnekin and Poyer 1990 for a discussion of this topic in the Pacific Island context).

We have been forced to develop increasingly sophisticated theories of identity because of the growing complexity of group relations. In a globalizing, transnational world, identity is a multilayered phenomenon. Social scientists must sort out ideas of "nationality," "community," "ethnicity," "race," "class," "gender," and other sorts of identity, which are connected in complicated ways, and which are constantly changing (see Alonso 1994 and Williams 1989 for reviews of the literature on these interlinked topics). Since the 1980s, then, anthropologists have studied ethnic identity as a "process" rather than a "thing." How do people come to see themselves as part of a group, and how do certain traits (such as language, appearance, or religion) become emblematic of that group? How does membership in certain groups confer privilege, while other groups are oppressed or constrained? How do people maintain and transform group identity in a context of international migration and globalizing culture?

In Micronesia, modern identity is complexly linked with foreign, as well as indigenous, ideas about culture. Islanders' views of themselves depend in great part on local understanding of what makes people alike and different, of "who we are," but it has also been shaped by Spanish, German, and especially Japanese and American ideas about what Micronesians are and should be. While the core of their identity depends on uniquely Micronesian ideas about people, land, kinship, and community, Micronesian identity has also been shaped in response to what colonial powers have told them about themselves, and in response to the structures that these foreign administrations have established to rule them.

In discussing cultural identity and ethnicity in the Pacific Islands, Linnekin and Poyer (1990:11) argue that Oceanic concepts of identity differ from those of Western cultures, that they "consistently emphasize context, situation, performance, and place over biological descent."

> in ascriptions of personal and local group identity, certain higher-level presuppositions are shared throughout Oceania: that people can voluntarily shift their social identities, that a person can maintain more than one identity simultaneously, and that behavioral attributes—such as residence, language, dress, participation in exchanges—are not only significant markers but are also effective determinants of identity. Moreover, fundamental Oceanic premises about the acquisition of cultural identity may persist in social relations even in the face of major political and economic changes, and in spite of the introduction of Western-influenced ethnic categories. (Linnekin and Poyer 1990:9)

This means that what Islanders evaluate when establishing someone's identity is whether that person acts like a member of a given community. Having ancestors who belong to a certain island population does not mean that one is automatically a member of that community, unless a person validates that identity through his or her behavior: living in a certain place, following local expectations about behavior, acting like a true kinsman, and so on. This contrasts with both Western and Japanese ideas about identity, which tend to give "blood" the priority in deciding someone's ethnic affiliation. Since past rulers have sorted Micronesians into ethnic categories and treated them according to the administrators' ideas about those ethnic categories, Micronesians, in turn, have added foreign ideas about identity to their own Oceanic concepts.

## Micronesian History and Identity

Another important difference between Micronesian and foreign ideas about identity is that indigenous Micronesian identity centers on the local community (that is, most people see themselves first as members of a small local group). Yet, at the same time, events of the past century have also engaged them in a broader regional and global discourse about identity. Even before Japanese rule in 1914, the Spanish, Germans, British, Americans, and other foreigners had sorted and grouped Micronesians through formal policy and informal interactions. The more-recent Japanese, and then American, bureaucracies entered an island world already organized by indigenous Oceanic ideas and by eighteenth- and nineteenth-century European racial categories. The fact that colonial regimes drew boundaries around Micronesia and governed it by a single set of rules does not mean—here or anywhere else in the world—that people within those borders shared a single identity. But when foreign colonial administrative frameworks were imposed, Islanders had to deal with foreign models of ethnic ascription and ranking.

It may be that peoples who are governed by a unitary order acculturate to its vision and create, over time, a shared identity. Successful empires operate that way. The Japanese sought to integrate Micronesians into Japanese society—albeit as "third-class" members. The United States, on the other hand, though constantly encouraging programs of American culture, politics, and language, never seriously sought to absorb Micronesia into its national sphere. Allied victory in the Pacific war meant, for Islanders, a shift between colonial rulers who differed greatly in their intentions toward Micronesians and in their view of Micronesian identity (Poyer 1999:198–200).

The Japanese era created educational, medical, legal, and economic programs for Islanders, but Japan also encouraged its own citizens to emigrate to Micronesia. By the 1930s, Japanese, Okinawans, and Islanders constituted a ranked hierarchy, with the Japanese holding the highest status. Despite sometimes close personal relationships between Japanese officials and Islanders, status differences were always marked. The Japanese cultivated some groups of Islanders and disprivileged others. For example, children of Japanese men and Micronesian women were privileged in education and jobs, and Chamorros on Yap held economic privilege over Yapese. Just before the war, large numbers of Korean laborers were imported for military construction, and during the war many people moved in response to labor demands. Wartime labor emphasized ethnic ranking, with tasks and living areas often assigned by ethnicity. During the war, scarce food was apportioned by ethnicity on some islands. For example, on Kosrae, Japanese officers got the best food, enlisted men and Korean and Okinawan laborers received less food and less-favored food, and Kiribati prisoners of war received the least and worst. (Kiribati people from the British colony of the Gilbert and Ellice Islands were treated as prisoners when the Japanese invaded the Gilberts, now Kiribati [see Poyer, Falgout, and Carucci 2001:180].)

After the war, the United States repatriated Japanese, Okinawans, and Koreans. Areas that had held thousands of Japanese civilians before the war, and tens of thousands of troops during the war, were now occupied by a few thousand, or even a few hundred, Micronesians. The United States stationed large numbers of troops in only a few places (such as Kwajalein and Saipan). Micronesians elsewhere encountered few Americans. And though the first encounters between Islanders and American servicemen encouraged fraternization, regulations and American custom soon restricted contact. Racial segregation—separate residences, recreation sites, and pay scales—became a fixture of the American colonial era. (Nonetheless, most Micronesians felt that Americans were more informal and egalitarian than the Japanese.) Americans also brought with them their own pattern of racism and competitive pluralism, the ethnic model most familiar in American public politics. In the United States, ethnic groups identified themselves as a "voting bloc" to compete for political and economic power. In the first decades of U.S. rule, administrators sought to identify the ethnic groups of Micronesia, and established attitudes toward (or stereotypes about) these groups (Poyer 1999). They imposed more rigid ethnic categorization than Micronesians themselves used, and established political structures based on the U.S. model that led to Micronesian communities organizing themselves to some extent like political parties in the United States.

Both Japanese and American colonial orders distinguished among island populations, but they also grouped Micronesians into a single unit ("tomin," "kanaka," or "Micronesians") to set them apart from their own citizens. Micronesians at times have accepted and even promoted this broad identity, but they have also maintained the significance of local identities, variations in custom and language that have been codified and expressed as political strategies. Each region of Micronesia—indeed, each of the islands, and parts of islands—has its own identity. This is as true today as it was in the years before World War II, and the salience of local identities continues to shape Micronesian life.

## Micronesian Identity and Global Politics

During the 1960s and 1970s, as the people of Micronesia began to examine their future political options, Micronesians educated in American schools and colleges and influenced by the identity politics of that era actively explored questions of community and national identity. This was a time when ethnic groups in the United States claimed a more public voice and argued for a new politics of identity to replace the "melting pot" (for example, African-American political activism). These were also the years when Micronesian leaders pondered different visions of the political future. Islanders sought to define new national identities, to create a pan-Micronesian identity, and at the same time to manage local and regional identities within these wider units (see Petersen 1999).

Because they thought political unity should be accompanied by a shared sense of identity, American administrators sought to cultivate national sentiment, to enculturate a new generation of leaders with a sense of "Micronesian-ness." The region's public high school (Pacific Islands Central School) and private Xavier High School integrated students from across the region. They invented commemorative days (such as U.N. Day) and symbolic gestures (a Micronesian flag, an anthem) and published materials intended to create a sense of shared identity. The shared use of English as a common language (a role previously played by Japanese) also created bonds among younger Islanders from different regions. But as the dissolution of the Trust Territory came under serious discussion in political negotiations, anthropologists and others familiar with the region insisted on the continuing significance of local identities. For example, while administrative boundaries included outlying atolls in the political units headquartered on the large islands of Yap and Pohnpei, people on those atolls had distinct identities and different political goals than people on the large islands (Petersen 1999; Poyer 1999). Although Saipan had served as headquarters for the Trust Territory, the Chamorros of the Northern Marianas saw themselves as having a very different future path from the less-acculturated Islanders to the east. By the time negotiations for ending the Trust Territory were underway, it was clear that Micronesia would not emerge from them as a single nation.

Behind the present facade of unity, peoples of the Trust Territory display a welter of opposing identities deeply rooted in Micronesia's geography, traditional cultures, and history of contact with the rest of the world. Only in recent years, when confronting the United States on political and economic issues, have some islanders come to regard themselves keenly as "Micronesians," employing a label that symbolizes their status as territorial citizens seeking emancipation. Otherwise, individuals will on occasion identify themselves as residents of a certain district—as Ponapean, Marshallese, or Palauan—but such denotations generally lack strong feeling and commitment to other members of the named reference group. In the face-to-face interaction of daily life, identities are colored with a greater emotion and sense of belonging to social groups that are distinctive in beliefs, sentiments, and behaviors. Examples are island villages, clans, lineages, kindreds, classes, and collectivities based on shared language, religion, occupation, or proprietary rights. (Mason 1974:225)

In this statement, Mason points to the two most salient levels of Micronesian identity—the global and the local—and the relative lack of commitment to intermediate levels of political identity. Over the past half-century, Micronesians have reaffirmed their commitment to local communities but have struggled with the need to create sociopolitical structures at the regional and national levels. In the negotiations that accompanied the breakup of the Trust Territory in the 1970s to 1990s, the islands separated into new political entities based partly on longstanding cultural and linguistic distinctions, partly on the historical contingencies of colonial administrative boundaries, and partly on the strategic potential of each island region.

Micronesians used their geographic position in the global military picture—a lesson learned in the hard school of the Pacific war—to negotiate their post–Trust Territory status (Firth 1989; Hezel 1995:325–367). The Northern Marianas, the Marshall Islands, and Palau were the areas of greatest military interest to the United States and were able to negotiate separately from the eastern and central Carolines. The people of the Northern Marianas, with a history of active acculturation during the Japanese and American eras, sought a close relationship with the United States. In 1975–1976, these islands entered a commonwealth agreement, granting the United States control over foreign affairs and defense in exchange for internal autonomy and favorable economic arrangements. Similarly, U.S. military needs in the Marshalls allowed for negotiation of a separate Republic of the Marshall Islands (RMI) in 1986. Reparations for nuclear testing effects and contracts on existing U.S. military bases in the Marshalls have provided funding for some residents, and the RMI government has pursued foreign investment and its own develop-

ment projects. Palau, like Guam and the Northern Marianas, is a potential rollback site for U.S. forces in Asia and has potential as a naval base. The rest of the Caroline Islands, though, had no distinctive strategic value to the United States. Palau negotiated a separate agreement (as the Republic of Belau, in 1994), while the rest of the Carolines banded together in a Federated States of Micronesia (FSM) in 1986. The FSM, the RMI, and the Republic of Belau (see Nero, Murray, and Burton, chapter 14) are in "free association" with the United States, meaning that they are members of independent nations but involved in a unique relationship that gives the United States certain powers in their territories (see Michal 1993). In exchange, these states receive money and services from the United States. Despite these innovative political arrangements, the Micronesian islands continue to struggle economically.

As people who suffered greatly in the Pacific war, Micronesians find themselves in an ironic position. To maintain political independence and gain financial support, they must continue to link themselves with the military needs of global powers. The decision for free association with the United States—exchanging economic resources for strategic rights—comes with the price of continuing to involve themselves in the world's military network. (We might think of this as the opposite of the Swiss, whose economy has in the past depended on neutrality.) In the postwar years, Micronesian islands have served the United States as locations for military bases, sites for testing weapons systems, a fallback and buffer for military dangers in East Asia, a support base for the war in Vietnam, and a locale for secret CIA activities. Micronesians serve in the U.S. armed forces.

From the 1930s—for more than half a century—Micronesians' lives have been shaped in the context of the global military situation. Micronesians are actively engaged with the implications of this history, as can be seen in their concerns about weapons testing on Kwajalein, nuclear testing in French Polynesia, and nuclear vessels in the region. They watch U.S. foreign policy with an eye to their own interests. They know their homes are potential bases for military action in any part of the world, particularly Asia. For example, we conducted interviews about World War II during the Gulf conflict, and found Micronesians very concerned about the potential danger, as in earlier years Micronesians had worried about the impacts of the Korean War and the war in Vietnam (Lessa 1950:16; Spoehr 1954:94; Rogers 1995). Micronesians worry that U.S. military action anywhere in the world might lead to the use of their islands as bases. Their perception of their own safety is inextricably connected with their position in worldwide military strategy. It is impossible for Micronesians to consider their own identity in isolation from global events.

## WAR, HISTORY, AND MODERN IDENTITY

Research into identity in the anthropological and sociological literature demonstrates that it is contextual, situational, flexible, ever changing, responsive to historical circumstances. If identity is contextual, what happens when context changes as dramatically as it did for Micronesians at the end of the war? In a few short years, the islands had changed physically by destruction and transformation of its natural resources and economic infrastructure, and Micronesian society was changed by the war's effects on leadership, land ownership, gender roles, and interaction with Japanese and Americans.

When Micronesians today reflect on the twenty seven prewar years of peaceful Japanese rule, they sometimes speak of it as an economic golden age. Historians of the region (for example, Hatanaka 1973–1974; Peattie 1988) describe the Japanese mandate as successful in providing basic education, health, and public order, with an economic program that benefited Islanders and expanded their opportunities to engage the wider Pacific region. Yet the mandate's economic projects were aimed at benefiting the Japanese, not Islanders. Immigration and loss of land threatened Micronesians' well-being, racial policies limited their achievement, and acculturation policies harmed local cultures.

Micronesians today also evaluate the decades of American rule. They see America as the most powerful military force today and thus as an important ally and protector. They are cautious about certain aspects of American culture that they have found problematic in the Micronesian context (for example, questions about democracy and the role of traditional chiefs, about personal and religious freedom, or about American popular culture). But at the same time they embrace economic and educational opportunities opened by on-going links with the United States (Poyer, Falgout, and Carucci 2001: 340–347).

If Micronesians' opinions of the conflicting powers that have shaped this century in the Pacific are ambivalent, they are certain of one thing: Their present and future is inevitably linked with global geopolitics. And their sense of themselves, their identity as Micronesians, as Pacific Islanders, and as members of specific island communities is linked with this strategic position. The people of Enewetak, for example, lived through a devastating battle of the Pacific war and the use of their home for atomic testing. Out of this raw material of historical suffering, they have crafted an understanding of their place in the world expressed in a lengthy ritual, *Kurijmoj*, integrating Christian and indigenous symbolism and centering on themes of community identity and power. In the annual ritual, they recount their experience of apocalypse through song, dance, and story, and they reaffirm their endurance as a cultural community (Carucci 1997, 2001).

## CONCLUSION

Some years after the war, anthropologist John Fischer wrote:

> Persons not thoroughly acquainted with the languages and cultures of the islanders often fail to realize the degree of difference between many of the islands and the feeling of separateness that accompanies these differences. Even where there is considerable cultural similarity, as among the five petty states of Ponape or

among the islands of Truk Lagoon or of the Mortlock group, the people of these formerly independent communities do not all consider that their cultural similarity inevitably implies that they should be politically united. (1957:181)

Yet they are united as new nations, and their economic future depends on negotiating with the United States through the political entities established as a result of strategic concerns. Like all peoples, Micronesians experience their identities in multiple layers. The most significant, for most Micronesians, continue to be the local level—where kinship, land rights, and traditional political order such as chiefly titles secure the individual's place in the social system—and the global—where the major questions of Micronesian economy and political order are decided. Micronesia's historical experiences under Japanese and then American administration created political and economic structures that link island communities into broader units, but the efficacy and meaning of those units have not yet become integrated into a sense of personal or group identity. A person will think of herself or himself as "Ngatikese" or "Yapese" or "Enewetak," rather than "Federated States of Micronesia citizen" or "Marshallese."

This region is still in the early stages of nation building, a creative symbolic and practical endeavor that has come under close study in recent years (see Foster 1991 for a review of the cultural process of nation building). But unlike regions that created national polities and identities in earlier centuries, or even decades, Micronesians are engaging in this process in a postmodern world. They are not alone: "Today, state-level politics is the most potent factor in the ongoing transformation of Pacific cultural identities" (Linnekin and Poyer 1990:11). Islanders define themselves in terms of who they are as members of indigenous cultural communities, but also in terms of their nation's position in the global game of military strategy. They are "Kwajalein people" or "Chuukese" or "Palauans," with strong commitments to local land, language,

and kinship, but they are also people whose lands have been and may continue to be locales of war.

The geopolitical power currents that generated and resolved the Pacific war also organize the postwar context of Micronesia's new nations. World War II was not their fight, but the suffering and transformation that resulted from it is very much their own. Today, they are building new national and regional communities from the experience of the war, and investing these identities with meaning by creating shared understandings of its significance.

## NOTES

1. Hezel (1983, 1995) provides the most comprehensive overview of Micronesian history. Readers are also referred to bibliographies of Micronesia (Marshall and Nason 1975; Goetzfridt and Wuerch 1989). Peattie (1988) examines the Japanese era in Micronesia in detail. This overview also relies on the description of the war years in Micronesian in Poyer, Falgout, and Carucci (2001). Most official and popular histories of the Pacific war focus on Allied and Japanese strategy and experiences; summaries that focus on the Micronesian region include Richard (1957a, 1957b, 1957c) and Morison (1951, 1953). Wartime experiences of Pacific Islanders, including Micronesians, are presented in Carucci (1995), Falgout, Poyer, and Carucci (1995), Poyer (1995), and articles in volumes by Lindstrom and White (1990), White (1991), and White and Lindstrom (1989; especially Carucci 1989; Falgout 1989; Nero 1989; Poyer 1989). For immediate postwar research, see articles in Kiste and Marshall (1999).

2. See Poyer, Falgout, and Carucci (2001:316–329) for details and references on wartime destruction in Micronesia.

3. For details of Japanese military construction in each region of Micronesia, see Hezel (1995:217–241), Peattie (1988:230–310), and Poyer, Falgout, and Carucci (2001:33–116).

4. Rogers (1995:194–210) describes the impact of U.S. military actions on Guam in 1944–1945.

5. For Guam, see Rogers (1995:214–217, 229–232) and Souder (1971:105–106).

6. Much has been written about the Marshall Islands relocations; for example, Carucci (1997), Kiste (1977), and Richard (1957c:511–556). On relocation in the Marianas, Peleliu, and Chuuk, see cites in Poyer, Falgout, and Carucci (2001:324–325).

7. This review of Micronesia's postwar economy is derived from the longer discussion in Poyer, Falgout, and Carucci (2001:289–314). See also the discussion

of Micronesia's postwar economy in Hezel (1995:249–251, 64–270) and Hanlon (1998), a critical study of American development efforts and discourse in Micronesia.

8. Peattie (1988:308) gives a total of 147,000 Japanese, Koreans, Okinawans, and Taiwanese repatriated from the South Pacific, of whom 52,000 were civilians. See also Hezel (1995:249–250) on repatriation.

9. On postwar Saipan, see Spoehr (1954) and Farrell (1991:504).

10. On postwar Palau, see Ballendorf (1988), Barnett (1949), Useem (1946b:89; 1952; 1949:107–110), and Vidich (1980[1952]:268–269, 285–290).

## REFERENCES

Alonso, Ana Maria. 1994. "The Politics of Space, Time and Substance: State Formation, Nationalism, and Ethnicity." *Annual Review of Anthropology* 23:379–405.

Ballendorf, Dirk A. 1984. "American Administration in the Trust Territory of the Pacific Islands, 1944–1968." *Asian Culture Quarterly* 12(1):1–10.

———. 1988. "The Japanese and the Americans: Contrasting Historical Periods of Economic and Social Development in Palau." *Asian Culture Quarterly* 16(4):55–63.

Barnett, Homer G. 1949. *Palauan Society: A Study of Contemporary Native Life in the Palau Islands*. Coordinated Investigations in Micronesian Anthropology (CIMA) Report No. 20. Washington, D.C.: Pacific Science Board. Reprinted n.d. Eugene: Department of Anthropology, University of Oregon.

Bowers, Neal M. 1950. *Problems of Resettlement on Saipan, Tinian, and Rota, Mariana Islands*. CIMA Report No. 31. Washington, D.C.: Pacific Science Board.

Carucci, Laurence Marshall. 1989. "The Source of the Force in Marshallese Cosmology." In *The Pacific Theater.* Geoffrey M. White and Lamont Lindstrom, eds. Pp. 73–96. Honolulu: University of Hawai'i Press.

———. 1995. "From the Spaces to the Holes: Ralik-Ratak Remembrances of World War II." *Isla: A Journal of Micronesian Studies* 3(2), Dry Season:279–312.

———. 1997. *Nuclear Nativity: Rituals of Renewal and Empowerment in the Marshall Islands*. DeKalb: Northern Illinois University Press.

———. 2001. "From the Elaboration of Practice to the Practice of Elaboration: Reflections on 'The Tenth Day' on Enewetak Atoll." *Journal of Ritual Studies* 15(1):67–79.

Embree, John F. 1946. "Micronesia: The Navy and Democracy." *Far Eastern Survey* 15(11):161–165.

Falgout, Suzanne. 1989. "From Passive Pawns to Political Strategists: Wartime Lessons for the People of Pohnpei." In *The Pacific Theater.* Geoffrey M. White and Lamont Lindstrom, eds. Pp. 279–297. Honolulu: University of Hawai'i Press.

Falgout, Suzanne, Lin Poyer, and Laurence M. Carucci. 1995. "'The Greatest Hardship': Micronesian Memories of World War II." *Isla: A Journal of Micronesian Studies* 3(2), Dry Season:203–221.

Farrell, Don A. 1991. *History of the Northern Mariana Islands*. Saipan: Public School System, Commonwealth of the Northern Mariana Islands.

Firth, Stewart. 1989. "Sovereignty and Independence in the Contemporary Pacific." *The Contemporary Pacific* 1(1/2):75–96.

Fischer, John L., with Ann M. Fischer. 1957. "The Eastern Carolines." HRAF Behavior Science Monograph. New Haven, Conn.: HRAF Press.

Foster, Robert J. 1991. "Making National Culture in the Global Ecumene." *Annual Review of Anthropology* 20:235–260.

Gale, Roger W. 1979. *The Americanization of Micronesia: A Study of the Consolidation of U.S. Rule in the Pacific.* Washington, D.C.: University Press of America.

Glazer, Nathan, and Daniel P. Moynihan. 1975. *Ethnicity: Theory and Experience.* Cambridge: MIT Press.

Goetzfridt, Nicholas J., and William L. Wuerch. 1989. *Micronesia 1975–1987, a Social Science Bibliography.* New York: Greenwood Press.

Hanlon, David. 1998. *Remaking Micronesia: Discourses over Development in a Pacific Territory.* Honolulu: University of Hawai'i Press.

———. 1999. "Magellan's Chroniclers? American Anthropology's History in Micronesia." In *American Anthropology and Micronesia.* Robert Kiste and Mac Marshall, eds. Pp. 53–79. Honolulu: University of Hawai'i Press.

Hatanaka, Sachiko. 1973–1974. Culture Change in Micronesia Under the Japanese Administration. Programme of Participation No. 4, UNESCO.

Hezel, Francis X., S.J. 1983. "The First Taint of Civilization: A History of the Caroline and Marshall Islands in Pre-Colonial Days, 1521–1885." Pacific Islands Monograph Series No. 1. Honolulu: University of Hawai'i Press.

———. 1995. *Strangers in Their Own Land: A Century of Colonial Rule in the Caroline and Marshall Islands.* Honolulu: University of Hawai'i Press.

Kiste, Robert C. 1977. "The Relocation of the Bikini Marshallese." In *Exiles and Migrants in Oceania,* Michael D. Lieber, ed. Pp. 81–120. Honolulu, University of Hawai'i Press.

Kiste, Robert C., and Suzanne Falgout. 1999. "Anthropology and Micronesia: The Context." In *American Anthropology in Micronesia: An Assessment.* Honolulu: University of Hawai'i Press.

Kiste, Robert C., and Mac Marshall, eds. 1999. *American Anthropology in Micronesia: An Assessment.* Honolulu: University of Hawai'i Press.

Lessa, William A. 1950. The Ethnography of Ulithi Atoll. Coordinated Investigations in Micronesian Anthropology (CIMA) Report No. 28. Washington, D.C.: Pacific Science Board.

Lindstrom, Lamont, and Geoffrey M. White. 1990. *Island Encounters: Black and White Memories of the Pacific War.* Washington, D.C.: Smithsonian.

Linnekin, Jocelyn, and Lin Poyer. 1990. "Introduction." In *Cultural Identity and Ethnicity in the Pacific.* Jocelyn Linnekin and Lin Poyer, eds. Pp. 1–16. Honolulu: University of Hawai'i Press.

Marshall, Mac and James D. Nason. 1975. *Micronesia, 1944–1974: A Bibliography of Anthropological and Related Source Materials.* New Haven, Conn.: HRAF Press.

Mason, Leonard. 1974. "Unity and Disunity in Micronesia: Internal Problems and Future Status." In *Political Development in Micronesia.* Daniel T. Hughes and Sherwood G. Lingenfelter, eds. Pp. 203–262. Columbus: Ohio State University Press.

McGrath, William A., and W. Scott Wilson. 1971. "The Marshall, Caroline and Mariana Islands: Too Many Foreign Precedents." In *Land Tenure in Oceania.* R. Crocombe, ed. Pp. 172–191. Melbourne: Oxford University Press.

Michal, Edward J. 1993. "Protected States: The Political Status of the Federated States of Micronesia and the Republic of the Marshall Islands." *The Contemporary Pacific* 5(2):303–332.

Morison, Samuel Eliot. 1951. *A History of United States Naval Operations in World War II.* Vol. 7. *Aleutians, Gilberts, and Marshalls: June 1942–April 1944.* Boston: Atlantic, Little, Brown.

———. 1953. *A History of United States Naval Operations in World War II.* Vol. 8. *New Guinea and the Marianas: March 1944–August 1944.* Boston: Atlantic, Little, Brown.

Nero, Karen L. 1989. "Time of Famine, Time of Transformation: Hell in the Pacific, Palau." In *The Pacific Theater.* Geoffrey M. White and Lamont Lindstrom, eds. Pp. 117–147. Honolulu: University of Hawai'i Press.

Peattie, Mark R. 1988. *Nan'yo: The Rise and Fall of the Japanese in Micronesia, 1885–1945.* Honolulu: University of Hawai'i Press.

Petersen, Glenn. 1999. "Politics in Postwar Micronesia." In *American Anthropology and Micronesia.* Robert Kiste and Mac Marshall, eds. Pp. 145–195. Honolulu: University of Hawai'i Press.

Poyer, Lin. 1989. "Echoes of Massacre: Recollections of World War II on Sapwuahfik (Ngatik Atoll)." In *The Pacific Theater.* Geoffrey M. White and Lamont Lindstrom, eds. Pp. 97–115. Honolulu: University of Hawai'i Press.

———. 1995. "Yapese Experiences of the Pacific War." *Isla: A Journal of Micronesian Studies* 3(2):223–255.

———. 1999. "Ethnicity and Identity in Micronesia." In *American Anthropology and Micronesia.* Robert Kiste and Mac Marshall, eds. Pp. 197–223. Honolulu: University of Hawai'i Press.

Poyer, Lin, Suzanne Falgout, and Laurence M. Carucci. 2001. *The Typhoon of War: Micronesian Experiences of the Pacific War.* Honolulu: University of Hawai'i Press.

Richard, Dorothy E. 1957a. *United States Naval Administration of the Trust Territory of the Pacific Islands.* Vol. 1. Washington, D.C.: Office of the Chief of Naval Operations.

———. 1957b. *United States Naval Administration of the Trust Territory of the Pacific Islands.* Vol. 2. Washington, D.C.: Office of the Chief of Naval Operations.

———. 1957c. *United States Naval Administration of the Trust Territory of the Pacific Islands.* Vol. 3. Washington, D.C.: Office of the Chief of Naval Operations.

Rogers, Robert F. 1995. *Destiny's Landfall: A History of Guam.* Honolulu: University of Hawai'i Press.

Souder, Paul B. 1971. "Guam: Land Tenure in a Fortress." In *Land Tenure in Oceania.* R. Crocombe, ed. Pp. 192–205. Melbourne: Oxford University Press.

Spector, Ronald H. 1985. *Eagle against the Sun: The American War with Japan.* New York: Free Press.

Spoehr, Alexander. 1954. *Saipan: The Ethnology of a War-Devastated Island. Fieldiana: Anthropology.* Vol. 41. Chicago: Natural History Museum.

Useem, John. 1945. "The Changing Structure of a Micronesian Society." *American Anthropologist* 47(4):567–588.

———. 1946a. "Americans as Governors of Natives in the Pacific." *Journal of Social Issues* 2(3):39–49.

———. 1949. "Report on Palau." Co-ordinated Investigations in Micronesian Anthropology (CIMA) Report No. 21. Washington, D.C.: Pacific Science Board.

———. 1952. "South Sea Island Strike: Labor Management Relations in the Caroline Islands, Micronesia [Angaur]." In *Human Problems in Technological Change: A Casebook.* Edward H. Spicer, ed. Pp. 149–164. New York: Russell Sage Foundation.

———. 1946b. *Report on Yap and Palau. U.S. Commercial Company, Economic Survey of Micronesia,* Report No. 6. Honolulu: U.S. Commercial Company. Mimeo.

Vidich, Arthur J. 1980[1952]. *The Political Impact of Colonial Administration.* New York: Arno Press. (Reprint of "The Political Impact of Colonial Administration." Ph.D. dissertation. Harvard University, 1952.)

White, Geoffrey M. 1991. "Remembering the Pacific War." Occasional Paper No. 36. Honolulu: Center for Pacific Islands Studies, University of Hawai'i.

White, Geoffrey M., and Lamont Lindstrom. 1989. *The Pacific Theater: Island Representations of World War II.* Honolulu: University of Hawai'i Press.

Williams, Brackette F. 1989. "A Class Act: Anthropology and the Race to Nation Across Ethnic Terrain." *Annual Review of Anthropology* 18:401–444.

# 19

# Tradition Sells: Identity Merchandise in the Island Pacific

**Jocelyn Linnekin**

*University of Connecticut*

This chapter examines links between transnational consumer capitalism and the representation of cultural identities in the contemporary Pacific Islands. Many historians and anthropologists have pointed out that texts about history, custom, and tradition enter into the construction of modern cultural and national identities.[1] Graphic symbols displayed on material goods also communicate messages about culture and human groups. Because of their immediate visual impact, these images may convey ideologies and stereotypes more effectively than texts, and they reach a much wider audience. In the Pacific Islands there is a growing market for what I call "identity merchandise"—consumer goods that depict islanders and cultural artifacts in evocative ways. In this chapter I will discuss Pacific cultural identities by examining the icons and symbols found on mass merchandise that is sold in shopping malls and local discount shops. This merchandise celebrates particular ethnic identities, but it also communicates a message about the nature of human groups in general. Clearly, culture and tradition "sell" in the contemporary Pacific.

A burgeoning literature in anthropology and cultural studies addresses the communicative functions of material items, cross-culturally and historically.[2] Once dismissed by anthropologists as vehicles of Western cultural corruption and inauthenticity (Miller 1995), consumer goods are now analyzed as powerful media for conveying public meanings. In industrial and postcolonial societies, consumption is inseparable from consumerism, for the denizens of modern society must engage with competitive and entrepreneurial markets in order to acquire the mundane articles of daily life. The historical analysis of consumerism has thus broadened into the study of mass culture in advanced capitalist societies (see Baudrillard 1981; Featherstone 1982; Kellner 1983; Dunn 1986; Garnham 1993). In the European context, Veblen (1953), Braudel (1973), and Bourdieu (1984) document how consumption patterns have come to function as indices of class. Particularly since the late 1960s, material culture has also become a venue for modeling group distinctiveness and "tradition," in industrial nations as well as on the capitalist periphery. Garnham (1993), Handelman and Shamgar-Handelman (1993), and Kemper (1993) have authored comprehensive articles addressing the public symbolism of cultural identities in the context of national ideology.

As the literature on modern mass culture attests, consumer markets now expedite the global circulation of identity symbols. In the past decade cultural symbols and representations of ethnic paragons have become increasingly popular on consumer goods in the Pacific Islands. Island retail markets large and small, metropolitan and rural, now feature identity merchandise—products that represent cultural groups by means of graphic archetypes and purportedly traditional motifs. These items typically display stylized physical exemplars and cultural icons in conjunction with slogans asserting ethnic power, purity, cultural authenticity, and "tradition." Significantly, such products are bought primarily by local people; they are sold in village stores and in back-street urban outlets where tourists are rare. In Hawai'i these goods can be found at outdoor flea markets, as well as at Woolworth's and J. C. Penney's. The popularity of identity merchandise in the Pacific and elsewhere can be attributed to the worldwide resurgence of micronationalism and the ubiquity of primordial claims in national-level politics around the globe. However, local economic history is also part of the explanation for the growing demand. In the Pacific Islands as in other colonial settings, forms of capitalism such as plantation agriculture and its successor, tourism, commoditized the labor and lifeways of indigenous peoples.[3]

Identity merchandise portrays human cultural groups rather like species in the Linnean taxonomic scheme: as discretely bounded natural populations distinguished from one another by particular essential characteristics. Sugar planters in Hawai'i operationalized precisely this model when they recruited successive cohorts of laborers from Asian and European nations. Each ethnic group supposedly embodied a different temperamental type, and the planters sought (in vain) for the perfect combination of docility and industriousness. It does not seem coincidental that a market in identity products now flourishes in a former plantation colony where cultural groups and local culture have been objectified as entities with market value. The graphic representations on identity merchandise purvey a primordialist, naturalistic model of cultural identity—a paradigm that closely approximates the popular Western ideology about the nature of human groups (Handler and Linnekin 1984; Handler 1985; Linnekin and Poyer 1990).

Historians of mass consumption and consumerism argue compellingly that marketing and advertising affect the buyers' self-perceptions, aspirations, and social values (Ewen and Ewen 1982; Fox and Lears 1983; McCracken 1988). The search for new markets—capitalist expansion—therefore has the potential to influence not only the graphic content of designs on consumer goods but also the ways in which people conceptualize themselves and others. Such effects are difficult to measure, and anthropologists frequently caution against assuming that Western ideological models necessarily supplant indigenous ones in colonized societies. However, it is striking that in Hawai'i—an archetypal plantation colony turned tourist destination—many local people today objectify culture and essentialize ethnicity in ways that echo nineteenth-century plantation stereotypes. Furthermore, the prevalent local model of distinct, quasi-racial groups defined by primordial land of origin is entirely in accord with tourist industry representations and with indigenous Hawaiian nationalist rhetoric (Handler 1984, 1988; Linnekin 1997). In the consumer society of modern Hawai'i, many local people have become collectors of objectified culture (see Clifford 1988)—but, unlike Western collectors of indigenous art and objects, Hawai'i residents collect artifacts and icons of their own culture.

## SOVEREIGNTY POGS

I will first examine a seemingly improbable venue for messages about tradition and identity, a genre of consumer goods that sparked a

**Figure 19.1** "Local" symbols on island nostalgia pogs

frenzied collectible market in Hawai'i and, to a much lesser extent, on the mainland. The focal objects were "milk caps," the small cardboard disks that were once used as tops on glass quart-size milk bottles (Figure 19.1). In its functional form the milk cap was held together with a staple and had a slotted tab that was pried up to remove the cap. Milk caps were typically printed with the dairy name and contents of the bottle, and were sometimes used to advertise the dairy's other products. Most Hawai'i residents refer to milk caps as "pogs." An acronym for passion-orange-guava, POG is the trademark name of a juice drink produced by one of the local dairies. Various local theories were proposed to explain how milk caps came to be called pogs. POG drink did not originally come in glass bottles, but in the early stages of the fad milk caps advertising POG were very plentiful. In any event, pog is the emic label and I will use it as such.

The children's game played with pogs involves stacking one or more, printed side up, and then vigorously throwing a "hitter" pog onto the stack. The thrower then wins the pogs that have been flipped over. At the height of the game's popularity in Hawai'i (circa early 1993), children were so preoccupied with playing and trading pogs that some schools banned them. Other schools printed their own pogs and used them as behavioral incentives and fundraising items. What started as a children's game quickly mushroomed into an adult craze similar to the mania for Beanie Babies. The pog frenzy was a sudden

economic boon for local designers, artists, printers, retailers, and fundraisers. Initially, many of the pogs in circulation were replicas of dairy milk caps and the printed designs were fairly rudimentary. Consumer demand sparked an efflorescence in creative design, however, and within a couple of months pogs were transformed into a collectible item.

Applying the baseball-card logic, many local adults believed that the pogs would someday increase in value several times over. The appreciation potential of the different varieties was hotly debated and speculative investor newsletters appeared. Local stores quickly opened pog sections where adult buyers usually outnumbered children. Pog kiosks sprang up in shopping malls, and designers and printers rushed to keep up with the demand for new and more elaborate designs. There was also a brisk market in "real," "authentic" pogs—that is, ones that had purportedly been produced for use as milk bottle covers. (Glass milk bottles, incidentally, have not been used or produced in Hawai'i for decades.) These were sold for several dollars each. Some consumers preferred the "authentic" style pogs, even if they were replicas, and looked for the characteristic staple and pull-up tab. If the tab was actually pulled up, however, the pog was less valuable, rather like a baseball card with a dog-eared corner or a Beanie Baby with the ear tag removed. However, most designers saw the staple and tab as impediments to artistic elaboration and all but the purists soon eliminated them.

Several months into the craze, nearly every local business and fundraising organization was selling or giving away its own trademark pogs. McDonald's produced a series of commemorative milk caps, a different one for every McDonald's restaurant in Hawai'i, and gave away a pog with each combination meal. Customers were encouraged to attempt to collect the entire set. For manufacturers and merchants, the incentive was obvious: Pogs could be quickly and cheaply printed in runs of several thousand and sold for many times over their production cost. Cheap pogs could be bought for twenty-five cents, but the more elaborate and artistic items sold for several dollars each. Even a design that was relatively expensive to produce, such as a sepia reproduction of a nineteenth-century photograph, could be sold at a profit of several hundred percent. Testimonials of fantastic windfalls abounded in local media, and people wondered if they could cash in on the appreciation before the fad waned. A logical development in marketing was to produce a series of pogs with different designs that were thematically and stylistically linked, so that buyers were motivated to collect all of them.

The role of pogs in cultural representation goes beyond their content and design, however. Pogs and the milk cap game were held to be a unique Hawai'i tradition. As reported almost daily in local newspapers during the milk cap craze, the origin, significance, and appeal of pogs are rooted in the lore of the sugar plantations. On the plantations the immigrant grandparents and parents of today's schoolchildren could not afford store-bought toys, so for amusement they devised a game using the humble milk cap. Pogs are therefore not only part of Hawai'i's plantation heritage but a reminder that the descendants of those poor laborers had realized the American dream. Pogs, in short, symbolize and encompass Hawai'i's favorite public scenario of ethnic advancement through hard work. Not surprisingly, in the competition to produce new designs manufacturers found that "traditional" motifs sold well. The Milk Cap Craze pog shown in Figure 19.1 includes several locally significant references and images. The block print in the background is a fabric pattern locally called *palaka,* a Hawai'ian word possibly derived from the English "block." The pattern is an old New England cotton design that is advertised in a mainland mail-order curtains catalog as "Sturbridge plaid." It was probably introduced during the early nineteenth century by missionaries, merchants, and/or whalers. When used today for aloha shirts and dresses, *palaka* fabric invokes old Hawai'i and insider sensibility. "Hanabata days" is a Hawai'i pidgin expression that means "runny nose days" and refers to childhood. "Kaki mochi" are Japanese *arare* or sweet rice crackers, a favorite local snack.

**Figure 19.2**    Icons of (masculine) Hawai'ian identity

Other pogs reproduce locally evocative symbols, particularly of indigenous Hawai'ian culture (Figure 19.2). In my estimation the greatest creative efflorescence took place precisely in the pog designs that represented and celebrated Hawai'i's past and Hawai'ian identity. Since the Hawai'ian renaissance of the 1970s, the helmet pictured has become the quintessential public symbol of Hawai'ian identity and communal strength, connoting spiritual power, mystery, and cultural revitalization. In the iconography of identity merchandise, ethnic strength is virtually always expressed through masculine images, a point I will return to below. The ubiquitous gourd helmet has been incorporated into the logos of numerous T-shirt lines with titles such as "Kapu—Forbidden Territory" and "Local Boyz Rule." It is typically combined with motifs such as pit bull dogs and fanciful weaponry. Indeed, this icon is popularly described as "the Hawaiian warrior helmet." At swap meets and shopping mall kiosks entrepreneurs sell reproductions made from polished coconut shells and dyed chicken feathers in a wide range of sizes and color schemes. These are favored ornaments for the rear-view mirrors of automobiles and pick-up trucks in Hawai'i. Ironically, early foreign visitors observed the gourd helmet only once, on the island of Hawai'i, and it almost certainly was not worn during warfare. John Webber, the artist on Cook's third voyage, produced two engravings of helmeted men who were described as priests of the god Lono. While the gourd helmet appears to have had a minor place in ancient Hawai'ian society, in twentieth-century Hawai'i its image has acquired new symbolic significance as a prominent cultural and political icon.

The Hawaiian Strength series, of which the Mana Piha Supreme pog shown in Figure 19.2 is number eleven, features loincloth-clad males in different bodybuilder poses, each wearing the warrior helmet. The figures are captioned with Hawai'ian words for strength, or with terms for task-based roles in the precapitalist society, such as "*Hoe Wa'a*—Canoe Paddler." By identifying the figures according to occupational roles, however, the series communicates a strikingly modern model of labor specialization, wherein an individual is identified exclusively through one kind of work. Collectors could buy the pogs separately or purchase the series in a single sheet, shrink-wrapped and not punched out.

*Mana*—a famous Polynesian concept—is perhaps best translated as "efficacious power," and *piha* means "full-blooded" or "pure." The design graphically and explicitly equates ethnic potency and strength with full-blooded power. Like many such designs, the Hawai'ian Strength images appeared first on T-shirts and were adapted for reproduction on pogs. In Hawai'ian identity merchandise the pit bull dog is almost as popular an image as the Hawai'ian warrior helmet as the graphic archetype of intimidating force. A typical pog design from Master Graphics, known locally for its popular T-shirts in the masculine power genre, depicts the silver head of a pit bull, mouth agape with sharp teeth, against a black background.

The pog craze coincided with the commemoration of the one-hundredth anniversary of the overthrow of the Hawai'ian monarchy, and the event provided the theme for new market lines of pogs. The Native Hawaii pog in Figure 19.2 uses a petroglyph figure to symbol-

**Figure 19.3** Queen Lili'uokalani, the last monarch, from a series marking the centennial of the overthrow

ize and celebrate indigenous identity; in this example the "1993 100 year" notation is minimally related to the design, however, and seems almost a marketing afterthought. More elaborate and artistic commemorative pogs portray Queen Lili'uokalani, the last monarch, as well as other nineteenth-century Hawai'ian chiefs (Figure 19.3). This sepia-tinted reproduction photograph of the queen is surrounded by the legend, "Learn the Truth, Respect the Culture," a political invocation to learn the facts about the overthrow of the monarchy. One of a series portraying Hawai'ian chiefs, this pog has a tab like an authentic functional milk cap, as well as the notation, "printed in Hawai'i." Both of these details seem to be design inclusions intended to enhance the aura of authenticity. The tab is a physical reminder of the pog's historical roots and identity. "Printed in Hawai'i" is an assurance of local provenience. At the height of the craze, pogs began to be imported from Taiwan and Hong Kong, where they could be produced less expensively than in Hawai'i. Most collectors viewed the imports as cheap and inferior, in part, I suggest, because the designs did not include locally meaningful symbols.

In Hawai'i pogs were tangible icons of past life-ways, hence the plethora of cultural representations in the designs and their popularity among adult collectors. Months after Hawai'i schoolchildren had lost interest in the game, pogs spread to the mainland. *Newsweek* (Seligmann and Gordon 1995:55) explained the activity as "based on a traditional Hawaiian game." On a trip to the east coast a year after the craze had waned in Hawai'i, I found pogs on sale in New York City's F. A. O. Schwarz toy store and at kiosks in shopping malls. At that time, the pogs at F. A. O. Schwarz appeared to have no takers; the mall kiosks were somewhat more populated. The patrons were all children and, in contrast to the Hawai'i selection, there was little variation in the artistic quality or price of the pogs. Instead of being carefully packaged in shrink wrap or offered as sets in full sheets, the pogs were simply jumbled together in bins. Some displayed the logos of Hawai'i high schools and an occasional warrior helmet or *palaka* print, but the mainland selection featured primarily the mass-produced pogs imported from Asia.

The prevalent designs were colorful but crude, featuring dinosaurs, samurai, Power Rangers, cartoon characters, or abstract patterns. I wondered what the mainland children made of them. In November 1994 the Bloomington, Indiana *Herald-Times* described pogs as "the latest gradeschool fad to hit the Midwest" (Denny 1994: D1). A schoolgirl interviewed for the story explained their appeal: "I like 'em because they have such neat pictures on them. . . . They're fun to collect and play with." In the mainland collecting trade, however, pogs are now referred to as "failed collectibles" because no adult demand materialized for them, by negative contrast with the fantastically successful Beanie Babies.

The enthusiasm that drove Hawai'i's pog market stemmed precisely, I suggest, from the object's local significance, which empowered the humble pog as a vehicle for narratives about tradition. The perceived link to local culture and the ability of graphic designers to elaborate and juxtapose locally evocative symbols made pogs a collectible craze in Hawai'i, albeit a short-lived one. About a year after it had begun, just as every small business in every Hawai'ian town was giving away cheaply

produced logo pogs, the fad was dead. The kiosks in shopping malls closed and collectible card shops were caught with thousands of unsold pogs. Liberty House, Hawai'i's upscale department store, put out boxes of them, offered at ten for a dollar. Only the mass-produced or imported varieties were dumped on the market in this way, however. The more artistically designed, heirloom-quality pogs—made in Hawai'i and celebrating local tradition—are still stored away in people's homes, waiting for the appreciation that grows with time.

## IDENTITY FASHIONS

Many of the motifs used on pogs appeared first on lines of apparel (Figure 19.4). This is particularly true of designs representing traditional culture and ethnic paragons. The primary venue has been T-shirts, which in Hawai'i and the Pacific Islands seem to function as personal communicative media more than they do in the mainland United States. The explicit identity fashions that began to appear in the 1980s, such as the Hawaiian Strength T-shirts, are traceable to lines of T-shirts that appeared locally in the 1970s. In the competition to produce distinctively Hawai'ian beachwear and surfer fashions, some entrepreneurs began featuring ethnic and pidgin in-jokes on shirts. Lines such as Cane Haul Road were particularly popular with Hawai'i's young people, who looked forward to the appearance of new designs. The 1970s also witnessed the Hawai'ian renaissance, entailing both cultural revival and increased activism for Hawai'ian rights and self-determination.

Since the mid-1980s the subtle local jokes—which were not ethnically exclusive—have been overtaken in popularity by explicitly celebratory group identity messages and hypermasculinized images of power. The current identity fashions explicitly equate the hypermuscular male physique with group power, strength, and tradition. Whether the shirt proclaims "Hawaiian strength" or "Filipino power," the images and slogans are largely the same. A few distinctive symbols or

**Figure 19.4** "Canoe paddler," from a series depicting "traditional" Hawai'ian roles

artifacts are included in the design to index cultural particularity, rather as one would distinguish similar bird species on the basis of small but significant anatomical details. Paradoxically, the identity images are hybrid in content at the same time that they present highly essentialized ethnic types. The content of the representations is often highly syncretic, juxtaposing cultural symbols from a variety of sources. The similarities of representational style and message are common to a number of different designers and manufacturers; the commonalities evidently reflect the fact that such portrayals sell.

In Hawai'i identity fashions are worn primarily by Hawai'ian men and boys. Ikaika, the name of one popular series of shirt designs, means strong or powerful and is a popular name for Hawai'ian boys. Shirts such as the one shown in Figure 19.4 celebrate male tasks and roles, such as canoe paddler. There are a few Hawaiian Strength shirts aimed at women; one depicts the volcano goddess Pele. However, identity is not only gendered but is overwhelmingly masculinized in this merchandise.

Stuart Hall notes that this is true of most marketing strategies in consumer capitalism: "certain forms of modern advertising are still grounded on the exclusive, powerful, dominant, highly masculinist . . . imagery, of a very exclusive set of identities" (1997:31). Women are largely absent from Pacific identity fashions. Most of the shirts that do depict women portray them in a highly stylized and sexualized manner, rather like the original Barbie doll; in the United States, most girls and women would be unlikely to wear these designs. For example, one line of shirts contains the word *kapu*, "taboo," next to a thin, voluptuous, leggy, and scantily clad female who resembles most Polynesian women only in that her hair is dark. The figure is very similar to the representations of women that one sees on the mud flaps of large trailer trucks.

With their bold and overstated messages, the shirts have an obvious appeal and function at a time when Hawai'ian sovereignty is a pressing public issue (Figure 19.5). The hypermasculine images juxtapose traditionalized symbols with modern images of

**Figure 19.5**   Icons and slogans of Hawai'ian sovereignty

machismo to send a graphic message about the reclamation of political power. In the design shown in Figure 19.5, the helmeted Hawai'ian warrior is associated with total sovereignty and *mana*. On another T-shirt, ravening pit bulls are held back by a steroidal, helmeted Hawai'ian warrior. The image is captioned, "TRADITION." The entrepreneurial process by which the designs are created gives full play to artistic license and creative innovation. T-shirts in Hawai'i have been produced by individuals working out of their homes and carports, and by family-run businesses. Much as neighborhood print shops experimented with their own series of pogs, store-front silk screeners have produced small lots of shirts for sale at swap meets and locally owned discount stores. After identity fashions became more popular, they began to appear in mass retail outlets such as J. C. Penney and Sears.

I asked an amateur graphic artist to explain a shirt depicting the god Lono wielding fire, captioned "Lono maku." Lono is conventionally associated with peace, rain, and fertility, and I knew of no Hawai'ian word or godly epithet corresponding to *maku*. My informant opined that the designer had simply truncated the Hawai'ian word *makua*, "parent," because it looked better. Judging by the shirts most often seen in Hawai'i's schools and neighborhoods, the most successful identity designs selectively combine evocative reminders of the cultural past with contemporary symbols of intimidating force—snarling pit bulls with studded collars, rippled muscles and iron-pumping poses, big-wheeled trucks, motorcycles, tyrannosaurs, and sword-and-sorcery crossbows.

The same imagery is used to appeal to other groups recognized as systematically disadvantaged in Hawai'i. Although there are lines of T-shirts featuring Chinese and Japanese motifs and in-jokes, I have never seen apparel touting Chinese, Japanese, or *haole*, "white," strength. As with the Hawai'ian identity fashions, bodybuilder-type muscularity is featured as a symbol of ethnic group assertiveness, and the pit bull appears as a generic macho icon (Figure 19.6). "Pinoy" means a Filipino from the Philippines, as opposed to one born elsewhere. Thus Filipinos in migrant communities—or, as we now say, living in diaspora—are encouraged to draw their "spirit" from the land of their warrior-like ancestors. Yet the Filipino figure's loincloth is very similar to that of the Hawai'ian warrior; the headband and choice of weapon are the only details used to signal Filipino ethnicity. In the small logo on the front of the shirt, a Hawai'ian-style petroglyph figure holds a spear and a dagger. On the Samoan strength shirt in the same series, the logo depicts a nearly identical petroglyph figure holding only a spear.

In counterpoint to the highly essentialized ethnic images are invocations of "Jawaiian" strength. Jawaiian was first used in Hawai'i to denote a genre of music that added reggae rhythms to the local string-band sound. A hybrid mix of Caribbean, Hawai'ian, and

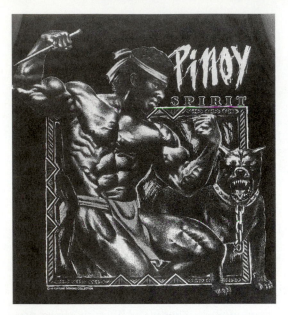

**Figure 19.6**    The "native-born" Filipino as paragon

**Figure 19.7**    "Jawaiian" iconography mixes Rastafarian, counter-cultural, and crudely drawn Hawai'ian symbols

mainstream pop styles, the music became extremely popular in the 1980s and early 1990s, as did merchandise labeled Jamaican style and featuring Bob Marley and Rastafarian symbols. The Jawaiian label was eventually extended from music to a variety of consumer goods, again illustrating how consumer markets drive design innovation and the distribution of identity symbols. Jawaiian stretches the appropriateness of the term "identity" because it is an ambiguous and amorphous category. The symbols used on Jawaiian goods are wildly syncretic. The logo on the front of the Jawaiian shirt shown in Figure 19.7 features the Ethiopian lion. Jawaiian imagery constructs a transnational identity by invoking the countercultural unity of oppressed peoples; a hybrid mix of symbols is used to link Hawai'i with Africa and the Caribbean. Some of the shirts proclaiming Hawai'ian sovereignty feature a background of "liberation colors," which derive from the Ethiopian flag and since the 1960s have been associated with African-American identity apparel in the mainland United States. These colors are experiencing a marketing comeback in the current era of micronationalism. The epitome of hybrid designs, the shirt in Figure 19.7 pictures the helmeted Hawai'ian warrior, the Ethiopian lion, the Egyptian ankh, the profile of Africa, the peace symbol, Scorpio, and a marijuana leaf. I purchased this shirt, along with many others celebrating Hawai'i identities, in a retail store frequented by local residents in Pago Pago, American Samoa.

Identity fashions have become increasingly popular in Western and American Samoa. Hawaiian Strength shirts are frequently seen on Apia's main street, worn by women as well as by men. Other designs picture stylized Samoan images—a man with a Samoan *pe'a* (full-body tattoo), a *taupou* or village maiden in ceremonial dance costume—or celebrate Manu Samoa, the Western Samoa national rugby team which won the 1993 world championship in seven-a-side rugby. In one Manu Samoa design, captioned "Pride of the Pacific," a male figure with a *pe'a* strikes a biceps-flexing pose and holds a rugby football instead of a weapon. The Hawai'ian and Samoan "power" shirts feature the same generic tapa cloth design in the background, and the pattern seems only slightly altered for the Pinoy spirit shirt. Other shirts seen in Pago Pago and Apia depict archetypal Samoan cultural figures in association with slogans such as "Samoa *moni*" ("real Samoan"), "*tōtō* Samoa" ("Samoan blood"), and even "*tōtō* Samoa *moni*" ("real Samoan blood"). One shirt in the Samoa *moni* series features an idyllic tropical island scene on the back: a thatched house on a beach, with palm trees and hibiscus. The indigenous Samoan style of *fale* (house) construction, however, features open sides with the roof supported by wooden columns. The house in the real Samoa shirt reflects an artist's imagining of a generic island culture.

Beyond the Western core states and their satellites, it is questionable whether the appeal of identity merchandise derives from the content of the message or from the association of these goods with Euro-American metropolitan society. Many scholars have documented the historical and present-day appeal of Western trade goods, from the iron adzes and colored fabrics of the earliest exchanges to today's boom boxes and VCRs. Tracing the history of mass imagery in America, Ewen and Ewen (1982:45–46) describe the significance of American goods as "magical objects" and "carriers of fantasy" to people in postwar Europe. Rural Americans experienced much the same sense of longing—and awareness of relative deprivation—in the face of mass images of consumer goods. Philibert and Jourdan write that in Vanuatu, Western consumer goods "are valued for their symbolic significance as agents of cultural change and social power rather than for their actual utility" (1996:66). Though of marginal practical use in daily life, the refrigerators and electric lights "are material proof of the social equality between villagers and Europeans, since they signify equal competence in the modern world" (1996:66–67).

In Tonga and Samoa, over half of the national income derives from migrant remittances. Electronic appliances and consumer goods found in Samoan villages are usually gifts from relatives living in New Zealand, Australia, or Hawai'i. In the 1990s a busy trade in Western consumer goods has developed in Apia, the capital of Western Samoa. More and more young Samoans are sporting ethnic identity T-shirts from Hawai'i—even those proclaiming "pinoy" or "Jawaiian" strength. Ironically, the rise of consumerism has occurred during a time of straitened economic circumstances, the result of two devastating cyclones in the early 1990s and an on-going taro blight that nearly wiped out the country's major export crop. Yet a few years after the cyclones, the residents of the island of Manono in Western Samoa demanded an electrical generator when they elected their member of parliament. Now the island has electricity, but it is switched on only at night and is primarily used to power lights, televisions, and VCRs. However engineered these wants may seem to Western intellectuals, people in cash-poor nations associate such conveniences with modernity, technology, wealth, and progress, and they want them, perhaps just as much as their American counterparts do.

## THE GLOBALIZATION OF DIFFERENCE

In a recent symposium volume on globalization and cultural representation, Anthony King comments that "the degree to which cultures are self-consciously 'different' is an indication of how much they are the same" (1997:153). Ironically, even as cultural diversity is celebrated in the Pacific Islands, graphic representations of group identity are becoming increasingly homogeneous in consumer markets and, arguably, in peripheral nations generally. In the current era, micronationalist assertions of group difference are promulgated globally at the same time that popular culture is taking on an increasingly transnational, albeit hybridized, character. Such promotion, of course, did not originate with manufacturers and merchants. Today's capitalist entrepreneurs are responding to the endemic international vaunting and mobilization of ethnic identities. In most cases reported in the international media, the rhetoric of modern ethnic assertiveness replicates the Western taxonomic, biogenetic paradigm of human differences. The most powerful selling point of this merchandise may be not any particular ethnic affiliation but identity itself: the very fact of belonging to *some* marked cultural group.

When cultural representations are used to market mass merchandise, then consumption patterns, fashion, and entrepreneurial creativity enter into the public conceptualization of cultural identities. Through a largely entrepreneurial and opportunistic economic process, the symbolism of cultural identity is becoming increasingly internationalized, as capitalist consumer markets distribute identity products across political borders. Motifs seen on the sidewalks of Washington, D.C., appear on apparel sold in the markets of Pago Pago. The profit incentive, competition, and responsiveness to consumer demand spur fast-paced creativity in graphic representation. Market demand encourages successful designs to be distributed widely. In the quest for novelty and originality, traditions are invented; cultural motifs are creatively fashioned, refashioned, and recombined to maximize visual and emotive appeal.

Apparel designs have in common with advertising the property of indiscriminate communication. Both media broadcast visual messages to an audience of strangers. Whether or not identity fashions are initially purchased because of their content, the messages are conveyed when the garments are worn in public. By associating the cultural past with ethnic distinctiveness and power, these fashions communicate the primordial basis and the exclusivity of modern identities. The designs seek to convey a sense of authenticity and boundedness by invoking tradition, even though they represent tradition as a hybrid mix of selected artifacts and symbols. Steroidal hypermuscularity is equated with ethnic group strength; women are largely excluded from the iconography. Essentialist metaphors of "blood" and "purity" are categorically associated with power and effectiveness. Human groups are portrayed as primordial, unambiguously bounded, biologically self-perpetuating entities maintaining separate cultural traditions.

In essence, tradition sells. Ever opportunistic and innovative, manufacturers, designers, and retailers are marketing cultural identities and, in the process, are marketing ideas about cultural identity in general. Representations of the past—many of them syncretic and highly inventive—are deployed to symbolize the primordial distinctiveness of ethnic groups, and the driving force behind this creativity is the pursuit of profit. In an increasingly globalizing postcolonial world, essentialist and exclusivist notions of ethnicity are purveyed to international consumers and, in many locales that Wallerstein (1974) would classify as the periphery of the world system, people are buying.

Although identity images sell, they sell for different reasons in different places. In contrast to Bosnia and Rwanda, cultural diversity in the Pacific is usually invoked in relatively benign ways. State-level and international celebrations of cultural traditions are ubiquitous in public discourse, festivals, and regional movements, such as the voyaging canoe revival that spread from Hawai'i's *Hokule'a* to nearly every Polynesian island group. In Hawai'i essentialist and primordialist notions of ethnicity are profoundly embedded in discourse at all levels of society—government, schools, media, entertainment. Ethnicity is not only constantly foregrounded in Hawai'i but is publicly celebrated on a daily basis in innumerable contexts. Items of local apparel have long been bundled with social meanings and have communicated subtle distinctions of class, culture, and insider knowledge. The current designs have emerged in a context of increasing political action by Hawai'ians accompanied by intense public debate about Hawai'ian sovereignty. As was the case in the mainland United States during the late 1960s, activism by one group tends to spark a general resurgence of ethnic thinking. Contemporary political activism in Hawai'i emphasizes ethnic distinctiveness over the state-promoted ideology of *aloha*, and consumer markets have responded rapidly to this new spirit of the times.

Pacific Islanders do not, of course, necessarily internalize the paradigm of cultural identity that founds primordialist images on consumer goods, nor do they share the same motives for wearing them. For people on the periphery, Western goods in themselves are weighted with meanings such as desirability, cosmopolitanism, wealth, and technological superiority. Although of vital concern in Hawai'i, sovereignty and nationalism are not presently salient local issues in the Samoas. (Western) Samoa has been independent since 1962, and there is no significant separatist movement in American Samoa. Here the identity messages appear minimally relevant, or are they merely ahead of the political curve? The fact remains that essentialist images of group distinctiveness have become popular on transnational consumer goods precisely during an era that has witnessed the global resurgence of micronationalism. This international political trend has heightened consciousness of ethnic identities even in postcolonial Pacific Island nations where sovereignty activism is largely a thing of the past. When a Samoan wears a Filipino strength T-shirt, she or he is at one level proclaiming, "I too have a 'culture.' I am culturally marked. I am not plain vanilla or nondescript, like the *palagi*" (whites).

The producers of identity merchandise are responding to perceived market demand, but as they attempt to read the prevailing *zeitgeist*, they also innovate, exaggerating and intensifying the messages of cultural boundedness and species-like differentiation. As the amateur graphic artist phrased it, they "try to go a little further" with each new design. The designers, manufacturers, and distributors are not state sponsored, affiliated with a political organization, or cognizant of hegemonic intentions; apolitical and autonomous, they are merely pursuing individual entrepreneurial goals, as are the Samoans who sell Samoan Strength T-shirts in stalls in the Apia market. At least one multinational corporation has also attempted to use the identity boom as a marketing tool. In American Samoa about five years ago, I purchased (and have kept) a can of Pepsi emblazoned with the slogan "Keep American Samoa clean . . . Fa'amama Amerika Samoa." The words are arranged around a line drawing of a young Samoan male chief in ceremonial dress, wearing a headdress of human hair and coconut fronds and holding a *nifo 'oti,* a steel killing knife modeled after pre-European war clubs made of wood. It is the sort of picture that can be found in nineteenth-century accounts. Foreign observers and ethnologists such as Augustin Kraemer photographed Samoans in "typical" cultural poses; men were usually portrayed with insignia of rank and/or warfare, and women were photographed with bare breasts. Thus a soft drink can is used to market both the product and Samoan cultural distinctiveness. Apparently, the subliminal message is that it is *fa'aSamoa,* culturally Samoan, to drink Pepsi—and to dispose of garbage properly. But the message is also that being a cultural creature is something to be celebrated.

A few years ago a graduate student at Hawai'i gave me a "Poseable Hawaiian Action Figure"—a plastic doll about six inches tall— that she had purchased at the Bishop Museum's Shop Pacifica. The package is emblazoned with the title "The Hawai'ians" in red and yellow, the socially and ritually high colors of the indigenous society, and with the adjectives, "The Original" and "Bendable." According to the package, "the set" includes two figures, "authentic detailed reproductions of the ancient Hawai'ians": "Ali'i, the Chief, King, and leader of the Hawaiian people," and Laka, "the goddess of the hula." The figures are marketed by a Honolulu company but are made in China. The cardboard backing card positions the dolls against a stylized volcano spewing red and yellow lava. The "Ali'i" doll, which I have, displays rippled abdominal muscles and wears representations of the garb associated with high-ranking Hawai'ian chiefs: a *lei niho palaoa,* whalebone neck ornament; a red and yellow cloak; and a helmet. The marketing copy on the back of the package states:

The beautiful people of the island state of Hawaii, the paradise of the Pacific, greet you with aloha (pronounced phonetically: A—Low— Ha), which means hello, goodbye and love. . . .

Our unique Hawaiian culture is rich in folklore. Our ancient Hawaiian gods and goddesses beckon you to Hawaii to enjoy our volcanoes, forests, mountains and our world famous sandy beaches.

The manufacturing date on the package is 1993—the height of the pog craze in Hawai'i—suggesting that, because of the dynamic quality of entrepreneurial capitalism, the production of identity merchandise is contagious. The package copy nicely illustrates the link between touristic representations—in this case, the selling of a place and a culture—and the commoditization of the people themselves. Tourists and other patrons of the museum's shop can now take home not only cultural souvenirs but reproductions of "the other" people. With these "Authentic Hawai'ian Figures," the indigenous people of the islands are thus enabled to collect themselves. An argument could be made that, for an Island child, playing with these dolls may be positive and empowering, as toy manufacturers might claim for "G. I. Joe" and other action figures. But when I showed the doll to a Hawai'ian graduate student, she examined it for some time, looked perplexed, and finally said quietly: "I think I'm insulted."

## CONCLUSION

Messages on consumer goods—at once innovative and responsive to popular preconceptions—may have far-reaching though subtle effects on public consciousness and conceptualization. There is likely to be a dialectical relationship between marketed representations and public understandings of cultural identity. Judging from the identity products sold in the Pacific Islands, the consumer market reflects *and* communicates the idea that cultural groups are natural categories of the same structural type, distinguished from one another by minor details of content. This segment of public culture promulgates one—arguably, Western—paradigm of group identity, but this paradigm has the potential to become part of a self-evident, globally prevalent "common sense" about the makeup of humankind. The transnational distribution of identity merchandise encourages people to assert cultural difference, but to conceptualize this difference *in the same way.*

## ACKNOWLEDGMENTS

This article reflects observations made during research trips to the Pacific Islands between 1972 and 1997, and during my residence in Hawai'i from 1984 to 1997, when I was on the faculty of the University of Hawai'i. Thanks go to my students for perspectives on local identities, and to my children, Benjamin and Abigail Fay, for empirical data on pogs. I am particularly grateful to Isaako Vaisagote and his family in Faleū, Samoa, for their hospitality. Preliminary versions of this essay were presented at the 1993 NEH Summer Seminar hosted by the Program for Cultural Studies of the East-West Center, Honolulu, at the 1994 annual meeting of the American Anthropological Association, and at a University of Connecticut Anthropology Department Colloquium in 1997. I thank Virginia Dominguez, Miriam Kahn, and Geoff White for comments. Geoff White generously shared documentary material on milk caps, and Lisa Gollin gave me the "Hawaiian Action Figure."

## NOTES

1. Some basic sources in this ever-growing literature include: Keesing and Tonkinson 1982; Anderson 1983; Linnekin 1983, 1991, 1992; Hobsbawm and Ranger 1983; Handler 1984, 1985, 1988; Handler and Linnekin 1984; Herzfeld 1985; Babadzan 1988; Hanson 1989; Keesing 1990, 1991; Dietler 1994.

2. See, for example, Douglas and Isherwood 1979; Appadurai 1986; Miller 1987, 1995; McCracken 1988; Rutz and Orlove 1989; Fine and Leopold 1993; Miller ed. 1995; Howes 1996.

3. Some theoretically significant sources in the anthropological literature on tourism and cultural commoditization are: Greenwood 1977, 1982; Adams 1984, 1990; MacCannell 1984, 1989; Volkman 1984, 1990; Smith 1989; Picard and Wood 1997.

## REFERENCES

Adams, Kathleen M. 1984. "Come to Tana Toraja, 'Land of the Heavenly Kings': Travel Agents as Brokers in Ethnicity." *Annals of Tourism Research* 11:469–485.

———. 1990. "Cultural Commoditization in Tana Toraja, Indonesia." *Cultural Survival Quarterly* 14(1):31–34.

Anderson, Benedict. 1983. *Imagined Communities: Reflections on the Origin and Spread of Nationalism.* London: Verso.

Appadurai, Arjun, ed. 1986. *The Social Life of Things: Commodities in Cultural Perspective.* Cambridge: Cambridge University Press.

Babadzan, Alain. 1988. "Kastom and Nation Building in the South Pacific." In *Ethnicities and Nations: Processes of Interethnic Relations in Latin America, Southeast Asia, and the Pacific.* R. Guideri, F. Pellizzi, and S. Tambiah, eds. Pp. 199–228. Houston: Rothko Chapel and University of Texas Press.

Baudrillard, J. 1981. *For a Critique of the Political Economy of the Sign.* St. Louis, Mo.: Telos Press.

Bourdieu, Pierre. 1984. *Distinction: A Social Critique of the Judgement of Taste.* Cambridge: Harvard University Press.

Braudel, Fernand. 1973. *Capitalism and Material Life 1400–1800.* Miriam Kochan, translator. Glasgow: Fontana/Collins.

Clifford, James. 1988. "On Collecting Art and Culture." In *The Predicament of Culture.* Pp. 215–251. Cambridge: Harvard University Press.

Denny, Dann. 1994. "New Kids' Craze Hits Town." *The Herald-Times* (Bloomington, Indiana). November 22:D1.

Dietler, Michael. 1994. "'Our Ancestors the Gauls': Archaeology, Ethnic Nationalism, and the Manipulation of Celtic Identity in Modern Europe." *American Anthropologist* 96:584–605.

Douglas, Mary, and Baron Isherwood. 1979. *The World of Goods: Towards an Anthropology of Consumption.* London: Allen Lane.

Dunn, Robert. 1986. "Television, Consumption and the Commodity Form." *Theory, Culture & Society* 3(1):49–64.

Ewen, Stuart, and Elizabeth Ewen. 1982. *Channels of Desire: Mass Images and the Shaping of American Consciousness.* New York: McGraw-Hill.

Featherstone, Mike. 1982. "The Body in Consumer Culture." *Theory, Culture & Society* 1(2):18–33.

Fine, Ben, and Ellen Leopold. 1993. *The World of Consumption.* London & New York: Routledge.

Fox, Richard Wightman, and T. J. Jackson Lears, eds. 1983. *The Culture of Consumption: Critical Essays in American History, 1880–1980.* New York: Pantheon Books.

Garnham, Nicholas. 1993. "The Mass Media, Cultural Identity, and the Public Sphere in the Modern World." *Public Culture* 5:251–265.

Greenwood, Davydd. 1977. "Culture by the Pound: An Anthropological Perspective on Tourism as Cultural Commoditization." In *Hosts and Guests: The Anthropology of Tourism.* Valene L. Smith, ed. Pp. 129–138. Philadelphia: University of Pennsylvania Press.

———. 1982. "Cultural 'Authenticity.'" *Cultural Survival Quarterly* 6(3):27–28.

Hall, Stuart. 1997. "The Local and the Global: Globalization and Ethnicity." In *Culture, Globalization and the World-System: Contemporary Conditions for the Representation of Identity.* Anthony D. King, ed. Pp. 19–39. Minneapolis: University of Minnesota Press.

Handelman, Don, and Lea Shamgar-Handelman. 1993. "Aesthetics versus Ideology in National Symbolism: The Creation of the Emblem of Israel." *Public Culture* 5:431–449.

Handler, Richard. 1984. "On Sociocultural Discontinuity: Nationalism and Cultural Objectification in Quebec." *Current Anthropology* 25:55–71.

———. 1985. "On Dialogue and Destructive Analysis: Problems in Narrating Nationalism and Ethnicity." *The Journal of Anthropological Research* 41:171–182.

———. 1988. *Nationalism and the Politics of Culture in Quebec.* Madison: University of Wisconsin Press.

Handler, Richard, and Jocelyn Linnekin. 1984. "Tradition, Genuine or Spurious." *Journal of American Folklore* 97:273–290.

Hanson, F. Allan. 1989. "The Making of the Maori: Cultural Invention and Its Logic." *American Anthropologist* 91:890–902.

Herzfeld, Michael. 1985. *Ours Once More: Folklore, Ideology, and the Making of Modern Greece.* New York: Pella.

Hobsbawm, Eric, and Terence Ranger, eds. 1983. *The Invention of Tradition.* Cambridge: Cambridge University Press.

Howes, David, ed. 1996. *Cross-Cultural Consumption: Global Markets Local Realities.* New York: Routledge.

Keesing, Roger M. 1990. "Creating the Past: Custom and Identity in the Contemporary Pacific." *The Contemporary Pacific* 1:19–42.

———. 1991. "Colonial History as Contested Ground: The Bell Massacre in the Solomons." *History and Anthropology* 4:279–301.

Keesing, Roger M., and Robert Tonkinson, eds. 1982. "Reinventing Traditional Culture: The Politics of Kastom in Island Melanesia." Special issue. *Mankind* 13(4).

Kellner, Douglas. 1983. "Critical Theory, Commodities and the Consumer Society." *Theory, Culture & Society* 1(3):66–83.

Kemper, Steven. 1993. "The Nation Consumed: Buying and Believing in Sri Lanka." *Public Culture* 5:377–393.

King, Anthony D. 1997. "The Global, the Urban, and the World." In *Culture, Globalization and the World-System: Contemporary Conditions for the Representation of Identity.* Anthony D. King, ed. Pp. 149–154. Minneapolis: University of Minnesota Press.

Linnekin, Jocelyn. 1983. "Defining Tradition: Variations on the Hawaiian Identity." *American Ethnologist* 10:241–252.

———. 1991. "Cultural Invention and the Dilemma of Authenticity." *American Anthropologist* 93:446–449.

———. 1992. "On the Theory and Politics of Cultural Construction in the Pacific." *Oceania* 62:249–263.

———. 1997. "Consuming Cultures: Tourism and the Commoditization of Cultural Identity in the Island Pacific." In *Tourism, Ethnicity, and the State in Asian and Pacific Societies.* Michel Picard and Robert E. Wood, eds. Pp. 215–250. Honolulu: University of Hawai'i Press.

Linnekin, Jocelyn, and Lin Poyer. 1990. "Introduction." In *Cultural Identity and Ethnicity in the Pacific.* J. Linnekin and L. Poyer, eds. Pp. 1–16. Honolulu: University of Hawai'i Press.

MacCannell, Dean. 1984. "Reconstructed Ethnicity: Tourism and Cultural Identity in Third World Communities." *Annals of Tourism Research* 11:375–392.

———. 1989. *The Tourist.* New York: Schocken.

McCracken, Grant. 1988. *Culture and Consumption: New Approaches to the Symbolic Character of Consumer Goods and Activities.* Bloomington: Indiana University Press.

Miller, Daniel. 1987. *Material Culture and Mass Consumption.* Oxford: Basil Blackwell.

———. 1994. "Consumption and Commodities." *Annual Review of Anthropology* 24:141–161.

Miller, Daniel, ed. 1995. *Acknowledging Consumption.* London: Routledge.

Philibert, Jean-Marc, and Christine Jourdan. 1996. "Perishable Goods: Modes of Consumption in the Pacific Islands." In *Cross-Cultural Consumption: Global Markets, Local Realities.* David Howes, ed. Pp. 55–73. London and New York: Routledge.

Picard, Michel, and Robert E. Wood, eds. 1997. *Tourism, Ethnicity, and the State in Asian and Pacific Societies.* Honolulu: University of Hawai'i Press.

Rutz, Henry J., and Benjamin S. Orlove, eds. 1989. "The Social Economy of Consumption." Monographs in Economic Anthropology No. 6. Lanham, Md.: University Press of America.

Seligman, Jean, and Jeanne Gordon. 1995. "Is It 'Game Over' for Pog Players?" *Newsweek,* January 30:55.

Smith, Valene L., ed. 1989. *Hosts and Guests: The Anthropology of Tourism.* 2nd ed. Philadelphia: University of Pennsylvania Press.

Veblen, Thorstein. 1953. *The Theory of the Leisure Class.* New York: New American Library.

Volkman, Toby Alice. 1984. "Great Performances: Toraja Cultural Identity in the 1970s." *American Ethnologist* 11:152–169.

———. 1990. "Visions and Revisions: Toraja Culture and the Tourist Gaze." *American Ethnologist* 17:91–110.

Wallerstein, Immanuel. 1974. *The Modern World-System.* New York: Academic Press.

# 20

# Cannibalizing, Commodifying, or Creating Culture? Power and Art in Sepik River Tourism

## Eric Kline Silverman

*DePauw University*

Over the past few decades, perhaps no area of the Pacific has proven to be as alluring to tourists and travelers as the Sepik River of Papua New Guinea. And with good reason: the Sepik is associated with the legendary research of Margaret Mead, tales of cannibalism and headhunting, towering spirit houses with mysterious visages, exotic art, dramatic rituals, dangerous crocodiles, and, of course, glimpses of the waning Primitive. The unique mystique of the Sepik has an enduring position in the romantic imagination of the West. Why not visit?

Well, one reason not to do so is the common assertion that tourism inevitably, and solely, erodes the authenticity, autonomy, creativity, and power of local people. MacCannell (1992:27) speaks to a widespread scholarly and popular opinion when he claims that "relations between tourists and recent ex-primitives are framed in a somewhat forced, stereotypical commercial exploitation model characterized by bad faith and petty suspicion on both sides." This view allows local people only one significant pursuit in the touristic encounter: money. In all other respects, tourism is apparently meaningless.

In this chapter, I challenge this view by focusing on the touristic encounter in the Eastern Iatmul village of Tambunum, a middle Sepik River community in Papua New Guinea that is a popular tourist destination. My foil is the widely seen film *Cannibal Tours,* which, as I detail, portrays tourism as a process that only disempowers local people and erodes from their lives all genuine, meaningful dimensions of their culture.[1] In my view, however, tourism is often a context in which local Pacific people exercise subtle forms of power and resistance, and artistically express novel and hybrid concepts of personal, ethnic, national, and transnational "modern" identities.

## CANNIBAL TOURS

No more persuasive evidence exists of the detrimental effects of tourism, and the arrogant buffoonery of Western visitors, than the 1987 film by Dennis O'Rourke, *Cannibal Tours*. The film follows a group of affluent yet astonishingly naive American and European tourists as they travel along the Sepik River aboard the *Melanesian Explorer* cruise ship. We see these intrusive visitors sunning themselves in bikinis aboard the ship, zipping along the river in small speed boats, and wandering through several Sepik communities. They incessantly snap photos of local people, hand out cigarettes and perfume as though they were rare treasures, offer embarrassingly foolish comments, applaud staged dances by the natives, purchase handicrafts, and comport themselves with such an awkwardly arrogant insouciance that the viewer can only squirm.

Interspersed throughout this voyage are comments by specific tourists, on whom the camera focuses. A trio of Italians muse about the differences between the Primitive and the Modern. Do the local people live in harmony with nature? Are they satisfied with their lives? Must the West, like missionaries, teach these people a modern lifestyle? An American woman bemoans the loss of authentic primitive art due to, of all things, tourism! A German man is obsessed with cannibalism. The tourists, we might say, are intent on validating themselves and Western Civilization as exalted or bereft through comparison with stereotypical notions of primitive people. Either we have much to teach them, or much to learn.

Local people, when they are not immobilized by the tourists' camera lenses, also speak—but to rather different issues. A man bemoans the loss of sacred objects and, somewhat abashed, recalls the naivete of his grandparents who looked upon the first Europeans to sail the Sepik as ancestral ghosts. An angry woman shouts about her lack of money and the miserliness of tourists. Young boys sing a missionary song. Elder men complain that white visitors buy so few handicrafts and snap photos without paying. Generally, local people

in the film are baffled by the entire touristic enterprise. Why do these white people travel here? Where do they get their money? Indeed, the "primitive" people in the film are eminently concerned with practical matters and money while, ironically, the Westerners are captivated by fanciful notions about the world. In sum, the film portrays the clash between Western desire for an authentic primitive and local anguish at the lack of modernization and money. We empathize with the plight of local people who are now forced to prostitute their culture in order to earn a few dollars, and we are embarrassed at the tourists, and hence at ourselves whom they represent, for so shamelessly buying into it.

*Cannibal Tours* may be the most successful depiction of the contemporary Pacific for popular audiences. It was enthusiastically reviewed in *The New York Times* (August 23, 1989) and *The Nation* (September 4/11, 1988) and played at the 1988 Margaret Mead Film Festival and the 14th Annual Seattle Film Festival. Scholars, too, have discussed the film (for example, Cohen 1988; Bruner 1989, 1991; Errington and Gewertz 1989a; MacCannell 1990, 1992; Coiffier 1991; Young 1992). *Cannibal Tours* is shown in introductory anthropology classes as well as courses on the Pacific Islands, visual anthropology, colonialism and postcolonialism, tourism, culture change, the politics of tradition and ethnicity, and recreation management. That one can purchase online term papers about the film attests to its importance in the undergraduate curriculum.

The film, we will see, was made to be a moral allegory about late twentieth-century Western traveling. In this respect, *Cannibal Tours* makes no pretense to ethnographic veracity. Still, most viewers, in my experience, especially students, assume that the film portrays with *some* accuracy the contemporary lives of Sepik River dwellers whom tourists now visit. Perhaps the most telling moment in the film occurs when an elderly village man states equivocally that "we are living between two worlds." But the film ultimately says little about this man's liminal identity. Indeed, *Cannibal Tours*, like many scholarly discussions about the film, does as much to erase or deny the empowerment of local people as the tourists that it so earnestly reproaches! To be sure, many facets of tourism are unsavory and humiliating. But is this all tourism has to offer? Unfortunately, most people are unable to answer this question, at least for the Pacific, since most studies of tourism essentialize the West and the Rest. The pure primitivism of local people, be it of the Hobbesian or Rousseauistic variety, is invariably corrupted by the vapidity of Western culture and over-whelmed by the onslaught of capitalism. In this simplistic framework, tourism is a process that exclusively erodes cultural authenticity. By thus foregrounding passive submission to Western hegemony, we are unable to appre-hend moments of genuine cultural creativity, and thus incapable of understanding the complexity of "living between two worlds" in the contemporary, village-based Pacific.

## MODERNIST ANGST

The tourists in *Cannibal Tours* voyage to Papua New Guinea in order to recapture the lost qualities of a raw, primal humanity—unfettered sensuality, aggression, artistry, beauty, and so forth. The narrative structure or diagesis of the film, as summarized by O'Rourke himself in an interview with Lutkehaus, concerns two quests worthy of Joseph Conrad:

> The first and obvious one is rich and bourgeois tourists on a journey into their own packaged version of the "heart of darkness" into the inte-rior, up the mysterious Sepik River. The second journey (the real text of the film), is a metaphys-ical one. It is an attempt to discover the place of "the Other" in the popular imagination. It af-fords a glimpse at the "real" (mostly unconsid-ered or misunderstood) reasons why "civilized" people wish to encounter the "primitive." The situation is that shifting terminus of civilization, where modern mass culture grates and pushes against those original, essential aspects of hu-manity; and where much of what passes for "val-ues" in Western culture is exposed in stark relief as banal and fake. (Lutkehaus 1989:427–428)

According to O'Rourke, tourists are awash with the existential angst of modernity that arises from displacement, alienation, unful-filled dreams of progress, and "the failure of Christianity. . . . We've had two world wars, the nuclear bomb, and the holocaust" (O'Rourke, cited in Lutkehaus 1989:428). Thus they—we, actually—look to primitive people for something Real, Truthful, and Primal. But when tourists arrive in the Sepik, alas, the primitive they desire has disappeared beneath the sheer power, and the mecha-nized brawn, of "modern mass culture."

If O'Rourke traces the origins of "cannibal tourism" to the postmodern condition of "loss," the noted theorist of tourism and cul-tural studies, Dean MacCannell,[2] embraces a psychodynamic explanation:

> modern civilization was built on the graves of our savage ancestors, and repression of the pleasure they took from one another, from the animals and the earth. I suspect our collective guilt and denial of responsibility for the destruction of sav-agery and pleasure can be found infused in every distinctly modern cultural form. (MacCannell 1992:25; see also MacCannell 1990)

Yet, in the Sepik at least, tourism affords Westerners no expiation for the sins of modernity. Local people, claims MacCannell (1992:26) after viewing *Cannibal Tours,* are ac-culturated exprimitives or, worse, performa-tive primitives. True, they continue to dance and sing. But these touristic parades are inau-thentic since they mirror European desire for Otherness (see also Bruner 1991:244). In-deed, *Cannibal Tours* implies that the only au-thentic rituals in the Sepik today are those of the tourists themselves! *They* are the real sav-ages. By contrast, villagers champion the bourgeois logic of rational utilitarianism. They seem so, well . . . , *Western.* Yet these Papua New Guineans are pragmatic, implies the film and MacConnell, only because their authentic culture has been steadily ravaged by colonialism, missionaries, capitalism, and, now, tourism.[3]

*Cannibal Tours* and MacCannell (1992) laudably critique (neo)colonialism and primi-tivist ideologies that continue to dehumanize "tribal" peoples. It is not this moral vision that I contest. But the film and many discussions of tourism reproduce an equally Eurocentric ideology by portraying the inhabitants of the Sepik River as irreducibly passive and disempowered—as children, to be honest. True, as O'Rourke intimates in the lengthy quotation which I discussed above, the intent of the film is not to present Sepik people in the full actuality of their current lives. His goal is to comment on the West. But O'Rourke's allegorical tale can only be sustained by depicting contemporary Sepik people in a particular way: a primitive people who have "fallen from grace." Moreover, one can assume that O'Rourke believed that he was, at some level, presenting an accurate portrayal of the contemporary Sepik lest his own film be as "mythic" as the touristic imagination he mocks. If, by contrast, local people are in some sense deriving "authentic" meaning from tourism, then the narrative collapses.

All too frequently, as evidenced by *Cannibal Tours*, critical reflections on tourism unwittingly write over indigenous meanings and concepts, much like the tourists who are so commonly denounced. Indeed, the touristic myth of primitivism is matched by the scholarly myth that tourism is structured solely by economic asymmetry. While the tourists of *Cannibal Tours* foolishly characterize Sepik art in terms of "baroque" curves and Modigliani, MacCannell (1992:25–30) calls Iatmul flute music a "concerto" and likens local people to Donald Trump! (He also repeatedly refers to the inhabitants of the region as Papuans, which in all respects is wrong.) MacCannell even suggests that the allure of the Sepik for tourists (and anthropologists) arises from a denial of our "violent, homoerotic, and cannibalistic impulses," and a "displaced anal sadism which is a strong, albeit necessarily denied, component of western culture and consciousness. A side benefit of New Guinea ethnography is free psychoanalysis" (MacCannell 1992:36–37). This may be true. To some extent, I concur. But it tells us *nothing* about the local experience of tourism. It is valid, of course, to discuss tourism in terms of Western woes, as per *Cannibal Tours*. My objection begins only when the focus on those woes denies local people their cultural authenticity, creativity, agency, and meaning.

## THE TOURISTS: NEOCOLONIALISM, AND ROMANTICISM

*Cannibal Tours* opens with a statement of biblical force (see Exodus 2:22), literally written in black and white: "There is nothing so strange, in a strange land, as the stranger who comes to visit it." The first scene consists of a deep panning shot of the ocean and coastal jungle. We hear Mozart, the spinning of a shortwave radio dial, and the mention of Henry Kissinger in a BBC news report. The message is clear: Even here, in the seemingly pristine Sepik, we can sense the inexorable penetration of Western power.[4]

Dichotomies recur throughout *Cannibal Tours*. Dugout canoes silently glide before the chugging tourist ship. Passive local children pose for aggressive European adults. And the symphonic melodies of European "High Art" or Mozart overpower the bamboo flute tones of "Primitive Art." Yet the sonorous presence of Mozart in *Cannibal Tours*—a German musician, after all—alludes not only to European gentility and genius, but to something more ominous and tragic in recent European history. Indeed, the frequent splicing into the film of black and white photographs from the 1884–1914 German protectorate of New Guinea implies that tourism is a form of colonialism, with all of its violence and domination. The old photographs of "authentic" natives in the film are accompanied by the melancholy tones of bamboo flutes. But the sounds of Mozart always frame the daguerreotypes of colonialism *and* the contemporary scenes of tourists zipping along the river in speedboats. Veiled allusions to the Holocaust and explicit references to colonialism make for a powerful moral statement. But it is flawed, inappropriate, and ultimately ethnocentric precisely because Western moral concerns are allowed to eclipse local cultural assertions.

The antihero of *Cannibal Tours* is a German man obsessed with cannibalism and thus, like most tourists, captivated by dreams of the past, rather than the realities of the present.[5] (For most Sepik people, cannibalism and headhunting are bygone practices, rarely discussed unless prompted by inquisitive visitors.) With his olive-green outfit and bush hat rung with a band of tiger skin, this man is the Ur-tourist, a Great White Hunter who embodies Rosaldo's (1989) "imperialist nostalgia." In *Cannibal Tours*, this man is a fool, but a dangerous one since he evokes the memories of World War II (MacCannell 1992:26). (One of my students, in fact, drawing on the popular American TV sitcom *Hogan's Heros*, called him "Sgt. Shultz.") But in so obviously figuring a German as "a cipher for all that is evil in the West" (Dan Jorgensen, personal communication, 1995), and by omitting any glimpses of Australian visitors, *Cannibal Tours* succumbs to the level of moralistic stereotyping which, when spoken by the tourists, it scorns.

*Cannibal Tours* also features an Italian trio for whom the natives are "truly living with nature . . . the experts assure us they are satisfied . . . happy . . . and well-fed." Nature "provides them with . . . the necessities of life, they don't have to worry about thinking of tomorrow." (This conversation about naturally satiated primitives contrasts with a previous scene in which the German tourists chat about cholesterol and dieting while partaking of a hearty breakfast.) Utopian sentiments aside, we also hear that local people "don't really live . . . more like vegetating . . . apathy . . . indolence." They are unproductive, in other words, and thus in need of a proper moral education: "We must teach them and go into their villages," one of these tourists says, "to educate and to stimulate them to behave different."

The film tends to deny the Italian woman a voice but certainly not a presence. She coyly flirts with the camera, which shortly thereafter focuses on a bikini-clad sunbather.[6] O'Rourke (cited in Lutkehaus 1989:428–429) wants to critique the ideology of sexuality in the myths of primitivism and tourism. But the film conveys this message through a male gaze that represents female sexuality in terms of the body alone, specifically, breasts and buttocks, of which we see quite a lot in *Cannibal Tours*. Indeed, the next series of shots consists of a crocodile drifting in the water, a colorful parrot, and carved house post images of phallic-nosed spirit faces and an ancestress with prominent genitals. But the film provides no context concerning, say, local cosmology and gender. As a result, the carved images make sense only in terms of the preceding shots of natural beauty, danger, and speechless female bodies. While the roving eye of the camera repeatedly focuses on female tourists and bikinis, every Sepik woman wears a modest "meri blaus." Ironically, *Cannibal Tours* inverts the gaze of *National Geographic* (Lutz and Collins 1993:115–116) by inscribing passive sexuality onto the bodies of women who are white (or tan) and modern rather than black and native. Still, the film retains a phallocentric gaze that is reminiscent of classical primitivism (see Solomon-Godeau 1989; Rony 1996).[7] It privileges the desire of white, heterosexual men.

The "ecstatic moment" of *Cannibal Tours*, writes Lutkehaus (1989:428), is the penultimate scene, filmed in slow motion to the sounds of Mozart, lit by a Sepik sunset. On the deck of the ship, their faces painted in swirling patterns by men from Tambunum village (Bruner 1989:440), the tourists perform what O'Rourke calls a "hyper-real . . . dance of death" (cited in Lutkehaus 1989:428). They prance, twirl, grimace, and parade. A burly man has removed his shirt and assumes the stance of a boxer. MacCannell remarks, "It is so profoundly embarrassing that no one can even tell him that he is making an ass of himself. The New Guineans could not have done him better" (1992:33). True. But in the film, this dance by the tourists is the *only* genuine ceremonial display in the Sepik today. Its appalling antithesis is the earlier scene where two Iatmul boys awkwardly sing missionary songs. Furthermore, local people in *Cannibal Tours* have no interest in romanticizing their alters (K. Barlow, personal communication, 1996). This is the prerogative of moderns, who thereby reveal themselves to be the true primitives. Whereas natives have lost their culture and desire only, as one Sepik man says, "to purchase trousers," tourists acquire primitive faces and triumphantly dance to the mythic beat of their own delusions.

Finally, the credits are interrupted by an American couple—a stereotype, it turns out, of Jewish New Yorkers—who clasp mock phallocrypts ("skin bilong kok," O'Rourke tells them), climb into a small propeller airplane, and disappear into the empyrean haze. The camera, by remaining behind on the grass airstrip, subtly positions itself in the "native's point of view." In the end, tourism reduces Sepik people to "emasculating trophies" (M. Rohatynsky, personal communication, 1996) of a successful voyage up the proverbial heart of darkness.

*Cannibal Tours* raises a key question that it refuses to answer: What would a critique of tourism look like that was itself not touristic? For most critics and analysts of tourism, local people are the antithesis of Westerners. In *Cannibal Tours,* tourists are driven by fantasy, sexuality, ethnocentrism, and missionary zeal. They are naive romantics, wealthy dilettantes, objects of prurient interest, insufferable excursionists, and neo-Nazis. By contrast, the exprimitives are simply pragmatic and decorous. Conrad's Kurtz said it best: "the horror, the horror."

## TOURIST ART

In *Cannibal Tours,* tourism is an inauthentic experience that denies local people their agency and forces them to commodify their culture into banal dances and crass trinkets which, to add insult to injury, the tourists never buy enough of anyway. Any potential for meaningful action is muted by the relentless pursuit of money. I now want to offer a contrasting view of Sepik tourism that, much as Gewertz and Errington (1991) argue for the nearby Chambri, acknowledges local creativity.

The tourists in *Cannibal Tours* incessantly photograph local people and purchase objects. They embody the power of European acquisitiveness (Clifford 1988; Thomas 1991).

This way, again, tourism is the latest stage in a long history of colonial exploitation and trauma.[8] But Sepik people *do* exercise self-conscious agency in creating their contemporary identities. Eastern Iatmul commonly deliberate the parameters of custom or *kastom,* and they frequently appeal to "culture" and "tradition" during totemic debates, village moots, and ritual preparations. Tourism, then, has not diminished local intentionality.

Nor has tourism eroded tradition through the introduction of alien practices and objects. After all, Margaret Mead (1938) noted a generation ago that Sepik societies trafficked extensively in cultural forms. The structures and categories of Iatmul villages, she recognized, were highly labile; they allowed for a discordant culture. Foreign objects, ideas, and behaviors were retained even though they were unable to be fully integrated into the local cultural system and its logic (Mead 1938:163; 1978:70). Hybridity, then, is an authentic and traditional quality of Sepik cultures. In the 1930s, European buttons were carefully pressed into the shell applique on spirit masks called *mai.* Today, young men sporting military fatigues and American T-shirts decorate these very same objects (Figure 20.1). During ritual, elder women dance in shirts that advertise "Greenwich Tennis Club" and "Disco Momma." This may offend European sensibilities about what constitutes a genuine, proper Sepik ritual. But no such difficulties, or contradictions, torment local people. Nor do these hybrid presences alter the efficacy of ritual, which may even, as in the case of the six-month long *mai* festival of 1989–1990, be staged for tourists as much as for local inhabitants of the region.

Eastern Iatmul are prolific creators of "tourist art." When tourists and art dealers arrive in Tambunum, thousands of objects may be displayed along the main village path in an informal and often playful, transnational, and polyvocal market. The shapes, colors, and styles include napkin rings and eight-foot-tall sculptures, carved animals and baskets, rattan figures, and pottery. We can, like the self-proclaimed "exponent of

**Figure 20.1**    A young man primes a *mai* mask while dressed in military fatigues and a T-shirt decorated with the American flag and the Statue of Liberty.

**Figure 20.2**    A man displays his touristic carvings. Of particular note is the center object, a multi-facial mask, and the mask at the left, which ambiguously depicts a crocodile emerging out of the mouth, or being eaten by it.

primitive art" in *Cannibal Tours,* bemoan that it would be "too bad if they . . . deviate . . . and work for tourism as such." The irony of this statement is obvious to all viewers (see also Price 1989; Errington 1994; Steiner 1994; Root 1996). But *Cannibal Tours,* rather than challenging this cliché, implies that tourist art is a meaningless source of money and frustration for local people—mere economic inequality and tawdry commodification.

In my view, tourist art in Tambunum expresses new concepts of self and ethnicity (see also Errington and Gewertz 1989b; Gewertz and Errington 1991; Silverman 1999). Carvers strive to create unique objects that reflect their identity as egocentric or autonomous individuals rather than sociocentric members of

a descent group. Men combine traditionally separate motifs into new forms, and carve mythological images that were not heretofore lent a visual expression. Tourist art also expresses traditional modes of identity. Men refrain from carving the totemic beings of other descent groups, and they depict sociocentric personhood by hewing multifacial masks (Figure 20.2, center) which juxtapose a large countenance with multiple selves.

Through tourist art, moreover, Eastern Iatmul continue to import, transform, and export anew alien cultural forms. They visit the villages of other language groups and town markets in order to purchase masks, pots, and ornaments which, often after modification, they offer at a profit to tourists and dealers.

Some carvers, in the search for novel and unusual aesthetic forms, acquire formal entitlement to reproduce and sell the art styles that are characteristic of other Iatmul and non-Iatmul villages—say, by drawing on distant affinal relations (Silverman 2001a). Women, too, participate in this process. They duplicate the baskets associated with the Murik of the Sepik Estuary, and loop long-fringed "Madang style" bilums or string bags. Tourism, we might say, sustains local notions of artistic "copyright," and encourages men and women to seek ways of borrowing aesthetic styles without violating traditional notions of cultural (and intellectual) property rights.

On many tourist masks, gaping maws ambiguously devour, disgorge, excrete, and give birth to creatures such as crocodiles. In the context of tourist art, the crocodile symbolizes pan-Iatmul and pan-Sepik ethnicity rather than, as in "traditional" art, the totemic ancestors of specific descent groups (Figure 20.2, carving on the left). Men also carve variations of the national emblem of Papua New Guinea (Figure 20.3, carving on the right), often in combination with biblical and Christian slogans. These works translate the abstract and modern notions of nationhood and citizenship (see Gewertz and Errington 1991) into localized, even individualized, expressions. My point here is that tourist masks draw on traditional idioms of self and society to represent the emergence of new social and personal identities.

Eastern Iatmul also sign their tourist carvings with Christian and sometimes totemic names, thus mediating between tradition and modernity through literacy and "graphicalization" (Gewertz and Errington 1991; O'Hanlon 1995). Likewise, women weave the acronym "PS" into baskets (Figure 20.4), which signifies in the national language of Papua New Guinea, called Tok Pisin, regional identity as "Pikinini Sepik" or "Child of the Sepik." On one carving (Figure 20.5), a crocodilian symbol of Iatmul ethnicity confronts a stylized bird-of-paradise that evokes the national emblem. Both figures are encircled by tokens of literate personhood and provincial identity: names, date, the phrase "P[ikini] S[epik]

**Figure 20.3**   A touristic mask with a "traditional" face surmounted by the national emblem of Papua New Guinea

Country," and a reference to the Wewak Post Office. Because tourist art is a relatively recent aesthetic medium, it is particularly appropriate for expressing new concepts of ethnicity such as "Sepik," "Papua New Guinea," and even "Iatmul," a term coined by Gregory Bateson in the early 1930s.

Touristic carvers also derive artistic inspiration from Melanesian art catalogs and guidebooks. This way, at least one type of mask, forgotten since the era of German colonization, was reintegrated back into the local repertoire in the late 1980s (Silverman 1999). Of course, this development confounds any simplistic notions of cultural authenticity, and the idea that tourism erodes tradition. Here, we might say, tourism revived it! The very same year, a tourist guesthouse was

**Figure 20.4**   A woman named Tupwa holds a basket into which is woven the letters PS for Pikinini Seik, or "Child of the Sepik." This basket, on which are attached a few kina banknotes, was a gift to the author, who earlier presented his nephew (standing behind Tupwa) with a chicken as part of the general exchanges that occur between mothers' brothers and their sisters' children.

**Figure 20.5**   A stylized version of the national emblem of Papua New Guinea in which a bird-of-paradise confronts a crocodile. This naturalistic "conversation" between tradition and modernity is encircled by the carvers' names, date, and location.

constructed across the river from the main village, which precipitated a complex dispute over the ownership of the land (Silverman 2001b). The feud, however, concerned symbolic power and not money, and it reinforced rather than denounced the role of totemism in the prestige hierarchy of the village.

All told, tourism in Tambunum fosters the emergence of complex identities that blur the local and global. On tourist art, Tambunum villagers express themselves as Iatmul, regional Sepiks, egocentric and sociocentric selves, capitalists, Christians, Papua New Guineans, and Tok Pisin writers and readers.

From this perspective, I turn again to *Cannibal Tours,* this time with an eye (and ear) toward moments of touristic resistance to visitors.

## GHOSTLY EUROPEANS

The portrayal of modern tourism in *Cannibal Tours* conjures the popular ethnographic spectacles of the late nineteenth and early twentieth centuries wherein "primitive" people were put on public display for curious Americans and Europeans. (For example, a Philippine village was erected at the 1904 St. Louis Exposition, featuring the so-called "Igorots"; a man from the Belgian Congo named Ota Benga was displayed at the same event, as well as the American Museum of Natural History and the Monkey House at the Bronx Zoo.) Instead of "savages in cages," though, the natives in *Cannibal Tours* are displayed in their own habitat. Moreover, they speak. Yet local people in the film talk exclusively about cultural malaise and stifling encompassment by the world system. Like many discussions of tourism, O'Rourke thus deconstructs the mythic "Savage Other" by concocting an equally fictitious image: the fallen primitive.

I now want to suggest that local utterances in the film are more complex and multilayered, or heteroglossic, than they first seem. Sepik people in *Cannibal Tours* insinuate modes of cultural authenticity and resistance that contravene the explicit narrative of the film and its commonplace vision of touristic tragedy. The first indigenous voice in the film recalls the frightened response of nineteenth-century Iatmul when they initially encountered Europeans: "the spirits of our dead have come back! . . . They went and got a new face and skin." He continues: "So now, when we see tourists, we say about them: The dead have returned." Nevertheless, "we don't seriously believe they are our dead ancestors . . . but we say it!" (in Tok Pisin, "mipela save makim tok nating").

These statements, which are common across Melanesia and the Pacific, seem to ridicule the innocence of a previous generation (see Bruner 1991:247). But in my experience, Iatmul do *not* mock their ancestors. They may reflect on the material impoverishment of the past, sigh with compassion, and feel "pity" (*miwi,* or "tarangu" in Tok Pisin)—but not shame.[9] Perhaps, then, our Iatmul interlocutor was parodying the *tourists?* After all, Westerners lack many of the moral characteristics that define adult personhood such as generosity, vernacular speech,

competence in the river, and the skillful ability to paddle canoes. The association of tourists with death is a satirical reflection on what it means to be human (see Strathern 1992). It is an instance of counterdiscourse rather than self-denigration (see also Errington and Gewertz 1989b:49–51). Like ghosts, Europeans are marginal and dangerous, sometimes cooperative, often powerful.

Like ghosts, too, Europeans are white. In local conception ideology, paternal semen and maternal blood respectively congeal into the hard skeleton and soft organs. The former is the final embodiment of death, and so ghosts are said to be as white as paternal bones. Furthermore, Eastern Iatmul myth and funerary rites are populated by numinous beings who slough old skin and regenerate a new epidermis. Contrary to the narrative of *Cannibal Tours,* it is no childish gesture to call Europeans "dead ancestors." It is a complex linguistic and cultural act that conceals multiple meanings. On the one hand, it mocks the humanity of the tourists by associating them not with persons but with ghosts. On the other hand, it categorizes Europeans according to Iatmul notions about the body.

Another local man speculates that tourists "must be wealthy . . . their own ancestors made the money . . . now they can travel . . . we don't have money so we stay in the village." If the tourists paid higher prices for carvings, "I could go on that ship." The issue here is unmistakable: White people are rich and powerful; Iatmul are poor and disenfranchised.

Or is it? These statements, too, are multi-faceted. Many Papua New Guineans hold the postcolonial state, not tourists, accountable for their economic woes. Indeed, this man wonders aloud if the tourists aren't given money by their government. From this perspective, the Western privilege of tourism is symptomatic of a wider crisis of legitimacy concerning the Papua New Guinean nation (see Clark 1997). The memory of colonial humiliation sometimes coexists with nostalgia for Australian rule. But the narrative of *Cannibal Tours* does not enable viewers to hear the range of possible and often contradictory meanings in local comments.

Many indigenous voices in the film seemingly express bewilderment about the tourists. Yet local people are not so naive. "Touris" is a recent ethnocategory that contrasts with missionaries, government administrators, patrol officers, health workers, artifact buyers, and anthropologists. Tourists, it is understood, want to see the localized culture which, as I indicated earlier, is self-consciously articulated as "culture." Furthermore, several Eastern Iatmul have traveled to Australia, often in conjunction with tourism trade shows, and two men in the 1990s spent several months at Stanford University and the greater San Francisco Bay area helping to carve the Papua New Guinea Sculpture Garden (Silverman 1997). They, too, like their European touristic counterparts in the Sepik, toured an unfamiliar environs in order "to see" exotic places and things. They, too, returned home with souvenirs and photos. But in *Cannibal Tours,* and the common view of tourism, local people lack the self-reflexivity and knowledge that is so often attributed only to Western visitors.

## SHELLS, BEADS, AND MISPLACED BANKING METAPHORS

One indigenous person in *Cannibal Tours,* a woman, is particularly aggressive and strident. She berates the camera because "we hurry down here with things for the tourists, but the tourists only look, they don't buy. . . . we village people have no money—we need it! [for school fees, she later implies] You white people! You have all the money . . . not us 'backward' people" (*kanaka* in Tok Pisin). She code-switches during these comments, that is, shifts between speaking her vernacular tongue and the national language of Papua New Guinea. But she prefers the former. As a middle-aged Sepik woman, her reluctance to speak English or even Tok Pisin is not surprising. For her generation, language is gendered, especially when older women speak to European men. Her vernacular speech also seems to challenge the filmmaker himself. She wants to be heard, but she also wants to exclude the filmmaker from her discourse.

"I'm talking in my dialect," read the subtitles, "and he [O'Rourke] doesn't seem to hear." O'Rourke, of course, is a "white person" who traveled, moreover, on the *Melanesian Explorer.* Regardless of how *he* perceived his identity, local people would have immediately associated him with tourists and touristic desires. O'Rourke, then, is not so much filming the problem of tourists in this scene: He is part of the problem himself.

This resentful Sepik woman deploys additional rhetorical strategies. She refers to Papua New Guineans in Tok Pisin as the "parents" of Europeans. This figure of speech is unrelated to her chronological age. In one cosmological tale, Eastern Iatmul say that Europeans, who are the mythological children (or younger siblings) of Papua New Guineans, fled the Sepik in a canoe laden with advanced technology. According to Iatmul norms, younger siblings and children have unrestricted access to the possessions of their parents and older siblings. But Europeans exceeded the limits of morality when they hoarded the wealth of their "parents." What were the Papua New Guineans doing while the Europeans monopolized communal technology? Eating. From one perspective, this signifies that local people are indeed lazy when compared to industrious Europeans. From another perspective, however, it suggests that local people forge sociality through generosity and feasting while Europeans are greedy. This way, the angry woman in *Cannibal Tours* appears to position tourists and filmmaker alike in a state of moral dependence on their Papua New Guinean "parents," and thus accuses *all* Europeans of violating the ethic of reciprocity within the parent-child relationship.

Moreover, she may reside in Angoram, a multiethnic administrative *town* born of the colonial experience. Angoram is not a traditional *village* populated by a single linguistic group and enmeshed in a common web of kinship and morality. If this woman does reside in town, then she may likely require cash for daily subsistence. We do not know from the film what access she has to gardens, fishing lagoons, sago palms, and so forth. Viewers can only react to her diatribe with a "gut feeling" rather than insight. Her wanting for money becomes emblematic of a wider regional predicament wherein all Sepik people are destitute because of tourism. But this image is inaccurate. In fact, many people in the middle Sepik remain in villages rather than migrating to urban centers precisely because tourism ensures a steady source of cash. The absence of tourism, then, would do more to erode village-based life than the presence of tourists! Finally, we have no way of knowing if this woman's vitriol was spontaneous or the result of relentless badgering by the cameraman, whose lens was surely as intrusive as that of any tourist. In sum, there is no self-evident or singular way in which to interpret this woman's comments, nor tourism itself.

For several years, I wondered if O'Rourke, like Kauffmann (1988:269) in another Sepik society, was unable to film in some locations because he did not reach agreement with local people. Imagine my surprise, then, to read in a recent essay by O'Rourke (1997:41) that he *did* encounter anger and distrust in one Sepik village, Kanganaman, "the place where the redoubtable American anthropologist, Margaret Mead, had done a lot of her famous work. The villagers were angry, they told me that they resented how she had profited from them." Mead, however, never conducted ethnographic research in this community. Something else was going on in Kanganamun. But the film contains no hint of the incident.[10] Had it done so, we would have likely seen another side of tourism, one where local people are far more assertive than we are otherwise led to believe.

I want to offer a final comment about the angry Sepik woman's invective in *Cannibal Tours*. This time, I am interested not in the film per se but in some erroneous suggestions by MacCannell (1992:30) in regard to the bead and shell necklaces that she has displayed on the ground before the tourists. MacCannell sees a "deeply ironic movement of the camera" as it focuses on these objects which, of course, she is hoping to sell. This "irony" hinges on his false assumption that these touristic ornaments are "strings of shell money."[11] They are not. What's more, MacCannell writes that the Sepik woman "knows herself to be positioned like the Western banker, trading in currencies under unfavorable exchange conditions. The tourists think they are buying beads." But that is *exactly* what the tourists are purchasing! I am not denying the presence of "unfavorable exchange conditions" in some touristic encounters. But I see no irony here. It is misleading, if not downright silly, to equate this woman and her necklaces with Western bankers and currency.

I do, however, perceive some irony in Tambunum village where men peddle World War II Japanese occupation notes and old Australian money to tourists. This way, they transform colonial history, Western nostalgia, and monetary symbols of European domination into valid Papua New Guinean currency.[12] In this instance, tourism is ironic, but this irony works in favor of local people, not against them.

*Cannibal Tours* is particularly noteworthy because it allows local people to speak and even dialogue with the filmmaker (see Bruner 1989; Lutkehaus 1989; Young 1992; Mascia-Lees and Sharpe 1994). In this sense, the film is somewhat collaborative—shaped by the intentions of the people it portrays, who are thereby allowed to exercise their subjectivity. They are not, therefore, objectified. But however much Sepik people speak in the film, they are never permitted to articulate fully or freely the circumstances of their contemporary lives. In the end, then, they *are* objectified. The selective interviews rely "on the audience's assumption that the authority of the speakers validates the authority of the entire structure" (MacDougall 1995:245). We hear, or read from the subtitles, a great deal of what MacDougall (1995) calls "testimony" and "implication" but little "exposition." In this manner, local voices in the film seem to authenticate a single ideological construct: the fallen primitive. It is only when *Cannibal Tours* is placed into a context furnished from outside the film itself—as I am trying to do— that the ideology of its narrative, and the local voices within it, begin to unravel.

Almost all the voices in *Cannibal Tours* are men: indigenous, Western, filmmaker. With the sole exception of the local woman who yells at the camera, women are passive and speechless bodies. By contrast, local men are generally inquisitive and reflective, albeit to a lesser degree than the tourists, who are allowed far greater discursive freedom than Melanesians. Since Iatmul interlocutors tend only to *respond* to specific questions posed by the filmmaker, they appear less assertive and capable of engaging in contemplative thought than the tourists (relatedly, see Kulick and Willson 1992; Weiner 1992: 104–105). For example, O'Rourke repeatedly asks local people why they want money. It seems an innocent enough question. But it ignores the last two centuries of history and reduces Papua New Guinean adults to the status of innocent, wide-eyed children, gaping at cash and miraculous commodities. I am reminded of the South African apartheid-era film *The Gods Must Be Crazy*, where a softdrink bottle, tossed out of the window of an airplane, lands at the feet of a bewildered native.

## THE POWER OF LANGUAGE

All Tok Pisin statements in *Cannibal Tours* are paraphrased into English subtitles. Tok Pisin is highly beguiling. It appears to be a simple language of descriptive phrases and limited vocabulary—like tourism itself. But underneath this grammatical facade lurks a vast range of subtleties which can only be understood in terms of regional dialects, social framing, and broader contextual cues. *Cannibal Tours*, however, translates Tok Pisin utterances with little regard for connotative nuance.

One man suggests that tourists want to see if "*mipela* [we] *sindaun gut*," which the film translates "if we are civilized." Yet *sindaun gut* connotes a general sense of well-being and not, at least not self-evidently, a notion of civilized civility. Another man says, "*mi no ken askim ol touris.*" We read, "I *can't* ask the tourists." "I *shouldn't* ask them," however, would have been more commensurate with Iatmul uneasiness about questioning the motivations behind a person's decisions.[13]

Finally, we learn that village leaders "had to obey" (*harim*) the missionaries. This may be true. But the verb *harim* evokes a range of meanings from simple listening to forceful heeding. As Dan Jorgensen (personal communication, 1995) remarks, "the cumulative effect of such slippage is to portray local folks as having less grasp of what's going on than they do, of being de-culturalized and more powerless vis-à-vis Europeans than their words indicate."

Most indigenous voices in *Cannibal Tours* speak with confusion, naivete, sadness, resignation, anger, and pathos. "Not only do tourists take photos of the village without paying," says one elder man, "but they make them into postcards—my own child spent money on a postcard of *my* house, which he sent me!" When local people stop talking, the camera often lingers on their silent faces; several men finish their comments with "*toktok bilong mi pinis*," "I have nothing more to say." When tourists are quiet, it is not because they have exhausted their discourse but, rather, because they are enthralled by the jungle or preoccupied with taking photographs. With the exception of one irate woman, local people are passively frozen by the camera. Only the tourists actually move. Not only does this overall portrayal irk many Papua New Guineans who view the film, but tourists have often commented to me that the inhabitants of Tambunum village are particularly assertive. Yet *Cannibal Tours* fails to "see" and "hear" these voices and behaviors. Most of the scenes do not occur in Tambunum, but in other villages, despite the fact that Tambunum is a touristic center of the region. Moreover, to repeat, the camera fails to capture moments of local assertion. The film does not, then, simply present local speech and action as it happened during tourism. Rather, it re-presents particular types of conversation and behavior.

Most local people who talk in *Cannibal Tours*, too, reached adulthood during the colonial era. Missing are the voices of youth whose postcolonial aspirations and discontentments are tied to the English language, formal schooling, urban employment, the lure of luxury goods, the promise of a middle-class lifestyle, rock and roll music, and romantic love (see Gewertz and Errington 1991; see also Gewertz and Errington, Chapter 16). Their voices, like the hybrid imagery on tourist art which I interpreted earlier, are not easily forced into an overall dichotomy that sees a primordial culture of purity waning beneath the sheer magnitude of a debased modernity. Younger voices, too, often tend to be a bit more outspoken, aggressive, and sexually audacious. Here is a brief example.

I was chatting with some men in the lower village one day when the tourist ship arrived. As I was walking along the main village path, a young man hurried past me with a small woodcarving that he wanted to show to the female tourists in particular. As he rushed up the path, he spun toward me, flashed the carving, and said with a malevolent grin "*tumbuna cunt.*" It was a stylized rendition of female genitalia. (Since these tourists were American, I thought it best to walk in the other direction lest I be called upon to intercede in what promised to be an awkward encounter!) Later, one tourist remarked that she found some of the younger men to be crude and intimidating. I'm sure they were.

The tourist guesthouse which stands across the river from the village is decorated with splendid mythological images, many of which highlight quite vividly erotic themes. A snake slithers into a vagina, and ancestral phalloi are prominent. Tourist woodcarvings are also embellished with hypertrophic genitals, and local men enjoy joking about the desire for, and trysts with, female tourists and European women in general. A competitive ethos colors all forms of sexuality in Eastern Iatmul culture (Silverman 2001c). Conversely, all forms of competition, especially to men, and all forms of desire, are eroticized. These themes do not pertain solely to tourism and Western women. Here, we might say, young men are simply translating nontouristic modes of interaction into a touristic encounter. At the same time, some Eastern Iatmul men are also intentionally seeking to shock Western women in order to reassert the local masculinity. It is, to be sure, a complex interaction.

Yet indigenous assertion, with the sole exception of an irate women, is entirely lacking in *Cannibal Tours*. (Recall, too, that sexuality in the film is associated only with tourists. Local people are far too modest.) Instead, we perceive a formerly warlike and ritualistic people, evidenced by the black and white photographs from the early twentieth century, conquered by modernity, and humiliated by tourism.

## OFF-CAMERA, OFF-SHIP

In one scene, a Iatmul man cryptically alludes to the totemic relationship between river waves, cloud formations, and decorative motifs on the cult house facade (see Bateson 1936 [1958]:230–231). This is virtually the *only* moment in the film where there is a focus on a contemporary belief or practice that is not directly tied to tourism. Yet this instance of nontouristic authenticity vanishes in the translation of the man's later assertion that "we have nothing sacred [*tumbuna samting*] anymore." All ritual objects, we read, were pilfered by Germany, England, and Australia. Here, "tumbuna" is an adjective that signifies sacredness. But "tumbuna" also connotes antiquity. In fact, the man's next utterance of *tumbuna samting* is translated as "old" rather than "sacred objects." As a noun, *tumbuna* refers to grandparents, distant relatives, and nonhuman ancestors such as totemic beings. This scene suggests that local people have been stripped of their genuine sacred culture. But this message, which ultimately denies local people their agency and creativity, arises from the narrative framing of the film and its overall allegory. It is not intrinsic to the statements themselves.

For Iatmul, in fact, sacredness is a nonmaterial quality that is largely transferred to an object through the bestowal of a totemic name. An old object, lacking a name, can be *tumbuna* in terms of age while a new object can be *tumbuna* in terms of magical sacredness. In short, the village has not been stripped of all its *tumbuna* objects, just its precontact ones. This is significant, to be sure, but not quite as decisive as the film implies.

Sepik men resent the many tourists and dealers who seek to bargain and to negotiate the prices of art and handicrafts. They dislike the persistent request for a "second" and "third" price. As local men say, they are allowed no such courtesy in the many stores in town. There, you have but one option: Pay the stated price, or move on. Consequently, village men may inflate the initial or "first price." More significantly, carvers adroitly weave tales about their touristic crafts in order to "authenticate" the price. Great antiquity can be readily simulated by soaking objects in the river and then smoking them like fish. Fictions of ancient rituals are enhanced when a seller quietly invites a tourist into the shadows of a house and then carefully unwraps an object. Local people, too, on their own initiative, stage open-air markets of objects when the tourists arrive in the village. Tourism, I am suggesting, does permit local agency and assertion.

Nearby Iatmul and non-Iatmul communities judge Tambunum to be one of the wealthiest villages in the region precisely because it is so frequently visited by tourists. Consequently, trading canoes from around the Sepik steadily voyage to the village laden with fruits, vegetables, betel nut, shells, clay pots and fire-hearths, smoked meat, baskets and net bags, and other items. Tourism has enabled Tambunum to maintain its position as a riverine entrepot. Many of these objects are resold, in fact, to tourists, often after some artistic modification. Likewise, men and women from nearby villages walk to Tambunum in order to gamble at all-night card games. Eastern Iatmul, who equip themselves for these competitions with magical spells and charms, are only too happy to oblige. Many competitors, too, also walk to the village with their own masks and carvings, which they themselves peddle to tourists. In this respect, it would be false to view tourism as a context that pits local people against Europeans.

In fact, tourism intersects with traditional trade and warfare rivalries and expands the horizon of regional exchange networks. Likewise, tourist art is rarely created entirely from local materials. Men procure paints, shells, styles, feathers, shoe polish, and so on from different areas of the Sepik region, both villages and towns. In this respect, tourist art is a wholly authentic cartographic representation of contemporary Sepik socioeconomic space.

The nearby Chambri, write Gewertz and Errington (1991), may alter the timing and pace of male initiation ceremonies so tourists can pay for the "right" to gaze at this "authentic" Sepik ritual. These rites transform youth into adults. Today, adult male personhood is a status that includes competence with modernity, for example, the ability to acquire cash and commodities, and to interact capably with Europeans and tourists. Tourism, then, reshapes a premodern ritual so that it remains relevant to contemporary lives rather than anachronistic. True, tourism instances a new form of hierarchy. Traditionally, Sepik hierarchies were based on what Gewertz and Errington (1991) call "commensurate" differences. Despite inequities in power and prestige, all members of the community were essentially equal. Tourism, and modernity more generally, entail "incommensurate" differences wherein people are fundamentally unequal. Nonetheless, tourism does not prevent local people from acting with genuine intention, meaning, and strategy.

## ARGONAUTS OF THE SEPIK?

The boat featured in *Cannibal Tours* is the *Melanesian Explorer,* a steamship that first sailed the Sepik in 1980. It was replaced in 1988 by the *Melanesian Discoverer,* a luxurious catamaran cruiser that is berthed at the Madang Resort Hotel, which is the main facility of the Melanesian Tourist Services. This company is owned and operated by Jan and Peter Barter, who are naturalized Australian-born citizens of Papua New Guinea. The names of these two tourist vessels, it is true, by invoking notions of exploration and discovery, do invite visitors' fantasies (D. Jorgensen, personal communication, 1996). But the *Melanesian Discoverer,* it should be noted, maintains a fairly extensive video and ethnographic library. In this respect, the tourist ship does provide the means whereby visitors can begin to contextualize their experiences of the Sepik. Whether or not visitors choose to do so is, of course, their own prerogative. Viewers of *Cannibal Tours,* however, are offered no such opportunity within the film itself of extending their gaze.

The tourist ship is a multifaceted institution along the Sepik. But *Cannibal Tours* overlooks much of this complexity. A world of interaction, for example, occurs between the vessel and local people. Because much of this activity is located at the stern of the vessel, and away from the tourists, it is largely concealed from their view—and from O'Rourke's viewfinder. The crew dispenses medical and school supplies at Sepik villages, purchases fruit and vegetables, and provides transportation along the river and sometimes to the coastal city of Madang. Several Sepik people are employed at the Madang Resort Hotel. For a period in the late 1980s, too, the crew reimbursed individual claims that the wake of the ship damaged dugout canoes. The tourist ship, then, does not merely ferry visitors throughout the region. It has a more complex relationship to local communities.

In the 1990s, Peter Barter won a seat in parliament, largely due to the successes of his touristic enterprises and locally perceived largess; shortly thereafter, he attained several cabinet posts. My point here is not to exonerate or justify the *Melanesian Discoverer* but, again, to suggest only that the tourist ship has a complex presence in the Sepik, one that is not so easily judged as exclusively disruptive or, for that matter, wholly beneficial. On the maiden voyage of the *Melanesian Discoverer,* for example, Tambunum villagers spontaneously danced for Peter Barter an honorific ceremony known as *naven* (Bateson 1936/1958; Silverman 2001c). In the film, however, the status of the tourist steamer is akin to that of the warship in Conrad's *Heart of Darkness:* an alien, intrusive vessel of folly and imperialism. It is a compelling portrayal, to be sure, but one that is unidimensional since it neglects all that goes on behind the tourist ship.

## CONCLUSION

My goal in this chapter was to argue that tourism affords Sepik people opportunities for asserting various forms of cultural hybridity, resistance, and aesthetic innovation. I can think of no more apt a conclusion than the words of one tourist as recounted by O'Rourke himself (1997:41–42). During the filming of *Cannibal Tours,* O'Rourke presented videocassette copies of his previous films to Sepik villagers "as a gesture of sincerity." He returned a few weeks later on the *Melanesian Discoverer.* As the ship was departing from one village, a tourist proudly waved one of the videotapes: "Guess what! A young man was selling your films and I bargained him down from 50 kina to 20 kina!"

Clearly, the tourist made out like a bandit, and the young Sepik man was robbed of his integrity and money. Or was he? How can we understand this transaction? An act of resistance? A moment of indigenous creativity and entrepreneurship? A repudiation of Western morality? A comment on O'Rourke's film? It is entirely ambiguous—and certainly complex. And so, too, I have argued, is Sepik tourism.

## ACKNOWLEDGMENTS

Fieldwork in 1988–1990 was graciously funded by a Fulbright Award and the Institute for Intercultural Studies; related support was granted by the Department of Anthropology and the Graduate School, University of Minnesota. The Wenner-Gren Foundation for Anthropological Research and DePauw University generously enabled a return visit in June–August 1994. My thoughts on *Cannibal Tours* benefited from conversations with Andrea Wohl, David Lipset, Dan Jorgensen, Stephen Leavitt, Karen Brison, Keith Nightenhelser, Kora Korawali, tourists, students at DePauw University, and an Internet dialogue about the film in November–December 1996 among members of the Association for Social Anthropology in Oceania (N. Maclean, M. Rohatynskyj, M. Evans, S. Srivastava, K. Barlow, J. Ruoff, M. McCutcheon, and J. Barker). I am also grateful for the hospitality of Jan and Peter Barter, and the crew of the *Melanesian Discoverer.* Finally, I extend my inevitably unreciprocated gratitude to the people of Tambunum. Of course, I alone am responsible for the text and tone of this article.

## NOTES

1. Ideally, this chapter will be read in conjunction with a viewing of *Cannibal Tours,* especially in the classroom.

2. MacCannell (1992:71, footnote 12) writes about a San Francisco newspaper article in which a Sepik man tells the reporter, who traveled on the *Melanesian Discoverer,* that Margaret Mead once studied in his village. Now there is another anthropologist in the community. During the reporter's visit, however, this new anthropologist was spending some time in town. The tour director facetiously added that the young anthropologists must phone his mother monthly to reassure her that he has not been eaten by cannibals. MacCannell labeled this unnamed anthropologist an "authentic postmodern attraction." I am flattered.

3. Two rejoinders to the longstanding tradition of using (fictitious) images of Pacific Islanders to examine Western morality is the 1999 film *Taking Pictures* by McLaren and Stiven (see the Filmography) and McCall's (1994) notes on the Hollywood film *Rapa Nui,* which was produced by Kevin Costner. During the filming of *Rapa Nui,* local people were offered US$25 per appearance—a gratuity that was increased to $36 for women who bared their breasts.

4. The invocation of Kissinger in the film recalls his infamous statement about Micronesia: "There are only 90,000 people out there. Who gives a damn?" (These comments were featured on the American CBS television program *60 Minutes,* in a segment titled "Who Gives a Damn?" which aired on December 23, 1979.) Kissinger sits on the board of directors for Freeport McMoRan Inc., which operates the enormous Freeport gold and copper mine in Irian Jaya. The mine has been implicated in human rights violations, environmental devastation, and official Indonesian policies concerning the erosion of Melanesian cultural identity in western New Guinea.

5. Morris (1996) ties the current fascination with cannibalism in popular, pseudoethnographic film to intensified capitalist consumption and bodily fetishes such as "urban primitive" tattoos, dieting, fitness, and natural cosmetics and clothing.

6. See Teaiwa (1994) for the role of the bikini bathing suit in the sexualized trivialization of Pacific history.

7. Mulvey (1975) and Kaplan (1983) explore the male cinematic gaze. *Cannibal Tours* is not the only film by O'Rourke to raise questions about sexual morality (Berry, Hamilton, and Jayamanne 1997).

8. Douglas (1996) traces the history of large-scale tourism in Melanesia to the early twentieth century. Other sources on Sepik and Melanesian tourism include Farrell (1979); Cohen (1982); Macnaught (1982); Errington and Gewertz (1989b); Schmidt (1990); Coiffier (1991); Gewertz and Errington (1991); Milne (1991); Michaud, Maranda, Lafreniere, and Cote (1994), and, relatedly Linnekin (1997) and Adams (1998).

9. Some Sepik societies, however, do internalize colonial and missionary racism, and view their past as immoral (Smith 1994; Brison 1996).

10. O'Rourke's comments about Margaret Mead are as stereotypical as his comments about tourism!

11. MacCannell cites early twentieth-century reports compiled by Quiggin (1949:172*ff.*), which do not concern the Sepik but rather the Papua Gulf, to the effect that these "strings of shell money" are "worth the value of between two and ten months of labor." This claim is groundless and wholly misleading.

12. On the eve of independence in 1975, Sepik people were trying to sell newly minted Papua New Guinea kina coins, which were pierced in the middle to resemble shells, for three times the Australian exchange rate (Griffin, Nelson, and Firth 1979:230).

13. Another man reports that his forefathers *pulim meri,* which O'Rourke translates as "raping women" but which could equally mean "seducing women." MacCannell, too, addresses language in the film, but with bizarre conceptual peculiarities that I cannot understand; for example, tourists speak metaphorically whereas "primitives speak metonymically" (1992:44) and "the language of the Iatmul people is filled with concrete images of violence. . . . The language of the tourists is filled with repressed violence" (1992:46). Of course, neither MacCannell nor O'Rourke understand the Iatmul language.

## FILMOGRAPHY

McLaren, Les, and Annie Stiven. 1996. *Taking Pictures.* Video. 56 minutes. First Run/Icarus Films, New York.

O'Rourke, Dennis. 1987. *Cannibal Tours.* Australia. 77 minutes. Direct Cinema Limited.

## REFERENCES

Adams, Kathleen M. 1998. "More Than an Ethnic Marker: Toraja Art as Identity Negotiator." *American Ethnologist* 25:327–351.

Bateson, Gregory. 1936 [1958]. *Naven: A Survey of the Problems Suggested by a Composite Picture of the Culture of a New Guinea Tribe Drawn from Three Points of View.* 2nd rev. ed. Stanford: Stanford University Press.

Berry, Chris, Annette Hamilton, and Laleen Jayamanne, eds. 1997. "*The Filmmaker and the Prostitute: Dennis O'Rourke's 'The Good Woman of Bangkok.'*" Sydney: Power Publications.

Brison, Karen J. 1996. "Becoming Savage: Western Representations and Cultural Identity in a Sepik Society." *Anthropology and Humanism* 21:5–18.

Bruner, Edward. 1989. "Of Cannibals, Tourists, and Ethnographers." *Cultural Anthropology* 4:439–449.

———. 1991. "Transformation of Self in Tourism." *Annals of Tourism Research* 18:238–250.

Clark, Jeffrey. 1997. "Imagining the State, or Tribalism and the Arts of Memory in the Highlands of Papua New Guinea." In *Narratives of Nation in the South Pacific.* Ton Otto and Nicholas Thomas, eds. Pp. 65–90. Amsterdam: Harwood.

Clifford, James. 1988. *On Collecting Art and Culture. The Predicament of Culture.* Cambridge, Mass.: Harvard University Press.

Cohen, Erik. 1982. *The Pacific Islands from Utopian Myth to Consumer Product: The Disenchantment of Paradise.* Centre des Hautes Etudes Touristiques, Serie B, No. 27.

Cohen, Hart. 1988. "Swinging Through the Jungle." *Filmnews* (March 1988):14–15.

Coiffier, Christian. 1991. "'Cannibal Tours,' l'Envers du Decor. Mani Bilong Waitman." *Journal de la Societé des Oceanistes* 92/93:181–187.

Conrad, Joseph. 1899[1988]. *Heart of Darkness.* Norton Critical Edition, Rovert Kimbrough, ed. New York: Norton.

Douglas, Ngaire. 1996. *They Came for Savages: 100 Years of Tourism in Melanesia.* Lismore, Australia: Southern Cross University Press.

Errington, Frederick, and Deborah Gewertz. 1989a. "Review of Cannibal Tours." *American Anthropologist* 91:274–275.

———. 1989b. "Tourism and Anthropology in a Post-Modern World." *Oceania* 60:37–54.

Errington, Shelly. 1994. "What Became Authentic Primitive Art?" *Cultural Anthropology* 9:201–226.

Farrell, Bryan H. 1979. "Tourism's Human Conflicts: Cases from the Pacific." *Annals of Tourism Research* 6:122–136.

Gewertz, Deborah B., and Frederick K. Errington. 1991. *Twisted Histories, Altered Contexts: Representing the Chambri in a World System.* Cambridge: Cambridge University Press.

Griffin, James, Hank Nelson, and Stewart Firth. 1979. *Papua New Guinea: A Political History.* Victoria: Heinemann Educational Press.

Kaplan, E. Ann. 1983. "Is the Gaze Male?" In *Powers of Desire: The Politics of Sexuality.* A. Snitow, C. Stansell, and S. Thompson, eds. Pp. 309–327. New York: Monthly Review Press.

Kauffmann, Christian. 1988. "Reflections on Art, Crafts, and Ethnographic Documentation in a Papua New Guinea Society." *Visual Anthropology* 1:263–273.

Kulick, Don, and Margaret E. Willson. 1992. "Echoing Images: The Construction of Savagery Among Papua New Guinean Villagers." *Visual Anthropology* 5:143–152.

Linnekin, Jocelyn. 1997. "Consuming Cultures: Tourism and the Commoditization of Cultural Identity in the Island Pacific." In *Tourism, Ethnicity, and the State in Asian and Pacific Societies.* M. Picard and R. E. Wood, eds. Pp. 215–250. Honolulu: University of Hawai'i Press.

Lutkehaus, Nancy Christine. 1989. "'Excuse Me, Everything Is Not All Right': On Ethnography, Film, and Representation: An Interview with Filmmaker Dennis O'Rourke." *Cultural Anthropology* 4:422–437.

Lutz, Catherine A., and Jane L. Collins. 1993. *Reading National Geographic.* Chicago: University of Chicago Press.

McCall, Grant. 1994. "Rapanui Images." *Pacific Studies* 17:85–102.

MacCannell, Dean. 1990. *"Cannibal Tours." Visual Anthropology Review* 6:14–23.

———. 1992. *Empty Meeting Grounds: The Tourist Papers.* London: Routledge.

MacDougall, David. 1995. "The Subjective Voice in Ethnographic Film." In *Fields of Vision: Essays in Film Studies, Visual Anthropology, and Photography.* L. Devereaux and R. Hillman, eds. Pp. 217–255. Berkeley: University of California Press.

Macnaught, Timothy J. 1982. "Mass Tourism and the Dilemmas of Modernization in Pacific Island Communities." *Annals of Tourism Research* 9:359–381.

Mascia-Lees, Frances E., and Patricia Sharpe. 1994. "The Anthropological Unconscious." *American Anthropologist* 96:649–660.

Mead, Margaret. 1938. "The Mountain Arapesh, Part I: An Importing Culture." Anthropological Papers of the American Museum of Natural History, Vol. 36.

———. 1978. "The Sepik as a Culture Area." *Anthropological Quarterly* 51:69–75.

Michaud, Jean, Pierre Miranda, Luc Lafreniere, and Ginette Cote. 1994. "Ethnological Tourism in the Solomon Islands: An Experience in Applied Anthropology." *Anthropologica* 36:35–56.

Milne, Simon. 1991. "Tourism Development in Papua New Guinea." *Annals of Tourism Research* 18:508–511.

Morris, Rosalind C. 1996. "Anthropology in the Body Shop: Lords of the Garden, Cannibalism, and the Consuming Desires of Televisual Anthropology." *American Anthropologist* 98:137–150.

Mulvey, Laura. 1975. "Visual Pleasure and Narrative Cinema." *Screen* 16:6–18.

O'Hanlon, Michael. 1995. "Modernity and the 'Graphicalization' of Meaning: New Guinea Highland Shield Design in Historical Perspective." *The Journal of the Royal Anthropological Institute* 1:469–493.

O'Rourke, Dennis. 1997. "Beyond Cannibal Tours: Tourists, Modernity and 'The Other.'" In *Tourism and Cultural Development in Asia and Oceania.* Shinji Yamashita, Kadir H. Din, and J. S. Eades, eds. Pp. 32–47. Bangi: Penerbit Universiti Kebangsaan Malaysia.

Price, Sally. 1989. *Primitive Art in Civilized Places.* Chicago: University of Chicago Press.

Quiggin, A. Hingston. 1949. *A Survey of Primitive Money: The Beginnings of Currency.* London: Methuen.

Rony, Fatimah Tobing. 1996. *The Third Eye: Race, Cinema, and Ethnographic Spectacle.* Durham, N.C.: Duke University Press.

Root, Deborah. 1996. *Cannibal Culture: Art, Appropriation, & the Commodification of Difference.* Boulder, Colo.: Westview Press.

Rosaldo, Renato. 1989. *Culture and Truth: The Remaking of Social Analysis.* Boston: Beacon Press.

Schmidt, Jurg. 1990. "The Response to Toursim in Yensan." In *Sepik Heritage: Tradition and Change in Papua New Guinea.* Nancy Lutkehaus et al., eds. Pp. 241–244. Durham, N.C.: Carolina Academic Press.

Silverman, Eric Kline. 1997. "Art, Authenticity, and Other Transnational Dilemmas: Lessons from Sepik River Tourism, Shona Sculpture, and the New Guinea Sculpture Garden at Stanford University." Paper presented at the annual meeting of the American Anthropological Association, Washington, D.C.

———. 1999. "Tourist Art as the Crafting of Identity in the Sepik River (Papua New Guinea)." In *Unpacking Culture: Art and Commodity in Colonial and Postcolonial Worlds.* Ruth B. Phillips and Christopher B. Steiner, eds. Pp. 51–66. Berkeley: University of California Press.

———. 2001a. "From Totemic Space to Cyberspace: Transformations in Sepik River and Aboriginal Australian Myth, Knowledge and Art." In *Emplaced Myth: Space, Narrative and Knowledge in Aboriginal Australia and Papua New Guinea Societies.* Alan Rumsey and James F. Weiner, eds. Pp. 189–214. Honolulu: University of Hawai'i Press.

———. 2001b. "Tourism in the Sepik River of Papua New Guinea: Favoring the Local over the Global." In *Local Perspectives on Global Tourism in South East Asia and the Pacific Region.* H. Dahles and T. van Meijl, eds. Special issue. *Pacific Tourism Review* 4:105–135.

———. 2001c. *Masculinity, Motherhood, and Mockery: Psychoanalyzing Culture and the Iatmul Naven Rite.* Ann Arbor: University of Michigan Press.

Smith, Michael French. 1994. *Hard Times on Kairiru Island: Poverty, Development, and Morality in a Papua New Guinea Village.* Honolulu: University of Hawai'i Press.

Solomon-Godeau, Abigail. 1989. "Going Native." *Art in America* (July 1989):119–129, 161.

Steiner, Christopher B. 1994. *African Art in Transit.* Cambridge: Cambridge University Press.

Strathern, Marilyn. 1992. "The Decomposition of an Event." *Cultural Anthropology* 7:244–254.

Teaiwa, Teresia K. 1994. "bikinis and other s/pacific n/oceans." *The Contemporary Pacific* 6:87–109.

Thomas, Nicholas. 1991. *Entangled Objects: Exchange, Material Culture, and Colonialism in the Pacific.* Cambridge, Mass.: Harvard University Press.

Weiner, Annette B. 1992. "Trobrianders on Camera and Off: The Film That Did Not Get Made." *Visual Anthropology Review* 8:103–106.

Young, Katherine. 1992. "Visuality and the Category of the Other: The Cannibal Tours of Dean MacCannell and Dennis O'Rourke." *Visual Anthropology Review* 8:92–96.

# 21

# "Killing Time" in a Postcolonial Town: Young People and Settlements in Port Vila, Vanuatu

**Jean Mitchell**

*University of Prince Edwards Island*

> The uses of a tax haven are really only limited to the imaginations of the taxpayer (and non taxpayers), their accountants, lawyers and other preferred advisors. (http://www:Vanuatu.Net.Vu/vanuatuonline directory.html)

Killing time (*Kilem Taem*) is an expression that many young people living in the town of Port Vila, Vanuatu use to describe the ways in which they pass their time when they cannot find work. Some young people also use the expression, *sperem pablik rod* (SPR), which literally means "hitting the road," to signify their unemployed status in the settlements where they live around Port Vila. Vanuatu is the Y-shaped archipelago located in the southwest Pacific that was known as New Hebrides from the time of Captain Cook's visit in 1774 until independence in 1980. The islands had been jointly administered by French and English colonial officials from 1906 through an arrangement known as the Condominium. The island nation whose citizens are called ni-Vanuatu has about 113 distinct indigenous languages and an extraordinary diversity of cultural practices often referred to as *kastom*. Bislama, the lingua franca, has been crucial in linking islanders and today it is generating new ways for young people to talk about their lives.

Since the establishment of a tax haven in Vanuatu in 1971, there has been rapid urbanization marked by urban settlements that now ring the capital (Connell and Lea 1994). With independence there has been a steep rise in the number of young people leaving school with the expectation of finding work in the wage economy in town. Vanuatu is a young nation with a very young population. According to the 1999 census, almost 43 percent of the total population of 186,678 is less than fifteen years of age and 69 percent of the population is less than thirty years of age (Government of Vanuatu 2000). This demographic profile is particularly evident in the settlements around Port Vila where there are large numbers of children and young people and very few old people.

The settlements are a new kind of spatial and social configuration. They differ from the rural and peri-urban villages around Vila where residents are, for the most part, traditional landowners living on their own land. In contrast, the people in the increasingly crowded settlements are living on land that belongs to someone else. Tenancy arrangements are often insecure, and the issue of land in urban areas is highly contested and volatile (Rawlings 1999a). Many young, unemployed people living in settlements ironically suggest that their work is "killing time" or, in Bislama, *wokem kilem taem*. In this chapter, I shall argue that killing time encodes new spatial and temporal practices in this postcolonial town that attracts tourists and off-shore capital, the restless media of modernity and globalization.

Killing time is an evocative practice. It draws attention to a number of important contemporary issues related to generation and youth (Jourdan, 1995a, 1995b; Gewertz and Errington 1996; Comaroff and Comaroff 1999, 2001; Sykes 1999) and globalization (Hannerz 1989; Appadurai 1990, 1996; King 1997; Tsing 2000). It also raises issues related to the nature of postcoloniality "which necessarily follows and is highly engaged with colonialism" (Thomas 1994:195). For many young people living in Port Vila twenty years after independence, postcoloniality may well mean that the memory of the independence struggle has receded while, "global capitalism in its latest avatar dominates" (Mishra and Hodge 1994:288). The impact of global capitalism is important to consider for it appears to "include and to marginalize in unanticipated ways, to produce desire and expectation on a global scale and yet to decrease the certainty of work" (Comaroff and Comaroff 2000: 298). The growing importance of consumption and the exclusion of young people from "work and wage" must be kept in mind when considering their lives and the ways in which they are fashioning new spatial and temporal practices. Focusing on the practices of "killing time" and *sperem pablik rod* shows the ways in which these processes are played out in the day-to-day life of young people in a town that began as a colonial creation.

This chapter is based on my fieldwork in Vanuatu that was undertaken between 1996 and 1999 in the settlement of Blacksands, near Port Vila. I did not plan to work with young people, but while living in the settlement, I was forced to seriously consider their lives, their talk, and their practices. During my fieldwork I established the Vanuatu Young People's Project (VYPP) with the Vanuatu Cultural Centre in 1997 with the idea of providing a forum for young people to speak about their lives.[1] The director of the Vanuatu Cultural Centre, Ralph Regenvanu, recognized the important changes taking place in town and among young people and has been instrumental in ensuring that the Vanuatu Cultural Centre undertakes research as well as advocacy with, and on behalf of, young people. The project began with research on young people in Port Vila and, as part of the project, more than 1,000 young people were interviewed by other young people. The project also created a video entitled *Kilem Taem*[2] based on the research undertaken by the young people. The aims of the video and research were to provide young people with a chance to speak and to document the increasing complexity and difficulty of their lives in town. It is important to point out that in Port Vila young people as a social category do not comprise a homogenous group but rather are highly differentiated. This chapter concerns those young people who are largely unemployed and are growing up in settlements such as Blacksands.

I shall argue that the practices of killing time represent a reworking of both spatial and temporal meanings among the postcolonial generation, many of whom are among the first to grow up in town or to spend long periods of time in town. Exploring the sociocultural processes through which such meanings are constructed is important for it shows the ways in which people "produce themselves as spatiotemporal beings and the space-time of the larger world" (Munn 1992:106). This is a useful way to approach the issue of globalization, which may be defined as "a set of projects that require us to imagine space and time in particular ways" (Tsing 2000:351).

Harvey has argued that the shift to "flexible accumulation" (1989:58) effects a compression of time and space through the development of new forms of production, circulation, and consumption. The process of globalization also entails "the radical intensification of relations between geographically separated spaces to a structurally transformative movement of people, things and ideas across cultural and national borders" (Lederman 1998:427). Globalization may be usefully viewed as a "shared historical process that differentiates the world as it connects it" (Gupta and Ferguson 1992:16).

While the practices associated with killing time are wide-ranging, I shall examine those that cohere around the visual. These include "eye-shopping" (window-shopping), video watching, and tourism as they provide examples of the ways in which the processes of globalization both "connect" and "differentiate." These activities also provide a locus for "imagination as social practice" that is central to global cultural processes (Appadurai 1996:31) and to the reworking of spatial and temporal meanings. I shall begin by locating the practices of killing time within a broad framework. This necessitates sketching the transformation of Port Vila from colonial planter town to postcolonial tax haven and the emergence of chronic unemployment, as well as urban settlements whose residents are increasingly referred to as "squatters."

## PORT VILA: FROM PLANTER TOWN TO TAX HAVEN

As a colonial community, Port Vila owes its origin to the French coconut planters' and traders' decision to place their economic interests there in the 1880s and 1890s (Rodman 1999, 2001). This area, which previously had not been settled, was claimed by Ifira Islanders who lived on the small island located near the harbor. With the establishment of the British/French Condominium in 1906, Port Vila became the site of the colonial administration. There were concerted efforts to have ni-Vanuatu recede from view as the town was created as a "white space" (Rodman

1999:1). Formal regulations and colonial practices restricted the movement of Islanders to and within the town for a number of years, and having work was a precondition for Islanders to be in town. For example, in 1918 the Joint Regulation No. 1 entitled "The Unemployed Natives Regulation" was issued, and it permitted unemployed Islanders to stay in town for only fifteen days before being sent back to their villages (Bedford 1973:55). From the beginning it was participation in wage work that gave Islanders the right to be in Port Vila.

This idea that residency in Vila is linked to work is rooted in colonial experience, but it continues to inform contemporary life in town. Indeed, some authorities currently concerned with the issue of unemployed young people believe that directives should be invoked to control the movement of young people to and in Port Vila. Thus, while marked as a "white space," Port Vila was also a space where some Islanders came to work in the wage economy. This enabled their acquisition of commodities and money that could be used to enhance or extend kin and exchange relations. A pattern of circular migration linked the villages to sites of wage employment in the towns of Port Vila and Santo and on plantations throughout the archipelago, as Islanders (primarily men) went away to work and then returned to their villages (Bedford 1973). However, this pattern has been changing over the past few decades as is evident in the growth of settlements in town (Haberkorn 1989). Clearly the idea of circular migration no longer fully explains the complex relationship between place and wage labor and between urban and rural areas. Port Vila has changed from being a place where people went to find work but were expected to recede from view to being a place where many young people do not work and are visible killing time. It is important to link this development to the wider processes that have been shaping Port Vila over the past few decades. While it is generally believed that the young people who live in Port Vila have just migrated to town, our research with young people found that many had accompanied family members to town as children or had been born in town. Thus, the current issue of unemployed young people in town is imbricated in longstanding changes shaped by colonial and postcolonial processes. Many of the criticisms leveled at young people hinge on the idea that they must work if they live in town. However, this perception fails to acknowledge that there is a new generation of young people who have been growing up in town with their families and that there are not enough jobs available to keep pace with population growth.

Globalization, according to Appadurai,

marks a set of transitions in the global political economy since the 1970s, in which multinational forms of capitalist organization began to be replaced by transnational, flexible and irregular forms of organization, as labor, finance, technology, and technological capital began to be assembled in ways that treated national boundaries as mere constraints or fictions. (1998:228)

This process of globalization is evident in the creation of a tax haven in Vanuatu. A tax haven is a jurisdiction that levies no (or very low) direct corporate or personal income taxes and is used by foreign individuals or corporations to avoid or alleviate the tax burden in their own country. In 1971, as the independence movement was building in the former New Hebrides (Vanuatu), British officials took steps to create an off-shore banking center or tax haven. As Rawlings noted, Port Vila became "redefined as a new entrepot for the circulation of massive amounts of global capital" (1999b:1). McKnight has summarized Vanuatu's success in attracting international capital as follows:

Vanuatu has set out to become an international investment center and tax haven. It imposes few business taxes, has no currency or exchange controls, and companies are not required to have their records open for public scrutiny, so complete secrecy can be maintained. As a result, more than 1,000 international companies maintain registered offices in Vanuatu, and many firms that offer legal, accounting, and financial services have been attracted. (1998:194)

In off-shore banking centers, production, "seems to have been superceded by less tangible means of generating value by control over such things as the provision of services, the means of communication and above all the flow of finance capital" (Comaroff and Comaroff 2001:295). Value is increasingly generated "by the market and by speculation" and these new markets and monetary instruments are aided by space-time compression (Comaroff and Comaroff 2001:300). These processes seem to detach financial realms from "real production" and to sever the processes of production from consumption. This point is important in understanding the context in which young people are killing time in Port Vila.

With the establishment of the tax haven in Port Vila, not only capital but also tourists and commodities in duty-free shops became part of everyday life. Interconnections created through the intense circulation of commodities, people, and ideas are central to the "new globalism" (Tsing 2000:336). Tsing, however, cautions against "over valorizing connection and circulation" for the market model that undergirds globalization and promotes the equalities of circulation may also justify "policies of domination and discrimination" (Tsing 2000). Massey had argued this point earlier when she wrote:

Different groups and different individuals are placed in very distinct ways in relation to these flows and interconnections . . . some people are more in charge of it than others; some initiate flows and movement, others don't: some are more on the receiving end of it than others; some are effectively imprisoned by it. (1991:27)

It is important to pay attention to the ways in which differences and disparities are produced and enforced in this era of intense circulation, interconnectedness, and flows. From this perspective, an examination of the situation of young people in Port Vila settlements in connection with the establishment of the tax haven is instructive.

## Banks, Hotels, and Settlements

The effect of the creation of the tax haven was "electrifying" (Forster 1980:371). The quiet town of Port Vila was transformed into a "boom town" as thirteen overseas banks opened, tourism took off when hotels of international standard were constructed, airline services increased, and cruise ships added Vila as a destination on Pacific routes. The expatriate population increased within a short period of time, occupying expensive new housing subdivisions that reshaped the landscape in and around Port Vila (Forster 1980:371). Thus, in the midst of efforts to forge a national territory and to loosen the hold of colonialism, Vanuatu (then the New Hebrides) was plunged into an even more complex and spatially differentiated global capitalist order that internationalized the state even before it had become nationalized.

The British administration claimed that the tax haven would provide employment and capital and thus spur the country's economic growth (Sope n.d.:48). However, Sope has argued that the establishment of the tax haven meant that commercial development has been concentrated in Vila and has only benefited the Europeans who live there. Most of the large sums of money passing through the banks were not available locally, as the money coming in goes out again to the overseas parent companies of the local companies (Sope n.d.:49). Recently, Rawlings (1999b) has pointed to the large sums of money domiciled in various Vila-based banks, finance houses, and trustee companies in contrast to the government's meager budget to fund basic needs such as health and education in the country. Based on his fieldwork in the village of Pango located outside of Vila, Rawlings describes some of the profound disjunctures in the lives of those people who worked in the finance and the service industries that expanded with the establishment of the tax haven and tourism.[3] The quotation at the beginning of this chapter suggests that "the uses of a tax haven . . . are only limited by the imagination." However, this formulation only serves to raise the vast differences in the

form and content of "imaginative practices" in the tax haven. "Global flows" are experienced differently by the nontaxpayers and their coterie of ancillary professionals and the employees described by Rawlings (1999b) and by the young people I knew. In the discussion of killing time below, I shall suggest how global flows inform imaginative practices of young people in ways that both connect and differentiate.

## Urbanization

Urbanization, as mentioned, has been rapid over the past few decades. In the ten years from 1979 to 1989, the population of urban Vanuatu grew at 5.1 percent per year compared to a rural population increase of 2 percent a year (UNDP 1996:30). According to the 1999 census, the urban population growth rate is now 4.2 percent, which is still considerably higher than the rural growth rate of 2.2 percent. The boom in the construction of hotels, banks, and other buildings and the jobs it created drew people to Vila for work. The population of Vila grew rapidly after legislation to transform Vanuatu into a tax haven and this, according to Connell and Lea, demonstrates how government policies affect migration and urban growth patterns (1994:40). Opportunities for earning cash have declined in a number of rural areas and access to land also appears difficult in some islands. This is evident in the high rates of migration from the island of Tongoa and the other Shepherd Islands, as well as from the islands of Tanna and Paama. These islands are experiencing land pressure and rapidly growing populations. Ward has noted that "the driving forces now reshaping Pacific Island economies, societies, polities and geographies have their sources in urban areas" (1998:22) and yet, urban areas are rarely studied.

Port Vila had been a small town for a long time. In the 1930s Port Vila had only about 1,000 people and by the end of the 1970s it had a population of 14,600. The 1999 census recorded the population of Port Vila at 29,356. The urban population now represents

21.5 percent of the total population of Vanuatu. The rapid urbanization has resulted in the development of settlements that are overcrowded and without access to basic services such as water, sanitation, electricity, and good roads. Houses in settlements are constructed from sheets of corrugated iron that can be readily disassembled and relocated. As noted, there is little security of tenure and people must be prepared to dismantle their houses quickly if the landowner wants the land back. The long-term settlement of islanders in town has been rendered complex not only by colonial and postcolonial developments but also by the traditional landowning patterns, which discourage permanent settlement by nonlandowners. Settlements are generally believed to be transitory and temporary.

Our research with young people in Port Vila showed that many young people are living in crowded settlements where it is difficult to find space. This is one reason why young men are so visible in town, as they often spend time in public places away from their crowded places in the settlements. Our research showed that at least 64 percent of the 1,000 young people interviewed lived with five or more people, often in small, crowded spaces. For many families living in settlements in crowded rooms without water and electricity, rent can take up to half of their family income (UNDP 1996:30). People in the settlement where I lived struggled to pay for their rented rooms and food, as well as for school fees for their children.

Unemployment is a widespread problem in town. A study of Blacksands in 1995 found that 55 percent of the population was unemployed and many of those working earned 10,000 VT (US$68) or less per month (Bong 1995). Actual average wages cannot be estimated because there is no income tax, but the minimum wage is 16,000 VT (US$110) per month. Low-income families must spend a higher proportion of their income on highly taxed imported food, rents, and essential items such as kerosene than do higher-income families. The high cost of living that accompanied high levels of inflation led to the teachers' strike and

the public service strikes of 1993 (Bong 1995). Currently, in some settlements, access to gardens has offset some of the ill effects of unemployment because gardens are used as a food supply as well as a way to augment income through food sales at the market. However, access to garden land is conditional on its availability. The increasing difficulties of obtaining permission from the traditional landowners and the rapid growth of Port Vila are steadily reducing access to gardens.

Settlements, as noted, are a new kind of space in Vanuatu. They reflect both the movement of people from the various islands to town and the fact that some people are now staying in town for longer periods of time. A new generation is growing up in town and in the settlements where people from different islands and cultures are living in very close proximity for the first time. Settlements are becoming increasingly stigmatized as sources and sites of transgression and crime, as is increasingly evident in newspaper reports in Port Vila. However, settlements also reflect the inequities within the country. There were notable differences between ni-Vanuatu and non ni-Vanuatu income and, for example, in 1989 the per capita income of expatriates was eighteen times higher than that of ni-Vanuatu. Rates of income growth have also been different; for example, expatriate per capita GDP increased between 1986 and 1989 while ni-Vanuatu per capita GDP fell during the same period (UNDP 1996:36). Over the past several decades the growing visible disparities between low-income settlement areas and the wealthier and largely expatriate areas of Port Vila have added to the volatility of the urban situation (UNDP 1996:30).

Coming to terms with the business of killing time means coming to terms with the changing demographic structure, as well as postcolonial economic and educational choices. The young age structure of the population ensures that the expectations and aspirations of young people will continue to have an enormous impact on the country for many years to come. The aspirations of these young people have been shaped by their experience of being the first generation to grow up in an independent nation where formal education and full-time wage employment are increasingly important. Settlements in Vila will continue to grow as the town is seen as the major employment center and thus it will continue to attract school leavers who are looking for work. However, young people are routinely admonished by authorities for being underemployed in town and are told "to go back" to their islands where they have land. But, as Patrick noted in the video *Kilem Taem,* "living conditions, water and sanitation are very difficult for people living in town. But it is not something to be resolved by going back to the islands because many of these children and young people were born in town." The large qualitative survey undertaken by the Young People's Project in 1997 found that more than 37 percent of the thousand young people interviewed had been born in Vila or had lived in Vila more than ten years. About 28 percent of those interviewed had never even been to their island villages (VYPP 1999:17–18). The official line on youth migration has been that the young people come from the villages for the excitement and the "bright lights" of town. However, some of the key findings that emerged from the research in Port Vila are that many young people are concerned about finding work, that they are closely allied with their families, and that many are not just recent migrants. This finding is at odds with the common perception that there is an unemployed "youth" problem because young people are "drifting" into town. While it is true that young people are coming to town, it is extremely important to recognize that the process of urbanization is on-going and has been for some time. I shall now turn to a discussion of killing time and the marginalization of young people from the wage sector.

## KILEM TAEM AND SPEREM PABLIK ROD: KILLING TIME AND HITTING THE ROAD

If the new settlements have become the place of many young people, then killing time has become their occupation. My experience of living in a settlement in Port Vila has forced me to recognize the urgency of understanding the changes pertaining to urban youth and their refashioning of ideas related to space and time. A number of authors have called attention to the issue of youth and identified generation as a critical factor in understanding contemporary change, conflict, and cleavages (Gewertz and Errington 1996; Comaroff and Comaroff 1999:203; Sykes 1999; Ward 1999; Durham 2000). In Melanesia, Strathern (1975) was among the first to draw attention to how the experience of young people living in town provided an important set of symbols about urban areas. In the Solomon Islands, Jourdan (1995a, 1995b) has described the lives of young people who are unemployed and known as *Masta Liu* and the ways in which they are shaping social change in Honiara. Such young people, she argues, "have been pushed to the fringes of urban economic life but the responses they give to marginalization stress cultural agency as a means to find one's urban identity and social space" (1995a:203).

The marginalization of young people and the ways in which they exercise agency against this background of exclusion are important to recognize. Comaroff and Comaroff have linked the emergence of "global youth cultures of desire, self expression, and representation" (2001:307) to "their relative marginalization from the normative world of work and wage" (2001:308). Sykes has described the lives of young people known as *raskols* (rascals) in urban Papua New Guinea (PNG), arguing that their "relations are made through consumption rather than through labor" (1999:158). Young men who are *raskols* in town, she argues, are alienated from both the kin and wage economy in PNG, and their lives, rife with violence, "document the darker side of modernity" (Sykes 1999; see also Roscoe, chapter 3).

It appears that with global capitalism there is a "nonclass of non workers" (Gilroy 1994:412) and in Port Vila this is evident in the discourses of killing time and *sperem pablik rod* (SPR). Some young people, especially in the settlement where I conducted research, referred to themselves as members of the *Sperem Pablik Rod Kompani* (Hitting the Road Company). Not working rather than working is the bond that binds the unemployed young people, who ironically called themselves the SPR company—"the biggest company in Vanuatu," whose speciality is killing time. With this ludic gesture, young people pointed to the unsatisfactory nature of their lives, ruefully linking their situation to the world of business enterprise, as well as to an earlier time when the idea of company was used to describe contingents of men going off to work on plantations throughout the archipelago.

Daniel, a young man who is unemployed in Vila, explained in the video *Kilem Taem,* "SPR is just a simple word that young people invented." As Daniel says, "every morning when we wake up we walk the streets until dark; tomorrow is the same, everyday, walking along the road." While Daniel claims the expression of SPR for young unemployed people, others have suggested that it gained currency in Port Vila after the 1993 public servants' strike. The strike meant that a large number of people who were gainfully employed in the government found themselves suddenly unemployed. However, over the past few years SPR has become increasingly associated with the unemployed young people who are living in town away from their island of origin. Young people are "hitting the road" and walking about in town, and in so doing they are reconfiguring ideas about place as well as reclaiming space for themselves. Frazer (1985) noted the importance of young people's walkabout in Honiara and pointed to the traditional basis of young people's incessant walking about in town, linking it to a longstanding island practice that facilitates an intense sociality among islanders. In Port Vila, SPR signifies unemployment and efforts to pass the day in town. Urban space is "claimed" as it is mapped and invented through young people's occupation and movement (De Certeau 1984). Walking, naming, narrating, and remembering are the ways in which space is claimed. Such spatial practices subvert and resist the marginaliza-

tion implicit in killing time in town: "The pedestrian's walking about is the spatial acting out of place, creating and representing public space rather than being subject to it" (Low 2000:19). The practices of killing time and the newly fashioned identity of SPR challenge deeply held notions of place in Vanuatu. The idea of place, as noted, is often conflated with identity as expressed by the idea of *man ples,* which is a condensation of place and person in Vanuatu (Rodman 1992; Jolly 1994). But not all young people identified with the idea of SPR, and its use, or aversion to its use, became a way to flag differences among them in Vila.

The desire for work in the wage sector is strong among young people. In the survey undertaken by the Young People's Project it was found that most young people wanted to work, but all found it very difficult to find paid employment in town. Of the more than 1,000 young people interviewed, 36 percent were working while 64 percent were not working (VYPP 1999:36). Larger numbers of young women were found to be working and this reflects the trend of increasing female employment since the late 1970s (Haberkorn 1989). The growing participation of women also indicates the current importance of the service industry in Port Vila. Young women often find work in stores or restaurants, and as domestic help in Port Vila. Most of the young people interviewed who reported working for wages worked as domestic help (23 percent), in stores (13 percent), and in hotels and restaurants (10.5 percent). Some of the young men worked in construction, gardening, or in kava bars (see Marshall, chapter 12).

In our many discussions with young people in Port Vila, we found that their main preoccupation was with finding work. They were concerned with the unavailability of work or that the available work was short-term, contingent, and service-oriented. Finding work often seemed impossible, for even the construction work that many young men sought as unskilled laborers was becoming hard to find. When asked to identify their main problems in the survey undertaken by the Young People's Project, young people invariably reported finding money, work, food, and a place to sleep as their main problems. As one young man said, *no wok, no mani, no kai kai* ("No work, no money, no food"). Clara, a young woman from central Vanuatu, explained the situation in the following way:

> Many young people nowadays do not have jobs. . . . I have found that there are many problems when I mix with my peers but the worst problem for them and for me is unemployment. In our two towns, Port Vila and Santo, a lot of school leavers who have not been able to make it, just drop out and do nothing. Unemployment is the biggest problem that young people face today in Vanuatu. So I think that if there is no employment, there should be other opportunities to keep our young people occupied.

Most young people who attended secondary school believed that they would find work in town in the wage economy. Indeed, a number of young people explained that they were expected to find work in town in order to pay for school fees for younger siblings. Having higher education has been equated with finding a good salaried job to assist those family members who often make sacrifices to pay for their school fees. Many young people do not have an opportunity to go to secondary school as there are not enough places for everyone and the cost of school fees can be prohibitive for many families. Usually pragmatic decisions are made by parents as to which children will continue their studies and who will stay in the village.

Young people also come to town to work because there are few opportunities for earning cash in most villages. Self-employment in both rural and urban areas has proven to be difficult, for young people lack access to the capital needed to start businesses. There are also other significant constraints such as access to land, marketing, and transportation that render creating or finding employment in rural areas difficult. In recent years kava cultivation has become an important source of income generation on some islands such as Pentecost and Santo; however, smaller islands that already experience land pressure cannot benefit from the demand for kava.

Most young people with whom we worked in Port Vila who believed that they would get work after finishing school felt frustrated, alienated, and helpless. Their perspective reflects the growing importance of the cash economy and consumption, but it also signals the dilemma of many small, newly independent Pacific countries which have been experiencing slow economic growth and high population growth rates. Vanuatu, with its economic model of development (of which the tax haven is part), is increasingly incorporated into a global system that is failing to meet the aspirations of many of the young generation.

The young people who did work in Port Vila frequently found their conditions of work difficult. Many of the young people interviewed were paid less than the minimum wage, and there was often a large turnover in jobs as young people left unsatisfactory jobs with poor conditions and low pay. Jonas explained that "the manner of the bosses is tough and they don't give a chance to the young people" (*fasin blong ol bos i strong tumas mo i no givim janis long ol yang fala*). Many young people told me, "I have run away from work" (*mi i bin ronwe finis long wok*). This was often delivered as a terse statement of agency. Others felt they could not leave their work as their families were so short of money in town. It is now important to briefly turn to the construction of killing time as a gendered practice.

## THE GENDER OF KILLING TIME

Young people kill time in any number of ways and places: walking around town, eye-shopping, playing sports, playing cards, talking, and swimming. However, killing time is primarily associated with males in Port Vila. Young males kill time, it seems, while young females are more often engaged in domestic work. Young women are often asked to come to town from their villages to help out their families who are working in Port Vila. They, in effect, subsidize the low wages of their relatives by working as domestic helpers (house girls) for their families. Child care, cooking, washing, and cleaning are tasks that fill the days of many girls and young women, especially those who have only been to primary school and have little chance of finding paid employment. Janet, a young woman living in the settlement of Ohlen, explained, "every morning, we wash up, clean the house then take clothes down to the river and wash. We wash at the river about three times a week. Girls do a lot in helping their mothers at home while the boys do very little or nothing at all." Carolyn, who conducted research with young people as part of the Young People's Project, explained:

> The girls stay at home and do the tasks at home and they do not have the free time to walk about whereas young men and boys have plenty of time to see their friends and hang around in the streets. Many young women who were interviewed told us that they came from the island to stay with families or relatives in town to work as a house helper. What we found mostly is that girls do not have the freedom of walking about or killing time in the same way as boys do.

The gender of killing time is not just about the sexual division of labor in town. As Sam, who works in the Young People's Project, explained, "Young men have much more chance to make the decisions they want to make, but young women don't have too much choice." The movement of young women to, and within, town is much more tightly controlled by parents, elders, and chiefs than are the movement and activities of young men. There are still restrictions placed on young women's movement and travel even though women have been coming to town in increasing numbers. Ideas about, and resistance to, women's travel are related to male and female connection to place (Bolton 1999b:48). In Vanuatu there has been resistance to women's travel outside of the designated roads of marriage. With the exception of travel for marriage, women have been less mobile than men. Travelling, an important route for the acquisition of knowledge and goods, has often been monopolized by men.

Urban space, as suggested, was created as a white space (Rodman 1999), but it was also created as a male space. Women are now, seemingly, challenging the incontestable maleness of urban space by travelling to Vila and attempting to claim some space for themselves. As Haberkorn explained, mobility "in the 1960s and 1970s appeared to have been the domain of single, young men but there has been a shift in husband-wife mobility and a greater incidence in the mobility of unmarried young women" (1989:41). Haberkorn described how employment opportunities for unskilled female labor expanded at a faster rate than similar jobs for men; with the increased movement of women to town, "urban kin filled the roles of employment brokers and moral guardians" (1989:142). This has meant changes in the relationship between town and villages and between males and females. Today there is an on-going discourse about women's travel and behavior in town, often depicted as a new and dangerous development. The resistance to women's travelling can, perhaps, be understood by the recognition that "as men move into a world opened up by colonial and postcolonial trade and politics, women become visible reminders of the enduring norms of social conduct" (Strathern 1988:77). There appears to be a need to control the mobility and behavior of women for they are "often constructed as the cultural symbols of the collectivity's honour and as its intergenerational reproducers of culture" (Yuval-Davis 1997:67).

Blocking young women's travel is very much a part of life today. During my first trip to the island of Tanna early on in my fieldwork in 1996, a group of young women boarded the passenger ship returning to Vila. But the parents and chiefs summoned the police to remove the young women from the ship. This has happened in other places. During her fieldwork in the late 1970s, Jolly commented on the desire for "holding women tight" in the village (1987:136) and resistance to their travel. Today, young women are travelling to town and have greater visibility in the wage economy. They are increasingly seen to be exceeding the bounds of "acceptable" behavior in town by "forgetting" kastom or adopting Western ways. Much more such criticism is leveled at young women than at young men. The gender of killing time and the broader issues related to gender and globalization need far more consideration in Vanuatu.

## KILLING TIME—TROUBLE IN TOWN AND FORGETTING KASTOM

Representations of young people as SPRs and the practices of killing time became highly contested during the course of my fieldwork. Leaders in town frequently urged young people to go back to their land in the islands instead of walking about aimlessly in town. Some churches forbade young people to call themselves SPRs. There were concerted efforts by church and government leaders to displace and transform the meaning of SPR. Instead of *sperem pablik rod,* young people were urged to redefine SPR as "special productive resources." This new formulation, promoted by church and political leaders, resonates with the discourses of economic reform and good governance that have become the staple concerns of development agencies and donors. This campaign, aimed at appropriation and displacement, suggests the important challenges posed by the practices related to SPR and killing time.

SPRs and killing time are often linked to trouble, as Iris, a young woman of seventeen years from Blacksands, noted: "I don't like the word SPR: SPRs cause a lot of problems. When they have nothing to do they do bad things such as stealing." Leah, a young woman who grew up in town, explained the connection between having no work and trouble. "SPR is the result of no work, if we have education and jobs, our lives in villages and towns will improve and we will live a happy life. If we work with the government it will help us by giving jobs to get money so we don't have to go around stealing and causing trouble." Many young people were acutely aware that they were seen as troublemakers. As Marilyn explained, "I think some of the older people look at youths as trouble makers like SPR, wasting time, stealing, drinking and causing problems." The trouble, such as

stealing, caused by some young people often results from their desire to consume despite their exclusion from the wage sector.

Killing time is often framed in terms of the loss of respect for kastom. Sykes described the alienation of young men in Papua New Guinea and the conditions that contribute to it by examining the excessiveness in their consumption habits (Sykes 1999:158), which is often facilitated by stealing. The young men, called rascals (*raskols*), are said to be alienated because "they exist without the sentiments of shame (*sem*) and the habits of respect" (1999:164). In Vanuatu, not having shame and losing respect are also believed to be symptomatic of the young, urban generation. Denny, a young man living in town, described this in terms of the difference he perceived between an "island boy" and a "town boy." He said: "An island boy has respect whereas the town boy does not have respect and outside influences cause young people to lose respect. Vanuatu people have a lot of respect but we are losing this."

In Denny's formulation, the loss of respect is linked to "outside influences" that animate desire for things and experiences from "outside." Annie, a young woman from Malekula, also suggested that "when we are in town there is no respect" (*taem yumi stap long taon i no gat respec*). Annie links the lack of respect with the ways in which young people "forget kastom" in town. "We, all of us young people, who are staying in town, we are forgetting our kastom" (*yumi fulap ol yangfala stap long taon yumi forgettem ol kastom blong yumi*). Kastom refers to a complex set of practices that has been defined as

> a way of summing up what the ni-Vanuatu understand to belong to themselves and to their place, in opposition to all that contact with other people and other places has introduced into their way of life. Kastom is thus, a flexible term used to denote a category of knowledge and practice, the content of the category is left largely undefined. (Bolton 1999a:1)

Kastom stands in sharp contrast to the "outside influences" to which Denny referred. During the course of the research project with young people, we found that kastom provided many young people with a means to critique life in town that appears to be increasingly shaped by outside influences. Kastom for many young people still provides a compelling reference point for the fashioning of spatiotemporal identities in Port Vila. In contrast, Gewertz and Errington, in their study of Chambri youth in Papua New Guinea, concluded:

> The anxieties and frustrations of alienation and of intergenerational conflict attendant on modernism were both vented and neutralized in a context in which the traditional was rendered symbolic rather than binding, and in which the traditional was not considered necessarily compelling in any of its particulars but was instead defined as a matter of personal albeit often collective—choice and appreciation. (1996:49)

In Vanuatu, memory, space, and time are encompassed in the relational practices of kastom. For example, from Annie's perspective, losing respect and "forgetting kastom" in town have devastating consequences. As she explained, "I won't know my brother; I won't know my kastom; I won't have any place to go now" (*mi no save hu i brata blong mi, mi no save kastom blong mi, mi no gat ples long go noaia*). Forgetting kastom is a very common way to formulate the dangers of staying in town and the nature of alienation in town. Young people who are killing time in town are frequently reminded that as ni-Vanuatu they are not "homeless people" or illegitimate children (*picinni blong rod*). They are frequently reminded that they have land and gardens in their islands. It is not surprising that gardening as a practice of place is evoked to offset the alienating experience of killing time in town. The activities associated with gardening in a person's own place involve people

> in temporalizations which go on in a landscape invested with the remembered ancestral events. These past events may be momentarily "out of focus" but they may also be brought into "focal awareness" as in narrative commentaries often evoked by topographic features. Another kind of temporalization is then formed in which

present activities become "charged" with the ancestral past, and the ancestral past with the present. (Munn 1992:114)

Young people are, then, much less likely to forget kastom when in their own place in the island that is also, of course, removed from the field of outside influences. The young person's village place is seen as the site of "true" or authentic kastom, and this is evident in Bonnemaison's contention that "Melanesian identity will remain alive as long as the forms of mobility remain dominantly circular" (1985:61), that is, connected to its own place in the village. Church elders, chiefs, and officials who lament the phenomenon of young people killing time in Vila urge them "to go back" to their own place. Instructing young people to go back to their island villages may be read as both a temporal and spatial directive. "Why don't young people go back (in time) to villages?" Young people who are in town killing time and hitting the road create a rupture in the narrative of place, movement, and the purpose of work. The urban practice of killing time as a strategic temporalization "illuminates ways in which time is not merely lived but constructed in the living" (Munn 1992:109).

Killing time may be seen as a shift in temporalization related to socioeconomic changes, and as such, it may be considered as one of a series of transformations that have occurred since European colonization. As Munn explained, missionization and colonization commodified time, and by this process the person and daily activities were brought into "a wider world order" (Munn 1992:110). The body is also implicated in these processes of spatiotemporalization, for as Munn explained, "the body is not only the fundamental means of tacit temporalization or spatiotemporalization but also part of the vital means of constant movement back and forth between the self and world time" (1992:109). This resonates with the new practices connected to hitting the road and claiming space through walking and narrating as described above. Space is the "practiced place"; its acting out is "in a sense articulated by the ensemble of movements deployed within it" (De Certeau 1990:117). Place, as mentioned, has long been a locus of identity in Vanuatu (Bonnemaison 1985, 1994; Lindstrom 1990; Rodman 1992; Jolly 1994; Bolton 1999b). However, place, like time, has been reshaped and as Rodman argues it is "fragmented and multilocal in construction" (1992:94). She explains:

> This is evident in the commodification of land, its use for cash cropping that relies on foreign markets, the use of media and newspapers to talk about land and national identity, the construction of an urban identity in terms of a place one no longer lives in and so on. (1992:94)

The establishment of the tax haven is yet another example of the ways in which place is reshaped. The movement of islanders to town and the movement of the town deeper into the global economy as it was transformed from planter town to a postcolonial tax haven and tourist destination are inextricably linked. This movement is important in understanding contemporary life in Port Vila. It also suggests that the distinction frequently made between global forces and local places can "obscure the ways in which place making and force making are both local and global that is both socially and culturally particular and productive of widely spreading interactions" (Tsing 2000:352). This is evident in the development of settlements which have grown rapidly as islanders have come and stayed in town for longer periods of time with the boom in employment opportunities and with the rising expectation of employment that accompanied the initial establishment of the tax haven. If ideas of global and local are being reconfigured, the idea of place remains important to young people, even to those who have not seen their island place. It is important to recognize "that place, body, and environment integrate with each other; that places gather things, thoughts and memories in particular configurations; and that place more an event than a thing, is characterized by openness rather than by a unitary self identity" (Escobar 2001:143). It is important, therefore, as Escobar cautions, not to allow the discursive erasure of place as so often happens in theories of globalization.

Space-time compression and imagining space and time in new ways (Tsing 2000) are central to globalization. The practices related to SPR and killing time within this context may be seen as a reworking of space and time. Comaroff and Comaroff have examined the new prominence of youth on a global scale and have argued that the signifying practices of youth "flourish with space-time compression" (2001:308). Space-time compression is related, as Harvey (1989) argued, to flexible accumulation, changes in technology, the intense acceleration in the circulation of commodities, and the deepening penetration of exchange values. Forces such as new media technologies, the manufacture and consumption of consumer goods, advertising, new leisure practices, and the acceleration of time are increasingly important everywhere. All of these, according to Feldman, create "the implosion of perceptual simultaneity—the abutment of persons, things, and events from a plurality of locales, chronologies, and levels of experiences once discrete and separate" (1994:407). This, argues Feldman, results in a "commodification of perception" (1994:406) and "new temporal and spatial coordinates" of perception (Feldman 1994:407). These processes related to the space-time compression are integral to understanding how spatiotemporal identities are being configured in postcolonial towns even in seemingly "far off places" such as the Port Vila. For globalization is indeed a process that connects as it differentiates, as the following discussion will show. Killing time implicates the body, the gaze, and consumption, all of which reshape "temporal and spatial coordinates."

## CONSUMING IMAGES

For young people, going to Port Vila is framed frequently in terms of the visual, whether the starting point is an island village or a peri-urban settlement. In explaining why they want to go to Vila, many young people said, "I only want to look" (*mi wantem lukluk nomo*). The desire for looking and seeing was often linked to hearing stories about Vila. As George Siaka from Tanna explained in the video *Kilem Taem,* he had heard many stories from people who had been to Vila; they said, "Oh, if you go to Vila you see so many things." Several practices of killing time privilege the visual—looking and seeing as a way of consuming images—bearing in mind that globalization involves a multiplication of images and an animation of desire.

## Videos—Inculcating Visual Realism

The transnational images of violence central to the action video are an important globalizing force inculcating the "priority of visual realism" (Feldman 1994:406) and the gendered gaze. Watching action videos has become a staple of killing time in Port Vila. In addition to the cinemas in Vila, many settlements have makeshift cinemas featuring a VCR and television, the owner of which goes into town each day to get new videos for public viewing in the settlement. Cinema was first introduced by the Americans during the Second World War when at that time there were fifty-four cinemas putting on different shows every night (MacClancy 1981:109). Of course, when the war ended, only a few cinemas remained in Port Vila and Santo. Today, however, the advent of the video cassette and VCRs has greatly expanded accessibility. But even now video watching is confined to the two major towns and the administrative centers on each island, since electricity is not widely available on the islands. Generators are often used to run the videos in settlements as they are in some places on the islands.

Watching videos is one of the most important ways in which young people, and particularly young men, pass the time. In the survey undertaken by VYPP, it was found that 57 percent of those surveyed had seen a video in the past week. A large number of this group reported that they often see four or more videos per week. It was also found that many more young men regularly watch videos than do young women (VYPP 1999:69). Young men, as noted, have considerably more freedom of movement and can, therefore, more

easily go off to town to the cinema or to some other public space for video watching (see Jourdan 1995b).

Exposure to global media through cultural forms such as movies, videos, and VCRs are discursive fields that are acquiring a new primacy in the imagining of both possible selves and possible communities under conditions of late capitalism (Appadurai 1996). Cinema watching, according to Connerton (1989), is imbricated in social practices that he calls inscribing and incorporating practices that are linked to collective identity, memory, and the body. In the following passage he explains the significance of cinema watching:

> In cinema, I am simultaneously in this action and outside of it, in this space and outside of this space, having the power of ubiquity, I am everywhere and nowhere. The inscriptional practice of cinema makes possible, and is in turn made possible by, the incorporating practice of the cinema spectator. (1989:78)

"Incorporating practice" refers to the sedimentation of collective memory in bodily postures. He further explains that:

> The cinema inscribes; but it could not be a practice of inscription if it were not also, in a specific sense, an incorporating practice. What is incorporated is an ocular convention: the identification of the object with the camera. During the cinema performance spectators duplicate the action of the projector, their eyes behaving as it were like search lights. (1989:78)

Watching action videos may be regarded as part of the "remolding of everyday sensory orientation" (Feldman 1994:407), and violent media provide images for self-fashioning that are powerful and persuasive for young males. Ben, one of the researchers in the project, explained: "The movies the young people watch are mostly action movies. The favorite action videos feature Rambo with Sylvester Stallone, Steven Segal, Jean-Claude Van Damme and Bruce Lee." Some young people explained, however, that action videos are popular because it is easier to follow the story lines of these videos, as many do not understand the language in the videos. Ben further explained how some young people utilize such images. He said, "I think the young people like these types of movies because they learn some ways of fighting that they may use when they go to night clubs." Such videos may be seen as instrumental in "creating new cultures of masculinity and violence" (Appadurai 1996:41).

## Tourists as Spectacle

The ways in which the tourist gaze (Urry 1990) searches out and constructs the exotic other is now well documented. When I lived in the settlement of Blacksands, cruise ships came regularly to Port Vila. They docked at the harbor and hundreds of tourists disembarked to spend the day in town. In Blacksands, I began to notice that some young people from the settlement also set out to go to town "to look at the tourists." As Lauretta explained to me, it was an opportunity to look at "white people and their ways" (*Ol waetman mo fasin blong olgeta*). Indeed, many of those cruise ship passengers did offer a spectacle. By the end of the day in Vila, many of the tourists would crowd into a bar on the main street called "Ma Barkers." Some of the passengers would drink, get drunk, pour beer over each other, and dance, spilling out onto the street. They routinely provided a show for young people who went to town to watch them. At the end of the day, when Lauretta returned to the settlement, she would relate her rendition of some of the tourists' behavior. She often drew attention to the male-female behavior of the young tourists (such as holding hands) that she found to be extremely amusing. The interaction between the males and females and the way in which tourists dressed and acted provided images about Western romantic relationships and other Western ways.

In addition to watching tourists, some young people from Blacksands also performed "traditional" dances and songs for tourists. In a clearing near the entrance to Blacksands at the main road, a group of mostly young dancers from the island of Tanna performed for busloads of tourists on the days when the cruise ship came to town. Similarly, young men from the central island

of Tungariki who lived in Blacksands learned some traditional dances in order to perform at a tourist hotel every week. Their aim was strategic in that they wanted to generate some income for their groups. But performing the dances also gave them, as many young men who grew up in town mentioned, a chance to learn their kastom dances.

The community from the island of Futuna in Vila had also created a kastom village in nearby Erakor to provide tourists with a look at traditional culture from their island. It was an ambitious project that started in 1994. Money generated was often sent to the island and in turn, Islanders sent material items such as baskets and mats to be sold to tourists. The person who started this project had worked with tourists for Tour Vanuatu. He explained, "I started asking myself why tourists come to Vanuatu and then I realized that culture was very important. In just two years by mid-1996, 11,500 people had seen it (the kastom village) and the young boys use their talents."

Benjamin, a young man from Futuna, was enthusiastic about the ways in which the performances for tourists provided a means for young men to learn about their own culture. The kastom village for tourists provided a way for people to gaze at their own cultural practices. While it appears that such enterprises commodify kastom, the situation is somewhat more complex. The construction of the traditional village in Vila provided the young people from Futuna living in a nearby crowded area of town with a temporal and spatial reminder of how Futuna is, has been, or might have been. The island of Futuna and its villages may well be seen as the true source of kastom ways, but the proxy kastom tourist village with its proximity to the daily lived space linked the increasingly disparate rural and urban lives.

The ways in which young men and women return the tourist gaze certainly does not enmesh tourists and young ni-Vanuatu in a relationship of mutuality. However, it does suggest that young people return the gaze and are enmeshed in consuming as well as providing images and spectacle. It also underlines the way in which young people pragmatically fashion their experiences of tourism in various ways that make sense to them.

## Eye-Shopping

In the video *Kilem Taem,* Daniel explained that he came to town for the purpose of "eye-shopping," or looking at the things in the shop windows. Many young people "just walk around eye-shopping." Many, like Daniel, admit, "I don't have money to buy anything." It is not so unusual to see young men with "SPR slave" or "squatter" written on their purposely tattered T-shirts peering into the windows of duty-free shops in Vila. Eye-shopping places young people in the world of commodities and desire. Consumption in an era of globalization has become "a privileged site for the fabrication of self and society, of culture and identity" (Comaroff and Comaroff 2001:299–300).

Appadurai has also suggested that consumption has been wrongly understood "as the end of the road for goods and services, a terminus for their social life, a conclusion to some sort of material cycle" (1996:66). Consumption, according to Appadurai, must be located within a temporal framework. In his view "consumption creates time but modern consumption seeks to replace the aesthetics of duration with the aesthetics of ephemerality" (1996:85). The aesthetic of ephemerality, linked to "the pleasure of the gaze and the manipulability of the body," produces new sets of practices which involve "a radically new relationship among wanting, remembering, being and buying" (Appadurai 1996). The practice of eye-shopping, a staple of killing time, privileges consumption while recognizing that it often must be denied or deferred. "Being and buying" are intensely problematic for young people unemployed in settlements yet living in a tax haven where the supply of commodities is seemingly endless and invariably out of reach. Eye-shopping as an imaginative social practice is powerful.

The link between the formulation of young people as social problems and consumers (Durham 2000) is very often forged when young people steal. In Port Vila, theft and break-ins fuel "a growing concern that young people were becoming lawless and the rate of crime was increasing" (*Vanuatu Trading Post* 1997). The settlements were increasingly seen as sites of lawlessness and young people as agents of lawlessness. Stealing may become an extension of looking, especially when consumption seems severed from production and commodities are beyond the reach of young people, but well within the scope of their imagination. Eye-shopping animates desire, as Jacki explained:

> Because we have no work we hit the road all over the place. Sometimes we (young people) look at something that we would like to have but we have no money to buy it so we go and steal it.

While globalization is characterized by intense circulation and flows, Tsing has urged us "to attend to the missed encounters, clashes, misfires, and confusions that are as much part of global linkages as simple 'flow'" (2000:338). From this perspective young people may be seen to interrupt the "flow" when they steal. Understanding that these episodes represent the "clashes" and "misfires" of global linkages draws attention to the transformation of actors in the global and local interface. Consuming images with its concomitant primacy of the visual and animation of desire is one way in which young people exercise agency, and young people make outside influences their own as they rework notions of personhood, space, and time.

## CONCLUSION

In Vanuatu the practices of killing time and hitting the road signify the emergence of an urbanizing generation who are forging new spatial and temporal meanings. It was important, I argued, to locate these new spatial and temporal meanings within the wider context of globalizing strategies that both connect and differentiate. The importance of understanding how these practices are produced through gender differences was also discussed. The emergence of settlements represents an important reconfiguration of space in town and is now crucial in shaping the lives of young people growing up there. In some important ways, killing time represents a very specific encounter with modernity and global strategies. The process of reconfiguring space and time has been shaped by colonial as well as postcolonial developments. Current spatial and temporal meanings cannot be separated from those processes and from the intense circulation of commodities, people, and ideas which typifies so much of what is now meant by globalization. However, the practices of young people encompassed in SPR and killing time may be read as counternarratives and counterperformances that disrupt the smooth articulation of circulation, connections, and flows that are said to be so central to global strategies. Moore has reminded us that "however globalized and fragmented the contemporary world is said to be, individuals and collectivities still engage with it and live meaningful lives, they hack a sense of self and meaning out of disparate circumstances." (1999:16). The young people whom I met in Port Vila are deeply engaged in producing new meanings and practices that confront, resist, and accommodate the dissonance generated by the inclusions and exclusions, as well as the connections and differences, that characterize their lives in a postcolonial town.

## ACKNOWLEDGMENTS

I would like to recognize the work of the many young people involved with the Vanuatu Young People's Project. I particularly wish to thank Emily Niras and Sam Obed for their friendship and to acknowledge their hard work and commitment that have sustained the project. The research undertaken for this chapter was supported by Social Sciences Humanities Research Council of Canada (SSHRCC). I also want to acknowledge the support of CUSO (Canadian University Services Overseas) in my work with the Vanuatu Young People's Project.

## NOTES

1. The Vanuatu Young People's Project is now an integral part of the Vanuatu Cultural Centre (VCC) under the direction of Ralph Reganvanu. Support from the VCC's staff and from the fieldworkers has been unstinting. Funding and support from the government of Vanuatu, AUSAID, Save the Children Australia, UNICEF, New Zealand, and CUSO have enabled the project to undertake research, video documentation, and programs for young people since April 1997. I was fortunate in working on the first round of research with Carolyn Bani, Emily Buleigh, Patrick Gilu, Ben Narai, Emily Niras, Linda Niras, Selena Haggai, and Sam Obed. Heidi Tyedmers worked on the project as a CUSO volunteer. Roger Barang, Vivian Lyich, and Annie Nichols have also worked on the project. Emily Niras has headed the project since 1998.

2. The video *Kilem Taem* was based on the research undertaken by young people. The video was funded by UNICEF and AUSAID and the film makers were Jan Cattoni, Randall Wood, and Anthony Mullin. A number of young people, the staff of the Young People's Project, as well as Jacob Kapere from the Vanuatu Cultural Centre worked on the video.

3. According to the *Islands Business* magazine (1999) the Reserve Bank of Vanuatu reported that Vanuatu's gross income for Port Vila's accountancy, trust company, legal, and banking firms totaled about US$20.36 million in the first three-quarters of 1998. Of 228 finance centre employees, 210 were locals and 18 were expatriates. The finance centre spent US$15.53 million locally with local employees earning US$2.64 million. Finance centre businesses paid US$1 million rent and the government received about US$1.73 million in fees, import duties, and other revenues generated by the centre's presence.

## REFERENCES

Appadurai, Arjun. 1990. "Disjuncture and Difference in the Global Cultural Economy." *Public Culture* 2(2):1–24.

———. 1996. *Modernity at Large: Cultural Dimensions of Globalization*. Minneapolis: University of Minnesota Press.

———. 1997. "Dead Certainty: Ethnic Violence in the Era of Globalization." *Public Culture* 10(2):225–247.

Bedford, R. D. 1973. *New Hebridean Mobility: A Study of Circular Migration*. Publication HG/9. Research School of Pacific Studies. Canberra: Australian National University.

Bolton, Lissant. 1999a. "Introduction." In *Fieldwork, Fieldworkers: Developments in Vanuatu Research*. Theme issue. *Oceania* 70(1):1–8.

———. 1999b. "Women, Place and Practice in Vanuatu: A View from Ambae." In *Fieldwork, Fieldworkers: Developments in Vanuatu Research*. Theme issue. *Oceania* 70(1):43–55.

Bong, J. J. 1995. Blacksands Settlement Research Project. Unpublished paper.

Bonnemaison, Joël. 1985. "The Tree and the Canoe: Roots and Mobility in Vanuatu Societies." *Pacific Viewpoint* 26(1):30–62.

————. 1994. *The Tree and the Canoe: History and Ethnogeography of Tanna*. Josée Pénot-Demetry, translator and adaptor. Honolulu: University of Hawai'i Press.

Comaroff, John L., and Jean Comaroff. 1999. "Occult Economies and the Violence of Abstraction: Notes from the South African Postcolony." *American Ethnologist* 26(2):279–301.

————. 2001. "Millennial Capitalism: First Thoughts on a Second Coming." *Public Culture* 12(2):291–343.

Connell, John, and John Lea. 1994. "Cities of Parts, Cities Apart?" *The Contemporary Pacific* 6(2):267–308.

Connerton, Paul. 1989. *How Societies Remember*. Cambridge: Cambridge University Press.

De Certeau, Michel. 1984. *The Practice of Everyday Life*. Berkeley: University of California Press.

————. 1990[1980]. *L'Invention du Quotidien 1. Arts de Faire*. Paris: Gallimard.

Durham, Deborah. 2000. "Youth and the Social Imagination in Africa: Introduction to Parts 1 and 2." *Anthropological Quarterly* 73(3):113–120.

Escobar, Arturo. 2001. "Culture Sits in Places: Reflections on Globalism and Subaltern Strategies of Localization." *Political Geography* 20:139–174.

Feldman, Allen. 1994. "On Cultural Anesthesia from Desert Storm to Rodney King." *American Ethnologist* 21(2):404–418.

Forster, R. 1980. "Vanuatu: The End of an Episode of Schizophrenic Colonialism." *Round Table* 280: 367–373.

Frazer, Ian. 1985. "Walkabout and Urban Movement: A Melanesian Case Study." *Pacific Viewpoint* 26(1): 185–205.

Gewertz D., and F. Errington. 1996. "PepsiCO and Piety in a Papuan New Guinea 'Modernity.'" *American Ethnologist* 23(3):476–493.

Gilroy, Paul. 1994. "Urban Social Movements, 'Race' and Community." In *Colonial Discourse and Postcolonial Theory: A Reader*. Patrick Williams and Laura Chrismas, eds. Pp. 404–442. New York: Columbia University Press.

Government of Vanuatu. 2000. *The Vanuatu National Population and Housing Census Report*.

Gupta, Akhil, and James Ferguson. 1992. "Beyond 'Culture': Space, Identity and the Politics of Difference." *Cultural Anthropology* 7(1):6–23.

————. 1996. *Culture, Power, Place in Explorations in Critical Anthropology*. Durham, N.C.: Duke University Press.

Haberkorn, Gerald. 1989. "Port Vila: Transit Station or Final Stop? Recent Developments in Ni-Vanuatu Population Mobility." Pacific Research Monograph No. 21. National Center for Development Studies. Canberra: Australian National University.

Hannerz, U. 1989. "Notes on the Global Ecumene." *Public Culture* 1(2)66–75.

Harvey, David. 1989. *The Condition of Postmodernity*. Oxford: Blackwell.

Jolly, Margaret. 1987. "The Forgotten Women: A History of Migrant Labour and Gender Relations in Vanuatu." *Oceania* 58(4):119–139.

————. 1994. *Women of the Place: Kastom, Colonialism and Gender in Vanuatu*. New York: Harwood.

Jourdan, Christine. 1995a. "*Masta Liu*." In *Youth Cultures: A Cross-Cultural Perspective*. V. Amit-Talai and H. Wulff, eds. Pp. 201–222. London: Routledge.

————. 1995b. "Stepping-Stones to National Consciousness in the Solomon Islands Case." In *Nation Making: Emergent Identities in Postcolonial Melanesia*. Robert J. Foster, ed. Pp. 127–149. Ann Arbor: University of Michigan Press.

King, Anthony D. 1997. "The Global, the Urban and the World." In *Culture, Globalization and the World-System*. Anthony King, ed. Pp. 149–154. Minneapolis: University of Minnesota Press.

Lederman, Rena. 1998. "Globalization and the Future of Culture Areas: Melanesianist Anthropology in Transition." *Annual Review of Anthropology* 27:427–449.

Lindstrom, Lamont. 1990. *Knowledge and Power in a South Pacific Society*. Washington, D.C.: Smithsonian Institution Press.

Low, Setha M. 2000. *On the Plaza: The Politics of Public Space and Culture*. Austin: University of Texas Press.

MacClancy, Jeremy. 1981. *To Kill a Bird with Two Stones*. Port Vila: Vanuatu Cultural Centre Publication No. 1.

McKnight, Tom. 1998. *Oceania: The Geography of Australia, New Zealand, and the Pacific Islands*. Englewood Cliffs, N.J.: Prentice Hall.

Massey, Doreen. 1991. "A Global Sense of Place." *Marxism Today*. June 26–27.

Mishra, Vijay, and Bob Hodge. 1994. "What Is Post (-Colonialism)?" In *Colonial Discourse and Post-Colonial Theory: A Reader*. P. Williams and L. Chrisman, eds. New York: Columbia University Press.

Moore, Henrietta L., ed. 1999. "Anthropological Theory at the Turn of the Century." In *Anthropological Theory Today*. Henrietta Moore, ed. Oxford: Blackwell.

Munn, Nancy D. 1992. "The Cultural Anthropology of Time: A Critical Essay." *Annual Review of Anthropology* 21:93–123.

Rawlings, Greg. 1999a. "Foundations of Urbanisation: Port Vila and Town and Pango Village, Vanuatu." In *Fieldwork, Fieldworkers: Developments in Vanuatu Research*. Special issue. *Oceania* 20(1):107–130.

————. 1999b. "Villages, Islands and Tax Havens. The Global/Local Implications of a Financial Entrepot in Vanuatu." *Canberra Anthropology: The Asia Pacific Journal of Anthropology* 22(2)37–50.

Rodman, Margaret C. 1992. "Empowering Place: Multilocality and Multivocality." *American Anthropologist* 94:640–656.

————. 1999. "Portentous Splendour: Building the Condominium of the New Hebrides." *History and Anthropology* 1–34.

————. 2001. *Houses Far from Home: British Colonial Space in the New Hebrides.* Honolulu: University of Hawai'i Press.

Sope, Barak. n.d. *Land and Politics in the New Hebrides.* Suva: The South Pacific Social Sciences Association.

Strathern, Marilyn. 1975. *No Money on Our Skins: Hagen Migrants in Port Moresby.* New Guinea Research Bulletin No. 61. Canberra: Australian National University.

————. 1988. *The Gender of the Gift.* Berkeley: University of California Press.

Sykes, Karen. 1999. "After the 'Raskol' Feast: Youths' Alienation in New Ireland, Papua New Guinea." *Critique of Anthropology* 19(2):157–174.

Thomas, Nicholas. 1994. *Colonialism's Culture: Anthropology, Travel, and Government.* Princeton, N.J.: Princeton University Press.

Tsing, Anna. 2000. "The Global Situation." *Cultural Anthropology* 15(3):327–360.

United Nations Development Program (UNDP). 1996. *Sustainable Human Development in Vanuatu.* Suva: United Nations.

Urry, John. 1990. *The Tourist Gaze: Leisure and Travel in Contemporary Societies.* London: Sage.

*Vanuatu Trading Post.* 1997. "Police Destroy Youth's 'Black Waif' Band Dream." May 14. No. 244, P. 2.

Vanuatu Young People's Project (VYPP). 1999. *Harem Voes Blong Yangfala Long Vila Taon.* Vanuatu: Vanuatu Cultural Centre.

Ward, Gerard R. 1998. "Urban Research in the Pacific Islands: A Brief Review." *Development Bulletin* 45:22–26.

Ward, Michael. 1999. "Keeping Ples? Young Highland Men in Port Moresby, Papua New Guinea." M.A. thesis. Australian National University.

Yuval-Davis, Nira. 1997. *Gender and Nation.* London: Sage.

# 22

# South Seas Confidential: The Politics of Interethnic Relationships in Colonial Samoa

**Paul Shankman**

*University of Colorado*

The people of Polynesia have a reputation for sexual permissiveness, and this reputation, sometimes exaggerated and sometimes misunderstood, has contributed to our own fascination with sex. Our images of tropical isles, blue lagoons, and swaying palms in the beautiful South Pacific are intimately linked with ideas about sexual paradise. But how realistic are these images? And how much of island life do they gloss over?

Today the cultures of Polynesia are rapidly being transformed by globalization. Images of the islands are effectively promoted by the tourist industry, the most recent form of globalization to come to the South Pacific. Along with their laptops and sunscreen, tourists also bring fantasies about sexual paradise. Yet people seeking erotic adventures may be in for a rude awakening. Current travel guides to the region warn tourists about the risk of AIDS and other STDs, about becoming involved in relationships that may unintentionally lead to marriage, and about beautiful island transvestites who look so much like women that unwary visitors may find themselves in compromising positions. Furthermore, many Islanders are well aware of misleading Western images about their private lives and actively resent them. So there is a major disparity between image and reality.

Where did these misleading stereotypes come from? Long before contemporary tourists arrived looking for paradise, other global forces were at work, changing Islanders' lives in very personal ways. In the eighteenth and nineteenth centuries, the earliest contacts between the West and Polynesia were between European men and island women. After many months at sea, Polynesia must have seemed like paradise to these weary voyagers. Although we may imagine European-Polynesian relationships as brief romantic liaisons between love-starved ship's crews and lusty maidens—a kind of South Seas version of "Temptation Island"—they were not always temporary and fleeting. Marriages, families, and children were also involved. A variety of

377

European men had relationships with Polynesian women, including beachcombers and castaways, plantation owners and laborers, traders and whaling crews, as well as colonial administrators and foreign soldiers. These relationships had social and political dimensions, along with sexual and romantic ones.

This chapter explores the politics of interethnic unions in Samoa,[1] the most traditional of Polynesian cultures. Samoa has generally been viewed as homogeneous, stable, enduring, and resistant to Western incursions, at least until relatively recently. Yet by the late nineteenth century, colonial Samoa was already an ethnically stratified, multicultural society. Even then Samoans were no longer isolated and living separately from Europeans. A small but significant group of European men, Samoan women, their children, and their descendants had become an interface between the two groups.

Some part-European children and descendants of interethnic unions became plantation owners, traders, businessmen, civil servants, and important political figures. Yet simply having a European father did not automatically make one part of the colonial elite. Many children of interethnic unions were raised as poor, landless "half-castes" who came to be regarded as a major problem by colonial administrators in the twentieth century. They had different rights and resources than Samoans, and fewer rights and resources than Europeans. In the l930s, one colonial official described this group in the following manner:

> Half-castes form the great social problem of the country; their number rapidly increases . . . they are almost without exception unemployable except in low grades of work. It is apparent that the problem of the half-caste will become increasingly acute, and a class of poor half-castes already in existence and growing in number will develop and exist on the borderline of extreme poverty—a menace to the Samoan and the European. . . . It would not be fair to the Samoan in whose interests the islands are governed and the preservation of whose race is considered to be our duty, to give the half-caste the same status as the native with regard to

land. On the other hand, the half-caste can never be expected to rise as a class to ordinary European level. The half-caste must be left to sink to his own level in the scale of humanity and become in time a hewer of wood and a drawer of water for the rest of the community. (in Keesing 1934:463)

For colonial authorities, interethnic unions and their descendants became a pressing political issue. These relationships and the children they produced were not part of an inclusive, democratic society in which people were treated equally. Instead, they marked a divided stratified society in which interethnic unions threatened the colonial order.

This chapter focuses on three periods in the history of interethnic unions in colonial Samoa: the missionary period, the period of German and New Zealand colonial rule, and World War II, each with its own distinct pattern of interethnic unions. During the missionary period in the nineteenth century, unions between European men and Samoan women were common and acceptable. But in the early twentieth century, with the arrival of centralized colonial power, interethnic unions were regulated, restricted, and even banned. Then, during World War II, the presence of the American military occupation, involving tens of thousands of servicemen, altered the dynamics of these unions once more, allowing many interethnic relationships. So, within a relatively short span of time, interethnic relationships went from being acceptable to being unacceptable and then becoming acceptable once again. Why were these relationships so complicated? Why were they so important to both Samoans and Europeans? And how did Samoans view Europeans who became their spouses and/or partners?

## THE SAMOAN SYSTEM OF COURTSHIP AND MARRIAGE

Our own perceptions of sex and marriage color our perceptions of other cultures. In America, young adults spend several years of their lives living independently before they marry. The average age of first marriages for

American men today is over twenty-seven and for women it is over twenty-five. As a result, there is a long interval of time between leaving home and getting married; the outcome is a "singles culture" in which sex is a matter of individual choice. As young adults establish independent lives, sex and marriage are no longer closely related. Moreover, interethnic or inter-"racial" relationships and marriages are no longer taboo. These recent developments are very different from the way that Americans thought about sex, marriage, and interethnic unions only a few decades ago. They are also very different from the way Samoans viewed sex and marriage when the first Europeans arrived in the eighteenth century.

In traditional Samoa, young men and women lived with their extended families in villages, each family headed by a chief or *matai*. Young people served their chiefs and did not make many independent choices. Sex and marriage, especially for young women, were under the authority of the family and, ideally, marriage partners were not a matter of choice. Yet there was a period in late adolescence when young Samoans could discretely engage in sex. These relationships often led to marriage, and were very much a part of the Samoan system of courtship and marriage.

Samoans had extensive restrictions on potential marriage partners, but when visiting other villages and districts young people were allowed and expected to seek sexual partners as potential spouses. In pre-European Samoa, there was a tradition of marrying outsiders at both the chiefly level and at lower-ranking levels. Prior to European arrival, high-ranking Samoans intermarried others of rank from Tonga and Fiji as a means of forging political alliances, increasing their prestige, and sometimes of necessity when no suitable high-ranking Samoans were available.

Traditionally, Samoan marriages took two forms. Chiefly marriages were arranged and involved the elaborate and formal exchange of gifts between high-ranking families. The brides were expected to be virgins (*taupou*), and at their marriages there was a public virginity-testing ceremony. High-ranking chiefs could have multiple wives, and they could

leave earlier marriages in order to wed new *taupou* or other women. Intervillage visiting was often an occasion for pursuing courtship of new *taupou* and others, as well as for affairs.

For chiefly families, sexual relationships and marriage arrangements were a means of upward mobility. The higher the chief's title, the more important the marriages. Because the Samoan political system was not centralized, consisting instead of shifting, warring alliances, chiefly marriages were essential to alliance formation. Daughters of chiefs were used in cementing these alliances, and high-ranking families were especially concerned with controlling their daughters' sexual conduct so that it might be most effectively used in the service of family interests.

A second form of marriage, common for people of lower rank and often the result of intervillage visiting parties, was elopement or *avaga*. A couple would elope secretly, usually to the husband's village, and begin living as husband and wife. This was a publicly accepted form of marriage, although it was not arranged by the respective families nor did it involve an exchange of gifts; such an exchange might take place after time had passed and tempers had settled. As with chiefly marriages, these unions were of varying duration. If they broke up, the wife and children usually returned to the wife's village and her family. Flexible kin relationships allowed her children and descendants to be fully incorporated into their mother's kin network, while retaining connections to their father's family.

## EARLY EUROPEANS AND CHRISTIAN MISSIONARIES (1830–1900)

During the early years of European settlement in the nineteenth century, traditional forms of visiting, courtship, and marriage provided culturally approved means for facilitating interethnic unions. Samoan historian Malama Meleisea reports that

> There were several instances recorded when Samoan men accompanied by women greeted visiting ships. It was the explicit customary role

of the *aualuma* [the organization of unmarried women] of the *nu'u* [village], led by ladies of rank, to welcome and entertain guests, with the implicit expectation that some matrimonial connections between visitors and hosts would result. For those of lower rank the connection might begin with eye contact between eligible young men and women and be pursued further during evening festivities (*pōula*). In the case of the *taupou*, the highest-ranking maiden of the *nu'u*, it was made clear that she was available to be courted as a wife by important chiefs. (1987:157)

The first Europeans to settle the Samoan archipelago were beachcombers and castaways. These men had practical skills, such as boat building, the use and repair of guns, and knowledge of the wider world, that were of real value to Samoans. So families gave their daughters in marriage to these men, some of whom had multiple wives, as well as mistresses and/or lovers.

As additional European men—missionaries, traders, and planters—settled the islands, Samoans realized that these recent arrivals were far more prestigious than the beachcombers, who eventually fell into disrepute. High-ranking marriages were arranged with many of these new and comparatively wealthy foreigners, and there were other, less visible relationships. The part-European descendants of these relationships became the *'afakasi* population, sometimes known as "half-castes," "mixed race," "mixed-blood," "local Europeans," or "part-Samoans."

Since there was no centralized colonial government in Samoa until 1900, missionaries, rather than secular officials, were often the most important European representatives involved in trying to regulate sexual conduct. First arriving in the 1830s, missionaries viewed many aspects of Samoan sexual conduct as a major barrier to conversion to Christianity. They were shocked by sexually explicit songs and dances, among other forms of alleged "immorality." Missionary John Williams witnessed one such "night dance" in the 1830s that he described as follows:

> The young virgin girls taking the lead they now enter the house entirely naked & commence

their dance. The full-grown women then follow after. Then come the old women all of whom are entirely naked. During their dancing they throw themselves in all imaginable positions in order to make the most full exposure of their persons to the whole company. . . . During the whole of the time of performing the females are using the most vile, taunting, bantering language to the men. (1984:247–248)

From the missionaries' perspective, such "indecent" practices demanded immediate reform. Yet missionaries were also impressed by more sedate dances, the formal courtship of *taupou* by chiefs, and the intricate system of chiefly etiquette and protocol. They regarded Samoans as "savages," but more "noble" than other so-called "primitives," and therefore worthy of Christianity. Missionaries praised the recognition given to the ceremonial virgin. At the same time, they deplored related practices such as polygyny, the role of the unmarried women's group in intervillage visiting, the ease of sexual access in living arrangements, adultery, prostitution, public defloration of ceremonial virgins, tattooing, minimal dress, erotic dancing, and sexually explicit singing.

Missionaries made reform of Samoan sexual conduct their highest priority and, in some ways, were surprisingly successful. Yet with so few missionaries, they could not realistically attempt far-reaching changes overnight. And there were many more temporary European visitors interested in vice than missionaries interested in virtue. The Reverend A. W. Murray noted that during the mid-nineteenth century as many as six whaling ships with "lawless" crews of thirty each could anchor at any one time in the port of Apia:

> There they were—men of our own colour, speaking the same language with ourselves, and some of them our own countrymen, and claiming to be Christians, while giving themselves up to the most shameful immoralities, and telling the natives all manner of lies, so far as they could make themselves understood . . . we mourned over the moral havoc they wrought, and the influence in drawing the people away from schools and services. (1876:41)

Such crewmen were interested in short-term sexual relationships, which the missionaries condemned. But Protestant and Catholic missionaries also attempted to discourage most marriages between Europeans and Samoans. Samoans, however, were quite capable of assessing their marriage prospects and would accept or reject European partners on their own. As historian Richard Gilson found,

> The L.M.S. [London Missionary Society] generally opposed marriage of Samoans to Europeans, unless the latter were deemed to be of "good character" and intended to remain in the group or, if leaving, to take their families with them. Such conditions determined whether or not a European might be married in church. Sometimes the mission had sufficient influence to prevent *fa'aSamoa* [*avaga*] marriage of foreigners but if not there were still considerations of rank and exchange to be satisfied. A man who had neither valuable service nor *'oloa* [marriage goods] to offer could not marry into a high-ranking family, if he could marry at all. And unless he continued in good standing in the community, his wife might desert him. . . . That does not necessarily mean, however, that foreigners were wholly deprived of female company." (1970:143ff)

When it came to relationships with European men, Samoans valued these unions despite missionary disapproval, and missionaries had no legal authority over either Samoans or Europeans. Europeans often took advantage of Samoan visiting relationships and, misunderstanding Samoan customs concerning courtship and marriage, gave Samoan women a poor reputation throughout the South Pacific.

Short-term interethnic unions were particularly common in the European area of the port town of Apia, the second busiest port in the region. In the latter part of the nineteenth century, Europeans and a growing group of poorer, rowdy part-Europeans clustered in an area called "the Beach," known throughout the South Pacific for its grog shops and dance halls. Prostitution, gambling, and drink were all available, much to the missionaries' dismay. Writing in 1892, the

author Robert Louis Stevenson, who lived in Samoa at the time, lamented that until recently, "the white people of Apia lay in the worst squalor of degradation" (1892:26). The port town was referred to as a "little Cairo" and a "hell in the Pacific." Samoans were supplying dancing girls and were rumored to be giving women in exchange for muskets.

These short-term unions were not a major concern for Samoans, who believed that desirable traits from another group could be acquired through conception of a child and that those traits were fixed at conception. Having been transmitted, the traits would eventually become evident as the child matured, whether or not the non-Samoan parent was present. This belief helps explain why "mixed race" children were so readily absorbed into Samoan families. For a number of Europeans, however, "race mixing" had a very different meaning. They believed that these unions led to dysgenic "mongrelization" of the children, bringing out the worst traits of each group.

## THE PART EUROPEAN POPULATION UNDER GERMAN RULE (1900–1914)

By the late 1800s, "the Beach" was becoming more "civilized." The European population had grown from only 55 in 1855 to almost 400 by the turn of the twentieth century. When the Germans took formal political control of Samoa in 1900, the pattern of interethnic relationships, along with a growing number of children and descendants, was becoming more formal and more hierarchical. The arrival of the German administration coincided with two more general trends occurring throughout the colonies. First, more European men—planters, managers, and others—were bringing their European wives with them to the islands; they no longer needed Samoan wives. And, second, during the late nineteenth and early twentieth centuries, new ideologies of racial superiority were arriving in the islands. The increasing number of European men and women, now primarily German, as well as these new ideologies, promoted "racial" separation.

The German colonial administration wanted to protect Samoans from an influx of lower-class Europeans and, at the same time, protect resident Germans (some of whom were large plantation owners in the islands) from the dangers of "race mixing" with Samoan women. One of the first tasks of the new government was to clarify who was European—more specifically who was German—and who was not. In 1903, the administration passed laws defining the categories and rights of Europeans, part-Europeans, and Samoans. Children of legally recognized European-Samoan marriages could be classified as nominal Europeans, having the status of resident aliens in the islands. That is, they were considered citizens of their European father's country of origin. Illegitimate part-Europeans, however, were legally prohibited from inheriting their father's property and obtaining European status. Thus there came to be two types of part-Europeans.

These two types were the result of differing European attitudes about children of mixed parentage. On the one hand, a number of European fathers wished to separate their children from full Samoans by giving them special legal status, and they began doing so as early as the 1840s. The German regime recognized these marriages and legitimized their offspring. On the other hand, there were many more European fathers who had brief relationships with Samoan women or had *avaga* marriages, who were not permanent settlers, and/or who did not wish to acknowledge their children by a Samoan mother. So while some part-European children were officially registered and recognized as nominal Europeans, most children of interethnic unions were not.

To determine how many people had legitimate claims to European status, the German regime conducted a census. At the turn of the twentieth century, there were 391 Europeans in Samoa on a permanent or semi-permanent basis out of a total population of about 33,000. They constituted 1.2 percent of the total population in 1906. The legal part-European population was 2.4 percent of the

population, while almost 90 percent of the remainder were considered full Samoans. Although part-Europeans were a very small percentage of the total population in the legal sense, they were part of the much larger "mixed-blood" population. One study estimating that, by the 1930s, more than 30 percent of the population had some "mixed-blood" (Keesing 1934:456). If this figure is at all suggestive, interethnic relationships were far more common in reproductive terms than in legal terms.

Legitimate part-Europeans had more rights and privileges than illegitimate half-castes. They went to special schools where they learned a European language, were subject to a separate set of laws (allowing more and better education, permitting alcohol consumption, for example), were more often involved with the cash economy as planters, traders, or government officials due to their education, and had a separate political status that allowed them to vote as individuals.

In contrast to the small legal part-European middle and upper class, the impoverished, landless, illegitimate, Apia-based mixed-bloods were disliked by both the European and legitimate part-European communities. Marriage became a marker of social status. A number of European men, including government officials, took half-caste wives or mistresses and lost status as a result. There were also many men who thought of themselves as legitimate part-Europeans but were not legally so, and they could not inherit their father's property and social position. This meant that they could not marry European women, only part-European or Samoan women. Part-European women fared little better. They "faced the choice of casual sexual relations with white men (who were titillated by the mythical belief of the time that the natives were 'hot blooded'), in the hope of eventual marriage; or marriage with other part-Samoans; or, in the rarest of circumstances, marriage to Samoans—towards whom they had been taught to feel some degree of superiority" (Meleisea 1987:161). The children of all of these types of interethnic unions were "mongrelized" in the eyes of

Europeans as a result of race mixing, and were often downwardly mobile.

Although the German colonial administration frowned on European-Samoan unions and passed legislation to discourage them, as a practical matter, this proved difficult. German men constituted almost half of the European population in Samoa at the turn of the century, and there were a number of pre-existing German-Samoan unions. German settlers with Samoan wives and part-European children quickly protested government restrictions, stating that Samoans were not racially "inferior" and that a number of part-Europeans were prosperous planters and traders crucial to the colonial economy, rather than wayward half-castes. One German member of the Association of Racial Hygiene, trying to spread his racial views in the islands, had to be taken into protective custody to prevent his being tarred and feathered in public. On the other hand, some German-Samoan parents were so concerned about discrimination against their offspring in Germany that they sent their children to school in America and New Zealand, fearing insults and intimidation in their European homeland.

A related problem for the German regime developed around Samoan-Chinese and Samoan-Melanesian interethnic unions that resulted from the importation of Chinese and Melanesian men to meet labor shortages on the large plantations. Although interested in preserving Samoan "racial purity" as well as their own, the German colonial administration realized that the colony's prosperity depended on cheap plantation labor that Samoans would not do, and when European planters demanded additional Chinese "coolie" laborers, the administration agreed. In 1903, Samoa began importing more than 2,000 indentured Chinese male laborers, who were forbidden to bring their wives. Soon Chinese outnumbered Europeans and legal part-Europeans. Considered inferior and often treated badly, the Chinese were temporary laborers, unable to own land, and required to return to China on completion of their contracts. Officials assumed that such constraints would limit Chinese-Samoan rela-

tionships. When it became clear that interethnic unions were occurring and children were being born, the German administration passed laws prohibiting Chinese laborers from even setting foot in Samoan houses as well as forbidding Samoan women from entering Chinese quarters. These laws were only partially successful in preventing interethnic unions, and Chinese-Samoan unions would pose a major problem for the subsequent New Zealand colonial regime.

## THE NEW ZEALAND COLONIAL REGIME (1914–1962)

Samoa would have remained a German colony except for the outbreak of World War I. New Zealand peacefully took over the islands in 1914 as a temporary military operation under nominal British authority. In fact, Samoa was the first German territory to be occupied as a result of World War I, and it remained a peaceful refuge from the ravages of war. But the racially based colonial hierarchy that the Germans had established would intensify under the New Zealand regime.

After World War I ended, the demography of Samoa changed markedly. Not only were New Zealand soldiers repatriated, Germans who had been held in Samoa during the war were deported. In 1914, of the roughly 600 Europeans in the islands, 373 were Germans. In 1920, after the war, most Germans were deported, significantly altering the European population. Only Germans with Samoan wives were allowed to stay, and this was due to the intervention of their wives with the government. More significant was the great worldwide flu epidemic of 1918, which devastated the Samoan population, killing almost 20 percent of Samoans and undermining support for the New Zealand occupation.

In 1920, New Zealand received an exclusive League of Nations mandate to govern Samoa, but Samoan opposition to colonial occupation was already galvanizing. The new regime was paternalistic and not well prepared to govern the islands, as the flu epidemic demonstrated. In protest against the colonial policies of New Zealand, the *Mau* (or opposition) was formed; it was the first anticolonial movement of the twentieth century to ask for self-governance. The *Mau* became a large, very popular political organization headed by a mix of full Samoans, part-Europeans, and Europeans with Samoan wives. The administration, viewing the *Mau* as a threat, responded by increasing its military presence.

In 1928, seventy-four New Zealanders were imported for the newly created Samoa Military Police. Their presence did not really impede the activities of the *Mau,* but these New Zealanders did become involved in a number of interethnic unions. Many of the Samoa Military Police had been unemployed servicemen and were not well thought of by the European community in Samoa, including middle-class women. These men therefore sought relationships with Samoan women. Yet they would soon discover that there was a broad colonial statute prohibiting marriage to a Samoan by *any* temporary immigrant or sojourner to the islands. They were thus unable to marry the only women available to them. George Westbrook, a long-time resident of the islands whose wife was Samoan and who himself was a participant in the *Mau,* wrote: "A few, I believe became attached to those women with whom they were intimate and would have married them. Others abused the hospitality of those who entertained them and seduced their daughters" (in Field 1984:126).

Other New Zealand colonial public servants also were interested in interethnic relationships. The senior New Zealand administrator at the time recommended that his "white" staff in the Office of Native Affairs be given the opportunity to find female companionship away from Samoa in order to avoid the possibility of interethnic unions in the islands. As for those New Zealanders already married to Samoans, he felt they should be forced out of the service because they had "lowered" themselves to the level of their wives, occasionally referring to some of these women as "whores." In fact, officials in interethnic marriages were often not promoted nor were they and their wives invited to official functions where European couples were present. In the small European community in the islands, they became outsiders.

The rationale for preventing these marriages was described in some detail by a senior administrator, who warned of their harmful effects on the European male:

> His outlook is a gloomy one, for after the first flush of romance is past he quickly realizes that he has made a serious error, that his physically attractive young wife is mentally unsuited to make him a help-mate or congenial companion, while his half-breed children serve to remind him that he is permanently isolated from that which is so dear to the white man—his home and native country. With no hope of leaving the tropics and little prospects [sic] of his half-caste children becoming a credit and honour to himself owing to the drawbacks from which they suffer on account of the uneugenic mating of the parents, the European father finds himself drawn back into the Native or semi-Native circle, and ultimately gives up the struggle to maintain the prestige of his race. (in Field 1984:122)

Like the German regime before it, the New Zealand administration in Samoa reiterated the dangers of tropical temptation for European men, viewing the islands' influence as corrupting, while stressing the necessity of close and continuing contact with the home country for the maintenance of European morale. Association with Samoans was officially discouraged because it was equated with "going native."

## THE CHINESE QUESTION

During the German and New Zealand colonial regimes, interethnic unions between Europeans and Samoans were disapproved, tightly regulated, and in the case of temporary European visitors banned altogether. But interethnic unions between Samoans and Chinese proved even more problematic. The economic difficulties associated with running large plantations continued after World War I, and the Chinese question that had arisen under the Germans continued as New Zealand became the colonial authority in the islands.

When New Zealand occupied Samoa under British auspices at the outset of World War I, there were almost 2,200 Chinese laborers, while Melanesian laborers numbered another 878. Like the Germans, New Zealanders were deeply concerned about the racial "pollution" of Samoans by the Chinese and Melanesians. German laws against Chinese laborers entering Samoan houses and against Samoan women entering Chinese laborers' quarters were revived by the New Zealand regime in 1917. New Zealanders also began efforts to return these laborers to China and Melanesia almost immediately. By 1918 the number of Chinese remaining in Samoa was only 838; the number of Melanesians had been reduced to 200. Nevertheless, in 1920 the colonial administration, now entirely in New Zealand hands, was still troubled by the specter of race mixing, and the regime imposed a strict law forbidding Samoan-Chinese marriages altogether. Government officials also encouraged Samoans to endorse their views of the Chinese "race menace," and a number already had done so independently.

Newton A. Rowe, a New Zealand district officer in Samoa during the mid-1920s, believed that even a reduced number of Chinese could cause racial "contamination" and were "Samoa's most present menace" (1930: 269–270). He estimated that Samoan-Chinese children numbered between 1,000 and 1,500 out of a total population of about 40,000. Despite harsh restrictions on the interaction of Chinese men and Samoan women and the outright ban on intermarriage, *avaga* marriages were taking place, children were being born, and these unions presented "no difficulties at all" for Samoans (1930:271). Rowe was upset that the Samoan custom of living together as a married couple was subverting legal efforts by the government to prevent these relationships, and that Samoans themselves were active participants in what he thought was the "demise" of their own "race." He was also frustrated that government warnings to Samoan-Chinese couples were ignored and that the law banning these interethnic marriages was not strictly enforced.

Samoan-Chinese relationships were not only banned by law, they were also frowned upon by Christian churches which had not missionized the Chinese because they were only temporary laborers. Why then were Samoans interested in these relationships? From a colonial perspective, as Rowe recounts, Chinese husbands treated their wives well and were reliable providers. "The main attraction of living with the Chinese is that the coolies give the greater part of their money to the women, who are allowed to live in complete idleness, the Chinaman even doing such housework as is done" (Rowe 1930:271). Colonel Tate, a senior New Zealand administrator, suggested that "Samoan women recognize the Chinese as better husbands than Samoan men" (in Meleisea 1987:172). Rowe also noted that family interests played a role, remarking that

> For their attitude in the matter the parents of the girls are perhaps to be blamed. But there is something of the procurer and procuress in most parents. And an alliance with a foreigner is likely to be beneficial to a family in Samoa. (1930:271)

Although repatriation of Chinese laborers was a priority for the New Zealand regime, like the German regime before it, the administration needed to preserve the economic viability of the large plantations, and so importation of Chinese men was resumed and continued until 1934. More Chinese-Samoan relationships developed. In 1939 there was an administrative crackdown on these unions when thirty-four Chinese-Samoan couples were arrested. The men were sentenced to three months in prison and the women three days. After other arrests, some men were deported to China; their Samoan wives were not allowed to go with them because they were not legally married. In contrast, European-Samoan unions were disapproved by the New Zealand regime and were forbidden for temporary settlers, but couples were not arrested, prosecuted, jailed, or deported. Of the Chinese-Samoan couples who remained in Samoa, their relationships would not be legally recognized until 1961, just before

Samoa became the first independent country in the South Pacific; this was also when their children became legitimate in the eyes of the law.

## INTERETHNIC RELATIONSHIPS DURING WORLD WAR II (1942–1945)

The pattern of racial exclusivity and discrimination established by the German colonial regime and its regulation of interethnic unions between Europeans, Chinese, Melanesians, and Samoans intensified under the New Zealand rule. But in the early 1940s, while Samoa was still a New Zealand colony, World War II came to the Pacific. The war years were a period of major change in the islands, including a dramatic increase in interethnic unions. Tens of thousands of American military personnel occupied Samoa from 1942 through 1945, overwhelming the local New Zealand presence as well as the Samoans. The Americans became the *de facto* colonial presence in the islands, and their agenda was quite different from New Zealand's.

W. E. H. Stanner, an anthropologist and postwar observer, described the situation as follows:

> Before the main body of troops moved to forward areas in 1943–44 there may have been as many as 25,000 or 30,000 troops in Western Samoa at any one time. The turnover, of course, was much higher because of transfer of units and movement of reinforcements. The troops were dispersed throughout the islands, many defended zones were constructed, and there was an enormous temporary building programme. The troops concentrated in camps or bivouacs along the coastline, in the main areas of native settlement, so that segregation was impracticable. . . . The Samoan islands experienced immensely heightened activity, intimate contact with Europeans en masse, and economic "prosperity," all in a degree greater than in any previous period in their history. (1953: 325–326)

The military needed Samoan labor and Samoan products; 2,600 Samoans were initially employed by the Americans. Samoans also quickly became effective small traders, restaurant and café owners, and brewers of crude but potent alcohol, leading to increases in Samoan income. Historian Mary Boyd comments that

> Wine, beer and spirits were manufactured from cocoa washings and sold at great profit. Gambling, drinking, promiscuity, and prostitution flourished. Samoan relations with the Americans were notably more friendly, hospitable and generous than with New Zealanders. (1969:185)

In terms of Samoan culture, "some native ceremonies were cheapened, and in cases debauched, to attract gift-bearing Americans. A few *matai* [chiefs] appointed new *taupo* virgins, as often as not girls lacking the technical attributes, to assist hospitalities" (Stanner 1953:326). More generally, "during the military occupation men fraternized very freely with native people, approaching them, accosting them, using their houses as sprawling huts, doing violence to one cherished courtesy after another with complete indifference. The barriers were down, and easy association became epidemic" (Stanner 1953:327–328).

Wartime interethnic unions were common. Stanner states:

> A great deal of sexual promiscuity occurred between Samoan or part-Samoan women and American troops. Responsible Samoans said that actual prostitution was restricted to a very small group of women. Romantic, at least friendly, relationships were very common. One mission society reported that in Upolu alone there were 1,200 known instances of illegitimate children by American soldiers from Samoan girls. The official statistics were not revealed, but put the number of known illegitimate children much lower. Only a few incidents were caused by the jealousy of Samoan men, and not much was made of them by either side. Some villages were said to have set up a special curfew for their girls, and at Falefa (near Apia) no troops except officers on business were allowed to enter *fale* [houses]. With troops so widely dispersed in an area so densely settled it is impossible to prevent familiar association.

Many soldiers regularly visited girlfriends within the villages, by no means only with single intention, but the entrance-gates to the airport, it was said, became known among Samoans as "the gates of sin." At least one *matai* [chief] was summarily expelled from his church congregation and from the society of the village on suspicion of procuring girls for prostitution. (1953:327)

The well-known author James Michener reports in a discrete but detailed manner his own participation in one such relationship. As a lieutenant, Michener was responsible for base security. Early in his western Samoan tour, he found a base where, during the day, sixty to seventy-two American men were on duty, whereas at night there were only six. Concerned about security, Michener learned that military vehicles took the men to villages at dusk, where they were dropped off to meet with their Samoan girlfriends for the evening. Michener saw first hand that these evening arrangements were openly welcomed by the Samoans. In the morning, servicemen were picked up and returned to their base. Michener himself was invited by a high-ranking Samoan chief to enter into such a relationship with his daughter and father her child (1992:38–40). As a result of his involvement, Michener felt so compromised that he never reported these relationships to his superior officers.

After the war and after the Americans had left, the New Zealand colonial government continued to discriminate against "mixed-bloods," including the children of Samoan-American unions. In fact, Samoa had the least tolerance for "mixed-bloods" in all of western Polynesia. And this would become a pressing issue as Samoa prepared for political independence in 1962. How could all the people of the islands be considered equal citizens of a new nation when discrimination, inequality, and special rights had pervaded colonial society? As political independence approached, these issues were openly addressed and partially resolved. Today interethnic unions and marriages are no longer issues for the independent state of Samoa because there are no sanctions against them.

Independence also meant a reworking of the separate ethnic identities that had been created by colonial society. These identities shifted in complex and unforeseen ways. As power shifted to Samoans, some legal part-Europeans became Samoan, taking Samoan names and chiefly titles, as well as representing their Samoan constituents in the Samoan parliament. On the other hand, as economic opportunities opened up abroad, many Samoans were willing to give up their newly gained Samoan citizenship for the opportunity to migrate overseas. In one seminal case, a Samoan woman who wanted to migrate to New Zealand filed a lawsuit, claiming that she was in reality a New Zealand citizen because she had been born under New Zealand colonial rule. She ultimately won her legal battle in the 1980s, and this landmark decision allowed large numbers of Samoans to migrate to New Zealand, where many retain dual citizenship.

As Samoans have become part of the global economy, they have taken advantage of employment opportunities abroad. In fact, most Samoans no longer live in the islands. Since the 1960s, they have migrated in large numbers to New Zealand, Hawai'i, the U.S. mainland, Australia, and over three dozen other countries. More than half of all Samoans now live permanently overseas. Intermarriage has facilitated some of this migration. Once abroad, though, Samoans continue to have a very high rate of intermarriage. In Hawai'i, for example, roughly 40 percent of Samoans have married non-Samoans. Samoan women have tended to marry whites, blacks, Hawai'ians, and part-Hawai'ians, while Samoan men have tended to marry Hawai'ians, part-Hawai'ians, and whites (Franco 1987:8). These relationships are creating new questions about what it means to be "Samoan" in the twenty-first century.

## CONCLUSION

If the rules and regulations concerning interethnic unions could be so easily discarded in the late twentieth century, why were they so important during the colonial period? The answers are straightforward. Colonial rule was based on alleged European superiority and actual European political control. Half-castes were not considered true Europeans, while Samoans were considered colonial subjects rather than genuine citizens. Moreover, Europeans wished to exploit the resources of the islands and pursue a policy of separate development for Europeans as distinct from Samoans. The existence of a substantial population of mixed-bloods raised questions about who had rights to land, property, and citizenship. It also raised questions about racial purity. So colonial concerns about who was "white" and who was "native" were not just academic questions; they were about control and power. Seemingly harmless procedures like legal categorization and the census became tools to enforce inequality. Control of interethnic sex and marriage, as well as the legal classification of children and descendants, were fundamental to the mission of the colonial state in Samoa and elsewhere in the colonial world.

The history of interethnic unions in Samoa highlights how rapidly political circumstances can change the way interethnic unions are viewed. In the nineteenth century, these unions were allowed and encouraged by both Samoans and Europeans before political consolidation under the Germans. But in the early twentieth century, these same unions became regulated, discouraged, and punished, Chinese-Samoan unions even more so than European-Samoan unions. When the Americans overwhelmed the islands during World War II, the New Zealand colonial regime could not effectively control them, and interethnic unions dramatically increased. These changing patterns of interethnic unions, sometimes occurring over a very brief period, demonstrate that the boundaries established by colonial authorities were not precisely fixed but flexible, at least to some extent. Finally, with the decolonization of Samoa in 1962, much of the stigma on these unions was lifted. Just as the spread of colonial authority had restricted interethnic unions in Samoa and elsewhere, the demise

of colonialism and the globalization of democracy helped lift these restrictions.

In America today, we view colonial attitudes and laws about race, sex, and intermarriage as hopelessly outdated. We sometimes ask how, in the twentieth century, people could justify the arbitrary regulation, punishment, and banning of interethnic unions. Yet in our own country laws prohibiting interracial marriages were widespread until very recently. Many states had antimiscegenation laws until a 1967 Supreme Court decision ruled them unconstitutional. At one time, laws against interracial marriages were on the books in forty of forty-eight states. In Alabama, the following law remained in the state's constitution until the year 2000; it stated that: "The legislature shall never pass any law to authorize or legalize any marriage between any white person and a Negro, or a descendant of a Negro." In 2000, Alabamans repealed this law by a vote of 60 percent to 40 percent in favor of equal treatment of all marriages and their descendants (Sengupta 2000:WK p. 5).

Our own history of the regulation of interethnic relationships mirrors Samoa's. And reminders of this not-so-distant past crop up in unexpected places. During World War II, when American servicemen were happily involved in relationships with Samoan women, Americans back home were deeply disturbed by the thought of interethnic marriages and the children of these unions. In his best-selling book about the war, *Tales of the South Pacific*, James Michener included a story line about a European-Polynesian union and their children, upsetting many American readers. The year was 1947. When Rodgers and Hammerstein turned Michener's novel into the Broadway musical *South Pacific*, they retained the controversial themes of forbidden interethnic unions and the children they produced. They wanted to remind Americans of how much prejudice there still was in America. *South Pacific* became one of America's favorite musicals and is still performed today. Yet that particular story line seems dated, especially in light of so many intermarriages in both real life and the media. What was once taboo provides us with a window on just how far we have come in our own attitudes about interethnic relationships.

## ACKNOWLEDGMENTS

This chapter is revised from a longer article entitled "Interethnic Unions and the Regulation of Sex in Colonial Samoa, 1830–1945" originally published in the *Journal of the Polynesian Society* 110(2):119–147. Revised article reprinted with permission, courtesy of the editor, Judith Huntsman.

## NOTE

1. In this chapter, Samoa refers to the country and area formerly known as Western Samoa. In 1997, the parliamentary government of Western Samoa approved changing the country's name to Samoa.

## REFERENCES

Boyd, Mary. 1969. "The Record in Western Samoa to 1945." In *New Zealand's Record in the Pacific Islands in the Twentieth Century*. Angus Ross, ed. Pp. 115–188. London: Longman Paul Limited.

Field, Michael J. 1984. *Mau: Samoa's Struggle against New Zealand Oppression*. Wellington: A. J. & A. W. Reed, Ltd.

Franco, Robert. 1987. *Samoans in Hawaii: A Demographic Profile*. Honolulu: East-West Population Institute. East-West Center.

Gilson, Richard P. 1970. *Samoa 1830–1900: The Politics of a Multi-Cultural Community*. London: Oxford University Press.

Keesing, Felix. 1934. *Modern Samoa*. London: Allen and Unwin.

Meleisea, Malama. 1987. *The Making of Modern Samoa*. Suva, Fiji: Institute of Pacific Studies.

Michener, James A. 1947. *Tales of the South Pacific*. New York: Curtis Publishing Company.

———. 1992. *The World Is My Home*. New York: Random House.

Murray, Reverend A. W. 1876. *Forty Years' Missionary Work in Polynesia and New Guinea from 1835 to 1875*. London: James Nisbet.

Rowe, Newton A. 1930. *Under the Sailing Gods*. New York: Putnam.

Stanner, W. E. H. 1953. *The South Seas in Transition*. Sydney: Australasian Publishing.

Sengupta, Somini. 2000. "The Color of Love: Removing a Relic of the Old South." *New York Times* (Sunday, November 5, 2000). WK P. 5.

Stevenson, Robert Louis. 1892. *A Footnote to History: Eight Years of Trouble in Samoa*. London: Cassell & Company, Limited.

Williams, John. 1984. *The Samoan Journals of John Williams, 1830 and 1832*. Richard Moyle, ed. Canberra: Australian National University Press.

# 23

# Pushing Children Up:
# Maternal Obligation, Modernity,
# and Medicine in the Tongan Ethnoscape

**Heather Young Leslie**

*University of Hawaii*

In October of 1991, a witty, hard-working, and generous Tongan woman named Vasiti ʻAholelei suffered either a cerebral hemorrhage or cardiac arrest and died. Vasiti had spent her last day weaving a fine *kie* mat destined for exchange with a New Zealand-based woman she had never met. She had eaten a large mid-day meal of pancakes, manioc, coconut cream, and mango and then, because she did not feel right, lay down to rest. Despite pleas from her kinswomen, she died just after dusk.

Three days before, and only after repeated requests from the island's nurse, Vasiti had overcome her dread of traveling the open ocean and had visited the doctor at the small hospital on a neighboring island. Two days before her death, Vasiti, her weaving partners, and I had a conversation about that hospital visit. She began the conversation by asking me what "high blood" was, what "180 over 130" meant, and whether it really was necessary to quit smoking and stop eating as she pleased. Finally, she had asked, would she really have to take the pills she had been given, every day, for the rest of her life?

In the same year, a younger, more active, and less acerbic (but equally witty and hard-working) woman named ʻAna Seini Taufa was also looking forward to the exchange with her New Zealand partners. ʻAna Seini had amassed an impressive stock of pandanus textiles, a feat of skill and physical endurance necessitated mostly by her six children's school fees that she and her husband needed to pay. Such energy and industry were expected of any mother in her middle years, but ʻAna Seini was remarkable in that she had succeeded in living up to the ideal. In 1999, however, she stubbed her toe, and sepsis from the infected cut spread up her leg. The dynamic and seemingly healthy ʻAna Seini was diagnosed with diabetes mellitus type II and her leg was amputated just below the knee.

A few years prior to ʻAna Seini's amputation, the man officially responsible for the health care system both she and Vasiti encountered

390

retired from his position as Minister of Health. Dr. Sione Tapa is a small, steely man who is discrete yet candid. Fiercely committed to personal integrity, devotion to duty, and the value of higher education, everything about Dr. Tapa was "first." He was a star athlete and the first-ranked student in his graduating year in Tonga, the first Tongan to receive a university degree in medicine, the first indigenous Director of Medicine, and the first commoner (nonchiefly) Minister of Health. It was he who steered Tonga's medical services into the twentieth century and incorporated Tonga into the international health community. In addition to ensuring that Tonga had a medical system that aligned with the principles promoted by the World Health Organization (WHO), Tapa also encouraged participation in international health trials with organizations such as the Atlanta Center for Disease Control (for example, a smallpox vaccine jet gun intended for Africa). As a member of the world community, and as a beneficiary of overseas consultants' advice, it was, he said, "only fair for Tongans to contribute to these researches" (personal interview, 10/08/99). After more than forty years of service, Tapa now lives a quiet, unassuming life punctuated by travel (and visits with foreign academics). Well travelled, well educated, exacting yet gracious, as comfortable in London, Geneva, or Auckland as in Nuku'alofa, Sione Tapa epitomizes in his very person a modern member of what I shall describe as the Tongan global ethnoscape.

These three individuals I have described offer the means for contemplating at the level of everyday life (and death) the ironies, ambiguities, opportunities, and tensions created by the interconnections which characterize globalization in the Pacific. I am especially interested in the experience of globalization, and its concomitant aspect "modernity," in relation to gender and health. These examples come from the kingdom of Tonga, a central Pacific nation that has continually attempted to position itself as a fully participating member of the global society, while espousing rhetoric which has variously privileged pe-

ripherality, nationalism, traditional Polynesian culture, and modernity.

Contemporary Tonga is a society cross-cut on the one hand by discourses of tradition and kinship, and on the other by the perceived benefits of modernity and participation in the global economy. In this chapter I want to make three points about the experience of globalization in Tonga and for Tongans. The first point relates to the interconnection of globalization, modernity, and the Tongan ethnoscape (I outline what I mean by globalization and the Tongan ethnoscape in the next section). The second relates to biomedicine's role in the development of a modern Tongan nation and in the national agenda of global participation. The third point focuses on globalization and modernity as experienced by outer island women like Vasiti and 'Ana Seini.

I begin with a discussion of globalization, ethnoscapes, modernity, discourse, and hybridity. These factors, I argue, are intrinsically interconnected. Medicine, as a modernist, hybridizing discourse, offers a particularly salient example of those interconnections. I then look more closely at the ways in which medicine and health have figured as strategies in the modernizing of the Tongan nation, and Tonga's relations with a globalized world. Sione Tapa figures as a significant example in this case. Finally, I return to consider how the Tongan reach for modernity and position in the context of globalization is experienced by individual women (like Vasiti and 'Ana Seini) living in smaller villages.

## COMPLEX CONNECTIVITY, GLOBALIZATION, AND TONGAN MODERNITY

Globalization is characterized by what John Tomlinson (1999) calls "complex connectivity." As a theory, the concept of globalization—and related concepts such as transnationalism (see Lee, chapter 8, and Macpherson, chapter 10), internationalism (Marcus 1993), modernity (Giddens 1990; Appadurai 1996), and even the world system (Wallerstein 1976)—emphasize to some degree or another the interconnectedness of people, goods, ideas, and practices across national and ideological boundaries. Much of this literature focuses on political and economic forces, tensions of diasporic and "home" place identities, technologies for travel and communication, and resultant forms of social relations. Such relations depend on various technologies—telecommunications media and airplanes in particular—which help to establish and maintain social contacts across great distances, but within very short time spans. The latter can lead to the sense of a "shrinking world" and fears of a loss of authentic traditions and homogenization of cultures. This is sometimes described as the inevitable result of modernity.

Being "modern," as Anderson (1983) has so clearly described, was offered to those of the burgeoning colonial (European) empires as a kind of imagined, homogeneous identity which seemed to transcend national borders. The importance of both imagined belonging and cross-national connectivity is clearly argued in the work of Appadurai, who identifies media and migration as the two major diacritics in any theory of modernity (1996:3). The notion of globalization, which is described as both evidence of and the pathway to modernity, and the notion of modernity, which is described as inherently globalizing (see Giddens 1990; Tomlinson 1999:107) forms a rather tautological relation in the literature, a circularity of mutual construction. However theorized, it is the flow of ideas and practices, movements (or deterritorialization) of groups of people, and the various forms of connectivity (including products and communications) that are the key characteristics of a globalized, modern world.

I think of Tongans both in-country and those who are part of the transnational diaspora abroad as an "ethnoscape." Ethnoscape is a term coined by Arjun Appadurai (1991) to refer to people living anywhere on the globe, who think of themselves as being linked by virtue of a particular homeland or ancestry. More than just a diaspora, or relocated persons, an ethnoscape includes the ideas and practices and political, eco-nomic, and cultural influences which the members bring to bear on each other and the places they are living. An ethnoscape is intrinsically connected to globalization, hybridity, and modernity, and a key aspect of any ethnoscape is mobility.

Tongans form an ethnoscape in which, to rephrase Appadurai (1991), the warp of stable communities, kinship, and residence that characterize the traditional system and the actual everyday life of most residents "is shot through with the woof of human motion, as more persons and groups deal with the realities of having to move, or the fantasies of wanting to move" (Appadurai 1991:192). This notion of stability cross-cut and overrun by the potential of movement describes contemporary Tongan society very well. There is one exception: the "woof of human motion" that Appadurai flags as new (especially for postcolonial peoples) is neither new, abnormal, nor particularly startling for Tongans. As 'Epeli Hau'ofa (1993) points out, Tongans have always understood themselves as groups of people simultaneously mobile in space and time, yet stable through ties of kinship, and as legitimate actors within a social framework that extended beyond their (current) geographical territories. The European contacts and resulting ventures of guest working, illegal overstaying, lusting for foreign commodities or experiences, and the economic or educational emigration which have characterized Tonga through the twentieth and into the twenty-first century are just the most recent set of deterritorializations for the Tongan people. This is a people whose ancestors discovered and populated many, many islands in the largest ocean on the globe, and then through trade, invasion, marriage, treaties, and/or religious proselytization repeatedly interacted with many of those Pacific societies. Tongans' history of "complex connectivity" is at least 2,900 years long, according to the most recent archaeological evidence for the oldest site in Tonga (Burley and Dickinson 2001).

Today it is accurate to say that every Tongan family has at least some kin living overseas. Much of this stems from the emphasis on education, which began early in the twentieth century as a type of prestige gesture among elite families. But it was quickly adopted by non-elites as a strategy for economic and social success. Today, good parents are those who support their children's studies and prioritize their education. Such parents hope that their child will receive a scholarship to study overseas, perhaps in New Zealand, Australia, Canada, the United States, or Japan. They fully expect the educated child to get a salaried job, settle overseas somewhere, and send remittances back to his or her family in Tonga. This is the way in which contemporary Tongans are expected to "help out the family" (see Evans 1997; Small 1997; and Lee, chapter 8). But this often results in having fewer people left to carry on life in the smaller villages.

This "brain and labor drain" has, among other things, helped to keep population levels within Tonga stable at about 97,000 persons. While fueled in part by investment in education, migration has also resulted from a desire for freedom from traditional obligations and controls of chiefs, perceived shortages of land, and a desire to travel and to gain new experiences. I say perceived land shortage, because while the area around the capital of Nuku'alofa and the main island of Tongatapu is experiencing a huge population boom, Ha'apai is depopulated, land is overfallowed, and it is labor, not land, that is in short supply (Evans 1997).

But deterritorialization is not unidirectional. Appadurai has argued that while deterritorialized people—as members of an ethnoscape—transfer ideas, images, goods, and experiences to one another, deterritorialization also disconnects people. He called it "one of the central forces of the modern world" that loosens the "bonds between people, wealth and territories" (Appadurai 1991:192–194). Tonga may be an anomaly (though I doubt it), but it is clear that in the Tongan ethnoscape, deterritorialization has not *necessarily* loosened the bond between people, wealth, and territory. Rather, the relocation of large portions of families has resulted in complicated flows of traditional gift items like textiles and food but also ideas,

such as Tongan-style Methodism, to overseas communities of expatriot Tongans. In exchange, in-country residents receive nontraditional wealth such as currency, trucks, VCRs, and freezers, but also scholarships, opportunities for 'eva—travel abroad—and ideas about national decision making and political representation. As Chappell (1999) notes, while not necessarily enabling democracy, transnationalism is affecting Tongan politics insofar as exposure to republican and parliamentary systems overseas has led to calls for reform of the current monarchy in Tonga. Furthermore, Gordon (n.d.) argues that the Tongan presence in the Church of Latter Day Saints (Mormons) is changing the character and representation of Mormonism, in the United States and elsewhere. A predominantly white American institution, the Latter Day Saints have had to reframe some of their early teachings connecting skin color, godliness, and right to authority, for example.

While the globalization experience of deterritorialization and complex connectivity is not new for Tongans, Appadurai's point about the scale of the movement and the forms through which ideas and people move is an important one. In Tonga, there is no isolated village where globalization is not evident. Vasiti and 'Ana Seini, for example, have experienced the "woof of human motion" first hand: They may have spent their whole adult lives on tiny Kauvai, but they thought about moving, they communicated with relatives who moved, and they sent things to and received things from overseas locales. During their lives, events such as world wars, the rise and fall of copra markets, and economic recessions, as well as anti-immigrant attitudes in places like the United States and New Zealand, ramified through the village. They affected when and where they went to school, and whether their husbands or brothers would get a guest visa, find work overseas, and send money home to help with school fees or annual church donations.

Appadurai's list of modern forces affecting an ethnoscape includes shifts in international capital, changes in production, technology, or consumers' needs, national violence, policies on immigration, and technologies of communication and travel. To that, I would add internationalization of social policies, and, in particular, attempts to create a globally uniform level of individual health. Examples of the latter include the International Sanitary Convention of 1892 (designed to interrupt the spread of cholera), the antimalarial campaigns of the 1950s, and the World Health Organization's (WHO) "Health for All by the Year 2000" campaign that began in 1977.

The push for "global health" (WHO 1981) represents one conduit of connectivity, one source of ideas and practices explicitly associated with being modern and part of the international community. "Health for All" is the term for an altruistic campaign first promoted by the World Health Assembly in 1977, and officially launched by the WHO in 1978. Its objectives were classically modernist: Use scientific (medical, social, economic) knowledge to tame the vicissitudes of both nature and social disadvantage, in order to achieve the humanitarian ideal of an end to unnecessary human suffering and a democratization of health at the level of every citizen. The "Health for All" strategy involved nationally set strategies, policies, and plans for action. One of the effects of the "Health for All" strategy was to precipitate a worldwide development of national medical systems focused around primary health care, professional and public education, health promotion campaigns, and internationally homogeneous health policies and legislation. Examples of the latter range from lists of reportable diseases to strategies for the professionalization of traditional birth attendants. The "Health for All" campaign also encouraged various means for monitoring and evaluating success within the local population, based on internationally accepted indicators. Just a few examples of the kinds of data—sources of capillary knowledge—collected on all the nations of the world in compliance with international protocols include maternal and infant death rates, hospital usage, reportable diseases (such as influenza, malaria, measles, smallpox, and diarrhea), breast-feeding, education levels by sex, and standards for nurse training and certification.

One way to interpret this nexus of practicing, thinking, and talking about health would be as a discourse characterized by complex connectivity which accretes, among other things, a corpus of experts, certain forms of knowledge, and disciplined bodies. This is an analysis based in poststructuralist, and especially Foucauldian, critiques of knowledge production (for example, Foucault 1972, 1974, 1980). I want to make the case that this type of analysis is as valid in Tonga as in other modern settings. However, because Foucault's *œuvre* was clearly focused on European knowledge, and especially texts, it might be considered inaccessible to societies like Tonga that have only very recently begun to compile written records. As in other Pacific nations, Tongan history and culture has been recorded mostly in oral forms (genealogies, stories, titles, site names, dances, and songs). While some of the older material has been recorded in travel narratives (Mariner 1991[1818]) and ethnographic reports (for example, Collacott 1971[1928]; Bott 1982; Gifford 1985[1929]), for Tongans, this corpus of knowledge is still mostly publicized in ritual, in ceremony, and in speech events (for example, radio programs, church sermons, title investitures, and kava drinking circles). How justifiable, then, is it to apply a poststructuralist focus developed for textual analysis to a setting where much that takes place is still oral? Lindstrom (1990:15) has shown that it *is* possible to "stretch the post-structuralist agenda so that it speaks to a non-textualizing society," such as those of the Pacific. As he argues in an analysis of ni-Vanuatu knowledge production, discourse is mostly talk. In Europe, talk was recorded in texts. In oral societies like Vanuatu (or Tonga), it is recorded mostly in speech events. I would add that for Foucault, a discourse is more than just talk. It includes the speakers and listeners of talk, both of whom are essential to any speech event.

Foucault's insight was that a discourse produces *something*. This is true of Pacific societies as well as European ones. Whether written or oral, influences and minute (or "capillary") subjugations of human beings are immanent in the social relations of a discourse. Foucault (1980) referred to this as power/knowledge, a term intended to demonstrate that discourse produces "knowledge" and such "knowledge" is productive of powerful relations. Such relations of power, whether they be between Parisian physicians and their clientele or Pacific island chiefs and their kin, are basically inherent "in the simple details of living one's life according to the dictates and expectations of local culture" (Lindstrom 1990:17). Borofsky's (1987) analysis of Pukapukan knowledge production is a good example of how everyday discussions and speech events produced a new form of social organization (the *akatawa*) that was accepted and believed to be traditional.

I am aware that when applying Foucauldian insights to Tonga, it is important to remember that, as most studies of the postcolonial have shown, local culture has a tendency to display indigenization of aspects of colonial power. One clear example of this in Tonga is the way in which the current monarchy mimics the structure of nineteenth-century British aristocracy as much as it represents paradigmatic Polynesian chiefly formations. Appadurai connects this blending of colonial forms of power and emergent local traditions to experiments with modernity (1996:90). As he sees it, blended or "hybrid" cultures evolve along with the interconnections that characterize globalization. In some ways, then, hybridity epitomizes modernity.

Hybridity is an important concept, not just for understanding what it is to be modern, but for understanding Western biomedicine. In theory, biomedicine is based in rational, scientific objectivity and motivated by humanistic principles. In practice, biomedicine has demonstrated a tendency to claim whatever therapies prove efficacious (herbal, diet, massage, surgery, acupuncture, shamanic rituals) as part of its scope, and the propensity to be motivated as much by capitalist profitability as humanism. This hybrid nature of biomedical practice (previously described as its cosmopolitanism; see Leslie 1976) is part of what makes biomedicine a prototypic example of a modernizing discourse. In addition, there is

what Foucault called medicine's totalizing "gaze," by which he meant its ability to systematically create the objects of which it speaks (see Foucault 1972:49, 1974[1973]), and finally, there is the dependence on ideas of scientific rationality which underlie biomedicine's claim to authority. Because science is always thought of as modern, biomedicine's rhetoric of scientism—most currently promoted through emphases on "evidence-based practice"—allows it to lay claim to a perpetual modernity. Biomedicine's modern cachet is not to be underestimated. Certainly, health discourse and attendant practices have been one means through which Tonga has actively participated in a modernizing process.

But what is it to be modern? And what is it to be a modern Tongan? One way to try to define this is to look at access to and use of material, particularly technological products. But I would argue that this is a limited version. One of the hallmarks of modernity, notes Latour (1993), is scientific rationalism: the creation of knowledge in which science investigates and catalogs the natural world. Such an endeavor, a discourse wherein a totalizing gaze is applied and subjects are constituted as they are described, requires a mental leap of faith in which science and nature are separated. To be modern, in this usage, is to be clear about what is fact and what is fiction, to keep the categories discrete, and to avoid muddled or *hybrid* thinking. However, Latour argues, while supposing a separation of science and nature, modernity actually erects equally false categorizations and typologies. In other words, even the so-called modern people are subject to hybrid thinking and thus have never really been modern (Latour 1993). Barley's (1988) analysis of medical technicians' magical thinking, including "letting the machine rest" and "speaking gently to it" in the face of CT scanner machine breakdown is a perfect example. Equally relevant examples from Tonga include the registered nurse who informs a patient that traditional medicine is not to be trusted and then reties the red belly string the woman is wearing under her clothes to protect her infant from *tevolo* (spirit attack), or the Tongan student who fasts before an exam in the hope that God will recognize the sacrifice and reward her with a good mark. Belief in electrons and neutrons, even though they have never actually been visualized, is a form of hybrid thinking typical of moderns.

I think of modernity as the espousal of enlightenment principles, including the value of education and the relevance of rational thinking based on the separation of nature and culture. It is also consciousness of a multiplicity of societies, lusting for exotic commodities and a vision of a "world of progress and production" (Baudrillard 1998). From this perspective, Tonga has consistently sought after what might be called the status of being modern while retaining the flavor and functions of tradition. The result of this agenda according to some analysts has been a "compromise culture" (Marcus 1978, 1980). However, the interconnections that characterize the modernity of the contemporary Tongan ethnoscape are much more complex than religion and tradition. I would suggest that Marcus's description of the syncretism of Christian and classical Tongan practice is better understood as part of the on-going "invention" or "figuration" (from Wagner 1975, 1986) of Tongan culture, what Gordon (1998) refers to as indigenous modernity. Latour's (1993) recognition of the links between hybridity and modernity are more helpful for thinking through the amalgam of traditional culture (called *'ulungana fakatonga*) and contemporary practice (called *anga fakatonga*) that is the essence of indigenous modernity in Tonga today. Contemporary Tongan culture is not characterized by compromise, but by hybridity, and modernity in Tonga is not just about commodities but about forms of interconnections and ways of thinking and attitudes (that is, thinking as a "modern"; explicitly trying to be modern).

Latour (1993) has noted that modernity is linked to identity. Pointing to the way in which being modern is constructed through a structural (imagined) opposite, Latour argues that modernist thinking claims rationality and objectivity in contrast to the irrational, "superstitious" thinking of those who are *not* modern. The latter are variously termed "sav-

ages," "primitives," or "natives." Again, very subtly, modernity is linked in a similar process to nationalism. Latour notes that nationalist statements (speech acts, slogans, public campaigns) pull on science and scientific knowledge for authenticity and for inspiration of national identities. The American and Russian automobile industry, space race, and Cold War messages are particularly salient examples of rhetorical linkages of scientism and national identity. Like other science-based forms of knowledge, biomedicine, with its claim to being modern and scientific, can be seen as a natural ally to nationalism and the emergence of a modern identity. This is particularly evident in Canada, where universal health care and the highest caliber of biomedicine are fundamental to notions of Canadian identity.

Thus, if one of the parameters of globalization is willing and active participation in the flows of ideas and practices (that complex connectivity identified by Tomlinson [1999]) and if we recognize biomedicine as one public practice that pulls extremely effectively on notions of modernity and science, then it follows that we must pay attention to the ways in which medicine and health have figured as a strategy in the modernizing of Tonga's national identity, and especially in the political strategies of the Tupou dynasty.

## MODERNITY AND MEDICINE IN TONGA

The actions of the late Queen Sālote Tupou III, who reigned over Tonga throughout most of the twentieth century, provide a particularly clear example of cultural hybridity and the use of medicine and health discourse in statecraft. The same types of political strategies are also evident in the actions of her son, the current monarch, King Tāufa'āhau Tupou IV.

Within Tonga, Queen Sālote is remembered as having both enlisted and resisted British guidance in developing her nation and preparing it for independence from its protectorate status. She is also renowned for having championed (and reinvented) Tongan traditions such as the royal kava circle, poem and song compositions, the wearing of the *ta'ovala* (woven waist-mat), and for her ability to position herself as the authority of all genealogies. All of these held particular importance in the construction of a national Tongan identity vis-à-vis both foreigners and Tongans. While generally demonstrating adherence to official forms of Tongan tradition and custom, her son King Tāufa'āhau is publicly associated with an agenda to modernize the nation through monetization, enabling of out-migration, and a love of sports. Less well recognized is the way both monarchs seized on health and medicine to craft Tonga's position vis-à-vis the international, global milieu. Three examples, all related to medicine, are offered as illustration of the fact that, despite being located on the geographic and economic periphery of the world system, Tongans have not been shy about their capacity to participate within the world system. They have in fact made transnational contributions, insofar as they have affected those living outside of Tongan borders, in material, if generally unheralded, ways. The three examples provided here indicate that Tonga has actively participated within the international society, has consistently thought of itself as a nation that could participate globally, and has espoused and sought to acquire public evidence of modernity.

In 1924, the late Queen Sālote asked a simple question, one that was eventually to prove instrumental in establishing a medical school dedicated specifically to training Pacific Islanders. She was speaking to Sylvester Lambert, a physician funded by the Rockefeller Foundation to combat hookworm in Pacific populations. Lambert had been trying to convince the Rockefeller Foundation to fund a medical school for Pacific Islanders. The school was to be located in Suva, Fiji, and was envisioned as a major expansion of a training program that was training indigenous Fijians about sanitation, first aid, and vaccinations. It was a risky proposal, insofar as some doubted that blacks had the intelligence to study medicine (Lambert 1941). The proposal had generated a lot of enthusiasm among colonial civil servants in Fiji, Samoa, Tonga, and elsewhere who were faced with the logistical problem of getting European doctors to stay in the civil service. But the little medical school was not sufficiently grandiose for the Rockefeller Foundation, which doubted that the expense would be worth the population to be helped and criticized the curriculum for being insufficiently rigorous (Heiser 1924). Lambert was meeting with the queen to give her the sad news that the Rockefeller funding request had been denied, and so the idea of a school to train Pacific islanders to be doctors would have to be abandoned. Queen Sālote asked why the Pacific island nations could not pay for their own medical school to train their own people in modern medicine (Lambert 1941:211, 282). It seems that neither Lambert nor the colonial officers had considered the idea of a self-funded program based on a partnership contribution model. Queen Sālote's suggestion revived the project. The Central Medical School, which eventually became the Fiji School of Medicine, was subsequently established in 1929, with Tonga contributing and guaranteeing the fees of an annual complement of four students.

The school came to be a model within the then British Commonwealth for the training of natives in medicine, proving among other things that non-Europeans could learn the skills required to practice modern medicine, and opening the doors for other, similar programs. This school, which students from across the Pacific still attend, has since graduated at least 1,000 professionals in medicine, dentistry, pharmacy, and allied health areas. Lambert's claim was that without the support and confidence of Queen Sālote, the school would never have eventuated. The investment that Tonga made in the establishment of the school and the training of medical personnel is clearly an example of the nation operating in a transnational context and demonstrating the skills to be an equal partner in planning and decision making. But it is also, I suggest, evidence that Queen Sālote recognized the necessity of creating her own cohort of professionals (in this case doctors) if she was to maintain the claim that Tongans were capable of managing their own national affairs. She sought to safeguard her islands from colonization or annexation such as her father (King Tupou II) had almost suffered, and which all other Pacific nations had experienced.

In the same time period, as a response to the aftermath of the world influenza epidemic of 1918, the queen established a national radio station in Tonga. While initially the radio was intended as a means of communicating emergency information, it quickly came to be used for (among other things) health promotion messaging and lectures about Tongan tradition. This is a direct example of one of Appadurai's diacritics of modernity (1996:3): the importance of communications media, and the motivation of health needs in the dissemination of modernity and in the invention of an imagined, national, indigenous identity (Anderson 1983; Appadurai 1996).

A third example of Tonga's direct, active, and material participation in events with international ramifications relates specifically to the "Global Health for All by the Year 2000" campaign. The impetus for the campaign came from the World Health Assembly held in 1977, and the campaign was officially launched in 1978 at the WHO conference at Alma Ata. Among the 134 participating countries' representatives at the conference were Drs. Sione Tapa and Laumeesi Malolo, two indigenous Tongan physicians, both trained originally at the Fiji School of Medicine, and both with postgraduate training overseas. But it was not just their presence in Alma Ata to which I point when noting Tonga's direct participation in an event of this nature.

As described above, Dr. Sione Tapa was the first Tongan to obtain a degree in medicine from a medical school that was not designed for natives. While the Fiji school had been preparing numerous Pacific Islanders to be medical officers, it transpired that they were not considered good enough by European and American practitioners' standards to be "real" doctors. Fiji graduates' professional titles began as "native medical practitioner." The first Indo-Fijian to graduate was awarded the title of "Indian medical practitioner." Eventually, in a move to be less racially insen-

sitive, the professional designation changed to "assistant medical practitioner." The graduates of the medical school in Fiji were considered acceptable to work as medical officers in their own nations, or in other Pacific nations, but they were still regarded as inferior to European physicians, especially insofar as management and important decisions were concerned. Their certificates and experience were not considered to be the equivalent of university degrees, and as natives they were generally considered unsuitable for positions of authority. It was usual for the "native medical practitioner" to work under the authority of a European chief medical officer.

Tapa changed all this by virtue of his academic excellence and zeal for learning. After he graduated from the program in Fiji, he studied for the New Zealand school certificate and was then granted admission to the university medical school in Dunedin. He was selected as a candidate for medical training and supported specifically throughout the several years of his advancement through schools in Fiji, New Zealand and other overseas locations by the then crown prince and prime minister, the current ruler King Tāufa'āhau. Tapa drew the royal's attention because of his participation in sports, as well as his high graduation marks. He became the hope of the Tongan privy council for an indigenization of modern medical practices in Tonga and indeed, despite the misgivings of the colonial medical officer in the kingdom at the time, became the first indigenous director of medicine. He eventually became the first commoner (nonmember of a chiefly family) minister of health.

Tapa was the architect of Tongan medical practices for twenty-six years. He was instrumental in framing government health and sanitation policies, in planning and managing the complement of medical services and personnel (practitioners and nurses). He suggested renaming the Department of Medicine the Ministry of Health, he collaborated with international researchers and consultants, did postgraduate studies in Europe, and arranged for Tonga to become a member nation in the WHO (after which he participated in its meetings annually). If anyone can be credited with aligning Tonga's health system firmly along modern medical principles (as outlined by the WHO), it was Dr. Tapa.

Prior to Tonga's independence (1970), Tapa was the Tongan representative to the WHO under the British. He was, he says, well known by WHO people because of the various training sessions and research projects in which he had participated. Upon Tongan independence, as director of health, Tapa prepared Tonga's bid to join the WHO. This occurred in 1975. He continued to serve as Tonga's representative to the WHO in 1976 and 1977. In 1977, Tapa was asked to sit as president of the World Health Assembly. The WHA is the international body that governs the WHO. Its mandate includes determining overall budgets and setting major policy directions. 1977 was the year when the idea that "every individual in every country of the world should be able to attain the level of health necessary to lead a socially and economically productive life" was drafted at the WHA. It was, for Tapa, a time of great promise, when health was to be achievable by anyone:

> WHO had . . . begun, you know, a sort of basic health service, previous to this idea, you know? Some call it a slogan. I don't believe it's a *slogan*. It's very important, the idea of health being unified, you know, so that it can be achieved by all. . . . You see, it referred really to the citizen of a country. . . . I remember the resolution [I was president of the WHA at the time] . . . and the wording—important words—is: the "attainment by every citizen" . . . *Citizen*, see, by *every citizen*, of a socially and economically productive life. This was the gist of the thing (Sione Tapa, personal interview, 10/08/99. Italics indicate vocal emphasis during the interview.)

As president of the WHA, Tapa was instrumental in drafting the resolution that became what is probably one of the most widespread and influential (nonmilitary) international political actions: the "Global Health for All by the Year 2000" initiative. It is hard to speculate on the degree to which Dr. Tapa brought a specifically Tongan influence to the WHA resolution on global health for all citizens.

But it is true that the democratization of health access is congruent with traditional Tongan notions of sympathy, generosity, and love—called *'ofa*—the things that ideally characterize social behaviors. *'Ofa* implies that one has the responsibility to act kindly and generously toward others, and that a resource such as food (or access to health) should be shared.

In the same interview, Tapa noted with some regret that this was a time "when there was talk of a new international economic order . . . a new health order," but one which was negatively affected by the actions of the oil cartels, beginning in 1973. As Tapa recalls it, "the price of oil went up, and of course that affected economic development throughout the world, but especially in developing countries" (10/08/99). The extra expense of crude oil meant that donor nations stopped giving money to recipient nations, and poorer nations had to spend money on fuels that would otherwise have gone into better health services, research, and promotion programs. In hindsight, the "new international health order" that Tapa looked forward to did not necessarily eventuate as he (and many others) hoped. Nevertheless, it is clear that for over two decades global health problems received major political, academic, and economic attention, and that many nations accepted the principle of access to primary health services at minimal or no cost.

The simple details of "living one's life according to the dictates and expectations of local culture" (Lindstrom 1990:17) must necessarily precipitate a previously unprecedented amount of complex connectivity, particularly in the context of a hybrid, modern, globalizing nation promoting medical training, health, and culture (in radio programming and international health forums). That connectivity takes the form of the transnational exchanges of ideas about services, policies, practices, and priorities that, while focused on health, had ramifications throughout Tongan society. Excellent students were sent overseas to study and to bring back skills and ideas. Government departments and procedures had to be established. The hybrid nature of the Tongan civil service encompassed both European and Tongan employees but also ideas and practices.

These examples (medical training, radio, and the WHO) are also indications of a small, supposedly underdeveloped nation actively aiming to be modern and to participate as an active player in the global community. The same examples also gainsay the implication that political and economic influences only flow *into* a small nation state, rather than into and out of those peripheral sites (see Chappell 1999).

What I have described so far are but a few accomplishments of which Tonga, as a nation seeking recognition as a modern member of the global society, can be proud. The argument and examples to this point indicate that Tonga is a modern nation and that it is clearly inaccurate to characterize Tongans who are in-country as somehow less modern than anyone living outside of the country. The nation's modernity is clearly evidenced in the clear espousal of humanist philosophies (that is, free medical services), the use of education and biomedicine as an envoy to modernity, and the relevance of scientific medicine within the nation-building process. However, as I discuss in the next part of the chapter, gendered prescriptions for behavior that are linked to notions of what it is to be a "traditional Tongan mother" mean that the effects of the modernizing process have had different ramifications for women. This may be particularly true for women of Ha'apai, like Vasiti and 'Ana Seini.

There remains a sense across the Tongan ethnoscape that Ha'apai people are the most-traditional, the least-sophisticated, the least-modern members of the ethnoscape. For many, the stereotype of Ha'apai is of those who simply follow "the Tongan way." The question I turn to next is how do these so-called traditional people of the nation (as exemplified by women in the outer island villages of Ha'apai) experience the globalized, modernizing nation state that is represented by the Tonga of Sione Tapa? Is that most modern of tropes, "health for all," a reality for village women like Vasiti and 'Ana Seini in the year 2000?

## TRADITION AND MATERNAL OBLIGATION

Vasiti and 'Ana Seini (see Figure 23.1) lived all of their adult lives on the coral atoll known locally as Kauvai, one of the many scattered islands in the Ha'apai region of Tonga. Ha'apai encapsulates a number of contradictions. On the one hand, it occupies a certain position of centrality as the nation's geographic center, as the historic land base of the chief and warrior who founded the current dynasty, and as a kind of romanticized center of traditional Tongan culture. Ha'apai is described by Tongans living in the capital as *the place* where real Tongan traditions are *still* practiced. Similar statements are made by overseas Tongans for whom the *idea* of traditional Ha'apai is just as significant as its reality.

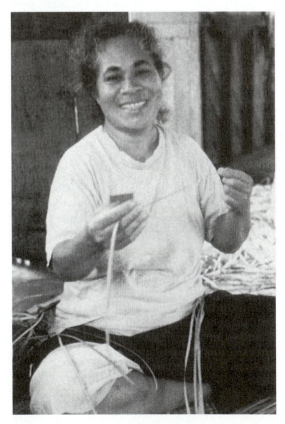

**Figure 23.1**    'Ana Seina Taufa, Photographed in 1992

But Ha'apai's broadly scattered and small, mostly low-lying islands, weak infrastructural links, and high levels of out-migration serve to keep the region, and islands like Kauvai, at the economic and political periphery of the nation. Yet, this peripheralization does not mean that Kauvai islanders have no experience with the processes, practices, and effects associated with globalization. The numerous ramifications of globalization, resulting from the complex connectivity which Ha'apai people experience, include dietary changes (toward fatter, sweeter, and saltier foods) and the loss of children or whole families from the village for education or through migration. Connectivity is created in many ways, including overseas telephone calls, letters, and gifts of foreign currency (from kin who have relocated); overseas excursions to New Zealand, Australia, or California; magazines, sports teams, and radio programs from overseas; consumer goods (traditional and foreign); and numerous health and development campaigns, many of them focused on mothers' roles and practices.

The emphasis on mothers and children that pervades much of the international health promotion initiatives and is redeployed in Tonga is echoed in traditional Tongan emphases on mothers' work. Tongan kinship is based on a bilateral kindred model with some skewing according to maternal and paternal sides of ego's kindred, whereby paternal kin are higher ranked and hold greater authority. According to Tongan idioms of kinship, a mother and her kin are structurally responsible for "pushing her child up," and thereby making a child socially healthy (Young Leslie 1999; see also Spillius 1958; Bloomfield 1986; Moengangongo 1988; and Morton 1996 for descriptions of mothers and health). Mothers do this by living lives considered to be morally and socially appropriate, demonstrated through publicly recognized industry, and the production and deployment of barkcloth and/or pandanus mats intended for gifting. Ceremonial occasions such as weddings or funerals call for maternal kin to donate this type of traditional women's wealth (and the best of those gifts are passed on to the receiver's paternal kin). But everyday social relations are maintained by smaller gifts, usually of food or (between men) kava. 'Ana Seini's industry in making and stockpiling so much women's wealth (pandanus mats) made her a very good mother, indeed.

In the same system, and because of the traditional skewing of gifting and obedience obligations, father and father's kin are said to "push you down" because their authority is supposed to be unquestioned, and because they must be given the best of your wealth. While fathers are traditionally responsible for providing a family's food and shelter, making children healthy and teaching them how to be Tongan is, by default, the work of mothers and, by extension, a child's maternal kin. This is referred to as the *fatongia oe fā'e,* the maternal obligation.

Therefore, in the traditional idiom, mothers are considered to be transmitters of cultural practices and protectors of traditional culture, called *'ulungaanga fakatonga.* A child who is not behaving properly, and thus is considered to be socially, physically, or spiritually unwell, is described as *ta'e mohe 'ofi*—one who did not sleep close. This is a serious criticism of the mother and refers to her failure to sleep near her children and to teach them (through bedtime stories) the important cultural information that is supposed to help any Tongan know his or her place, duty, and personal obligations (that is, genealogies and rank-based behaviors).

The contemporary international health discourse, however, places mothers in a different, if still pivotal, position. Within the health discourse, mothers are in some ways the targeted subjects of programs aimed at modifying their daily practices. Messages focused on improving public health and productivity, aimed at ensuring Tonga as a nation that is in line with other modern nation states, target mothers by emphasizing breast-feeding, vaccination promotion, and nutrition. Mothers therefore act as front-line workers, interpreting these internationally framed and locally disseminated health promotion messages and carrying out the instructions of nurses, doctors, nutritionists, and media-based educators, most of whom assume that women are the domestic managers for the family. This assumption may hold true in the urban Tongan setting, but it does not necessarily apply in the more subsistence-based outer islands. There, men generally select what food is available for eating on a daily basis according to what is available (from their gardens, livestock, or the ocean). Historically, cooking was considered unsuitable for women because it is dirty work. Today, men effect the family's nourishment, at minimum on a weekly basis, insofar as they still do much of the cooking for the Sunday meal, because this often includes slaughtering a piglet and building an *'umu* (earth oven).

Women in general, and mothers in particular, are targeted because demographic and epidemiological research has shown that a range of family-centered factors contribute to declining levels of morbidity and mortality, and to increasing levels of productivity and health (Cochrane et al. 1980, 1982; Garenne and van de Walle 1985; Caldwell 1986; Simons 1989; Lindenbaum 1990; Rubinstein and Lane 1990; van de Walle 1990; Lane and Rubinstein 1996). They include nutrition, employment, girls' education, access to primary health care services, fertility control, and access to clean water. Based on this research, maternal education has been hailed as a particular development goal (and marker) because of its direct, positive effect on child survival (Cochrane, O'Hara and Leslie 1980; Herz and Measham 1987) and on reduction of birthrates. Lower birthrates have an indirect effect on women's and children's survival (Herz and Measham 1987; Lane and Rubinstein 1996).

Examples of global initiatives originating from agencies such as UNICEF and WHO that have influenced Tonga's health promotion campaigns include Better Maternal Child Health through Family Planning, Safe Motherhood against Maternal Mortality, the Task Force for Child Survival, and Strategies for Encouraging Mothers to Have Children Immunized (see Evans et al. 2001:6). Philanthropic agencies with globalizing agendas have adopted the same maternal emphasis. In

1989, for example, the Ford Foundation sponsored an Interdisciplinary Workshop in Ahmedabad, India on Mother's Education and Child Survival (Simons 1989). Material from these workshops and initiatives is housed in the library of the main hospital in Tonga, right next to the office of the WHO representative and accessible to hospital staff as well as students at the nursing school located on the same grounds. One of the major specialties within the Tongan medical workforce, and the only nursing specialty recognized and paid for by government funds, is "maternal-child nurse." Under Sione Tapa, maternal and child survival has been taken very seriously.

For women living on Kauvai, survival is generally assumed, but "living well" is a different matter. The neologism for health, *mo'ui lelei*, glosses as living well, and in everyday (that is, nonclinical) settings, this term indexes living well through the maintenance of appropriate social relations, what is referred to as *va lelei* (Young Leslie 1999). Living well requires far more than compliance with medical and health promotion messages. In a survey I conducted with all the mothers (eighty-one women) in the village where I lived on Kauvai, no one indicated that she made her children healthy by the activities associated with health promotion measures. Neither inoculation, balancing the nutritional component of their food, nor complying with the advice of the local maternal child health nurse were mentioned as a means to ensure a healthy child. Instead, mothers cited cleanliness, obedience, prayer, eating freely, and maternal behavior as keys to a healthy child.

Overall, living well for women depends on fulfillment of their maternal obligation. Part of her obligation is to enrich her family. This is referred to as *fakakoloa* (making/to be like wealth). *Fakakoloa* can mean obtaining material provisions and commodities or weaving pandanus mats or beating barkcloth, but it also implies the active creation of a moral and social setting necessary for children to develop into good, healthy Tongans. Good Tongans are persons who display the traditional social characteristics of love and generosity (*'ofa*), duty to family (*fatongia*), respect (*faka'apa'apa*), mutual aid (*feitokoni'aki*), and obedience (*talangofua*) to those of higher rank (including God). A woman who is competent at *fakakoloa* not only produces ceremonially vital textiles, she knows how to deploy those valuables—when to give what to whom—in various life passage events, and does so in such a way that the family benefits. Gifting benefits can derive through release of an obligation incurred by a previous gift, creation of a future obligation, or elevation in social status gained by the distribution of a large amount of wealth (that is, pandanus mats).

Polynesians are famous for their generosity and the magnificence of their gifting. Indeed, Polynesian gifting played a major role in the development of Mauss's now classic theory of reciprocity and social structure (Mauss 1990[1925]). The pre-Christian Tongan social formation at the point of European contact was one based on a flow of tribute toward centrally located paramount chiefs, with the redistribution of prestige goods back to local chiefs, played out through the idiom of kinship. Gifts are gendered, and the names reflect this. Pandanus mats and barkcloth are both forms of ceremonially significant textiles. These textiles, called as a class *koloa,* are produced, given by, and associated with women. Kava, pigs, and garden produce or *ngoue* (the generalized term for the root crops grown by men, with special reference to yams [ *'ufi*] and taro [ *talo*]) are associated with men. While precontact ceremonial and exchange activity was controlled by the chiefly and socially elite women, now nonchiefly Tongans also engage in such forms, and the ceremonial uses of *koloa* have come to be iconic for traditional culture of all strata of Tongans. Today, events such as birth, first and twenty-first birthdays, marriage, school graduation, travel overseas or return from travel, taking a title (for example, a noble or a minister of the church), death, and serious demonstrations of gratitude or affection are marked by presentations of women's textiles. For overseas members of the Tongan ethnoscape, prearranged exchanges of the sort that Vasiti was preparing for on the day of her death are one of the best ways to stay connected with kin or villages in Tonga.

Production of the textiles (pandanus mats and barkcloth) required by members of the ethnoscape wishing to live as cultural Tongans is a multipronged way for mothers to push up their children. By producing and properly deploying their textiles, women demonstrate to neighbors and kin that they are industrious, have knowledge of *'ulungaanga fakatonga* (Tongan culture), and the ability to properly engage in prestige and ceremonial gifting. By exchanging these textiles with women overseas, village women are also able to maintain or create social linkages across the oceans that may prove beneficial later, when children leave Tonga on scholarships or to find work. The return gifts of cash women receive from their overseas partners help women pay for other necessities required by children and families engaged in a modernizing society, such as school fees and attendant costs (books, uniforms, and so on), overseas travel, house improvements, and church donations.

Thus, despite Gailey's (1987) contention that the missionization period resulted in women's textiles being relegated to secondary economic importance, *koloa* continues to play a significant role in contemporary social practice. In addition to its uses in ceremonial presentations, as a means for tying the ethnoscape together, and as a source of otherwise scarce cash, women's textiles are used as a source of emergency funds and as collateral in bank loans (Young Leslie 1999; see also Horan 1998; Schoeffel 1996). There are few sources of cash on islands like Kauvai. Food is mostly self-produced from gardens, livestock (mostly pigs, goats, and horses), the reef, and the ocean. The only people with paid employment are the elementary school teachers, the nurse, and elected town officers. Cash comes from the episodic sale of agricultural products, copra, or fish, and women's textiles. *Koloa* therefore has a particularly gendered function in the modern economic system. In the absence of any other source of income for women living on the outer islands, it is the key element in an overseas exchange system perpetuated between women in which Tongans of the ethnoscape exchange *koloa* in return for cash or commodities.

But women's textiles are not the most frequently gifted items. Food is the way in which good social relations are managed between kin and neighbors on an everyday level. It figures prominently in greetings, such as *ha'u tau kai*—come let us eat—and the most frequently asked question to visitors is *na'a ke kai*—Have you eaten? To be stingy with food is one of the worst social sins possible. The term for greediness is *kai po'uli*—eating in the dark. A surplus of food is always desirable and within the village plates of extra portions of cooked foods flow back and forth between neighbors each Sunday, and between some households daily. The historic ceremonies of first fruits gifts to the highest-ranking chief, the Tu'i Tonga, included, in addition to textiles and other durables, massive amounts of prestigious foodstuffs—garden, animal, and ocean-based produce.

Today, feasting and displays of large amounts of food are still very important, and every ceremony at which textiles would be exchanged includes a feast. On Kauvai, where most people are Methodist, the first week of each new year is marked by feasts, sometimes two a day, at which the entire community will be fed by one extended family. Families elect to give a feast, often in honor of a deceased loved one, but most frequently, the New Years' feasts are named in honor of a young child. Such feasts are called *feilaulau*—a sacrifice—and the intention is clear: A family offers a feast for the eyes of God, in the hope that He will reciprocate with blessings for their child. The offering is witnessed by their community (the guests) and, most important, accepted and praised by the representatives of the church and local elites (for example, chiefs and other ministers). Food production, then, is one way in which men demonstrate their capabilities and fulfill their responsibility to their families.

Access to food, especially prestige foods, is important in traditional Tongan constructs, and evidence of that access, in the form of large bodies, is equally important. As for most Polynesian people, large, corpulent (and motionless) bodies are indices of personal and familial rank and power, tangible embodiments of contemporary and historical access to resources. In many ways, each body can be read as evidence of a genealogy, a kindred's ability to fulfill social obligations. A large body potentially signifies sacred and chiefly connections. In other words, social weight is demonstrated physically. The kinship system ranks sisters above brothers and while wives are subordinate to their husbands, women enjoy relatively high social status in Tongan society in general. The way in which women *literally* embody familial prestige and demonstrate social status is through consumption of food. Women feel social pressure (and then freedom) to be large bodied. This begins in the teenage years as girls go through puberty, and becomes full-fledged as young women begin to consider marital opportunities (Tupoulahi 1997).

Men probably do not get as obese, mostly because of their work and athletic activities. This begins in secondary school, where the curricula generally include sports and periods of work in the school gardens involving hoeing and other forms of farm labor required to produce the crops that feed the students. This type of physical labor traditionally carries on throughout a man's life, although the move toward an urban, waged labor force is contributing to more male obesity. Farming in Tonga is hard work, and requires the expenditure of a great deal of energy, helping men to better utilize the calories they consume. Farming is very clearly not women's work. Women are expected to remain still, indeed to stay seated whenever possible. Their prototypic forms of labor, whether barkcloth beating, weaving pandanus mats, doing child care or laundry, is done sitting down. Schoolgirls participate in some active sports—netball for instance—but this stops as soon as they leave school and must begin to behave like proper adults.

The principles of status as demonstrated through bodily comportment are the same for chiefs and highly ranked persons as for women in general. So men who acquire titles, salaried employment, or prestigious social positions often become obese as well. Partly this is because they tend to be in situations where they are presented with high-calorie foods (for example, at feasts) more frequently than are lower-status men. But it also seems to be because body size symbolizes, for both women and men, desirable individual characteristics such as high personal rank, maturity, wealth, and sophistication (Tupoulahi 1997). In the final sum of things, obesity signifies success and good social relations.

Modern Tonga has a problem now with obesity. This problem is exacerbated by two factors: gendered assumptions about work and the large body as an icon of good social relations, and the influx of high-fat, imported foods related to (in part) the king's monetization program. This was an effort to increase the flow of foreign funds into Tonga, and to stimulate a waged labor force, initiated in the late 1970s as part of a development and modernization agenda. Along with other imports came cheap, high-fat meats (corned beef, mutton flaps, and turkey tails), highly sugared drinks (soda pop), candies, and other junk foods that very quickly were adopted into the regular diet. They have become mainstays at daily meals, as well as icons of (cash) wealth at feasts. The cultural propensity toward overeating and public demonstrations of "pushing one's child up" by demonstrating success through consumption of imported foods, combined with inappropriate diets and decreased levels of physical exertion, are combining to make modern Tonga a nation of the obese. The legacy of globalization in Tonga as in other parts of the Pacific is becoming one of morbidity and mortality rather than connectivity.

Doctors I interviewed in Tonga (1999, 2000, and 2001) were keen to discuss the problem of obesity, and the resultant morbidity issues resulting from poor diet and eating habits: cardiovascular and circulatory problems, certain neoplasms, and, very significantly, diabetes. At the Tongan Medical Association conference in September of 2001, the major causes of death—eating-related non-communicable diseases (NCDs)—were the focus of attention for most presenters and participants. For men and women, cardiovascular problems such as the hypertension and

heart disease experienced by Vasiti are the greatest killers in modern Tonga. Presenting a comparable picture, an unpublished analysis by Crowley (n.d., circa 2000) suggests that 48 percent of all deaths in Tonga are due to cardiovascular disease, neoplasms, and diabetes. Overall, the top five causes of death are modern lifestyle-related diseases (see Figure 23.2). In Tonga, as in other parts of the Pacific, people are dying from "the good life" (Zimmet et al. 1990).

While data analyzed in the Ministry of Health Report does not consistently reflect gender differences, it is clear that there are sex-based differences in suffering and death in Tonga. Tongan physicians suggest that any gender parity that might seem to exist in the statistics on eating-related NCDs is equivocal. Anecdotal evidence indicates that secondary complications, such as the sepsis and possible amputation that can affect noninsulin-dependent (or adult onset) diabetics, more severely affect women. Why this is so is not yet clear, although most physicians I spoke with surmised it is because women's inactivity, greater levels of obesity, and natural propensity to higher body fat make them more susceptible to infections. What is clear is that 'Ana Seini Taufa, the middle-aged mother described at the beginning of this chapter, is just one of many who found themselves being treated at the special diabetic clinic at Vaiola Hospital. And like others, she had to learn to use crutches and wheelchairs (a real trick on rural roads and in villages with few roads at all!). In 1999, there were 1,463 diabetics registered at Vaiola (up from 1,336 the previous year) and they made 10,881 visits to the clinic. Material presented at the Tongan Medical Association conference in 2001 indicates that these numbers have risen again, and are expected to continue to rise. Diabetics make up the largest cohort by far of any of the special medical clinics set up by the Ministry of Health (see Figure 23.3).

While data exist (accessible to the Ministry of Health and the Central Planning Department) which could clarify the sex-linked differentials in diabetes morbidity, it has yet to be analyzed or published. Nevertheless, the

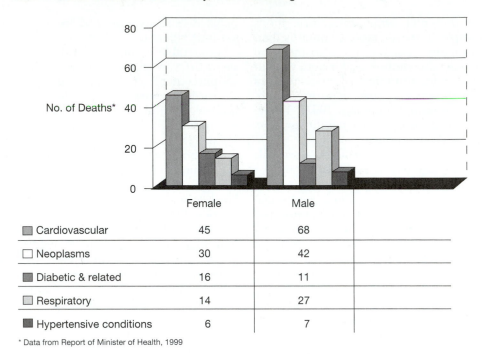

| | Female | Male |
|---|---|---|
| ▨ Cardiovascular | 45 | 68 |
| ▢ Neoplasms | 30 | 42 |
| ▮ Diabetic & related | 16 | 11 |
| ▨ Respiratory | 14 | 27 |
| ▮ Hypertensive conditions | 6 | 7 |

\* Data from Report of Minister of Health, 1999

**Figure 23.2**    Tonga: Top Five Leading Causes of Mortality (by Sex)

anecdotal and collateral evidence and available ethnographic research (for example, Young Leslie 1999; Tupoulahi 1997) suggest that individuals whose personal status means they have social expectations associated with prestige are most likely to be those who are obese (that is, women and elite males—chiefly men, church ministers, and government employees). The cultural etiquette that high-status persons should be mostly immobile and large bodied has its counterparts: hypertension, heart disease, circulatory problems, and the ailment that plagues the crown prince and several other members of the social elite, gout. These problems, of course, increase with age (see Table 23.1).

I have argued thus far that the social expectations of gendered roles and the public demonstration of appropriate social relations mean that women are more likely to become and stay obese. Moreover, the spinoff effects from this embodiment of familial and traditional ideals has health (and death) ramifica-

**Table 23.1**    Tonga: Obesity and the Rate of Diabetes (by Sex).

| | Obese | Diabetes | Age 30+ |
|---|---|---|---|
| Men | 10.9% | 0.8% | 3.7% |
| Women | 39.1% | 2.3% | 9.4% |

*Source:* Data from draft: Tonga Report on the Economic Costs of NCDs.

tions that disproportionately affect women. I have suggested that it is not just tradition (*anga fakatonga*) that underlies this skewing of illness burden. Part of the problem lies in the easy availability of low-quality and dangerous food substances.

Evans et al. (2001) have analyzed food preferences, knowledge of nutrient value, and food selection factors in Tonga. They compared factors based on island groups, age, and gender and found that, among other things, the current consumption patterns actually contradict food preferences

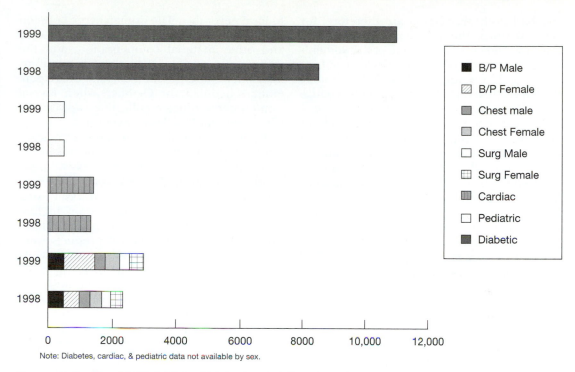

Note: Diabetes, cardiac, & pediatric data not available by sex.

**Figure 23.3**   Special Clinic Visits, Vaiola Hospital (Data from Report of the Minister of Health, 1999)

and knowledge about nutritional value. Food choices were best explained by accessibility, particularly cost and convenience. On reading their data, it becomes clear that cultural ideas about eating are also involved. This includes the fact that for Tongans, having *kiki*, something special to perk up a meal of starches (for example, taro, yam, manioc), is desirable. *Kiki* tends to enhance the flavor—usually because of its fat content—and makes a meal interesting. *Kiki* can include traditional treats like pork, fish, or any other meat, which today includes imported, high-fat foods such as mutton flaps, turkey tails, and sausages. It is no coincidence that the term for "fat", *ngako,* is also the term for food that is tasty. Having *kiki* in a meal is also an implication of access to wealth.

There is another aspect of social and personal conduct that impinges on women, and has ramifications for their share of the national morbidity statistics. Personal status and

"good breeding" is demonstrated not only in bodily bulk but also deportment—how one moves. Symbolically, stillness and silence, like girth, index chiefly status. Women, ideally, should move gracefully, sit (especially when indoors), eat well and in quantity, and not spend unnecessary time out of doors.

The cultural prescriptions on deportment, labor, and eating can combine in particularly dangerous ways for women: Even when they are working hard, women are not expending all the calories they consume, because weaving is not an aerobic activity. Also, sitting for long periods impedes the circulation of the lower limbs, raising the risk of thrombosis and reducing oxygenation of the tissues (which increases risk of infection). Finally, diets high in imported foods further predispose women to obesity and the attendant health risks.

Men's work is garden work, and women's work is within the domestic space. Weaving and barkcloth production are therefore, for many reasons, the paradigmatic traditional labor for Tongan women. One of the women's (especially mothers') key duties to her family is, as 'Eva Feimo'efi'afi said in a public church address one May morning, to produce these items: "*Ko e fakakoloa 'o e fāmili 'oku fai 'e he fā'e*" ("The wealth of the family is made by the mother"). When describing the duties of the mother, 'Eva referred to a gamut of duties, from domestic chores to ensuring children's Christian education, but emphasized that women represented the wealth of a family by virtue of their industriousness and their ability to produce women's wealth— pandanus textiles and/or barkcloth. Such production makes it possible, as described above, for women to fulfill their maternal obligations.

However, not all women can make *koloa,* or have it when they need it. Overseas Tongans in particular depend on their kin and contacts in Tonga for their *koloa* (see also James 1997 for a related perspective on the overseas exchanges). The monetary wealth available to overseas members of the ethnoscape means they have greater opportunity to participate in gifting and greater impetus for competition in public prestations. This, in combination with overseas Tongans' desire to help the family, has meant that thus far, there has always been a market for the exchange of *koloa.* The exchanges (*katoanga*) between women of Kauvai and Tongans from Honolulu, Auckland, and California that I have seen and been privy to the planning of, involve, as does any other gift exchange, initial gifts, counter gifts, and a great deal of public celebration and merriment. *Katoanga* exchanges are arranged usually between kin or migrated village residents and a contact person or "chair" on Kauvai. It is not unusual for other members of the overseas ethnoscape who hear of the impending *katoanga* to request admission so that they too can acquire the pandanus mats required for ceremonial gifting. A *katoanga* takes about a year to complete. Each woman is matched to a partner (one in Kauvai, one overseas) and it is not unusual, as in the case with Vasiti, for exchange partners

to have never met. The women agree between themselves as to sizes and appropriate cash and other material compensation, and the weavers get started. Often there is a halfway installment, and the final exchanges are generally scheduled for October, when Kauvai women need to begin collecting cash for the Christmas and New Year's expenses.

While the Ministry of Finance historically tended to ignore this source of income at the national level, the *katoanga* were essential for villagers on Kauvai. In 1992, for example, in the village where 'Ana Seini and Vasiti lived, weaving income represented the highest single source of cash to the village. Men's sales of fish and agricultural products were worth approximately 14,000 *pa'anga* while women's pandanus products brought in approximately 19,000 *pa'anga* (Young Leslie 1999). (The *pa'anga* was then worth approximately US$0.75). According to Niuatoputapu's health officer, women's weaving represents the only source of cash for the family today (Vaka'uta 2001). From a recent visit to Kauvai (August 2001), I can confirm that for many residents on outer islands (like Kauvai and Niuatoputapu), the means to elevate the family's social and material status, to "push up" their children, continues to rest, ultimately, on *koloa* production.

Education was and continues to be a key strategy for familial success, as has been discussed by many (see Lee, chapter 8). But education costs money. Even though well subsidized by the government at the elementary level and the churches at the secondary level, there are still fees, books, and uniforms to pay for. Overseas funded scholarships for university are available, but not everyone is a top student who can win a scholarship. In families with seven children (the norm on Kauvai) and few or no ways to earn cash other than through the sale of products of their own labor, women create the "wealth of the family" mostly by weaving. While women do sometimes take some of their textiles to the market in the hopes of a sale, on Kauvai, the preferred means of marketing their pandanus mats is through the commissioned exchanges called *katoanga.* It was this type of exchange that Vasiti was preparing for the day she died.

There is one other health problem connected to traditional practices and production for the wider ethnoscape—the spinal distortions and consequent back pain that are associated with being a life-long weaver. In death, Vasiti's body, misshapen by curvature of the spine, indicated the exigencies of life lived to the hybrid tune of both tradition and modernity. She resisted travelling to the hospital because the small boats on the open ocean scared her, but also because of her back problems. Vasiti had difficulty walking any distance, and she was not alone in this complaint. Of the twelve women over the age of sixty living in the village when I first went there in 1991, six, all life-long weavers, were unable to stand upright because of severe curvature of the spine.

While not a reportable item according to WHO formulas and so not recorded in national health statistics, back pain associated with weaving is one of the top complaints dealt with by the health officer from Niuatoputapu, Mr. Vaka'uta (reported at the Tongan Medical Association conference, August 2001). The type of spinal deformation I saw on Kauvai is probably not new; evidence of arthritic changes exists in the Tongan archæological record. Spennemann (1990) notes arthritic changes evident in the spines of individuals recovered from a burial dated at 1200–1500 A.D. The changes observed in the female bones are consistent with stresses related to severe and frequent periods of bending; Spennemann speculates as to the role of women in the precontact economy that would cause such spinal changes. He considers shell fishing, barkcloth beating, and gardening labor and concludes that the most likely cause of the arthritic changes was food production. Unfortunately, he did not consider the bodily changes that take place from years of weaving, a form of labor which, far more than barkcloth production, requires hours of sitting and leaning forward at the waist, and which reshapes women into hunchbacks.

Culturally competent persons can "read" the social body, Vasiti's world laid out on her skin, and in her hands, eyes, and misshapen back, but also they can see her stocks of (self-made) textile wealth and extensive kin network. From a Foucaultian perspective, her body is a site of disciplines based in ideals and routines for daily practice that substantiate a political ideology: that of the contemporary yet traditionally Polynesian Tongan nation. Vasiti's body was a product of her daily practice, practices she engaged in for familial, ceremonial, and fiscal reasons, and we can read her life's priorities—including the things she has been willing to sacrifice—in her body.

Imagine Vasiti at her death, a moment thick with implications for any discussion of globalization—if we know what we are seeing. Picture her, wearing a faded polyester dress made in Hong Kong, lying on a prestigious, self-made mat called a *fala,* in her small house. That house was built of plywood stamped "BC Timber products" (referring to British Columbia, Canada), and its purchase was subsidized by the Commonwealth of Nations as hurricane relief in 1982. The mat was commissioned by a New Zealand woman for her daughter's wedding and traditional wealth exchanges. When she died, Vasiti was surrounded by the three junior kinswomen who regularly wove with her and a young anthropologist who had, until recently, worked as a registered nurse in a hospital intensive care unit in a major Canadian city. On his way to her side was a Methodist minister who had studied, among other things, Greek philosophy in Fiji and Australia. Her relatives in California were telephoned with the sad news, and people in the next village were informed by a young man riding a bicycle made in Taiwan. Thus ended the life of one sixty-plus-year-old woman who lived her entire life on a tiny atoll in the middle of the Pacific Ocean. But living on an atoll in the middle of the Pacific Ocean did not mean living a life disconnected from the rest of the world.

## CONCLUSION

In this chapter I have described the Tongan experience of globalization, and its concomitant aspect modernity, in relation to gender and health. I focused on three themes: what it means to be a modern Tongan, the role of biomedicine in the strategic framing of Tonga as a modern nation, and the ramifications for women of the current embrasure of modernity in a globalizing Tonga.

To understand the Tongan experience of globalization, I argued, is to recognize that Tongans are, and perhaps always have been, embracing and combining ideas, attitudes, and behaviors which we now associate with modernity. The image of Tonga as a place "lost in time," the "last Polynesian kingdom"—stereotypes that are evidenced in both tourist brochures and the nostalgic remembrances of ethnic Tongans living overseas—are romantic views which ignore the scope of most Tongans' international interconnections, both historical and contemporary. In other words, it is a mistake to think of Tonga as simply "traditional Polynesia," and in-country residents as simply traditionalists, people who cling to old-fashioned behaviors in opposition to what we might call modern ways. I say, therefore, that Tongans are as modern as anyone else. A heretofore unrecognized and yet key point of evidence for Tonga's early embrasure of modernity and equal participation with the global community is the state-sponsored emphasis on medical services for and by Tongans, and Tonga's active participation in a global strategy of "Health for All."

The other main theme in this chapter was that women, as *mothers,* are nodes at which the ambiguities and tensions of traditional and modern, global and local are realized. While modernity and globalization have been beneficial to some members of Tonga—people like Sione Tapa—its experience has been different for other segments of the society, women like Vasiti and 'Ana Seini. Traditionally, maternal family members view themselves as responsible for cultural and domestic reproduction, a process which depends heavily on women's work as mothers, textile producers, and exchangers, and which includes the production of children's health. Within this context, contemporary village women walk a fine line. On the one hand, they are expected to "live well," embodying Tongan culture and tradition, and raise healthy Tongan children. On the other hand, as mothers, Tongan women are expected to support a socialization and educational program which encourages their children to become a part of the wider Tongan ethnoscape, with most eventually leaving Tonga to join the overseas diaspora.

Despite a state-level espousal of modernity (symbolized in this instance through medical services), the overall experience of global participation has been painful for village mothers. On the one hand, there has been increased access for sons and daughters to overseas education and work, high demand for the ceremonial textiles village women produce, new varieties of material goods and foods, and new sources of social prestige. On the other hand, embracing modernity has meant shrinking villages, smaller village networks, increased personal social responsibilities, dispersed families, and susceptibility to debilitating conditions such as diabetes, circulatory diseases, and arthritis. Ultimately, the intersection of modern ideals with traditional emphases on maternal roles in the context of the Tongan diaspora of the last four decades (see Lee, chapter 8) means that women's physical health is often sacrificed in the interests of their children's social health and future in a globalized society. Mothers raise the children who move overseas and become the market for the traditional goods which the mothers produce. The children become the sources of the remittances upon which the modern Tongan economy is based, remittances that are motivated by feelings of love and nostalgia for the (now unhealthy) mothers who have remained behind.

Some of the perceived benefits of participation in the modern, global society are advanced education and health services. However, fulfilling the diverse expectations required to achieve modernity yet retain the traditions that make Tonga unique leaves village women at risk to particular forms of morbidity and death.

## ACKNOWLEDGMENTS

In writing this chapter I have benefited enormously from the generosity and rigorous attention of (alphabetically) 'Ana 'Akauola, 'Ana Seini Taufa, Aara Suksi, Andie Diane Palmer, Caroline Tupoulahi Fusimalohi, Cecily Devereux, Julie Rak, Kerry James, Laumeesi Malolo, Leslie Butt, Loutoa Fifita, Malakai 'Ake, Nancy Pollock, Selina Fusimalohi, Sione Talia'uli, Sione Tapa, Tamar Gordon, Toa'ila Ngalu, and Vili Maea Malohi. I am grateful to His Majesty's Cabinet and to the Minister of Health, the Hon. Viliami Tau Tangi, for permission to conduct research in Tonga. Victoria Lockwood has provided an exemplary model of editorial finesse, insight, and patience. Funds from the Social Science and Humanities Research Council, International Development Research Centre, and University of Alberta (Canada) made the research possible, and enthusiasm from an audience at the University of Hawai'i helped encourage me to publish this material. This chapter is dedicated to the memories of Vasiti and Vili 'Aholelei, and to the futures of Mavae Ngalu, Lea'ae'ofa Fusimalohi, and Ceilidh Evans.

## REFERENCES

Anderson, Benedict. 1983. *Imagined Communities: Reflections on the Origin and Spread of Nationalism.* London: Verso.

Appadurai, Arjun. 1991. "Global Ethnoscapes: Notes and Queries for a Transnational Anthropology." In *Recapturing Anthropology: Working in the Present.* Richard G. Fox, ed. Pp. 191–210. Santa Fe: School of American Research.

———. 1996. *Modernity at Large: Cultural Dimensions of Globalization.* Minneapolis: University of Minnesota Press.

Barley, Stephen R. 1988. "The Social Construction of a Machine: Ritual, Superstition, Magical Thinking and Other Pragmatic Responses to Running a CT Scanner." In *Biomedicine Examined.* Margaret Lock and D. Gordon, eds. Pp. 497–540. Boston: Kluwer.

Baudrillard, Jean. 1998. "The End of the Millennium or the Countdown." *Theory, Culture & Society* 15(1):1–9.

Bloomfield, Siosiana. 1986. "It Is Health We Want." Unpublished M.A. thesis. University of the South Pacific, Suva.

Borofsky, Robert. 1987. *Making History: Pukapukan and Anthropological Constructions of Knowledge.* Honolulu: University of Hawai'i Press.

Bott, Elizabeth, with Tavi (Preben Kauffman). 1982. *Tongan Society at the Time of Captain Cook's Visits: Discussions with Her Majesty Queen Sālote Tupou.* Wellington: The Polynesian Society.

Burley, D. V., and Dickinson, W. R. 2001. "Origin and Significance of a Founding Settlement in Polynesia." *Proceedings of the National Academy of Sciences* (98): 11829–11831.

Caldwell, John. 1986. "Routes to Low Mortality in Poor Countries." *Population and Development Review* 12(2):171–220.

Chappell, David. 1999. "Transnationalism in Central Oceania: A Dialectic Between 'National' Polities and Polynesian Diasporas?" *The Journal of the Polynesian Society* 108(3):277–303.

Cochrane, S. H., J. Leslie, and D. J. O'Hara. 1982. "Parental Education and Child Health: Intra-Country Evidence." *Health Policy Education* 2(3/4):213–248.

Cochrane, S. H., D. J. O'Hara, and J. Leslie. 1980. "The Effects of Education on Health." World Bank Working Paper No. 405. Washington, D.C.: World Bank.

Collacott, E. E. V. 1971[1928]. *Tales and Poems of Tonga.* Honolulu: Bernice P. Bishop Museum. Reprinted by Krauss Reprint Co.

Crowley, Steven. n.d. Draft: Tonga Report on the Economic Costs of NCDs. Ministry of Health, Nuku'alofa. Unpublished manuscript.

Evans, Mike. 1997. "Gifts and Commodities on a Tongan Atoll: Understanding Intention and Action in a MIRAB Economy." Ph.D. dissertation. McMaster University.

Evans, Mike, Robert Sinclair, Caroline Tupoulahi-Fusimalohi, and Viliami Liava'a. 2001. "Globalization, Diet and Health: An Example from Tonga." *Bulletin of the World Health Organization* 79:856–862.

Foucault, Michel. 1972. *The Archaeology of Knowledge and the Discourse on Language.* New York: Pantheon Books.

———. 1974[1973]. *The Birth of the Clinic: An Archaeology of Medical Perception.* Alan Sheridan, translator. New York: Vintage Books, Random House.

———. 1980. *Power/Knowledge: Selected Interviews & Other Writings 1972–1977.* Colin Gordon, ed. New York: Pantheon Books.

Gailey, Christine. 1987. *Kinship to Kingship: Gender Hierarchy and State Formation in the Tongan Islands.* Austin: University of Texas Press.

Garenne, Michel, and Francine van de Walle. 1985. *Knowledge, Attitudes and Practices Related to Child Health and Mortality in Sine-Saloum, Senegal.* International Population Conference, Florence. Vol. 4. Ordina: Liège.

Giddens, Anthony. 1990. *The Consequences of Modernity.* Cambridge: Polity Press.

Gifford, Edward Winslow. 1985[1929]. *Tongan Society.* Bulletin No. 61/Bayard Dominick Expedition. Honolulu: Bernice P. Bishop Museum. Reprinted by Krauss Reprint Co.

Gordon, Tamar. 1998. "Border-Crossing in Tonga: Marriage in the Field." In *Families in the Field: Constructing New Models for Ethnographic Research.* Juliana Flinn, Leslie Marshall, and Jocelyn Armstrong, eds. Pp. 130–141. Honolulu: University of Hawai'i Press.

———. n.d. *Mormons and Modernity in Tonga.* Durham, N.C.: Duke University Press, forthcoming.

Hau'ofa, 'Epeli. 1993. "Our Sea of Islands." In *A New Oceania: Rediscovering Our Sea of Islands.* Eric Waddell, Vijay Naidu, and Epeli Hau'ofa, eds. Pp. 2–16. Suva: School of Social and Economic Development, University of the South Pacific.

Heiser, V. G. 1924. Letter from V. G. Heiser, International Health Board of the Rockefeller Foundation, to Dr. S. Lambert. Colonial Secretary Office files, National Archives, Suva, Fiji.

Herz, Barbara, and Anthony Measham. 1987. *The Safe Motherhood Initiative: Proposals for Action.* World Bank Discussion Papers No. 9. Washington, D.C.: World Bank.

Horan, Jane. 1998. "The Production of Textile Koloa as 'Development' in the Kingdom of Tonga." M.A. thesis. University of Auckland.

James, Kerry. 1997. "Reading the Leaves: The Role of Women's Traditional Wealth and Other 'Contraflows' in the Process of Modern Migration and Remittance." *Pacific Studies* 20(1):1–27.

Lambert, S. M. 1941. *A Yankee Doctor in Paradise.* Boston: Little, Brown.

Lane, Sandra D., and Robert A. Rubinstein. 1996. "International Health: Problems and Programs in Anthropological Perspective." In *Medical Anthropology: Contemporary Theory and Method.* Carolyn F. Sargent and Thomas M. Johnson, eds. Pp. 396–423. Westport, Conn.: Praeger.

Latour, Bruno. 1993. *We Have Never Been Modern.* Boston: Harvard University Press.

Leslie, Charles, ed. 1976. *Asian Medical Systems: A Comparative Study.* Berkeley: University of California Press.

Lindenbaum, Shirley. 1990. "Maternal Education and Health Care Processes in Bangladesh: The Health and Hygiene of the Middle Classes." In *What We Know About the Health Transition: The Cultural, Social and Behavioural Determinants of Health.* John C. Caldwell, Sally Findlay, Pat Caldwell, Gigi Santow, Wendy Cosford, Jennifer Braid, and Daphne Broers-Freeman, eds. Pp. 425–440. Canberra: Australian National University.

Lindstrom, Lamont. 1990. *Knowledge and Power in a South Pacific Society.* Washington, D.C.: Smithsonian Institution Press.

Marcus, George. 1978. "Status Rivalry in a Polynesian Steady-State Society." *Ethos* 6(4):242–269.

———. 1980. *The Nobility and the Chiefly Tradition in the Modern Kingdom of Tonga.* Wellington: The Polynesian Society.

———. 1993. "Tonga's Contemporary Globalizing Strategies: Trading on Sovereignty Amidst International Migration." In *Contemporary Pacific Societies: Studies in Development and Change.* Victoria S. Lockwood, Thomas G. Harding, and Ben J. Wallace, eds. Pp. 21–33. Englewood Cliffs, N.J.: Prentice Hall.

Mariner, William. 1991[1818]. *An Account of the Natives of the Tonga Islands.* Compiled and arranged by John Martin. London: John Murray. Reprinted by Vava'u Press, Nuku'alofa: Tonga.

Mauss, Marcel. 1990[1925]. *The Gift: The Form and Reason for Exchange in Archaic Societies.* New York: W. W. Norton.

Moengangongo, Mosikaka. 1988. "Tonga." In *Pacific Women: Roles and Status of Women in Pacific Societies.* T. Tongamoa, ed. Pp. 59–65. Suva: Institute of Pacific Studies, University of the South Pacific.

Morton, Helen. 1996. *Becoming Tongan. An Ethnography of Childhood.* Honolulu: University of Hawai'i Press.

Rubinstein, Robert A., and Sandra D. Lane. 1990. "International Health and Development." In *Medical Anthropology.* Thomas Johnson and Carolyn Sargent, eds. Pp. 367–390. New York: Praeger.

Schoeffel, Penny. 1996. *Sociocultural Features of the Economic Systems of the Pacific Islands.* Manila: Asian Development Bank.

Simons, John. 1989. Cultural Dimensions of the Mother's Contribution to Child Survival. Ford Foundation's Interdisciplinary Workshop on Mother's Education and Child Survival. Ahmedabad, India: Ford Foundation.

Small, Cathy. 1997. *Voyages: From Tongan Villages to American Suburbs.* Ithaca, N.Y.: Cornell University Press.

Spennemann, Dirk. 1990. "Changing Gender Roles in Tongan Society: Some Comments Based on Archaeological Observations." In *Tongan Culture and History.* P. Herda, J. Terrell, and N. Gunson, eds. Pp. 101–109. Canberra: Department of Pacific and Southeast Asian History, Research School of Pacific Studies, Australia National University.

Spillius, Elizabeth. 1958. *Report on a Brief Study of Mother-Child Relationships in Tonga.* Nuku'alofa, Tonga: Central Planning Department. Unpublished manuscript.

Tomlinson, John. 1999. *Globalization and Culture.* Chicago: University of Chicago Press.

Tupoulahi, Caroline. 1997. "The Socio-Cultural Antecedents of Obesity in Tonga." Ph.D. dissertation. Flinders University, Australia.

Vaka'uta, Kolotau. 2001. Health Officer's Report, Niuatoputapu and Niuafo'ou. Public presentation, Tongan Medical Association Conference, Nuku'alofa, Tonga.

van de Walle, Etienne. 1990. "How Do We Define the Health Transition?" In *What We Know About the Health Transition: The Cultural, Social and Behavioural Determinants of Health.* John Caldwell, Sally Findley, Pat Caldwell, Gigi Santow, Wendy Cosford, Jennifer Braid, and Daphne Boers-Freeman, eds. Health Transition Series 2(1):xiv–xv. Canberra: Health Transition Centre, Australian National University.

Wagner, Roy. 1975. *The Invention of Culture.* Englewood Cliffs, N.J.: Prentice Hall.

———. 1986. *Symbols That Stand for Themselves.* Chicago: University of Chicago Press.

Wallerstein, Emanuel. 1976. *The Modern World System: Capitalist Agriculture and the Origins of the European World Economy in the Sixteenth Century.* New York: Academic Press.

World Health Organization (WHO). 1981. *Global Strategy for Health for All by the Year 2000.* Geneva: World Health Organization.

Young Leslie, Heather. 1999. "Health: Tradition, Textiles and Maternal Obligation in the Kingdom of Tonga." Ph.D. dissertation. York University.

Zimmet, Paul, S. Serjeantson, G. Dowse, and C. Finch. 1990. "Killed by the 'Good Life': The Chronic Disease Epidemic: Adverse Effects of Life-Style Change in Developing Pacific Nations." In *What We Know About Health Transition: The Cultural, Social and Behavioural Determinants of Health.* John Caldwell, Sally Findley, Pat Caldwell, Gigi Santow, Wendy Cosford, Jennifer Braid, and Daphne Boers-Freeman, eds. Pp. 275–284. Canberra: Health Transition Centre, Australian National University.

# 24

# The Transformation of Person and Place on Enewetak and Ujelang Atoll

**Laurence Marshall Carucci**

*Montana State University*

In a March 2001 edition of *Newsweek,* fears of an epidemic spread of mad cow disease derived from cattle in Britain to humans at the far ends of the earth was brought more centrally into the consciousness of American readers. Underlying fears of death from a latently manifest disease lies a story of how radically agricultural production has been transformed under capitalism. If the Eurocentric age of exploration gained substantial impetus with sailors seeking more viable trade routes to India, a much-expanded market economy leads to a condition where animal fodder from Britain is consumed by livestock at the far reaches of the globe. Thence, we fear, the problem is spread to unsuspecting humans who are dependent for their diet upon incredibly intricate and extensive networks of intermediaries and exchanges. Of course, nothing is new about this knowledge. Indeed, at the societal level, Emile Durkheim used the interdependent character of complex societies to set them apart from so-called primitive societies with much less elaborated divisions of labor (1933[1893]). The twentieth century only brought to consciousness the increasingly global character of interdependence under capitalism. This chapter explores what happened to people in one such small-scale society that has been radically transformed by manipulation and victimization as a pawn in the nuclear age.

The residents of Enewetak Atoll, one of two outlying atolls in the current-day Republic of the Marshall Islands, have long held their geographic location to be, simultaneously, a blessing and a curse. Prior to the years of frequent European contact, their isolation made voyaging a particular challenge but, at the same time, it protected them from successful incursions by chiefly-dominated regimes from the Rālik and Ratak atoll chains of the Marshall Islands (see Figure 24.1). While missionaries and traders began to frequent most parts of the Marshall Islands during the second half of the nineteenth century, their influence was minimal on Enewetak until well into the twentieth century. German government entrepreneurs tried to encourage Enewetak residents to plant coconut trees and enter the copra trade in the 1890s, but local people say that they consumed the sprouted coconut

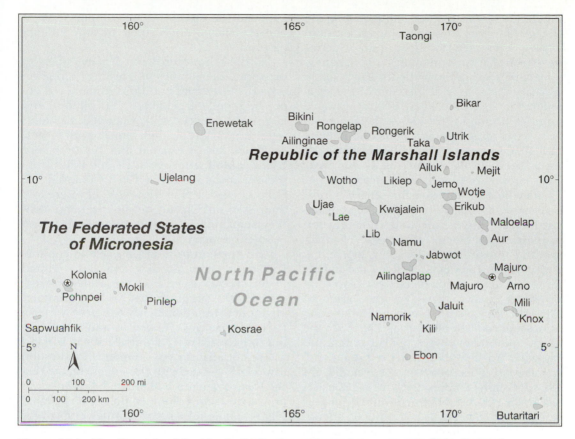

**Figure 24.1**    The Republic of the Marshall Islands and immediate surrounds (L.M. Carucci)

seedlings and offered the Germans drinking coconuts filled with urine when they returned to check on planting progress.

The first major lifestyle changes came when representatives of the American Board of Commissions for Foreign Missions arrived on Enewetak in the 1920s, soon followed by Japanese traders who, by 1940, had three small stores on Enewetak trading rice, tea, and other staples for copra (dried coconut). The Japanese agenda of economic development and exploitation for their *uchi Nan'yo* (inner South Seas), as well as plans for migration and settlement (Peattie 1988), certainly altered the course of everyday life on Enewetak. Copra production came to have a central influence on daily life, and expectations for trade goods became routine. At the same time, people felt exploited by Ijimarijen, the major trade store manager, who often tried to cheat people as they exchanged their copra for trade goods. He also schemed to dispossess local people of their land, a case that, ultimately, reached the courts in Pohnpei, the governing center of that era. In large part, however, Enewetak's isolated location and relatively desiccated environment kept it on the fringe of Japanese imperial designs until war loomed on the horizon.

The import of Enewetak's ambivalent location changed substantially with the beginning of the Pacific war. Enewetak was developed as a second-order defensive military base by the Japanese military. Then, late in 1943, Enewetak, some 3,000 miles southwest of Hawai'i, was selected as a site worth fighting for by

Allied troops, who adopted an island-hopping strategy to bypass and isolate Japanese troops as they attempted to move quickly across the North Pacific and attack the Japanese homeland. During the battle for Enewetak in February 1944, over 20 percent of the local population lost their lives, leaving a fragile group of about 140 residents. Japanese soldiers were entirely eradicated. For military strategists, Enewetak offered the advantage of being within flying distance of Guam, Truk (now known as Chuuk), and several other Japanese-held locations in the central part of Micronesia. Virtually overnight, the atoll was transformed from an under-construction Japanese military facility to a major Allied airbase and transshipment location. Remaining villagers from Enewetak, Meden, and Enjebi, the atoll's three major islets, were placed on two small "native islets" on the fringe of Enewetak and placated with generous food rations and cast-off military supplies. With the atomic bombs that obliterated Hiroshima and Nagasaki, World War II came to a rapid end. In Enewetak eyes, however, the war did not end; it simply changed its form (Carucci 1989). The United States continued nuclear testing after the war, and Enewetak offered United States military officials an ideal site from which to monitor the first round of tests on Bikini Atoll (see Kiste 1974).

The course of daily life for Enewetak people was entirely disrupted during this period when they lived on the fringe of their own atoll. While people could still fish, virtually every tree or bush on the major islets had been leveled during the battle. Military rations, at first in abundance, then in ever-decreasing quantities, were provided in lieu of local foods. Daily subsistence routines, house construction, gender relations, and education were substantially altered. Moreover, personal friendships with military personnel developed into exchanging partnerships. Handicraft and shells and promised sexual liaisons were exchanged for special foods, cigarettes, alcohol, and highly valued American clothing. Between 1944 and 1947 local people developed the idea that American wealth was inexhaustible and, somewhat naively, they took full advantage of the opportunity to become clients under their wealthy military patrons.

By 1947, however, United States plans to expand their nuclear testing program brought to a rapid end this remembered era of high-ranked chiefly distribution and largesse (Carucci 1989). Enewetak residents were moved from their small native islets on Enewetak to isolated and resource-poor Ujelang Atoll, approximately 130 miles from their homeland (Tobin 1967; Conard 1992; Carucci 1980, 1997). Although they were told their stay on Ujelang would be temporary, they remained in that location for the next thirty-three years.

The decision to move Enewetak people to Ujelang seemed entirely logical to United States officials since it fit the oversimplified, paternalistic program that the United States envisioned for their newly acquired western Pacific territories. Indeed, a national desire not to be seen as a colonial power in a world where colonialism was coming into question came face to face with the extant reality that the former Japanese Mandated Territory was now a de facto colony of the United States. High-ranking military authorities lobbied for annexing these lands as part of the United States. Instead, the region was designated a "strategic trust" to be governed by the United States under the auspices of the United Nations. A self-serving "hands-off" policy prevailed, in which the residents of the Trust Territory of the Pacific Islands were to be returned to a "traditional lifestyle" that predated the era of Japanese development and, perhaps, even the era of German governance before that. This hands-off policy placed the economic and political future of the people of the western Pacific at substantial risk.

From the beginning, United States strategic interests in these small islands and atolls were of prime concern. Used as a stepping-stone to eradicate the "Yellow Menace" (the Japanese) during the war, the region was transformed into a buffer against "Red" incursion (the Soviet Union) during the Cold War. In late 1947, the now-convoluted character of Enewetak, geographically isolated yet militarily central, proved to be a tremendous advantage to military authorities and an equal disadvantage to its indigenous inhabitants. Enewetak people simply got in the way of plans to expand the nuclear testing program. Out of fear that the all-powerful American military officials might kill them if they did not agree, the community moved to Ujelang. There, they would be forced to live as the United States envisioned them, as true primitives on the margins of an adequate subsistence. (This 1940s American image of primitive marginality was soon found to be misguided by Sahlins [1972] and Lee [1979] in the 1960s.) By separating Enewetak people from Enewetak, the place, the United States greatly elaborated the "central::peripheral" contradiction. Internationally, Enewetak became even more recognizable. At the same time, placing its inhabitants in exile on Ujelang, the United States both demonstrated and greatly enhanced the political marginality of the community that found itself silenced by its colonially constructed isolation.

With their exile on Ujelang, Enewetak people experienced a life of suffering that was far more tragic than traditional. Since the atoll had only a fraction of Enewetak's resource potential, people soon encountered conditions of incredible hardship. Many Ujelang islets, including the main residence islet, were strewn with large blocks of coral rubble as a result of a severe typhoon that struck the atoll in the 1860s. These lands were marginally productive when Enewetak people first arrived. Only following major community planting efforts and years of waiting did local land foods—pandanus, breadfruit, and coconut—become modestly produced. Life on Ujelang placed the community into cyclical famines that lasted for over fifteen years. It also created an incredible psychological burden on the community whose very sense of identity was vested in Enewetak lands.

For Europeans and Americans, it may be difficult to understand how a group of people can experience psychological trauma as a result of being moved to another place. But for most of us, land is treated as just another commodity. It is alienable, and to move from house to house and one parcel of land to another is nearly as common as purchasing a new automobile. For Marshall Islanders in general, and Enewetak people in particular, land is an integral part of a person's sense of who they are in the world and how their life makes sense as part of a certain culture. Special Marshallese words like *kapijukunen* and *lāmoran* express this deeply seated linkage to land. Not only is land hypervalued because it is scarce, but it is also extremely highly valued because it represents the collective labor of generations of people who have worked the land, transforming it from bush into habitable space. The concepts of *bed,* "staying or remaining (on)," and *jukjuk im bed,* "making a living and remaining (on)," capture the importance of perpetual occupation that leads to the unification of land and person. Both a person's labor and physical person, at death, are embedded in land in a manner that erases any distinction Europeans or Americans might make that would separate the person from the family land that he or she inhabits. Whereas Europeans live and die, Enewetak people are the visible snippet of an active group of relatives who share a totem-like identity, a clan or *jowi*. Not only does that group represent the continuity of life from ancient times until the current day (*jowi*), it is equally manifest in the family land that is the realization of generation upon generation of continuous occupation that has made untended earth into soil through toil. The physical substance of those who work the land is also, after death, embedded in the most elemental fragments of that soil.

When Enewetak people were moved to Ujelang in 1947, this sense of communal origin, of land as the visible representation of centuries of human labor, was lost. The markers in the landscape that served to codify the history of Enewetak, from the moment it became a meaningful primordial location, became distant locations for Ujelang residents. These historical markers were still imaginable in the minds of those old enough to remember, but no longer were they connected with the community, no longer continuously reshaped by Enewetak labor. No longer could these landmarks be used by people, on a moment-by-moment basis, to conjure up a sense of their proper place in a world that was fashioned of and by Enewetak locations and Enewetak historical occurrence (see Carucci 1999 for further discussion of these concepts).

Even as Enewetak identities were transformed on account of forced alienation from their homeland, people's bodies were also altered. Through their residence on Ujelang, through the consumption of the products of the land and sea, Enewetak people were changed into riUjelang (the people of Ujelang). While people told proud stories of the exploits of their Enewetak forebears, being an Ujelang person came to be equated with hardship and suffering.[1]

Given the way in which landscape and humans enliven one another and exchange life's substance back and forth like alternate generations, it was predictable that, some thirty years later, after returning to their homeland, people once again would be changed into Enewetak people. After a time, however, these new Enewetak people realized they were quite different from their predecessors. They returned to a land so transformed in physical contour and productive capacity that people soon began to refer to it disparagingly as "the New Enewetak." Many locations were unrecognizable, and the sequence of historical tales that made sense out of Enewetak in 1947 no longer fit the new landscape. This New Enewetak was manufactured by Americans, a floating fortress in the sea, devoid of the contours and landmarks that had once made it home. Recontoured into a small plateau that could support a large airstrip, most of Enewetak islet's rich surface soil was mixed with sand from the dredged lagoon reef flat to manufacture fill for the runway. When I first viewed Meden in 1976, the large habitation islet next to Enewetak, it bore rusting residues of a small city that had housed 10,000 nuclear testing personnel. Like Enewetak, it was fortified with cement, paved over in great slabs of concrete, a token coconut, ill-maintained, here and there, the shoreline rigidly demarcated in vulnerable

areas by cement sea walls to prevent the sea from comingling with the soil. Following the cleanup in 1978 and 1979, several other islets were also stripped of all vegetation and much soil to eliminate radioactivity.

The New Enewetak was an American military landscape bearing only the most distorted remains of its earlier Enewetak sensibilities. The footsteps of Etao, the cultural trickster, as he made his primordial escape from Enewetak to Bikini, were now partly obliterated. The reef shelf, from under which the first elfkin-like *menanune* stepped prior to the appearance of true humans, a location near the shore on the ocean side of Jeptan, was altered. Sacred religious sites, where deified coconut and pandanus trees once stood on the leeward end of Enewetak islet, had been leveled and buried under new layers of now-foreign earth. It *was* a new Enewetak in 1980, an Enewetak that no longer had the culturally evocative qualities that made Enewetak (the place) and Enewetak (the people) synonymous before the arrival of the Americans. With no viable land foods, limited access to sea foods, and little certainty of occupying the land parcels of their ancestors, people came to inhabit polyglot bodies so unrecognizable that they began to refer to themselves and their residence location with the epithets *jorāān* and "damage" (the approximately equivalent English term).

Such rapid and radical changes caused inhabitants of the New Enewetak to see themselves in disjointed and alien forms. To trace this embodied anomie, I begin with an analysis of longstanding cultural and historical factors that made the move to Ujelang so traumatic. Next, I present local stories of suffering and an analysis of a 1952 diet recall log recorded by Jack Tobin, district anthropologist in the Marshall Islands throughout much of the 1950s and 1960s. Finally, the diet and lifestyle changes that have accompanied the community's repatriation on Enewetak are discussed. I rely on multiple sources of information to construct the account, including historical sources, the recollections of Ujelang and Enewetak people from 1976 until the current day, and Tobin's diet records.

To situate the idea of an alienation from a person's own self, it is first necessary to ask what it means to an Enewetak person to be "one with the land." In one sense it means that the unity of land and person is deeply embedded in the collective consciousness. Not only is knowledge of the land shared by each community member, that knowledge goes back in Enewetak people's minds to the first days of existence on the face of the earth. Elder Enewetak people say that Enewetak people have resided there since the beginning of time. Whereas the residents of Kwajalein, for example, tell of a time when they arrived on the atoll from Namu (Carucci 1997), Enewetak people talk about clan members from Enewetak and Runnit islets as having been there "since the first moment." If Enewetak people were Jews, it is as if they are still living in the Garden of Eden, that original place where life on earth began.

Moreover, even though ideas about the relationship between food and identity have, of necessity, changed, my discussions with the oldest members of the Ujelang community in the 1970s made it clear that the land is embedded in persons through the products of a particular place. In eating the products of their atoll and of the land parcel that they have worked with their own hands, people take on characteristics of that place. The very core of a person's identity is given at birth by the mother, who transmits her clan essence directly to her offspring. This sacred essence must be protected and, in part, it is protected by food tabus. For a member of the "shark clan" on Enewetak, eating shark is absolutely tabu. In precisely the same way, a person cannot eat foods from her or his own land parcel that are too close to the burial grounds of immediate ancestors. But, in the estimate of Enewetak elders, eating foods grown from the soil of more-ancient ancestors is far from harmful; it is empowering. Other than the tabus around the core clan essence, it is proper and good to consume the products of a person's own land and labor. Indeed, it is dangerous to do otherwise. From the opposite perspective, eating food from foreign places and food prepared by foreign hands is

always risky. People gain strength and avoid danger by consuming the products of their own land and the fruits of their own fishing labor: fish from collectively owned Enewetak waters. And, of course, working the land is a way of investing their own persons in the land. In a logically complementary way, eating the products of the land in which they have embedded their own being is a good thing. It completes the circle of unity that makes a person one with the land and one with his or her ancestors who have been, and continue to be, part of the same land since the beginning of time.

It is certainly true that not all foods are created equal for Enewetak people. Not only are land foods and sea foods (staples and complements) quite different in character, they also embed complementary properties in human bodies. Land products contribute to internal characteristics of the body, like strength, stamina, and elements of demeanor, whereas sea foods shape external characteristics such as beautiful skin and glistening hair. And, while on Enewetak both men and women have equal rights to reside and subsist on either the land of their father or their mother, women are more closely associated with the land and land foods and men are more closely associated with the sea and foods from the sea. Therefore, not only clan identity but things like gender and beauty are linked to how, what, and where they eat.

The move from Enewetak placed people at risk since they had to consume foods from lands that, for most of the community, were foreign. The risk was greater for women, and particularly for pregnant women, who are constantly enjoined to remain close to home and eat familiar foods. In the 1970s it was considered dangerous for a pregnant woman to consume foods from Kalo and the other leeward islets of Ujelang (which were frequented by foreign spirits from Kapiliñ [the Caroline Islands]). A pregnant woman also placed herself at risk by journeying outside the reef or traveling to Majuro in the Marshall Islands, for here, too, she would be forced to venture into the men's domain, and consume foreign foods. These dangers must have been particularly great when Enewetak people were first moved to Ujelang.[2] The very person that one would become was unlike anything known in the past. Cast out of their ageless Garden of Eden, people had to eat foreign fruits and invest their energies in foreign lands with largely unknown histories and dangers. Given the doubly integrated way in which Enewetak cosmology allowed people to develop meaningful identities in relation to a communal history that they had inscribed in the landscape (a history that was then embedded in individual members of the community by consuming products of that land), it is little wonder that the move to Ujelang was extremely traumatic.

## THE MOVE TO UJELANG

In most locations in the Marshall Islands, early experiences after the war are remembered in very positive terms but, on Enewetak, the stories of this time are already tinged with ambivalence. Thankful to be alive after having survived the strafing and invasion of the atoll, local people also lost control of their atoll when they were placed on the small "native island" of Aoman. They were fed and given clothing but restricted in mobility. They eventually received permission to expand their settlement onto neighboring Bijili and to fish the waters along the northern fringe of their atoll, but land foods were virtually nonexistent. Months passed. VJ day merged into the support mission for nuclear testing on Bikini.[3] Enewetak people were moved to Meik on Kwajalein during one series of atomic tests, then back to Aoman and Bijili. The course of daily life was further disrupted. Still in awe of the Americans, still recalling with fear their recently demonstrated power, and still mourning their dead, local people felt they had no choice but to honor the wishes of military commanders. In comparison to the times that would follow, this era is recalled in relatively positive terms. People were fed, clothed, and given tools and materials to build homes and canoes. Yet people did not control their own lives. They could not sail from place to place at will. They could not subsist on their land. Indeed, the very contours of that land changed shape as they returned in awe to visit it. In the words of Obet, who was in his late teens at the time of the battle:

> The Americans were quite unlike the Japanese. The Japanese had struggled for months to build an airstrip (on Enjebi), but the Americans built one in three days. . . . And each time we went to visit (Enewetak islet), there was something new, they would have already built another building, or a piece of land had been moved from here to over there. It was a thing of amazement. However, Enewetak would never be the same. In those times (1944–1947), they were changing (it) around, destroying some things and making others. Everything was different.

Late in 1947, when Enewetak people received news that they must move to Ujelang, the community was thrown into chaos. They did not dare confront these awe-inspiring foreign chiefs. Local residents were told that their move would help to promote the cause of peace for all humankind. How could they say "no" to military leaders who had leveled their homeland with hundreds of tons of bombs and shells? In confusion and out of fear, local people agreed to leave. Aluwo, a storyteller of about fifty, recounted the event for me in 1977:

> So Ioanej and Ebream, they returned from the gathering, along with some of the elders to tell the rest of the people what (the Americans) had revealed. They said that the white people had told them we would have to move, to leave Enewetak. The women began to shriek, as if someone had died, and children began to cry. "Where would we go, back to Meik?" "No, they said it would be to a 'new island.'" . . . When they came back . . . they said we would go to Ujelang. And then, again, Ioanej and those folks came back to inform us, and when we asked where, they said, "Ujelang." And some of the women began shrieking and the children crying. And the old ones like Lūkwojeni and Ijo and Jorim, they said, "It will never be O.K. It is far too small and damaged: rocks only. That place is nothing more than a wild bush-atoll (*ailiñ uaan*)." They knew on account of the

stories they had heard from . . . Enewetak people who had lived on Ujelang during German times. . . . On this occasion, only Ernej was happy because it was his homeland, because he was really from Ujelang. It would not be a foreign place; and he ran off to tell his younger sibling (Jonni).

The military time line was short. Enewetak people arrived on Ujelang less than two weeks after they were asked to leave their homeland. Arriving at their new island just prior to Christmas, they celebrated Christmas Day with extremely mixed emotions. From their throats (the seat of emotions for Marshall Islanders) came counterpoint songs scripted to evoke happiness, yet embedded in those same throats were the yearnings and moans of a people wrenched from their ancestors and their homes. "Normally infused with joy, the entire event is recounted as 'a *Kūrijmōj* thrown off in sadness.' Most people longed for a time in the near future when they could return home: they remained on Ujelang for the next thirty-three years" (Carucci 1997:5).

On Ujelang, the 139 Enewetak people who had been fortunate enough to survive the war at least had a minimal sense of bearings. During German times, a few Enewetak people were brought to Ujelang to work on the copra plantation that had been planted on expropriated Ujelang lands. Some years later a small group of Ujelang people who had left their atoll in disgust after working their own lands for the benefit of others returned (via Pohnpei and the Marshall Islands) to Enewetak, to marry into families they knew from the Ujelang plantation days. While these ties with Ujelang were useful to the newcomers in ascertaining potential resource areas, Enewetak people's knowledge of the place was superficial. In the words of one consultant:

When we first moved here to Ujelang, we did not know anything. But Joseph and his fathers (Ernej and Jonni) they showed us around and told us various things—oh, that the surround fishing location was there to the windward and the most productive coconut toddy trees were there or there, in Jenete (a series of land parcels) and . . . and those sorts of things.

And they showed us where the local deities had lived, and other things. But all of this (latter) knowledge was meaningless (of no value) to us, since these were gods of ancient Ujelang people, not of Enewetak people. Some people felt these spirits were dangerous and they were afraid of them, but after a few years it became clear that they would not damage us.

Exploring the atoll like tourists with a guide, Enewetak people began the process that would soon transform them into "the people of Ujelang." But they could not, in the course of thirty-three years, develop the fully grounded history that, over hundreds or thousands of years, had embedded them in the soil, the wave patterns, and the atmospheric conditions of Enewetak. Making the best of their experience of exile on Ujelang, people began to develop a historical consciousness suited to their new place, but in this endeavor, they could only encounter a sense of cultural ambivalence. This was true because, for the two generations that people spent becoming Ujelang people, the detailed knowledge and experience required to maintain and elaborate upon their collective consciousness as Enewetak people were necessarily set aside. Borrowing an apt scene from the Old Testament, Ujelang people spoke of themselves as one of the Lost Tribes of Israel, wandering in isolation from their homeland.

The shift from the U.S. Navy governance to governance as part of the Strategic Trust Territory administered under the United Nations by the United States occurred in 1951. With this shift, local people began to feel a sense of stagnation and abandonment. The stagnation resulted from funding cutbacks; Kiste notes that the entire Trust Territory budget was capped at 7.5 million dollars (1993:71). It also resulted from the U.S. commitment to a hands-off policy that, years later, would result in claims that the United States was trying to maintain a "human zoo" (Heine 1974). The sense of abandonment during this era was felt in greatest measure on Ujelang, the most peripheral area of the Marshall Islands. Some 630 miles from Majuro, Ujelang had limited contact with the district center and received little support from the Trust Territory government. When Enewetak people were told they would have to leave their home atoll, they were also told that the move would be temporary and that the Americans would continue to watch over them. Not surprisingly, on Ujelang they came to feel that they had been totally abandoned. For a period of time, the Navy maintained a weather station on the atoll that kept people supplied with entertainment if not much food, but, with the departure of the Navy, serious hardship and suffering became even more apparent. In thinking back on this era, people recall that the earliest times of hardship began around 1950 or 1951. Up until that time, life on Ujelang was satisfactory, since the products of land and sea had not been harvested for over a decade and somewhat more food was available. Throughout the remaining years of the 1950s, up until the late 1960s, however, the community was mired in despair, living through frequent periods of famine and having given up all hope of being returned to Enewetak. Not until 1969, a year after local people became so disillusioned that they staged a "strike" to raise public awareness of their dismal living conditions, did the sense of futility on Ujelang begin to abate (Asselta 1971). Even after that time, hunger was not unknown.

Many forms of evidence indicate how serious the suffering was on Ujelang during these years. First, there are many similar stories that elders told during my stay on the atoll from 1976 through 1978. While stories of suffering are innumerable, those that were repeated again and again focus on a number of core incidents. They include famine and hunger, near-starvation and death from illness, food shortage and the limitations of the environment on Ujelang (fishing/collecting), the polio epidemic, the measles epidemic, the rat infestation, the strike, and then an easing of suffering during the 1970s, but with continued homesickness and desire to return to Enewetak.

In a recent article (Carucci 2001), I argue that the stories Enewetak people tell today of suffering on Ujelang lack the kind of depth, elaboration, and emotion that stories of the same events had in the 1970s. This is entirely logical, since the experiences of those events are far more remote than they were in 1976–1978. At that time, people still knew what it was like to be hungry. Having just lived through a severe food shortage in the first months of 1978, it was easier for people to remember what it was like to live within a body that had already begun to reject the conditions of its own existence.

The following story about life on Ujelang in the 1950s and 1960s is a modestly elaborated version recounted by a woman in her early forties. She recounted the story as we sat in her house near the end of the food shortage that lasted from late January through March, 1978:

Well, perhaps we (endeared, inclusive) are very hungry now with people sailing here and there throughout the atoll to search for food, and with everyone digging arrowroot, consuming *pikūkkūk* (an arrowroot-based Ujelang food), and scraping coconuts too unripe for harvesting from their shells with their teeth (because the fully mature, copra-stage coconuts are gone), and with everyone eliminating shit so watery it evaporates or seeps into the sand, with many people sick and some of the babies nearing death, but things are still O.K. The young ones call this a famine (*ñita*), but in comparison with the times of the past, this is just a severe hunger.

(Meditates) . . . Those times previously were difficult days on Ujelang, for then, the times of hunger, of real famine, were more frequent than the times of health. God have mercy on us (*kapokwekej*). Many children and old ones died as a result of those times of danger. Tebij, that man who is the grandfather of Paul and Mahten, well, he was one of those who died on account of the famines. And infants, well there were so many who disappeared (died), you could not count them. Their stomachs stuck out like they were bloated, and you would never think that they were hungry. Full; as you looked at them you would think they were very full. But, in fact they were hungry. And their stomachs were soft all the time, and when they defecated, it was just water, hot foamy water that winnowed away into the sand. Just like nowadays. But they would get hot fevers, then cold chills: hot fevers, then cold and sweaty. And then, in just a moment, they would be gone. Dead, they would never move again. Their life was gone. And, in those days, the wailing across the village was constant. We grieved, but there was hardly time to feel sorry for those who died, for we had to try harder and continue working or else all of the others would die as well.

So, you see, when Tebij died, some members of his family had to pause and prepare for the funeral. Some women grieved, and a few of the men had to dig the grave. But, at the same time, while the men dug, others had to remain in the sea and collect food. They had to redouble their labors because they would then fish for themselves and their own family as well as for the family of that other one, the one who had died. And, as you know, they were already in the sea from some time prior to the appearance of the sun until the sun once again dove (into the sea in the evening). There was no breakfast. The children would wake up crying, and they would never stop crying on account of their hunger. They would scrape coconut with their teeth until their stomachs were slightly filled but, at times, even the supply of coconuts was exhausted. You could scrounge around Jabōnbok (the windward-most tip of Ujelang) until you were exhausted and find only one, perhaps two. Even the immature copra-stage nuts on the tallest coconuts in Jabōnbok were gone, for the young men had already climbed them and stripped away their fruits.

And so, the infants would just cry, because there was no milk at their mothers' breasts. Only the smallest quantity (of milk), but it was of no use because it was so watery—like rainwater. And the women would have to make *aojek*, an arrowroot-based jello, often just with water because there were no drinking coconuts, just to keep the infants from crying. If it was a good day, perhaps a woman's husband would come home by noon with a few fish, or if (he) had bad luck, perhaps a few clams. And, as you know, during these times of famine, fishing is very difficult. Everyone is in the sea from morning until night, and even on Enemanōt or Kalo

(the islets furthest from Ujelang islet) there are inadequate numbers of fish. And even the fish that remain are easily frightened.

(*LMC: So what did you do during these times, since your husband was away, working?*) Well, there were times when he was here, but most of the time we experienced even greater misfortune. Sometimes that fellow, my mother's husband, would bring us fish. Tiny grouper of a sort, for as you know, he always likes to fish for small grouper along the reef shelf. Or my (extended) siblings, would bring the remains of some clams or fish after they had divided and kept a portion for their own children. But we were truly unfortunate. Many days we had only arrowroot jello. And then, when the arrowroot was all exhausted on Ujelang, because we had no way to sail (to an outer islet), then I would make soup from *markinjojo* (leaves of a bush plant, *Vigna marina*), or we would cut *liok* (pandanus runner roots), and I would boil them, and we would chew on them like sugar cane. The thing is, they had no content. They have a bitter taste, but if you chewed on them and chewed on them, just like a piece of pandanus, they would seem to fill you up. It was better than nothing. The children would stop crying, and we would have an opportunity to go and search for some other food.

You know, this was an era of great sadness, for even though Ujelang people are known for their generosity and caring, it was very difficult to be kind when we were starving. And those of us who lived in the center of town had an even greater hardship for, if you caught some fish, or found an unripe pandanus hidden on the ocean side of Āne-koñe, how is it that you could get it home without being stingy? You had to walk through town to get home and yet, every time you would encounter your relatives, with their children crying and still crying more out of hunger, you could not *not* give them some of your food item. And so, by the time that you arrived home, there would be only a little remainder to share with your own children, even though you had been fortunate in your food gathering that day. Those on the fringes of the village, they were a little bit luckier. But still, they too had to share. Their families continued dying and dying as well. So, we all became hungrier and hungrier together.

Life on Ujelang before was extremely difficult. Many people became ill and, because, they had no strength, many died.

The context of telling this story on Ujelang atoll gives it a sort of reality that is hard to remember after nearly twenty years of life on Enewetak. At the time this story was told in 1978, following a typhoon and then a tropical storm, we lived through a four-month period without a supply ship. The final six weeks of this period were termed *ñita,* "famine" or "starvation" by Ujelang people, though the contours of this food shortage were nothing like the periods of famine in the 1950s. In those days, people recall that it was not uncommon for "nearly a year" to pass between supply ships, and Jack Tobin (personal communication), searching through incomplete stevedores' records many years later, found periods of over eight months between the visits of supply ships. Even those records, however, did not record the availability of supplies on board and, being at the end of the delivery line, it was not uncommon for supply boats to arrive on Ujelang to purchase copra with little or nothing in the hold for sale.

Again, the environment on Ujelang and the atoll's small size worked to place local people in an impoverished state. One man, now dead, recalled:

The field trip ships never wanted to come to Ujelang because there was so little copra. We would even climb the trees to throw down nuts that were not yet copra-stage nuts, but there were never enough. The entire atoll would produce less than Enjebi alone. Ninety ton, and that was just the ocean side (of Enjebi) for, you see, is it not the case that Enjebi is really deep (wide from lagoon to ocean)? Well, during Japanese times, just on Enjebi (a main islet in the northern sector of Enewetak) we would compete to make copra, and it could produce far more than all of Ujelang.

(*LMC: What could you make on Ujelang?*) Well, if things were good, 50 ton, maybe 60.

And then, things just got worse (on Ujelang). For when the ship did not come, we got really hungry. You could not make as much copra because you needed to eat the copra-stage nuts, and drink the drinking coconuts. And even when the ship came, it would have no food, for it would already have travelled around *Kapinmeto* (the central western atolls), and all of the supplies were gone. One time there was only tabasco, and cloth. White: all of the colored fabrics were gone!

So then you would make 20-some (tons), maybe 30. And it would take maybe five or six months, if not more (to recover), because you already drank all of the drinking coconuts, so there would be no *waini* (copra-stage nuts).

Fishing was equally difficult during the frequent times of food shortage:

As for the men, well, we were in the ocean from before dawn until dusk. Who says anything like "breakfast"? There was a single meal, after fishing, if life was treating you well, and by that time night had already arrived. And if you were not fortunate, there would be no fish. Nothing! Or sometimes, just a few *mejānwōd* (small clams). Every day, from one month to the next, all of the men would be in the ocean (gestures: from dawn to dusk). Each man had to really struggle, for the children were hungry. They would wake up crying, and that night, when you returned (from fishing) they would still be crying. It was truly a thing of pity. The men tried so hard fishing that all of us had red hair. You would think we were white men! But our hair was really frizzy and stiff (brittle). We were in the ocean all of the time, and in the bright sun our heads were cooked like lobsters in an earth oven.

While local people attribute men's blond hair to baking in the sun, the discolored, frazzled, brittle characteristics are classic signs of malnutrition. Other stories about children and babies confirm this interpretation. One woman, for example, says:

Well, we really craved fish, because fishing was very difficult since all of the men were in the sea every day, and the fish became very easily spooked. My daughter had small children then . . . scarcely more than infants, and their skin was very bad. The least scratch, and their skin would really be damaged, for their food objects were inadequate. The fish was never adequate to repair the wounds, and so all the time their skin was damaged. They just ate arrowroot and sprouted coconut, arrowroot soup and arrowroot bread. It is funny, because when I was a child all of the people thought I had such beautiful skin, shiny and without blemish. But here (on Ujelang), there was not enough fish, and so my grandkid's skin was badly blemished and their hair also lacked beauty. It was like strands of coconut husk, red and stiff, not reflective and green (with blue-green highlights).

Hardship affected all aspects of daily life. Even the simplest of supplies had to be obtained locally. For example, entire days were spent boiling seawater for salt:

Do you see that spot where the coral rock protrudes into the lagoon? . . . When I was a youth my siblings and I used to come there with my mother and the other women to boil ocean water. We would boil sea water from morning until night for two or three days. Those of us who were children would gather and bring wood onto the coral rock, and the women would keep the fire blazing and bring sea-water. It was a lot of work. Nevertheless, in those days, all the time you would go until the salt (supply) was exhausted, because there were so few (supply ship) trips.

The extremely marginal conditions on Ujelang had substantial effects on the day-to-day organization of the community. Not only were people's efforts fully dedicated to subsistence, the lack of contact with the wider world, the lack of supplies and communications that had been fairly dependable during the Japanese era, had substantial effects on medical care, education, and even on church membership. One resident recalls with some humor the inverse relationship between church membership and the availability of cigarettes:

Well, in those days smoking was really a joke, because the cigarettes would be quickly exhausted. . . . People always used (small-cigarette) pipes because there were so few cigarettes. The ship still would be pulling up its anchor, and the men who smoked already had cut their cigarettes (into small segments for the cigarette pipes). And if there was even one (liquor) bottle of (cigarette) pieces, a man was in luck, because money was so scarce. And after just a little time, the smokers would dig up their (hidden) bottles of cigarettes, and the cigarettes would be gone. Then cigarette yearning would appear, and the people who smoked would be digging under house platforms to seek out the remaining shreds of tobacco. After that, they would go out and smoke leaves (from bush plants) for a while. But they were worse than bad, very bitter.

Oh, life during those times was ironic because after their cravings, the smokers would all repent and become members of the church. Yeah, all of those bad guys (i.e., non-church members) would repent . . . and the number of church members would really increase. And then, after some months, a ship would appear, and all of the smokers would fall from grace.

## QUESTIONS OF SCALE

The psychological impact of living and working on foreign lands served as a major source of impoverishment in people's lives on Ujelang. But there are also ecological reasons that account for the suffering that people experienced on Ujelang. Indeed, both Enewetak and Ujelang are outliers, and Enewetak is only slightly closer to Majuro. Nevertheless, on Enewetak, people had access to a plethora of resources from land, sea, and air. The atoll is large, 378 square miles, with 2.7 square miles of land. In contrast, Ujelang's lagoon is less than 1/13 the size, with 27.5 square miles inside the fringing reef and 1.2 square miles of land. The reef space, which bears a direct relationship to fishing potential, is also vastly greater on Enewetak, about seven or eight times the reef space on Ujelang. In terms of small islets suited to birds and turtles, Ujelang has only a triad of true bird islets, Bokenenelapemen and Kidinen in the far northwestern quadrant of the atoll, whereas Enewetak has four series of such small islets with, perhaps, eight times the subsistence potential of the Ujelang islets. Clams constitute a dependable food source that becomes especially important in times of nutritional stress; Enewetak is a renowned source of giant clams (*kabur*) and abounds with other smaller varieties of clams. Ujelang has no giant clams, only substantially smaller species, the largest, *dimooj*, being five to ten times smaller than giant clams.

While the land areas of the two atolls are more comparable in size than the seafood and bird exploitation areas, with Enewetak having a bit over twice as much land area, the quality of the land is not at all comparable. As mentioned, Ujelang was the site of a major typhoon in the 1860s and much of the land on the main islet and the downwind islets fringing the southen half of Ujelang (where most of the land lies) is covered with piles of coral rubble. From the time that Enewetak people first arrived until their return to Enewetak in 1980, "burning rocks" was a common occupation. Rather than burning trash and cleared brush in one standard location as in other parts of the Marshall Islands, Ujelang people moved the fires from spot to spot across their land parcel, and rolled large blocks of coral into their fire pits to split the boulders into smaller pieces. Within the village space, thirty years of burning reduced the chunks of coral to fragments one to eight inches in diameter. But, with the exception of a tiny garden just to the leeward side of the center of town (where Japanese had imported topsoil from Pohnpei), even the village lands were extremely unsuited to agriculture. Outside of town, coral cobbles are much larger, although years of labor transformed these rocks from small boulders to chunks from six inches to two feet in diameter.

In the course of three decades, Ujelang residents replanted the entire atoll with new coconuts to replace unproductive trees from German times. They planted large numbers of pandanus and breadfruit, but the adverse conditions made such endeavors extremely arduous, and local people recall that it was not until well into the 1960s that the breadfruit trees began to produce any significant amount of fruit. In 1947 there were only four breadfruit trees on Ujelang, and those not very productive trees on the windward end of the main islet. There was also a paucity of pandanus, a land food that had been central

to people's lives on Enewetak. On Ujelang, people recall that initially there were only *edwaan*, "wild bush pandanus," and even these were in short supply. The food records collected by Jack Tobin during a visit in 1952 show that even immediately after the arrival of a supply ship, people were living largely on coconut, arrowroot, a few squash, and variable quantities of seafood and birds. This diet compares very poorly with what they had available on Enewetak immediately before the war.

## TOBIN'S 1952 UJELANG DIET

Not only is the story of Ujelang people's suffering recorded in their stories, the diet records kept by Jack Tobin, Marshall Islands district anthropologist, during his 1952 visit to the atoll provide a second source of evidence. Tobin also recorded a second, less-complete diet survey in 1957. Tobin's food records offer the tremendous advantage of having been collected on the spot during a time when the patterns of day-to-day life and the availability of foods on Ujelang was far different than in the 1970s and 1980s. At the same time, Tobin's notes on dietary consumption are less complete than we might like. Rather than tracking the food each person consumed, he records only foods prepared for each family (that is, of a group that eats together), along with the number of children and adults in each of these food consumption groups. Moreover, Tobin asked people what they ate during the day rather than tracking actual consumption. As has been shown, this diet recall method is less than ideal. Finally, Tobin does not record actual weights of food prepared or consumed. Nevertheless, Tobin's dietary records give us the best available picture of subsistence practices and consumption patterns on Ujelang in the 1950s. An analysis of Tobin's food records, with considerable assistance from Mary H. Maifeld, a registered dietitian who has worked with Enewetak people for over two years, yields the following conclusions:[4]

The caloric intake in this diet suggests that an average adult in the fifteen sampled families consumed about 1,300 calories per day, a very marginal intake as judged by United States Department of Agriculture (USDA) or World Health Organization (WHO) standards. (Averages for active adults should be 2,538 kcal/person/day.) Based on guidelines used to establish children's consumption levels for U.S. Recommended Dietary Allowances (ages three to fourteen years), Ujelang children were calculated to ingest 78 percent of the adult average, or 1,014 calories per day. USDA school food service guidelines indicate that children should consume 1,977 kcal/child/day. It is also important to note that a *keemem* on Friday of the week of Tobin's visit overinflates nutrient levels for the entire week's records. The *keemem*, "first birthday party," is a major festive event when the family of a one-year-old child provides large quantities of feast foods for the entire community. The community welcomes and blesses the infant and, in ancient times, this was the time when children were given a name and an identity in the community. In October 1952, some families obtained over half of their entire caloric intake for the week from this one meal. It appears likely that the *keemem* Tobin recorded had been postponed until the arrival of the supply boat. Most of the European food in people's diet was obtained from the *keemem*.

Of several possible sources of bias that might make Tobin's diet unrepresentative of a typical week, only one proved significant: the presence of the islandwide first birthday celebration on Friday night. Another major source of dietary variation derives from the monthly and yearly fishing cycles. Tobin's diet was collected during the dark of the moon (October 14–19), however, the second most desirable part of the lunar cycle for fishing. Similarly, in terms of the yearly fishing cycle, the diet was collected at a midway point between the most difficult winter months (December to February) and the highly productive wet season fishing times.

If a correction factor is included in Tobin's diet to adjust for the *keemem* (first birthday celebration), the diet becomes more reflective of an "average weekly consumption," but the levels of dietary intake are even less adequate. According to birth records I collected in the 1970s, there were nine births in 1951. Concomitantly, nine *keemem* would have been celebrated in 1952. On average, one *keemem* would have been held every six weeks. When Tobin's diet is corrected for this infrequent feast, the average Ujelang adult consumed 916 kcal/day, only slightly more than one-third of the United States daily recommended calorie level for an adult. At 78 percent of the adult average, children would have received 712 kcal/day![5]

In spite of the extreme marginality of Tobin's 1952 diet, this was not a time Ujelang people would call *ñita*, "famine." By local definition, famines begin well after all imported foods are exhausted, when local foods become extremely hard to find. Such true famines occurred frequently in the 1950s and 1960s, but Tobin's food records were not made during an extreme food shortage. Rather, this food record was inscribed soon after a supply ship had delivered the district anthropologist to Ujelang Atoll.

Other evidence also shows that Tobin's diet does not reflect famine conditions. For example, famines are described as periods when a single daily meal was eaten, with leftovers saved for early the following morning. In Tobin's diet, people consume two or three meals each day of the week. Even though caloric intakes in Tobin's 1952 diet are well below acceptable levels for the maintenance of good health, no true "starvation foods" are recorded (pandanus runner roots, heart of palm, *markinjojo* [*Vigna marina leaves*], and so on). Indeed, 8 percent of the food in this 1952 diet is imported. Finally, the dispersed pattern of settlement that typifies periods of extreme hunger was not in effect at the time Tobin recorded this diet. Beginning with Boas, anthropologists have noted this strategy of spreading out across the landscape to maximize food-gathering success (Lee 1979). Nine days after the end of the typhoon and tropical storm in December 1977/January 1978), Ujelang residents began to spread out across the atoll in order to better exploit available resources. In October 1952, the community was gathered as a unit in the main village on Ujelang islet. All of these clues provide strong evidence that Tobin's visit did not occur at a time that local people would have classified as *ñita*. There were many times when people experienced greater food shortages on Ujelang.

In terms of land foods, coconut, arrowroot, and squash provided the basic staples in the 1952 diet. Neither of the high-nutrient Marshallese staples, breadfruit or pandanus, appears in the diet records. The lack of pandanus and breadfruit in Tobin's records is the direct result of inadequate planning by the United States at the time Enewetak people were moved to Ujelang. As an old German coconut plantation, Ujelang had few of the subsistence plants that were common on most atolls. These tree fruits had been cut down since they detracted from the amount of land that could be dedicated to raising coconut. The pitiful supply of breadfruit and pandanus is constantly noted in the starvation stories of the 1950s told by Ujelang people. Only a few *edwaan* (an undesirable variety of bush pandanus) were available during the first ten years of residence. Breadfruit was also extremely rare until around 1962–1963 when the seedlings planted by Enewetak people had begun to mature. Only four breadfruit trees were growing on Ujelang when Enewetak people arrived in 1947. They were marginally productive trees that had little subsistence value for the displaced community.

Over the long run, the gross inadequacy of calories and high-quality protein reflected in Tobin's 1952 diet led to severely compromised health status. Under these conditions, people lost much of their ability to resist diseases. The result was precisely what occurred with the measles epidemic in 1963 when two apparently vigorous respected elders, Tebij and Elija, succumbed to the disease within a few days of one another. Three or four children also died at this time.

The nutrient deficiencies that people experienced on Ujelang reflect the difference between living on a small atoll like Ujelang and a location like Enewetak. When the United States moved the people of Bikini and Enewetak to allow for nuclear testing, President Truman promised to make them wards of the United States, and to treat them with honor and respect (see Kiste 1974 for information on Bikini). In fact, with the end of the Navy era, Ujelang people were left without support on a small, resource-poor atoll a fraction the size of Enewetak. The cycles of famine that the community endured provide strong evidence that the United States promises to promote the well-being of Trust Territory residents were broken.

Not only did Ujelang people's health status suffer as a result of the shortage of protein and calories, numerous nutrient deficiencies also align with conditions described on Ujelang. Indeed, even on Enewetak, where protein and calorie malnutrition have been largely eliminated, nutrient deficiencies continue to be a problem (the cause of these problems are discussed below). The nutrient deficiencies evident in Tobin's 1952 diet are substantial. The following table summarizes the nutrient levels for an "overall" average adult (averaging adult intakes in fifteen recorded families).[6]

While the array of nutrient deficiencies is broader than that presented here, including a variety of B vitamin-related problems, this example focuses on evidence for shortages of vitamins A and C, calcium, iron, protein, and the concomitant effects. In terms of adult dietary shortages, community members received an average of 51 percent of the U.S. Recommended Dietary Allowances (RDA) for calories. Fiber intake averaged 31 percent, iron 53 percent, vitamin A 23 percent, vitamin C 50 percent, calcium 24 percent, and protein 34 percent. In the two families at highest nutritional risk, adults received only 31 percent or 36 percent of the required calories, and much of this food came from a single meal, the *keemem*. Adult members of these two families received only 13 or 14 percent of the recommended fiber, 32 to 35 percent of the iron, 3 to 5 percent of the vitamin A, 19 or 36 percent of the recommended vitamin C, 11 or 19 percent of the calcium, and 25 or 34 percent of the recommended protein. Moreover, much of the protein was not obtained

**Table 24.1**   Average Nutrient Intakes for Adult Members of the Community

| 1952 Ujelang Diet | Average of 15 Families | US RDA Target Levels | % of Target |
|---|---|---|---|
| Calories | 1,300 kcal | 2,538 kcal | 51% |
| Cholesterol | 85 mg | <300 mg | 28% |
| Sodium | 315 mg | <3,000 mg | 10.5% |
| Fiber | 7.8 g | ~25 g (20–35) | 31% |
| Iron | 6.9 mg | 13 mg | 53% |
| Vitamin A | 232 RE | 1,000 RE | 23% |
| Vitamin C | 30 mg | 60 mg | 50% |
| Calcium | 283 mg | 1,200 mg | 23.6% |
| Protein | 43.3 g | ≥127 g | 34% |
| Carbohydrate | 215.4 g | 317 g | 68% |
| Total fat | 28.4 g | ≤85 g | 33% |
| Saturated fat | 10.9 g | ≤8.5 g | 128% |

from high biological protein sources, increasing the likely volatility of their health status. Even for the best-fed family in the village, the levels of vitamin A (43 percent), vitamin C (50 percent), and calcium (38 percent) are of serious concern, and protein (69 percent), fiber (63 percent), and sodium (just over 300 mg.) are very marginal. Average nutrient intakes for adult members of the community are described in Table 24.1.

Children, of course, are placed in an even more compromised situation, since their requirement for protein (which must help build new cells as well as repair worn and damaged cells) is much higher in relation to body mass than is the adult requirement. Similarly, calcium and vitamin A are particularly critical for proper bone development. Vitamin C works to cement developing cells together and is essential for healing wounds. Iron is important to build red blood cells as the body grows, and it also transports oxygen to the cells. Hence, children have higher requirements of each of these nutrients in relation to their body size than do adults; yet, on Ujelang, they suffered from inadequate levels of these crucial elements.

The averages described in Table 24.1, of course, obscure the specific intakes of any particular family. Adult members of the least-well-nourished family received only 31 percent of the needed calories, 13 percent of the fiber, 32 percent of the iron, 3 percent of the vitamin A, 19 percent of the vitamin C, 11 percent of the calcium, and 25 percent of the

protein recommended for healthy adults. The most-well-nourished family was *far* more well fed that any other family, receiving 93 percent of the needed calories, yet only 43 percent of the vitamin A and 38 percent of the calcium. The second most-well-nourished family is far more representative of the well-fed residents; adult members of this family received 60 percent of the calories, 36 percent of the fiber, 62 percent of the iron, 20 percent of the vitamin A, 40 percent of the vitamin C, 25 percent of the calcium, and 38 percent of the protein recommended for healthy adults. These figures give some idea of the serious and pervasive levels of nutrient inadequacy that were experienced on Ujelang, even during a period when people were *not* experiencing famine.

Stories of life on Ujelang provide little evidence that people died directly of malnutrition; nevertheless, they describe numerous signs of vitamin deficiency and malnutrition that point to a seriously compromised health status. The descriptions of life on Ujelang during the first Peace Corps years, and particularly the experiences of those volunteers who first arrived in the mid-1960s, are also telling. These are stories that, at least in three or four cases, I have heard recounted from both sides. The first Peace Corps volunteer came at a time when life was still extremely trying. He remembers clearly the infestation of rats that overran the atoll and, equally, the impossibility of hoarding his own food while hungry children gathered around him as he ate. Ujelang residents remember clearly the contradictions that this young man faced. In the words of one Ujelang person:

> Well, when (the first Peace Corpsman) first came to the island things were much worse than they are today (June, 1977). It was the time when the rats nearly took over this place (Ujelang). Everywhere you looked there were rats, maybe 100 rats for every person. It got so bad that you could never sleep. . . . Each night before bed, you had to bathe the babies, and wash your hands and face, and especially your ears and the children's noses, particularly if their noses were running, or the rats would come and chew on your fingers or your ears, or toes . . . until they were bloody. And for mature people it was a little better, but for children, they were so disturbed that they could not sleep, so we had to build boxes, and (the Peace Corpsman) said they were like coffins, for the small children to be able to sleep. It was a difficult time.
>
> (*LMC: So, what next?*) Well, after a while, some months or maybe a year, they sent some people to deal with the rats—some Marshallese (government workers). They came and tried cats and traps and then, finally, we had to poison them. And the dogs—as you know—now there are not any dogs on Ujelang . . . well, that is when they said "Kill the dogs! Eliminate them all!" . . . because the dogs were chasing the cats and killing them. So we killed dogs, and killed dogs, until they were gone. . . .
>
> (A third man joins the conversation.) . . . Yes, that is correct, there were two types of traps. The regular white people's traps that we tried, and then traps made of pipe that we made and put (the bait inside). (Third man: and don't forget the fees). Oh, yeah. (The government officials) also paid us a fee [bounty]: five cents a rat. (Third man: No, it was five cents for *two* rats). Wejej! Was it not five cents? . . . Anyway, those of us who were still somewhat older (unmarried) young men, we went trapping rats a lot until, in the end, they were better.

Another man recalls:

> Well, not only did they (the rats) damage your sleep. There were so many that they almost ate all of the drinking coconuts.

(*LMC: They would climb the trees?*) Yeah, sure, all the time. They climbed and exhausted all of the coconuts. Sometimes you would climb a tree to throw drinking coconuts and on an entire spathe there would be only one drinkable coconut. Or sometimes you would climb and throw coconuts down and, nothing. It was really bad. And the same with the copra stage nuts. They would eat the copra stage nuts until they were gone.

Another man recalls the internal conflict that was endured by the first Peace Corpsman:

> In those days, it was still the time when the government supply ships would stop coming and all of the people would be hungry, just as in previous years. And (the first Peace Corps), well, he still had a little food that he had stored his footlocker and locked. Not a lot, . . . just enough for him to eat a small amount, eat a small amount, and then see (things through until) the time of the ship. Nevertheless, when he cooked, the children would come and watch him cook, because in those times there was no one who was not hungry. And this man (the first Peace Corps), perhaps he really felt sorry for those children, because all of the time they came and watched him during eating times. So even while he was cooking he was crying; crying because he felt sorry for the children. And when he finished cooking, he said "Here!" and gave his food-class thing, a little rice or whatever, to the children, and went in his house still crying.
>
> (*LMC: and what did he eat?*) Just like you. He ate all of the food that we ate. A little at a time, a little at a time, and stayed alive.

My own experience on Ujelang, even in the mid-1970s, perhaps also lends credence to these stories of the past. In the 1970s, field trip ships visited Ujelang every two to four months and, with the exception of the single six- or eight-week famine, we seldom were totally out of food. Nevertheless, during my time on Ujelang I lost twenty pounds (from an already lean body), and experienced the sort of difficulties the young grandmother describes for her grandchildren's poor skin. The smallest scratch could take two or three months to heal, often becoming ulcerated and much larger than the original wound.

Seemingly fully healed wounds would later rupture, creating new scars that repaired very slowly from within. I did eat what everyone else ate, but having two purchasers from the ship meant that my family was able to stave off periods of food scarcity a bit longer than most. I also took a multivitamin every day during this twenty-five-month period on Ujelang.

During the famine, I moved from the village to my adopted family's land parcel on the windward end of Ujelang. Much as in the stories from the 1950s, there was seldom a time we were not hungry, and dawn until dusk was spent fishing, collecting, and processing or preparing food. We ate one meal per day, usually arrowroot, baked into unleavened arrowroot bread, or boiled into jello-like balls. In the morning we ate a few sprouted coconuts and drank a couple of drinking coconuts, these gathered by travelling further and further toward the windward tip of Ujelang. Most of a day was spent processing arrowroot, or walking to a "secret spot" where a far-from-fully-ripe pandanus might be obtained to boil and mix with the arrowroot. Every day also meant fishing at varied times of the day or night, depending upon the tides. On days we were unsuccessful, our arrowroot was complemented simply with a drinking coconut or, on more fortunate days, with a few small bites of clam. Every day we discussed moving to the other end of Ujelang, to Enelap or Enemanōt, for each day it became more difficult to find the minimum foods required to remain alive. Men of my age joked with me about the lethargy that, I believe, all of us must have felt. It was their theory that Americans needed more complements or meats than local folks required, and they knew we were all far short of these foods.

The 1978 famine eased when a field trip ship appeared in late February bringing 100 bags of rice. It was not enough to last for there were over 325 people on Ujelang at the time. Nevertheless, it helped us bridge the final weeks until a properly stocked field trip ship finally anchored at the atoll.

Even though Tobin's dietary records suggest that the time he describes was not a period of famine (and not even a time of hunger like that the community experienced in 1978), there is strong evidence that there were many cycles of famine in the 1950s and 1960s when conditions were far worse. These conditions were not the result of natural causes, but of political decisions made in Washington, D.C., of failed promises and a lack of oversight, forethought, or logical policies. At the very beginning of the atomic testing program, Bikini people had suffered through famine conditions when they were moved to Rongedik, an atoll much smaller than Bikini, but United States officials failed to properly recognize the critical balance between population and an atoll's established resource potential. In a report commissioned by the U.S. Commercial Company, Leonard Mason described many of the important details of life in the Marshall Islands, including matters of population and resources (Mason 1948), but this report did little to shape United States government policy. Those policies were governed, instead, primarily by a concern with United States strategic interests. While Jack Tobin forwarded several reports to Trust Territory of the Pacific Islands headquarters concerning the marginal conditions on Ujelang, those reports brought little change in United States policy. The daily lives of Ujelang people were simply not a major concern to officials in Washington, D.C.

Indeed, living on Ujelang and ingesting local foods transformed the community into "the people of Ujelang." But people's entire identity as "Ujelang folks" is tinged with recollections of suffering. And, if by eating Ujelang foods people truly came to exist as Ujelang people, having ingested the products of the soil, their bodies became ill-nourished and disease prone as a result of the paucity of foods and the inadequacy of nutrients contained therein. With this suffering in mind, it is not difficult to understand that Ujelang people never gave up on their dream to return to their homeland, a place that was rich in foods and equally enlivened by the embedded history of the community's own past.

## YEARNING TO RETURN HOME

One of the most difficult sources of psycho-cultural distress that Enewetak people faced on Ujelang was lack of any knowledge of when they might return to their home atoll. For much of the time they lived in exile, people thought that there well might not be an atoll to which they could return. When Enewetak people were told that they would have to leave their home atoll, it was their understanding that some day in the not-too-distant future, the United States would be finished using their atoll and they would be returned. Nevertheless, after the Mike test in 1952, a detonation of the world's first thermonuclear device, many Ujelang people became convinced that their atoll had been destroyed. One resident recalls the scene:

> After explaining the tests, he [Tobin, the district anthropologist] departed . . . on a boat belonging to the military people. We took only a few clothes and left everything else behind and closed up the houses because they said the trip would be fast. And still closer to evening, we . . . sailed in a southward direction for Kosrae and those parts. We spent the entire evening and all night at sea and sailed off, way off there to the south, and those ships are fast, not like the Marshallese vessels [trade boats], they do about fifteen or eighteen knots. And then early in the dawn we stopped, and drifted a bit, and floated with the bow of the boat to the windward, and then that man [the government representative] and the officers took us to the edge of the vessel and pointed off toward the north. Perhaps they had prearranged the time, for in just a little while we saw it. First like a cloud, white, but enlarging, up, away; then, as if they set ablaze the entire earth—colors: red, blue, purple, all colors of the rainbow, but stronger. Up higher and wider, until the entire sky to the north was filled with colors.
>
> And then they told us it was Enewetak, one of the bombs, and we began to be sad, for we knew it was gone. After some minutes, then we heard the sound, like thunder, but louder and it stayed. And we again saddened, for the sound revealed the truth: perhaps Enewetak was gone. And we did not hear talk of the atoll for many years, until recently, and it only revealed to us our own thoughts, that island, the island of ours, was gone. (Carucci 1989:89–90)

It was not until 1970 or 1971 that Ujelang people knew for sure that Enewetak was still in existence for, at that time, two respected elders were allowed to accompany a person, evacuated from Ujelang for medical reasons, on a trip that stopped at Enewetak. Local people recall that upon their return people were jubilant for they finally knew that Enewetak was still there, even though it had been radically changed by the Americans.[7] For eighteen years, however, people lived in fear that their homeland had, in all likelihood, been destroyed. Many people believed that when a group of "soldiers" came to offer a payment for Enewetak in 1954 the settlement was proof that the atoll was gone.

By the late 1960s, the community was becoming impatient, and their desire to return to their homeland was increasing. Above-ground nuclear tests were banned in 1958, yet there was still no talk of repatriation. After the strike to protest abominable living conditions on Ujelang in 1968 and word of the agreement to allow Bikini people to return to their home atoll, Ujelang residents sought legal council through Micronesian Legal Services to begin a formal appeal that would allow them to move back home. They sought a court injunction to end the Pacific Area Cratering Experiments on Enewetak, a set of tests that used high-intensity explosives to replicate the effects of nuclear blasts (Kiste 1976). With the testing halted pending an environmental impact statement, the community then sought to formally reestablish their claim to Enewetak. Finally, in September 1976, the rights to the atoll were transmitted back to the community. Nevertheless, it was not until they had actually returned to Enewetak in 1980 that the community fully recognized that it was not really their homeland to which they had returned but another place, a location they came to call "the New Enewetak."

As I have noted, the New Enewetak was a location of American military design, whose contours and landmarks were far different from Enewetak prior to the war. But it took people some years to realize that this place also lacked the very possibility of embedding Enewetak identity in its residents in the same way that it once had. Indeed, people began to refer to themselves as Enewetak people, but the elders soon questioned that identity. Two years after their repatriation many elders chose to return to Ujelang because life on Enewetak was so devoid of meaning. With the exception of fish, no Marshallese foods were available on the atoll and arable land on Enewetak islet was in short supply. This was because the topsoil had been mixed with sandy fill from the lagoon and chunks of coral from the reef, and was infused with the discarded residues of a military base. During the cleanup of Enewetak, much of the atoll was stripped of all vegetation, including the bush trees that provided a buffer to salt spray from the sea. Equally devastating, to bring the major islets within an acceptable range of radioactive residue, from six inches to the entire depth of topsoil had been removed from the residential islets. It would be over fifteen years before 30 percent of the coconut trees, the hardiest food crop, would even begin to produce fruit. Even today coconuts remain far from fully productive.

## SUBSISTENCE ON THE NEW ENEWETAK

As people were planning their return to Enewetak in the late 1970s, they relied on serious miscalculations that had been made in the Enewetak rehabilitation plan (Holmes and Narver 1973). In the government subcontractor's estimate, it would take five to seven years before local food trees would be productive. Yet the projection failed to account for the difficulty of rehabilitation on islets without topsoil and without any way to protect crops from high winds and salt spray. After having read the rehabilitation report, in one lively council meeting in 1977, people argued that they would be able to survive for five to seven years without local foods, relying solely on "white people's foods," if only they could be on their home atoll. People also failed to realize that, with only four of

forty-eight islets rehabilitated, they would have access to less land than on Ujelang. All land foods would have to come from the tiny segment of the atoll that stretched from Enewetak islet through Ananij. Other parts of the atoll could be exploited for marine resources. But without access to the resources needed to manufacture and maintain canoes, people were dependent on small outboard motor boats, and these craft required a fuel supply that, on Enewetak, was never adequate (Carucci 1995). In short, on the New Enewetak people were less internally mobile than they had been on Ujelang. While the atoll itself was much larger than Ujelang, the accessible portion was actually smaller, and the availability of local land foods was negligible. The community was forced into a condition of dependence that was largely beyond their own control. One of the most unforeseeable elements of the dependence had to do with food, for as outside foods necessarily were imported to replace the local crops that people could neither grow nor consume, the entire way that Enewetak people were "making" their own bodies was seriously altered.

As Enewetak people waited for new subsistence foods to grow, the bulk of the diet comprised European imports. In local terms, these "white people's foods" (or "USDA foods") could not transfer to people the same lifegiving qualities of local foods since they embedded qualities of local land and labor. No longer was it possible to literally unify Enewetak people with the soil, the sea, and the sky that make up that place through the consumption of its products.[8] At their core, people were being shaped by foods whose qualities they did not comprehend. Enewetak residents combined imported foods using the rules of their own nutritional theory (Carucci 1980, 1997). They expected the starchy foods to shape healthful internal characteristics of the body, and using complements (fish and other "meats"), particularly greasy complements, to add lustre to the body's exterior. With repatriation to Enewetak, however, nutrient-hollow imports (polished rice, white flour, granulated sugar) became the primary staples, and many of the imported complements were high-fat canned goods like spam, corned beef, and vienna sausage. The only local foods in the diet were limited supplies of sea foods, birds, and eggs. The insidious effects of eating foreign foods for over a decade transformed people into beings they neither understood nor had the ability to change. In an incredibly short time span, between 1980 and 1995, an entirely new array of so-called first world diseases was implanted in Enewetak people's bodies.

By placing the repatriated Enewetak community on USDA and supplemental foods, the United States solved problems of caloric malnutrition that the community had faced on Ujelang. Between 1980 and 1997, when problems with shipping again threatened Enewetak residents with food shortage, people had enough food. Nevertheless, new nutritional diseases that were unknown on Ujelang began to plague people on Enewetak. Borrowing terms from urban settlements on Majuro and Kwajalein, Enewetak people now spoke with increasing frequency of *tōñal,* "sweet," and *jaal,* "salt." In Euro-American nutritional terms, people were now at high risk for adult-onset diabetes, heart disease, and high blood pressure. Even though caloric malnutrition was gone, new forms of nutrient malnutrition became manifest. Each of these diseases was the result of people's dependence on imported foods that were high in fat and simple carbohydrates, and lacking in fiber and critical nutrients. The New Enewetak, lacking local staples on which people had depended for eons, placed people in a position where they could no longer use their own cultural logic to survive. Without any source of firewood for baking and braising foods, fried foods prepared on kerosene stoves became the norm. Along with the concomitant lifestyle changes, combining foods in accord with a Marshallese logic led not to health but to disease and death.

This common Pacific logic of food combination is well known (Carucci 1980; Pollock 1992). For Enewetak people, a food event requires a drink and a food, in combination. A quick visit to any local home will result in the offer of such a "snack," nowadays coffee or tea and a few Marshallese doughnuts. For a full meal, the food domain is further elaborated, with a complement added to the staple (starch-type food). Feasts are further elaborated by adding more foods and foods of higher rank. Given an adequate supply of *local* foods, this balanced pattern of combination works well to maintain health, since Marshallese staples such as pandanus and breadfruit are nutrient rich and many fish are high in heart-healthy Omega 3 fatty acids.

With the substitution of American imports for local staples, however, the situation shifts dramatically. Rice and flour do not contain the supply of nutrients found in breadfruit and pandanus. Europeans, long adapted to temperate climes, are accustomed to staples that store well through harsh winters but are low in nutrients. They have a different schemata in which the triad of "meat::starch::vegetable" provides a healthy solution to a diet that relies on low-nutrient staples. But again, in repatriating Enewetak people to a different homeland, one lacking all of the local foods that made people viable and healthy Enewetak residents, the United States asked them to divest themselves not only of the foods that made them into true Enewetak beings, but also of the cultural modes of combining those foods that have served them well for centuries. Americans who help administer the food programs in Micronesia have a simple answer to this dilemma: "Just eat the vegetables." There are a number of problems with this answer. First, the total number of canned vegetables shipped to Enewetak in the 1990s amounted to less than one can per person per week, far from the one or two cans per day required to meet dietary guidelines. More important, "just eating the vegetables" (a tactic that does not work very well even in Los Angeles or Chicago) requires Marshall Islands' residents to completely rethink their culturally validated system of combining foods and refashion it along a European model. This is hardly a culturally sensitive expectation, yet it is part of the reality on the New Enewetak.[9]

Unlike the 1950s and 1960s when the United States largely overlooked the nutritional needs of Ujelang people (resulting in malnutrition), since repatriation the United States has, in fact, attempted to respond to the conditions of repatriation by providing food. By providing American staples rather than Marshallese foods, however, Enewetak has been drawn more deeply into a web of transnational food dependence. Concomitantly, in spite of discourses about food "aid" or "assistance," people are now dying from the cure. Several Enewetak families have been severely affected by the death of family members from diabetes, and the number of residents suffering from the disease is proliferating. In contrast, adult-onset diabetes on Ujelang was unknown during the time I worked on the atoll in the 1970s. The diabetic conditions and deaths have resulted from a near 100 percent dependence on the USDA and supplementary food diet that is available on Enewetak, foreign food which is prepared in accord with deeply embedded Marshallese principles of food combination.

In 1998, Maifeld and I sampled daily dietary intakes of nearly sixty Enewetak residents. Of those residents, 74 percent either consumed a diabetes-prone diet or followed an eating pattern that was at borderline risk of developing diabetes.[10] One thirty-eight-year-old woman, for example, consumed 26.5 ounces of tea, 42 ounces of water, 2 ounces of evaporated milk, and 6 tablespoons of sugar (mixed into drinks), during one day. She had nearly 8 ounces of doughnut, a bit over 11 ounces of white rice, and 11 ounces of spam, tuna, and sashimi (raw fish). Of the total of approximately 100 ounces she consumed, about 65 ounces was liquid, 19 ounces were simple starches, 8.75 ounces were high-fat meats, 2.33 ounces were other meats, 3 ounces was sugar, and 2 ounces was evaporated milk. While men tended to consume more total food and drink, and while children typically consumed less, the balance of foods this woman ate are quite representative of the diabetes-prone eating patterns on the atoll.

## CONCLUSION

At the end of World War II, the United States worked hard to prove that it had no interest in becoming a colonial power. Yet the effects of American imperialism on the Enewetak community have been substantial. After having agreed to protect the interests of residents of Micronesia and having announced that they would watch over Enewetak people as wards of the state, the United States has, in fact, left Enewetak people to suffer through waves of famine and neglect on Ujelang. Subsequently, with promises to rehabilitate their home atoll, the United States has, to date, only rehabilitated a tiny section of Enewetak. Twenty-one years after repatriation, Enewetak still suffers from a very fragile environmental situation and still lacks the array of indigenous foods that could provide people with a healthful style of life. Therefore, in spite of the well-meaning intentions of the United States, the food program has solved one problem (preventing hunger during the period of rehabilitation), while creating another set of integrally related problems (such as heart disease, adult-onset diabetes, and the resultant deaths). And while it is possible to argue that "if people would only eat the (foreign) vegetables the U.S. has provided, there would not be a problem," this solution requires people to discard their own cultural practices in favor of others'. The United States has asked Enewetak people not only to eat foreign foods for twenty or thirty years, foods that are less desirable in many cases than are local staples, they have also been asked to combine foods as we would combine them, not in the local fashion that has proved viable for hundreds of years. This choice between giving up their cultural practices and facing severe physical debility or death (in the case of diabetes) is a form of suffering with which people have had to live since their return to the New Enewetak.

### Retrospective on the New Enewetak

In many senses, the suffering Enewetak people have endured since their return has been as great, if not greater, than their suffering on

Ujelang. The nature of their travails, however, has differed substantially from the 1950s and 1960s. On Ujelang, people suffered through destitution and extreme physical hardship as a result of the much smaller physical size and rocky conditions of that atoll and administrative negligence. People also struggled psychologically as a result of the separation from their homeland that also meant separation from their history, their primordial roots, their personal accomplishments, and their dreams and physical ability to be able to project a meaningful identity into the future.

Initially people were thrilled with the long-awaited return to Enewetak, yet that return has involved more-serious, though perhaps more-subtle, forms of oppression. Since their repatriation in 1980, Enewetak people have struggled with the bleakness of life on the New Enewetak, a place reminiscent of their homeland yet, in so many ways, a radically different location than the atoll on which people lived in the 1930s and 1940s. In this new landscape, stripped bare of the materials required for daily existence, most of the day-to-day activities of Marshallese life have been made irrelevant. Ironically, having been brought back to the physical skeleton of their homeland, the longstanding object of their desire, people were only able to witness first hand how desiccated, distant, and unrecognizable their mother place had become. The more people struggled to fulfill their desires of reunification with their primordial place, the more they recognized the foreignness of their home. It is this contradiction of the grandest scale that has become the source of despondency and frustration for Enewetak people. They cannot be at home in the very land that is their home. This is so because the contours of the land are no longer the same, its productive capacity is lacking, and, without local products, people have not been able to make themselves into "real Enewetak people." This is the grand contradiction of life on Enewetak. The community that many Marshall Islanders used to consider the most cohesive in the Marshall Islands has, in one generation, been thrown into disarray by placing them in a situation where their

most heartfelt desires could not possibly be realized.

In a recent work, James Clifford (1997) talks about the way in which metaphors of routes travelled are as critical as are roots traced even in what may seem to be the most isolated of cultural circumstances. Indeed, in the case of Enewetak, its very isolation served to make it an ideal stage upon which the mid-twentieth-century melodrama of nuclear testing could be carried out. Yet, having appropriated Enewetak lands for their own purposes, the United States soon abrogated their responsibility to care for the people of that place they so much desired. Reminded of those responsibilities in the late 1960s and 1970s, the United States responded with a modest compensation and an agreement to repatriate Enewetak people to their homeland.

Yet, as I have indicated, the contradictions of this repatriation are, in many senses, greater and the forms of suffering more deeply cynical than the original plan to place Enewetak people on Ujelang. While it is clear that Enewetak will never divest itself of the reconfigurations of the nuclear era, it is important that the long-awaited settlement for nuclear claims be completed. At the current time, the Nuclear Claims Tribunal has judged that it will take 341 million dollars to compensate Enewetak people for damages that resulted from the nuclear testing era.

While the tribunal was set up to adjudicate all nuclear-related claims in the Marshall Islands at the behest of the United States, the U.S. Congress must still allocate monies to pay for the claim. This settlement must be paid in order to restore as yet unrehabilitated sections of Enewetak atoll. Even though that land will never be the same, the settlement would allow the community to pursue its own future, not on an atoll of archaic contour and isolated circumstance, but in a world where centers and peripheries intermingle. That is a world where internal contours, as much as physical movements or thoughts, are shaped by forces that bring the most distant locations into intimate contact with the core of being.

## NOTES

1. At the same time, people tell a variety of empowering stories that describe the vagaries of having survived in such marginal conditions, conditions that required people to increase their cohesiveness and solidarity. Only through reliance on sharing and helping one another, they contend, could people have endured.

2. While we have no records of these earliest years on Ujelang, Bikini people, first moved to Roñdik, encountered precisely the sorts of problems derived from unsuitable foods and dangerous foreign spirit beings (Mason 1948).

3. The expansion of nuclear testing to Bikini and Enewetak are an incisive indicator of the shift in United States policy that led the nation from isolationism to its current rank as a "superpower" in the network of global exchange. During the war, nuclear tests were conducted in the American southwest. Following World War II, the Lilienthal Commission debated the advantages and drawbacks of continuing nuclear experimentation or "rebottling" the nuclear genie. With President Truman's decision to continue testing, Bikini (Pikinni) was chosen as the most viable nuclear testing location. Even though the United States was charged with protecting the best interests of the island residents of Micronesia, Bikini was viewed as an ideal test site on account of its isolation, small population, and the nearby existing military bases on Enewetak and Kwajalein that could be used for support (see Kiste 1974). Relocation onto isolated islets effectively silenced Bikini and Enewetak people. The residents of the desert southwest who lived downwind of test sites in the United States were more difficult to control.

4. Tobin's diet scenario is based on a one-week record of reported consumption among fifteen families (cookhouse groups) on Ujelang Atoll. Names indicate that those families sampled were from the Jitoen half of the community. Recipes used to convert foods to their constituent components were collected by Maifeld and Carucci among Ujelang and Enewetak households in the 1970s, 1980s, and 1990s. Mary H. Maifeld, M.S., R.D., analyzed the diets based on nutrient values found in *Food Values of Portions Commonly Used,* by Jean Pennington, *Composition of Foods* (U.S. Agricultural Handbook #8), and *New Pacific Nutrition,* by Nancy Rody. Food components were commonly added to the recorded diet to make an edible food. For example, in cases where Tobin recorded "flour: made into doughnuts," *jekero* (coconut syrup) was added as an ingredient. When *makmok* (arrowroot) was listed as "baked," drinking coconut liquid and *jekero* were added to make *pikūkkūk,* a common Ujelang recipe for unleavened arrowroot bread. Some additional calories are contained in these added products.

5. To correct for the presence of the *keemem* in the Tobin diet, Carucci and Maifeld averaged the *keemem* meal (which ranged from 2,900 to 3,300 calories per adult, depending upon family) with five generous evening meals of 1,200 calories per meal to come up with a six-week average Friday evening meal consumption for each family. Under this scenario, the least-well-nourished family had adult consumption levels of 634 kcal per day and the best-fed family had adult consumption levels of 1,464 kcal per day. The Ujelang adult average daily intake, corrected for the pattern of birthday parties in 1952, is 915.77 kcal per day.

6. While no one consumed the precise array of foods in the average diet, this hypothetical consumption pattern gives valuable information about the community norm. Of course, averages also obscure the specific activity patterns of any single family. One significant pattern that emerges is that family consumption patterns tend to be perpetuated from one generation to the next. Two of the three most marginal families in terms of food intake in the 1950s continue to be at high health risk in the 1970s, 1980s, and 1990s. (The third family at high risk of malnutrition moved away from the outer island situation.) Of course, families at risk from a U.S. nutritional standpoint may escape that high-risk situation as the structural and life-cycle contours of each family changes. On the other hand, consumption patterns often persist, and the families whose health status looks grim in Tobin's record were likely the most marginal for substantial periods of time on Ujelang. The long-term effects of calorie and nutrient malnutrition manifest themselves in physical symptoms that are most obvious and most severe among these families.

7. While people on Ujelang were thrilled to hear that Enewetak was still in existence, the changes the medical sojourners described were also baffling and disturbing. A long-time American worker on Enewetak showed the visitors a film of the nuclear tests and it was then that the visitors first realized that part of the atoll had been evaporated, that islands that were theirs had been destroyed, that the contours of the land would never again be the same.

8. The original rehabilitation plan included a vessel that the community could use to travel back and forth between Ujelang and Enewetak, transporting Marshallese food and people in both directions. This plan failed immediately when the boat that was provided, christened the "Wetak," proved too unseaworthy to navigate waters outside of the lagoon. The Wetak II was purchased to solve this problem but, while adequately seaworthy, it lacked cold storage to allow local foods to be shipped from Ujelang to Enewetak. Not until 1998 did the community obtain a ship with the characteristics required to allow for the importation of local foods from Ujelang.

9. Some suggest that dietary matters of this sort are a universal problem that has changed all Micronesians into Macronesians (Shell 2001). It is simply a feature of rapid culture change or of an omnipresent "thrift gene." These explanations are far too simplistic.

While similar effects can be found on Majuro or Epjē (Ebeye, Kwajalein), they are not commonly found among those residing on outer island locations like Ujae. And few of Majuro's residents are "true" Majuro people. Most people *choose* to live on Majuro. In the Enewetak case, people should have the right to choose to live on their own homeland and consume local foods in historically tested ways that work for them. The fact that Enewetak people do not have this choice is a direct result of their involuntary involvement in the nuclear testing program.

10. Enewetak residents are not unaware of the risk for diabetes, since Ms. Maifeld and Dr. Carucci have taught people about adult-onset diabetes and diabetes-prone diets since 1991. People are well aware that, during the time they must rely on imported foods, it is critical to combine fruits and vegetables with imported staples and complements and increase their exercise, in order to avoid being at risk for diabetes. Nevertheless, given the deep cultural embeddedness of the staple::complement pattern, most families have found the adjustment extremely difficult. For Americans, this might be comparable to forcing everyone to give up meat, potatoes, and vegetables for the raw fish, rice, and seaweed found in sushi. While some families could make these adjustments, many would find the changes neither desirable nor easy.

## REFERENCES

Asselta, Richard M. 1971. "Formal and Informal Learning in the Marshall Islands of Micronesia with Special Emphasis on the Culture of Ujelang Atoll." M.S. thesis. Western Connecticut State College.

Carucci, Laurence M. 1980. "The Renewal of Life: A Ritual Encounter in the Marshall Islands." Ph.D. dissertation. Department of Anthropology, University of Chicago.

———. 1989. "The Source of the Force in Marshallese Cosmology." In *The Pacific Theatre: Island Representations of World War II*. L. Lindstrom and G. White, eds. Pp. 73–96. Honolulu: University of Hawai'i Press.

——— 1995. "The Symbolic Imagery of Enewetak Sailing Canoes." In *Modern Pacific Seafaring*. R. Feinberg, ed. Pp. 16–33. DeKalb: Northern Illinois University Press.

———. 1997. *Nuclear Nativity: Rituals of Renewal and Empowerment in the Marshall Islands*. DeKalb: Northern Illinois University Press.

———. 2001. "Elision or Decision: Lived History and the Contextual Grounding of the Constructed Past." In *Cultural Memory: Reconfiguring History and Identity in the Postcolonial Pacific*. J. Mageo, ed. Pp. 81–101. Honolulu: University of Hawai'i Press.

Carucci, Laurence Marshall, and Mary H. Maifeld. 1999. *Ien Entaan im Jerata: Times of Suffering and Ill Fortune.* Majuro: Marshall Islands Nuclear Claims Tribunal, March 1999.

Clifford, James. 1997. *Routes: Travel and Translation in the Late Twentieth Century*. Cambridge: Harvard University Press.

Conard, Robert. 1992. Fallout: The Experiences of a Medical Team in the Case of a Marshallese Population Accidentally Exposed to Fallout Radiation. Contract # DE-AC02-76CH00016. Washington, D.C.: U.S. Department of Energy.

Durkheim, Emile. 1933. *The Division of Labour.* New York: Macmillan. (Originally published 1893.)

Heine, Carl. 1974. *Micronesia at the Crossroads*. Honolulu: University of Hawai'i Press.

Holmes and Narver, Inc. 1973. *Enewetak Atoll Master Plan for Island Rehabilitation and Resettlement.* (2 vols). Anaheim, Calif.: Holmes and Narver, Inc.

Kiste, Robert. 1974. *The Bikinians: A Study in Forced Migration.* Menlo Park, Calif.: Cummings.

———. 1976. "The People of Enewetak vs. the U.S. Department of Defense." In *Ethics and Anthropology.* M. A. Rynkiewich and J. P. Spradley, eds. Pp. 61–80. New York: John Wiley.

———. 1993. "New Political Statuses in American Micronesia." In *Contemporary Pacific Societies: Studies in Development and Change*. Victoria Lockwood, T. G. Harding, and B. J. Wallace, eds. Pp. 67–80. Englewood Cliffs, N.J.: Prentice Hall.

Lee, Richard. 1979. *The !Kung San.* Cambridge: Cambridge University Press.

Mason, Leonard. 1948. *Rongerik Report.* Honolulu: The Pacific Collection, Hamilton Library, University of Hawai'i.

*Newsweek*, March 12, 2001. Gersh Kuntzman, "American Beat: Let Them Eat Steak"; Geoffrey Cowley, "Canibals to Cows: The Path of a Deadly Disease."

Peattie, Mark R. 1988. *Nan'yo: The Rise and Fall of the Japanese in Micronesia, 1885–1945.* Honolulu: University of Hawai'i Press.

Pollock, Nancy. 1992. *These Roots Remain: Food Habits in Islands of the Central and Eastern Pacific Since Western Contact.* Institute for Polynesian Studies, Brigham Young University, Laie, Hawai'i. Honolulu: University of Hawai'i Press.

Sahlins, Marshall. 1972. "The Original Affluent Society." In *Stone Age Economics*. Pp. 1–39. Chicago: Aldine.

Shell, Ellen R. 2001. "New World Syndrome." In *The Atlantic Monthly* 287 (June 2001): 50–53.

Tobin, Jack. 1967. "The Resettlement of the Enewetak People: A Study of a Displaced Community in the Marshall Islands." Ph.D. dissertation. Department of Anthropology, University of California, Berkeley.

# 25

# Between Heaven and Earth: Missionaries, Environmentalists, and the Maisin

**John Barker**

*University of British Columbia*

The arrival of my wife and me in Uiaku village on the northeast coast of Papua New Guinea in November 1981 triggered a great deal of speculation. I had made contact with the local priest and village leaders through the good offices of the Anglican Church, and some of the people who met us were clearly familiar with the odd pursuits of researchers. Some fifteen years later I learned that some of the older people had speculated that we were returning ancestors who would hopefully rejuvenate the fortunes of the Maisin people (the language group that lived in Uiaku and surrounding villages). Others, perhaps more in tune with the national times, hoped that we would draw upon our vast business connections in "America" to bring development to the Maisin. These reactions were the kind we expected in light of what we had read and heard about New Guinea. What we did not expect was that the majority of villagers had already decided that we were missionaries.

Villagers were very concerned with what kind of missionaries we were. Although the Maisin had been dealing with missionaries since 1890, only one white missionary ever resided with them, and he had left after suffering an emotional breakdown some sixty years earlier. The Maisin were now second- and third-generation Christians and the Anglican Church itself almost completely localized. Still, some people obviously hoped that they were at last getting the white priest they had long hoped for. Others, observing that I did not seem at all priestlike, speculated that we were with the Summer Institute of Linguistics and had come to translate the Bible into Maisin, or that perhaps we were evangelists from one of the Pentecostal sects that had begun to make inroads into the Anglican religious monopoly elsewhere in the Northern Province. This last theory prompted intense discussion, for the Maisin had heard stories of how all-night Pentecostal revival meetings turned into sexual orgies. Some parents related their knowledge to us, clearly on to our tricks. Around the same time, I was approached by some young men who wondered, a little too hopefully, if I might be into gospel gatherings.

Anthropologists working in Papua New Guinea expect to encounter "strange" customs and "exotic" beliefs, by which we mean phenomena that we assume to be indigenous in origin, that make sense within the distinctive logic of a cultural "Other." We tend to be decidedly less impressed by things that look familiar—churches, schools, trade stores, and the like. Anthropologists have always studied such things, and in recent years these studies have become quite sophisticated, but usually as signs of the impact of outside agencies with which, as outsiders ourselves, we are already familiar. Like other anthropologists who have worked in the Oro Province in recent years, I could not help but be impressed by how central the church was in Maisin life in the 1980s, but I still perceived it largely as an import that duplicated Christian institutions elsewhere. So too, incidentally, did the Maisin. But Maisin notions about the nature of and their need for "missionaries" provided an early clue that much more was at work here. Christianity was an import, but one that Maisin had over the course of decades remolded to fit with their own cultural orientations, the contingencies of interacting with outsiders, and aspirations for social and economic improvement in their community. In greeting my wife and myself as missionaries, Maisin gave us our first clue that Christianity meant something different for them than it did for people in our own country.

The first part of this chapter traces the origins of the Maisin's understanding of missionaries. I then turn to a more detailed consideration of how they conceptualized the concept of missionary during my early fieldwork in the 1980s. The third and longest section of the chapter brings the story to the present. When my wife and I arrived in Uiaku in 1981, most Maisin longed for missionaries (of the "right" sort, of course) who would assist them in achieving political and moral unity and, thus united, economic prosperity. In the mid-1990s, this dream seemed to be coming true. The Maisin have gained practical and moral support from a wide variety of non-governmental organizations, most of them involved in environmental conservation. The activists do not think of themselves as missionaries, anymore than my wife and I did. They tend to view the Maisin as an autonomous indigenous people whose traditional ways of life are now threatened by the rapacious forces of multinational corporations, particularly logging and mining interests. I do not think that their perceptions are entirely wrong. I do want to suggest, however, that the Maisin have been dealing with outsiders for a long time. Their prior experiences necessarily shape their perception of and ways of dealing with the newcomers. And to a considerable extent, they are treating the environmentalists as if they were the long-awaited missionaries.

Before plunging into the narrative, however, I need to head off a possible misunderstanding. There often is, unfortunately, fierce rivalry between different groups that work in partnership with indigenous peoples. Often one group will claim to understand and represent the true interests of the indigenous group, accusing the others of serving their own selfish or ideologically driven interests. There is a longstanding rivalry of this sort between some anthropologists and missionaries, although their battles tend to pale when compared to the nasty sectarian sniping that occurs between missions and between rival environmental organizations. One could read what I write here as a putdown of the environmentalists who have arrived in large numbers in Collingwood Bay in recent years (see Figure 25.1). This is not my intention. I feel tremendous respect and gratitude for the generous time, energy, and imagination that these activists have put into direct assistance to the Maisin and to the development of projects meant to benefit the community. Indeed, I have joined their ranks, as we shall see. I do hope, however, that twenty years of researching and thinking about Maisin society and history have provided me with some insights that will be of interest and use to my new colleagues. I use the term "colleagues" here deliberately. I have myself become a missionary in the Maisin sense. And much of the analysis that follows has an autobiographical

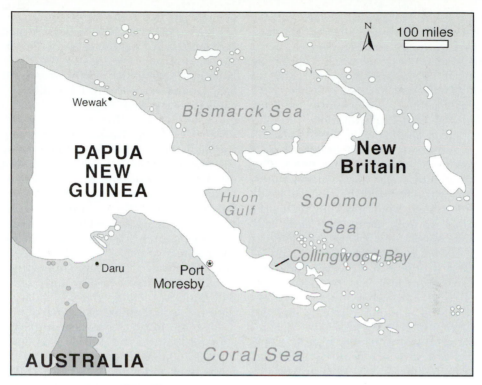

**Figure 25.1    Papua New Guinea**

undertone—it is an attempt to make sense of my own shifting relationship with the Maisin community.

## THE ANGLICAN MISSION

Numbering around 3,500 people, the Maisin occupy four village clusters along the southern shores of Collingwood Bay on the eastern edge of Oro Province. They are among the largest of the five language groups occupying the bay. The villages are divided into contiguous hamlets occupied by patrilineally related men who share rights to certain lands for gardening. Like their ancestors, villagers today get most of their food through subsistence gardening, fishing, hunting, and gathering. They rely upon the resources of the rainforest and mangrove swamps that surround their homes for much of their material culture, including houses, canoes, and mats. Villagers

eke out cash from periodic sales of copra and tapa cloth,[1] but Collingwood Bay today is an economic backwater, as it was through the entire colonial period. But the Maisin are not deprived, at least by typical rural standards in Papua New Guinea. They enjoy a relatively high level of education. Since the 1960s, a majority of Maisin has graduated from at least grade six and many have gone on to secondary and tertiary institutions. At least a quarter of the Maisin population have migrated to urban areas, most of them holding well-paying jobs in the public and private sectors. Their remittances, in cash and manufactured goods, has come to form a crucial subsidy for their village relatives. As we shall see, the Anglican Church bears a large responsibility for the present economic situation.

From the early nineteenth century to the present, Christian missions have been among the most ubiquitous and important agencies of change in the Melanesian region (Garrett 1982; Barker 1990a; Trompf 1991). The missionaries who sought converts from the western Pacific islands were primarily inspired, as are Christian missionaries everywhere, by the message of salvation embodied in the New Testament teachings and example of Jesus Christ and by Saint Paul's injunction to take that message to all the world. But the process of conversion has never been straightforward or entirely predictable (Burridge 1978). The missionaries interpreted the Christian message through the filters of their own cultural backgrounds, their languages, the theological orientations of their home churches, and their personalities. The historical contingencies of working in the Melanesian islands— the logistical support for the missions, the presence of other Europeans, the slow growth of commercial enterprises, and so forth— served to subvert a purely Christian message further. Last, but certainly not least, Melanesians reinterpreted Christian teachings and missionary initiatives in terms of their own cultural orientations and shifting understandings and aspirations. The missions have been enormously successful. Virtually all Melanesians belong to one or another of the churches that today form a central presence in the towns and villages (Ernst 1994). Yet this success has not resulted in a uniformity of culture and belief. To a considerable extent, Christian Melanesia continues to express its famed pre-Christian diversity.

In 1884 the British and German governments divided control over the eastern half of New Guinea and adjoining islands. Unbeknown to themselves, the Maisin along with others in southeastern New Guinea became subjects of the British crown in the new territory of British New Guinea, later to be ruled by Australia as Papua.[2] The London Missionary Society had been working along the southeastern coast since 1871 and was joined by Roman Catholic missionaries in 1884, but the northeast remained largely unexplored. The fledgling colonial administration, which was expected to pay its own way, courted missions as partners in the task of controlling and "civilizing" the tribal peoples of British New Guinea. In 1890 the administrator of the territory, William MacGregor, invited the Methodist and Anglican churches in Australia to establish new missions in the Papuan islands and along the north coast of British New Guinea respectively. Up until the 1950s, each of these four missions enjoyed a religious monopoly within their respective territories. They ran the schools, operated the hospitals, and often provided employment to converts on mission-run plantations and other commercial enterprises. As Papua New Guinea moved toward independence in 1975, the government took control of several of these services, notably education,[3] and the established churches began to face competition from a host of newly arrived Christian sects. Still, the Roman Catholic, United (formerly London Missionary Society and Methodist), and Anglicans remain among the largest and most influential churches in the country.

The Maisin first began encountering missionaries during the 1890s, when members from the newly founded Anglican mission made brief forays into Collingwood Bay from their base at Dogura, about eighty kilometers to the east.[4] In 1898, after a site in the Maisin village of Sinapa proved to be too swampy, the Anglicans established a district station at Wanigela, a few kilometers to the north of Maisin territory. Three years later, Percy John Money, an Anglican lay missionary, built a magnificent new station at Uiaku, entirely from native materials. It included a huge church capable of seating a congregation of 550 and a commodious school awaiting more than 200 pupils (Money 1903). The mission, however, was unable to find a white missionary to staff the Uiaku station and it never lived up to the ambitions that Money held for it. Except for a period starting in 1917, when a sensitive young Australian priest spent a miserable three years enduring drumming and pigs, the Maisin learned Christianity and the rudiments of reading, writing, and arithmetic from men who looked very much like themselves. The first of these teachers were New Hebrideans, recruited from the sugar plantations of Queensland. They were later replaced by Papuans, trained at the mission headquarters as teacher-evangelists, and eventually by Papua New Guinean priests.

The Anglicans were typical in this respect. Most missions in Papua at that time relied heavily upon Pacific Island converts to staff village schools and churches (Munroe and Thornley 1996). The Anglicans' method of missionizing was also a standard one for the time. Most of their efforts were geared to reproducing in the new village settings the liturgy, institutional structure, religious programs, educational system, and discipline of the home church in Australia and England. Although the church buildings and schools were built from the same bush materials as village houses, supervising missionaries made sure they were arrayed along straight neat paths, bordered by flowers, with the whole mission compound fenced off from surrounding villages. Indeed, school children spent a good deal of time building and maintaining these church structures as well as gardens to support the teachers. And although the teachers—particularly the first generation recruited from Queensland—often possessed only a rudimentary education themselves, district supervising missionaries regularly visited them to assure that at least the scheduled weekly rounds of teaching and preaching were maintained. Encouraged by the supervisors, many teachers made a fetish out of schedules, developing—if elderly Maisin are to be believed—elaborate forms of torture for pupils who came to class late. In the words of a senior missionary, the school and the church provided key environments within which to impart to children "a christian (sic) habit of life" (Gill 1929). If most children failed to grasp the intricacies of reading and writing from their school experience, they did at least gain a preparation in European orientations to time, to work, and to discipline.[5]

The Anglican mission, however, did differ from other missions in Papua in two key respects. First, the early bishops and most of the senior clergy were staunch Anglo-Catholics who embraced an ideal of Christian worship and belief modeled upon the medieval church. Many of the missionaries idealized Papua village life, perceiving in it values that

they feared were being eroded or destroyed in the West. Consequently, senior clergy were reluctant to authorize interference in local customs except where these clearly contravened Christian teachings, as in the case of polygyny, or basic human values, as in the case of cannibalism. The Anglican leaders imagined their church merging with a preexisting society rather than replacing it, to the benefit of both church and village. The Reverend Henry Newton, for instance, wrote that the church "is not to be a body distinct from the native life, but rather one that permeates the whole by its influence. . . . The Mission has not come . . . to change native life into a parody of European or Australian civilization" (Newton 1914:251; Wetherell 1977).

Some missionaries gained intimate knowledge of Papuan societies, but most remained quite innocent. This was probably just as well, because the mission possessed very few resources to change the social ways of villagers. This was the second major difference between the Anglicans and the other missions: They were profoundly poor. Constant shortages of cash and staff retarded the mission's expansion and left district missionaries and teachers heavily dependent upon villagers for most of their support. The Anglicans could not simply impose their version of Christianity and civilization. They required the cooperation—indeed, the active support—of villagers. Typically, the missionaries turned what many would see as a weakness into a virtue. The bishops and other leading clergy wrote scathingly of the materialism and corruption of Western countries, contrasting this with the "simple faith" of village-based Christianity. Some missionaries actively discouraged young men in the villages from signing up to work on plantations or in mines. Compared to other missions, the Anglicans developed very few commercial ventures of their own and provided little in the way of technical education for their students. Their economic policies, in other words, were consistent with their vision of a village-based Christianity.

Mission records indicate that the Maisin were usually very supportive of the mission (Barker 1987). The schools at Uiaku and

Sinapa (established in 1905) enjoyed large classes and steady attendance. The absence of a white missionary delayed baptism, but after 1911 large numbers of young people were deemed well prepared and accepted as fully baptized members of the church. By the early 1920s, around a third of the population, mostly graduates of the village schools, had become Christians. Church councils had been established in both Uiaku and Sinapa. Despite these indications of progress, however, European missionaries remained skeptical of the sincerity of many of the Maisin converts. They complained in particular about the unwillingness of converts to abide by the mission's strict marriage rules. But they also wondered, in the absence of a "strong" white missionary presence, whether Maisin commitment and understanding of Christianity ran very deep. For many Maisin, the presence of the mission may have been of greater significance than its message. The mission teachers were the villagers' most-common trade partners, a significant conduit of valued tobacco, steel tools, and other goods. The villagers likely perceived the labor and food they donated to the mission, their willingness to allow their children to attend school, and (albeit limited) tolerance of mission rules as "gifts" that created a moral relationship between themselves and the powerful white missionaries and their god.[6]

Collingwood Bay was absorbed quickly into the emerging colonial system with the arrival of the government and mission at the turn of the century. By 1915, most young Maisin men routinely left the area to work on plantations or mines elsewhere in Papua, returning after eighteen-month stints with valued manufactured goods. A few Maisin joined the police force at the district station on Cape Nelson and some went on to the mission headquarters to train as teachers. Most, however, settled back in the villages to resume a subsistence routine that predated the conquest.

This changed abruptly in July 1942, when Japanese forces landed near Buna and Gona villages on the central coast of the Northern District. All able-bodied Maisin men were soon after made to serve as carriers and laborers for the Australian and, later, American troops. As elsewhere in Melanesia, the Maisin were profoundly transformed by the experience. In the Kokoda campaign, they witnessed some of the most brutal fighting of the Second World War. They were touched by the friendly and egalitarian attitudes of Australian and American soldiers. Most significantly, they came back to the villages inspired by the idea that they themselves could construct a new way of life to achieve the material standards enjoyed by Europeans.

Ironically—for most Anglicans had been at best indifferent and often hostile to commercial development in Papua—the mission provided Maisin and other people of the Northern District with a model of how this might be achieved. After barely surviving a four-year stint as a Japanese prisoner of war, the Reverend James Benson returned to his former base at Gona village where, in collaboration with Samuel Ungega, a mission school graduate and former member of the Papua Infantry Battalion, initiated an experiment in Christian socialism: a village cooperative. Benson idealistically hoped that the cooperative would improve the diet of villagers while deepening their understanding of Christianity through the discipline of daily prayers and regular labor (Dakeyne 1966). The Gona cooperative attracted attention from across the district. Missionaries spread the word, as did a number of individuals who visited Gona. One of these, Samuel Garandi, returned to Uiaku in 1949 bearing new ideas and rice seed. Under the encouraging eye of the district missionary, the Maisin called a grand meeting at Uiaku to proclaim a new era of peace and prosperity. Leaders ritually broke a club and spear to signal the end of animosities between rival clans. The members of the Uiaku-Ganjiga Christian Cooperative Society then planted the rice, sending the first harvest to the missionaries at Wanigela (Barker 1996).

Although villagers took up the ways of Christian cooperatism with alacrity, the prayer meetings, seed blessings, and hard work clearing and planting produced meager results. They tried a series of cash crops, but many proved difficult to cultivate and even more challenging to get to distant markets. The cooperative leaders had little idea of how to handle "shares" villagers invested into the ventures or the rare profit that came in. Afraid of being accused of stealing money, most seem to have simply stashed the cash in their houses. Villagers rarely saw any return on their efforts. By the early 1950s, the mission had lost interest in the cooperatives and the local administrators, worried that the mission had touched off a potential cargo cult, were wary. Despite these setbacks, Maisin kept returning to the cooperative model. They had one major success. With the assistance of the district missionary, who agreed to open a bank account on their behalf, a group of Uiaku Maisin raised enough cash mostly through copra sales to buy materials to build a semipermanent church building, the first in southern Collingwood Bay. The church was consecrated in a major celebration in 1962 by George Ambo, the first indigenous Anglican bishop, who at the same time installed a Papua New Guinean priest to serve the Maisin. The Maisin surrounded the new church with a special fence made up of the tree emblems representing different clans, something that had never been done before. In doing this they signaled, as they had with the ceremonial breaking of the spear and club thirteen years earlier, the new unity of the Maisin people established through cooperative activities and the Anglican Church.

Twenty years later, witnesses to this event still considered it a defining moment (Barker 1993). For this generation of Maisin, the consecration of St. Thomas Church represented the climax of a carefully constructed exchange relationship. The Maisin had given the missionaries (and the Christian god) their prayers, their labor, and their children. In return, the mission had given them the gift of the cooperative. The relationship established, villagers had continued to shower God with prayers and labor. The church symbolized a unity that surmounted the petty squabbles and incessant gossiping that divided villagers. It also promised a future economic prosperity if the moral unity of the church community could be maintained.

The Maisin had a second reason to want to cultivate relationships with the missionaries during this period. In 1947, the Anglicans opened the Martyrs' Memorial School in the central part of the Northern District. In the early years, Martyrs' offered only a couple of grades beyond basic village school education but eventually it became a full-fledged high school, one of the first and still regarded as one of the best in Papua New Guinea. In 1956, the Anglicans added a second high school, Holy Name, to serve girls. Stimulated by the need to prepare students for these schools, and encouraged by the colonial government, the Anglicans also worked to improve the standards of village schools and advanced schools at the district stations. Long familiar with mission schools, the Maisin were well placed to take advantage of these enlarged educational opportunities. By the early 1960s, a majority of Maisin village school graduates were spending a portion of their late teens studying at one or another of the mission high schools. Many went with the express blessing of the district missionaries and other senior Anglican clerics. Most intended to become "missionaries" themselves. That is, they imagined themselves serving within the mission infrastructure that comprised most of the employment opportunities at that time in the Northern District. Even after they learned that there were other possibilities, working, for instance, within colonial administration, a large number opted to become priests, nurses, doctors, medics, and teacher-evangelists.

In the late colonial period, the Anglican mission came to enjoy an enormous influence over much of the Northern District. Many villagers like the Maisin looked to the Anglican missionaries for information on the nature of the outside world and guidance in dealing with the changes sweeping over the country at the time.[7] The extraordinary respect local people showed the mission during this period cannot be adequately explained merely as a response to the services—actual and hoped for—delivered by the church. The colonial administration also provided people with services and clearly had access to great power, yet administrative officers continually complained that the local people did not treat them with the same respect they accorded the missionaries.

Many hoped that by forming relationships with the mission, they would eventually gain access to the vast wealth and power enjoyed by white people. This would happen through an exchange of moral equals, an exchange that would preserve the moral integrity of local people through Christian faith while elevating their material way of life. This was the crucible in which Maisin formed the notion that I would encounter in the early 1980s, of the missionary as a necessary partner in facing the challenges of an expanding world.

## WE ARE ALL MISSIONARIES

The Anglican mission reached the pinnacle of its influence during the 1960s. The mission now administered a network of churches, schools, teacher and theological colleges, and medical clinics covering most of the Northern District, but it did so on a miniscule budget dependent mostly upon contributions from the colonial government and overseas supporters. The mission owed much of its success to its long association with villagers and the fact that it offered the majority of positions at that time for educated Papuans. This situation changed dramatically with the decision of the Australian government in the 1960s to fast-track Papua New Guinea for rapid independence. Graduates of Anglican schools now found their options enlarged as the administration practically overnight created a system of secondary and tertiary schools providing general and technical training in a variety of areas. To their immense frustration, missionaries watched many of their prize students lured into jobs in the government or public service—jobs that offered immensely better pay and heavier responsibilities than anything the mission could hope to match. The mission suffered an additional decline in influence when the administration established a set curriculum for village schools and, by the early 1970s, took responsibility for accrediting and paying teachers. The Anglicans remained nominally in charge of the schools, but limited their role to religious education. In most respects, days of the "mission" properly speaking were over. Almost all of the clerics were now Papua New Guinean, as were several bishops. In 1974, in recognition of this transformation, the Anglican Church of Papua New Guinea came into being as its own ecclesiastical independent province, no longer a missionary diocese of the province of Queensland, Australia.

The Maisin and other local peoples in the Northern District, as we have already seen, played a large role in defining the nature of Anglicanism—broadly, of the mission—in village society. Even as the institutional mission became a national church, beginning a slow decline, villagers continued to organize their societies and make sense of their relationships with the outside world in terms of their conception of the nature of the church and its mission. I had come to study the long-term impact of Christianity upon the Maisin. I quickly came to realize that they had localized an understanding of mission, drawing in equal parts upon received indigenous notions of moral and political action and their reinterpretations of missionary teachings.

In the early 1980s, the Maisin universally continued to refer to the Anglican Church of Papua New Guinea as a "mission." Although they were by then mostly third-generation Christians and served entirely by Papua New Guinean clergy and teachers, Maisin called the complex of classrooms, residences, playing field, and church at the center of Uiaku a "mission station." They did not associate the term "missionary" with the act of proselytizing. Instead, the term referred to those people and groups associated with and through the village church. Most major public events in the 1980s occurred on the grounds of the mission station, from saints' day feasts to independence celebrations at the school. Maisin regarded these, along with the routine tasks of maintaining station buildings, paying the priest's salary, and practicing traditional dances for upcoming church celebrations and fundraisers, as comprising "mission-side" activities. Much to my surprise, I found an abundance of "missionaries" resident in

Uiaku: retired clergy, lay evangelists, teachers, members of the Mothers' Union church group, and associates of Anglican religious orders such as the Melanesian and Franciscan Brotherhoods. Once, as I attended a church service in honor of "women's day," the head of the Mothers' Union volunteered that now, "We are all missionaries here."

To most Maisin, "missionary" referred to something more than offices and church pursuits; it implied certain attitudes and orientations. The missionary's main duty, according to the Maisin I interviewed, is to "care for" (*kaifi*) the people. They do this by giving the people *giu*—roughly, accurate knowledge and sound advice. Those people who "respect" the missionary and "hear" the *giu* live good moral lives. My informants saw the Bible as the major source of the *giu,* but they had a quite vague notion of its contents. They tended to speak of it in a general sense, as a kind of knowledge that clarifies understandings, dissipates confusion, and allows a person to perceive the truth. Christian faith, in their view, was based upon a fundamental relationship in which the missionary acts as a mediator between the truth as revealed by God and the people. Most of the Maisin represented this as a collective relationship. They saw the missionary as caring for all the people, not for individual sinners.

This last assumption was in accord with the paternalistic model of the relationship between the "father" priest and his congregation favored by the Anglo-Catholic missionaries. But it also reproduced indigenous assumptions about hierarchy. The Maisin, in common with many other coastal peoples in New Guinea, distinguished between two types of ranked clans and associated leaders, usually described as "peace" and "war" people (Chowning 1979; Hau'ofa 1981; Lutkehaus 1982). The Maisin thus distinguish between higher-ranking *kawo* and lower-ranked *sabu* clans. In the past, the *kawo* clans held the ritual prerogative of hosting feasts in their hamlets, feasts to which lower-ranked *sabu* clans brought food and danced. *Kawo* leaders had the responsibility of hosting intertribal feasts, building alliances between groups by sharing food and other gifts with outsiders. The *sabu,* in contrast, were said to be hot tempered—driven by their passions. They had the right to throw the first spear and thus initiate fighting.[8] In their oral traditions, the Maisin imagined the *kawo* as "older brothers" to associated *sabu* clans. Like older and wiser brothers, the *kawo* were supposed to temper their younger brothers' anger by offering sound counsel. When fighting occurred, they should make the first efforts to restore peace. Each type of clan had its own leaders. Maisin today refer to these leaders by the English term "chief," but this is rather misleading. The Maisin possessed no inherited political offices. Rather, the leaders of *kawo* or *sabu* clans tended to be senior but still physically vigorous men who attracted followers through their own demonstrated abilities in organizing feasts, conducting raids, and so forth.[9]

The Maisin likened the missionaries to *kawo* and themselves to *sabu.* Like many other Christian Melanesians, for instance, Maisin represented the arrival of white missionaries as a moment of episodic change. It was a transformation from a condition of Hobbsean violence to peaceful relationships, from an absolutist *sabu* state to *kawo* bliss. They more frequently applied the model to their contemporary situation, portraying the relationship between missionary and villagers, like that between *kawo* and *sabu,* as an exchange relationship. The missionary should dispense the *giu* and, in return, receive the respect, obedience, and material support of his dependent congregation, acting like proper *sabu.* The hope was to bring the two exchange partners into a perfect balance (*marawa-wawe*). From such balance, the Maisin believed, came not only peaceful relationships but also the bountiful blessings of both the Christian god and the ancestors.

It would be tempting but I think quite misleading to see this as an instance of cultural appropriation, as an indication, on the one hand, of the enduring power of Maisin culture and of a superficial grasp of Christianity, on the other. The distinction between "peace" and "war" leaders is quite ancient and widespread in coastal Melanesia, but I suspect that

Maisin notions of the opposition were strongly influenced and reinforced by mission teachings about the transforming power of Christianity. The Maisin formulation about missionaries is better understood as a historical product of a long conversation between Maisin and Anglican missionaries and teachers. It bears the traces not only of indigenous cultural categories but of Anglo-Catholic conceptions and the direct experience the Maisin had with the mission, particularly during the cooperative years of the 1950s and early 1960s.

The localized model of the mission provided Maisin with a framework within which to make sense of their current predicament. Most villagers at that time perceived themselves as poor and their communities as backwards and "dirty." They resented their growing dependence upon remittances from working relatives in town, but worried about how to find money to cover school fees, the priest's salary, and purchases of clothing and other manufactured goods that people now consider necessities. It was universally believed that the Maisin had only once achieved the desired state of *marawa-wawe,* of balance between the missionary and his congregation. The construction and consecration of the church at Uiaku in 1962 provided the model for the desired state. At village meetings and in private, Maisin conducted a great deal of soul searching to determine the reasons for their failure to bring economic riches— "development"—to the villages. Following the logic of the model, many blamed themselves for an assortment of lapses: People gossiped too much, did not provide generous offerings to the church and other public institutions, and were too "lazy" to work hard on community projects organized by village leaders. Overall, people did not listen to the *giu.* There was too much arguing and division and, as long as this was true, the Maisin villages would remain mired in poverty, sickness, and sorcery.

But the missionary model suggested that "missionaries" could just as easily be to blame for the sad state of things in the villages. As we have seen, most villagers could be viewed as missionaries of some kind or another. Maisin focused their criticisms on leaders whose connections to the church and to outside institutions and knowledge put them in the position to (ideally at least) dispense the kind of useful knowledge that would bring health and prosperity to the village. Village leaders were criticized for being lazy or greedy or sometimes for stealing money. But their worst fault, in the imagination of the people, was that they tended to favor their own relatives over others. A missionary, according to the model, brings unity by serving all. And this is probably why the most promising missionaries in the Maisin imaginings were outsiders who might stand above the incessant bickering of village family politics.

It is interesting to note that at this time many Maisin were quite critical of the bishops and leaders of the Anglican Church. Many villagers complained that the mission had failed to provide the people with plantations and other forms of economic development that might help lift them from their poverty. David Hand, then the Archbishop of the Anglican Church, provoked an outraged protest from village leaders in 1983 when, on a visit to Uiaku, he spoke out against a proposal to allow commercial logging in the rainforests behind the Maisin villages. Father David used to be a good missionary, I was told, but he had "forgotten" the people and no longer looked after their interests. Villagers were eager to do their part to bring prosperity. They needed new missionaries who would respond to their gifts and provide help. Hence the keen interest and anticipation when my wife and I first arrived in Uiaku late in November 1981.

## FROM SAVING SOULS TO SAVING THE RAINFOREST

The independence of Papua New Guinea and the creation of a national Anglican Church might have been expected to bring the era of the mission to a close. But in many parts of the country, including Collingwood Bay, missionary campaigns have in fact intensified in recent years. These new missionaries can be roughly divided into two groups, religious and secular.

The new religious missionaries, while all Christians (so far at least), differ from earlier Anglican evangelists in several respects. Most promote forms of Christianity focused upon individual salvation and morality. They challenge the older tendency to identify community unity with membership in the Anglican Church. Overt sectarianism began to appear in the early 1990s in the form of small congregations of Pentecostals, Jehovah's Witnesses, and Seventh Day Adventists, mostly made up of Maisin who had converted to these sects while living and working in urban centers and brought them back to the villages. But the old association between church and community was also weakening among the majority who still belonged to the Anglican Church. Encouraged by visits from Australian Charismatics, by the ready availability of popular gospel music on the radio and on cassettes, and by an expanded program within the Anglican Church to encourage youth "fellowship," young people in particular were embracing individualistic evangelical styles of worship and belief, leaving behind the established Anglo-Catholic traditions as stodgy and conservative.

On the other hand, the secular "missionaries" are made up mostly of environmentalists interested in conserving the great rainforests of Papua New Guinea. Environmentalists make up the largest part of a burgeoning group of nongovernmental organizations (NGOs) that has become a prominent feature of political life in Papua New Guinea since independence in 1975. Colin Filer estimates that, as of 1996, somewhere between 100 and 150 NGOs were operating in the country, a third to a half concerned with forest policy (Filer 1998:264). NGOs range from organizations with global reach, like Greenpeace and the World Wildlife Fund, to organizations run entirely by local villagers. They are largely staffed by national citizens, but many receive differing degrees of funding from international environmental organizations, national and international church bodies, foreign government aid agencies, and international development organizations like the World Bank. Many make use of expatriates for senior staff positions and as consultants.

This explosion of NGOs results from the conjunction of both local and global developments. Papua New Guinea has experienced a massive intensification of resource exploitation, mostly by transnational corporations, in the years since independence (Zimmer-Tamakoshi 1998). Large-scale mining, logging, fishing, and oil projects have brought funds to the country but also created serious social disruptions, pollution, and corruption. Papua New Guinea is unusual in that some 97 percent of the land remains under customary ownership, giving local peoples a fair amount of political influence over projects in their traditional lands. Many landowners have found it useful to work with and to create their own independent NGOs to attempt to influence government and corporate decisions on projects, to claim compensation for the damages incurred in past projects, or to work out conservation plans to protect lands from overexploitation. This same period has witnessed a rising concern, particularly in the industrialized world, with the impact of the global economy upon the world's forests, waters, air, and climate. The global conservation movement has taken many different forms—from organizations opposed to commercial developments to those working closely with them or in corporations attempting to "green" their image (if not always their practices). Papua New Guinea presented an enticing target for the movement, as the home of the largest remaining primary rainforest in Southeast Asia. The national NGO movement in general, and the conservation movement in particular, is thus the result of the synergy between both local and global developments. Global organizations looking to invest funds and expertise for conservation have found ready partners in the local NGOs.

Since the mid-1990s, the Maisin have been working with a host of both foreign and national conservationists attached to different NGOs. While these activists do not bring an overtly religious message and are not trying to build a church, it is clear that many Maisin visitors think of their relationship with them in ways that strongly resemble how villagers viewed Anglican missionaries in the 1960s. In other words, they imagine themselves in an exchange partnership with these outsiders, one that requires a unity of identity and purpose on the part of the community and a willingness on the part of the outsiders to connect villagers with outside sources of knowledge and wealth. In this section, I wish to assess the nature of this relationship from the point of view of the villagers. I also want to consider the implications for Maisin society of a growing separation of religious and community commitment.

First, I must justify my use of the term "missionary" to describe the environmental activists and their associates. This is a designation that I am applying. I have never heard Maisin call environmentalists "missionaries." I know that many of the activists who condemn the Christian missionary project in principle would be quite offended to be labeled as such themselves. There are, I readily admit, vast differences between the projects of most Christian missionaries and those of environmental activists. Yet I think the designation is helpful, if used cautiously, to remind us of the reality that, from the point of view of local villagers themselves, the foreign activists who arrive to work with them to save the rainforest bear a number of striking similarities to foreign missionaries who work to save their souls. And they treat them in similar ways.

There are a number of crucial commonalities between the religious and secular missions:

1. Foreign-sponsored agents, like missionaries or environmentalists, working with rural people in Papua New Guinea have a primary commitment to concerns that transcend localities and nationalities. Missionary agents usually perceive themselves as serving and often protecting the interests of local people from other outsiders bent on exploitation. This is because they assume that the real interests of local people are identical to the transcendent truth they wish to communicate. This assumed commonality is critically important for it helps legitimize the mission itself. Older missionary texts are replete with instances in which heathens beg missionaries to send them evangelists, to make them fully Christian. By the same token, environmental tracts often present "indigenous"

people as inherently conservationist. The missionary or activists thus present themselves as coming to protect and build upon a truth that is already present.

2. Foreign missionaries and secular activists who work intimately with members of rural communities are prime agents of *cultural* globalization. Different and conflicting as their ideological mandates might be, missions and environmental organizations share an underlying commonality reflected in their routine operations and organization. Both are international bureaucracies whose operations require fundraising, budgets, plans of action, and so forth. To the degree that they participate in the routine work of mission or environmental organization, local peoples gain a practical sense of the cultural logic of these global enterprises. This often is not entirely voluntary. That is to say, if members of a local community want to attract and hold a mission or environmental agency, they will be obliged to conform to some of the key values of the foreign group.

3. Local peoples often identify enthusiastically with the ideals of the outside agency. They want to be part of the global Christian community; they feel pride at being one of the "tribal" peoples who have the wisdom to save the rainforest. All the same, they bring their own cultural orientations and historical experience to these concepts and inevitably understand them in ways that differ, often profoundly, from the official understandings of the foreign agency. This provides fertile ground for both creative and destructive mutual misunderstandings. While the relationship between foreign agency and local people is fraught with inequalities, it is nonetheless a dialectical one, which eventually transforms both parties.

4. Once they enter the local scene, the projects initiated by foreign missions and activists alike become subject to local politics. In poor countries like Papua New Guinea, where the government provides few and often inadequate social services, independent organizations like the missions and larger environmental organizations may provide major material assets for the local communities lucky enough to attract them. Local leaders build their reputations by

attracting foreigners to "help" their communities. By the same token, these leaders are subjected to the constant criticism and intrigue that characterize the competitive ethos of village politics.

As a last point, I would add that I am using the term "missionary" in the elastic sense used by villagers in the 1980s. A missionary for the Maisin is not necessarily a proselytizer. While a few of the activists who have worked with the Maisin over the past few years hold their beliefs with something akin to religious fervor, most are very focused upon practical projects with specific benefits. I myself have now become a "missionary" in this, the Maisin, sense. I have raised money overseas to help Maisin defend their lands from logging and I recently led a delegation of Canadian aboriginal people and a film crew to the area to help publicize the Maisin cause and to promote a relationship that I hope will benefit both parties (see Figure 25.2). I have myself thus entered an

exchange relationship in which I am perceived (with some discomfort on my part) by many villagers as "caring for" them, much as a *kawo* leader must care for his *sabu* or an older sibling for a junior. I have thus finally become a missionary, and not a moment too soon.[10]

The Maisin came to the attention of environmental activists in the mid-1990s when villagers launched a public campaign, including prominent ads and interviews in the national newspapers, to prevent the national government from permitting commercial logging on their ancestral lands. Ten years earlier, Maisin leaders had actively courted logging companies, seeing this and the subsequent planting of commercial plantations as the best option for bringing economic development into the area. Most villagers at that time, however, voiced strong objections to any scheme that would pay higher taxes and royalties to the national and provincial governments than to the landowners. Villagers perceived this latest scheme, which had been

**Figure 25.2**   Canadian film crew

developed in secret between the government and a small group of urban-dwelling men claiming to represent Collingwood Bay, as little more than theft. There was now, however, an additional group, made up mostly of educated younger men in the towns, who had come to question the wisdom of clearing the forest itself. Sensitized by the squalor, poverty, and violence of the towns, these individuals—many of whom looked forward to retiring in the village—reminded people that the forest held many nonmonetary assets that would vanish with logging. The petitions, interviews, and ads presented a strong conservationist message along with the essential point that the Maisin alone would determine what to do with their lands.

The Maisin had already gained the important support of an activist from Greenpeace International. The public action to prevent logging attracted more support. The logging industry in Papua New Guinea had been the subject of innumerable complaints and a major government probe since the 1980s. Villagers around the country frequently complained that the logging companies had not given them promised compensation while racking up large profits for themselves (Filer 1998). The Maisin were quite unusual, however, in protesting a logging project before it even got off the ground. Their initiative attracted logistic and financial support from a number of international and national nongovernmental organizations (NGOs). Unfortunately, since 1994 the Maisin have had to call upon the support of their new allies to fend off additional development schemes, like the first launched without local consultation, which would result in the clearing of the forest on Maisin lands. Over the past two years, the Maisin have been involved in an expensive court battle with a land developer to contest a fraudulent "sale" of most of their forest lands.

Rejecting commercial logging did not mean rejecting economic development. At this time, several environmental groups were assisting rural peoples with small-scale development schemes meant to help them earn cash with a minimum of harm to the environment. In an odd echo of the origins of the cooperative movement in the late 1940s, a Maisin man employed at the Oro Butterfly Conservation Project in central Oro Province (as the Northern District had been renamed) returned to the villages to promote a scheme to form an "integrated conservation and development" organization (ICAD) to be run by the Maisin. The national Department of Environment and Conservation, with the prodding and financial assistance of international donors, had launched the first ICADs in 1993 (Filer 1998:246–248). The butterfly project, an endeavor sponsored by the Australian government to protect and commercially breed the rare Queen Alexandra birdwing butterfly, the largest in the world, had started in 1991 and then been reconceived as an ICAD (Filer 1998:254–255). It provided the basic model that was now presented to the Maisin villagers.

While clearly a creature of the environmental politics of the 1990s, from a local perspective the Maisin Integrated Conservation and Development group bears striking commonalities with the early cooperatives. Formally, it is an autonomous political body with its own elected officials and rules of procedure. Most villagers, however, regard MICAD as the embodiment of an exchange relationship between themselves and powerful outsiders (Figure 25.3). For their part, villagers give the "gift" of their time and attention to the efforts of environmentalists to teach conservation values and to conduct the necessary research on flora and fauna, as well as land tenure. The latter allows the Maisin land to be declared a conservation area under Papua New Guinea law. Most of these efforts have been conducted by Conservation Melanesia,[11] one of the larger national environmental NGOs that for several years worked exclusively with the Maisin and is now headed by a Maisin biologist (a graduate of the University of Papua New Guinea). In return, as it were, villagers have expected their partners to help develop enterprises that will bring cash into the villages.

**Figure 25.3**   Japanese environmentalists with Sylvester Moi of MICAD

Another striking parallel is the insistence by MICAD leaders and ordinary villagers alike that the organization must represent all Maisin and embody a consensus of the community. This is enormously difficult to achieve logistically and very expensive, especially as the Maisin insist that MICAD must include Uwe, an outlying Maisin-speaking village some thirty kilometers to the north of the main territory. Finally, Maisin leaders have again proven adept at deploying symbols of "traditional" identity in rituals meant to shore up the new partnership and local unity. The arrival of the Greenpeace flagship in Collingwood Bay in 1998 was marked by days of traditional dancing and community feasts. While the occasion was very different from the more limited church feasts I knew in the 1980s, let alone the feasts orchestrated by *kawo* clan leaders in the past, Maisin represented it as a statement of their common heritage. The joint effort simultaneously indicated their common endorsement of the new partnership with the environmentalists.

The partnership has been very productive during its short existence. In close consultation with village representatives, Conservation Melanesia has coordinated a multipronged approach to protecting the environment in Maisin lands. First, they have conducted independent surveys of flora and fauna in marine and forest environments and inventories of natural resources recognized and used by villagers. Conservation Melanesia has also organized a number of workshops meant to raise consciousness about environmental matters and landowners' rights in the villages. The main aim has been to establish the groundwork for the Maisin to declare their lands a conservation area, which would make it more difficult for the government to approve development projects there. Environmentalists have also played key roles in defending Maisin's rights over the future of their lands. They have given advice and funds on those occasions when villagers have had to fend off development projects.

They have also sponsored a number of initiatives to publicize the Maisin struggle to preserve the rainforest. Since 1995, small delegations of Maisin have traveled to the United States, Japan, Australia, and New Zealand to attend museum exhibitions featuring Maisin tapa cloth, to speak before audiences of environmentalists, and to seek out financial support for small-scale economic projects in the villages. As knowledge of the Maisin has spread, a steady stream of visitors have made the trek to Collingwood Bay. In 1999, both CNN and the Australian Broadcasting Corporation covered the Maisin story of resisting commercial logging. The story will receive even more attention as a subject in a fifty-minute documentary, *Shifting Ground,* aired on the internationally syndicated program *The Nature of Things* in early 2001.

Bringing sustainable local economic projects has proven more difficult. For many years now, the Maisin have sold tapa cloth both for a small national market (where it is used as traditional clothing in dances) and for tourists who purchase it in artifact stores in Port Moresby. Tapa has a number of attractions as a development project. Both the cloth and the dyes are made from fast-growing local plants so there is a minimal environmental impact. Further, the cloth is traditionally made by women, a target group that most of the Maisin's partners particularly want to support. A Greenpeace activist put in a great deal of effort to develop the international market for tapa while two Peace Corps volunteers, stationed in Uiaku, helped train Maisin to organize the local business and keep track of the costs and profits. These efforts resulted in a steady if still moderate increase in cash earned by villagers. Environmental groups have explored other economic options with the Maisin, including insect farming, with few results so far.

The environmentalists, through their very presence, provide Maisin with important material benefits. Visitors pay villagers for food and lodging and often leave behind gifts, adding to the remittance economy. In addition, partners have donated medicine, a satellite telephone, and (as a loan) a motorized dinghy. Conservation Melanesia assists MICAD with finances, including a bank account, lends money for those needing to travel to town, and provides a reliable alternative to the national post system.

Despite these achievements, the relationship between the Maisin and outside environmentalists has become increasingly stressful. The major victim of these differences has been MICAD, which seemed on the verge of collapse during my last visit to the area in July 2000. There are many points of tension, but I think that much of the stress can be understood in terms of the different ways Maisin and their environmentalist partners conceptualize their partnership. For the Maisin, the partnership represents, as we have seen, an exchange. For the environmentalists, much like the Anglican missionaries in the past, the partnership should be understood as a temporary alliance meant to bring about a permanent change in the indigenous society. While both parties are able to work productively together at first, eventually their differing perceptions create a clash that may be difficult, if not impossible, to resolve.

Exchange relationships are inherently unstable. While Maisin villagers have taken up the various initiatives proposed by environmentalists and MICAD leaders with enthusiasm, the initial periods of support have inevitably been followed by growing suspicions that things are not "fair," that someone is benefiting at the expense of everyone else. As gossip spreads, villagers quietly withdraw their support and the initiative falters. That MICAD has survived as long as it has is testament to the determination and diplomatic skills of a handful of leaders. But few Maisin can long withstand the growing whispers that they are pocketing money that rightfully belongs to the community or working only to benefit their own kin. It is hard to find individuals willing to serve on the MICAD executive board. Indeed, I have frequently heard members of that executive board express their conviction that their colleagues are only working for their own benefit. And many villagers, especially those most closely associated with MICAD, resent the fact that most of the international grant money that funds groups like Conservation Melanesia does not come instead directly to the villages, and that museum shops in Australia or the United States themselves make profits from selling Maisin tapa cloth. A new threat to Maisin land or a new project can overcome such divisiveness, but only for a short time. It soon returns leading Maisin to conclude, as they did with the old cooperatives, that their greatest weakness is their apparent inability to remain unified (to enter into that graced state of social amity, of *marawa-wawe*). Environmentalists are poorly equipped to deal with village politics. Most, when they first come to Collingwood Bay, are seduced by the beauty of the area, the generosity of the people, the apparent resilience and strength of Maisin culture, and the compelling nature of the story line of an indigenous "David" resisting the "Goliath" of the international trade in rainforest hardwoods. The first complaint everyone hears is that some villages, usually Uiaku, get all of the benefits. Trying to deal with this suspicion requires visitors to hold meetings in all of the Maisin villages, an exhausting task that, as it turns out, does only a little to overcome the problem. (See Figure 25.4 for a villager's idea of what is needed.) The longer they work with the villagers, the more likely it is that the visitor will hear accusations of favoritism, theft of money, and so forth. While villagers overwhelmingly direct their complaints against each other, and especially at the leaders of MICAD, eventually partners become aware that similar things are being said of them—that they are reaping huge financial benefits at the expense of the Maisin. At this point, they may feel some resentment over the Maisin's apparent lack of gratitude for the sacrifices the visitor has made or feel some guilt that not enough has been done.

Few if any partners perceive the politics of the village in terms of the cultural logic of exchange. Instead, most of the partners working with the Maisin tend to see these complaints as a reflection of a "culture of dependency," itself a product of the colonial period during which rural people came to see the mission and government as the source of material

**Figure 25.4** "My Environment," by Felix Jovisa

progress. They may dismiss the villagers' hopes for immediate material returns as "cargoism," an irrational belief that the mere presence of Europeans attracts wealth. Such mistaken beliefs can only be countered through education. The environmentalists aim to enhance the self-reliance of the local community, not make them even more dependent upon the outside economy that tempted them to allow the destruction of the natural environment in the first place.

In the past, the Anglican mission also labored to create self-reliant communities. While seeing villagers and village life as essentially good, the goal of self-sufficiency still required practical and moral changes. The new environmental "missionaries" do not build schools or preach every Sunday, but they do require the Maisin who work with them to learn the mysteries of rationalized surveys, planning, book keeping, and regular reports. Maisin leaders have assigned young men and women to these tasks, much like their own ancestors sent their sons and daughters to the mission school. But more overt attempts to transform village society can be met with resistance. Many of the Maisin's new partners, for instance, are ideologically committed to elevating the status of women. Maisin women enjoy a relatively high status by Melanesian standards. They lack the right to speak publicly or to inherit land, but they do make their opinions known through their brothers and husbands and suffer very little violence. Many of the activists working with the Maisin insisted on a much more visible role for women. In response, the Maisin formed a new women's organization, included women representatives in MICAD, and agreed that delegations headed overseas would include equal numbers of women and men. From the start, most Maisin men resented and resisted these changes, attempting to contain them to the times when valued partners were actually in the villages. By 2000 the resistance had become far more overt. In June, I led a group of five members of an aboriginal group from British Columbia on the first stage of a planned exchange between the Sto:lo First Nation and the Maisin people. The second part of the exchange is now on hold because of my insistence (on behalf of the financial donors) that half of the delegation be female. The (male) leaders of the Maisin villages insisted that women were too poorly educated, too shy, and unwilling to participate in public life and therefore only men should go. Several men politely but firmly protested to me and a female Sto:lo delegate against efforts of outsiders like ourselves to "change the culture," the first time I have ever heard this complaint made.

## CONCLUSION

Present-day Maisin have responded to the emergence of an environmental movement in Papua New Guinea much as an earlier generation did to the Anglican experiment with community cooperatives. In both cases, Maisin assumed that they required a partnership with powerful outsiders to secure community prosperity and political unity. The village cooperatives and MICAD both emerged as intermediary institutions meant both to unify the Maisin and to demonstrate a moral and political unity that the people believed was the essential requirement for the creation of prosperity. While the integrated conservation and development model has proven popular in many parts of Papua New Guinea, few groups have taken up the program with as much enthusiasm—and none with such spectacular results—as the Maisin. A review of Maisin history suggests that they were already searching for "new missionaries for old" in the early independence period. Given their generally positive experience with the Anglican mission, the Maisin may have been quicker to see the potential in building partnerships with environmentalists than other communities. While successful in the face of immediate threats to Maisin lands, the relationship is nonetheless a fragile one, balanced between two contradictory perspectives. The Maisin for the most part continue to view their relationship with outside partners according to the logic and politics of exchange while the environmentalists seek instead to create a short-term alliance that preserves and strengthens the Maisin's self-reliance. The relationship, based in part upon creative misunderstanding, demands adjustments on the part of both partners if it is not to break down entirely.

History repeats itself, but never in exactly the same manner or under the same conditions. The Maisin of the 1990s had far more education and a far greater sophistication about the outside world than did the men who initiated the Christian cooperative movement. And the environmentalists were not Christian missionaries, let alone anything like the Anglo-Catholic Anglican romantics who dreamed of recreating an imagined medieval theocracy in the jungles of Papua. Both the cooperatives and MICAD began as local social movements drawing ideological strength by virtue of an imagined exchange partnership with powerful outsiders. But in the case of the cooperatives, the Anglican mission was too poor and too insular to offer much practical support and Maisin were left to draw mostly from their own resources. In contrast, environmentalists have offered individual Maisin unprecedented access to institutions and organizations spread around the globe.

There are many other differences that one could point to, but perhaps the most important is this: In the early postwar period, the Anglican mission provided the Maisin with their major source of knowledge of the outside world and their major link to it. In those days, old people told me, they believed that Jerusalem and heaven were the same. The Anglican monopoly started to break down during the 1960s, as Maisin trained in mission schools suddenly found their skills and knowledge welcomed in the public service and government. By the early 1990s, Anglicanism had lost its monopoly within the villages and individuals became increasingly aware of different forms of belief, different approaches to the world. Some Maisin visited Jerusalem and returned to tell the people that it was really a city, much like other cities on earth. Many Maisin are still actively searching for "missionaries"— partners who will unite their communities, link them to the outside, and thus bring prosperity. But they no longer presume coherence between religious faith and political unity. Perhaps the time is not far off, as Maisin society becomes more individualistic, when the idea of a common partner for the Maisin people will cease to make sense.

## ACKNOWLEDGMENTS

I received funding for fieldwork in Papua New Guinea since 1981 from a variety of organizations, including the Social Sciences and Humanities Research Council of Canada, the Wenner-Gren Foundation for Anthropological Research, the National Geographic Society, the Overseas Ministries Study Center, and the Hampton Fund at the University of British Columbia. My thanks to all of these organizations. My debt to my Maisin hosts and friends is enormous. I hope that this, among my other attempts to make sense of their history and experience, makes a small repayment. I want to express a special thanks to Lester Seri of Conservation Melanesia and Lafacadio Cortesi for their frankness and patience in answering my many questions. This chapter represents my views and I take full responsibility for the interpretation offered here.

## NOTES

1. Tapa cloth was traditionally made across the Pacific Islands, usually from the pounded inner bark of the paper mulberry tree. Although Pacific Islanders have universally adopted Western clothing, a few groups in scattered parts of the Pacific still make tapa today for use in ceremonial exchange and as a form of tourist art. The Maisin may have begun selling their beautifully designed tapa cloths to visitors as early as the 1930s. By the early 1980s, they had found a niche in the small national artifact market for their cloth and, at this time, are the only group producing it for sale in the country.

2. The Australians took over German New Guinea during the First World War but elected to run it as a separate colony from Papua. Following the Second World War, the Australian government combined the two colonial adminstrations, leading to the creation of Papua New Guinea.

3. Since the early 1970s, the government has set the basic curriculum for the schools and provided most of the training and salaries of teachers. The churches, however, retain at least nominal control over most local schools and several secondary and tertiary schools in the country. Some churches, such as the Seventh Day Adventist and Roman Catholic Church, continue to largely finance and run their own school systems. Churches today still run a large portion of the national health system.

4. Wetherell (1977) provides an excellent history of the Anglican mission in colonial Papua. See Barker (1987) for a detailed account of early missionary activities in Collingwood Bay.

5. Scholars have long observed that Christian missionaries may influence indigenous cultures as much through the practical routines they establish for converts as through explicitly religious instruction. By participating in schools and churches, converts may gradually become accustomed to and even internalize the missionaries' own cultural orientations to such conceptual dimensions as time, space, work, and value (Smith 1982). Ironically, Western missionaries have been key agents of secularization in rural Melanesia, easing the incorporation of people into the hegemonic framework of global capitalism (Trompf 1977). This is by no means a simple process of cultural replacement, of missionaries forcing Western culture upon villagers, however. In their magisterial study of nineteenth-century Protestant mission activity among the Tswana in southern Africa, Jean and John Comaroff clearly demonstrate that even at the level of routine, local people resist, contest, and transform the cultural patterns missionaries work to

establish. In other words, they engage in a dialogue or a dialectic with the mission (Comaroff and Comaroff 1991; Comaroff and Comaroff 1997). In places like the Maisin villages, where missionaries had to work from a distance and through intermediaries, villagers played a larger part in determining popular Christian understandings and practices (Barker 1993).

6. This interpretation is supported by, among other things, repeated efforts by the Maisin to use the power of the mission to purge their villages of sorcery materials. In 1903, for instance, Money was startled when villagers presented him and the teachers with a large pile of "charms" to be destroyed (Barker 1990b).

7. An observer of the national election of 1972 reported that villagers in several parts of the Northern District assumed that the bishops of the Anglican mission would (and should) tell them which candidates to support (Jawodimbari 1976).

8. Maisin thus also refer to *kawo* and *sabu* clans as people who "respect the drum" (*ira ari kawo*) and who "respect the spear" (*ganan ari kawo*) respectively.

9. Although Maisin speak of "chiefs," anthropologists would classify their indigenous political system as a cross between a "big man" system, in which leaders largely achieve positions of influence, and a "great man" system, in which men gain renown through their ability to exercise certain activities (such as warfare, sorcery, or feasting), which are themselves inherited prerogatives passed down family lines (Godelier and Strathern 1991).

10. In 1998 when I was visiting the area to discuss the exchange and film, I'm told that a woman who had once been my wife's research assistant spoke up at a meeting I was not able to attend and said something close to the following: "Baka [my Maisin name] came here and lived with us for a long time, but he didn't do anything for the people. He went away. And then he finally thought about us. Now he is finally going to help us." The people who told me about this speech clearly thought it would please me. And they are probably right. After all, they do regularly speak of their own relatives working in town in such prodigal terms.

11. Like most of the larger national NGOs, Conservation Melanesia receives a considerable amount of its funding from foreign sources, notably the World Wildlife Fund and the Australian government. International organizations also provide Conservation Melanesia with expatriate experts to assist in developing conservation campaigns.

## REFERENCES

Barker, John. 1987. "Optimistic Pragmatists: Anglican Missionaries Among the Maisin of Collingwood Bay, Oro Province." *Journal of Pacific History* 22(2):66–81.

———. 1990b. "Encounters with Evil: The Historical Construction of Sorcery in Maisin Society, Papua New Guinea." *Oceania* 61(1):139–155.

———. 1993. "We Are 'Ekelesia': Conversion in Uiaku, Papua New Guinea." In *Christian Conversion: Historical and Anthropological Perspectives on a Great Transformation*. R. Hefner, ed. Pp. 199–230. Berkeley: University of California Press.

———. 1996. "Village Inventions: Historical Variations upon a Regional Theme." *Oceania* 66(3):211–229.

Barker, John, ed. 1990a. *Christianity in Oceania: Ethnographic Perspectives*. Lanham, Md.: University Press of America.

Burridge, K. O. L. 1978. "Missionary Occasions." In *Mission, Church, and Sect in Oceania*. J. Boutilier, D. Hughes, and S. Tiffany, eds. Pp. 1–30. Ann Arbor: University of Michigan Press.

Chowning, Ann. 1979. "Leadership in Melanesia." *Journal of Pacific History* 14:66–84.

Comaroff, Jean, and John Comaroff. 1991. *Of Revelation and Revolution: Christianity, Colonialism and Consciousness in South Africa*. Vol. 1. Chicago: University of Chicago Press.

Comaroff, John L., and Jean Comaroff. 1997. *Of Revelation and Revolution: The Dialectics of Modernity on a South African Frontier*. Vol. 2. Chicago: University of Chicago Press.

Dakeyne, R. B. 1966. "Co-Operatives at Yega." In *Orokaiva Papers. New Guinea Research Bulletin No. 13*. Pp. 53–68. Port Moresby and Canberra: New Guinea Research Unit.

Ernst, Manfred. 1994. *Winds of Change: Rapidly Growing Religious Groups in the Pacific Islands*. Suva: Pacific Conference of Churches.

Filer, Colin. 1998. *Loggers, Donors and Resource Owners*. Vol. 2. London and Port Moresby: International Institute for Environment and Development; National Research Institute.

Garrett, John. 1982. *To Live Among the Stars: Christian Origins in Oceania*. Geneva: World Council of Churches.

Gill, S. R. M. 1929. "Committee Appointed to Enquire into the Interrelationship Between Native Ideas and Christianity." In *Anglican Archives*. Port Moresby: University of Papua New Guinea.

Godelier, Maurice, and Marilyn Strathern, eds. 1991. *Big Men & Great Men: Personifications of Power in Melanesia*. Cambridge: Cambridge University Press.

Hau'ofa, Epeli. 1981. *Mekeo: Inequality and Ambivalence in a Village Society*. Canberra: ANU Press.

Jawodimbari, Arthur. 1976. "Politics of Confusion and Religion." In *Prelude to Self-Government: Electoral Politics in Papua New Guinea 1972*. D. Stone, ed. Pp. 492–503. Canberra: Australian National University.

Lutkehaus, Nancy. 1982. "Manipulating Myth and History—How the Manam Maintain Themselves." *Bikmaus* 3:81–89.

Money, Percy John. 1903. Letter of December 19, 1902. *Missionary Notes* 99(March 23, 1903):18–19.

Munroe, Doug, and Andrew Thornley, eds. 1996. *The Covenant Makers: Islander Missionaries in the Pacific.* Suva, Fiji: Pacific Theological College and the Institute of Pacific Studies, University of the South Pacific.

Newton, Henry. 1914. *In Far New Guinea.* London: Seeley Service.

Smith, Michael French. 1982. "Bloody Time and Bloody Scarcity: Capitalism, Authority, and the Transformation of Temporal Experience in a Papua New Guinea Village." *American Ethnologist* 9(3):503–518.

Trompf, Gary. 1977. "Secularisation for Melanesia?" In *Christ in Melanesia.* Pp. 23–52. Point Goroka: Melanesian Institute.

Trompf, Gary W. 1991. *Melanesian Religion.* Cambridge: Cambridge University Press.

Wetherell, David. 1977. *Reluctant Mission: The Anglican Church in Papua New Guinea, 1891–1942.* St. Lucia: University of Queensland Press.

Zimmer-Tamakoshi, Laura, ed. 1998. *Modern Papua New Guinea.* Kirksville, Mo.: Thomas Jefferson University Press.

# 26

# Converted Worlds, Converted Lives: History and Opposition in Agarabi Adventism

**George Westermark**

*Santa Clara University*

One of the dominant forces in the transformation of the Pacific Islands' cultures over the past five hundred years has been the expansion of global Christianity. From Guam in the seventeenth century to Papua New Guinea in the twentieth century, missionaries and their organizations introduced ideas and institutions that expanded the network of connections Pacific Islanders have with the rest of the globe. Along with commerce and colonialism, Christianity was one of the "Three Cs" of culture change in the region. Christianity is now incorporated fully into the lives of Pacific Islanders, both through the links to the worldwide system of Christian churches and the elaborations of local practice. It is the dynamic relationship between one church and its local situation that is the focus of this chapter.

On August 19, 1989, an extraordinary event occurred for Seventh-Day Adventists. The largest baptism of Adventists ever performed in the history of that church occurred at Keiya, a site outside the town of Goroka in the Eastern Highlands Province of Papua New Guinea. With some 200 pastors from around the country and the South Pacific region, over 4,000 converts were baptized in the rain-swollen waters of the Asaro River. This massive undertaking was part of a week's camp meeting where an estimated twenty thousand people were in attendance (PNG *Post-Courier* 1989). In part, these thousands were drawn to the meeting by the visit of the American international leader of the church, Pastor Neal Wilson, who would speak to those participating. The baptism, meeting, and leader's visit were evidence of the growth of Adventism in Papua New Guinea, as well as the significance of this country for this worldwide church movement.

Although the number of Papua New Guinean Seventh-Day Adventists expanded through the last decades of the twentieth century in members and churches, and they have a significant presence elsewhere in the Pacific, little has been written about this group. My aim in this chapter is to show how the growth in Adventist membership is affected by both a global religious system and by the local elaborations of the Adventist message in the Eastern Highlands. Only by setting the local interpretation of prevalent Adventist themes within a backdrop of international missionary efforts can we account for the shift in church membership in this region. Although I believe that Adventist teachings have a multifaceted appeal, drawing adherents for a variety of reasons, I will focus in particular upon how the long-term goal of salvation is structured by a specific historical consciousness (Ohnuki-Tierney 1990:4). Combining texts from both the Old and New Testaments, Adventist biblical interpretations serve as a unifying conceptual framework that articulates the linkages between the history of Papua New Guinea and the rest of the globe. Yet, even as it provides this global framework, it also outlines a guide for current individual action and advocates a doctrine of opposition toward other Christian groups. Because the past and present are joined in the truth claims of this group, and because their ideas link the global and local in critical ways, the historical aspects of Adventist doctrine explain the secular benefits of their ideology even as they associate them with the expected millennial events of the Last Days. In this way Adventism provides many Eastern Highlanders with "new answers and ways to live" (Hefner 1993:24), or "more integrated systems of meaning, personal autonomy, and more responsibility" (Cucchiari 1988:418; see also Saunders 1995), at a time of significant social transformation in Papua New Guinea. More broadly, the Adventist experience in the Eastern Highlands offers us another example of the complex ways in which peoples everywhere are using religion to respond to the stresses of modernity in this global age (Hefner 1998).

The ethnographic context for my examination of Adventist activities is that of the Agarabi of the Kainantu District. Making up about one-fourth of the district's population, they live in some thirty communities to the north and east of Kainantu town. Both the first Adventist missionaries to, and the first converts from, the highlands were associated with the Agarabi. The grandchildren of the first converts are now active church members, and with this long Adventist record, they have been fully engaged with the Adventist growth of the past decade.[1] I begin by outlining the phases of social change in this part of the Eastern Highlands.

## SOCIAL CHANGE IN AGARABI

Prior to the incursion of Australians and Europeans into the Eastern Highlands about seven decades ago, Agarabi life was centered on the demands of horticultural subsistence and shifting political alliance. With garden lands surrounding their often palisaded villages, the Agarabi organized their relationships through the idiom of patrilineal descent. Frequent conflict between communities led to the movement and recombination of community segments so that actual relationships were a complex blend of consanguinity, affinity, and residence. In this respect, they were similar to their neighbors in the Eastern Highlands (Watson 1983).

Agarabi oral traditions link their contemporary communities with a mythological and historical record of movement and change. In one narrative, a woman and a boy walk through their territory naming objects and places. Having walked down to the Markham Valley below the Eastern Highlands, the boy is initiated into manhood, the couple give birth to sons, and they gradually return to the Agarabi territory of today. Population grows, conflicts occur, and groups divide as the Agarabi move westward toward the site of Kainantu town. The details of these movements grow more precise as conflict, division, and movement collide with the European intrusion. It is at this stage that the Agarabi story connects with the unfolding of Adventist history, and the first phase of contemporary Agarabi social transformation begins.

Starting in the late 1920s, the transitions of the pre–World War II world included the extension of the Australian colonial realm to this region. Communities consolidated at the urgings of patrol officers, village boundaries were set, and warfare ended. Although the Lutherans were the first Christian group in the Kainantu area, the Adventists followed soon thereafter in the middle of the 1930s. The Adventist expansion into the highlands came with "generous financial aid and leadership from Australia and New Zealand" (Garrett 1997:36–37). With World War II came the first significant movement of Agarabi men outside their own territory as they worked as bearers for the troops. The postwar period speeded the process of economic change, bringing coffee production to their villages, and with it, a new economy forever linked to the world economic system. This second phase of social transformation also saw the first Agarabi Adventist converts in the 1940s, and their first journeys, in the 1950s, as lay evangelists to southern regions, which were then not under colonial control.

An improved Highlands Highway linked Kainantu to the coast in the mid-1960s, and because the road bisected the Agarabi area, all of the new social and economic changes entering the highlands came there first. This was the time when new political innovations were introduced, beginning with council government in 1960, parliamentary elections in 1964, national self-government in 1973, and independence from Australia in 1975.

The independence period might be said to mark the third phase of social transformation the Agarabi experienced over the last seventy years. What distinguishes this phase is the growing control of local and national institutions by Papua New Guineans. Innovations in local self-government were introduced (Westermark 1978, 1986). While subsistence gardening remained the primary source of food, various economic developments had an impact during this period. Cattle projects were seen by some as a source of new income (Grossman 1984). Small-holder coffee projects were encouraged by the government in the 1980s (Gimbol 1984). The competition for land stimulated by development led to the reworking of clan histories for legal purposes (Westermark 1997). Today, in those communities close to town, many Agarabi participate in wage employment in stores or with government departments. Some men even own stores in Kainantu. Cars and trucks have become more prevalent forms of village transportation, and they have increased villagers' movements between village and town.

The changes of this third phase were not all viewed as positive by Agarabi. As is the case elsewhere in the world, the inroads of foreign ideas and images led to conflict between generations, elders frequently complaining of the lack of industry and the promiscuity of the young. Alcohol became a serious problem in the villages, especially with the licensing of village clubs by the Eastern Highlands provincial government. Criminal activity, or "rascalism," emerged as a persistent problem in the last decade, affecting both villagers and townspeople (Goddard 1995; Hart Nibbrig 1992; Strathern 1992). Intercommunity conflicts, or "tribal warfare," persisted in the other highland provinces (Brown 1982; Podolefsky 1984; Strathern 1983, 1992), as well as in the Eastern Highlands (Westermark 1984). New diseases appeared as a pernicious factor in the Eastern Highlands. In the late 1980s, a serious epidemic of typhoid developed, which had the highest incidence in Kainantu, and was most deadly among the Agarabi.[2] In recent decades, therefore, Agarabi have had to adapt to the effects of rapid change, and, consequently, have sought new interpretive frameworks that would account for this transformation.

## ADVENTIST GROWTH IN THE EASTERN HIGHLANDS

Although the Keiya camp meeting was a dramatic event, an assessment of the significance of this mass baptism for Adventist growth must be situated within the broader field of Papua New Guinea and the South Pacific. Accurate determinations of church affiliation are difficult to make in this region, and we must approach such records with particular care. Nevertheless, Adventists are rather strict in allowing only those who have been prepared as adults and submitted to full-immersion baptism to become members (see Figure 26.1). They are just as stringent in

**Figure 26.1**    Agarabi village Adventist baptism

noting those they call "backsliders" for having fallen away from the church. Thus, the attention to and care for church affiliation records is taken seriously. Moreover, in comparing changes within the church between one decade and another, or between one area and another, we can at least assume a certain consistency.

The Pacific region is clearly an important one for the Adventists. In 1986, their South Pacific Division (SPD), which covers all the Pacific nations, including Australia and New Zealand, totaled 182,864 adherents from a population of nearly twenty-four million. In contrast, the Euro-Africa Division totaled just 266,541 members in a population of nearly 385 million.[3] Within the SPD, the Papua New Guinea Union Mission stands out as the largest and fastest-growing area. It is twice as large as the Australian and New Zealand membership combined (Garrett 1997:342). Their 1986 membership of 88,451 gave them nearly half the Pacific's Adventists. By 1989, PNG membership had grown to 108,000.[4] Church estimates point to a potential membership of 211,000 by 2000 (Steley 1988:102,

ftn. 4). Within PNG, the Eastern Highlands-Simbu Mission accounted for 30 percent of PNG's Adventists in 1986.[5] By 1989, their growth from 26,620 to 35,353 gave them one third of the country's Adventists. Although not all of those baptized at the Keiya meeting were from the Eastern Highlands-Simbu Mission, their numbers must have swelled again from the converts of that day.

The relative significance of these membership figures can be measured in another way by comparing them with other Adventists in the Pacific Islands outside Papua New Guinea, Australia, and New Zealand.[6] Ernst (1994:305–307) provides the number of Pacific church members of different Christian groups, dividing them between "The Historic Mainline Churches" (for example, the Anglican Church, the Roman Catholic Church), "Established New Religious Groups" (for example, Church of Jesus Christ of Latter-Day Saints, Seventh-Day Adventists), "The Most Recent Arrivals" (for example, Fiji Baptist Convention, Samoan Full Gospel Church), and "The Breakaway Groups from the Historic Mainline Churches and New Religious

Groups" (for example, Alleluia, Rewa Wesleyan Mission). As might be expected, the largest number of adherents are to be found in the first group, "The Historic Mainline Churches," with the Roman Catholics (504,813), the Methodist Church in Fiji (264,579), and the Anglican Church (154,240) being the three largest. From amongst the "Established New Religious Groups," however, it is the Adventists who have the largest membership with 94,593. This number, somewhat less than the Papua New Guinea membership, makes them the fourth largest church in this region and "the largest religious group from all the non-mainline churches in the Pacific" (Ernst 1994:49).

Still, official figures are only one way to measure growth. Observations of significant religious changes at the local level in Kainantu parallel these numbers. From a time in the late 1970s, for instance, when there was but one Adventist church in Kainantu town, Agarabi Adventists had established at least five churches in their villages by the end of the 1980s. In the community with which I am most familiar, two churches had been established in separate hamlets. We also can look to the reduction in the membership of other churches. In this same community, hamlets that had been for decades firmly aligned with the Lutheran church had, in the 1980s, converted to Adventism. Moreover, Eastern Highland Lutheran leaders were expressing concern at the reduction in their church membership by the end of that decade.[7]

## TRANSMITTING THE MESSAGE

Before turning to the elements of the Adventist ideology that have been found appealing to Agarabi and other Eastern Highlanders, the well-developed organization of this church must be described, since it is responsible for both transmitting their message and sustaining their converts. For over fifty years, Kainantu town, situated on the edge of Agarabi territory, has been the center of Adventist evangelization (Garrett 1997:36–37). Church members are proud to point to the bullet marks on the church's walls where the building was strafed

by Japanese planes during World War II. To the east of town, fully in Agarabi territory, is found an Adventist grammar school. In the Gadsup area, south of Kainantu town, is the training school for Adventist pastors at Omaura. During the 1980s, a youth activity center was added to the Kainantu church. Thus, in combination with the new village churches, the Kainantu area in general, and the Agarabi specifically, have had extensive and long-term exposure to the institutions of the church.

The identity of Adventists is reinforced in the groups and roles that members can participate in outside the ordinary realm of village activities. Within each of the churches, groups like the Women's Welfare Society, the Laymen's Society, and the Youth Choir offer social and recreational activities in addition to their church work. Church officers such as deacons, deaconesses, and church elders perform the duties of supervising seating in church, collecting offerings, and assisting with church service.

Worship activities occupy the time of Adventists beyond the Sabbath church meetings. Adventist booklets published in Pidgin guide daily prayer meetings in the morning and evening that can last forty-five to sixty minutes. During the course of the year, a special revival meeting might be held over several days where a pastor visits the village church members to discuss a special topic, such as marriage, child rearing, or the Second Advent. In such settings, the ideas preached daily by a church member, or each Sabbath by a lay evangelist, can receive more official validation. On occasion, camp meetings are organized with large numbers of the members of the district's churches gathering at the Kainantu town headquarters.[8] Smaller versions of the Keiya gathering, these events may mark the visit of a church official or the initiation of a new program. Through such gatherings, as well as the Bible study urged upon individuals, Adventist readings of the Bible can be kept in the forefront of members' minds, even as the traditions of the past and the events of the day are discussed.

Unlike the Anglicans described by Barker (chapter 25), who sought to merge with the village community, Adventists' stress on education and the rejection of old ways has meant that Agarabi Adventists have become both economic and political leaders in the institutions of town and government. Either through coffee or commerce, a number of these men became prominent and wealthy within the regional community, and thereby served as notable role models within the Adventist community.

While the local churches are today largely run by Agarabi church officials and Papua New Guinean pastors, outreach by the international church continues to be significant for the transmission of the Adventist message. The Keiya meeting, for instance, took vast coordination on the part of representatives from various levels of Adventist organization in Papua New Guinea, the South Pacific region, and the international church. Moreover, it was a prominent event that was part of a five-year, worldwide evangelistic campaign called "Harvest '90." Literature from the Papua New Guinea headquarters urged local leaders to adopt diverse evangelistic strategies: running branch Sabbath schools in non-Adventist villages; organizing song concerts, children's programs, and health talks; and

having church members help potential converts with work in village gardens. The Harvest '90 literature also touted the accomplishments being made annually within the local area and around the world. In this way, Agarabi church leaders learned that Adventists in Papua New Guinea had exceeded their recruitment goal for the campaign's first year by more than 1,000; they read that the international results had exceeded the recruitment goal by almost 100,000.

One noteworthy aspect of the campaign was the "Grow One" objective: Each church was being challenged to initiate at least one new church in their area during the five-year period. As a result, the campaign literature reported, 130 new churches had been started within the Eastern Highlands in one year. The expansion of the Adventists among the Agarabi and in the Eastern Highlands was, therefore, not just a local phenomenon. Part of a well-planned global movement fostered by the international church and implemented at the community level by innovative evangelistic techniques, the campaign gave added significance to both ordinary church activities and extraordinary events such as the Keiya meeting (see Figures 26.2 and 26.3).

**Figure 26.2**   Keiya gathering to hear Pastor Neal Wilson, International Adventist President, speak

**Figure 26.3**  The Pidgin sign at this Keiya meeting, "Hausat bai i pinis," refers to indicators for the end of the world in the last days

## OPPOSITION AND IDENTITY

As we will see, Adventist beliefs offer a distinctive blend of Christian themes. Their name indicates two fundamental beliefs: the Second Coming, or advent, of Jesus is imminent and worship on the seventh day, or the Sabbath, is essential. The latter belief is tied to a number of tenets of faith that they draw from the Old Testament (for example, diet prohibitions). Sabbath worship is linked to the Second Coming because Adventists believe that their adherence to the "true" teachings of the Bible will precipitate the events of the Last Days when Jesus returns to defend those who have been faithful to his teachings.

In understanding the appeal of Adventism in the Eastern Highlands, I believe we must examine how these teachings of Adventism structure a series of critical markers of opposition which are important for the transformation of personal and group identity. Studies of sectarian religious groups like the Adventists show that, on the one hand, their confrontational stance to the wider society may cause some social isolation, while, on the other hand, they offer a particularly appealing blend of doctrine and social bonding in changing societies. Both cohesion and purpose are strengthened among sectarians when they perceive themselves under attack by elements in the world (see McGuire 1992:162). Although sectarianism is not rare in Pacific Christian communities (Ross 1979; Gewertz and Errington 1993; Barker 1990; Ernst 1994; Tuzin 1989), the opposition theme is central to Adventist historical consciousness since it singles out certain memorable events reflective of the antagonism critical for the Second Coming.[9] Even as Adventist numbers grow so that the intracommunity hostility of the past is less prevalent (Westermark 1987), opposition toward the many other Christian churches in the area provides an ample target for this orientation.

Because Adventists believe that they are followers of the true Christian church, and because they feel that their rightness creates an antagonistic relationship with other churches, opposition is a strongly voiced aspect of the Adventist doctrine. As with other fundamentalist Christians, Adventists adhere to a strict reading of the teachings of Jesus. They give a unique turn to certain aspects of these teachings, however, which serves to clearly contrast them with other churches. It is this clear definition of religious identity that many Agarabi adherents have found appealing in their conversion to this faith. As one leading Kainantu Adventist put it: "Adventists place the hardest demands on their followers, but people like their teachings." Moreover, as these symbols of identification are linked to Adventist historical consciousness, they also have the attraction of demarcating a clear plan for living in the contemporary world as it approaches the Last Days.[10] Some of the most critical beliefs in this respect include dietary prohibitions, Sabbath worship, and reading the Bible.

Adventist teachings bring the search for salvation to an immediate and personal level through dietary prohibitions. These proscriptions are a unique feature of the Adventist doctrine that carries a tremendous symbolic load in highland cultures.[11] Emerging from statements by Jesus that he came to fulfill the laws of the Old Testament, Adventists avoid the consumption of pork in a region noted for its attachment to this animal. For the Eastern Highland Adventists, this clearly creates a definitive separation from their precolonial world, as well as from other Christians and non-Christians. The rejection of pork by Agarabi Adventists includes rejecting food that is cooked with pork in earth ovens. In the 1970s, some Adventists even were concerned about walking through their communities at night for fear of inadvertently stepping on the pig feces of animals owned by non-Adventists.[12] Although Adventist doctrine elsewhere in the world favors vegetarianism, this dietary preference has not been advocated in Papua New Guinea, as far as I know. As a result, cattle and goats have been raised by Adventists as an alternative to pork, and coffee earnings have allowed for the purchase of meats in town. Additionally, dietary rules motivated Agarabi to initiate some of the first cattle projects in the Kainantu District, and to continue to develop these projects in the 1970s and 1980s (Grossman 1984:57-58).

Concern for the state of the body in its relationship to the soul leads Adventists to avoid other substances. For Agarabi Adventists, some of their greatest temptations come in trying to reject tobacco and alcohol. Conversely, individuals attempting to end their consumption of beer have found that it was only by converting that they gained the strength to oppose the pressures from non-Adventists to drink. One fairly recent male convert described it the following way: "I was going out and spending my money on beer, and I was afraid I would be killed in a fight or a car accident. And I wanted to have my money to use for other business." A member of many years made a similar association: "Before I joined I threw away my money on drink and tobacco. Now I have lots of money and my family is well taken care of with a growing business." Given the prevalence of drinking and smoking among almost all adult non-Adventists, avoiding these substances is an obvious way to affirm group identity, as well as retain savings. The contrast between Adventists and non-Adventists was sharply drawn for me one Saturday morning as I walked along a village trail below the two adjoining hills where one Adventist church and the village club oppose each other. From one hill came the sound of church hymns and from the other traditional Agarabi singing by men remaining there from Friday night.

Dietary prohibitions are thus recognized to have more immediate rewards. The avoidance of smoking and drinking, and the healthy living he associated with it, led one of the first Agarabi Adventists to tell me that he had been influential in converting other Agarabi because they could see in his life "another kind of happiness." Yet, since participation in drinking can consume large amounts of monetary resources, not to mention the threat to employment for those who work in town, many Adventists also speak of the significance of this avoidance for their efforts to be economically successful in business.[13]

The most distinctive marker of Adventist identity is their commitment to the Saturday Sabbath. Some Agarabi Adventists have told me that the American founder of Adventism, Ellen White, saw in her earliest visions the Ten Commandments with the fourth commandment illuminated. She interpreted this to mean that, unlike most other Christians, Jesus never intended that the day of worship should be Sunday. The fourth commandment states that believers should keep the Lord's

Day holy, and since Jesus came to fulfill the laws, he intended that the Old Testament Sabbath should be followed. Her teachings caused the other churches to oppose her, especially because of her thoughts on the Sabbath. Some Agarabi Adventists say that the Catholic armies were sent to capture and kill her, but that she fled, hid in a cave, and was protected by a fog sent by God that covered the cave's entrance when the armies approached.[14]

More than any other belief or practice, this adherence to the Saturday Sabbath is cited by Adventists as the proof that they are the *true* church. When asked why they converted to Adventism, many Agarabi say they did so because of the Saturday worship. A meeting I attended in 1977 illustrates this commitment. A slide show of biblical sites was held at the Kainantu town church and put on by a highland Adventist from Goroka. He and a number of other highland businessmen had made a trip to Israel that year led by an Australian Adventist missionary. During his presentation, he highlighted one slide of an Israeli town on the Sabbath with shops and businesses closed following Jewish practice. The significance of these images for the Agarabi Adventists with whom I was sitting was clear: In the land of Jesus, Israelis, like Adventists in Papua New Guinea, worship on Saturday. A question that several in the audience asked was: Why had the other Christian churches attempted to mislead them into believing that Sunday was the Christian holy day?

While other ritual practices such as adult full-immersion baptism are different from other highland churches, it is the Sabbath that is seen to be the central source of opposition with other Christians. Moreover, it is this key tenet of their beliefs that Adventists cite as the future catalyst for the events of the Last Days.[15] Agarabi Adventist explanations for the Second Coming hold that other Christian churches, led by the Roman Catholics, will conspire with the world's governments to enact a law in favor of Sunday worship. Because the Adventists will remain faithful to the fourth commandment, they will be discriminated against in various ways in daily life.

When the other churches discover that these acts will not influence the Adventists, the churches and governments will move to destroy them. With the Adventists facing destruction, Jesus will return bringing salvation to God's chosen people.

Adventists' readings of the Bible give them a detailed framework for interpreting historical events leading to the Second Coming. Critical books like Daniel in the Old Testament and Revelations in the New Testament, which are filled with prophecies of what is to come, are used to provide the guide for this interpretation. It is here that Adventist historical consciousness enters into an understanding of both past and present events, for either type can be shown to be fully understandable only according to their framework. Agarabi Adventists strongly underline the fact that all this comes from the Bible as first introduced to them, not the altered and updated versions that some Christian groups have introduced.[16]

One unintended consequence of Adventist emphasis on reading the Bible has been that they had introduced schools and education to a greater extent than some other Christian groups.[17] As a result, some of the first Agarabi to achieve high school educations in the 1960s were Adventists, and these are the men who have gone on to take advantage of a variety of economic and political opportunities in later decades.

Clearly, Christian opposition, biblical symbolism, and the expectations of the Last Days of worldly existence are intertwined in Adventist discourse. Agarabi Adventists say that the attempt to discriminate against them will be introduced by forcing them in some way to be labeled with the potent number, 666. They interpret this to mean that during this period of discrimination, the number will keep them from participating in any form of business. The number has additional significance in that it is linked to the Beast, that demonic force described in Revelations that will lead to the persecution of the Adventists. Because Catholics figure prominently in the accounts of the Last Days, it is not surprising that 666 is "the number of a man," and that Adventists believe that it identifies the Pope.[18]

## HISTORICAL CONSCIOUSNESS, CONVERSION, AND SALVATION

Historical consciousness and conversion are interrelated in unique local ways with events of the past, present, and future. One prominent theme for Agarabi Adventists is the sense that Papua New Guinea, and the highlands in particular, is inextricably related to the unfolding of the Last Days. Adventist teaching suggests that salvation will come only when the word of Christ has been taught to all peoples; humans everywhere must have the opportunity to choose the "true road" before the last judgments are made in heaven. Agarabi Adventists realize that their region was one of the last reached by missionaries, and, therefore, Adventist work in the Eastern Highlands represents one of the important last events. Moreover, the Bible also says that knowledge will be great in the Last Days, and the expansion of education and technological knowledge in Papua New Guinea is seen as an example of the fulfillment of this prophecy. One Adventist pastor, for instance, took note in his sermon in Kainantu town of the hiring of a Papua New Guinean pilot by Air Niugini in the late 1970s. As he spoke to the largely Agarabi congregation, he pointed out how they had always felt that flying airplanes was only for whites. Now, with an indigenous pilot working for their national airline, he was convinced that they were soon to see the Second Coming.

Aspects of indigenous culture are cast in a new light by Adventist teachings. As with other Papua New Guinea Adventists (Josephides 1990:60), Agarabi frequently preach that many of their precolonial customs were part of a period of darkness or ignorance that now has been illuminated by Adventist teachings. Beliefs surrounding sorcery, marriage, and mourning are some areas where Agarabi distinguish a dark past from their current religious position. While sorcery has always been recognized as an evil, Agarabi say, it was only with the arrival of Adventists that they learned that this power had its source in Satan. Sorcery is not, therefore, rejected as a false belief, but is seen as an autochthonous reflection of the age-old, global battle between Good and Evil, God and the Devil. Agarabi Adventists point out the reality of sorcery, just as they do other sinful acts based in Satan. The perception of growth in the prevalence of sorcery in recent decades parallels the Adventist belief that evil will abound in the Last Days (Westermark 1981). In the 1970s, Agarabi Adventists suggested that, though they could not participate in the evils of sorcery, the presence of men in their communities who were still knowledgeable about this practice protected them from the active sorcerous attacks of their enemies. A decade later in 1989, the conversion of many of these men to Adventism was one explanation suggested for the deaths caused by the typhoid epidemic of the preceding years.

A number of traditional practices surrounding marriage and the family are opposed by Adventists. Polygyny has been rejected by Agarabi Adventists for many years, but more recently other family and marriage customs have been the scenes of contest and conflict. At the Keiya meeting, the religious suitability of Adventists paying bride-price was discussed in large group sessions and it was reported that the votes taken at the sessions favored ending the payments. Yet, in both individual and group discussions in their communities, many Agarabi Adventists also clearly recognized that the level of payment had been inflated in recent years, and they focused on the wealth lost through marriage arrangements that could be better used for business investments.

A prominent characteristic of Agarabi mourning ceremonies is the long-term visits of relatives of the deceased. Temporary structures are prepared for their lodging and food is gathered and cooked for their board during what might be a stay of more than a week. Some Agarabi Adventists argued that this custom reflected their pre-Christian past. Shorter periods of mourning would be more in keeping with expectations of the glories of the Second Coming. At other times, however, some Adventists cited the resources contributed to support the stay of visitors as a waste of money and time. While with both bride-price and mourning the most prominent rhetoric for change was whether or not these practices fit Adventist teachings, there was a recurrent subtext focusing on lost economic opportunities.

Many contemporary events are seen as either reflections of God's presence in the world or as indicators of the imminent return of Jesus. Of the former, for example, is one leading Agarabi Adventist businessman's belief that his success in the new small-holder coffee plantations was due to his practice of regular tithing. A lay evangelist attributes his recovery from a serious illness to God's plan for him to continue the work of conversion. Evidence of God's opposition to promiscuity was apparent for one Agarabi choir group whose truck crashed while on a journey to perform on the coast. The injuries the choir sustained were later said by some choir members to be the result of one young woman's hidden affair with a married man.

A variety of occurrences was cited by Adventists as signs of the approach of the Second Coming. In some cases, changes not directly attributable to human hands were seen as evidence for the unfolding of God's plan. Thus, news of phenomena like global warming or the AIDS epidemic were circulated by pastors and evangelists and were said to support prophecies from Revelations. More immediate in the Agarabi environment was the typhoid epidemic of the late 1980s. As it was most serious for the Agarabi, it was clearly related by them to Revelations' prophecies of the plagues that would come in the Last Days. A number of older Agarabi attributed their conversion to deaths associated with this epidemic.

New social problems also were associated with the coming millennium. Promiscuity among the young was frequently preached against, but noted as indicative of these Last Days. The growing consumption of beer, along with the violence it stimulated, was another indicator. Criminal activities on the roads and in the towns by so-called "rascal" gangs were one more proof that the time for Jesus' return was drawing near.

More significant than these other indicators, however, were the events in recent history

cited as revealing the opposition with other Christians that would precipitate the millennium. Just as with biblical interpretation, Adventists incorporate these stories into their own sectarian narrative that they use as evidence of the conspiracy against them. Some years ago, an Australian missionary working at the Adventist lay evangelist training center near Goroka was found shot to death. Although the police suggested that it was the act of local criminals bent on thievery, Adventists offered a different explanation. An Agarabi lay evangelist argued that the assassins had been sent by the Catholic leadership who were disturbed with Adventist conversion success. As the Adventist numbers grew larger, he explained, their religious victories would instill additional animosity toward them among other Christians. Since inroads on the Catholic stronghold in Simbu Province were increasing, the Catholics wanted to curtail the work of the training center. Evidence for the assassination theory was said to be the fact that the gun used in the murder was, based on the bullets found, one that had never before been seen in Papua New Guinea, thus supporting the alleged international element of the conspiracy.[19]

A similar story discussed by Agarabi Adventists was the fate of the prominent national leader from the highlands, Iambaki Okuk. Originally from Simbu Province, Okuk had shifted his residence for political reasons to his wife's district in the Eastern Highlands Province. Although he came close to becoming the Papua New Guinea prime minister, a serious illness led to his death in the 1980s. The frustration of his loss was deeply felt in both the Simbu and Eastern Highlands provinces where serious public rioting followed the announcement of his passing. Agarabi Adventists offered an alternative explanation for the events surrounding his demise.

A suspicious aspect of his end was believed to be that, after his death in Australia, his body was returned to Papua New Guinea for burial, but his family never saw the actual body; the casket, it is said, was buried without opening.[20] Later, a relative of Okuk's, who is a

Catholic priest, reported seeing him alive and captive in the Vatican. The explanation for this plot supposedly centers on the fact that the Catholic Church funded Okuk's campaign for prime minister, with the objective of imposing their rules after his victory, and he had threatened to reveal this fact. As with the murdered Adventist missionary, there is no confirmation of this story, but its mere existence highlights the extent to which Adventist ideology shapes the interpretation of significant current events, and how they, in turn, affirm the ideology.

In the weeks before the Keiya meeting, there was a flurry of preparation among Agarabi Adventists. Given that thousands would be baptized, and tens of thousands would be present, the church organization labored for months to develop its plan. The meeting came near the end of the five-year global Adventist evangelistic campaign, "Harvest '90." Added excitement was instilled in the Keiya meeting for Agarabi Adventists since the Adventist General Conference president, Pastor Neal Wilson, would be traveling from the United States to participate.

Shortly after the first Agarabi left for the Keiya meeting site, disturbing reports filtered back to the community where I resided. Carried secondhand by supporters who had gone by truck to Keiya to visit and to bring their relatives additional supplies, the reports suggested that potential assassins had been captured in the crowd. Later accounts further clarified these reports, describing how three men dressed as women had been discovered and pressured into revealing their intentions. They were said to have admitted to being paid by Catholic church leaders to eliminate Pastor Wilson. When I visited Keiya on the Sabbath occasion of the mass baptisms, security was tense, and I was stopped several times and asked about my identity and purpose. That I was approached with suspicion may have been linked to later reports I heard that on that afternoon two Europeans were sighted with guns in their possession. One was said to have been captured and taken to the police, but I was unable to learn anything more about the outcome of this event.

## CONCLUSION

In this chapter, we have seen the way in which the global influence of a Christian church has converted the lives of a highland Papua New Guinea people. Yet, as with other Pacific peoples, we have seen how the Agarabi and other Eastern Highlanders have taken the ideologies and structures of the Seventh-Day Adventists and interpreted them through their own cultural emphases. Although it has not been my goal here to compare the adaptation of Adventist belief elsewhere in the highlands, Papua New Guinea, or the Pacific, there undoubtedly are similarities. Still, if we are to recognize the importance of the indigenization of church beliefs in the Pacific (Barker 1990; see also Barker, chapter 25), then our studies of current patterns of religious commitment, even with fundamentalist groups like the Adventists, must be sensitive to the ways in which the appeal of particular doctrines are subtly altered by the nuances of local cultural reinterpretation.

While Agarabi Adventists do not stray far from church teachings, they have indigenized these teachings in the historical realm by attaching their own experience to the unfolding of the Adventist millennial account. Thus, interpretations of sorcery, marriage payments, and mourning customs as associated with the darkness located in their past become part of a narrative which includes the expansion of education and knowledge in this last site of Adventist evangelization. The realization that the Last Days could not unfold until the most distant reaches of the earth had been exposed to the truths of Adventist teaching adds greater significance to the Eastern Highland work for local Adventists. No longer is their position on the periphery of the world stage as it is geopolitically; rather, they are situated in the front rows, if not in the cast itself, of this global religious drama.

Representations of the past in Adventist beliefs also hold the key to salvation for many Agarabi and other Eastern Highlanders. Because their historical consciousness provides a ready framework for the interpretation of experience, various events become memorable as they can be situated in this structure of beliefs. Whether it be the effects of an epidemic, the murder of a missionary, or the publication of a Bible by a rival Christian group, the events take on added meaning for the signs they offer of the expected Second Advent. When stories touch on the central concern of opposition with other Christian groups, such as the rumors of assassination at the Keiya meeting or the abduction of Okuk, they are more noteworthy for their resonance with the anticipations of the Last Days.

Signs of the millennium, whether specifically linked to opposition or not, are transmitted through an array of formal and informal mechanisms structured by the church. Frequent worship led daily by local evangelists with Pidgin study guides provides a ready setting for the transformation of events into signs. Youth groups and women's groups offer settings for the communication of this information, as well as social affirmation. Dramatic gatherings such as the Keiya meeting create opportunities where the sinful society that surrounds Adventists can be preached against. They also create opportunities where the reconstruction of their own communities can be considered and voted upon, and where mass baptism can itself proclaim the success that Adventists see as moving them along the path already outlined in their historical model.

Moreover, Adventist teachings that call upon adherents to renounce many of their former foods and behaviors clearly offer a clear-cut personal reordering of experience. A boundary separates the new believers from those in their community outside the Adventist flock that allows them to resist many of the pulls associated with social dislocation. At a personal level, they may characterize their life course as a "new kind of happiness."

The motivations surrounding Agarabi Adventist historical consciousness are not, therefore, only millenarian in nature. The historical backdrop of Adventist teachings also entails much that is linked to day-to-day existence in the time that remains here on earth. The economic advantages that accrue to those who adopt this altered social calculus are undeniable. Ignoring contributions to family, marriage, and mourning obligations, or resisting the temptations of the village pub, may result in the accumulation of capital for investment. Turning to cattle project investments, at least in part due to dietary prohibitions, has led to economic benefits. The theological care for body and mind that Adventists preach on spiritual grounds may, ironically, be associated with the material success realized by members of this sectarian group. As a consequence, it is not surprising to find that many of the local Kainantu entrepreneurs are Adventists.

Adventist historical consciousness is certainly aimed at what it reveals about the Last Days. Yet the doors it opens are as much concerned with restructuring the present as they are with prognostications of what is to come. Since the practices of today ready Adventists for tomorrow, Adventist historical consciousness serves the critical role of justifying these social reconstructions, even as it accounts for current social transformations. Conjoining the past with the future in a prophetic narrative thereby provides a powerful message, one whose appeal offers both immediate and long-term rewards, both for individuals seeking to transform themselves and for groups searching for new collective identities. The meanings of that message articulate converted lives with converted worlds in the new reality of the contemporary Pacific Islands.

## ACKNOWLEDGMENTS

This chapter is a revised version of my article "History, Opposition, and Salvation in Agarabi Adventism," which was originally published in *Pacific Studies* 21(3):51–71, 1998. The revised article is reprinted with permission. I would like to gratefully acknowledge the support for my research from the following sources: National Science Foundation (1977–1978, 1989); National Institute of Mental Health (1977–1978); Bollingen Foundation (1977); Department of Anthropology, University of Washington (1977). An earlier version of this chapter was presented as part of a session on "Representations of the Past in the Pacific" at the annual meeting of the Association for Social

Anthropology in Oceania, San Diego, 1994. I wish to thank the other members of that session for comments on this chapter, particularly the session organizers, Lin Poyer and John Terrell. I also offer my thanks to the anonymous *Pacific Studies* reviewers of the article for their helpful suggestions. Most especially, I would like to thank the Agarabi Adventists who shared their thoughts and experiences with me.

## NOTES

1. Research for this paper comes from two periods of fieldwork in the Eastern Highlands in 1977–1978 and 1989. During these stays in an Agarabi community, I was able to learn much of the Adventist beliefs through participation in worship, interviews, and the study of local church records. Many Adventist friends in the community described their faith to me in some detail, and I had the opportunity to visit with Adventist acquaintances from other Agarabi villages. In 1989, I attended the Keiya camp meeting mentioned above, speaking with participants on site and with people after their return to the community. In the Kainantu area, I also heard the opinions of other Christian groups regarding the religious changes then occurring.

2. Personal communication from Dr. P. F. Howard, epidemiologist, Papua New Guinea Institute of Medical Research, Goroka, September 14, 1989 (letter in the author's files). See also Papua New Guinea *Post-Courier* 1990.

3. These figures are based on official Seventh-Day Adventist publications. The numbers cited for 1983 by Garrett (1997:342) and for 1988 by Steley (1989:617) parallel my work.

4. This figure was cited in a public speech at the Keiya meeting on August 19, 1989 by one of the Eastern Highland Adventist leaders of Australian origin (name unknown).

5. This religious division combines the Eastern Highlands and Simbu provinces. My concern in this chapter is primarily with areas of the former.

6. The figures cited by Ernst are described as follows: "The data presented in these tables is based on different sources such as official censuses, and published as well as unpublished church sources. The numbers given for 1992 are mainly based on Church Sources, field research carried out in the respective islands and extrapolations of growth rates in previous years" (1994:305).

7. The author attended a meeting with Eastern Highland Lutheran leaders held in Kainantu in August 1989, at which it was pointed out that the Lutherans had lost 5,000 members in 1988.

8. Camp meetings were an early part of Adventist practice in the United States. "They were a means of socializing within one's own 'culture,' developing unity, promoting revival and evangelism, and providing education in Adventism. They maintained and generated the Adventist ethos" (Steley 1989:26–27). In light of this quotation, it is interesting to note the reports from the Keiya meeting participants about the tears shed by many of them at the end of the meeting.

9. It is ironic that the more legalistic and sectarian orientation of Adventists before the 1950s, which still characterizes the beliefs advanced in the Eastern Highlands, has become much less doctrinaire in Adventism generally in recent decades (Steley 1989:35–51; see also Butler and Numbers 1987 and Samples 1990).

10. As Steley points out, this sense of rightness was a part of the nineteenth-century American origins of the Adventists within other Protestant churches: "[Adventists] came to view Protestantism, as well as Catholicism, as the 'Babylon' of the Apocalypse. Their separation was given eschatological significance and the cry arose 'Babylon is fallen . . . come out of her, my people'" (1989:4).

11. The centrality of health concerns in Adventist teachings developed as part of their "holistic" teachings on lifestyle (Steley 1989:13).

12. One more indicator in 1989 of the growth of Adventism in the community in which I lived was the absence of pigs, except for a few that were kept penned. Very few pigs were seen along the roads in the Agarabi area.

13. This pattern of economic commitment and success for Adventists has been noted elsewhere in Papua New Guinea (Garrett 1997), in the Pacific (Ross 1979), and in Latin America (Lewellen 1979).

14. It is interesting to note that this element of protagonists hiding in caves and being saved from discovery by a mysterious fog appears elsewhere in Agarabi oral tradition.

15. Steley (1989:8–9) points to the significance of the Sabbath for early Adventists: "Furthermore Sabbath observance was seen as the central issue about which the final conflict of earth's history would revolve as Sunday represented a counterfeit day of worship. The Sabbath supplied a standard by which God's people would be judged by heaven and earth in the last days prior to the Second Coming. The expectation of those events exerted a massive influence upon Adventist psychology and philosophy" (1989:8–9; see also page 34).

16. This criticism even applies to the new Pidgin Bible, *Buk Baibel,* which is said to have altered references to God's "Holy Day" to read Sunday. One lay evangelist explained to me that the publication of this first complete Bible translation in Pidgin was primarily supported by Catholics.

17. "The Seventh-Day Adventist Church conducted the second largest parochial school system in the world in 1986 with a total enrollment of almost three

quarters of a million students, including eighty-six colleges and universities" (Steley 1989:23).

18. The identification of the Beast with "the Papacy, apostate Protestantism and enforced Sunday observance" was part of the earliest nineteenth-century Adventist teachings (Steley 1989:6; see especially ftn. 16). Agarabi Adventists frequently cite a verse associated with this idea, Revelation 13:18: "Here is wisdom. Let him that hath understanding count the number of the beast: for it is the number of a man; and his number is Six hundred three score and six." Official church literature available to Agarabi Adventist lay evangelists shows that one of the Pope's titles, "Vicar of the Son of God," can, according to Adventist readings, be translated using numerical values for the Latin alphabet to total 666. These ideas also were included in an official primary-level Sabbath school lesson book used during June–July 1989 by Agarabi Adventists. Opposition between Adventists and Catholics has been noted elsewhere in Papua New Guinea (Josephides 1990:60; Papua New Guinea *Post-Courier* 1991).

19. At least one official note was taken of this account of the killing. A provincial magistrate based in Simbu Province referred for investigation to the Goroka provincial police commander allegations from an expatriate Seventh-Day Adventist pastor that three young men had confessed to being hired for the murder by an American Baptist missionary with money supplied by the Catholic Church and the Evangelical Brotherhood. Unfortunately, I do not know what conclusion, if any, was reached by this investigation (letter from R. Giddings, senior provincial magistrate, to provincial police commander, Goroka, RE: "Allegation of Conspiracy to Murder," February 9, 1990. Copy in the author's files).

20. In fact, Okuk returned to Papua New Guinea alive and died on November 14, 1986. His death led to severe rioting, especially in Goroka, capital of the Eastern Highlands Province, where there was much property damage. He was buried in Kundiawa on November 24 with about 10,000 mourners present (Paula Brown, personal communication).

## REFERENCES

Barker, John. 1990. "Introduction: Ethnographic Perspectives on Christianity in Oceanic Societies." In *Christianity in Oceania: Ethnographic Perspectives.* J. Barker, ed. Pp. 1–24. ASAO Monograph No. 12. Lanham, Md.: University Press of America.

Brown, Paula. 1982. "Conflict in the New Guinea Highlands." *Journal of Conflict Resolution* 26:525–546.

Butler, Jonathan, and Ronald Numbers. 1987. "Seventh-Day Adventism." In *Encyclopedia of Religion.* Vol. 13. M. Eliade, ed. Pp. 179–183. New York: Macmillan.

Cucchiari, Salvatore. 1988. "'Adapted for Heaven:' Conversion and Culture in Western Sicily." *American Ethnologist* 16(3): 417–441.

Ernst, Manfred. 1994. *Winds of Change: Rapidly Growing Religious Groups in the Pacific Islands.* Suva: Pacific Conference of Churches.

Garrett, John. 1997. *Where the Nets Were Cast: Christianity in Oceania Since World War II.* Suva: Institute of Pacific Studies.

Gewertz, Deborah, and Frederick Errington. 1993. "First Contact with God: Individualism, Agency, and Revivalism in the Duke of York Islands." *Cultural Anthropology* 8(3):279–305.

Gimbol, Christopher. 1984. "Group Coffee Development Projects: A Preliminary Survey of the 20 Hectare Blocks." Discussion Paper 88/3, Papua New Guinea Department of Agriculture and Livestock.

Goddard, Michael. 1995. "The Rascal Road: Crime, Prestige, and Development in Papua New Guinea." *The Contemporary Pacific* 7(1):55–80.

Grossman, Lawrence. 1984. *Peasants, Subsistence Ecology and Development in the Highlands of Papua New Guinea.* Princeton: Princeton University Press.

Hart Nibbrig, Nand E. 1992. "Rascals in Paradise: Urban Gangs in Papua New Guinea." *Pacific Studies* 15(3):115–134.

Hefner, Robert. 1993. "Introduction: Worldbuilding and the Rationality of Conversion." In *Conversion to Christianity: Historical and Anthropological Perspectives on a Great Transformation.* R. Hefner, ed. Pp. 3–43. Berkeley: University of California Press.

———. 1998. "Multiple Modernities: Christianity, Islam, and Hinduism in a Globalizing Age." *Annual Reviews in Anthropology* 27:83–104.

Josephides, Sasha. 1990. "Seventh-Day Adventism and the Boroi Image of the Past." In *Sepik Heritage: Tradition and Change in Papua New Guinea.* N. Lutkehaus, ed. Pp. 58–66. Durham, N.C.: Carolina Academic Press.

Lewellen, Ted. 1979. "Deviant Religion and Cultural Evolution: The Aymara Case." *Journal for the Scientific Study of Religion* 18(3):243–251.

McGuire, Meredith. 1992. *Religion: The Social Context.* 3rd ed. Belmont, Calif.: Wadsworth.

Ohnuki-Tierney, Emiko. 1990. "Introduction: The Historicization of Anthropology." In *Culture Through Time: Anthropological Approaches.* E. Ohnuki-Tierney, ed. Pp. 1–25. Stanford, Calif.: Stanford University Press.

Papua New Guinea *Post-Courier.* 1989. "History in the Making." August 21, p. 1.

———. 1990. "Typhoid Fever Update." June 28, p. 10.

———. 1991. "Religious Differences Spark Off Village Fighting." March 13, p. 3.

Podolefsky, Aaron. 1984. "Contemporary Warfare in the New Guinea Highlands." *Ethnology* 23(2):73–87.

Ross, Harold. 1979. "Competition for Baegu Souls: Mission Rivalry on Malaita, Solomon Islands." In *Mission, Church, and Sect in Oceania.* J. Boutilier, D. Hughes, and S. Tiffany, eds. Pp. 163–200. ASAO Monograph No. 6. Lanham, Md.: University Press of America.

Samples, R. 1990. "The Recent Truth About Seventh-Day Adventism." *Christianity Today* 34(2):18–21.

Saunders, George. 1995. "The Crisis of Presence in Italian Pentecostal Conversion." *American Ethnologist* 22(2):324–340.

Steley, Dennis. 1988. "Seventh-Day Adventist Sources for the Pacific." *Journal of History* 23(1):102–105.

———. 1989. Unfinished: The Seventh-Day Adventist Mission in the South Pacific, Excluding Papua New Guinea, 1886–1986. Unpublished dissertation. University of Auckland.

Strathern, Andrew. 1983. "Contemporary Warfare in the New Guinea Highlands—Revival or Breakdown?" *Yagl-Ambu* 43:135–146.

———. 1992. "Let the Bow Go Down." In *War in the Tribal Zone: Expanding States and Indigenous Warfare.* R. B. Ferguson and N. Whitehead, eds. Pp. 229–250. Santa Fe, N.M.: School of American Research and Advanced Seminar Series.

Tuzin, Donald. 1989. "Visions, Prophecies and the Rise of Christian Consciousness." In *The Religious Imagination in New Guinea.* G. Herdt and M. Stephens, eds. Pp. 187–208. New Brunswick, N.J.: Rutgers University Press.

Watson, James B. 1983. *Tairora Culture: Contingency and Pragmatism.* Seattle: University of Washington Press.

Westermark, George. 1978. "Eria Komuniti in Kainantu: Observations After Five Years." In *Decentralization: Observations After Five Years.* R. Premdas and S. Pokawin, eds. Pp. 91–97. Port Moresby: University of Papua New Guinea Press.

———. 1981. "Sorcery and Economic Change in Agarabi." *Social Analysis* 8:89–100.

———. 1984. "'Ol I Skulim Mipela:' Contemporary Warfare in the Papua New Guinea Eastern Highlands." *Anthropological Quarterly* 57(4):114–125.

———. 1985. "Court Is an Arrow: Legal Pluralism in Papua New Guinea." *Ethnology* 23(2):131–149.

———. 1986. "Church Law, Court Law: Competing Forums in a Highland Village." In *Anthropology in the High Valleys: Essays on the New Guinea Highlands in Honor of Kenneth E. Read.* L. L. Langness and T. Hays, eds. Pp. 109–135. Novato, Calif.: Chandler & Sharp.

———. 1997. "Clan Claims: Land, Law, and Violence in the Papua New Guinea Highlands." *Oceania* 67(3): 218–233.

# Photo Credits

**Chapter 7.** Page 124: reprinted by permission of Nestle S.A., Vevey (Switzerland). Page 127: courtesy of Robert J. Foster.

**Chapter 9.** Page 159: courtesy of Simon Foale.

**Chapter 12.** Pages 202, 204, 213: courtesy of Mac Marshall. Page 205: reprinted by permission of Eagle Family Foods.

**Chapter 19.** Pages 326, 327, 328, 330: courtesy of Jocelyn Linnekin. Pages 331, 332 (left and right): courtesy of Fortune Designs Collection.

**Chapter 20.** Pages 345 (left and right), 346, 347 (left and right): courtesy of Eric Silverman.

**Chapter 23.** Page 400: courtesy of Heather Young Leslie.

**Chapter 25.** Pages 451, 453, 455: courtesy of John Barker.

**Chapter 26.** Pages 463, 465, 466: courtesy of George Westermark.

# Index